# Global Empowerment
# of Women

# Routledge Research in Gender and Society

# Global Empowerment of Women

## Responses to Globalization and Politicized Religions

**Edited by
Carolyn M. Elliott**

Routledge
Taylor & Francis Group
New York   London

First published 2008
by Routledge
270 Madison Ave, New York, NY 10016

Simultaneously published in the UK
by Routledge
2 Park Square, Milton Park, Abingdon, Oxon OX14 4RN

*Routledge is an imprint of the Taylor & Francis Group, an informa business*

Transferred to Digital Printing 2008

© 2008 Taylor and Francis Group

Typeset in Sabon by IBT Global

*Library of Congress Cataloging-in-Publication Data*
A catalog record has been requested for this book

ISBN10: 0-415-95545-9 (hbk)
ISBN10: 0-203-99975-3 (ebk)

ISBN13: 978-0-415-95545-4 (hbk)
ISBN13: 978-0-203-93375-6 (ebk)

# Contents

# Preface

The authors represented in this collection were members of the Fulbright New Century Scholars Program (NCS) on Global Empowerment of Women. This group of thirty-one scholars from twenty-two countries met in three seminars over the course of the program year, 2004–2005, in addition to pursuing individual research projects. They worked on a broad variety of issues—from sexual autonomy, to marriage laws, to war and memory. Their research was located in many different spaces—villages, prisons, health clinics, and the International Criminal Court, among others. The task of the seminars was to draw on this research for collaborative projects to advance women's empowerment, and to formulate an overall research-based understanding of problems and possible solutions. At the first meeting the NCS scholars divided themselves into four working groups, organized by topic, that worked together throughout the project year. The statement that follows (the Scholars' Statement) is compiled from the scholars' collective statement and the subgroup conclusions that they summarized for presentation at a public meeting in New York in May 2005.

The Scholars' Statement provides a powerful, substantive critique of the structural impediments to women's empowerment agreed upon by scholars from both the North and the South. As a group, these scholars speak from long experience with research, both field investigations and theoretical formulations. Many of the group have also established careers as activists on behalf of women's and gender issues.

## SCHOLARS' STATEMENT

The implementation of neoliberal policies over the last twenty-five years has resulted in the dominant role of the market, greater openness to international trade and investment, and a reduced role for government in promoting population well-being. The focus of government policy is on individual strategies rather than collective responsibility. These processes are intertwined with continued violence against women, the feminization of poverty, transnational labor exploitation, and control of women's mobility.

The world has moved toward greater inequality within and among states as well as among women, even as women are achieving a degree of equality with men in some settings. Structural adjustment, privatization of state functions, and the expansion of market economies contribute to widening the gap between North and South, rich and poor, and men and women. Religious, ethnic, and national tensions obscure and justify material injustices. In this setting of increasing worldwide inequality, the path toward global gender equity is more difficult.

We support the substantial international commitments and conventions to advance women's equality made in such agreements as the Convention for the Elimination of Discrimination against Women (CEDAW), the Declaration of the United Nations' Conference on Human Rights, the Beijing Platform for Action, the World Summit on Social Development, and the Millennium Declaration. We are concerned, however, that the recently adopted Millennium Development Goals (MDG) are a step backward from the earlier United Nations-based initiatives that came out of the conferences on women and social development. These earlier recommendations were concerned not just with individual claims but also with broader questions of structural change that now appear to have been removed from the mainstream agenda.

We focus on understanding what changes in the global order mean for women and women's empowerment. Our work is guided by an explicit commitment to developing analytical and practical alternatives to contemporary global hegemonies. We address debates about globalization and global restructuring through the development of a critical transnational feminist framework for analysis and action.

Our research has identified many key sources and sites of women's empowerment. Empowerment has been a critical concept for the international women's movement, underscoring the effectiveness of women's activism in changing the world. We have discovered numerous ways in which women have transformed their lives. We have also found multiple instances of individual and institutional resistance to global trends that have negative effects on women. Further, our research confirms and exemplifies the power of women's collective action.

Yet we also recognize problems with the way empowerment has been defined, measured, and deployed. Notions of empowerment often emphasize individual rights without recognizing women's responsibilities to others. Empowerment has too often been used in instrumental ways to meet the goals of development programs rather than to transform structural and gender inequalities. There is also a tension between empowerment as a series of individual choices and the structural constraints within which those choices must be made. Choices that may appear self-defeating or self-endangering to an outsider may be rational within the situation a woman faces. Other problems arise when empowerment generates conflict among the several roles of women or between groups of women. The unevenness and inconsistencies of empowerment must be charted, within women's lives and across women's experiences.

## GENDER, GLOBALIZATION, AND GOVERNANCE

Our research deals with governance, understood to be a multifaceted political process that involves both public and private sectors in the determination of social and economic inequalities. While economic governance is generally posited in terms of states and markets, we broaden these concepts to include inequalities of power, production, and distribution. The research challenges the narrow understanding of economic governance inherent in the neoliberal paradigm.

Global restructuring has increasingly shifted governance processes to private institutions and international actors, which operate by market rules and are removed from democratic accountability. The policy of marketization—increasing reliance on markets for producing and distributing goods—is detrimental to poor people in general and to women in particular, for it ignores the critical contribution of social reproduction and the care economy to the capacity for production. The impacts of global restructuring include cutbacks in public support for the unwaged work crucial for family survival, increasing burdens on women. We are experiencing deepening inequality and jeopardy of the productive capacity in our societies.

## NEGOTIATING CITIZENSHIP AND DIVERSITY: GENDER, NATION, AND DIASPORAS

Studies of women's empowerment must take into account their membership in ethnic, national, and religious communities, be attentive to the contradictory roles of women in social and political conflicts, and investigate the complex relationships between gender, citizenship, and processes of social inclusion and exclusion. In particular, they need to examine how gender is used in the construction of national and ethnic identities.

Group rights are often prioritized over women's rights. Women accept, actively embrace, reject, or reconfigure their roles as symbols and markers of identity. While we can no longer assume that women are simply used as passive symbols of nationalism, in many instances women do function as bearers of culture, and the consolidation of national/ethnic identity takes place at the cost of their freedom and well-being. In highly charged situations where group identity is at stake, communities tend to react with increased concern about gender roles and seek to tighten control over women. At the same time it is necessary to acknowledge women's agency in each context, even if it is expressed in ways we may find difficult to understand.

Many women have found participation in liberation and resistance movements empowering. However, post-liberation results have often been contradictory, uneven, and disappointing. In situations of conflict, women and girls are affected in specifically gendered ways. Restoring to collective memory women's victimization, activism, and resistance can be the basis for new forms of democratic development and gender justice.

## RESPONSES TO VIOLENCE

Violence against women has been widely recognized as a pervasive global problem. It is an enduring impediment to the empowerment of women and, more generally, to social justice and peace. Cultures of violence are based on repression, denial, and manipulation. In the case of violence against women this is particularly acute. Historically women have been blamed, shamed, and silenced about the violence perpetrated against them, especially sexual violence. Silence surrounding gender violence contributes to the violence by maintaining it and exacerbating its traumatic impact on victims and the broader consequences for all women.

The identification, documentation, and validation of these crimes are a key to providing accountability and redress, and for achieving a more just truth. Providing a public space for breaking the silence and recording the testimonies of violence contributes to justice and helps to minimize the possibility of recurrence. Truth commissions have played this role in many post-conflict situations, but within these forums violence against women has been ignored or considered to be outside the commissions' purview. Women's participation in anti-war and resistance movements is also too often absent from public memory, leaving the impression that women were victims and supporters but never actors in the movements against war.

We propose that that truth commissions be designed to emphasize the empowering aspects of inclusion, recognizing women not only as victims, but also as leaders and agents. Debates about constructions of women as agents rather than victims pose a false dichotomy. Without denying the structural limits on this agency, and ignoring the pain and fear that accompany violence, we think it essential to recognize the resiliency and strength of women in the face of widespread violence. Women may be simultaneously victims, survivors, and agents of change. They may also be perpetrators of violence.

## SEXUAL AUTONOMY AND GLOBAL POLITICS: FEMINIST CRITIQUES OF HIV/AIDS INTERVENTIONS IN AFRICA

As the HIV/AIDS epidemic accelerates, it has become evident that the behavioral health and risk-reduction models used to understand and address the epidemic are inadequate because they ignore the complexities, contradictions, and tensions inherent in sexual decisions for many women around the world. These models incorrectly assume that populations are undifferentiated (by sex, class, age, or other factors), that males and females have equal control over their sexual health decisions, that individuals act autonomously and according to biomedical constructions of rationality, and that culture (usually read as "African culture") is an impediment to risk reduction. Such assumptions narrowly define the spread of HIV as a problem of individual choice and fail to account for the political, economic, and social contexts surrounding sexual health decisions. For example, condoms might not seem rational for a newly married couple for whom reproduction is an important family obligation and a public symbol of marital happiness. HIV/AIDS campaigns are so focused on risk that they do not adequately address desire or other emotions that motivate sexual behavior. We argue that designing appropriate campaigns requires an appreciation of local ideas of desire, including who can desire and who is desired. Feminist analyses show that intervention programs intended to protect public health may draw females further under the surveillance of local and global patriarchal structures, undermining their sexual rights and sexual autonomy.

## NOTES

1. The group included one scholar each from twenty-one countries of Asia, Latin America, Africa, Europe, and the Middle East and ten from the United States, two of whom were born and educated abroad. It was chaired by Carolyn Elliott, editor of this volume.
2. This statement is based on the presentation made and distributed at the public plenary of the New Century Scholars (NCS) Program in New York on April 28, 2005. It was made possible by the NCS program but reflects the views of the NCS Scholars, not the Fulbright Program nor the U.S. State Department. Editorial changes made in this statement for this publication have been approved by the authors in this volume.

# Dedication and Acknowledgments

This volume is dedicated to the memory of Alice Stone Ilchman. Alice had a favorite quotation from Edith Wharton inscribed on the wall above the books in her study:

> There are two ways of spreading light;
> to be the candle or the mirror that reflects it.

Alice did both, in public and private ways. Appointed by President Carter as Assistant Secretary of State for Educational and Cultural Affairs, she was responsible for the Fulbright program, U.S. libraries abroad, and the international visitor program. Alice was revered in the field of international education, for she worked long after her tenure in Washington to support Fulbright funding and articulate the significance of public diplomacy. While maintaining this important public stance, she also did the work of scholars in the interstices of Fulbright, reading piles of applications, sitting for hours on selection committees, and supporting scholars at work with enthusiastic appreciation of their contributions to scholarship and international understanding. The New Century Scholars Program on Global Empowerment of Women was privileged to have Alice Ilchman on our committee.

Alice was a candle and mirror also in higher education. She served Sarah Lawrence College as president for seventeen years and, through building the science center now named for her, led its emergence as a full-spectrum institution of excellence in liberal arts education. Alice attended commencements far and wide for family and friends, served on trustee boards, and led search committees. At her death she was the Director of the Jeannette K. Watson Fellows Program that placed New York City-based undergraduates in paid summer internships, offering them vision-expanding opportunities not broadly available in city institutions. Alice observed, "Talent is widely distributed but not widely recognized." She was enormously proud of her fellows and they blossomed in her light.

Alice was a feminist who largely worked inside institutions to make them work for both women and men. As Dean of Wellesley College, she provided critical nurturance to the Wellesley Center for Research on Women, now a major source of scholarship and advocacy for educational equity for women and girls. She was a trustee of Mount Holyoke College during the period of many women's colleges considering coeducation; Mount Holyoke did not change and is now thriving as a college for women. In the eighties Alice chaired the National Research Council's Committee on Women's Employment and Related Social Issues, and produced two research initiatives on work and family. Recently on her watch as search committee chair, the Public Broadcasting Corporation appointed its first woman president. All the while, Alice recommended women for positions in her extensive network and wrote many letters for students and colleagues.

Alice was also a dear friend, godmother to my daughter, loyal supporter, and witty commentator on life events. We shared tailors in India, a nanny in the US, and many adventures in conversation, reading, and travel. When my daughter needed a college and I was off in India, Alice took time from her own presidency to visit a college. When Alice needed internships for her fellows, I took three overnight flights in one week to Africa and India. Our sisterhood was personal and global.

For the possibility of writing this book, I wish to thank the NCS program, the U.S. Department of State, and the Council for International Education of Scholars (CIES). This program supported the scholars' research and the seminars, and provided crucial assistance in preparing the manuscript. At a time of so much difficulty in U.S. relations with the rest of the world, it is heartening that in one corner of U.S. diplomacy this open and fruitful program could proceed unfettered.

A number of individuals deserve special thanks: Micaela Iovine, then of CIES, provided administrative support. Jane Jaquette, Alice Ilchman, Deborah Rosenfelt, Molara Ogundipe, and Kathleen Cloud served on the selection committee. The Ford Foundation made possible the NCS seminar in India and the U.S. Educational Foundation in India arranged the India program. I am especially grateful to all the scholars who contributed to an exceptionally rich set of discussions that inform the volume, and the contributors who gracefully dealt with a fairly interventionist mode of editing in the name of creating a volume accessible for undergraduate classroom use. Deborah Guber, Associate Professor of Political Science at the University of Vermont, was an invaluable colleague as technical editor.

I also wish to thank Ben Holtzman for his friendly facilitation at Routledge Press, *Feminist Studies* for permission to reprint the Ewig article and *Political Geography* for permission to reprint the Silvey article, both without fees. Finally, I must acknowledge the Internet. Without the capacity to send manuscripts instantaneously back and forth between the U.S., Ghana, India, and wherever, we could never have attempted a project like this.

# Introduction
## Markets, Communities, and Empowerment

*Carolyn M. Elliott*[1]

The Scholars' Statement identifies two major concerns of international feminist scholarship and advocacy that are often seen as alternatives and in opposition: globalization and the politicization of religions. The scholars' investigations of gender violence and denial of sexual autonomy, as noted in their statement, trace the impact of these concerns in problem areas of special significance to women.

In agreement with a major trend of feminist research, the scholars offer a strong critique of neoliberal economic policy, a policy that privileges markets over states as generators of economic growth. While not uncritical of the resurgence of patriarchal practices and fundamentalist politics, the scholars appear more tolerant of religious and other expressions of identity than of markets. They argue that women may find spaces for empowerment and support for family functioning within community-based politics. In this they reflect criticisms of the North by many feminists in the South who identify neoliberal economic policy with imperialist ambitions.

The debate about globalization and politicized religions is situated in a tradition of political theory that contrasts individualist and communitarian approaches to modernity. These two ideas originate in different philosophical positions, one deriving from the conviction that individuals know their own preferences and interests best, the other from a concern for sustaining a common interest that may be neglected by self-maximizing individuals. In modern history, these positions were reflected in debates between liberals seeking to free society from medieval constraints on political and personal freedom, and conservatives wishing to preserve the stability of local communities.[2] Concerns for community in the face of industrialization led also to a left strand of communitarianism, the utopian socialists, that eventually generated Marxist socialism.[3]

The liberals were the modernizers historically, whereas the conservatives wanted to preserve the old order. In the contemporary politics of development, modernizers continue to be largely identified with classical or market liberal views, now called neoliberalism. The conservative position today is associated with religious politics, ethnic politics and, at the extremes, resurgent nationalism and fundamentalism. But it finds resonance on the left where communitarian visions have long challenged the liberal narrative.[4] Socialist communitarians have often allied with nationalist resistance to imperialism and westernization.

From the liberal conviction comes a concern for individual rights and a preference for limited government. Citizenship is conceived as equality among members in a political community that guarantees political and civil rights against intrusion by the state. In economic terms, this translates into a preference that the market allocate most resources, that individuals exercise choice, and that property rights be protected. Proponents of the market claim equality and inclusion, though markets often don't deliver on these ideals.

From the communitarian position comes a concern for social solidarity. Conservatives endorse leadership to articulate common goals and shape choices; they tolerate or espouse hierarchy and exclusion in the service of these goals. When conservatives use the language of rights, they often elevate the rights of groups to sustain their culture and protect their memberships over the rights of individuals to exercise choice. In the left form of communitarianism there is a strong commitment to equality, and a sharing of social benefits is privileged over civil, political, and property rights. All socialist communities that have existed in history have shared the conservatives' endorsement of leadership, often charismatic, to articulate and enforce an ambitious vision for the community.

This debate has now been elevated to the international stage. In economic terms, neoliberals emphasize freeing international trade from nationalist protection, arguing that international markets enable consumers to exercise choice. Proponents of local or national autonomy and those who object to international human rights agendas to protect cultural practices are drawing from a historically conservative position. Given human history to date, this position is inevitably anti-egalitarian in ways that can only be described as patriarchal.[5]

Where does feminism fit? Many feminists liked socialist communitarianism because it filled all their goals: equality, material improvements to meet people's needs, and community.[6] With Marxism largely off the agenda, the choice is narrowed to neoliberal capitalism (often linked with democracy) and various "neoconservative" and sometimes "multicultural" positions, from the pro-family, anti-abortion right in the U.S. to religion-based nationalism shaping political change in the Middle East, Africa, and beyond. The language of human rights draws from the liberal tradition; many feminists support rights-based arguments while rejecting the individualist understanding of agency and citizenship that underlies the rights perspective. Deeply critical of neoliberalism, international feminism contains many alliances between socialists and Islamists, left and right communitarians.

There are rich lines of feminist theory and research analyzing each of these positions. Feminist scholars have pointed out that liberalism and markets tend to disadvantage women who have the responsibility for children; their inadequate resources (educational, social, financial, and time) make it difficult for them to compete in the marketplace. Feminists point out that, politically, the liberal concept of citizenship derives from a distinction between public life and private life, which historically excluded women from public life and left them unprotected from abuse and exploitation in the household.[7] Moreover, the reluctance of classical liberals (now called neoliberals) to expand government means less support for health, education, and the community services women need to fulfill family responsibilities. However, because liberalism assumes equality and inclusion, it can be called to account for unfairness to women, with increasing success in many societies and in international norms.[8]

Given the problems that markets can generate—individualism, exclusion, and inequality—does a community-based politics provide a better setting for women's well-being? Conservative communitarians elevate and protect women but at the cost of their autonomy. They generally accept gender bias and provide rationales for institutionalizing and accepting it. As childbearers, women reproduce group members and, through marriage and production of "pure" or "impure" children, they sustain or violate group boundaries. Controlling reproduction means controlling women's sexuality, leading to constraints on their mobility. These restrictions are legitimated by conventional religious practices, ideals of women's purity, adulation of motherhood, and other patriarchal ideas. Women are also assumed to be the major transmitters of culture to children. Through their dress and in allegories, women are made into symbols of national difference.[9]

Today, an assessment of the meaning of community models for women must focus on religion, nationalism, and ethnicity, the three most important political expressions of community today. Many argue that women in various kinds of restrictive communities strongly embrace the ideals of their particular communities.[10] Women's lives are also embedded in relationships in which they feel responsible to others and make choices to protect them, often at the cost of their own autonomy. To many community-minded women, the concept of women's rights seems inappropriately individualistic and selfish, or utterly alien, imposed by international discourse emanating from Western culture. These communities may provide identity, solidarity, and spiritual sustenance, but the models make it difficult to argue for a universal understanding of women's basic rights. They leave feminists of the South vulnerable to attacks from those who associate women's rights discourse with the imposition of "westernization."[11]

The goal of this volume of essays is to identify possibilities for women's empowerment within this complicated matrix. The contrast between rights-based citizenship and identity-based communities provides a framework for considering this question. Empirical investigations of these models reveal that they are not nearly as distinct as theory would have it. The tensions, contradictions, and inconsistencies both within and between the liberal and community models may provide spaces for women to act.[12] But these tensions may also generate obstacles to empowering initiatives conceived elsewhere and subverted or transformed by local elites. Locating women's agency requires research in specific contexts with nuanced probing of differences in how agency arises and is expressed. The papers in this volume are the fruits of such endeavors.

## GLOBAL CONTEXT

The contemporary state of the international economy and global governance makes women's empowerment a challenge. NCS Scholar Isabella Bakker, whose previous work traced the gendered effects of structural adjustment, emphasizes the gendered impact of neoliberal governance, a process that has shifted many government functions to private institutions and international actors operating by market rules.[13] Because the market focuses on work for wages, and caring work is done "for free," the so-called economy of care does not enter into national economic accounts and is neglected in government policy. Pressures by international economic institutions to reduce inflation led many governments to cut back state expenditures on services that facilitate social reproduction, i.e., unpaid work largely done by women to maintain homes, care for children and dependents, and build social networks.[14]

Even where social services have not been cut, domestic policy goals have shifted from promotion of well-being to investment in human capital, leaving little room for recognition of women's contributions to the larger economy. Christina Ewig's study of health sector reforms in Latin America found that where health plans have moved to private providers, as in Chile, a poster child for the success of neoliberalism, women pay higher fees than men.[15] Their reproductive capacity is seen as a "risk" to private capital, not a benefit to society. Privatization may also pose risks to women's health, now or in the long term. Wendy Chavkin in this volume finds that in Canada and Europe, employed women who have postponed childbearing until the point of infertility are resorting to Artificial Reproductive Technologies (ART), an individualized technological solution to a societal problem of reconciling work and family life for women. A medical doctor, Chavkin worries that the lifetime effects of the required hormonal treatments are unstudied.

It is necessary, however, to distinguish the effects of specific neoliberal reforms from the impact of more general forces of globalization. Many of the outcomes the NCS scholars deplore, such as trafficking and exploitative migration as well as ethnic tensions and religious politics, would likely be occurring even if neoliberalism had not become dominant internationally. These outcomes owe as much or more to advances in transnational communications, the fall of the Soviet Union, and U.S. unilateralism as to economic policies. Finally, where neoliberal economic policy has hastened the spread of market capitalism but not otherwise affected government functioning, it appears that the main driver of change for women is modernization, a punishing process in every nation that has experienced it. Thus Meena Acharya argues from Nepal that the impact of globalization on rural Nepal is not a reduction of services, for the government had never provided them, but an escalation of the marketization of the village economy, eroding food security and propelling women to seek wage work in exploitative urban factories.[16]

Part of the phenomenon of globalization is the transnational spread of liberal ideas of citizenship and equality. The social movements and UN conferences that were instrumental in spreading these ideas, as well as in facilitating cross-national networks among activists, are products of global communication. They have generated debates about women's roles within societies and led to increasing commitments to women's rights, both nationally and internationally. Global communication has also facilitated the spread of Women Living Under Muslim Laws (WLUML), a twenty-year-old solidarity network of mostly Muslim women from seventy countries. Calling for equality, gender justice, and women's rights, and identifying themselves as human rights activists, Women Living Under Muslim Laws works within the communitarian model of religious-based society.[17]

But institutional support for equality norms remains weak. Research by NCS scholars show continuing unawareness, reluctance, or defining away of women's issues from the central concerns of national and international institutions. Julissa Mantilla in this volume traces the long and difficult history of getting post-conflict Truth and Reconciliation Commissions to recognize sexual abuses as within their scope and to understand that gender expertise is needed to deal with it. Maria Floro and Hella Hoppe analyzed contradictions between the UN-led statements on development and the policies of multilateral trade and financial institutions.[18] They report a growing effort led by the World Trade Organization and other financial institutions to coordinate macroeconomic policies, a goal labeled "convergence." The power asymmetry in favor of economic institutions over the human rights/social development agencies places commitments made to the Beijing Platform for Action and the UN Millennium Development Goals at risk.

Possible links between market reforms and the new conservatisms, especially resurgent nationalisms and fundamentalisms, must be theorized and examined. Many scholars have suggested that neoliberalism's focus on market individualism has destroyed any notion of the common good, other than the market, in many societies. The coincidence of pro-market forces and growing global inequalities has left an ideological vacuum now filled by theocratic alternatives. Similarly, the waning of workers' solidarity movements and the loss of the socialist vision sponsored by the Soviet Union have left space that is now filled by politicized religious organizations from evangelical churches to Hezbollah. Further, the NCS Scholars argued that neoliberal governance has had particularly negative consequences for women by encouraging governments to withdraw their commitment to collective remedies for social problems. Without state-sponsored services and safety nets for populations threatened by the dislocations of modernization, including globalization, religious organizations have stepped into the breach.

Contemporary history shows that as populations fear or experience loss of control over, or support from, their communities, they tend to reassert conservative ideologies that include controls over women. During political transitions and in diasporic communities, pressures to conform to traditionally defined gender roles increase and women's bodies become symbols of cultural integrity.[19] Rhoda Reddock in this volume observes the continuing insistence among the Indo-Trinidadian and Afro-Trinidadian communities on preserving separate regimes of personal law in Trinidad and Tobago. She attributes the continuation of four different marriage laws to the effects of competition among male elites at the end of colonialism. Apprehensive about their power in the new regime, elders of the various communities used marriage law to reassert ethnicity-based controls over women.

The impact of globalization on national communities has increased these effects. Agnieszka Graff's study in this volume of several Polish medias found that a rise in concern about masculinity accompanied Poland's integration into the European Union. Anxieties evoked by the prospect of losing the nation-state only so recently recovered from Soviet domination were expressed through images of feminized males and oversized dominant women. Similarly, Titia Loenen in this volume shows how the European Court of Human Rights abandoned its commitment to individual rights when confronted with Muslim teachers wearing headscarves in school. Making no attempt to investigate the meaning of headscarves to the individuals involved, the Court adopted an essentialized stance against what they thought to be religiously prescribed precepts in order to reaffirm European values. Ironically, the values the Court claimed to uphold were tolerance and gender equality.


## EMPOWERMENT AND GENDER

Empowerment was a strategy first proposed internationally in the 1980s by a group of activists from the South to challenge the hegemony of northern feminists in international discourse regarding women.[20] The term was quickly mainstreamed by international development agencies as a way of mobilizing women's well-documented commitment to family well-being for development goals.[21] In the course of this transition, women's empowerment has come to be associated with local grassroots, participatory initiatives that allow women voice but not necessarily power. This focus on the local leads to neglect of the structural constraints embedded in global and national institutions that limit the prospects for empowerment. Parpart, Rai, and Staudt suggests it "encourages a rather romantic equation between empowerment, inclusion, and voice that papers over the complexities of em(power)ment, both as a process and a goal."[22]

At its most nefarious, the empowerment of women has been co-opted as a neoliberal strategy to abdicate state responsibility for social provisioning and promote women's "self-help." Women are encouraged to form community associations to perform functions previously assumed by the state, such as the supervision of neighborhood water distribution.[23] Lynne Haney in this volume describes how this strategy has transformed the prison regimes of neoliberal states. These states have responded to economic marginalization by incarcerating social groups unable to provide for themselves, so prison populations have soared in countries most influenced by neoliberal governance. Inside prisons, "therapeutic communities" seek to "responsibilize," "entrepreneurialize," and ultimately hold prisoners accountable for social problems. Female inmates are subjected to penal programs that attempt to break them down in order to rebuild them in the name of empowerment.

Scholars reflecting on this mainstreaming have urged that women's empowerment be rescued from a future as a "motherhood" term by focusing on its core meaning: women gaining power to shape their own lives, their communities, their states and the international system (Parpart, Rai, and Staudt, 2002: 3). Empowerment may be defined as an individual's capacity to take control of her own life and resources; to make decisions about strategic life choices; to alter power relations that constrain her options, autonomy, and well-being; and to achieve her desired outcomes.[24] The concept is about a process of transformation, from being disadvantaged by power relations that shape choices and well-being into a position of being able to make meaningful choices. Power is central to the notion of empowerment.

To recapture the "hard-edge" notion of empowerment, it is useful to draw on the concept of gender.[25] Though this concept is still not fully accepted internationally, feminists have long used it to emphasize the social constructions of masculinity and femininity in contrast to the biological determination of sex (also now contested.) At its most potent, the concept of gender forces us to examine power relations between men and women in both intimate and social settings, and more recently to study cultures of masculinity. Gender as a feminist critique describes a governing code that favors masculinity, not necessarily men, over femininity. Like empowerment, it has developed a softer side, in this case incorporation of men's concerns for self-realization freed from hegemonic masculinity, along with opposition to women's oppression. The more potent conception of gender suggests that the empowerment of women offers a response to the norms and institutions of male domination.

It useful to discern three closely related dimensions of empowerment: individual capabilities such as health, education, knowledge, self-confidence, vision, etc.; institutional, cultural, and other resources that provide opportunities and constraints; and agency or processes through which choices are made and put into effect.

Enhancing the capabilities of women is a major focus of scholarship and development activity.[26] Increasing education and providing micro-credit loans have emerged as the major strategies. While they are often oversold as solutions or are too narrowly focused to achieve promised results, these strategies have clearly enhanced women's well-being to some degree. But without attention to the political and economic environment, as well as to cultural assumptions and discourses, in which women and men in poor communities seek power, empowerment strategies cannot reach their goals. Parpart, Rai, and Staudt call for "historically situated analyses of women's struggles to gain power in a world rarely of their own choosing" (Parpart, Rai, and Staudt, 2002: 17).

Third, studies of empowerment focus on agency. Empowerment means a woman, or a group of women, finding the power *within* themselves to make choices and act upon them to achieve results. Achievements—daughters in school, women-owned business, seats on village councils, control of fertility—are used by development agencies as indicators of women's empowerment.[27] Empowerment, however, involves not only observable action, but also meaning, motivation and purpose.[28] Too often development agencies see empowerment as only an instrument for reaching other goals, just as contraception can serve the goal of population control rather than women's choices.[29] When international development agencies provide "incentives" or pressure, program goals may be achieved, but without individual transformation it is not empowerment.

Monica Maher's piece in this volume provides a particularly vivid portrait of what individual and collective empowerment might look like. She describes the experience of the Dream Weavers in Honduras, a group that arose out of the realization by an economic cooperative that the women members needed to learn to visualize a different future for themselves in order to act on their own behalf.

The notion of empowerment must leave room for bad choices and anti-feminist politics. Women frequently join movements that appear hegemonic and masculine, supporting nationalism, religious politics, and even war. At the NCS seminar in India, the NCS Scholars were challenged by Indian feminists' reports of their struggle to understand the Hindu women who inflicted violence on Muslim women in the Gujarat riots of 2002. In interviews, Hindu women declared themselves empowered by participation in the rightist party that sponsored the riots.[30] We cannot assume that all women's movements are progressive and that women who have joined hegemonic movements are passive, seduced, or lacking in feminist consciousness. The Scholars' Statement challenges us to understand how women view themselves as they make these choices.

Although choice is the word generally used to denote the process of empowerment, it is in some ways misleading. "Choice" suggests a rational process of decision-making followed by overt action. This does not capture all the possibilities. To be useful in many contexts the notion of empowerment must include strategies of deception, subversion, passivity, and adherence as well as resistance and alternative-seeking.[31]

Like neoliberalism, the philosophy behind empowerment is a focus on the individual even if the barriers to empowerment are structural. Embracing a definition of empowerment, however, that rests on the notion of an autonomous individual or group pursuing their own goals without regard to the claims and needs of others would restrict the notion of empowerment to its narrow liberal meaning. As feminist scholars in both the North and the South have argued, this conception does not reflect women's commitment to relationships, especially responsibilities to children and community, and is not useful for understanding the lives of women—or of men.[32] Indeed, while concern for children may weigh more heavily on women's decisions, there are many parallels in the lives of men embedded in kinship networks, communities, and political groupings. We cannot assume that all decisions to forego some measure of independence to serve the needs of others are disempowering. We need a definition of empowerment that can travel into the worlds of community as well as that of individualism.

In this volume, Kawango Agot struggled with this issue as she sought to understand the thinking of widows in the Luo community of East Kenya. Upon the death of their husband, they commonly choose to be "inherited" by a male member of the husband's family despite awareness of the risk of HIV/AIDS. She argues that when basic survival and fulfilling responsibilities for children are at stake, the widows understand empowerment as access to means of survival. Without opportunity, their choice or agency cannot be considered empowerment, only strategic survival. But if the economic dependency that makes them vulnerable were addressed, the widows she studied would readily define empowerment in terms that do not include cultural conformity.

Lakshmi Lingam's study in this volume explores this issue in another situation of extreme duress, a poor agricultural district in India. She found that almost half of the loans made by women's micro-credit groups are used for agriculture, an area in which women exercise no decision-making. Women stated that their goal in using the new resources was not individual autonomy but contribution to household survival strategies, a collective view of the household but not necessarily an indicator of disempowerment.[33]

Transformational empowerment is usually collective. Changes in consciousness and individual agency may be the initial results of empowerment, but these cannot be transformative without larger scale institutional change that requires action on many fronts and at different levels. Processes that move from single actions to collective assertion of power, from private spheres to public arenas, from resistance to rule change are more likely to be transformative.

The concept of gender has structural and collective components that are useful for making empowerment a more useful term. Gender encompasses many domains in a person's life, and is shared across numbers of people. As such, it provides insights into the impact of structures and may provide a basis for collective action. Thus Chavkin argues, as noted above, that unawareness of the gendered structure of career-building results in the failure of European policy to deal with the demographic crisis resulting from postponed child-bearing. Even countries with policies that seek to support childbearing incorporate the male model of career by linking maternity benefit levels to salaries. This provides incentives to women to wait until they have reached high salary levels, at which point infertility is one of several increased risks.

Nicola Gavey in this volume draws on a gender analysis to critique Western models of treating rape victims. Because the treatment follows an individualistic approach, victims are seen as suffering from trauma akin to posttraumatic stress syndrome. The sociocultural bases of rape are downplayed, masking the need for a collective transformative response to gendered inequalities in power that make rape a common occurrence.[34]

Studies of links between masculinity and violence are a necessary adjunct to women's empowerment. How do men and women come to accept men inflicting violence on women as legitimate, as in many societies or among subgroups within them? Akosua Ampofo in this volume provides some insight into this question through her investigation of adolescent boys in Ghana. She finds that young male adolescents are often willing to consider sharing domestic work and decision-making about sexuality with girlfriends, but anticipate that the institution of marriage will provide them with authority over women. Although not many justify violence, most consider disciplining and instilling fear in their wives an appropriate way to deal with female disobedience.

The concept of gender violence, rather than violence against women, expands awareness of gender and violence to include violence against men. Shanti Parikh's work in this volume on statutory rape in Uganda finds that the two problems are closely linked. She shows how legislation intended to protect young girls from older "sugar daddies" has been coopted by parents seeking to prohibit daughters from having class-inappropriate boyfriends. Parikh argues that the legislation has served to reinforce the patriarchal system in Uganda in which old males have control over young men as well as women. Meanwhile the older men who were the intended targets of the legislation are able to buy their way out of court, leaving young men as the major recipients of punishment.

## MARKETS AND COMMUNITIES: NCS RESEARCH

Market capitalism, accentuated by globalization, has provided women workers with choices, resources, and elevated status at home that they did not have before. Four of the NCS Scholars examined women migrants working in urban factories or households abroad, in China, Nepal, Saudi Arabia, Spain, and the U.S. Esther Chow's interviews, reported in this volume, found that rural migrants working in South Chinese factories are generally satisfied with their jobs, while those who have returned to the village plan to go back to the work when possible. Migration enabled them to escape patriarchal constraints on marriage choices or living with an oppressive mother-in-law. Similarly, Gioconda Herrara reported that Ecuadorian immigrants to Spain and the U.S. enjoyed more decision-making authority at home due to the resources they were able to contribute.[35]

However, opportunities for women are severely diminished by patriarchy and gender biases that are compatible with market-driven development. Governments specifically recruit women as migrants because they are preferred by employers who see women as docile, low-wage producers. Women factory workers in Nepal are concentrated in low-pay, less-productive jobs with extremely unfavorable working conditions. As Meena Acharya concludes, women are integrated into the global system at the bottom as the most disadvantaged workers with no rights nor security of employment. One of the reasons women are available for this work in Nepal is that the continuing system of dowry makes families withdraw their daughters from education to avoid the higher costs of educated wives for the husband.[36] She concludes that the global marketplace in Nepal works hand in hand with restrictions on women's opportunities. For women to benefit from the market, the ideology of patriarchy must be confronted directly.[37]

Governments recruit women for domestic service abroad to relieve job pressures at home and to secure remittances. In the receiving country these migrants are inserted into racialized and gendered spaces in the labor force. Herrara's study of Ecuadorian women migrants to Spain and the U.S. found that the Catholic Church provides their main access to the larger society, acting as an employment agency for that preserve cultural identity. In these ways the church reinforces the boundaries of domestic workers and as a sponsor of the Virgin processions that preserve cultural identity. In these ways the church reinforces the boundaries of domestic roles rather than facilitating broader social mobility and civic participation.[38]

Governments may not provide migrant women workers with equal citizenship even within national boundaries. In China, the government recognizes two tiers of citizenship based on the household registration system established during the socialist period to control labor and population movement. The system distinguishes between urban locals and rural migrants in their rights to education, social insurance, and other services. It places much greater burdens on women than men because women are responsible for family maintenance and children's schooling and because they are vulnerable to gender-based abuse in spaces neglected by the state.[39] In Saudi Arabia, as Rachel Silvey reports in this volume, Indonesian women working as domestic servants are denied protection by the Indonesian government that recruited them, for the consulates abroad are loathe to offer shelter or other services in cases of employer abuse. The Indonesian government established a special airport terminal to protect them from hustlers preying upon their cash as they return home, but this has become a site of concentrated harassment. Silvey argues that monitoring the migrants in gender-specific ways at the terminal reinforces their subordinate gender and class status as less then rights-bearing citizens.[40]

Perhaps the most challenging critique is Lingam's study, in this volume, of micro-credit programs in South India. These programs are often hailed as a solution to the dual goals of empowering women and spreading capitalism to the poor.[41] She found micro-credit did offer the women limited ways of mitigating poverty and achieving some impact on village affairs. But the meager funds brought in by micro-credit programs do little to address the despair brought by drought and indebtedness in a region where small farmers had overinvested in commercial cropping encouraged by neoliberal agricultural policy. Numbers of farmers have committed suicide while most others dream of urban migration to escape the crisis in agriculture. The empowerment of women in a region that has been systematically disempowered has little meaning. Her study serves as a corrective to those who have argued that micro-credit is the silver bullet against poverty.

The disempowering effect of the global economy and its attendant liberal ideology is reported by the NCS Scholars working on HIV/AIDS in Africa. Because neoliberalism emphasizes individual solutions over community efforts, the focus of the international campaign against HIV is on individuals changing their behavior. This ignores women's limited control over their sexuality, which makes it impossible for them to refuse sexual relationships embedded in marital or community norms. The NCS Scholars argue, "The unrelenting spread of HIV in Africa is much more complicated than early sex, too much sex, infidelity, and lack of condom use."[42] Gender power relations and cultural expectations must be addressed in any proposed solution to the HIV/AIDS crisis.[43]

These scholars also analyzed the impact of global mass media in disrupting local patterns of sexual learning in Africa. Whereas young people formerly learned intertwined lessons about sexual risk and pleasure through a specific person in the kinship system, they are now inundated by messages of rampant sexuality. Global corporations working in African mines, oil fields, plantations, and tourism fuel a system of continual labor migration with long-term spousal separation, feeding the casual sex industry. The NCS Scholars argue that lack of corporate responsibility to the south has enabled companies to ignore their role in spreading HIV and responsibility to assist in ameliorating its effects (Epstein and Kim, 2007).

Three studies show how international sponsorship of values and policies supportive of women's empowerment has been thwarted or altered by local power structures. Parikh's study of statutory rape legislation in Uganda, discussed above, shows how global initiatives have been coopted to strengthen patriarchal controls over adolescents, both male and female. Ewig's study of family planning in Peru in this volume shows how President Alberto Fujimori used global feminist discourse about reproductive rights to cloak a traditional population control program. Claiming to be implementing the UN Cairo document on reproductive rights, he enlisted feminists to monitor the Peruvian program, a tactic that hid the program's abuse of poor indigenous women in family planning clinics. Ironically, feminist critics of the program eventually found an ally in the Catholic Church that is itself no opponent of patriarchy.

Haney, noted above, describes how the neoliberal version of empowerment in women's prisons is resisted by the Hungarian prison staff. They have reinterpreted the word empowerment to mean not self-management, but integration of inmates into the social institutions of work and family. Their program of social education, supervised labor, and assistance with personal needs was reminiscent of the state socialist system that has officially been replaced by capitalism. Prison officials explained to Haney that women had "special" needs and could not be treated like men.

In these various contexts, the Scholars' investigations revealed numerous gendered tensions within capitalism, deriving from the failure of capitalism to alter patriarchal values and the instrumental use of patriarchal structures to achieve capitalist goals. The opposition between markets and community, as set out in theory, looks much murkier on the ground.

What is the alternative? Does a politics based in community—religious, nationalist, ethnic, or socialist—promise support for women's functioning and address the hidden discrimination embedded in liberal politics? Several NCS Scholars examined various forms of community-based politics to evaluate this possibility.

Agot's paper noted above shows the costs to women of staying integrated into the Luo community in Kenya. Placing vulnerable widows under protection of a male may preserve their reputation and provide economic support but at the cost of autonomy and increasingly, health. However, many of these women describe themselves as choosing to be inherited, suggesting that choice has little meaning in a situation where options are few.

The NCS Scholars examined women's agency in the context of African masculinities. African women, they found, are generally portrayed as voiceless victims lacking agency, or acting agents lacking rationality. African men, on the other hand, are commonly depicted as hypersexualized, making interventions necessary to "save the African female from the Black male" (Epstein and Kim, 2007). The scholars argue that this formulation ignores the many reasons that women might choose sexual activity. Condoms might not seem rational to a newly married couple for whom reproduction is an important family obligation and a public symbol of marital happiness. Nor are they emotionally rational when condomless sex is seen as proof of faithfulness, romantic investment, and emotional commitment. These situations show how high the costs of relationships and community can be to women's health.

Can women make autonomous choices in highly charged situations where group identity is at stake? Loenen's examination of the headscarf ruling in Europe, noted above, found that the Court's decision assumes that women are passive bearers of culture and religion, ignoring the possibility that they individually make the choice to be active keepers of their community's identity. NCS Scholar Rabab Abdulhadi's research asked why women join national liberation movements, which are often seen as inherently masculinist, hegemonic, and given to using women as allegorical symbols of national difference.[44] Rejecting the view that women militants are merely dupes of charismatic men, she interprets the Palestinian movement as a social movement community offering space for many kinds of oppositional cultures, including women's collective action. Its fluid authority structure and boundaries enabled groups organized around various categories of difference to find greater equality and horizontal comradeship, a form of left communitarianism. Similarly, during the Eritrean War of Independence, women took on new roles and became engaged in public events according to NCS Scholar Amanuel Asghedom's study, a transformative change that far exceeded the level of transformation in the larger society.[45]

In post-liberation consolidation, still incomplete in Palestine, institutionalization of the national and collective identity has happened at the cost of women's autonomy. Radical grassroots groups pressing for large-scale transformation in Palestine have found an inhospitable environment, while in Eritrea women feel betrayed by the government's reluctance to provide mechanisms to sustain their new status. International organizations assisting in post-war reconstruction gave lip service to women's empowerment but failed to provide frameworks on the ground. The new international norms developed during the UN Decade for Women and subsequent conferences have not been honored in the Eritrean case, nor has left communitarianism survived in Palestine.

Established religious communities have generally been seen as patriarchal, but two scholars, both in this volume, documented women finding transformative potential in religion. As noted above, Maher shows how a feminist re-reading of the Bible enabled women to reject religious bases for male privilege and resist the growing feminicide in Honduras. Margot Badran reports in this volume how Muslim women activists in northern Nigeria organized legal defense teams well-equipped in Islamic jurisprudence to argue before higher shari'ah courts for acquittals of two women condemned to death for *zina* (adultery), winning acquittals in both cases. Muslim and Christian women coalesced around these cases within the Islamic court system, showing how activists of different religious affiliations can work together to promote gender justice.

A key resource for the empowerment was the leadership of feminist religious scholars in Islam and Christianity. Responding to the same social and intellectual currents that inspired the human rights claims of international feminism, scholarship in the textual origins of their faiths enabled the religious communities of women to articulate claims for equality and social justice in the language and doctrines of faith. It shows the shared commitment to equality between left communitarianism and liberal feminism.

The research also provides important insight into the possibilities of community-based politics. Contrary to the essentialism of interpretations often made by outsiders, communities are not homogeneous nor is their culture static. The experience of these women's religious communities show how identities like religion and culture may be renegotiated by women who have the space, collective solidarity, and intellectual resources to do so.

These examples provide the basis for new thinking about the nature of citizenship within community. The NCS Scholars suggested that the concept of citizenship be extended beyond the traditional notion of an individual's relationship to the state (NCS Scholars, 2005). Especially for women, there is no clear boundary between public and private domains, so confining citizenship to the public sphere fails to capture their experience or their goals. The scholars therefore defined citizenship as full and equal membership in a variety of collectivities: family, ethnic group, religious community, civil society, etc. Citizenship stands at the intersection of attention to gender, class, and ethnic inequalities. This provides a way of assessing women's membership in communities as well as in liberal democratic politics.

What have we learned about markets, community, and empowerment? This essay has emphasized the importance of context-specific investigation, but the following general points stand out.

Globalization—as trade, the spread of market-based production and new communication technologies—provides women access to universal human rights discourse and to notions of equal citizenship that are familiar in western societies. But market ideology fails to recognize work that is outside the market and ignores the unequal ways in which women enter the marketplace. The individualism inherent in the market perspective diminishes commitment to collective solutions, leaving each woman alone to solve her problems.

Communities provide women solidarity and support, but historically and today, women become symbols of national and cultural resistance at the price of their interests and personal autonomy. Socialist communities did not eliminate patriarchal values and resistance movements tend to drop support for transformative gender relations when faced with nation-building. Finally, community-based politics masks inequality and conflict over resources, shifting political discourse away from economics in favor of identity, and often charismatic leadership, over democratic representation.

This distinction between markets and community is a binary that does not adequately capture what happens in most women's lives. We have seen that market-based systems, such as neoliberal globalization, utilize patriarchal structures to recruit and discipline the labor force, while transnational networks of women in Muslim societies make claims for women's rights and reach out to international feminists. Setting out this binary has, however, provided a useful lens for discerning trade-offs and tensions which, left unacknowledged, create the worst situation for women. They are left with assumptions of equality that do not exist in market economics, socialist communities nor traditional communities.

The volume also critiques the binary between local and global that pervades the literature on globalization (Grewal and Kaplan, 1994). This literature tends to assign global or cosmopolitan modes to the global North and local communitarian ways of living to the global South. Within the global/local binary, local communities are generally seen to be more authentic, egalitarian, and humane. Neither generalization captures the complexities women face. We have seen how the language of human rights was used in Europe to essentialize Islam, and how local communities perpetuate class, gender, and other hierarchies. The conflicts among castes in India and ethnic groups in many societies challenge *prima facie* valorization of the local.

But let us not be disheartened by contrasting recalcitrant problems of the present with imaginary ideals—patriarchal traditions that truly value women; a role for the state requiring resources that state-run development cannot not produce; small scale economies that support large-scale societies; empowered women constantly on the alert to support claims for social justice. This volume provides some guidance for devising ambitious but workable strategies:

- Empowerment programs for grassroots women need to be supported by changes in the community and in structures in national and international arenas.
- Access to material resources must be accompanied by ideological challenge to the legitimacy of structures of domination, including gender, caste, ethnicity and class.
- Commitments to women's rights and equality by national governments, the UN system and transnational feminist movements within Islam and other international communities need to be supported by institutions, personnel training, budgets, and procedures for accountability.
- The costs of family and community-sustaining activities to women's health and well-being should be reduced by providing them with support and alternative ways of fulfilling their responsibilities. Such policies should be an intrinsic part of strategies to deliver equality in education, the workplace, and public life.
- Exploitation of workers in factory work and the informal labor market should be countered by promoting national legislation, international standards, and union organizing. Workers and communities severely disadvantaged by the new economy should receive support for the transition.
- Efforts to reconfigure models of community away from patriarchy and toward equality along the axes of gender, class, race, etc. deserve support and encouragement in local and national communities.
- Strategies to limit the spread of HIV/AIDS should incorporate recognition of gender inequality, sexual desire, and needs for intimacy.

Finally, let us reflect on often unadmitted tensions in feminist theory that are revealed by these studies:[46]

- We feminists argue for an increase in women's rights yet are critical of the market, which is associated historically and philosophically with the concept of individual rights.

- We argue against essentialism and tradition in favor of making individual choice and motivation a measure of the "rightness" of any policy or ideology, yet are critical of individualism as a basis for public policy.
- We argue against universalism in favor of "local understandings," without recognizing the fruitfulness of the conflict between them.
- We support the empowerment of women but criticize decisions of women who join right- wing movements
- We recognize that the consequences for women of choosing empowerment may be very high in personal terms, but are critical of micro-credit programs and employment opportunities that may provide them greater autonomy.

This is not to charge feminist theory with timidity or groupthink, but to set out an agenda of work and advocacy to make fine distinctions, evaluate moral choices, avoid false dichotomies and offer alternatives that can be achieved.

## ORGANIZATION OF THE VOLUME

The findings reported here emerge from several sources in the NCS program: Papers collected in this volume, summaries of individual research submitted to the program that did not result in papers for the volume but may be published elsewhere, and written reports by subgroups during the program seminars. The chapters that follow are all by scholars in the NCS Program, though not all the participants were able to contribute chapters. A listing of all the participants and their projects is at the end of the book. Except for two chapters, this material is being published for the first time.

This collection is noteworthy not only for the intrinsic interest of each piece but also for how effectively the chapters speak to the collective themes of the volume. This is the result of the many hours of discussion and joint drafting of statements during the meetings of the program. The coherence, if not agreement, is especially notable given the broad representation of scholars from almost every region of the globe. Among the NCS Scholars we found near unanimity about feminist goals. The most difficult discussions were about differences in interpretations of language arising from the political and feminist histories in various contexts. We found, for example, that the term "post-communist" carries different meanings and normative connotations in the various countries of Eastern Europe and is ultimately rejected by those that do not read their history as having been truly communist. Similarly, multiculturalism proved to be a contentious term because it is seen by the Arab diaspora in the U.S. as having validated their concerns, language, etc., whereas in the Caribbean it has been used to justify group hierarchies. All of us became more aware of how we have been individually shaped by the political histories of our communities and their trajectories of feminism.

As notable is the array of disciplines represented. The collection includes pieces by two lawyers, two public health professionals, a historian, and scholars of religion and cultural studies, as well as ten social scientists in six disciplines. These various disciplines draw on different bodies of theory, examine different kinds of evidence, strike different balances between theory and data, and use different methodologies and modes of presentation. The articles may be read for what they reveal about their disciplines as well as their substantive contributions to understanding of empowerment. What some readers may miss is the heavy emphasis on theory that has become standard in many disciplines. To make the collection accessible to undergraduates, the authors in this collection were specifically encouraged to downplay, though not neglect, the theoretical context of their problem and emphasize case study material.

The volume is divided into four sections that correlate with the four topical subgroups in which the NCS Scholars worked: Globalization and Neoliberal Governance, Politicized Religions and Citizenship, Gender Violence and Masculinities, and Sexual Autonomy and Global Politics. Due to the international nature of the volume, the references follow several different bibliographical styles.

## NOTES

1. I wish to thank the publisher's anonymous reviewers for many substantive comments that guided the introduction. Jane S. Jaquette and Margot Badran read several drafts and contributed immensely to the final result. Responsibility for errors and any provocation, reasonable or not, "engendered" by this essay is mine.
2. The term "liberal" is used here in the original sense of liberation, not the later U.S. usage identifying liberals with the welfare state. See Terence Ball and Richard Dagger, *Political Ideologies and the Democratic Ideal* (New York: Harper Collins, 1991).
3. Asher Horowitz and Gad Horowitz, *"Everywhere They Are in Chains:" Political Theory from Rousseau to Marx* (Scarborough, Ontario: Nelson Canada, 1988).
4. For a contemporary communitarian proposal for U.S. politics, see Michael J. Sandel, *Democracy's Discontents* (Cambridge, MA: Harvard University Press, 1996).
5. For a review of the reservations placed by states on the main human rights instrument for women, CEDAW, see Shaheen Sardar Ali, "Women's Rights CEDAW and International Human Rights Debates: Toward Empowerment?" in *Rethinking Empowerment: Gender and Development in a Global/local World,* eds. Jane L. Parpart, Shirin Rai, and Kathleen Staudt (NY: Routledge, 2002), hereafter cited in text as Ali (2002).
6. Jane Jaquette was very helpful in formulating an approach to left communitarianism in the essay.
7. Susan Moller Okin, *Justice, Gender and the Family* (New York: Basic Books, 1999); Naila Kabeer, *Reversed Realities: Gender Hierarchies in Development Thought* (London: Verso Press, 1994) has a good chapter on intra-household power relationships.

8. Margaret E. Keck and Kathryn Sikkink, *Activists Beyond Borders: Advocacy Networks in International Politics* (Ithaca, NY: Cornell University Press, 1998).

9. Nira Yuval-Davis, "Women, Citizenship and Difference," *Feminist Review 57* (1997): 4–28.

10. Valentine M. Moghadam, ed., *Identity Politics and Women: Cultural Reassertions and Feminisms in International Perspective* (Boulder: Westview Press, 1994).

11. Inderpal Grewal and Caren Kaplan, "Introduction: Transnational Feminist Practices and Questions of Postmodernity." *Scattered Hegemonies: Postmodernity and Transnational Feminist Practices* (Minneapolis: University of Minnesota Press, 1994): 17; hereafter cited in text as Grewal and Kaplan (1994).

12. See the discussion of "scattered hegemonies" in Grewal and Kaplan (1994): 17.

13. Isabella Bakker, ed., *The Strategic Silence: Gender and Economic Policy* (London: Zed Books, 1994).

14. Structural adjustment generally has three components: reducing inflation, privatization, and free trade. Neoliberal policy is not against social services per se. The policy opposes inflation, which is caused by state spending not backed up by taxes. In Asia, where inflation was not an issue, structural adjustment did not have the same drastic effects. (Personal communication with Jane Jaquette, January 2007.)

15. Christina Ewig, "Reproduction, Re-reform and the Reconfigured State: Feminists and Neoliberal Health Reforms in Chile." In *Social Reproduction and Global Transformations: From the Everyday to the Global,* eds. Isabella Bakker and Rachel Silvey (NY: Routledge, forthcoming).

16. For a contrary argument against viewing factory labor as exploitation see Linda Lim, "Women's Work in Export Factories: The Politics of a Cause." In *Persistent Inequalities: Women and World Development,* ed. Irene Tinker (New York: Oxford University Press, 1990).

17. Women Living Under Muslim Laws, "Plan of Action—Senegal 2006." WLUML Publications, accessed on the web, January 21, 2007. See also Valentine M. Moghadam, *Globalizing Women: Transnational Feminist Networks* (Baltimore: Johns Hopkins Press, 2005). Ali (2002): 69 discusses the commitment to international human rights instruments made by Islamic women parliamentarians in their Islamabad Declaration of 1995.

18. Maria Floro and Hella Hoppe, "Towards Globalization with a Human Face: Engendering Policy Coherence for Development." In *Social Reproduction and Global Transformation: From the Everyday to the Global,* eds. Isabella Bakker and Rachel Silvey (NY: Routledge, forthcoming).

19. "These pressures do not necessarily bring adherence to a fully conservative politics, however, as demonstrated by contrasting views of the market in Eastern Europe (pro-market) and Iran and the Taliban (market skepticism)." Jane Jaquette, personal communication, January 2007.

20. Gita Sen and Caren Grown, *Development Crises and Alternative Visions: Third World Women's Perspectives* (New York: Monthly Review Press, 1987). Margot Badran points out that U.S. feminists in the 1970s were holding conferences on women and power, and readily agreed with third world women at the 1985 UN Conference on Women in Nairobi in calling for women's empowerment.

21. Ruth Alsop and Nina Heinsohn, "Measuring Empowerment in Practice: Structuring Analysis and Framing Indicators." *World Bank Policy Research Working Paper 3510* (February 2005); hereafter cited in text as Alsop and Heinsohn (2005).

22. Jane L. Parpart, Shirin Rai, and Kathleen A. Staudt, *Rethinking Empowerment, Gender and Development in a Global/local World* (New York: Routledge, 2002): 3; hereafter cited in text as Parpart, Rai, and Staudt (2002).
23. Caroline Moser, *Gender Planning and Development: Theory, Practice and Training* (New York: Routledge, 1993).
24. Esther Chow, "Gender Matters," *International Journal of Sociology* 18 (September 2003): 443–60.
25. For the classic discussion of this concept see Joan Wallach Scott, "Gender: A Useful Category of Analysis." In *Feminism and History*, Joan Wallach Scott, ed. (Oxford: Oxford University Press, 1996).
26. Martha Nussbaum, *Women and Human Development: The Capabilities Approach* (Cambridge: Cambridge University Press, 2000).
27. For an extensive consideration of possible indicators, see Alsop and Heinsohn (2005).
28. Naila Kabeer, *Inclusive Citizenship: Meanings and Expressions* (New York: Zed Press, 2005).
29. Jane S. Jaquette and Kathleen A. Staudt, "Gender and Politics in U.S. Population Policy." In *Political Interests of Gender,* eds. Kathleen Jones and Anna Jonasdottir (London: Sage Press, 1998).
30. Tanika Sarkar and Urvashi Butalia, eds., *Women and Right-Wing Movements: Indian Experiences* (London: Zed Books, 1996).
31. Naila Kabeer, *The Power to Choose: Bangladesh Women and Labour Market Decisions in London and Dhaka* (London: Verso, 2000). See also James C. Scott, *Weapons of the Weak: Everyday Forms of Peasant Resistance* (New Haven, CT and London: Yale University Press, 1985).
32. Grace Clement, *Care, Autonomy and Justice: Feminism and the Ethic of Care* (Boulder, CO: Westview Press, 1996) explores the debate between the ethics of justice (equality and individualism) and care (relationships) in moral philosophy.
33. Sylvia Chant, "Contributions of a Gender Perspective to the Analysis of Poverty." In *Women and Gender Equity in Development Theory and Practice: Institutions, Resources and Mobilization,* eds. Jane S. Jaquette and Gale Summerfield (Durham, NC: Duke University Press, 2006); hereafter cited in text as Chant (2006).
34. Susan Brownmiller, *Against Our Will: Men, Women and Rape* (New York: Simon and Schuster, 1976) discusses the prevalence of rape.
35. Gioconda Herrara, "States, Work and Social Reproduction through the Lens of Migrant Experience: Ecuadorian Domestic Workers in Madrid" in Bakker and Silvey. Hereafter cited in text as Herrara.
36. Meena Acharya, "Global Integration of Subsistence Economies and Womens' Empowerment: An Experience from Nepal" in Bakker and Silvey.
37. Chant (2006): 101 makes the same point in her review of the field of gender and poverty studies.
38. Herrara.
39. Esther Ngan-ling Chow, "The Citizenship Divide: The Politics of Space and Activism: The Organizing of Migrant Workers in Urban China." Paper presented at RC-32, Research Committee on Women in Society at the ISA World Congress of Sociology, Durban, South Africa, July 2006.
40. The analysis of the terminal is in Rachel Silvey, "Managing Migration: Reproducing Gendered Insecurity at the Indonesian Border." in Bakker and Silvey.
41. Mohammed Younus of the Grameen Bank won the Nobel Peace Prize in 2006 for his work with micro-credit in Bangladesh.
42. Sexuality Health Group Final NCS Plenary Presentation, "Using Feminist Critiques of Human Rights and Sexual Autonomy to Assess and Inform HIV/AIDS Interventions," New York, April 2005.

43. Helen Epstein and Julia Kim, "AIDS and the Power of Women," *New York Review of Books* (February 15, 2007): 39–41; hereafter cited in text as Epstein and Kim (2007).
44. NCS Scholars, "Final Presentation: Negotiating Citizenship and Diversity: Gender, Nation, Diaspora," New York, April 2005; hereafter cited in text as NCS Scholars (2005).
45. Amanuel Andebrhan Asghedom, "The Impact of War on the Role of Women," unpublished paper presented to Fulbright NCS Program, April 2005.
46. I am indebted to Jane Jaquette for suggesting this line of thinking. Personal communication, January 2007.

# Part I
# Globalization and Neoliberal Governance

# 1 Competing Empowerments
## Gender and Neoliberal Punishment in the East and West

*Lynne Haney*[1]

Like many politicized terms, "neoliberalism" evokes multiple meanings and associations. Most often, it is understood as an economic project of deregulation, privatization, and marketization. Yet neoliberalism also encompasses particular forms of governance—patterns of power and regulation that shape, guide, and manage social conduct.[2] In fact, one distinctive aspect of neoliberalism is the way it combines and coordinates economic, political, and social programs. Along with economic deregulation come calls for the scaling back of state support and assistance; along with economic marketization comes a mandate to end many social programs and entitlements; and along with economic privatization comes a shift away from public responsibility and toward "self-governance." In this way, the socioeconomic projects of neoliberalism are frequently promoted as empowerment projects—that is, as designed to enhance the participation and freedom of everyone from women to immigrants to welfare recipients to prisoners to the urban poor.[3]

It is precisely this promise of empowerment that makes neoliberal forms of governance so effective and resonant. It is also what gives them their ability to travel across national borders and become integral to institutional change in a variety of contexts. This has certainly been the case in Eastern Europe, which has proven particularly susceptible to neoliberal claims of empowerment. In part, this is because they mesh so well with the post-1989 regional narrative of freedom. In this story, East Europeans weathered decades of state-socialist overregulation and paternalism before being freed to privatize, marketize, and self-govern. And while social scientists tend to resist the triumphant quality of this story, they have centered on the triumph of neoliberal policies and discourses. So the enactment of reforms to liberalize and privatize national economies are viewed as examples of the region's "rapid and strong embrace of neoliberalism"[4] and the scaling back of state is presented as an example of neoliberal welfare reform.[5] Even the rhetoric used by East Europeans to talk about the transition is framed as the victory of neoliberal narratives of the past and future.[6]

Yet just as neoliberalism is more than an economic project, its effects are felt more widely than in national-level policy and public discourse. By confining themselves to the world of policy analysis, expert discourse, and political rhetoric, social scientists have avoided venturing out into the messy, and often chaotic, lives of existing institutions. As a result, they have focused on explaining neoliberalism's regional triumph instead of deconstructing the complex meanings attached to it and the responses elicited by it. To understand the latter we would need accounts of diverse societal spaces and the concrete institutional interactions within them. And we would need to be open to the possibility that neoliberal models might be accepted or contested, reproduced or rejected in these spaces.

In this paper, I provide an account of one such space: the post-socialist penal system. Interestingly, the story I tell is not of the championing of neoliberal notions of empowerment but of doubting and being skeptical towards them. In fact, the degree of skepticism I uncovered surprised me. Having spent the better part of the 1990s analyzing the development of the Hungarian welfare system and the deep imprint neoliberalism left on it, I expected to encounter similar patterns in other state systems (Haney, 2002). Thus, when I began ethnographic research in Hungary's largest women's prison a decade later, I was prepared to find the reproduction of "neoliberal penality."[7] Signs of such reproduction appeared to be everywhere: from the huge increase in Hungarian incarceration rates to its media's fixation with crime and punishment to lawmakers' preoccupation with disciplining the seemingly undisciplined. Yet once I entered an actual carceral institution, I discovered a penal system that seemed like a throwback in time, operating as if it had been untouched by the global discourses on punishment. Thus I was left with a case not of the reproduction of neoliberal governance, but of its failure—a case not of the acceptance of neoliberal empowerment claims, but of their transformation and mutation. This paper describes what this mutation process looked like and what it implies for theories of gender and neoliberal governance.[8]

More specifically, the paper begins with an analysis of neoliberal penality in the U.S. and Western Europe—its emergence in the U.S. penal system and its migration to parts of Europe. I then describe the discourses and practices at work in the Hungarian penal system, revealing how they emphasized a form of rehabilitation that diverged from neoliberal punishment models and promises of empowerment. Hungarian prison officials countered these models and promises with their own notions of social empowerment that were drawn from state-socialist ideals of social integration and gender difference. Through a case study of a Hungarian women's prison, I draw out some of the complexities and contradictions too often obscured by narrow conceptions of neoliberalism—complexities that remind us how, as global forms of governance circulate across locales, they must be filtered through real institutions and how, in the process, they often evoke contestation and subversion.

## NEOLIBERAL EMPOWERMENT: INDIVIDUALIZATION
## AND RESPONSIBILIZATION

Although the contours of neoliberal governance are not always consistent or coherent, they are characterized by a few common features. At the level of state structure, neoliberal regimes often combine the public and private in new ways. Their policies and practices operate increasingly through private institutions and actors—as evidenced in the rise of for-profit welfare agencies, private or "faith-based" prisons, school "choice," and the privatization of social security. Neoliberal governance also works through intermediary associations, frequently disguised as "non-governmental organizations." As a result, we now have a slew of "community-based" groups taking responsibility for everything from education to social policy to policing to imprisonment. Political theorist Nikolas Rose (1999) articulates this shift best when he argues that advanced liberalism rests on "governance from a distance": By moving the state from the foreground to the background, it creates an impression of the state's disappearance. Yet this is merely an illusion. Neoliberalism is not a project of less government but of government redeployed—of governance through privatization and community.

Accompanying these new structures of governance is a distinctive governmental focus and agenda. Here too, Rose (1999) puts it quite well when he claims that contemporary governance seeks to "responsibilize" and "entrepreneurialize" its subjects. This is achieved through techniques that seem to emphasize autonomy and choice—or the need for self-inspection, self-management, and ultimately self-empowerment. Thus, the state identifies which social groups are unable to self-govern and then enmeshes them in policies and practices to teach self-preservation.[9] This is where entrepreneurialization comes in: State intervention becomes an enterprise in retraining and reskilling the seemingly untrained and unskilled. So rather than evaluating state policies in terms of their ability to alleviate social problems, justifications revolve around cost-benefit calculations. Do welfare-to-work programs give us more bang-for-the-buck than AFDC benefits did? Are alternative-to-incarceration programs more cost-effective than traditional imprisonment? Will private social security accounts give people the choice to better invest in their futures? Again, the goal is self-empowerment through the individualizing of social responsibility and the entrepreneurializing of citizens.

Because of its focus on retraining and reskilling, neoliberal governance has quite concrete implications for state institutions. These implications have been examined most extensively in the welfare arena, with numerous scholars analyzing the global scaling back of social assistance and entitlements as an example of neoliberal governance at work.[10] More recently, social scientists have begun to theorize neoliberal penality—that is, how state systems of punishment also reflect elements of neoliberal governance.[11] Recognizing that incarceration rates have soared in those countries most influenced by neoliberal policies, these scholars view imprisonment as a key technique of rule. While the social state may have responded to economic marginalization through redistributive policies, the neoliberal state does so by putting the marginalized behind bars.[12] In perhaps the clearest articulation of this argument, Wacquant claims that, in the United States, neoliberalism has bred the "penalization of poverty" through a carceral machine designed to neutralize those rejected by the deregulated service economy.[13] In doing so, U.S. penal institutions "contain the disorders produced by mass unemployment, the imposition of precarious salaried work, and the shrinking of social protection" (Wacquant, 2001: 3).

In addition to using incarceration as a response to social insecurity, neoliberal penality implies a particular approach to the socially insecure once they are imprisoned. If neoliberal governance does indeed seek to responsibilize and entrepreneurialize, where better to achieve this than in prison—where there is, quite literally, a captive audience? So just as welfare agencies in the U.S. now glorify personal responsibility and pathologize dependency, its penal institutions set out to teach the tools of self-governance.[14] As a result, we get prison programs to fix U.S. inmates' attitudes and psychological problems.[15] We get the introduction of private industries in U.S. prisons, even of private prisons, touted as cost-effective ways to enhance personal responsibility—or, as the California Joint Venture Program promised, to instill a "work ethic in idle prisoners" (California Department of Corrections, 1994). And we get the emergence of all kinds of counseling programs to address the many addictions that U.S. inmates presumably have, thus preparing them to be self-reliant upon release.[16] In these ways, neoliberal penality differs from rehabilitative corrections: by replacing the "social" with the "self," it shifts focus from inmates' social problems and societal integration to their personal pathologies and self-help. Neoliberal penality thus embodies and elaborates on key elements of contemporary governance. And it often does so by promising to empower those it targets.

This institutional focus on empowerment is particularly pronounced in U.S. penal institutions for women. Perhaps this is because female inmates are still viewed as less culpable than their male counterparts. Or perhaps it is because many find it distasteful to punish and condemn women. Whatever the reason, the discourses and practices of neoliberal empowerment pervade female penal institutions—from their use of "therapeutic communities" that emphasize inmates' "true selves" to their discourses of recovery that focus on freeing inmates from their addictions and vices.[17] Somewhat paradoxically, this has led to a convergence in the form and focus of male and female prisons. Once upon a time, the U.S. penal system constructed women's and men's problems as vastly different; it viewed women as having special needs that should be met through the "feminine" treatment of reformatories as opposed to the "masculine" handling of penitentiaries.[18] Yet with the new focus on self-governance and empowerment, this gendered logic has begun to break down. The result is what Meda Chesney-Lind (1995) calls "equality with a vengeance": a penal system in which women are also responsibilized, entrepreneurialized, and held accountable for societal problems.[19] Thus, like their male counterparts, female inmates in the U.S. frequently encounter programs that try to break them down in order to rebuild them, all the while claiming to empower them and instill self-esteem where there once was none.[20]

Without question, neoliberal penality originated in the U.S. penal system and finds its clearest contemporary expression there.[21] Yet, as with so many U.S. products, these penal policies and practices have become a key export, making their way east to Europe, north to Canada, and south to Latin America. Their channels of migration exemplify a key element of neoliberal governance: Less likely to be relayed through state-to-state exchanges, these penal models often travel through expert systems, think tanks, and NGOs. For instance, in one of the only accounts of this import-export process, Wacquant (2001) suggests that neoliberal penality entered Britain through workshops and training sessions organized by NGOs and academic groups.[22] Something similar occurred in France, where state-funded organizations brought in a similar cast of characters to hold training seminars and to produce reform proposals. And while the ultimate effects of these exchanges remain to be seen, Hannah-Moffat (2001) reveals that many of them were instituted a bit closer to their home: in Canadian women's prisons, which recently embarked on reforms designed to be more responsive to women's needs and increase their self-esteem. Her account of this reform process reads like a textbook case of neoliberal penality—with an NGO task force creating a reform program, appropriately called "Creating Choices," that gave rise to the governance of women through individualizing strategies and claims of empowerment.

Given that these channels of discursive migration seem to flow through Western Europe and North America in an almost unobstructed way, we might expect their circulation to be equally unrestricted in other regions—particularly in areas like Eastern Europe, which tend to be more vulnerable to global pressures. Indeed, since 1989 the floodgates of international exchange have opened and through these gates came U.S. and West European experts set on teaching East Europeans how to reform their social institutions. In Hungary, many of them were criminologists who held workshops on the theory and practice of neoliberal penality. Some of these exchanges did seem to shape national-level discourse about crime and punishment, prompting state officials to promise to get "tough on crime" and increase "personal responsibility." Thus, as in Western Europe and North America, the Hungarian signs seemed to point to the diffusion of neoliberal discourses of punishment.

Yet the real test of this diffusion is not simply whether neoliberal discourses surfaced in political appeals or ideological gestures—it is the extent to which they shaped penal institutions and practices. This is a much more difficult test as, at the institutional level, neoliberal punishment models must be filtered through the lives of real people and contend with their interests and imaginations. Do the concrete practices of the Hungarian penal system reflect the emphases of neoliberal penality? Do they try to individualize and entreprenualize their female charges? Do they promise to empower them? And do they imagine empowerment as self-management and self-governance?

## (POST)SOCIALIST EMPOWERMENT: INSTITUTIONAL REHABILITATION AND INTEGRATION

With these questions in mind, I set off to study the institutional practices of the largest women's prison in Hungary. Located in the small town of Kalocsa, the prison houses over 400 inmates, half of the prison system's female population. The prison is Hungary's only maximum-security facility for women.[23] It sits in the center of town, just off the main square, in an old baroque building. On the outside, there is no indication it is a prison. In fact, the building looks like it could be a museum. As I would come to learn, the prison did have museum-like qualities, displaying artifacts from a bygone era.

When I first entered the prison, I was immediately struck by the color of the inmates' uniforms: Some were blue, others green, and others had black and white stripes. Hastily, I assumed I had found my first piece of evidence of neoliberal penality, concluding that, like in some U.S. prisons, the uniforms denoted the inmates' crimes and security risk. Moreover, as in the U.S., I interpreted this color-coding as key way the prison categorized and controlled its inmates.[24] But by the end of the day, the first of many assumptions proved to be false: The inmates' uniforms did not designate their level of security but rather the kind of work they were engaged in. In effect, they offered a visual representation of inmates' positions in the prison's world of work.

Both of these initial observations—of the prisons' central location and of the inmates' uniforms—ended up being quite symbolic of the prison's institutional focus. From the highest- to lowest-level prison employee, I was told that the purpose of incarceration was to rehabilitate and empower. But their understanding of empowerment was quite different from the definition implied by neoliberal penality. Instead of emphasizing self-governance and self-management, the Hungarian prison staff stressed inmates' integration into the institutions of work and family. Moreover, they believed it was their job to be involved in all aspects of inmates' lives and relationships. For them, inmates' needs were social and their responsibility was to care for them. And they did this through practices that centered on wage labor and social education.

### Freedom through Work

Walking into the prison, I frequently felt like I was traveling back in time. The prison seemed like a relic of the state-socialist past—or at least of the past that is now remembered. The leader of the institution was the elderly male warden who claimed complete control over the facility, but who was actually clueless about its day-to-day workings. Under him was an administration encased in bureaucratic rules, but in which no one could keep track of all the official mandates. This administration oversaw a series of departments that promised to provide everyone with basic necessities, but the infrastructure was plagued with chronic shortages of resources and space. And the on-the-ground prison staff operated under a veil of formality and discipline, requiring inmates to stand at attention and ask for permission to pass in the hallway, but such discipline was constantly undercut in daily interactions of camaraderie and friendship. It was as if the prison functioned as a microcosm of the state-socialist system.

Of all its parallels with the past, perhaps the most striking was the prison's fixation on wage labor. Work was quite literally at the center of prison life. As under state socialism, participation in wage labor was defined as a right and an obligation—inmates were entitled and expected to labor. This focus on work was codified in national-level policies and laws. The Hungarian Penitentiary Code, first constructed in 1979 and amended in 1996, states that prison work must be provided to "help prisoners maintain their physical and spiritual strength, give them the opportunity to acquire and develop professional skills, and thus facilitate, after being released, the reintegration process into society" (Hungarian Penitentiary Code, Article 44). To further facilitate such reintegration, the Ministry of Justice introduced the Lenient Executive Rule (LER) that allows inmates with good behavioral records to work for wages outside of the prison.[25] Here too, the goal was to rehabilitate inmates through integration into the labor force.

Given this mandate, it was with some embarrassment that the staff admitted to me that only 65 percent of their inmates worked.[26] "It is unfortunate and unacceptable," a high-ranking officer explained to me. "Only those with health or behavioral problems should be excluded from work." Their inability to employ all eligible inmates acted as a benchmark for the staff to assess their practices against those of the past. Many staff members bemoaned the loss of their ability to secure a 100 percent employment rate in the prison—they had fond memories of the 1970s and 1980s when the system had great "hiring capacity" and could provide "jobs for everyone."[27] They believed this made the work of rehabilitation viable and rewarding.

The prison employment rate also became a way for the staff to interpret the limitations and constraints of the present. Like all Hungarian prisons, the Kalocsa facility was severely overcrowded—it operated at 180 percent capacity. Whenever the staff spoke about this issue, which they did quite often, they always related it to inmate employment. They didn't mind that overcrowding also led to constant shortages in resources and cramped cells—the staff was most concerned about its effects on inmates' access to work. "With so many women here, we can't find work for everyone," a counselor once explained to me as we walked by two inmates washing the same window. "There are only so many times they can wash the floor or clean the windows." Or, as another prison official put it, "At 100 percent capacity, we could do it. We could give everyone a job like in the past. But not now. This is very unfortunate, a real pity." Thus, full employment was a symbolic goal for many staff members—symbolic because wage labor was the centerpiece of their rehabilitative ideal of social integration.

Overall, inmates had access to two main types of work. First, there were jobs related to prison maintenance and upkeep. Inmates who held these jobs did everything from kitchen work to cleaning to laundry. Some inmates also did office work, staffing the well-stocked library or doing paperwork for administrators. Second, a small private company operated in the prison to produce apparel for state-sector workers. When the company opened in 1960, it made jumpsuits for industrial workers and uniforms for the police, and in 1990, it expanded production to include medical apparel. Interestingly, the company's glossy promotional catalogue makes no mention that it operates out of a women's prison or uses prison labor.[28] Instead, it promotes its merchandise as expertly made yet affordable. The inmates employed by the company worked on an assembly line; they cut material, sewed clothing, and packaged the final products. Surprisingly, these inmates made less money than those working for the prison, often as much as 50 percent less. But the pay was abysmal for both groups, ranging from $35 to $90 a month (all figures in U.S. dollars) prior to the mandatory deduction to offset the cost of imprisonment. At $25 for all workers, this deduction left many women with virtually no take-home pay. One staff member estimated that 75 percent of the inmates end up with about $10 a month after working full-time.

Clearly prison work did not carry with it significant financial gains. But it was accompanied by another kind of gain: the work structure formed the central hierarchy in the prison. Where an inmate worked was quite literally a statement about where she was located in this hierarchy. As a result, decisions about who got which jobs were a constant source of struggle and strife. Here, too, the state socialist analogy seems apt: Work within the prison, or "state-sector" jobs, were the most coveted not only due to their higher pay, but also because they were more secure and offered connections to those in charge. Yet in order to get such work in the first place, one needed connections. Over and over again, inmates reported that the best jobs were allocated on the basis of one's ability to butter up the bureaucratic machine as opposed to skill level or work experience (Tóth, Zentai, and Krizsán, 2005). And the staff often admitted to using work in this way, as a reward for those they liked or felt sympathetic to. At the other extreme, denying an inmate work was clearly viewed as a punishment. Those banished from the prison labor force and forced into the dreaded black-and-white striped uniform carried enormous stigma.

The stigma of the unemployed was not merely symbolic—it also implied their exclusion from the everyday life of the facility. Unlike U.S. women's prisons, which typically organize their days around meals, recreational time, or counseling sessions, this prison's daily rhythm was structured around work. The inmates were up at the crack of dawn, given a hearty breakfast, and then sent off to work for eight straight hours. After a late-afternoon meal, they rested and prepared for the next day's work. The staff allowed no exceptions to this schedule; all other prison activities revolved around the inmates' workday. I first encountered this non-negotiable schedule when I tried to organize the language classes I provided to the staff and inmates. While the staff's classes could be held during the workday, it was out of the question to do the same with the inmates' classes. Nor was it possible to hold their classes in the late afternoon after they had finished work, as this would cut into the time they needed to get ready for the following day's work. Fridays were also off-limits as the staff insisted that the inmates would be too tired to concentrate after a full forty-hour work week.

In fact, it was in my negotiations over the timing of my classes that I began to understand how work fit into the prison's rehabilitative agenda. The purpose of prison labor was not to retrain inmates or to teach them marketable skills—most of the staff realized the work they provided was far from marketable outside prison walls. Nor was work thought to be inherently gratifying or empowering—again, most staff members recognized how grueling and even degrading prison work could be, with one even describing it as "robotic" (Tóth, Zentai, and Krizsán, 2005: 17). Instead, prison work was meant to demonstrate the importance of contributing to the common good. As one staff member explained, work showed women how to "be useful" and not "die of boredom." It was a way of life, a method of structuring one's days to add to what another staff member called "the good of the whole." In effect, work was presented as a form of social integration—and thus critical to inmates' sense of empowerment upon release.

For instance, an issue of central concern to the prison staff was that the social security system failed to take into account the work inmates did while incarcerated. They believed this was unfair and subjected women to economic hardship later in life because a variety of welfare provisions—from unemployment benefits to maternity leave to family allowances to pensions—were linked to participation in the social security system. So instead of lobbying to demand an end to overcrowding or the creation of part-time work that might enable them to employ all eligible inmates, these staff members were more interested in revising the social security code to make prisoners eligible for work-related benefits. Such revisions were key to their empowerment ideal and to positioning work as a social entitlement and the foundation upon which inmates' future well-being rested.

In these ways, the prison used work to instill a sense of social responsibility as opposed to promoting personal responsibility. While this difference in focus may seem minor, it is actually quite significant. It is the difference between the logic of the social state and of the neoliberal state; it is the difference between viewing work as the basis of the social contract binding the state and its citizens and appropriating work as a technique of self-transformation.

When the Hungarian prison staff organized its facility around labor, they did not set out to entrepreneurialize the inmates or to turn them into enterprising women ready to market themselves upon release. This was not because the Hungarian staff was simply unaware of other approaches to prison labor: Many had encountered them in lectures by Western prison experts, training courses, internet chat rooms, and books. Some of them even felt compelled to explain their approach to me, assuming that as a U.S. researcher I would be unfamiliar with their version of rehabilitation. In doing so, they rarely presented their approach as superior to what they imagined occurred in the U.S. Instead, they insisted that the Hungarian context was different and thus required another approach. One counselor put it succinctly when we were discussing the inmates' work schedules:

"I know prisoners in America do not work so much as here. I understand that they have other things they must do with their time besides work. But you see, here in Hungary rehabilitation must still be about work. This must be its most important meaning for the women."

## Social Education and Intervention

Although the prison staff insisted that employment was essential to the empowerment of female inmates given the realities of Hungary, I remained suspicious. I kept wondering whether it might also be a way to cut back on the costs of staffing the facility. After all, this is often the function that prison labor serves in the U.S. I held onto this hypothesis until one day, during a language class in which the staff was reciting English numbers, the director of the prison's computer system claimed that he had "180 colleagues." I immediately corrected him, suggesting that the number he was looking for was 18. "No, no, there are 180 of us," he retorted. The others in the class nodded in agreement. Stunned, I blurted out that this put the inmate-staff ratio at almost two-to-one, which was unheard of in most U.S. and West European prisons. Again, everyone nodded. So much for my hypothesis about prison work as a labor-saving technique.

The key question then becomes why the prison needs such a large labor force, particularly as most inmates spend their days working. In part, the answer relates back to the state socialist analogy. Overall, there was tremendous redundancy in the facility, with two or three workers doing a job that could be done by one. There was also the enormous prison bureaucracy to attend to—countless regulations to be administered and reports to be completed. But beyond this, another more substantive reason was the reason for the high staff-to-inmate ratio: The staff saw it as their job to be intermediaries between the inmates and the social world. Herein lies the second key component of the prison's empowerment agenda—to provide inmates with "social education." On the one hand, this implied maintaining close supervision over the inmates' lives and relationships in order to teach them appropriate social behavior. Yet it also meant requiring that inmates rely on the staff for all of their needs, from the essential to the frivolous.

At the center of this institutional structure of social education were the twelve staff, called "educators," whose job it was to coordinate and administer inmates' needs. Upon entering the prison, each inmate was assigned to one of these educators and instructed to go to them with all requests. To facilitate this, request boxes were placed along the corridors of inmates' living quarters. Inmates dropped their written requests in these boxes and the educators responded to the inquiries the following day. The educators spent the bulk of their time sifting through the boxes; some had staff to help them with inquiries about prison regulations. Yet the educators preferred to handle the more substantive requests themselves because, as one put it, "this is the real work of rehabilitative."

More specifically, this work entailed becoming involved in inmates' relationships both inside and outside of prison. On the inside, educators acted as intermediaries among inmates and between inmates and staff members. When conflicts arose with other inmates, women were to go to their educators for advice. "When there's a fight or disagreement, they must come to me first. If I let it boil over, life here would be impossible," an educator explained to me. Some educators claimed to know intimate details about inmates' personality conflicts, love triangles, and work-related tensions. No problem seemed too minor to warrant educator intervention. For instance, Judit, an educator in my advanced English class, always spoke about an inmate who submitted a slew of daily requests, from inquiries about how to deal with an asocial cellmate to how to combat her sleeping problem to what color to dye her hair. In recounting these requests, Judit was never the least bit annoyed at being drawn into such matters. "Our female inmates have a lot of problems and need a lot of guidance," she noted. "I think more than you are used to in American prisons," she added.

Educators also served as critical links between inmates and the outside world. As in most countries, female inmates in Hungary received very few visitors. The situation was especially difficult for the women in the Kalocsa prison since it was quite expensive and hard to reach from other areas of the country. As a result, less than 50 percent of inmates reported regular visits (Tóth, Zentai, and Krizsán, 2005). The educators then saw it as their job to facilitate the maintenance of inmates' social ties, particularly with family members. So they arranged for monthly payments to be sent to inmates' children; they encouraged inmates to keep up their correspondence with supportive family members; and they advised inmates on how to deal with the stigma other family members might attach to them. Some educators even reported gathering information for inmates who were worried about problems their children had at school or with the police. Again, the goal was social education in preparation for social integration.

As important as what social education encompassed was what it excluded. In all my interactions and discussions with prison educators, there was never any mention of inmate therapy or counseling. Nor was there any talk of the need for programs to instill self-esteem or personal responsibility. Only after several inquiries did I learn that new inmates were given a short psychological test upon entering the facility. The test consisted of ten questions designed to detect if the inmate had suicidal tendencies. Following the test, inmates met for a few minutes with the sole psychologist in the prison and were instructed to contact him if they became suicidal. He admitted that inmates never contacted him. In his five years in the prison, he never held group therapy sessions or counseling programs for the general inmate population.

Instead, the prison psychologist spent his time in the two special wards. In a reversal of U.S. women's prisons, which tend to treat all inmates as plagued with some sort of addiction, this Hungarian prison cordoned off those thought to have drug and alcohol problems. The former were housed in their own ward, while the latter shared a ward with the mentally ill. Initially this separation perplexed me, but with time I began to see it as yet another example of the prison's emphasis on social rehabilitation. The decision to separate drug users and alcoholics from the general population, and from each other, seemed obvious and natural for the prison staff. On one hand, these inmates should not mix with non-users because, as one prison official put it, they were "not ready or able to become part of the whole." Nor should they be treated together because, as another staff member explained, the "environments of their lives are entirely different." In effect, these inmates were not classified according to their addiction *per se,* but according to the context in which they became addicts: Drug users were thought to be linked to others through the drug trade and networks, while alcoholics (especially female alcoholics) were said to be more likely to abuse alone. It was the social context that mattered most and formed the basis for their special classification.

It was also the social context that the staff highlighted in their treatment. The prison's approach to these special inmates seemed more like lifestyle counseling than addiction treatment inspired by Alcoholics Anonymous (AA)-.[29] For instance, in the alcoholics' ward the entire focus was on teaching women how to structure their days without alcohol. The staff posted daily schedules around the ward, accounting for every minute of every day. Absent were all the accoutrements of twelve-step programs that dominate "therapeutic communities" in U.S. women's prisons. "The big challenge here is filling the inmates' free time with productive things," a high-ranking official explained to me as he pointed to the inmates' artwork, lacework, and crochet that covered the walls of the ward. "We need to fight the anti-social effects of alcohol, and hobbies are a way to do this."

As in the prison's world of work, I uncovered few traces of neoliberal penality in its regime of social education. Inmates' resocialization did not imply teaching the tools of self-governance or self-management; it did not give rise to techniques to promote self-esteem or self-transformation. This "technology of the self" was nowhere to be found in the prison's discourses or practices. In its place was a kind of "technology of the social" that targeted and treated inmates' social relationships and insisted that women rely on others for their resocialization, and ultimately their empowerment. The prison's empowerment model must also be seen as a form of governance; its goal was to manage women's social conduct and to guide them toward appropriate behavior. In this way, its form of governance was also premised on particular ideas about gender and women's special needs.

## Governing Women as "Women"

The Hungarian prison staff had many images of how things worked in the U.S. penal system. Yet the image that affected them the most was the idea that the U.S. system treated women like men. They saw this as far from positive: Even the suggestion of gender-neutral treatment offended the prison staff. For instance, months before I began my research, some of the staff had seen a film about a maximum-security women's prison in Texas. The film's images continued to haunt them, leading some to admonish me for what my system did to its women. They were stunned by the what they perceived as the coldness of the prison's approach. They were impressed by all its high-tech equipment, but worried that it positioned women as robots. They could not fathom how the prison could isolate women and deny them social contact. Most of all, they found it unacceptable that the prison seemed to treat women like men, thus failing to acknowledge women's special needs and problems. This, they argued, was a profound form of disempowerment.

The staff's outright rejection of this approach to female inmates was clearly linked to their understanding of female criminality. This interpretation was first relayed to me during my initial meeting with the prison's warden and executive officers. When I asked these officials what kind of crimes the inmates had committed, one of them responded that they were "very serious crimes, often murder." The others immediately jumped in. "Oh, but not real murder. Most of the women killed family members," one explained. "Yes, their crimes come out of family conflicts. So they are not serious murders," another added. The warden nodded in agreement.

This interpretation of women as "not serious" criminals was echoed down the prison's chain of command. The staff repeatedly refused to assign individual culpability to the inmates. While they admitted that many inmates had done horrible things, they claimed that the women could not be held fully accountable for their actions because they were also victims. Some were victims of abusive men, others of neglectful families, and still others of the rise in poverty and unemployment. This construction of women as victims then collided with the notion of gender-neutral treatment: "How can you act the same to female and male inmates when the men are often the reason for the women's crimes?" an official pointedly asked me.

The staff's description of women as victims with special needs was so pervasive that it prompted the staff to create an institutional environment that was as "warm" and "homey" as possible. On many of the prison's wards, the walls were painted in pastel colors and while plants and flowers lined the corridors. The inmates' collective cells, which housed up to fifteen women, included a center table covered with flowered tablecloths and small fruit bowls. Despite the facility's severe overcrowding and shortage of space, the staff made room for a small inmates' kitchen to allow the women to maintain their cooking skills while incarcerated. "The inmates love this kitchen," an official remarked as we watched three of them bake bread one afternoon. "Some are really excellent cooks. It is good for them to do this [cooking] here since it reminds them what normal life is like." Maintaining this sense of normality was said to be necessary for inmate rehabilitation; in fact, it was central to what was considered their empowerment.

The prison staff clearly organized the facility to accentuate and enforce their particular type of femininity. It was not the form characteristic of nineteenth-century U.S. penal institutions and reformatories that emphasized the women's need to become respectable wives, mothers, or domestic servants. Nor was it the contemporary version of what could be called "neoliberal femininity," which enmeshes women in therapy culture and discourses of the self as routes to self-discovery and self-esteem.[30] Instead, like so many aspects of the prison, its version of mandatory femininity harkened back to key state socialist ideals, with all their tensions and contradictions: it heralded the values and virtues of women's labor, while requiring their domesticity; it emphasized the importance of women's integration into familial relationships, while recognizing their frequent victimization in those relations; and it idealized women's strength and perseverance, while denying them agency as victims.[31] The end result was an insistence on governing women as "women."

## RETHINKING NEOLIBERAL GOVERNANCE

From the perspective of the Hungarian penal system, it is difficult to sustain the common view of neoliberalism's regional triumph. Instead, the core elements of neoliberal governance—from its emphasis on individual responsibility to its responsibilizing tendencies—seemed absent from this system. In their place was an empowerment ideal of institutional integration through wage labor and social education. Among other things, the failure of neoliberal discourses of punishment to infiltrate this prison system raises important questions about how globalization operates in different international and national spaces. Too often, social scientific theories of neoliberal governance conflate intentions and effects, assuming that the articulation of neoliberal ideals necessarily leads to institutional reform. This is certainly true of analyses of neoliberal penality, which tend to equate the existence of neoliberal punishment models with their institutionalization. Yet there is another level that frequently remains unexamined; these discourses must be grounded in the lives of real people working in real institutions. And those receiving these transnational exchanges must be receptive and responsive to their messages. Our theories of neoliberal governance are far weaker when it comes to understanding and explaining what shapes this receptiveness.

To strengthen them, we need more analyses of the responses neoliberal models evoke in concrete institutional spaces. Clearly some state spaces provide fertile ground for the blossoming and flourishing of the neoliberal models—in post-socialist Hungary, the arenas of macro-economic policy and welfare provision come to mind. But there are other realms where the ground is not as fertile. As I suggested in this paper, the post-socialist penal system may be one such realm. There are several possible reasons for this. On the one hand, those in charge of this system had clear blueprints for how the world of punishment should work: They remained devoted to the ideals of societal responsibility and social integration, which kept them from psychologizing or responsibilizing female inmates. They were deeply committed to ideologies of gender difference and of female victimization, which kept them from individualizing or entrepreneurializing these women. What's more, these officials were able to retain the power to organize penal institutions to reflect their blueprints. So while it would be easy to dismiss their organizational responses as backward or even ignorant, this would be a mistake. It is far more revealing to interpret them as examples of how neoliberal models can fail to capture the imaginations or the interests of those they target.

It would also be a mistake to glorify their model of social empowerment. As I described in this paper, their model clearly acted to govern women. As a mode of governance, it was quite invasive, intruding on women's lives whether they liked it or not. It was quite educative, instructing women how to deal with all their relationships—and it was quite paternalistic, taking on the responsibility to care and educate women. As Cruikshank (1999: 69) points out, by their very nature state empowerment projects are power relationships—their object is to act on another's interest in order to bring them in line and to shape their conduct. The Hungarian version of empowerment certainly had this goal; it tried to make women's conduct consistent with particular ideals of wage labor, social integration, and gender. Its divergence from neoliberal empowerment was one of kind not degree—it simply acted on different interests, targeted different conduct, and tried to bring women in line with different ends.

Acknowledging the relations of power embedded in this model of social empowerment should not blind us to its political possibilities. It is important that this model acted on different interests and targeted different conduct—particularly for those of us interested in finding alternatives to neoliberal governance. In a world where an increasingly international chorus is singing the praises of personal responsibility and independence, it is encouraging that some state officials still speak of collective responsibility and obligation. In a world where discourses of personal responsibility give rise to policies of state retrenchment, it is encouraging that some policies still stress the state's responsibility in securing citizens' well-being. And in a world where policies of retrenchment often lead to practices to treat women's individual ailments and addictions, it is encouraging that some state institutions continue to prioritize women's social integration and relationships—even if we have to go to a women's prison in Eastern Europe to find such institutions.

## NOTES

1. I am grateful to many colleagues and friends for the helpful comments on earlier drafts of this chapter. In particular, I thank Micheal Burawoy, Carolyn Elliott, Christina Ewig, Wendy Chavkin, Jo Dixon, Ruth Horowitz, Gail Kligman, Jill McCorkel, Ann Orloff, Andras Tapolcai, and Herta Toth for their challenging and constructive thoughts on the ideas in this paper. I also thank Ferenc Kis and the Racsok Alapitvay (Bars Foundation) for helping me gain access to the Hungarian prison system.
2. Nikolas Rose, *Powers of Freedom* (New York: Cambridge, 1999); hereafter cited in text as Rose (1999).
3. Barbara Cruikshank, *The Will to Empower* (Cornell University Press, 1999).
4. Gil Eyal and Joanna Bockman, "Eastern Europe as a Laboratory of Economic Knowledge: The Transnational Roots of Neo-Liberalism," *American Journal of Sociology* 103, no. 2 (2004): 310.
5. Lynne Haney, *Inventing the Needy: Gender and the Politics of Welfare in Hungary* (Berkeley, CA: University of California Press, 2002); hereafter cited in text as Haney (2002).
6. Elaine Weiner, "No (Wo)Man's Land: The Post-Socialist Purgatory of Czech Female Factory Workers," *Social Problems* 52, no. 4 (2005): 572–92.
7. Loic Wacquant, "Deadly Symbiosis: When Ghetto and Prison Meet and Mesh. In *Mass Imprisonment: Social Causes and Consequences,* ed. David Garland (London: SAGE Publications, 2001); hereafter cited in text as Wacquant (2001).
8. The research this analysis is based on was conducted over a four-month period in 2004–2005. During this period, I not only collected an array of materials on Hungarian imprisonment trends and laws, but I conducted fieldwork in the country's largest women's prison, the Kalocsai Fegyház és Börtön. I spent two days a week in the prison, teaching English and creative writing classes to both the prison staff and inmates. On occasion, I also attended the prison's programs and classes. Together, these different activities allowed me to observe staff/inmate interactions and participate in the social life of the facility—thus arriving at a fuller understanding of its focus and organization.
9. There is, of course, an irony here as the project of "teaching" self-reliance is something of an oxymoron. Yet the idea is to show these "dependent" groups how to care for themselves in the future. For more on the ironic practices this gives rise to, see: Deborah Little, "Independent Workers, Dependent Mothers: Discourse, Resistance, and AFDC Workfare Programs," *Social Politics* 6 (1999): 161–202; and Sharon Hays, *Flat Broke with Children: Women in the Age of Welfare Reform* (New York: Oxford University Press, 2003).
10. Nancy Fraser, *Justice Interruptus* (New York: Verso, 1997); Jamie Peck. *Workfare States* (New York: Guilford Press, 2001); Sylvia Bashevkin, *Welfare*

*Hot Buttons: Women, Work, and Social Policy Reform* (Toronto: University of Toronto Press, 2002).

11. Pat O'Malley, "Volatile and Contradictory Punishment," *Theoretical Criminology* 3 (1996): 175–96; David Garland, *The Culture of Control: Crime and Social Order in Contemporary Society* (Chicago: University of Chicago Press, 2001); and Kelly Hannah-Moffat, *Punishment in Disguise: Penal Governance and Federal Imprisonment of Women in Canada* (Toronto: University of Toronto Press, 2001).

12. Katherine Beckett, and Bruce Western, "Governing Social Marginality: Welfare, Incarceration, and the Transformation of State Policy." In *Mass Imprisonment: Social Causes and Consequences,* ed. David Garland (London: Sage Publications, 2001); John Sutton, "Imprisonment in Affluent Western Democracies," *American Sociological Review* 69, no. 2 (2004): 170–89.

13. Loic Wacquant, "The Curious Eclipse of Prison Ethnography in the Age of Mass Incarceration," *Ethnography* 3, no. 4 (2002): 382l hereafter cited in text as Wacquant (2002).

14. At the same time, those who show little ability or willingness to learn these skills are then simply warehoused—left to serve their time with few educational or work-related programs. Thus, the penal system's practices of self-governance and of warehousing are two sides of the same coin. For more on the warehouse quality of contemporary penal institutions, see Wacquant (2002), also: Joe Domanick, *Cruel Justice: Three Strikes and the Politics of Crime in America's Golden State* (Berkeley: University of California Press, 2004; and Lorna Rhodes, *Total Confinement: Madness and Reason in the Maximum Security Prison* (Berkeley: University of California Press, 2004).

15. Kathryn Fox, "Changing Violent Minds: Discursive Correction and Resistance in the Cognitive Treatment of Violent Offenders in Prison," *Social Problems* 46, no. 1 (1999a): 88–103, hereafter cited in text as Fox (1999a); Kathryn Fox, "Reproducing Criminal Types: Cognitive Treatment for Violent Offenders in Prison," *The Sociological Quarterly* 40, no. 3 (1999b): 435–53; Mona Lynch, "Rehabilitation as Rhetoric: The Ideal of Reformation in Contemporary Parole Discourse and Practices," *Punishment and Society* 2 (2000): 40–65.

16. Lynne Haney, "Gender, Welfare, and States of Punishment," *Social Politics* 11 (2004): 3; hereafter cited in text as Haney (2004).

17. Fox (1999a); Haney (2004); also Allison McKim, "Getting Gut-Level: Punishment, Gender, and Therapeutic Governance." Paper presented at the Annual Meeting of the American Sociological Association, session on Gender and Incarceration (August 2006).

18. Estelle Freedman, *Their Sisters' Keeps: Women's Prison Reform in America, 1830–1930* (Ann Arbor: University of Michigan Press, 1981); Pat Carlen, *Women's Imprisonment* (London: Routledge, 1983); Nicole Hahn Rafter, *Partial Justice: Women, Prisons, and Social Control* (New Brunswick: Transaction Books, 1990); and Mark Kann, "Penitence for the Privileged: Manhood, Race, and Penitentiaries in Early America." In *Prison Masculinities,* eds. Don Sabo, Terry Kupers, and Willie London (Philadelphia: Temple University Press, 2001), hereafter cited in text as Kann (2001).
Of course, this special treatment was always race-specific. As numerous scholars have shown, African American women were never held up to these feminine norms. Instead, they were masculinized and subjected to harsh, punitive treatment. For more on the racial dynamics of this system, see: Angela Davis, *Are Prisons Obsolete?* (New York: Seven Stories Press, 2003) and Kann (2001).

19. Meda Chesney-Lind, "Rethinking Women's Imprisonment." In *The Criminal Justice System and Women,* eds. Barbara Price and Natalie Skoloff (New

York: McGraw-Hill, 1995). While the form and focus of this punishment model may be similar for male and female inmates, it often gets relayed in gender-specific ways. For instance, as in the welfare system, these strategies of individualization are frequently cloaked in promises to give women the autonomy and confidence they too often lack. Cloaking responsibilization tactics in pseudofeminist empowerment talk makes the former seem more positive and less punitive. And there is also some evidence that this gives it more support from the state actors, many of whom are women themselves, whose job it is to administer such programs. For more on this, see: Kelly Hannah-Moffat, *Punishment in Disguise: Penal Governance and Federal Imprisonment of Women in Canada* (Toronto: University of Toronto Press, 2001), hereafter cited in text as Hannah-Moffat (2001); also Kelly Hannah-Moffat, "Losing Ground: Gendered Knowledges, Parole Risk, and Responsibility," *Social Politics* 11 (2004): 3; and Haney (2004).

20. Jill McCorkel, "Criminally Dependent? Gender, Punishment, and the Rhetoric of Welfare Reform," *Social Politics* 11 (2004): 386–410; and Haney (2004).

21. The sheer size of the U.S. penal system underscores this point: Over 6.5 million U.S. citizens live under correctional supervision and over 2 million of them are in prison. There is also evidence that incarceration has indeed become a response to social insecurity. For instance, Western and Beckett (2001) found that the U.S. states with the highest imprisonment rates spend the least on welfare provisions. Moreover, the U.S. penal system does an impressive job responsibilizing and entrepreneurializing its subjects: Since the mid-1980s, the percentage of inmates in some form of counseling more than doubled, while the number of prisoners engaged in wage labor increased by over 80 percent. See David Garland, "Introduction: The Meaning of Mass Imprisonment" in *Mass Imprisonment: Social Causes and Consequences*, ed. David Garland (London: Sage Publications, 2001b) and Christian Parenti, "Rehabilitating Prison Labor: The Uses of Imprisoned Masculinities." In *Prison Masculinities*, eds. Don Sabo, Terry Kupers, and Willie London (Philadelphia: Temple University Press, 2001), cited hereafter in text as Parenti (2001).

22. Moreover, these workshops brought in notoriously conservative ideological exporters such as Charles Murray, Larry Mead, and William Bratton.

23. More specifically, roughly 30 percent of the inmates in this prison are under maximum security confinement while the remaining 70 percent are medium security. In actuality, this designation does not have much influence on an inmate's daily life or opportunities in the prison. Instead, it affects the length of her sentence—with maximum security prisoners doing more time. It is also possible for an inmate to change her security status if she has the support of the prison staff.

24. See Wacquant (2001) for a discussion of how color-coding works in the U.S. and has become a key technique of rule.

25. While important overall, the LER was not relevant in the Kalocsa prison as the law excludes all maximum-security inmates. Given the prison's classification as maximum security, the warden decided to deem all its inmates ineligible for LER.

26. Their use of the word "only" here was interesting given that these rates are more than double those found in U.S. and West European prisons. So although inmate employment rates are up in these other systems, they still rarely surpass 30 percent.

27. Herta Tóth, Violetta Zentai, and Andrea Krizsán. *Hungary Country Report: Women, Integration, and Prison.* Final report prepared for the EU Project "Women, Integration, and Prison" (2005): 17; hereafter cited as Tóth, Zentai, and Krizsán (2005).

28. Nor does it note that the models wearing the clothing in the catalogue are prison guards and officials. When I asked the head of the company why the catalogue made no mention that its workers were inmates, she looked at me like I was crazy, noting that this was a marketing tool and it was not fashionable to be a prisoner in Hungary. Here is yet another contrast with the U.S. penal system, which often advertises the products produced in prison as such. And the success of the "prison blues" jean company testifies to their marketability. For more on this industry in the U.S., see Parenti (2001).

29. This was true despite the spectacular rise of the Alcoholics Anonymous movement in Hungary. In fact, the head of the movement, Istvan Csanyi, now has his own television show and periodicals that are enormously popular. His techniques are far more confrontational and aggressive than the classic AA style, as he frequently subjects his "patients" to an onslaught of accusations and insults in order to "cure" them.

30. Although neoliberal femininity may not have surfaced in Hungarian prisons, it has certainly emerged in Hungarian culture. Perhaps the clearest example of it can be found in the national women's weekly magazine, *Nok Lapja,* which has been transformed into an Oprah-style self-help handbook. And if weekly installments are not enough, the magazine now holds weekend-long "femininity classes" in which they teach women the newest styles and grooming techniques, as well as practices of self-reflection, self-actualization, and self-discovery.

31. For more on these state socialist ideals, and their often contradictory messages, see: Susan Gal and Gail Kligman, *The Politics of Gender after Socialism* (Princeton: Princeton University Press, 2000).

# 2   Biology and Destiny
## Women, Work, Birthrates, and Assisted Reproductive Technologies

*Wendy Chavkin*[1]

In the last third of the twentieth century in the developed world, dramatic changes happened quietly in the ways people live their most intimate lives. Many women entered the labor force and deferred marriage and childbearing. Divorce rates rose as did single parenthood. Birthrates dropped below the level needed to replace the population, death rates declined, and people lived longer. While the details vary between and within countries, the general patterns hold true for highly developed countries. Similar changes are taking place in many developing countries as well.[2]

Some attribute the decline in birthrates to the advent of effective modern contraception and safe, legal abortion, both of which became available in much of the developed world in roughly the same time period. Others see these techniques as enabling people to control their fertility, rather than causing them to do so, and point to cases where births declined even when access to abortion and contraception were restricted, for example Poland. Some consider the trio of urbanization, women's education, and employment to be explanatory. Others ascribe this birthrate decline to the total cluster of concurrent changes. Whatever the bundle of social factors associated with declining birthrates, an important route is through delayed childbearing.[3] In twelve European countries where mean age at first birth increased by half a year or more from 1990 to 1999, fertility rates also decreased.[4]

The whole constellation of changes is called the "second demographic transition" by scholars. The decline in birth rates has led to a host of positive changes on both societal and individual levels—economic growth resulting from women's increased employment, improved health and education of children, benefits for women's health, and life opportunities. However, it has also resulted in shrinking the size of the working-age population whose labor supports the social and economic needs of both children and older, retired people. This in turn has profound implications for the tax base that funds social security and health systems.[5]

Therefore some governments have begun to worry about declining birthrates and tried to craft policies to sustain birthrates. These policy responses are diverse, revealing varied understandings of the factors underlying individuals' fertility decisions. Some try to promote couple formation—Singapore's government essentially runs a dating service through their sponsorship of "loveboats" and the Czech Republic offers priority access to scarce housing for young couples.[6] Others offer financial incentives, such as Putin's promise of $8,900 for a second child. Some acknowledge the costs associated with childrearing and provide cash grants or tax credits per child and subsidized child care.[7] Others design services to support domestic responsibilities of employed parents, such as parental leave at the time of birth, leaves to take care of sick family members, and flexible working hours.[8] A rare few encourage immigration to sustain population size.[9]

**Table 2-1.** Support for Earlier Childbearing

| Country | Support Given |
| --- | --- |
| Singapore | Tax rebates for women who have children by specified ages; priority access to housing to facilitate young couples' formation of independent households |
| Japan | Provision of home–based electronic continuing education and training for women on maternity leave |
| Czech Republic | Provision of low interest loans to newlyweds, with portions forgiven with each birth |
| South Korea | Offers households with more than 2 two children a 12–18 month bonus period in the national pension system for more pension benefits |
| Hungary | Allows deferment of mortgage repayment for borrowers who are buying a new house and expecting to have an additional child. This loan will be paid by the government at the time the child is born. |
| Sweden | "Speed premiums" whereby parents of more than one child are entitled to benefits without returning to work between births |

**Paternal Participation**

| Country | Support Given |
| --- | --- |
| Iceland Norway Japanese city Sweden | Mandate that fathers use portion of paid parental leave ("use it or lose it") |
| Czech Republic | Increase in the income level eligible for parental leave |
| Sweden | Individually based tax structure (rather than for family unit) that benefits two-earner family |

There is emerging agreement among many scholars and policy analysts that the policies most likely to support birthrates are those that enable men as well as women to participate in paid employment and in domestic and childrearing responsibilities. Through pragmatic recognition that birthrates have declined steeply when childbearing significantly reduces employment opportunities for women, or when work and home responsibilities are too burdensome,[10] such major international organizations as the European Union (EU), the Organization for Economic Co-operation and Development (OECD) and the United Nations (UN) have come to support "work-family reconciliation" policies.

Yet even the most extensive of these programs link benefits to salary levels and thus structurally encourage their citizens to have completed their education and training and to have attained stable employment before having children. This in turn reinforces delayed childbearing and thus fewer births. Table 2-1 shows some policy efforts to encourage early childbearing and paternal participation.

## DELAYED CHILDBEARING AND ASSISTED REPRODUCTIVE TECHNOLOGIES

While it may be socially advantageous to delay childbearing, the social and the biological are out of synch. There is a fairly short window of time of biological opportunity before women's ability to become pregnant and successfully carry to term begins to decline.[11] This window may be further compromised by other exposures, such as smoking or reproductive tract infections that can impede function of the fallopian tubes, or possibly by environmental exposures that may affect quality of sperm, or other factors that we do not yet understand.

The scientific evidence indicates that women's ability to become pregnant begins to decline by their late 20s and very sharply after the late 30s.[12] Women in their early 20s are about twice as likely to become pregnant as women in their late 30s. Spontaneous abortion—or miscarriage—rates also increase with age, due largely to age related increases in genetic abnormalities (Frank, et al., 1994; Dunson, et al., 2002). Many complications of pregnancy increase with maternal age, often because women acquire other age related health problems such as hypertension or diabetes.

Many experience this biological limitation unhappily and are demanding recourse to technological means of having babies: Assisted reproductive technologies (ARTs). The first" test tube baby" was born about a decade after the second demographic transition began. Since that time, ART use has skyrocketed, with between one and two million babies born worldwide (OECD, 2005).[13]

The term "ART" refers to a variety of techniques in which sperm and egg get together with the help of a laboratory. The most well known and widely used is in vitro fertilization (IVF) Other techniques include intracytoplasmic sperm injection (ICSI), gamete intrafallopian transfer (GIFT), zygote intrafallopian transfer (ZIFT), use of a donor egg or embryo, and surrogacy (or use of a gestational carrier). These techniques require hormonal stimulation of the woman so that she releases ova and later, to ready her uterus for pregnancy. The sperm and the ovum can come from the original couple or from donors.

While success ("take home baby") rates have been increasing, they are still quite low, at best in the low 30 percent range. The treatments are very expensive, time consuming, and emotionally taxing. They are associated with serious medical complications, many of which are the result of increased rates of twins and higher-order multiple pregnancies[14] such as triplets, quadruplets etc. Most of the risks associated with multiple births are because the births are more likely to be preterm and have low birth weight, and follow up studies indicate neurological and cognitive deficits in long-term survivors of multiple births of very low birth weight.[15]

There are also heightened risks to women who carry multiple pregnancies. Ovarian hyperstimulation syndrome is a fairly rare but serious complication for women undergoing hormonal fertility treatment. There are also biologically plausible reasons for concern about the long-term consequences of the hormonal manipulations involved in many ARTs, specifically whether they increase risk for reproductive cancers or earlier menopause. These questions have been inadequately investigated; few studies have been performed and they have been limited by sample size and length of follow-up time (Evans et al., 1995; Gleicher et al., 2000).[16]

For Europe, slightly less than a quarter of ART cycles result in live births. Approximately a quarter of these are multiple births. Success rates and multiple birth rates vary widely between countries.[17] In contrast, about a third of ART births in the U.S. are multiple births, compared to three percent in the general population. These statistics reflect differences in the practice of ART cycles, particularly in the number of embryos transferred to the uterus, which is lower in Europe than in the U.S. in an effort to minimize risk.


## POLICY DISSONANCE

National policies regarding the rise in ARTs are generally unrelated to policy efforts to stem birthrate decline or to support work and parenthood. If we take a look at several countries' policies in these arenas we will see that, despite a variation in approach, the commonality is non-integration of these issues.


### Sweden

Sweden has based its family and family-planning policies on the principles of universality and individual rights (Ministry of Health and Social

Affairs, 2003). Swedish abortion law was liberalized, along with America's, in the early 1970s, and contraception and abortion are publicly funded (United Nations, 2002). Sweden has pioneered the promotion of gender equity and the well being of children by formulating work-family reconciliation policies and providing structural incentives for men to participate in childrearing (see Table 2-1).[18] The latter resonates with longstanding feminist analyses of the relationship between the gender-wage gap and female assumption of domestic responsibilities. The Swedish total fertility rate (TFR) has often been amongst the highest in Europe although it declined in the early 90s when there was an economic recession and a retrenchment of benefits.

However, there is an unexamined discordance between the stated commitment to gender equity and work-family reconciliation, and the structural incentives to delay childbearing until salary level and career status are well established. In Sweden as well as elsewhere, the financial supports for childbearing are determined by salary levels, encouraging delay. As a result, maternal age at first birth and ART use have risen in Sweden. In 1992 the mean age for first marriages was 27.95 and at first birth was 28.87; a decade later it had risen to 30.5 and 30.3 respectively in 2003 (EUROPA, 2006) While Sweden makes ARTs readily available, it places health-related constraints on them. As early as 2002, Swedish guidelines limited transfers to two embryos and state-funded procedures to a single embryo. By 2003, the Swedish National Board of Health and Welfare restricted all ART procedures to single-embryo transfer (SET) except in exceptional circumstances.[19] During this time period the SET rate has risen from 25.1 to 72.7 percent without a change in the pregnancy rates (33.3 to 37.4 percent). As a result of this national policy, the twinning rate has decreased from 22.6 to 6.2 percent.

Swedish policy regarding ARTs is much less coherent than their general health or reproductive health policy. Sweden subsidizes and allows the normalization of these technologies despite their high cost, low efficacy, and understudied risks for women and children. The Swedish law stipulates that embryo transfer can only be completed in couples who are married or cohabitating, and requires the consent of the husband or partner. Either the sperm or the egg must be from one of the parents; both cannot be from donors.[20] The government covers the cost of one to three cycles, depending on the region of Sweden the couple lives in, but the wait for IVF in a publicly funded clinic can be anywhere from two to eight years.[21] Private clinics are available at a much higher cost but a much lower wait time. Thus Swedish policy regarding ARTs jumbles together cautious medical and conservative socially normative requirements, in contrast to their extremely liberal and tolerant family policies.

## Canadian Province of Québec

Québec has undergone rapid social transformation from a conservative Catholic tradition regarding family organization, gender, and reproductive roles to the current situation with high proportions of employed women, high rates of out-of-wedlock childbearing, delayed age at first birth and low birthrates.[22] Similar transitions have occurred in other Catholic countries, notably Spain and Italy. The provincial government of Québec has attempted various measures to increase population and support its residents' efforts to straddle their work and family obligations. The government has long encouraged immigration, particularly from Francophone countries, although recently it has added restrictive skill requirements. Interestingly, while immigrants' birthrates are initially higher, within less than a generation their rates quickly fall to the Canadian range.[23] The Québécois provincial government has also recently initiated universally subsidized childcare (initially $5 Canadian perday, now $7 Canadian perday) which has been so popular that there is an insufficiency of places.[24] The government is scurrying to increase slots and has raised the pay of day care teachers but still cannot keep pace with demand. The provincial government also offers various supplements to the moderate level of parental benefits throughout Canada.[25]

Canadian policies and provision of reproductive health care reflects a mixed bag of efforts to have rational and evidence-based policies and services, and efforts to appease public and private as well as liberal and conservative interests. For example, Canadian abortion law was initially liberalized in the 1960s, the same period when abortion liberalization transpired in much of the developed world, but retained restrictions that have since been deemed unconstitutional. Currently there is no specific abortion legislation, which on the ground means that some provinces deny or restrict funding, and consequently there is uneven access depending on geography and income.[26] Quebec's universal health insurance fully covers abortions under the Quebec Health Insurance Act.

The Canadian response to ARTs reflects a disconnect resulting when policy targets public but not private provision of medical care.[27] Recently passed legislation regarding ARTs ambivalently straddles the demand for it by consumers and physicians, and the countervailing evidence demonstrating high cost and low yield. A 2004 bill prohibits cloning, commercial surrogacy, and the purchase of gametes, but permits reimbursing egg or sperm donors for "expenses" accrued during the process. The bill also established a regulatory body to oversee ART and related research.[28] Ostensibly the bill is part of a strategy to improve reproductive health that includes prevention of STI's and environmental causes of infertility, increased access to contraception, support for parents, and public funding of ARTs. Meanwhile during the decade of debate preceding passage of the bill, private sector provision of ARTs increased quickly, with unregulated and varying policies regarding social eligibility. Lack of public funding means these privately provided techniques are now available only to those who can pay for expensive treatments.

Canada and Québec exemplify the perils of the halfway effort: the work-family reconciliation services are nowhere close to the level of the Scandinavian countries and the efforts to develop rational ethical cautious policy regarding ARTs has partially foundered because of the co-existence of an autonomous sector of private health care.

## Italy

The Italian case demonstrates a different set of forces at play. While Italy also liberalized abortion in the same time period as the other Western developed countries and publicly funds it (first-trimester abortion is free of charge, second-trimester abortion is permitted only if necessary to protect the health of the mother; conscientious objection allowed for physician refusers and is highly prevalent), in 2001 the government stopped providing direct support for contraception. The Italian state is a much more meager provider of social benefits in general and certainly of family benefits.[29]

Italy's TFR is one of the lowest in the world at 1.28 between 2000 and 2005.[30] In 2000 the mean age at first marriage was 27.4, and mean age at first birth was 30.3.[31] Maternity leave is publicly funded and cash bonuses are provided to young, working, low-income women at each birth. Paternity leave, however, is paid for by employers and only allowed if the mother is working, ill, or absent.[32] The low TFR is ascribed to the inadequacy of the benefits provided, the limited participation of men in domestic and child-drearing responsibilities, and the consequent burden for women who are expected to carry the load of paid employment and family care. ARTs took off in Italy without laws in place to regulate the practice. However, after intensive campaigning by the Catholic Church and Berlusconi government, a bill was passed in 2004 that practically banned the practice by imposing tight restrictions. Embryo research was prohibited and language in the bill ascribed human rights to the embryo; only married heterosexual couples are eligible; sperm and ova donation are prohibited; the creation of more than three embryos are prohibited; it is mandatory to implant all embryos; and destroying and freezing embryos is prohibited.[33] While testing the embryo for genetic disorders is allowed, it is required that all embryos be transplanted to the uterus, no matter what the results of the pre-implantation genetic diagnosis are (Nyoboe Anderson et al., 2004).[34] The media gave widespread coverage to the case of a couple seeking IVF who each carried the recessive gene for thalassemia. They were required by court order to implant any embryo created via IVF without a preimplantation genetic diagnosis, although she would be permitted to subsequently abort it if the fetus were later found to be affected.[35]

A coalition formed of labor unions, women's groups, gay activists, infertility patients, physicians, scientists, and left political parties successfully gathered a sufficient number of signatures to require a referendum on repealing the bill. However, after the Catholic Church intensively urged people not to vote, only 29 percent voted, an insufficient proportion to force repeal. A new government has recently been elected, and some coalition members expect another effort to repeal the bill. In the interim, many Italians reportedly seek treatment abroad, particularly in Eastern Europe. Nearby Slovakia has seen an increase in Italians seeking infertility treatments[36] and several private fertility treatment centers in the Czech Republic, Russia, Greece, and Austria have translated their entire website into Italian to facilitate Italian "reproductive tourists."[37]

## CONCLUSION: POLICY APPROACHES AND CONTRADICTIONS

Sweden, Iceland, and other Scandinavian countries are explicit in relating gender relations in both the public and private spheres and birthrates. They have a host of policies and benefit programs to further the well being of children, to increase gender equity, and to support both women and men in combining work and family responsibilities. The benefits provided are amongst the world's most generous.

Nevertheless, these policies do not appear to be based on an appreciation of the centrality of delayed childbearing in linking the phenomena of gender, unequal domestic responsibilities, unequal pay, declining birthrates, and ARTs. Sweden has allowed ARTs to develop on a separate track from their work-family reconciliation policies, rather than reconfiguring the latter to accommodate the constraints of reproductive biology. An example of such an alternative approach could include experimentation with unlinking work-family benefits from salary level in order to enable earlier childbearing without penalty.

Québécois work-family policies are based on similar analyses of gender, work, and family but the Canadian benefit levels are far below the Scandinavians,' even though Québec augments them. Nor has Québec addressed the delay in childbearing, employment, and benefit structures. While Canada has been unusual in its efforts to devise rational, cautious policy regarding ARTs, it has not grappled with the contradictions inherent in private health care alongside the public system. Thus the private provision of ARTs has essentially taken off like a runaway train while the slow deliberations took place in the public sphere.

Italian benefits for working mothers are meager and policies neither support fathers nor tackle the assignment of the domestic to women. The virtual ban on ARTs ignores the realities of European unification, reproductive tourism and the public health and medical perils of unregulated ARTs. Although Italian birthrates are amongst the lowest in the world, policies fail to address the contemporary realities of working women, the era of fertility control, or gender inequality in employment and domestic responsibility.

Some countries have devised policy components to support earlier child-bearing and paternal participation in childrearing, as shown in Table 2-1.

## SAMPLE POLICIES TO SUPPORT YOUNGER CHILDBEARING AND PATERNAL INVOLVEMENT IN CHILDREARING

However, most of these policies take place in the context of limited levels of benefits or limited efforts to reconcile work and family from a gender equality perspective. I argue that policies to promote gender equality must incorporate female reproductive biology into the design, to support earlier childbearing without sacrifice of career or salary and so that ARTs are well-studied and cautiously provided to ensure the health of women and future children. Feminists have long objected to the notion that biology is destiny. However, efforts to forge social equality must understand and address biology or fall short.

## NOTES

1. I am enormously grateful to the Fulbright Commission's New Century Scholars Program, to Carolyn Elliott and to the members of my cohort for their stimulating, thoughtful company. Many thanks to Drs. Karin Schenck-Gustafsson and Zsuzsanna Wiesenfeld Hallin, my hosts at the Center of Gender Medicine, Karolinska Institutet, Stockholm; to Professor Évelyne LaPierre Adamcyk, my host at the Department of Demography, University of Montreal; to Stefano Fabeni, JD, LLM, and Dr. Maria Gigliola Toniollo of the National New Rights Section, Confederazione Generale Italiana del Lavoro who convened a meeting for me with representatives of the pro-referendum coalition in Rome. I am very grateful to graduate research assistants Liza Fuentes and Molly Findlay for their help.
2. Clarence Lochhead, "The Trend Toward Delayed First Childbirth: Health and Social Implications," *Isuma* 1 (2000): 41–4.
3. Peter McDonald, "The 'Toolbox' of Public Policies to Impact on Fertility: A Global View," *Low Fertility, Families, and Public Policies*. Sevilla: European Observatory on Family Matters, 2000, hereafter cited in text as McDonald (2000); Ann Orloff, "Gender in the Welfare State." *Annual Review of Sociology* 22 (1996): 51–78.
4. Hans-Peter Kohler, Francesco C. Billari, José Antonio Ortega, "The Emergence of Lowest-Low Fertility in Europe During the 1990s," *Population and Development Review* 28 (2002): 599–639.
5. Colleen M. Fox, "Changing Japanese Employment Patterns and Women's Participation: Anticipating the Implications of Employment Trends," *Manoa Journal* 3 (1994): 1–5.
6. OECD, "Babies and Bosses: Balancing Work and Family Life," *Policy Brief* (Paris: Organisation for Economic Cooperation and Development, 2005), hereafter cited in text as OECD (2005); Library of Congress, "Czechoslovakia—Health and Social Welfare," *Country Studies* (Washington DC, Library of Congress, 2006).
7. C.J. Chivers, "Putin Urges Plan to Reverse Slide in the Birth Rate," *The New York Times,* May 11, 2006, late edition; Guy Laroque, and Bernard Salanié,

"Fertility and Financial Incentives in France," *CESifo Economic Studies* 50 (2004): 423–50.

8. Jody Heymann, Alison Earle, Stephanie Simmons, Stephanie S. Breslow, and April Kuehnoff, *The Work, Family, and Equity Index: Where Does the United States Stand Globally?* (Boston, MA: The Project on Global Working Families, 2004).

9. Herbert Brücker, "Can International Migration Solve the Problems of European Labour Markets?" *Economic Survey of Europe* (Geneva, UN Economic Commission for Europe, Economic Analysis Division, 2002).

10. McDonald (2000); Karen Oppenheim Mason, and Ann-Magritt Jensen, eds., *Gender and Family Change in Industrialized Countries* (New York, Oxford University Press, 1995); Constance Sorrentino, "The Changing Family in International Perspective," *Monthly Labor Review* 113 (1990): 41–58; Jean-Claude Chesnais, "Fertility, Family, and Social Policy," *Population & Development Review* 22 (1996): 729–39; Francis G. Castles, "The World Turned Upside Down: Below Replacement Fertility, Changing Preferences and Family-friendly Public Policy in 21 OECD Countries," *Journal of European Social Policy* 13 (2003): 209–27.

11. David B. Dunson, Bernardo Colombo, and Donna D. Baird, "Changes with Age in the Level and Duration of Fertility in the Menstrual Cycle," *Human Reproduction* 17 (2002): 1399–1403; hereafter cited in text as Dunson, et al. (2002).

12. O. Frank, P. Bianchi, and A. Campana, "The End of Fertility: Age, Fecundity and Fecundability in Women," *Journal of Biosocial Science* 26 (1994): 349–68, hereafter cited in text as Frank, et al. (1994); Dunson, et al. (2002).

13. Fernando Zegers-Hochschild, "The Latin American Registry of Assisted Reproduction. In *Current Practices and Controversies in Assisted Reproduction*, eds. Effy Vayena, Patrick J. Rowe, and P. David Griffin (Geneva: World Health Organization, 2004).

14. M.I. Evans, L. Littmann, L.S. Louis, L. LeBlanc, J. Addis, M.P. Johnson, and K.S. Moghissi, "Evolving Patterns of Iatrogenic Multifetal Pregnancy Generation: Implication for the Aggressiveness of Infertility Treatments," *American Journal of Obstetrics and Gynecology* 172 (1995): 1750–5, hereafter cited in text as Evans, et al. (1995); Norbert Gleicher, Denise M. Oleske, Ilan Tur-Kespa, Andrea Vidali, and Vishvanath Karande, "Reducing the Risk of High-Order Multiple Pregnancy After Ovarian Stimulation with Gonadotropins," *New England Journal of Medicine* 343 (2000): 2–7, hereafter cited in text as Gleicher, et al. (2000).

15. Tracy Shevell, Fergal D. Malone, John Vidaver, T. Flint Porter, David A. Luthy, Christine H. Comstock, Gary D. Hankins, Keith Eddleman, Siobhan Dolan, Lorraine Dugoff, Sabrina Craigo, Ilan E. Timor, Stephen R. Carr, Honor M. Wolfe, Diana W. Bianchi, Mary E. D'Alton, for the FASTER Research Consortium, "Assisted Reproductive Technology and Pregnancy Outcome," *Obstetrics & Gynecology* 106 (2005): 1039–45.

16. See also: H. Klip, F.E.V. Leeuwen, R. Schats, and C.W. Burger, "Risk of Benign Gynecological Diseases and Hormonal Disorders According to Responsiveness to Ovarian Stimulation in IVF: A Follow-Up Study of 8714 Women," *Human Reproduction* 18 (2003): 1951–8; Reija Klemetti, Tiina Sevon, Mika Gissler, and Elina Hemminki, "Complications of IVF and Ovulation Induction," *Human Reproduction* 20 (2005): 3293–300; A. Venn, L. Watson, J. Lumley, G. Giles, C. King, and D. Healy, "Breast and Ovarian Cancer Incidence after Infertility and In Vitro Fertilisation," *Lancet* 346 (1995): 995–1000.

17. A. Nyoboe Anderson, L. Gianaroli, and K.G. Nygren, "Assisted Reproductive Technology in Europe, 2000," Results generated registers by ESHRE, *Human Reproduction* 19 (2004): 490–503.
18. Division for Gender Equality, "The Equal Opportunities Act is Now More Stringent," *New Life: A Gender Equality Magazine for New Parents* (2001).
19. Pia Saldeen, and Per Sundström, "Would Legislation Imposing a Single Embryo Transfer be a Feasible Way to Reduce the Rate of Multiple Pregnancies after IVF? *Human Reproduction* 20 (2005): 4–8.
20. Swedish In-Vitro Fertilization Act, 1988: 711.
21. E.G. Hughes, and M. Giacomini, "Funding In-Vitro Fertilization Treatment for Persistent Subfertility: The Pain and the Politics," *Fertility and Sterility* 76 (2001): 431–42.
22. David K. Foot, Richard. A. Loreto, and Thomas W. McCormack, "Demographic Trends in Canada, 1996–2006: Implications for the Public and Private Sectors." In *Canada in the 21st Century* (Ottawa: Industry Canada Research Publications, 1998); Michael S. Pollard, and Zheng Wu, "Divergence of Marriage Patterns in Quebec and Elsewhere in Canada," *Population & Development Review* 24 (1998): 329–56.
23. Minister of Industry, "Canada's Demographic Situation: Fertility of Immigrant Women," *The Daily*. Statistics Canada, 2003.
24. Michael Baker, Jonathan Gruber, and Kevin Milligan, "Universal Childcare, Maternal Labor Supply and Family Well-Being," NBER Working Paper No. 11832 (December 2005).
25. Kevin Milligan, "Quebec's Baby Bonus: Can Public Policy Raise Fertility?" *Backgrounder* (Toronto: C.D. Howe Institute, 2002).
26. United Nations, *Abortion Policies: A Global Review* (New York: Population Division of the United Nations Secretariat, 2002).
27. Éric Montpetit, "Public Consultations in Policy Network Environments: The Case of Assisted Reproductive Technology Policy in Canada," *Canadian Public Policy* 29 (2003): 95–110.
28. CBC News Online, "The Assisted Human Reproduction Act," *Indepth: Genetics and Reproduction* (Canadian Broadcasting Company, 2004).
29. The Clearinghouse on International Developments in Child, Youth and Family Policies. *Issue Brief*. New York: Columbia University (Spring 2002): Table 1:Maternity, Paternity, & Parental Leaves in the OECD Countries 1998–2002. http://www.childpolicyintl.org/issuebrief/issuebrief5table1.pdf (accessed April 12, 2006).
30. United Nations, *World Population Prospects: The 2004 Revision and World Urbanization Prospects: The 2003 Revision* (New York: Population Division of the Department of Economic and Social Affairs of the United Nations Secretariat, 2004).
31. EUROPA. Population and Social Conditions. Eurostat, 2006. http://epp.eurostat.ec.europa.eu/ (accessed June 26, 2006).
32. EUROPA. The European Job Mobility Portal (EURES). http://europa.eu.int/eures/main.jsp?acro=lw&lang=en&catId=490&parentId=0 (accessed June 26, 2006).
33. V. Fineschi, M. Neri, and E. Turillazzi, "The New Italian Law on Assisted Reproduction Technology," Law 40/2004, *Journal of Medical Ethics* 31 (2005): 536–9.
34. John A. Robertson, "Protecting Embryos and Burdening Women: Assisted Reproduction in Italy," *Human Reproduction* 19 (2004): 1693–6.
35. Fabio Turone, "New Law Forces Italian Couple with Genetic Disease to Implant all their IVF Embryos," *BMJ* 328 (2004): 1334.

36. Martina Grenova, "Slovakia's Booming Fertility Tourism," *Insight Central Europe*, 2 June 2006.
37. Sanatorium   Helios.   http://www.sanatoriumhelios.cz/index_italian.html (accessed July 8, 2006); East Coast Assisted Parenting. http://www.russians-urrogacy.com/ (accessed September 7, 2006); Kosmogonia. http://www.kos-mogonia.gr/italian/italian/main.htm (accessed September 7, 2006); Istituti di Medicina della Riproduzione ed Endocrinologia. http://www.ivf-institut.cz/IT/default.htm (Accessed September 7, 2006).

# 3  Socio-Economic Transformation under Globalization

## The Case of Nepalese Women

*Meena Acharya*[1]

This paper shows how markets integrate and sometimes intensify traditional gender and other social discriminatory structures. The central question posed is whether the globalization process, with its accelerated market penetration and dichotomization of material and social reproduction, is empowering or disempowering for women in the context of economies such as Nepal. This is an economy that is just emerging from the subsistence stage with many other social divisions existing alongside gender. We shall find that globalization tends to transplant and perpetuate these divisions and the hierarchies in which they are embedded.

## CONTEXT

Although the Nepalese economy has been virtually open to the India due to its long open border and the 1950 Treaty of Peace and Friendship, economic liberalization in Nepal officially began in 1985 and accelerated after 1990. The process was wide and deep, affecting all sectors and adhering to a minimalist government philosophy.[2] Economic reforms encompassed internal and external sectors.

When the reform process started Nepal was at an early stage of capitalist development as characterized by production for the market. Its economy was largely subsistence agriculture and manufacturing units on the small-village level producing goods for the everyday needs of the villagers. This economy had already started to erode with the opening of the hinterlands by roads during the sixties and seventies, enabling slow penetration of factory-made goods from India and Nepal into the village economy. Still, in 1981 agriculture contributed about 60 percent of Gross Domestic Product (GDP) and primary products constituted 75 percent of exports. In 1984–1985,[3] at the household level about 67 percent of the income was derived from household enterprises and 61 percent from agricultural enterprises. Wages and salaries were only 26 percent of household income.[4]

Liberalization accelerated the process of market penetration as subsidies and other protections for agriculture, irrigation and domestic industries were withdrawn.[5] Rapid socio-economic transformation ensued, benefiting some and marginalizing others. By 2001, the contribution of agriculture to GDP had come down to 38 percent. Exposure of the economy to the external sector was greatly increased. Foreign trade increased from 24 percent of GDP in 1985–1989 to 40 percent in 2000–2003.

But the impact on the growth rate was not dramatic. Real GDP growth rate hovered at about 5 percent during the 1990s, showing no improvement over the 1980s. Agricultural growth rate slowed after globalization while the non-agricultural sector including manufacturing grew faster.[6] Reduction in the contribution of agriculture to the GDP was not matched, however, by a concomitant reduction of its role as an employment provider, which remained at 66 percent in 2001. The armed insurgency, which spread like fire during the 1990s in the face of increasing disparities, further slowed down economic growth and made problems worse. Only remittance income sent from external employment has kept the economy going. This income was sufficiently large to reduce the overall poverty level from 42 percent in 1996 to 31 percent in 2004.[7]

Liberalization severely reduced the viability of commercial agriculture. After the withdrawal of subsidies for fertilizer and other inputs, Nepali agriculture could not face competition from subsidized Indian products. Agriculture also declined because of a diminishing availability of free land for new cultivation. Better protection of national forestland and the introduction of community and lease forestry from the early-1980s have further reduced the availability of grazing land, eroding the viability of small livestock-raising for generating some cash income by poor households. This process has paralleled the 16th-century enclosures in England.[8]

Further, as land holdings were divided and subdivided among landed households and larger landholders started to put their land to alternative uses such as forestry and fruit farming, the demand for agricultural labor declined. Progressive penetration of the hinterlands by roads and mass-produced factory products has destroyed the market for goods made by the traditional service castes in the villages. Large numbers of landless service castes lost employment.

The nature of the household economy also changed substantially. By 2003, the share of farm income in the household had been reduced to 47 percent and the wage income share had risen to just 28 percent. Men started to look for alterative avenues of employment and income, migrating to urban areas within the country, to India, and overseas. The percent of households receiving remittances increased from 23 percent in 1995–1996 to 32 percent in 2003–2004. Seventy-six percent of these remittances were from workers employed in India or other countries.[9]

These simultaneous processes have intensified existing disparities and created new ones: between men and women, between urban and rural areas, between the hills and Terai[10] areas, between migrant and non-migrant households, between well educated and not-educated, and among people of various castes/ethnicities.[11]

What impact are these processes having on the productive and reproductive roles of women? Has women's access to income, economic resources, and sources of knowledge increased much in relation to men? How are women from various caste and ethnic groups being incorporated into the emerging class formation? Do their changing roles lead to their empowerment vis-à-vis men and the international power structure in general?

A rich series of studies from the early 1980s has investigated the economic impacts of globalizing capital on women in various contexts.[12] These issues have been explored by many feminist authors in South Asia also.[13] Most of these authors focus, however, only on economic impacts. Moreover, they deal primarily with more advanced developing countries and areas where market penetration was already deep. They have tended to be concerned more about the withdrawal of the state than about the effects of deeper market penetration in the hinterlands. In countries like Nepal with many remote and difficult-to-reach regions, market penetration is more important than withdrawal of the state, which was never there as a service provider anyway. I will examine the impact of market penetration in the specific context of globalization on women's lives in totality, covering economic, social, and political dimensions.

## DATA SOURCES

Major data sources for this analysis are the Nepal Census (1991 and 2001), family budget and living standard surveys (1984–1985, 1996–1997, and 2003–2004) and recently completed DFID/World Bank Studies on Gender and Social Analysis. Macro-level data provide background information on structural changes in the economy and overall social and human development indicators. At the micro level, household and individual data for twenty-five households, twenty-five men, and twenty-five women, from two village surveys in 2004 have been compared with 1978 studies of the same villages. Information on a total of 50 men and 50 women factory workers from Kathmandu provides the basis for examining the process of their direct incorporation in the global production chain.

## OVERALL IMPACT ON GENDER

The Human Development Index (HDI) combines per capita income, life expectancy, and educational attainment to provide a summary indicator of population well being. Nepal has made substantial progress in human development in the last two decades; from an HDI of 0.328 in 1981 to 0.526 in

2005. The gain was slightly faster during the 1980s than during the 1990s. In the first half of that decade the increase was only 0.27 points.[14]

The Gender Development Index (GDI), which compares female to male attainments on the same dimensions of per capita income, life expectancy, and education, increased from 0.328 in 1991 to 0.511 in 2005. This shows that during the l990s female-to-male disparities have been reduced faster than the overall gains. Both life expectancy and educational achievement have increased more for women than men. Yet in 2005 the GDI remains 15 points below the HDI, indicating continuing disparity between men and women. Moreover, the Gender Empowerment Index, which compares women to men in terms of access to positions of power along with earned income, education and life expectancy, was only 0.391 in 2004 (Table 3–1).

These achievements were not distributed equally between the urban and rural populations. Nor have all development and ecological regions prospered at the same rate. In the less developed regions gender disparity on these indicators is much higher.

Deciphering these overall indicators into economic, political, and social components reveals the complex, often contradictory processes at work. While women's well being has improved, the manner in which they have been inserted into the global economy has not led to much empowerment.

Table 3–1. Regional and Urban/Rural Distribution of HDI and GDI, 2001

| Regions | HDI | GDI | GEM |
|---|---|---|---|
| *Nepal* | *0.471* | *0.452* | *0.391* |
| Urban | 0.581 | 0.562 | 0.425 |
| Rural | 0.452 | 0.430 | 0.365 |
| *Eco-cultural-zones* | | | |
| Mountains | 0.386 | 0.363 | 0.356 |
| Hills | 0.512 | 0.498 | 0.408 |
| Terai | 0.478 | 0.450 | 0.372 |
| *Development Regions* | | | |
| Eastern | 0.493 | 0.475 | 0.382 |
| Central | 0.490 | 0.467 | 0.407 |
| Western | 0.491 | 0.477 | 0.395 |
| Mid-westernWestern | 0.402 | 0.385 | 0.363 |
| Far-westernWestern | 0.404 | 0.377 | 0.368 |

*Source:* HMG/ UNDP, 2004

## ECONOMIC ASPECTS

### Income and Property

In terms of purchasing power parity dollars,[15] women's earned income is only half of what men earn. Using this measure, in 2005 men earned PPP$1868 while women earned PPP$949. Women's wages lag behind men's as well.

In property ownership women lag further behind. As per the 2001 Census, women in very few households owned property by themselves. About 11 percent of households reported some land in female legal ownership. Similarly only 5.5 percent of households had a house in a woman's name. Only 7.2 percent of households reported female livestock ownership, in-spite of multiple credit institutions funding this activity for women. Households having all three—house, land, and livestock—under female ownership constituted a paltry 0.8 percent. Almost 83 percent of households had no property under women's legal ownership. This contrasts sharply with 88 percent of the households owning their own house, nearly 71 percent having animals, and 76 percent having their own farm in the district of residence[16]. On the average, female-headed households had only 0.50 hectares of farm land compared to 0.78 hectares held by the male-headed households.[17]

Despite the cultural differences between the Indo-Aryan and the Tibeto-Burman groups and within each of these groups on matters related to gender, land is inherited universally in all communities from the father to the son and women lag far behind men in access to economic resources.[18] Not much change occurred in this system in last twenty to twenty-five years. Legal changes in the early 2000s made it a bit easier for unmarried daughters to inherit parental property and ensured a daughters right to claim support for survival on equal footing with her brothers. It also made a woman's rights to property more secure in her afinal (husband's lineage) household by removing the conditions that she had to be 35 years old and completed fifteen years of married life to claim her deceased husband's property. However, as before, a daughter had to return her share of property to the natal (house of her birth) household after marriage. Only in 2006 has the newly reinstalled Parliament withdrawn this requirement. Similarly a woman may claim her husband's property only on certain conditions. Thus, the institution of marriage is still the major determining factor for her rights to claim, own, use, and control property.

In spite of the plethora of credit programs, women's access to institutional credit is still marginal. Even in 2004, women clients account for less than 2 percent in the total outstanding credit from banks and financial institutions.[19] Women's access to institutional credit has been consistently lower than that of men, irrespective of ecological regions, urban or rural areas, and ethnicity and caste (Acharya, 2000).

## Economic Opportunities, Occupational
## Status, and Working Conditions

The proportion of economically active women in Nepal has always been high compared to other South Asian countries (Acharya, 2003b). Economic activity rates of both men and women in rural and urban areas and in all ecological and development regions have increased between 1991 and 2001. However, more rural men and women are economically active than urban men or women. Urban rural differences are much higher for women. Thus the trend observed internationally that the shift in production processes from the household to the market in the early stages of capitalist development tends to reduce women's role in the economic activities is visible in Nepal as well. While 58 percent of rural women were economically active in 2001, only 38 percent of urban women were reported so. This shows declining economic opportunities in the comparative male-female perspective, although it is expanding in absolute terms. A large group of women are being converted into pure consumers and housewives.

Several factors hinder women's participation in the labor market when production activities are externalized from the household to the marketplace. Participation in the market as elementary workers is usually not acceptable to middle-class households, unless it becomes economically necessary for the household. Also, with industrialization the spatial separation of reproduction (reproducing human beings) from production of goods and services becomes inevitable, and women with young children have difficult choices to make: give up their visible economic work, take their children to workplace, or leave them without good care and supervision. The choice often imposed by social expectations is for mothers to give up their visible productive role if family finances allow.

Moreover, women from the rural labor class who work in the labor market lack the necessary educational prerequisites to work in the modernized sectors. Consequently, the majority of women in both the agricultural and non-agricultural sector are employed in the non-formal sectors where work schedules are more flexible and the workplace is more compatible with children.[20] A high proportion of these workers are in knitting, cutting threads and cleaning, packaging garments, and carpet weaving.

Women's relative concentration in agriculture is also notable, despite the transfer of some women workers from home-based, local-market-oriented production to factory-based, export-oriented production and tourism-oriented service sectors. In 2001, women constituted 48 percent of the agricultural and 34 percent of the non-agricultural labor force. The representation of women workers in agricultural wage employment increased dramatically from 25 percent in 1991 to 50 percent by the early 2000s, indicating the deteriorating situation of small farmer-households that could no longer survive on their own cultivation. However, in the better-paid, non-agricultural sector of wage employment, the proportion of women has remained at about

18 percent since 1991 despite expansion in carpet and garment industries and services. Opportunity for non-agricultural employment for women in relation to men seems to have increased much faster in the pre-globalization period between 1981 and 1991, when it had increased from 14.5 to nearly 19 percent (Acharya, 2003b).

In terms of wages, women are concentrated in low-paying, less-productive, low capital-intensive jobs (CBS/NPC, 1999). Most of the labor regulations are sidetracked by employing women at piece rates.[21] Overall at the national level, in terms of daily wages women earned about three-fourths of what men earned both in agriculture and non-agricultural sectors (CBS/NPC, 2004). In agriculture this ratio declined from four-fifths in 1996.

Detailed studies show appalling conditions of work in many industrial units, particularly in carpets and garments, the country's major exports, and the main sectors of women's manufacturing-sector employment (Appendix 3–1). A survey conducted between 2005 and 2006 of fifty men and fifty women factory and hotel workers in Kathmandu shows that all female and 80 percent of male carpet weavers earned less than US$40 a month. In the export industries of carpets and garments, nobody earned more than US$80 a month. About 70 percent of workers were paid on piece basis, which means there is no job security, provision for leave, or other facilities. The carpet workers were mostly migrants from rural areas, lived in factory provided dormitories with four workers plus children in one twelve-by-twelve-foot room, and took their children to work. They came from landless or near-landless families with less than 0.05 hectares of land.

Both pay scale and working conditions in the export industries seemed to be much worse than either in food or hotels, whose products were more domestic-market and tourism- oriented. In contrast to exports, the domestic industries employed 97 percent of their women workers on a permanent basis and provided legally required leaves and other facilities. Workers were more evenly distributed between urban and rural origins, migrants and non-migrants and caste/ethnicity. The differences between the export and domestic industry show how traditionally discriminatory structures are transferred into the globalized factory space.

Overall, a larger proportion of women workers were in the lowest earning brackets than men, despite longer work experience. On the average those at the lower end of the pay scale, both men and women, worked longer hours. Men and women had similar number of years in the lowest- and highest-earning brackets, but women had less education in the US$40–80 earning bracket.

Though women did not fare as well as men, they were less likely to complain. Only 20 percent of the women workers interviewed in the carpets and 30 percent of all women workers were not happy with the working conditions, while much higher percentages of men expressed dissatisfaction. This suggests women feel a higher level of insecurity because of lack of alternative work opportunities.

Given the scarcity of employment opportunities within Nepal, external migration (to India, the Gulf countries, and other countries) is being used as a coping mechanism. Historically not much employment-oriented external female migration was recorded despite some trafficking for commercial sex work, mostly to India. In recent years, particularly since the mid-1990s, both voluntary and forced (trafficking) female migration has increased rapidly. Most of the increased female migration, as male migration, is for employment. Women have also started to seek employment beyond India. Though complete recent figures on total women migrants are not available, a recent UNIFEM/NIDS (2006) estimates slightly more than 78 thousand women worked abroad between 2005 and 2006, of which more than half worked in the Gulf countries.[22]

## SOCIAL ASPECTS OF EVOLVING PATRIARCHY

### Education

Nepal has made significant gains in education. Male literacy among the age group of six and above has increased from 34 percent in 1981 to 65 percent in 2001. Similarly, the female literacy rate among this age group has more than trebled, from 12 percent in 1981 to 42.5 percent in 2001. Neverthless, disparities persist. Gender parity in school enrollment has not been achieved even at the primary level (SAHAVAG, 2006). The higher the educational level, the lower the number of women with comparable educational degrees. For example, while the number of women with primary education was 77 compared to 100 men with the same level of education in 2001, the number of women with secondary school and higher degrees was only 43, and with graduate and higher degrees only 23. These ratios have not improved in the last decade. Among the 6-to-25 age group, out of the total student population girls constitute 43 percent.

Besides gender, urban/rural location, regions of residence, and above all, caste and ethnicity are important factors governing educational access. Higher caste groups have much better access while the Dalits of the Terai have the lowest access to education (Table 3–2). Between 1991 and 2001, the Terai Dalit women with just an 11-percent literacy rate in 2001 had made the least progress among Hindu women, while Muslim women have made no progress even in basic literacy.

Gender disparity is visible in all castes and ethnicities, and more so in the Terai groups despite the better facilities in Terai areas. This indicates a higher level of gender discrimination within the family in these areas. Urban-oriented groups (Newar/Thakali) and Other Hill Janajati groups have the highest female-to-male ratios in educational attainments beyond literacy.

In the Indo-Aryan communities (caste groups), the ideology of the purity of female body described by Bennett (1993) still rules supreme. It is a matter

Table 3-2. Literacy Rates and Educational Attainments of Population Six Years and Above by Caste/Ethnicity, 2001

| | | | Literacy | | SLC and above*** | | BA/BSC and above*** | |
|---|---|---|---|---|---|---|---|---|
| | Caste\ Ethnicity** | % increase in F literacy rates | Female | F/M* ratio | Female | F/M ratio | Female | F/M ratio |
| I | Hindu caste groups | | | | | | | |
| 1 | Brahmin/ Chhetri | 19.2 | 55.9 | 72.5 | 2.5 | 46.0 | 0.3 | 20.5 |
| 2 | Terai Middle Caste | 13.2 | 26.3 | 42.4 | 0.5 | 20.3 | 0.1 | 11.2 |
| 3 | Hill Dalits | 17.1 | 31.8 | 65.4 | 0.1 | 32.3 | 0.0 | 19.5 |
| 4 | Terai Dalits | 7.5 | 11.5 | 36.1 | 0.1 | 18.7 | 0.0 | 17.1 |
| II | Janajatis | | | | | | | |
| 5 | Newar/ Thakali | 14.5 | 62.6 | 77.9 | 7.4 | 61.8 | 1.5 | 43.6 |
| 6 | Other Hill Janajatis | 18.1 | 42.3 | 71.4 | 0.6 | 50.5 | 0.1 | 30.6 |
| 7 | Terai Janajatis | 18.7 | 31.5 | 53.1 | 0.2 | 19.7 | 0.0 | 8.3 |
| III | Muslims | 0.8 | 11.4 | 31.5 | 0.3 | 12.1 | 0.1 | 10.1 |
| | *Total* | *16.9* | *42.5* | *65.8* | *1.5* | *43.6* | *0.2* | *22.9* |

Source: TPAMF, 2005
*F=Female; M=Male
** For group composition see Appendix 3-2 and footnote 10.
*** SLC = 10th class completers; BA/BSC = who have completed 14 years of education either in humanities or science

of honor for the family to marry off their daughters, giving rise to practices like dowry/Tilak.[23] After marriage, the bride is transferred to the new home. The natal home may not claim any part of her earnings nor does she have any responsibility to them. She also forfeits all rights to property in the natal household. These practices mean that the natal household receives no benefit for the costs of educating daughters. Once a girl is married, procreation, children, and household responsibilities take the first priority in her life because her status in the household rests on her success in such matters. All of her economic and social rights depend on whether she can gain footage in the new household. Therefore daughters are socialized to make marriage their first livelihood option and priority. The whole system is structured so that it hampers women's access to education, health resources, and advancement in career jobs. Unfortunately, certain features of this system are strengthened rather than weakened under global consumerism. There are increasing demands for dowry/Tilak, which greatly hinders girl's access to higher education.[24]

## Sex Ratio, Life Expectancy, and Health Status

The sex ratio of men per 100 women netted of migratory trends reflects the overall social status of women. In Nepal, the overall sex ratio had changed in favor of women during the 1980s, reducing from 105 in 1981 to 99.5 in 1991. But it has slightly increased in favor of males to 99.8 in 2001. This could be a statistical error or an evidence of increasing female fetus abortion, as in India. The comparative access of boys and girls to health resources is clearly reflected in the mortality rate of children less than the age of five, which is 104.8 (per thousand) for boys and 112.8 for girls, showing discrimination against girls. The population ratio in favor of males increases from birth to until the age of fourteen, after which it declines because of male migration. Although the life expectancy of women has improved to 60.7, slightly surpassing that of men, it is still one of the lowest in the region.

Women's access to services related to family planning, pregnancy and delivery is increasing. Contraceptive prevalence rate has reached 39 percent in 2001 from 29 in 1996.[25] Total fertility rate (RFR) has declined to 4.2 while the maternal mortality rate per 100,000 deliveries has come down to 415 (Acharya, 2003b). Nevertheless these rates are still high even by South Asian standards. Moreover fertility reduction is largely accounted for by women using contraceptives or sterilization. A high proportion of men, 69 percent, continue to think that sterilization is equal to castration in 2001 (MOHP, et al. 2001).

As in education, there is a large difference in the access to services by various groups of population. For example, while it takes only 20 minutes to get to the source of contraceptive devices in Central Development Region, it takes 60 minutes in the Mid-Western Region. Differential access to reproductive health services and the caste and gender problems involved is illustrated by a study of three administrative areas in the FarWestern border district of Darchula. A total of 144 cases of prolepses, an easily remedied condition, were found, with the incidence of disease highest among women from Dalit and poor families. None of the local health institutions, from village to district hospital, were aware of the situation, while the district was full of public notices about STD and HIV/AIDS risk (SAHAVAGI, 2006), a stark example of dissonance between local problems and global remedies.

Other studies have also pointed out such differences in access (DFID/ World Bank, 2005). Brahmin/Chetri[26] and Newar women tend to have

**Table 3-3.** Selected Indicators on Access to Health Services by Caste and Ethnicity, 2005

| Caste/Ethnicity | Receiving antenatal care | Knows ways to avoid AIDS (2001) | fully immunized children under 5 years | | | Contra-ceptive user % |
|---|---|---|---|---|---|---|
| | | | Boys | Girls | Difference | |
| Brahmin/ Chetri+ | 63.2 | 43.9 | 61.2 | 60.2 | 1.0 | 40.5 |
| Terai middle castes | 77.4 | 11.9 | 60.0 | 50.7 | 9.3 | 33.9 |
| Dalits | 55.6 | 27.0 | 50.7 | 52.7 | -2 | 28.1 |
| Newars | 71.5 | 57.8 | 70.5 | 68.2 | 2.3 | 44.4 |
| Hill Janajati | 46.7 | 43.5 | 58.2 | 55.6 | 2.6 | 36.9 |
| Terai Janajati | 55.3 | 34.8 | 44.0 | 40.0 | 4.0 | 51.3 |
| Muslim | 60.3 | 9.3 | 58.1 | 55.7 | 2.4 | 12.6 |
| *Total* | *57.1* | *37.8* | *61.5* | *57.2* | *4.3* | *38.3* |

Source: DFID/World Bank, 2005, CBS, 2004 NLSS and MOHP,et. al, P/HMG, et. al, 200

higher access while Dalits, Terai middle caste and communities in remote areas tend to have lower access (Table 3–3). While urban Newar women had higher access to all services and HIV/AIDS awareness, Hill Janajati had lower access to antenatal care and Dalits were much behind other groups in AIDS awareness and among the family planning users. The case of Muslims is surprising. While they have higher access to antenatal care, they are far behind in terms of AIDS awareness, family planning use, and child immunization. Such differences in availability and use of services may be attributed to higher gender discrimination among the Terai middle castes and Muslims. This shows the crucial role of cultural factors in women's access to health and education.

## Violence against Women

Violence, in the domestic as well as in the public arena, is still used extensively to establish domination over women of all ages, from fetus to old age.[27] SAMANTA (2005) reported beating, slapping, or kicking, pulling hair, verbal abuse, use of a stick, knife, or *khukuri* (Nepali sword) causing injury to the head and other parts of the body, burns including acid burns, etc. as common forms of physical violence.[28] Even pregnant women were not spared such violence. Forms of cultural violence, such as dedicating women publicly to goddesses or gods (*deuki*); condemning whole groups of the population to commercial sex-work (*badini*); discrimination against widows; child marriage; the knee-burning ceremony in some communities; and banishment of women to cowsheds during menstruation and delivery (*Chaupadi*) are still prevalent. One-third of urban women and 25 percent of men thought it was acceptable for a husband to beat his wife for any reason— for example, burning food, an argument, going out without informing the husband, neglecting children, refusing to have sex, etc (MOHP, et al, 2001).

Domestic violence may increase as erosion of the household economy increases women's need to work outside the family economy. As women enter the work market, their mobility and assertiveness increase. In a society dominated by the patriarchal value system, this assertiveness may result in domestic conflict. Moreover, expectations and demands for dowry/Tilak also increase the risks of violence against women in the household.

Women are facing new risks of violence as they come out of the secluded life into public places such as streets, the workplace, and police custody. The recent political situation of insurgency and counterinsurgency has also endangered their personal security severely. Displacement caused by the insurgency, poverty, and lack of adequately paying jobs at home are forcing an increasing number of women to move out of their usual habitat and fall in the trap of sex traders. Globalization of the market for the sex workers has made this trade very lucrative. Younger and younger girls are reported to be lured to this trade, overtly or covertly (New ERA, 1998).

## ACCESS TO THE POLITICAL POWER STRUCTURE AND EMPOWERMENT

Legal equality is necessary for empowerment and political equality. In Nepal women still face inequities in the constitution and the laws. The Constitution of the Kingdom of Nepal (1990), although seemingly non-discriminatory and protective of women, is fundamentally discriminatory against women in such basic rights as citizenship. Until recently a mother's citizenship did not entitle her children to Nepalese citizenship at all, which was based solely on the father's line of descent. Moreover, the constitutional provision for "equality without discrimination" applies only to the application of law, not to the discriminatory laws themselves. Even after the 2002 amendments to the Civil Code, there were still 275 discriminatory provisions in the Constitution, laws, acts, and regulations[29] relating to inheritance, ownership and disposal of property, marriage and family, legal and court proceedings, trafficking and sexual abuse, employment and education. Women's mobility is restricted by laws regarding night employment. The ban on the migration of women to employment in the Gulf countries was still in effect until recently. Even adult women needed the consent of a guardian to receive a passport until this was struck down by the Supreme Court in 2005.

The citizenship and a few other laws have been changed in November 2006. These changes make easier for women to get citizenship for her children if she can prove that the child has a Nepalese father, but Nepalese descent along the mother's line is still not recognized. Children of a Nepalese woman marrying a foreigner may obtain only naturalized citizenship, and that only on conditions which may be difficult to prove. The requirement that a married daughter had to return the property to the natal household after marriage has also been lifted. Marital rape and sexual harassments have been recognized as crimes.

Women's access to positions of power, political or otherwise, has not improved much in the last 10 to 15 years. The 1990 Constitution contained a legal mandate that political parties ensure that 5 percent of the candidates are women, but women still have not been able to be represented by more than 6 percent of the current House of Representatives. In the earlier Panchayat Parliament women had a similar level of representation, suggesting the new provision is ineffective. Women candidates have often complained that political parties allocate them constituencies that are difficult to win. The cabinets formed in the last decade have not included more than two women or given important positions to them, barring one or two exceptional cases. One female member in twenty to fourty-five ministers has been the rule. In 2005 women constituted less than 10 percent of the Central Committee members of the major political parties.

In 1997 there was a major breakthrough. Twenty percent of all seats in village assemblies were reserved for women, bringing a significant proportion of women into grassroots politics. There is also a provision that at least one woman and one representative from Dalits/Janajatis will be nominated by the executive bodies of the Village/Municipality Board and District Councils, members of which are elected by the respective assemblies. Still in the district councils, women constituted only 1.5 percent even with such mandatory nominations. The higher the position, the lower the female representation. Moreover, due to the fact that they are nominated and not elected as other members, women are less effective (SAHAVAGI, 2006). A bright spot in this scenario is the Parliamentary Declaration of May 30, 2006 promising a 33-percent reservation for women in all organs of government. However, its implementation is still shaky.

The problem of low representation of women in the government administration in general, and in the decision-making levels in particular, has been equally endemic. Women constitute less than 10 percent of the total government staff. Not much effort has been made to change this position in the last decade. One woman each has been appointed to the Supreme Court, NPC, and PSC among the constitutional bodies. The Civil Service Administration Act (1998) has made some concessions for women, on entrance age (five years), the probationary period (six month) and waiting period for eligibility in promotion (one year) since 2002 (SAHAVAGI, 2006). But these changes have had little effect. Further, caste and ethnicity emerge as the major differentiating factor in access to positions of power and decision-making roles (DFID/World Bank, 2005).

As to the process of empowerment, with the democratic changes in the early 1990s women have been mobilized extensively into groups by various NGOs/INGOs, government programs, and political parties. One study found more than 200,000 community groups engaged in various activities in the country. Another study covering about 2000 men and women from sixty villages of different parts of the country found that women were much empowered in terms of their mobility and voice in household decision-making compared to a previous 1978 study.[30] Nevertheless compared to men, they had less confidence in availing of the government/NGO provided services, police, and courts, even though a larger percentage of women were group members than men. My findings from two current village case studies confirm this pattern (Acharya, 2006).

The impact of discriminatory ideology and structures was manifest in the structure of group membership and empowerment. Bennett and Gajurel (2004) note that women from high Brahmin/Chetri castes were much more empowered in terms of their access to services and confidence in dealing with law enforcement agencies or service providers than women from other ethnicities and castes. Dalits were the most disadvantaged.

## CONCLUSIONS

Though the overall human development indicators suggest that women have gained much under globalization, the process of empowerment has not gone very far. On the economic front, the move of poor, rural women and men to factory work in labor-intensive export industries has given them some alternative source of income and widened the scope for individual choice. However, the old discriminatory structures and international competition have combined to keep their working conditions inhuman. Women are more disadvantaged than men on these jobs.

Although the changes in the structure of the economy had started earlier, government interventions had been made to protect local industries, subsidize small agriculture, education, health, and other social services. Under the current global restructuring, government interventions are supposed to facilitate the market and not limit its scope. This involves privatizing major public resources and activities (in Nepal, for example, forests, transport, and other public enterprises) and withdrawing almost all kinds of subsidies and privatizing all sectors. This process has usually accentuated the existing inequalities along with creating new ones (Acharya, 2003a). Old social discriminatory structures have been shifted to the modern jobs as well. New class formation is not destroying the old gender or social divisions, but fortifying the older social divisions and creating new ones. To the differences between the social classes are now added the differences between highly

**Appendix 3-1.** Work Conditions and Pay Scale by Industry (in Percent)

| | Carpets | | Carpets + garments = export | | Noodles + hotels | | All | |
|---|---|---|---|---|---|---|---|---|
| | Men | Women | Men | Women | Men | Women | Men | Women |
| **I. Total number of workers (Number)** | 39 | 61 | 46 | 54 | 74 | 26 | 64 | 36 |
| | *(66)* | *(104)* | *(117)* | *(138)* | *(648)* | *(230)* | *(831)* | *(472)* |
| Total interviewees Number of Interviewees | 10 | 10 | 20 | 20 | 30 | 30 | 50 | 50 |
| **Percent by pay Pay Scale\1** | | | | | | | | |
| *1000–3000* | 80 | 100 | 40 | 70 | 10 | 10 | 18 | 34 |
| *3001–6000* | 20 | — | 10 | 30 | 67 | 50 | 60 | 42 |
| *6001–9000* | — | — | 40 | — | 20 | 23 | 16 | 14 |
| *9001 and above* | — | — | 10 | — | 3 | 17 | 6 | 10 |
| **II. Mode of Payment** | | | | | | | | |
| *Daily Wage / Piece Rate* | 80 | 100 | 65 | 70 | 33 | 3 | 42 | 32 |
| *Temporary/ Permanent* | 20 | — | 35 | 30 | 67 | 97 | 58 | 68 |
| **III. With Training** | 2 | 5 | 25 | 55 | 9 | 40 | 28 | 46 |
| **IV. Level of Satisfaction** | | | | | | | | |
| *Satisfactory* | 10 | 30 | 10 | 20 | 10 | 10 | 10 | 14 |
| *Good* | 40 | 50 | 60 | 50 | 37 | 60 | 46 | 56 |
| *Not good* | 50 | 20 | 30 | 30 | 53 | 30 | 44 | 30 |
| **V. Living quarters Quarters** | | | | | | | | |
| *Home* | — | — | — | 10 | 60 | 73 | 36 | 48 |
| *Factory-provided* | 90 | 70 | 60 | 35 | — | — | 24 | 14 |
| *Other* | 10 | 30 | 40 | 55 | 40 | 27 | 40 | 35 |

Source: Field survey

1/ Nepalese Rupees 70.35 = US$1

**Appendix 3-2.** Caste/Ethnic Groupings and Their Proportion in Total Population, 2001

| Caste/Ethnicity | Percent |
|---|---|
| *Caste groups Groups (1+2+3+4)* | *57.5* |
| 1. Brahman/Chhetri = Hill Brahmin, Chhetri, Thakuri, Sanyasi; Terai Brahman (Terai), Rajput, Kayastha, Baniya, Marwadi, Jaine, Nurang, Bengali, | 32.8 |
| 2. Terai Middle Castes = Yadav, Teli, Kalwar, Sudhi, Sonar,Lohar, Koiri, Kurmi, Kanu, Haluwai, Hajam/Thakur, Badhe, Bahae, Rajbhar, Kewat, Mallah, Nuniya, Kumhar, Kahar, Lodha, Bing/ Banda, Bhediyar, Mali, Kamar, Dhunia | 12.9 |
| 3. Hill Dalits = Kami, Damai,,Sarki, Gaine, Badi | 7.1 |
| 4. Terai Dalits = Chamar, Musahar, Dhusadh/Paswan, Tatma, Khatway, Bantar, Dom, Chidimar, Dhobi, Halkhor, Dalit/ Unidenified Dalit | 4.7 |
| Janajatis (5+6+7) | 42.7 |
| 5. Newar/Thakali | 5.5 |
| 6. Other Hill Janajatis = Magar, Tamang, Rai, Gurung, Limbu, Sherpa, Bhote, Walung, Byansi, Hyolmo, Gharti/Bhujel, Kumal, Sunuwar, Baramu, Pahari, Advasi Janajati, Yakkha, Chhantal, Jirel, Darai, Dura,. Majhi, Danuwar, Thami, Lepcha,,Chepang, Bote, Raji, Hayu, Raute, Kusunda | 23.0 |
| 7. Tarai Janajatis = Tharu, Dhanuk, Rajbanshi, Tajpuriya, Gangai, Dhimal, Meche, Kisan, Munda, Santhal/Satar, Dhangad/ Jhangad, Koche, Pattarkatta/ Kusbadiya, | 8.7 |
| 8. Muslim, Churoute | 4.3 |
| 9. Unidentified /others Others | 1.0 |
| 10. Total | 99.9 |

Source: TPAMF, 2005

educated and not educated, those who are computer literate and educated at private English schools and those with low-quality education, those from rural societies and the more advanced urban societies. All of these differences combine to produce new classes of divisions between very rich capitalists and poor or unemployed workers.

Globalization is not only an economic process. It is a multidimensional process encompassing all aspects of life, economic, political, and social. In its current phase it involves unfettered market penetration and global consumerism together with advocacy for democracy, gender equality, and inclusion.

However, the ideals of democracy and gender equality are translated in practice only to a limited extent. The emphasis has been on integrating women into the system as new economic agents, to prepare them for industrial employment with minimal literacy and schooling levels, and to maintain the viability of small farm households in the face of male migration by supplementing their incomes through social mobilization and micro- credit/micro-enterprise promotion. Legal-formal and informal discrimination persists in economic and social fields, which hinders women in the exercise of political rights. Globalization has incorporated some of the patriarchal features of subordination to intensify exploitation.

Empowerment is not only about a little mobility, a little voice within the household in mundane matters of what to purchase and what to cook, or a little education and health access. It is an ongoing, multidimensional, and dynamic process, encompassing all spheres of life: the political, the economic and the social/religious. The final goal of empowerment is to transform the ideology and practice of domination and subordination. It means challenging and transforming existing power structures, systems and institutions that have upheld and reinforced this discrimination in order to gain access and control over material and knowledge resources.[31] Despite increased political awareness, the results of surveys suggest that Nepal has gone little beyond rhetoric in translating this consciousness into substantial change in gender status. Viewed from this perspective Nepalese women have gained little power. With the shift of material production from the household to the public arena, they might be losing the power they had.

## NOTES

1. I am grateful to the Fulbright for selecting me for the New Century Scholars program for 2004-5, which gave me chance to renew my knowledge base and build a network of like-minded researchers from around the world, and resources to go back to the village for the field study. Similarly I express my gratitude to the IDCP at Clark University for accepting me as a scholar and providing all of the facilities at the university. Professor Barbara Slayter, William Fisher, and many others in the University and the IDCP deserve my special thanks for the warmth they showed me. Special thanks are also due to Professor Carolyn Elliott who led our group successfully through the year. I also like to express my appreciation to the Asmita Group, without whose help it would not have been possible to complete the field study in such a short time.
2. Keshab P. Acharya, Nara Bahadur Thapa, and Shiva Sharma, *Economic Liberalization in Nepal: Sequence and Process* (Kathmandu, Nepal: OXFAM GB-Nepal, 1998).
3. Nepal's fiscal year is mid-July to mid-July. For example, 1984–1985 means these figures are for the period between mid-July of 1984 to mid-July of 1985.
4. Nepal Rastra Bank. *Multipurpose Household Budget Survey: A Study on Income Distribution, Employment and Consumption Patterns in Nepal* (Kathmandu, Nepal: Nepal Rastra Bank, 1988).
5. See the following for a detailed discussion on this process of market penetration and its implications for women: Meena Acharya, *Labor Market Developments*

*and Poverty in Nepal: With Special Opportunities for Women* (Kathmandu, Nepal: Tanka Prasad Acharya Memorial Foundation, 2000), hereafter cited in text as Acharya (2000); Meena Acharya, "The Economic Foundations of the Current Socio-Political Crisis in Nepal." In *Nepal Tomorrow: Voices and Visions,* ed. D.B. Gurung (Kathmandu, Nepal: Koselee Prakashan, 2003a), hereafter cited in text as Acharya (2003a).

6.  Meena Acharya, Yuba Raj Khatiwada, and Shankar Aryal, *Structural Adjustment Policies and Poverty Eradication* (Kathmandu, Nepal: Institute for Integrated Studies, 2003).

7.  World Bank, Poverty Trends in Nepal between 1995–1996 and 2003–2004: Background Paper for Nepal Poverty Assessment (Kathmandu, Nepal: World Bank). Unpublished mimeograph, May 12, 2005); hereafter cited in text as World Bank (2005).

8.  Karl Polanyi, *The Great Transformation* (Boston: Beacon Press, 1957).

9.  Central Bureau of Statistics/NPC, *Nepal Living Standards Survey, 2003/2004,* vols. 1 and 2 (Kathmandu, Nepal: HMG, 2004); hereafter cited in text as CBS/NPC (2004).

10. Nepal has three ecological belts, high mountains, the hills, and the Terai plains, and five development regions, which are inhabited by people of different ethnic/cultural groups. While analyzing these groups in 1981, we (Acharya and Bennett, 1981) classified them into two major groups, Indo-Aryan and Tibeto Burman, on the basis of their racial origin and the socio-cultural space accorded to women. On the basis of women's participation in the labor market, decision-making roles within the household, and greater freedom in marriage and sexual matters, we concluded that the Tibeto-Burman group was more egalitarian towards women as compared to Indo-Aryan groups, who idealized seclusion of women. According to the 2001 census, there were 100 ethnic/caste groups and subgroups in the country, of which Indo-Aryan caste groups constituted 57 percent and Janajatis (Tibeto-Burman and Terai ethnic groups) about 37 percent. The religious minorities—Muslims, Sikhs, Christians, and others—accounted for 4 percent. About one percent did not report their ethnicity/caste or religion. All three groups are divided into multiple subgroups. Traditionally the Hindu high castes—Brahmin, Chetris, and Newars—have exercised power in Nepal and have highest access to resources and education, while the Dalits and certain tribal groups have been most disadvantaged, with lowest access to power structure, resources, and education. See Meena Acharya and Lynn Bennett, *An Aggregate Analysis and Summary of 8 Village Studies: The Status of Women in Nepal,* vol. 2, part 9 (Kathmandu, Nepal: CEDA, 1981); hereafter cited in text as Acharya and Bennett (1981).

11. World Bank (2005); NPC/UNDP, *Nepal Human Development Report 2004: Empowerment and Poverty Reduction* (Kathmandu, Nepal: United Nations Development Program, 2004); DFID/World Bank, Citizens With (Without) Rights: Nepal Gender and Social Exclusion Assessment, final draft (Kathmandu, Nepal: DFID/World Bank, June 2005), hereafter cited in text as DFID/World Bank (2005); Tanka Prasad Acharya Memorial Foundation, *Analysis of Caste, Ethnicity and Gender Data from 2001 Population Census in Preparation for Poverty Mapping and Wider PRSP Monitoring,* a report submitted to DFID, Kathmandu. Unpublished mimeograph, 2005.

12. Janet W. Salaff, *Working Daughters of Hong Kong* (Cambridge: Cambridge University Press, 1981); Liisa North and John D. Cameron, *Rural Progress Rural Decay: Neoliberal Adjustment Policies and Local Initiatives* (Bloomfield, CA: Kumarian, 2003); Fauzia Erfan Ahmed, "The Rise of the Bangladesh Garment Industry: Globalization, Women Workers, and Voice," *NWSA*

*Journal* 16, no. 2 (2004): 34–45; Christa Wichterich, *The Globalized Woman* (London/New York: Zed Books, 2002); Shirin M. Rai, *Gender and Political Economy of Development* (Cambridge: Polity Press, 2002); Saskia Sassen, *Globalization and Its Discontents* (New York: The New Press, 1998); Nancy Folbre, *The Invisible Heart* (New York: New York Press, 2001); Isabella Bakker and Stephen Gill, *Power, Production and Social Reproduction: Human Insecurity in the Global Political Economy* (New York: Palgrave Macmillan, 2003).

13. Nirmala Banerjee, ed., *Indian Women in a Changing Industrial Scenario* (New Delhi: Sage Publications, 1991); Radhika Balakrishnan, ed., *The Hidden Assembly Line: Gender Dynamics of Subcontracted Work in a Global Economy* (Bloomfield, CT: Kumarian Press, 2002); Naila Kabeer and Ramya Subrahmanian, *Institutions, Relations and Outcomes* (New Delhi: Kali for Women, 1999).

14. UNDP, *Human Development Report* (New York: United Nations, 2005).

15. The Purchasing Power Parity dollar (PPP$) is a unit specifically devised and used by the World Bank for measuring comparative actual incomes of various countries. It is not equal to the U.S. dollar. While income in U.S. dollars is simply Nepalese Rupee income converted at the prevailing exchange rate, the PPP$ compares the purchasing power of each currency in its own country with the purchasing power of the U.S. dollar in the U.S.

16. The information on household farmland collected in 2001 Census includes all farmland under a household's cultivation in the district, excluding rented out land and land in other districts under its ownership. Therefore it is not quite comparable with women's ownership, but in Nepal rented out and rented-in land constitutes a small proportion of the total farmland.

17. Meena Acharya, "Changing Gender Status—Achievements and Challenges." In *Population Monogram of Nepal* (CBS Kathmandu Nepal, 2003b); hereafter cited in text as Acharya (2003b)

18. Acharya and Bennett (1981); Jeannette D. Gurung, ed., *Searching for Women's Voices in the Hindu Kush Himalayas* (Kathmandu, Nepal: ICIMOD, 1999).

19. SAHAVAGI, *Gender Equality and Empowerment of Women: An Update.* Submitted to UNFPA, Kathmandu, forthcoming in 2007; hereafter cited in text as SAHAVAGI (2007).

20. Central Bureau of Statistics/NPC, *Nepal Labor Force Survey* (Kathmandu, Nepal: HMG, 1999); hereafter cited in text as CBS/NPC (1999).

21. GDS/FES, *Women in Garment Industries* (Kathmandu, Nepal: GDS/FES, 1997); GEFONT, "Search for Alternatives" (Kathmandu, Nepal: GEFONT, 2003).

22. UNIFEM/NIDS. *Nepali Women and Foreign Labour Migration* (Kathmandu UNIFEM/Nepal Institute of Development Studies, 2006).

23. Dowry is given to daughters and, in principle, is her property. This practice prevails in the Hill communities. Tilak is given to the bridegroom or his family, on which the girl has no claim even in principle. In Terai communities both dowry and Tilak prevail.

24. Meena Acharya, "Global Integration of Subsistence Economies and Women's Empowerment: An Experience from Nepal." In *Globalization, Governance and Gender,* eds. Isabella Bakker and Rachel Silvey. NY: Routledge, forthcoming. Hereafter cited in text as Acharya (2006); Nirmala Banerjee, "Between the Devil and the Deep Sea: Shrinking Options for Women in Contemporary India." In *The Violence of Development,* ed. Karin Kapadia (New Delhi: Kali for Women, 2002); Karuna Chanana, "Female Sexuality and Education of Hindu Girls in India." In *Sociology and Gender,* ed. Sharmila Rege (New Delhi: Sage Publications, 2003).

25. MOHP/HMG, New Era and ORC Macro, *Nepal Demographic Health Survey* (Kathmandu, Nepal, 2001); hereafter cited in text as MOHP, et al. (2001).
26. Currently we do not use the terms "high caste" Brahmin/Chetri or "low caste" for Dalits, as they are considered derogatory to the Dalits. It is a question of political correctness.
27. SAATHI and the Asia Foundation, *A Situation Analysis of Violence Against Women and Girls in Nepal* (Kathmandu, Nepal, 1997); New ERA, *A Situation Analysis of Sex Work and Trafficking in Nepal with Reference to Children,* October 1996. Submitted to UNICEF, Nepal (mimeo), 1998; hereafter cited in text as New ERA (1998).
28. SAMANTA, *A Study on Linkages between Domestic Violence and Pregnancy* (Kathmandu, Nepal, 2005).
29. FWLD, *Shadow Report to CEDAW Monitoring Committee, Nepal* (Kathmandu, Nepal: Forum for Women, Law and Development, 2003).
30. Lynn Bennett and Kishore Gajurel, *Negotiating Social Change: Gender, Caste and Ethnic Dimensions of Empowerment and Social Inclusion in Rural Nepal* (Kathmandu, Nepal: World Bank, November 2004); hereafter cited in text as Bennett and Gajurel (2004).
31. Kamala Bhasin and Dhar Sunita, *Joining Hands to Develop Women Power, a Report of a South Asian Workshop on Gender and Sustainable Development* (Koitta, Bangladesh, 1998); Meena Acharya and Puspa Ghimire, "Gender Indicators of Equality, Inclusion and Poverty Reduction for Measuring Program/Project Effectiveness," *Economic and Political Weekly* 40, nos. 44 and 45 (2005): 4719–28.

# 4 Empowerment of Women Migrant Factory Workers in South China

## Opportunities and Contradictions

*Esther Ngan-ling Chow*[1]

Responding to global economic restructuring, the international division of labor, and world economic integration, China began economic reforms in 1978 to move into a freer market economy. One of the major outcomes has been massive waves of workers hastening from rural to urban areas and from city to city in search of a better life. This internal migration has been propelled by the macro force of industrialization, which has created job opportunities and incentives motivating people to move from less-developed to more prosperous regions within China. In the past, migration tended to favor men, who left home to seek jobs elsewhere to support family at home. Despite the fact that the number of women migrants has been increasing not only in China but also worldwide, much more is known about factors influencing men's migration than about those influencing women.[2] To fill this literature gap, my study focuses primarily on women's migration experience in China as compared to that of men.

Three research questions guided my inquiry: In what ways is migration gendered? How is gendered migration related to the meaning and practice of empowerment for migrant women workers? What social and cultural contexts may facilitate their development of empowerment in the migration process and what major contradictions in this regard have emerged from their migration experience? How gendered migration bears on workers' lives depends on the historical and contextual specificities of a given country. China, as a rapidly developing county with a huge, floating migrant population in major cities, provides a unique case study for examining women's and men's experience as migrant laborers.[3]

A perplexing question is whether migration is empowering for women given the stresses of factory work and survival in a new urban environment. Existing literature on empowerment tends to focus on the process by which women's agency fosters capability building, autonomy, and making choices and how these qualities influence their subsequent attitudes and behavior (e.g., fertility choices and reproductive health). While these topics are of interest, I argue for the study also of the social construction of empowerment: examining the major conditions, both institutional and ideological, that set parameters influencing the extent to which empowerment potential is developed, articulated, and circumscribed in the migration process.

The purposes of this paper are to explore the engendering nature of migration, to contextualize the conditions under which women migrant workers' empowerment develops in South China, and to examine how these women experience major contradictions inherent in the processes of migration. I will first discuss how I use the empowerment concept and then examine the structural and ideological conditions under which women migrants may or may not empower themselves. I will present evidence of women's developing self-empowerment in two phases of migration—before and during migration. Finally, I will discuss how women are constrained by the contradictions that are inherent in the migration process and will sum up how these women assess their position in the labor market.

## CONCEPTUALIZATION OF EMPOWERMENT

Empowerment is a complex, multifaceted, and fluid concept which has evolved over time since the late 1970s and early 1980s. Relevant discourse has gradually identified multiple conceptual meanings.[4] In this study, I define empowerment as a process of capacity building to take control of resources, to make decisions about strategic life choices, and to challenge the power of gender regimes[5] that constrain one's options, autonomy, and well being while seeking to achieve desirable life outcomes.

Central to the concept of women's empowerment is the building of their inner strength from the bottom up rather than by a top-down process imposed on them externally. Power is understood as "power within," or self efficacy; "power with," or the capacity to organize with others toward a common goal or struggle; and the "power to" effect change for oneself as well as for a group (Rowlands, 1995). Empowerment is both a goal in itself and a process that leads to other achievements and outcomes. The specific outcomes of empowerment are to meet "practical and strategic needs and interests"[6]—basic needs for everyday survival (e.g., shelter, food, sanitation) and strategic needs for change in unequal power relations and oppressive social structures that subordinate women. These outcomes may also bring about transformations for women as well as for some men who are disadvantaged because of their class, race/ethnicity, age, nationality, sexual orientation, and other differences. Empowerment has two main dimensions: "self" for individual women and "collective" with others for mobilization and action. The ultimate goal of women's empowerment is the transformation when women, individually and collectively, engage in self-examination, voice their needs and interests, and become active agents to change power relations and social inequality. Given space limitations and the complexity of the concept, this paper focuses on the findings and analyses regarding individual empowerment.

## SOCIAL AND CULTURAL CONTEXTS OF
## EMPOWERMENT AND MIGRATION

Fundamental to women's empowerment is the relationship between agency and structure and between individual and society.[7] I argue that empowerment embraces both sides of this coin, necessitating a contextualized understanding of the structural base that shapes the conditions, the processes, and the consequences of women's empowerment. Some feminist scholars argue that women's empowerment requires systemic transformation (e.g., Sen and Grown, 1987; Batliwala, 1994; Bisnath and Elson, 2003)[8] of institutions that support the "inequality regime" (Acker, 2006) of which the gendered power regime is a constitutive part. If empowerment has emancipatory potentials, it is important to interrogate structures and ideologies that support asymmetrical power relations derived from gender, class, race/ethnicity, nationality, and other differences. In this study, I make a distinction between power as embodied in structures (e.g., the state, the economy, and the family) and power as inherent in ideologies (i.e., belief and values). These forms of power reinforce each other, prescribing the behavior of women and men, justifying existing gendered arrangements, and perpetuating unequal power relations.

This study explores how three major institutional domains—the family, the economy, and the state—shape individual migration decisions, processes, and outcomes, particularly women's empowerment. Most of the existing literature on these subject matters focuses on the individual and household levels. A common assumption is that the migration decision represents an individual's rational choice. Jacob Mincer advances a theory of family migration which views the household as a socioeconomic unit for which migration is a responsive adaptation.[9] All family members are involved in using migration as a strategy for family survival in order to maximize resources while minimizing risks and costs of migrating. Although this household model compensates for the tendency to see the household as a passive unit,[10] the model is grounded on the shaky assumption of a monolithic household based on consensus and without conflicting interests and diverse experiences among its members. The fact is that the migration experience is found to be gendered by women's and men's various contrasting interests and expectations, resulting in their different migration experiences.

Women are increasingly participating as laborers in the economic migration process.[11] A number of empirical studies have shown that market access or labor force participation has cross-culturally and positively affected women's influence in household resource allocation, decision-making, and personal autonomy.[12] Some researchers caution that women may be empowered in one area while not in another, depending on social or cultural setting, household characteristics, gender ideology, and social networks.[13] Social construction of traditional gender roles greatly determines the image of women, their types of work, degree of their freedom for movement, taboos for women (e.g., *purdah* practices), and the value of womanhood.

Social network theories have pointed out that social capital in terms of ties and contacts is an important enabling factor, mediating between the individual migrant and macro changes.[14] The presence of family members, kin, friends, and even acquaintances provides social connection, personal influence, information about sending and receiving places and the likelihood of obtaining jobs, thus reducing the costs and the risks of migration, settlement, and bargaining with families.[15]

Finally, I incorporate the role of the state in examining the interplay between capitalism and patriarchy. Besides China's powerful assertion of macroeconomic policies, it also regulates population growth (e.g., the one-child policy) and migration flow (e.g., the *hukou* policy to restrict labor) and deprives citizen of entitlements at the place of destination (this will be explained below). Also, in partnership with transnational corporations (TNCs) and local firms, the state and local governments determine, directly or indirectly, the ways in which women and men enter the segmented labor market, the kinds of jobs they do (e.g., women's or men's work), and the rewards they may receive (e.g., fringe benefits), laying the material bases for the workers' social existence at the micro level. Although previous feminist scholarship[16] has examined the primacy of capitalism and patriarchy, my study adds the significant impact of the state and its politics on the economy, the household, and the workers' personal experience.

## THE STUDY

This exploratory study uses survey and field research as well as two kinds of interviews—face-to-face and in-depth—to observe and measure women migrant workers' empowerment as shaped by various institutions and ideologies in the manufacturing sector of Guangzhou and nearby areas.[17] The combined approaches provide empirically quantitative data as well as allow women to give voice and meaning to these data.

I conducted the survey by using quota sampling, controlling for two main factors—firm ownership and size—inside and outside of the Lotus Special Economic Zone (SEZ).[18] Once factories were selected and entry permission was given, workers were chosen by gender and by rank (i.e., high, middle, or low) according to their approximate proportions within that factory.[19] Survey interviews used a semi-structured questionnaire that ensured that certain data were collected while presenting an opportunity to clarify and probe regarding questions that less educated workers would not be able to answer in writing. Within each factory, a subsample of workers, two-thirds of them women in each case, was selected for in-depth interviews. Survey interviews lasted about one to one-and-a-half hours, whereas in-depth interviews took two to four hours for completion. Both were administered in Chinese, mostly in the factories, worker dormitories, and public places at times and locations that were most convenient for workers. The study included

268 workers from three types of firms—joint-venture, foreign-owned, and locally owned respectively—in the survey analyses and forty-six in-depth interviews from the field research in the qualitative analyses.

Because empowerment is a goal as well as a process, I explore the development of three components of empowerment—access to and control of resources (i.e., travel costs, loans, social capital, income disposal), strategic choice decision-making (i.e., the migration decision, job search or change), and dealing with gender regimes of the family, the firm, and the state in the two phases of before and during migration.[20] The survey provides most of the direct and some proxy measures of empowerment, which are supplemented and deepened by the in-depth interview data.

## ECONOMIC REFORMS AND FEMINIZATION OF LABOR

From its inception in 1949, socialist China's closed system had resulted in economic stagnation and backward development. By 1978, China had shifted from centralized state planning to a free-market economy and had embarked on economic reforms including foreign investment, industrial restructuring, and establishment of special economic zones (SEZ). The main purpose was to achieve modernization and industrialization by stimulating regional economic development, revitalizing local markets, and reducing poverty. By 1980, zones in Guangzhou of South China had attracted many foreign-invested enterprises with a high labor demand, especially in the manufacturing sector, creating employment opportunities sufficient not only for locals but also for migrant workers from afar.

One striking phenomenon is the gendered nature of the migration.[21] Great numbers of workers originating from the rural areas poured into the new economically prosperous regions in search of a better life. Their numbers far exceeded those in the local labor force ready to work in unskilled, low-ranked, and low-paying jobs. While migration in the north had tended to favor men, women migrant workers outnumbered men in South China. Government-sponsored labor outsourcing programs in some rural areas may contribute to the mounting number of women workers in the manufacturing industries. By the mid-1990s, it has been estimated that approximately six million migrant workers had concentrated in the Guangzhou area and on the Pearl River Delta and that two-thirds of these were women.[22]

In my non-state sector sample, 91 percent of workers employed in the manufacturing firms were migrants. Among these, 63.8 percent were women and 36.2 percent were men, percentages that reflect the actual sex composition of the local labor force in that industry. Migrant workers' mean age was twenty-five years old, and 82 percent of them were single. In comparison to their male counterparts, women workers tended to be younger, more often single, and with fewer years of education, half having completed only junior high school or less.[23] Very few workers (two to three percent) migrated before 1990. The year of 1993 marked a drastic increase in labor migration and subsequent labor force entry (over 10 percent per year). Two-thirds of the workers originated from rural areas and one-fourth from small towns. Half of them were from other parts of Guangdong province, while 30 percent were from outside the province (such as Guangxi, Hunan, and Sichuan provinces).

## PRE-MIGRATION PHASE: MAKING THE DECISION

Who made the decision to migrate for jobs to urban areas in South China? Why did they make this decision? In both my survey and field samples, about three-fourths of the workers said that they had made the labor migration decision, a strategic life choice, by themselves. Table 4–1 shows that gender differences in this decision-making are statistically significant. While women were more likely than men to "usually or mostly" make the decision by themselves (75 percent and 70 percent respectively), men had a greater tendency than women to either consult or jointly decide with other family members on labor migration. These findings appear inconsistent with family migration theory which views the household rather than the individual as determining the migration decision.[24] We should examine what is different in the historical and social contexts of China that lead to this difference in migration decision-making.[25]

Some clues are provided by the different women's and men's responses to survey questions asking them to select the five most important factors in their decisions concerning whether and where to migrate. "Search for Better Job Opportunity" (82 percent) topped the list for both men and women, followed by "Have Relatives/Friends at the Destination" (46.5 percent), "Lack of Local Job Opportunity" (45 percent), "Look for Educational Opportunity," (27.8 percent), and "Need Better Living Conditions" (17.2 percent). Although both genders equally considered working to be important, men workers were more practical than women workers in thinking about finding jobs that would support the family, provide educational opportunities, and improve their living conditions. Women workers, who were younger than the men, scored higher on "Have Relatives/Friends at the Destination" (48 percent vs. 34.6 percent) and "Self Exploration" (5.1 percent vs. 2.7 percent). These findings show a slightly higher tendency for women than men to consider migration as a form of personal growth through discovery of the world away from home. At the same time, women were more likely than men to choose a destination where they could rely on relatives and friends for assistance.

Among several explanations, state control plays the most prominent role in appropriating labor from the rural areas and subsequently shaping household options and individual motives regarding migration. The state's appropriation of labor was accomplished by using a *hukou* policy

**Table 4–1** Migration Job Decision and Work Attitudes by Gender (N=268)

|  | *Total* | *Men* | *Women* | X *Squares* |
|---|---|---|---|---|
| *Labor Migration Decision* |  |  |  |  |
| Mostly/Usually by Family Member | 4.5% | 2.8% | 5.4% | 13.08, p<.01 |
| Jointly Decided | 22.3 | 27.4 | 19.7 |  |
| Usually Decided by R | 24.1 | 35.6 | 18.4 |  |
| Mostly Decided by R | 49.1 | 34.2 | 56.5 |  |
| *Importance of Working* |  |  |  |  |
| Utmost Importance | 29.2% | 35.4% | 25.6% | 3.34, ns |
| Very Important |  | 49.6 | 46.9 | 51.2 |
| Fairly Important |  | 15.6 | 21.4 | 19.3 |
| Unimportant |  | 1.9 | 2.1 | 1.8 |
| *Reason of Migration* |  |  |  |  |
| Search for Job Opportunity++ | 82.2% | 93.5% | 76.9% |  |
| Have Relatives/Friends at Destination | 46.5 | 34.6 | 48.0 |  |
| Lack Local Job Opportunity | 45.0 | 51.7 | 44.4 |  |
| Look for Educational Opportunity+ | 27.8 | 43.6 | 22.9 |  |
| Need Better Living Conditions+ | 17.2 | 31.0 | 13.5 |  |
| Family Reallocation with Parent/Spouse | 11.9 | 16.2 | 10.2 |  |
| State/Military Assignment | 9.1 | 16.2 | 7.1 |  |
| Self-exploration | 5.6 | 2.7 | 5.1 |  |
| Natural Calamity at Home | 2.7 | — | 3.4 |  |

Note: ++ Chi-Square value is statistically significant at equal or greater than the .002 level.

+Chi-Square value is statistically significant at equal or greater than the .05 level.

and a labor outsourcing program. Originating in the mid-1950s, *hukou,* a residence registration system, requires all persons to register their place of residence as determined by their birthplace or their parent's residence. This system was first set up as a geographical division of labor between rural and urban areas. It became a control mechanism for regulating rural-to-urban movement and a status marker for de-legitimizing rural migrants from becoming legal residents of urban China. Without urban *hukou,* rural migrants as transient laborers must apply for a temporary work permit enabling employment in the cities, but not offering the same entitlements as those received by urban citizens. Because of high urban demand for labor in the 1980s, the Chinese government proclaimed labor outsourcing to be a strategy for poverty reduction in certain rural areas. This strategy, while broadening household's economic options and income resources, also diminished the power of the patriarchal family to control its members.

Another factor influencing rural migration has been the response of the transnational corporations (TNCs) and local firms, which use the social construction of gender to economic advantage for both profit-making and efficient management. Materially, to cut production costs, they perceived women to be a cheaper labor source than men. Ideologically, they stereotyped women workers, characterizing them as manually dexterous, docile, meek, and thus easy to manage and suppress should labor unrest occur. Labor contracts offered by manufacturing firms to local governments stipulated that they sought predominantly women workers. Because this new reality of preference for women gave them the socioeconomic advantage, local governments and even parents were readily convinced to let their daughters go. As interviewee Yuen Chun explained,

> When the local government announced the labor outsourcing plan, my brother and I applied right away. As you may know, it costs us one hundred *yuan* [Chinese currency unit] each to submit our applications. If you are chosen, you will pay five hundred more for the travel, accommodations, and processing fees. I felt lucky being chosen in the first group of two hundred applicants, mostly women, going from my village. . . . . It took us three days and two nights to get to Dong Quan by train and buses. I had a job placement waiting for me when I arrived. . . . . Well (she exclaimed), my brother was not so lucky and he was told that the factories did not need that many men to operate machines. The bosses like women workers to do most of the simple things like making toy parts.

Another explanation for the Chinese pattern of migration lies in the changing nature of the patriarchal household and village community.[26] In an agrarian society, farming depends primarily on men as the key labor source, although women often work side-by-side with men in the field. In the prereform era, male dominance in the rural household, parents' authority over their offspring, preference for sons, and restrictions against women traveling afar limited these women's options to migrate. When China's economic reform abolished the commune system in 1978, the peasants' reliance on small plots of allotted land for subsistence production became insufficient. Stagnant growth, surplus labor, lack of industry, natural disasters, and a bad harvest created inadequate food supplies, unemployment, and poverty. The political economy of the post-reform era, however, has created new material and ideological conditions for some rural women, albeit discrimination against them remains.

The opportunity to enter the factory door in a free labor market has meant an additional income source and a rising social status for the household as well as for the employed women.[27] These women were also tempted by tales of a "gold mountain" of economic prosperity in the south that promised a fortune to workers, families, and villages. While parents at first tended to keep their elder sons with them for old-age security, they were more willing to let their daughters and younger sons join temporary labor migration because the state *hukou* registration system restrictions against permanent urban residency would offer some degree of guarantee of their return. Once parents had begun to reap the benefits of their offspring's migration, these and their other children—regardless of their birth order and whether they were key or surplus labor—were relatively free to migrate in the early 1990s.

In cases of family opposition, rural women attempted strategies such as manipulation, subversion, and resistance to deal with patriarchal constraints against their migration. It was particularly difficult when their villages did not organize labor outsourcing programs. One women worker, Pui Han, confessed that she instructed friends to participate in a manipulative scheme by painting a rosy picture for her parents of working in a factory of South China. Her parents took their words for it and allowed their daughter to move with her friends to search for factory job in the south.

Resistance to parent's objections was difficult because individual women often did not have the resources to undertake such a long journey without support from family and kin. An exception was Yuen Ling, who told this story of how she rebelled:

> When I asked my parents whether I could accompany my friends to Guangzhou to work, they flatly rejected my proposal. In spite of their objections, I left with my friends the next day without packing many of my belongings. After I arrived in Guangzhou, I called home to tell them where I was. However, my first job was terrible . . . I somewhat regretted that I had not listened to my parents' advice. But I was stubborn in sticking to my own decision. It would have been shameful to have gone home with empty hands, don't you agree?. . . . . After two years of struggle, I got a better job and was promoted to a line supervisor. Now my parents are so proud of me having a good job . . . and have almost forgotten my disobedience in running away from home.

On the one hand, these migrant women workers were brave, audacious, and tenacious in exerting their agency to make a key decision for migration at a critical period in their late adolescence or early adulthood and in rounding up resources (e.g., savings, gifts, and loans) for this risk-taking adventure.

On the other hand, in the interviews they also expressed the perplexity of mixed emotions of excitement and anxiety they had experienced as they confronted their uncertain destinies ahead. Discussion in the next two sections will make the reasons apparent for these contradictory emotions.

## DURING MIGRATION: THE DEVELOPMENT OF INDIVIDUAL EMPOWERMENT

The migration process itself presents a new socioeconomic reality that is both enabling and challenging to migrant workers, especially women. I report on four interrelated dimensions of individual empowerment—economic, educational, social, and psychological.

### Economic Empowerment

Wage employment means economic power. It has enabled migrant workers to become "rice" earners, contributing members of households with a strong sense of their own economic independence. In the post-reform era, both genders were free to sell their labor in the urban industrialized areas where jobs are abundant. Cash income had become a critically important form of economic gain for many poor rural women.[28] One worker, Honjing, explained her changing economic situation: "I like neither schooling nor farming. After I dropped out from junior high school, I was idle for three years. Being the youngest one with three older siblings, I was not expected by my family to do much farm work except during harvest time. . . . . If I liked, I would raise a few chickens. . . . . Frankly, I was not much use in the household. Now I am preoccupied with work to earn 'big' money that I had never dreamed of earning before. I can't wait for pay day every other week." While Honjing actually was receiving only modest remuneration, by her standard in comparison with rural earnings, her factory wage seems generous to her.

Table 4-2 shows that women workers tended to have lower wages than men because they were concentrated in what are commonly known as "women's jobs," performing simple, unskilled, manual tasks with low rank and pay. Assembly-line jobs were held by 82 percent of women workers in contrast to 62 percent of men. The gender wage gap was found to be statistically significant, with women earning just 77 percent of what men did.

The central question is whether migrant workers have the power to decide how to dispose of their income. Although men workers' decision making in the amount of income disposal was controlled slightly more by their parents or parent-in-laws, no substantial gender difference was evident in such control. Regardless of gender, only about one-fourth of workers said that all or more than half of their wages were controlled by their parents or parent-in-laws. Slightly more than one-third of the workers decided to

Table 4-2 Frequency Distribution of Income Disposal and Allowance by Gender (N=268)

| Main Variables | Total | Men | Women | Statistics |
|---|---|---|---|---|
| *Job Rank* | | | | |
| High | 10.7% | 16.1% | 7.7% | $X^2$=12.72 |
| Middle | 14.1 | 21.5 | 10.1 | p<.002 |
| Low (assembly-line) | 75.2 | 62.4 | 82.2 | |
| Wage (mean Yuan) | 782 | 916 | 711 | t=3.96 |
| US $ Equivalence | $95 | $112 | $87 | p<.001 |
| *Amount of Income Disposal* | | | | |
| All by Parents/In-Laws | 6.2% | 7.3% | 5.6% | $X^2$=3.2, ns |
| Half by Parents/In-Laws | 20.2 | 22.0 | 19.4 | |
| Less than Half by Parents/In-Laws | 39.0 | 36.6 | 40.0 | |
| All by R's Disposal | 34.6 | 34.1 | 35.0 | |
| Amount for Monthly Allowance (in Yuan) | 180.49 | 244.25 | 148.26 | t=4.30 p<.001 |

Note: ns—statistically insignificant at greater than the .05 level.

let their parents or parent-in-laws control less than half of their wage while another one-third reported no parental control of earnings.

Although parents and relatives might have instructed that remittances should be, and are expected to be, sent home, the plain fact is that this was difficult because these workers earned meager wages. After deducting expenses for housing, food, and other life necessities from their paychecks, workers on average could save half or less of their wages. They could not send large remittances home even if they felt obliged to do so. Being dutiful working daughters and wives, women workers tended to spend less and save more than men. While working sons and husbands were expected to contribute more financially to the family, they seemed to negotiate better with the patriarchal household, keeping more back for personal allowances (29 percent more than women workers).[29]

## Social Empowerment

This dimension refers to the enabling force that strengthens or weakens the migrant's social relations and their position in social structures. Through wage employment and breaking away from one's family, the migration process reshapes the notion of personal autonomy. Breaking away means gaining a relative degree of freedom from the geographical boundaries of one's hometown, from the patriarchal control of one's family, from the bondage of kin and neighbor, and from the scrutiny of local officials. Through migration, workers became "urban floaters," invisible in a large sea. The newly experienced sense of freedom, like a breath of fresh air, can exist as long as a migrant is away from home. As a 17-year-old Leung Tsz happily remarked: "My life here is quite different from living at home. I feel free to make friends with whomever I want. If I don't tell, no one in the village knows how much I actually earn, save, and spend. As long as I send some money back home, my parents and brother will not and cannot interfere in my life here, even if they want to. Though I am quite free and independent, I have learned to discipline myself and have remained obedient to my parents. It is a choice that I have to make."

While workers enjoy their relative autonomy and self-reliance, migration is also sometimes used as an escape from an unhappy marriage, family conflicts, pressure from parents to marry, and or involvement in farm production. Yin Chun, a 21-year-old woman worker from Sichuan province who had been employed in a factory for four years, complained about low wages and boredom at work. In spite of this, she planned to remain in Guangzhou for the time being. She explained, "I do not want to go back home now. Perhaps I'll look for another better job and work two or three more years. My parents constantly nagging me to marry and to have a family really annoy me." Postponing marriage and family was often justified by workers' continuing ability to send remittances home, thus increasing their own social status and well-being as well as that of their families in the eyes of other villagers. Building a new, preferable brick house has become a status symbol in rural China, a parents' dream (sometimes the worker's dream as well) fulfilled through the migration of their offspring's labor.

The migratory movement from the rural areas has transplanted workers socially, economically, and to some extent politically into the new social milieu of South China. Social capital, such as network ties accessible through direct and indirect social contacts, becomes critically important in the processes of mobilizing resources to cover migration costs, to obtain or change jobs, to adjust socially in the place of destination, and to deal with sickness and other urgent problems.

The social gains of making new friends and building networks were critically important to many of the migrant women workers. Workers tended to form cliques according to the closeness of previous social relations, ranging from kin relations to those from the same place of origin, schoolmates, friends, and acquaintances. Those who originated from the same village, town, or province called each other "*lao xian,*" which means "clansman" or "clansperson," and formed mutual support networks offering help, trust, and understanding. They helped each other solve financial, social, and emotional problems. Thus respondent Yuen Ling from Hunan province expressed her heartfelt thanks to her "*lao xian*," who had sneaked her into the factory dormitory illegally and had shared meals with her for over a month when she was unemployed after quitting her first highly exploitative job. Such alliances enabled the migrants' everyday survival.

## Educational Empowerment

Contrary to the common belief that migrant workers of humble rural origins are naïve and ignorant, and are coming to South China to "dig for gold," a significant number of the migrant workers I interviewed are better character-ized as "explorers," "pioneers," and "innovators." Men tended to be more highly educated and trained than their female counterparts and hence better able to obtain mid- or high-level jobs. While half of women workers in this study had junior high school or less education and 41 percent a high school education, another 4 percent had some vocational training and 4.7 percent either some college or a college degree. Thus 10 percent of the migrant women were able to secure mid-level jobs (e.g., line supervisor, quality control staff), and a few attained even higher positions (e.g., assistant manager, division head). Liu Fung, the Director of the factory's Research and Development divi-sion, was one such exceptional case. She told her story as follows:

> I believe that if I put my mind into doing my work, eventually I will succeed. One key is to actualize my potential in the workplace. Being trained in a technical college as a mechanical engineer, I was hired in the R & D division. After one year, I designed a way to bypass two steps in the production line. The general manager of the factory was so pleased with how such a design saves production costs. When I was up for my two-year job evaluation, I was promoted to the Director position of this unit when the post was vacant.

Although the majority of migrant workers were not so fortunate as to have had many years of schooling and training before entering the factory, they sought occupational knowledge and skill acquisition in their jobs. As Table 4–1 shows, 44 percent of men and 23 percent of women workers claimed "look for educational opportunity" as one of the main motives for their migration. Many told me of their yearning for new knowledge and skills training. Some had a futurist outlook and looked forward to job mobility. A few women used their limited time to enroll in computer train-ing, bookkeeping, and business management courses at night after a full day of factory work. As respondent Chin-Kuan put it, "Money is not every-thing, you know. I want to learn new things and get some skills as much as possible while I am working doubly hard in this firm. Many of us do not want to be line workers forever. We *must* examine our situation and find ways to improve our lots."

## Psychological Empowerment

Migrant workers have not only transgressed geographic boundaries, but have also transformed their selves and subjectivities. The women migrant workers I studied have psychologically empowered themselves by recognizing their self-worth, building their self-confidence, and taking control of their lives. Relatively speaking, migration has offered them opportunities to see and to know more of the world than those do who have stayed behind. This personal growth and exploration has given them self-respect, pride, maturity, and resiliency as they have exerted their independence away from home. At the same time, some acknowledged that they might sometimes need parental advice and care, particularly when they are sick. Yuen Ling, a line supervisor, blossoming into a smile, said, "Being a factory worker is like being an 'iron girl.'[30] We can be firm, tough, and hardworking as an example for other girls in the village. I consider that I am more useful as a person than I originally thought. With a strong spirit to overcome difficulty, I believe that I may achieve my dream of being a manager someday!"

At the micro level, a major indicator of psychological well being is satisfaction in various aspects relating to work, living, learning, personal, and financial situations. These are subjective and evaluative measures of well-being to understand the over-all outcomes of their migration as workers experienced their empowerment. In the survey, workers were asked, "Having moved here, in general, how satisfied are you with . . . ?" Table 4–3 reports the results for the six dimensions of satisfaction on a Likert-type scale consisting of four response categories—"very satisfied," "satisfied," "dissatisfied," and "very dissatisfied." On the average of the six dimensions of satisfaction, 65

Table 4–3 Dimension and Degree of Work Satisfaction (N=268)

| Dimension of Work Satisfaction | Degree of Work Satisfaction | | | |
|---|---|---|---|---|
| | Very Dissatisfied | Dissatisfied | Satisfied | Very Satisfied |
| Work Condition | 1.6% | 21.6% | 69.2% | 7.6% |
| Living Environment | 1.4 | 21.3 | 64.3 | 13.9 |
| Personal/Social Relation | 0.8 | 15.6 | 75.3 | 8.2 |
| Educational Opportunity | 4.6 | 32.1 | 55.7 | 7.6 |
| Family Financial Contribution | 15.6 | 35.5 | 39.3 | 9.5 |
| Saving | 20.7 | 38.3 | 27.7 | 13.3 |

percent were either "Satisfied" or "Very Satisfied," whereas 35 percent of workers were either "Dissatisfied" or "Very Dissatisfied" with their current job situations.

Workers' responses of satisfaction fell into two general patterns. On the one hand, 83 percent of the workers were satisfied with the social relationships they had developed in their personal lives, and nearly three-fourths of them were satisfied with their working and living conditions. On the other hand, 37 percent of them were very much dissatisfied with the educational and training opportunities at their job and did not think that they had learned much. The majority of workers were also either highly dissatisfied or dissatisfied with the amount they were able to contribute to family finances and personal saving (51 percent and 59 percent respectively). No gender differences were found on any dimensions of workers' satisfaction responses. Because it was evident that one-third of the workers were dissatisfied with aspects of their work and personal life, some discussion of the contradictions of wage employment and its disempowering potential in the migration process is in order.

## CONTRADICTIONS OF EMPOWERMENT AND CITIZENSHIP

The experience of migration is paradoxical for many migrants. What they find to be empowering in one migration stage may become less so in another stage, and what is considered empowering in one context may be disempowering in another, even at the same stage of migration. These paradoxes reflect the mixed (positive and negative) consequences of labor migration at the macro level and the disabling and enabling aspects of migration at the micro, individual level.

While migrant workers gained economic power and independence, they simultaneously confronted new forms of dependence as a result of the interaction among the waged labor market, patriarchal control, the managerial regime, capital production, and state power in the migration process. The majority worked long hours in poor working conditions, were placed on the bottom rung of the job ladder, and performed dead-end jobs for low pay with few fringe benefits and limited security.[31] With a zeal for learning, they wondered whether their assembly-line work would offer them much occupational knowledge beyond a minuscule, monotonous, and manual skill.

Occupational segregation by gender increased the negativity for women. Jobs were designated primarily either for women or for men,[32] which erected barriers limiting training and job mobility. While most women workers tended to think that they were on equal employment footing with their male counterparts, some men workers tended to stereotype them.[33] One male worker, Wing Tak, argued that men's work was worth more than women's, offering an essentialist viewpoint regarding femaleness and maleness. He proudly remarked, "Men workers can do what women do in this factory. And yet women can't do men's jobs. The plain fact is that we men do heavy, dirty, difficult, and sometimes dangerous tasks as machinery operators or construction workers." Mao Tse Dong's widely known slogan of the 1960s, "The times have changed; men and women are the same. What men can do, women can do too," seems to have fallen by the wayside in the recent rush away from socialism toward a free-market economy.

Furthermore, adjustment to new urban areas has created new social and psychological dialectics for migrant workers. The women have experienced a greater degree of personal autonomy, becoming relatively free from familial obligations and exercising self-determination in daily decision-making. But prejudice by local residents against migrant workers because of their differences in dialects, customs, and food habits have augmented the migrants' personal agony, social maladjustment, and occasional homesickness.[34] The transformation of personal identity from a rural peasant to urban factory workers has challenged worker's evolving self and subjectivity. Hence, the migrant's social and urban identity is a transient one that will eventually revert back to that of peasant upon their returning home.

At the corporate level, migrant workers increasingly were under the control of managerial regimes. To prevent migrant workers from hopping from one factory to the other, managements of the different firms set up control mechanisms and punitive measures to keep workers in place. For example, a high security deposit (usually one month's wage), submission of a work permit and other identification cards, and deferred wage payment were common tactics used by employers and managers to deter workers from leaving. Any workers who did not comply with factory regulations were free to go, but they sometimes had to forgo their security deposits and wage payments. If workers damaged product parts, produced below quota, or took excessive break time, they faced payroll deductions.

Although workers might have been aware of their economical dependence on the factory as exploited laborers and their positioning in the labor market, they resisted passively in their everyday life. The fact is that most migrant workers did not have the time or energy to become involved in labor organizing and feared being laid off or identified as trouble makers. Only very few in recent years have begun to organize and participate in NGOs and grassroots groups to deal with pressing labor issues and problem.[35]

State policy provides an additional set of contradiction relating to the use of *hukou* (the residential registration system) and the labor outsourcing program. The key problem is that the state continues to use the *hukou* policy to regulate population movement, separating urbanities from peasantry and stipulating different citizenship entitlements for each group. This dualistic system creates what I have called a "citizenship divide," because this spatial demarcation between urban and rural citizens creates a class-based distinction which results in second-class citizenship for migrants (Chow 2006). Not only are rural migrants concentrated in lower-paid jobs with few or no fringe benefits, but they are also excluded from arrays of state-provided welfare benefits and services, including education, medical care, and even affordable housing in some areas. In addition, migrant women workers face problems involving reproductive health service delivery, gender-based violence against women, human trafficking, and the sex trade. These depletions of citizenship are due to the state-engineered *hukou* policy, preventing migrant workers from enjoying equal rights and full entitlements.[36]

A labor outsourcing program, another way the state appropriates labor, became popular from late 1988 to 1991 as a way to manage massive, uncontrolled rural-to-urban migration. It lost its effectiveness when migrants flowed spontaneously through social networks and other market channels. However, migrant workers as a transient labor force with temporary work permits were essentially a cheap labor source appended to the urban labor market only so long as they were needed to serve capitalist interests sanctioned by the state.

## WOMEN MIGRANT WORKERS' ASSESSMENT

A key question is whether rural migrants think labor migration has been good for women migrant workers. Although they have experienced mixed outcomes, about two-thirds of the women respondents thought that the overall results were, relatively speaking, more positive than negative. Economic migration had generally met their basic needs and permitted them to experience some degree of socio-economic empowerment, though more was desired. The women migrant workers felt that they were more confident, less timid, and more self-reliant than they had been before departing from their homes of origin.

They also unequivocally agreed with the men that higher wages were at the top of their wish lists. They knew that they were exploited laborers, but were willing to accept these jobs. When faced with strategic life choices—staying in the rural area vs. relocating to the urban area, doing self-sufficient farm work vs. relying on paid employment, and subjecting themselves to parental supervision vs. a factory's managerial regime—their logic seemed to be, "A good job is better than a bad job; a bad job is better than no job." As one migrant woman worker, Lai Hua, summed up the situation, "Yes, it is a tough life, engaging in everyday struggle in a strange and alien land. At least I have a job here for which I receive pay. The last time I returned to my village, for three months, I felt so awful that I basically got not a single penny by sitting around at home and looking at the leaking roof and dried mud wall."

On the whole, the migrant workers' abilities to challenge the unequal relations of power embedded in different gender regimes—in the family, the economy, and the state—remain weak and uneven. Under strong state control, the possibility for the workers to join in collective solidarity is hopeful, but the prospect for labor resistance is still bleak.

## CONCLUSION

In this study, I have raised three research questions for social inquiry and provided both quantitative and qualitative data gathered by survey and field research in south China to address these questions. The three research questions are: In what ways is migration gendered? How is gendered migration related to the meaning and practice of empowerment for migrant women workers? What social and cultural contexts may facilitate the women workers' development of empowerment in the migration process and what are the major contradictions emerging from their empowerment experience?

First, I have explained the extent to which labor migration is gendered, for the experiences of women and men share some commonalities but diverge in various respects. Instead of looking at the women migrant workers as socio-economically marginalized, I place them at the center of analysis and use their male counterparts for subgroup comparison. I found that regarding the migration decision women were permitted to make such a move more readily than their male counterparts because rural sons, especially first ones, are the lifeblood of the patriarchal family, human labor power in the agrarian society, and the providers of family support and old-age security. Regardless of gender, the majority of workers tended to make individual decisions for rural-to-urban migration. My finding in this study is inconsistent with research results based on family migration theory which have treated migration as a household strategy for survival.

Second, I have explored the meanings and practices of empowerment using a multi-faceted concept that consists of four interrelated economic, social, educational, and psychological dimensions. Economic empowerment is of paramount importance, yet women migrant workers also reaped the benefits of self-reliance, personal exploration, some degree of autonomy, expansion of social ties, experiential enhancement, and psychological satisfaction, offering those rewards beyond monetary measures. Every women migrant worker displayed empowerment to some varying degree since each was driven by different motives to undertake the bold step of migrating. By and large, the women were conscious of their migration decision-making and anticipated certain outcomes, for the good or for the worst, as they entered the paid labor market.

The third question asks what major social and cultural conditions may empower women migrant workers and what contradictions are inherent in the migration process that may disempower these workers. In the forgoing analysis, I have articulated the complex relationships between structure and human agency, reflecting the socio-cultural contexts through which women's empowerment and gender relations develop in and through the interaction of social, political, and economic institutions, buttressed by the dominant ideologies. Specifically, my analyses reveal how this dynamic interaction and its reconfiguration produce shifting bases of enabling potentials for women migrant workers' empowerment at the two stages of before and during migration. The power base of control shifted from the private domain of the patriarchal family in the rural area to the public domain of the labor market, the firm, and the state. In other words, women migrant workers were slightly freer from the control of their families, and at the same time, they had begun to subject themselves to control by the labor markets in which and the firms at which they were employed. The state patriarchy has taken a fair amount of power from the patriarchal family by exerting control over labor appropriation through its policies and programs. However, state control is counteracted by such market forces as privatization and liberalization of capital, labor, trade, and finance.

Empowerment is dialectical and paradoxical. What constitutes empowerment in one context may be disempowering in another. Participation in markets will not necessarily empower women migrant workers. Instead of assuming from neoliberal thinking that the free market empowers women, a high priority should be placed on interrogating ways in which social structures and ideologies situate women and men differently in gender hegemonic regimes, on contesting contradictions in women's and men's unequal relationships, and on examining ways in which women migrants may foster empowering potentials. I suggest rethinking the potentials and limits of women's self-empowerment, framing it in the larger sociocultural and political contexts, relating it to asymmetrical, gendered power dynamics at both the structural and the individual levels. Future study should address the prospects for women migrants' collective empowerment as a bottom-up process transforming individual actors, challenging gendered relations of power, and building grassroots people-centered communities toward the goal of claiming these workers' basic human rights as citizens.

## NOTES

1. This paper reports part of major findings from a research monograph in progress. The project was originally supported by the Funds for the Advancement of the Discipline in Sociology from the American Sociological Association and the National Science Foundation, which provided seed money to lay a foundation for the survey research. I later secured a research grant from the Fulbright New Century Scholars program to undertake part of the fieldwork. Special thanks go to Cai Guo Xuan, Yu Chun Zou, Yu Huang, Ray-May Hsung, and Chi-Kwan Ho for their support in the early stages of data collection in South China. I also thank Carolyn Elliott and Elaine Stahl Leo for reviewing an early draft of this paper.
2. INSTRAW (International Research and Training Institute for the Advanced of Women), *The Migration of Women: Methodological Issues of the Measurement and Analysis of Internal and International Migration* (Santo Domingo, Dominican Republic: United Nations, 1994), 43; United Nations Population Fund (UNFPA), *State of World Population 2006: A Passage to Hope, Women and International Migration* (New York: UNFPA, 2006), 22.
3. Strictly speaking, migrant laborers are "floating population" (*liudong renkou*) in Chinese, which refers to people who do not have *hukou* status to be in the

city. To migrate means to obtain a new official household registration permit to reside in their current place of residence. In 1982, however, the Chinese Census began to count as migrants all those who had been living in a location different from their place of permanent registration for a year or more. The 1993 Chinese Census followed the same rule in tabulation of migrants. I use the terms "migrant workers" and "floating population" interchangeably in this paper.

4. Savitri Bisnath and Diane Elson, "Women's Empowerment Revisited," *Background paper, Progress of the World's Women* (UNIFEM, 2003). http://www.unifem.undp.org/progressww/empower.html (accessed October 2006), hereafter cited in text as Bisnath and Elson (2003); Marilyn Carr, Martha Chen, and Renana Jhabvala, eds. *Speaking Out: Women's Empowerment in South Asia* (London: IT Publications, 1996); Naila Kabeer, "Reflections on the Measurement of Women's Empowerment." In *Discussing Women's Empowerment: Theory and Practice,* Sida Studies No. 3. (Novum Grafiska AB: Stockholm, 2001); Anju Malhotra and Mark Mather, "Do Schooling and Work Empower Women in Developing Countries? Gender and Domestic Decisions in Sri Lanka," *Sociological Forum* 12, no. 4 (1997): 599–630; Linda Mayoux, "Tackling the Down Side: Social Capital, Women's Empowerment and Micro-Finance in Cameroon," *Development and Change* 32 (2001): 435–464; Martha Nussbaum, *Women and Human Development: The Capabilities Approach* (New York: Cambridge Press, 2000). Zoe Oxaal with Sally Baden, *Gender and Empowerment: Definitions, Approaches and Implications for Policy,* Bridge Report No. 40. (Sussex: Institute of Development Studies, 1997); Jo Rowlands, "Empowerment Examined," *Development in Practice 5*, no. 2 (1995): 101–7, hereafter cited in text as Rowlands (1995); Gita Sen and Caren Grown, *Development, Crises, and Alternative Visions: Third World Women's Perspectives* (New York: Monthly Review Press, 1987); hereafter cited in text as Sen and Grown (1987); Nelly P. Stromquist, "The Theoretical and Practical Bases for Empowerment." In *Women, Education and Empowerment: Pathways Towards Autonomy,* ed. Carolyn Medel-Anonuevo. Report of the International Seminar held at UIE. (Hamburg ,Germany and Paris: UNESCO, 1995).
5. I would prefer to use "inequality regime," Joan Acker's (2006) term designed to be inclusive of all forms of inequality including gender, but in this study I will focus on the different gender regimes that are structurally embedded in different social institutions such as the family, the firm, and the state. Joan Acker, "Inequality Regimes: Gender, Class, and Race in Organizations," *Gender & Society* 20 (August 2006): 441–464; hereafter cited in text as Acker (2006).
6. Maxine D. Molyneux, "Mobilization Without Emancipation? Women's Interests, State, and Revolution in Nicaragua," *Feminist Studies* 11 (1985): 227–54.
7. Anthony Giddens, *Central Problems in Social Theory: Action, Structure and Contradiction in Social Analysis* (London: Macmillan, 1979).
8. Sen, Gita and Caren Grown. *Development, Crises, and Alternative Visions: Third World Women's Perspectives* (New York: Monthly Review Press, 1987); Srilatha Batliwala, "The Meaning of Women's Empowerment: New Concepts from Action." In *Population Policies Reconsidered: Health, Empowerment and Rights,* ed. Gita Sen, A. Germain, and L.C. Chen (Cambridge, MA: Harvard University Press, 1994). Bisnath, Savitri, and Diane Elson, "Women's Empowerment Revisited," Background paper, Progress of the World's Women (UNIFEM, 2003). http://www.unifem.undp.org/progressww/empower.html (last accessed October 2006).
9. Jacob Mincer, "Family Migration Decisions," *Journal of Political Economy* 86 (1978): 749–73.

10. Gramsmuck, Sherri and Patricia R. Pessar, *Between Two Islands: Dominican International Migration* (Berkeley: University of California Press, 1991), hereafter cited in text as Gramsmuch and Pessar (1991).
11. Although women laborers may pursue migration for marriage, my study focused on economically motivated migrants. Neither was migration to advance entrepreneurial or business interests a concern of this study.
12. See Brooke A. Ackerly, "Testing the Tools of Development: Credit Programmes, Loan Involvement, and Women's Empowerment," *IDS Bulletin* 26, no. 3 (1995): 56–68; Elizabeth Frankenberg and Duncan Thomas, *Measuring Power*, Food Consumption and Nutrition Division Discussion Paper No. 113 (Washington, DC: International Food Policy Research Institute, 2001); Syed M. Hashemi, Sidney Ruth Schuler, and Ann P. Riley, "Rural Credit Programs and Women's Empowerment in Bangladesh," *World Development* 24, no. 4 (1996): 635–53, hereafter cited in text as Hashemi, et al. (1996); Naila Kabeer, "Women, Wages and Intra-Household Power Relations in Urban Bangladesh," *Development and Change* 28 (1997): 261–302; Shireen J. Jejeebhoy, "Women's Autonomy in Rural India: Its Dimensions, Determinants, and the Influence of Context." In *Women's Empowerment and Demographic Processes: Moving Beyond Cairo*, eds. Harriet Presser and Gita Sen (New York: Oxford University Press, 2000); Anne Marie Goetz and Rina Sen Gupta, "Who Takes the Credit? Gender, Power, and Control over Loan Use in Rural Credit Programs in Bangladesh," *World Development* 24, no. 1(1996): 45–63; Sherri Grasmuck and Rosario Espinal, "Market Success or Female Autonomy? Income, Ideology, and Empowerment Among Microentrepreneurs in the Dominican Republic," *Gender & Society* 14 (April 2000): 231–55; Sidney Ruth Schuler and Syed M. Hashemi, "Credit Programs, Women's Empowerment, and Contraceptive Use in Rural Bangladesh," *Studies in Family Planning* 25, no. 2 (1994): 65–76.
13. Hashemi, et al. (1996); Sunita Kishor, "Empowerment of Women in Egypt and Links to the Survival and Health of Their Infants." In *Women's Empowerment and Demographic Processes: Moving Beyond Cairo*, eds. Harriet Presser and Gita Sen (New York: Oxford University Press, 2000).
14. Nan Lin, *Social Capital: Theory and Research* (New York: Cambridge University Press, 2001); Douglas S. Massey, et al., "Theories of International Migration Theory: A Review and Appraisal," *Population and Development Review* 20, no. 4 (1993): 699–751.
15. Monica Boyd, "Family and Personal Networks in International Migration: Recent Developments and New Agendas," *International Migration Review* 23 (Autumn 1989): 638–70; Gramsmuck and Pessar (1991); Pierrette Hondagneu-Sotelo, *Gendered Transitions: Mexican Experience of Immigration* (Berkeley, CA: University of California Press, 1994); Shawn Malia Kanaiaupuni, "Reframing the Migration Question: An Analysis of Men, Women, and Gender in Mexicom," *Social Forces* (June 2000): 1311–48.
16. Lourdes Beneria and Martha Roldan, *The Crossroads of Class and Gender* (Chicago, IL: University of Chicago Press, 1987); Maria Mies, *Patriarchy and Accumulation on a World Scale* (London: Zed Books, 1986).
17. Guangzhou is the capital of Guangdong province, and Dong Quan on the Pearl River delta is the nearby county included in the study.
18. Lotus SEZ is a pseudonym used to protect the regional identification of the economic zone studied.
19. Not all the firms allowed my research team to select a stratified random sample as originally planned or gave us a complete list of workers for random selection. Factory ownership was differentiated as state-owned, foreign-owned, or joint-venture/locally owned, and factory size was classified as large or small.

We ended up approaching firms that were willing to cooperate. We were able to use these stratifying factors to set quotas for sample selection to ensure some degree of representativeness.

20. My survey data reported here covers only the two before and during migration phases when migrant women workers were on the move. Only a panel research design would permit a time-series study comparing the same migrant sample over time in the migration process.

21. Esther Ngan-ling Chow, "Economic Reforms, Gendered Migration, and Women's Employment in the Manufacturing Industries of South China: A Preliminary Analysis," Paper presented at the World Congress of Sociology, sponsored by the International Sociological Association, Montreal, Canada, July 1998.

22. Phyllis Andors, "Women and Work in Shenzhen," *Bulletin of Concerned Asian Scholars* 20, no. 3 (1988): 22–41; Shen Tan, "At the Pearl River Delta: The Relations of Women Migrants to Foreign Invested Enterprises and Local Government," Paper presented at the Annual Meeting of the American Sociological Association in San Francisco, 1998a.

23. Similar findings were reported by Tan Shen (1998b) and her research team in a national study of peasant out-migration conducted by the Chinese Academy of Social Sciences in 1994. Shen Tan, "Gender Differences in the Migration of Rural Labor," *Sociological Studies* 1 (1998b): 70–76.

24. Tan Shen reported a similar finding in her 1998 survey that found little support for the family migration theory. Migrants made individual decisions based on self-motivation (unpublished paper, Chinese Academy of Social Sciences).

25. Esther Ngan-ling Chow, "The Feminization of Survival: Is Migration a Household Strategy or an Individual Rational Choice?" Paper presented at the Mid-Year Meeting of the Sociologists for Women in Society in San Juan, Puerto Rico, 2006; hereafter cited in text as Chow (2006).

26. Ellen R. Judd, *Gender and Power in Rural North China* (Stanford, CA: Stanford University Press, 1994); Rachel Murphy, *How Migrant Labor Is Changing Rural China* (Cambridge: Cambridge University Press, 2002); Judith Stacey, *Patriarchy and Socialist Revolution in China* (Berkeley, CA: University of California Press, 1983).

27. All-China Women's Federation, *A Review of the Social Status of Women in China* (Beijing, China: New World Press, 1995).

28. Esther Ngan-ling Chow, "Gendered Migration, Politics, Space, and Citizenship of Women Migrant Workers in South China." *Gender, Place, and Culture* (special issue "Seeking Gender Justice: Reflections, Dialogue, and Strategic Action," forthcoming), hereafter cited in text as Chow (forthcoming).

29. Male migrant workers allotting more income for family remittances were those who had higher ranking and better-paid jobs. In using the same sample, my further analysis shows that 14 percent more men than women migrant workers contributed more than half their income to family finance in terms of remittance (33.7 percent and 19.5 percent respectively) because the former tended to have higher ranking and better-paid jobs. Esther Ngan-ling Chow. "Paid Work, Income Control and Remittance: Empowering Migrant Workers in South China." Paper presented at the Annual Meeting of the American Sociological Association, New York City, 2007.

30. "Iron girl" was a classic heroine during the Mao era of China in the1950s and 1960s .

31. Human resource management systems and practices (HRM) varied greatly by firm type. State-owned enterprises provided a better package of wage and other welfare benefits than other firm types. Nowadays, with China's

economic development still in transition, some variations in wages and benefits can be found within the same firm type.

32. Karyn A. Loscocco and Xun Wang, "Gender Segregation in China," *Sociology and Social Research* 76 (1992): 118–26.

33. A few women in the study shared this man worker's view of the appropriateness of different jobs and occupations for women and men.

34. Migrant women workers were called "*da gong mei*" and men workers "*da gong jia*" by the local people of Guangdong. Both were derogatory labels which identified them as working-class girls or boys. In contrast to the mild Cantonese cuisine, the Sichuan diet is mostly spicy and hot.

35. One factory which I studied had two labor strikes before I arrived at the site. Each strike only lasted for two to three days. Strong state control made it difficult for labor resistance to surface for observation at the time of investigation, although labor unrest was sporadically reported in the media. See Chow (forthcoming).

36. A few women interviewees brought up the issues of accessibility and affordability of health care-delivery services near their factory compounds. I was told that they had to pay at higher medical fees for such health services than locals in the urban hospitals or clinics.

# 5 Transnational Domestication

## State Power and Indonesian Migrant Women in Saudi Arabia

*Rachel Silvey[1]*

Feminist approaches to political geography argue that the dynamics of gender and difference should not be conceptualized independently of the state. Rather, formations of gender, race, and ethnicity should be understood as mutually constitutive elements of capitalist state power and process.[2] Such inclusive feminist views of the state are relevant to understanding the roles of the Indonesian New Order (1966–1998) state and the Kingdom of Saudi Arabia (1899 to present) in shaping the migration of Indonesian female domestic workers to Saudi Arabia. Indeed, between the early-1980s and the late-1990s, both states have put policies in place that have contributed directly to rapid, large-scale increases in the numbers of Indonesian women workers migrating to Saudi Arabia.[3] Both states' sets of policies for migrant domestic workers fall under the broader rubrics of national economic development, with Indonesia focused on creating employment and generating foreign exchange through remittances, and Saudi Arabia's economy benefiting from the provision by migrant workers of social reproduction at low cost. In addition, the practices of the Indonesian state's migration apparatus, and the Saudi state's regulation of women's mobility, as well as both states' lack of regulation of domestic work, have contributed to the gender-specific exploitation and abuse faced by migrant women.

Yet the gendered efforts of states do not mechanistically produce given patriarchal-capitalist outcomes. Rather, as Jessop argues, the state is "the site of struggles and rivalries among [its] different branches."[4] Indeed, in recent years, social activists based primarily in Indonesia have pressured the Indonesian state to stop sending women migrants to Saudi Arabia until better protections are in place, and they have succeeded in pushing the two states to begin to develop a bilateral agreement on the protection of domestic workers abroad.[5] Attention to their actions contributes to understanding the role of the state inasmuch as "[s]tate power ... depends on the forms and nature of resistance to state interventions—both directly and at a distance from the state" (Jessop, 1990: 269). Focusing on the activities of NGO activists is aimed analytically at developing a "society-centered" concept of the state that, parallel to approaches in feminist scholarship, expands and reframes that which counts as political. In the case of migrant domestic workers, it has been NGO activists that have challenged the "walls of silence"[6] surrounding the abuse of migrant women in "private" domestic spaces, and identified the state's "public" silences as policy gaps that have in some cases served broader state interests and reproduced existing social hierarchies.

This chapter is divided into five sections following this introduction. The first section reviews the literature on feminist theories of the state and discusses the relevance of these views for understanding gendered international migration. Second, the paper describes the recent migration and employment patterns of Indonesian domestic workers in Saudi Arabia, and traces the New Order state's role in prompting and conditioning women's overseas migration. The third section examines the Saudi state's role in producing the demand for these migrant workers, and its complicity in permitting the abuses that migrant domestic workers often face. The fourth section explores how migrants have circumvented and ignored state regulations in a range of ways, and how migrant NGO activists have pressured the Indonesian state to internationalize protections for migrant workers. The conclusion argues that a feminist reading of state power in relation to the Indonesia-Saudi migration circuit reveals the gender politics in the interconnections between the production of gendered subjects, domestic labor, the nation, and transnational migration. In addition, it illustrates the limitations of the state in protecting migrant women workers in transnational context, and discusses the necessity of non-state entry points and spatial strategies for improving women migrants' rights.

## FEMINIST THEORIES OF THE STATE AND INTERNATIONAL MIGRATION

Most research on gender and migration—whether it is concerned with internal, international or transnational mobility—has focused on the changing roles of women migrants' within the family, the household, and the labor market, without paying much attention to the roles of states.[7] The exceptions have tended to view the state primarily as a policy-making set of institutions that generate the legal regulations that structure citizenship, immigration, childcare, and work.[8] Here, I am interested in extending this work to analyze the state in terms of the tensions and contradictions that characterize gender policy and ideology in transnational context, and examining the ways that the dynamic elements of the broader state apparatus influence the gendered discourses and policy exclusions that contribute to shaping migrants' identities and possibilities.[9]

This analytical approach to the state parallels key conceptual assumptions put forth by feminist theorists of the state.[10] First, there is agreement among these authors that the state does not represent a unified or coherent set of interests, and that states are based on processes of negotiation rather than fixed power relations. Therefore, even if state power ultimately operates in support of patriarchal privilege, it does so through a series of ongoing struggles and bargains in which subordinated groups play active roles. Such a conceptualization of the state also raises a point that is crucial to understanding the gender politics of the geography of domestic labor: The sites, spaces, and scales through which domestic workers are controlled and empowered are not fixed, nor are they shaped solely by the disciplinary power of the state. Rather, this very geography is an arena that is struggled over, entered into by activists, and affected by the political agency of domestic workers and non-state actors.

Second, feminist theorists see gender relations and norms as constitutive of—rather than just coincidental to—states and state policy. In the Indonesian case, and specifically in Java, where the majority of migrants to Saudi Arabia originate, women have historically carried out the majority of both paid and unpaid domestic work.[11] This norm has then been reflected and refashioned in the New Order state's policy decision to promote women's employment in domestic service. However, norms have different implications for the state when they are expected to travel transnationally. The Indonesian state's ideologies of feminine domesticity and motherhood, state feminism, and state paternalism raise different stakes for the state when they are applied to transnational migrants in Saudi Arabia than they do in relation to women still living in Indonesia. Whereas domestic workers' rights were not a widely contested political issue within Indonesia's national boundaries, in the Saudi context, they have emerged as a political flashpoint.

The manipulation of gendered labor and gendered spaces was integral to both the New Order and the Saudi states' efforts to produce the developmentalist social orders within their respective national territorial boundaries, and it became a critical arena of political action through which the states could be pressured. Feminists emphasize two additional features of the state as vital for examining gender. First, as Rai points out, states actively engineer national economic development in gender-specific manners.[12] The New Order and the Saudi states actively promoted particular roles for women in economic development and social change through a variety of educative state institutions. In Gramscian terms, these would be the (gendered) strategies of cultivating the consent on which state hegemony depends. As explored further below, a central goal of the Indonesian New Order and the Saudi states' education and service campaigns was to socialize and encourage low-income women to play the roles of supportive mothers and wives in families and serve as contributors to national economic development through particular forms of participation in the labor market.[13] Second, the effects of the reach of the state into women's lives are complicated and incomplete. State officials and brokerages themselves sometimes recruit, manage and document migrants illegally, alongside and sometimes within the state's formal migration apparatus. State officials as well as informal brokers perpetrate gender-specific abuses of migrants. The lack of state capacity to protect these women is not a coincidence. Rather, it is reflective of class-, nationality-, and gender-specific norms about tolerable crimes and acceptable victims.

As the literature on migrant domestic work has shown repeatedly, the state shapes gendered subjects, labor markets, migration patterns, and family formations in ways that lead to the construction of domestic work as a woman's job that garners low wages, provides little security and few benefits, involves high rates of multiple forms of abuse, and offers only slim chances of occupational mobility.[14] The Indonesian and the Saudi states' lack of policy regulating the terms and conditions of domestic employment, both within and beyond their national borders, contributes to the continued exploitation and abuse of migrant workers. In sum, these feminist conceptualizations of the state are relevant in two main ways to the analysis of the New Order and Saudi states' roles in shaping female domestic workers' international migration. First, investigating the geographic dimensions of contestations over migrants' rights may contribute to feminist analyses of the state by showing how state power relies on struggles over gendered spaces and scales, and not just gendered subjects and institutions, as is often assumed. Second, in that the New Order actively encouraged the international migration of women as part of its development agenda yet failed to provide protection for migrants at either end of the migration chain, it opened itself up to criticism by activists able to capitalize on the ambiguous role of the state in transnational context. The remainder of the article explores each of these aspects of state power, state policy, and recent activism directed at the Indonesian state, beginning in the following section with an analysis of the Indonesian New Order state's role.

## THE INDONESIAN STATE MIGRATION
## APPARATUS AND GENDER IDEOLOGIES

There are a number of direct ways in which the Indonesian New Order state bureaucracy has shaped women's migration to Saudi Arabia. Beginning in 1983, the Indonesian government began permitting private agents from Middle Eastern countries to recruit Indonesian nationals to work abroad.[15] Indonesia's ambassador to Saudi Arabia at the time expressed enthusiasm for the prospects of labor export because, as he saw it, overseas employment meant jobs for unemployed Indonesian nationals as well as crucial foreign exchange that he expected would come in the form of remittances (Robinson, 1991). In the first year of recruitment, 47,000 fully documented workers left Indonesia for Saudi Arabia, and these numbers continued to climb rapidly.[16] Between 1980 and 1984, the Indonesian government recorded 55,976 migrant nationals with work contracts destined for Saudi Arabia.[17] Between 1984 and 1989, the number rose to 223,579, and increased again to 384,822 in the following five-year period. The majority (59 percent) of all documented overseas workers from Indonesia between 1989 and 1994 chose to migrate to Saudi Arabia[18]; two-thirds of the migrants were women; and more than 80% of these women were estimated to work as domestic servants (Amjad, 1996: 346; Chin, 1998: 103).[19] Indonesian institutions and programs aggressively promoted this movement of women domestics overseas (Hugo, 1995: 282). First, the state's Department of Manpower (DEP-NAKER, Departemen Tenaga Kerja) made efforts to improve the overseas perceptions of Indonesian labor, setting up programs that were largely oriented towards training women in domestic service skills. Second, in 1984, the state developed a unit within the Department of Manpower, named Pusat AKAN (Antar Kerja Antar Negara, Center of Overseas Employment), that was organized to monitor and regulate overseas workers. The stated goals of the Pusat AKAN were: "(1) to expand employment opportunities of Indonesian workers; (2) to increase the income of Indonesian workers; (3) [to] increase national income through foreign exchange revenue, and; (4) to foster closer relationships among Indonesia and other countries."[20] In that the training programs targeted women, the efforts to increase employment and income promoted women's labor migration in particular. Bolstered by the Pusat AKAN, the Department of Manpower aimed to send more workers abroad each year. Between 1994 and 1999, the goal was to send 1,250,000 workers overseas (Spaan, 1999: 158). In order to facilitate this process, the state's Manpower Department licensed formal recruitment agencies (Perusahan Jasa Tenaga Kerja Indonesia, PJTKI, or the Indonesian Labor Force Service Businesses), theoretically intended to support migrants as they arranged their overseas employment and completed the application process for overseas contract workers.

However, the agencies required that potential migrants fill out numerous documents, which were then circulated for approval through several different levels of government, making the process time-consuming and frustrating for potential workers (Hugo, 1995). The many detailed forms that were required were unclear to most applicants (Hugo, 1995), and at this stage of the application process, migrant candidates were vulnerable to the corrupt dealings of officials responsible for processing their applications (Spaan, 1999: 161). Women applicants faced gender-specific forms of exploitation, including sexual harassment, sexual abuse, and rape.[21] The Manpower Department also imposed age and marital status requirements for overseas migrants, which further differentiated potential migrants' options by sex. Men who applied to work in Saudi Arabia were required to be 18 years old, while women had to "either be married (in which case they need[ed] permission from their husband) or 25 years of age at a minimum" (Spaan, 1999: 158). Women with children under one year of age were not eligible to apply (Spaan, 1999: 158), and unmarried women under 25 were only permitted to work abroad if they received parental permission.

In these direct ways, the state's migration apparatus discouraged many potential migrants from formal registration, and in so doing created the conditions under which more women than men sought illegal migration channels. Low-income people's interest in bypassing the formal documentation procedures led to rapid growth in the business of unregistered migration brokers.[22] Indeed, informal brokerages have become widespread in Java's rural areas, growing into a sizeable industry that encourages and in many cases prompts illegal overseas migration. The labor recruiters and middle-men or brokers (*taikong* and *calo*) have advantages over the migrants in terms of financial resources, knowledge of the destination area, and relatively complete information about both the migration process as well as the overseas work that is available. All of these advantages serve to perpetuate the existing privileges of recruiters and the vulnerability of both women and men migrant candidates. Further, some recruiters, like some government officials, sexually harass and demand sexual services from female migrant candidates in particular (Tagaroa and Sofia, 2002).

The direct influence of the state's migration apparatus and the unregulated migration brokers' effects on women's migration are not easily disentangled. Indeed, state officials who work for the Pusat AKAN and the PJTKI often do little to enforce government policies, and some of the state-sanctioned brokerages themselves exploit the vulnerability of migrant candidates. In addition, some highly ranking civil servants own and operate labor brokerage companies. In these ways, the Indonesian state can be understood to be implicated—both directly and through its lack of regulatory capacity—in producing the conditions under which overseas domestics migrate and work.

In addition, several New Order (1965–1998) institutions, including Dharma Wanita (Women's Duty) and the PKK (Pembinaan Kesejahteraan Keluarga, Family Welfare Guidance), have produced and reinforced ideologies aimed more generally at spatially and socially domesticating women.[23] Indeed, women's roles as mothers and wives devoted to the maintenance of a stable, nurturing, domestic environment were central to the state's vision of an orderly and morally controlled nation. Yet the state's production of idealized bourgeois femininity as naturally linked to the home and hearth (Robinson, 1991) was complicated in the state's own promotion of class-specific gender ideologies that encouraged low-income women's separation from kin in certain situations.[24] In order to work as a domestic in Saudi Arabia, most migrants leave their families, including their children in many cases, behind in Indonesia. Thus, the family regimes under the New Order that promoted the domestic workers' departure from kin were considerably more flexible than the state-promulgated ideal of the middle-class nuclear family.

The flexibility in state ideology was predicated on the state's reformulations of ideal womanhood depending in part on the ways that particular class categories of workers were sought to be incorporated into specific labor market niches. For instance, in the 1970s, the government's "women and development" campaign actively encouraged women to labor in both the wage earning sphere and the domestic sphere, or to play the "dual roles of women" (*peran ganda wanita*),[25] and to migrate, as long as their mobility did not interfere with their domestic duties. The government's strategy a decade later for promoting labor migration to the Middle East was similar (Hugo, 1995), as the state's dominant vision of idealized femininity was translated into a migratory income-earning woman for the sake of the "national family's" larger goal of economic development, a process of transnational domestication. That is, the New Order promoted low-income women's multiple domestic and transnational roles, and framed the remittance-sending migrants as "heroes of national development" (Robinson, 2000).

By the 1990s, the New Order's gender discourses had begun to change, reflecting the household arrangements and political voices of the growing number of professional women in Indonesia (Sen, 1998). As Sen (1998: 45) points out, a key policy shift, evident in the 1993 GBHN (Garis Besar Haluan Negara, or the Broad Outlines of State Policy) began "to define gender equity not only as women's access to jobs but also in terms of men's shared responsibility for looking after children." But, she continues, the silences in the 1993 GBHN were perhaps more significant than the principles directly addressed in the document. That is, although the new document emphasized both women's and men's roles in the education and moral guidance of children, it made no mention of domestic work or of physical reproductive labor more generally. The absence of attention to the real labor of childcare and housework was, Sen (1998: 45) suggests, a reflection of the domestic division of labor in most middle- and upper-class households within Indonesia, where "physical work is performed largely by domestic servants." Low-income women's gender-specific needs and issues, and those of domestic workers in particular, were still not addressed in the state's principles.

The New Order's gender ideologies have shifted to meet the needs of the state in relation to changing constituencies (i.e., the growth of the middle class and the rise of the "femocrats" in the state bureaucracy (Sen, 1998) and to encourage transnational capital accumulation. In addition to idealizing the woman as "wife-and-womb" through the programs of a number of state institutions, the state has sought to ideologically incorporate low-income women into the poorly protected transnational migrant labor force. By the 1990s, state policy had begun to represent middle-class women's gender equity interests, but the struggles of women who work as domestic servants remained absent from official policy. These silences, along with the direct institutional efforts to prompt low-income women's overseas migration, shaped the conditions of domestic workers labor abroad, as did policies implemented by the Saudi state, explored in the following section.

## THE SAUDI STATE'S ROLE

Since the early 1980s, the Saudi state's immigration policies have been explicitly geared towards the "Saudisation" of the labor market, aiming to replace foreign workers with Saudi nationals.[26] However, strict immigration control and widespread repatriations of undocumented workers over the last two decades have nonetheless coincided with a continuing heavy reliance on foreign workers in both highly skilled positions and the service sector[27] as well as persistently high levels of immigration of Indonesian domestic workers.[28] The Saudi state's inclusion of Saudi women in higher education, its selective and partial incorporation of women in the labor force, and its formal restrictions on women's mobility fuel the demand for domestic workers and isolate these migrants from one another in the homes of their employers. At the core of Saudi immigration policy are strict limits on the length of immigrants' stays, with contracts for domestic workers ranging from six months to three years.[29] The limits on foreign labor provide the state with labor market flexibility, allowing it to respond to political pressures and structural changes in the economy through deportations or temporary informal permissiveness towards undocumented immigrants.[30] Given the difficulty and expense of obtaining or renewing a visa as previously mentioned, many immigrants work in the country without documentation, making them a particularly exploitable segment of the labor force.

In addition to the state's immigration and lack of domestic labor policies, several specific Saudi-state policies focused on women have underpinned the growing demand for domestic workers. First, since the 1960s the Saudi state has strongly promoted the education of girls and women. The number of women students in Saudi colleges and universities doubled between 1983 and 1993, and then more than doubled again by the year 2000,[31] marking for the first time a female majority in higher education. These education policies have led to Saudi women's increasing involvement in non-domestic activities, drawing growing numbers of women away from their families' domestic spheres for coursework and other meetings associated with their academic pursuits. Saudi women's increasing absence from the home has thus—in conjunction with the on-going construction of domestic work as women's work—increased the dependence on foreign domestic workers. In addition, the Saudi state is itself the largest employer of women,[32] subsidizing women's careers in education and health care positions in particular. The entry of large numbers of Saudi women into the public sector in the 1970s was tied to a growing demand for domestic servants.

Since the early 1980s, the dramatic decline in Saudi oil revenues has led to a reduction in the state's provision of public sector employment, decreases in state subsidies for education, and a fall in the per capita GDP from US$18,800 in 1981 to US$6,700 in 1995. These pressures have served as incentives for Saudi women to enter private sector employment to supplement their families' falling incomes. Since the 1990s, Saudi women have increasingly participated in professions once largely closed to them, including journalism, advertising, broadcasting, and architecture (Doumato,1999: 569).

In addition to contributing to the creation of the demand for domestic workers, the Saudi state's gender policies have also played a role in structuring the conditions of domestic employment. Most fundamentally, the Saudi state legally requires the segregation of the sexes outside of the home and imposes restrictions on women's mobility. Government policies also forbid women to drive and to board airplanes alone without written permission from a male relative (Doumato, 2000). The morals police (the *mutawaa'in*), who are the patrolmen for the state's Committee for the Promotion of Virtue and the Prevention of Vice (Hai'at al-amr bi al-ma'ruf wa al-nahia 'an al-munkar), seek out and discipline women who are alone in cars, women who are dining in restaurants with men to whom they are not married, and women who are not dressed in the *hijab* (Doumato, 2000). In addition, the state has created legal impediments to abortion and birth control, encouraging a high fertility rate (i.e., 6.25 children per woman, among the highest in the world) and large families with domestic needs that women are expected to fulfill (Doumato, 1999: 580). In these ways, the state is directly involved in controlling unaccompanied women's mobility, defining women's ideal roles within families, and producing a demand for domestic service. Also, these laws contribute to the isolation of domestic workers, making it difficult for them to seek support or develop advocacy organizations.

State policy is strongly influenced by the Council of the Senior Ulama (religious scholars), which is the most powerful religious political force in the country and sets the tone and direction of national debates (al-Rasheed, 2002). Indeed, the monarchy of the Saudi Kingdom rules in an informal but deeply entrenched partnership with the Council, engaging the *ulama* in the formation of public policy. The Council offers *fatwas* (religious/legal opinions) that it sees as necessary for societal well-being as well as ones to provide religious legitimacy to decisions that the monarchy's rulers have already made. As is the practice of any group of religious leaders, the Council draws selectively upon the scriptures, interpreting the Hadith (Sayings of the Prophet Mohammad) and the Qur'an in ways that reflect their own and the monarchy's various and sometimes conflicting priorities at a given time. The Council's members subscribe to Wahhabism, a school of Islamic thought that specifically rejects reformist teachings.

In that the *ulama* are involved in shaping the state's control of the different spaces available to women and men in Saudi Arabia, they are also key actors influencing the spaces available to Indonesian migrant domestic workers. Further, the political import and specific mobilizations of Islamic teachings are particularly salient for understanding the Indonesian state's lack of interference in Saudi Arabia's national affairs, because the political and religious leadership in Indonesia tends to grant superior, authentic status to Saudi Arabian Islam and to defer to Saudi ulamas' interpretations of religious texts.[33]

However, while religious interests play an influential role in the Saudi state, they are by no means monolithic, immutable, nor similarly expressed across regions of the country. Moreover, while *fatwas* and the rules that stem from them may in some cases provide justification for particular state policies, there is a great deal of flexibility in the interpretation and enforcement of specific laws. Indeed, some religious opinions provided by the *ulama* "serve more as ventilation for conservative frustrations than as restrictions to be taken literally" (Doumato, 1999: 579). Further, there are active Muslim and non-Muslim feminist and non-governmental organizations in Saudi Arabia that oppose the dominant state interpretations of Islam.[34] Thus, while Islamist politics are an important dimension of Saudi state power, they also play a role in opposition to the state, and gender ideals and restrictions are represented in a range of various ways within these different interpretations. Moreover, most recently, Saudi "[w]omen and girls have taken possession of public spaces that did not exist a generation ago" (Doumato, 2003: 239), and they too have invoked reworked religious rationales in support of their mobility and transgressions of dominant norms. Such caveats about the role of religion are important in order to counter Western feminist perspectives on gender in the Middle East that inaccurately construct Muslim women as the uniquely religiously subordinated Other and imply a homogeneity within and across majority Muslim populations.[35] Challenging Orientalizing stereotypes of Muslim women is particularly crucial in light of recent mobilizations of "the Afghan woman problem" for international political gain.[36]

Overall, then, in recent decades the Saudi state's efforts have invited "experimentation" with the gendered social order, yet also enacted legal provisions beginning in the 1990s "to redraw the boundaries, to reaffirm the lines between women and men" (Doumato, 1999: 578). Within this context of contradictory impulses and policy change emanating from the state, Saudi households have increasingly employed Indonesian migrant domestic workers (Pujiastuti, 2000). Despite the national recession, the middle and high income, urban, educated segments of the Saudi population have continued to reap the rewards of the national material transformation of the 1970s, and many expect a range of services, including domestic service, to be available to them. The Saudi state's legitimacy rests in part on ensuring the continued availability of such markers of modernity and economic development (al-Rasheed, 2002). Yet, as the following section explores, migrants have employed a range of means to circumvent state controls on them, and activists have called on particularly the Indonesian state's gendered claims to legitimacy and moral authority to pressure both states to provide greater protection to overseas migrant workers.

## ENCOUNTERING THE STATE: CIRCUMVENTION AND ACTIVISM

There are a range of ways in which women migrants adapt to, accommodate, or seek to circumvent state policy regarding their mobility and the gender norms that the state produces about them. In addition, a growing number of NGOs have organized actions to pressure the Indonesian state in particular to provide better protection to overseas migrants. When women avoid contact with the state's migration apparatus, they participate, albeit unwittingly, in reaffirming the state's lack of regulatory capacity. When activists pressure the state, they contribute to shaping the issues for which the state is held accountable. Women migrants' circumvention of formal bureaucratic procedures reveals key geographic, ideological, and practical limits to state power, which Indonesian NGOs, buffeted by a strengthening of civil society more generally, have demanded that the New Order and Saudi states address.

Migrants are often unaware that the informal brokers' practices, and therefore their own migration, are illegal (Tagaroa and Sofia, 2002). When they enlist for overseas work with an informal broker, their actions are not intentionally aimed at subverting state policy, but they are doing so nonetheless. Riani, who had returned from Saudi Arabia, spoke about the reason she allowed an informal sponsor to process her visa documentation for her: "I didn't know how to deal with it. I was glad when it [visa processing] was dealt with [for me], just picked up like that. Yeah, I just waited to be called, and let the sponsor deal with it" (Tagaroa and Sofia, 2002: 107). In Riani's case, the sponsor's work did not set her up for problems overseas, but in other cases the middlemen who fill the vacuum left by the state's inadequate migrant apparatus exacerbate migrant candidates' vulnerability. For instance, a woman named Kodriah who was interviewed after returning from Saudi Arabia, said, "My sponsor and my agent let me know that working in Saudi Arabia was nice, the salary was large, and the work was light, only washing like I usually do every day" (Tagaroa and Sofia, 2002: 68). After arriving abroad, however, she discovered that the sponsor and agent had neglected to mention the restrictions on mobility that she would face in Saudi Arabia. The recruiter had been able to hinge his message on the state-sanctioned normalization of low-income women's domestic work, and the limited information provided by the state had shaped the context within which he was able to manipulate Kodriah.

There are also a number of ways that women migrants have endeavored to alter their situations after arriving in Saudi Arabia, effectively moving beyond the reach of either states' immigration apparatus. Specifically, many women break their contracts when they face abuse, overwork, or lack of payment in the homes of their employers.[37] The Indonesian embassy in Riyadh reports that between 300 and 500 Indonesian women per day can be found waiting at the embassy for assistance, and that the majority of these women lack formal documentation and have run away from abusive situations in the homes of their employers (Tirtosudarmo, 2000). One recent study found that in response to various abuses, 75 percent of return migrants had cut short their stays, broken their contracts, and returned home earlier than planned (Pujiastuti, 2000). In addition, many women have acted in self-defense, as evidenced by the numerous reports of women hitting their bosses or forcefully defending themselves against various forms of abuse (Tagaroa and Sofia, 2002). Finally, some who have returned to Java decide never to attempt overseas migration again. As one return migrant, Mariya, said, "I don't want to work overseas again, I've felt enough hellishness. I worked to make money, but what I got was suffering" (Tagaroa and Sofia, 2002: 107).

In response to information about these abuses, beginning in 1984, a growing number of NGOs (e.g., Solidaritas Perempuan, Kalyanamitra, and later The Center for Indonesian Migrant Women) publicly protested the Indonesian state's inadequate protection of overseas women workers. These NGOs have directed public attention to migrant women's issues through encouraging the media to provide prominent coverage of cases of mistreatment, excessively heavy workloads, sexual harassment, and rape. News magazines have published regular reports on the increasing numbers of women who have mysteriously disappeared, been murdered, sentenced to death, or committed suicide in Saudi Arabia (Ananta et al., 1998). NGOs have circulated graphic depictions of the wounds caused by assaults on migrant women's bodies, and have cultivated widespread public opposition to the treatment these women are receiving. They have pressured the state to protect migrants from abuses such as non-payment of wages, confinement to the place of work, and work overload (Adi, 1995). Strategically, they have drawn on the Indonesian state's own paternalist discourses of idealized femininity and domestic roles in order to pressure the state to internationalize its accountability.

Within Indonesia, the maltreatment of Indonesian domestics was viewed as a national "embarrassment" (Hugo, 1995: 289), particularly for the elite (Ananta et al., 1998), who joined NGOs to pressure the state to change their regulatory procedures. In 1996, the Indonesian Ministry of Women's Affairs argued that the government should stop sending housemaids altogether.[38] In addition, the Minister of Manpower proposed that beginning in 1999, Indonesia would not send any "unskilled" workers abroad, suggesting that such a change in regulation would prevent further abuse of Indonesian domestics.[39] This proposed "solution" did not satisfy the activists, who argued that prohibiting women from entering overseas domestic service jobs would not stop their migration, and would serve instead to increase the numbers of unprotected migrants who would continue to seek employment abroad regardless of the regulations. According to the activists, the Indonesian state's efforts to control migration and simultaneously neglect labor regulation in Saudi domestic employment reveals the state's prioritization of particular elite constituents' concerns about national identity above concerns for worker welfare.

The New Order faced pressure to address the situation of overseas domestics as a result of the increase in media attention, the growth of women's NGOs working in support of overseas workers' rights, and the voices of politically influential Indonesian Islamic leaders in opposition to the situation of overseas women workers (Tirtosudarmo, 2000). In particular, while the New Order's gendered order was linked to an idealized domesticated femininity within its territorial boundaries, it has refused to extend protection to the working women whose domestic labor makes it possible for wealthier women to live this image both within Indonesia and abroad. These class-based contradictions in state gender ideology which had gone relatively without remark within Indonesia (but see Sen, 1998) became powerful points of contention in the context of transnational migration.

## CONCLUSIONS: TRANSNATIONAL SUBJECTS OF STATE POWER

Many studies of recent Indonesian history have detailed the coercive and repressive features of the New Order state. Massacres led by the military, extralegal killings and torture, and ongoing human rights abuses were all part of the Suharto regime's bloody legacy[40] as was the sexual victimization, torture, and terrorization of women who posed a threat to the state (Sunindyo, 1996). Similarly, foreign analyses of the Saudi state have tended to focus on the repressive nature of the monarchy's strategies of rule, or if generated within the Kingdom, they have primarily reflected state propaganda (Al-Rasheed, 2002). But, as this case study has aimed to show, it has not been direct military intervention or overt state repression that has prompted women to make up the majority of Indonesian migrants working in Saudi Arabia. Nor can women's migration be understood to have resulted solely from gendered push and pull factors in the labor market as distinct from the cultural struggles around gender and state migration policy specifically linking Indonesia and Saudi Arabia. In order to see how this gendered migration stream has taken shape, it has been necessary to examine both the direct and the less direct mechanisms of state power, and specifically the state's role in constructing gendered mobility, idealized feminine identities, and transnational domestic labor niches. The Indonesian and Saudi states have not coincidentally neglected the protection of domestic spaces and migrant workers' rights. Rather, the lack of regulation of domestic service, inasmuch as it increases the exploitability of migrant workers, plays a productive part in maintaining and reinforcing the privileges of the Saudi and the Indonesian elite. Also, the migration of Indonesian domestic workers to Saudi Arabia both reflects and reinforces the two countries unequal positions in the global political economy.

Indonesian women migrants leave family and nation to become domestics, and yet they do so under the rubric of self-sacrifice for family and nation. Therefore, when returned domestics and activists from non-governmental organizations have protested on behalf of the female migrants in Saudi Arabia, they have rallied the Indonesian state's own paternalism behind their cause, casting the state as the set of actors and institutions that must protect the nation's citizens—and particularly women—abroad, and thereby protect its national status and pride. In effect, activists call upon the migrant female body as a vessel and emblem of the nation itself, thus extending and reimagining the territory in which the state is held responsible for its citizens. In addition, NGOs, along with Indonesian state officials, have pressured the Saudi state to generate a set of bilateral agreements protecting the rights of Indonesian nationals abroad (Nakertrans, 2003).

Understanding the constitutive role of counter-hegemonic activism moves analyses away from too deterministic a view of the state and its relationship to women migrants. This approach has allowed examination of the roles that migrants and activists play in relation to, and not solely as a result of, state policy and power. Taking these migrants' and activists' practices and voices seriously is part of the broader feminist geographic project of "starting from these informal spheres in which women and men are marginalized under global capitalism as a strategic way of revealing how informal economies of production and caring subsidize *and constitute* . . . neo-liberal states."[41]

The New Order and the Saudi states have come to look the way they do—relieved of particular responsibilities and held accountable for other stakes to legitimacy—in part because of their interplay with insurgent voices. Although the territorialized state promoted Indonesian women's overseas migration, this migration stream and the activism associated with it have called into question the geographic scope of the Indonesian state's responsibility for its nationals.

There still remains the thorny question of what states ought to do to provide better protection to women migrants, and what in particular a feminist perspective would define as the ideal normative role of the state. This analysis—which has pursued a deliberately inclusive notion of politics and the state—suggests that because women's migration and overseas labor is affected by a wide range of educative efforts and formal policies, as well as extralegal activities and gaps in policy and information, any strategies for addressing these problems must be equally wide-ranging in order to be effective. Lobbying the state alone, even if effective in changing labor policies, will not lead to success in protecting migrant women workers. Beyond changing state policy for domestic workers, this analysis suggests that specific ideologies—and particularly the construction of a domestic sphere as "private," "informal," and as the site where particular women belong—should themselves be challenged. State power relies on deployments of particular gendered spaces, subjects, and scales, but it is also through these constructions that it can be challenged.

## NOTES

1. Reprinted with minor revisions with permission from *Political Geography* 23, no. 3 (2004): 245–64. I thank the Fulbright New Century Scholars Program for support to continue this work, Lembaga Ilmu Penelitian Indonesia for research permission, and Maria Hartiningsih, Carla June Natan, Monica Ogra, Alison Mountz, Caroline Desbiens, Margaret Walton-Roberts, Dylan Clark, Cindy Fan, Lynn Staeheli, and three anonymous reviewers for insightful commentary. I alone remain responsible for any shortcomings. The research

on which this article is based was carried out under NSF grant SBR-9911510. That funding is greatly appreciated.

2. cf. Eleonore Kofman and Linda Peake, "Into the 1990s: A Gendered Agenda for Political Geography," *Political Geography Quarterly* 9, no. 4 (1990): 313–36. For reviews of feminist political geography more generally, see *Space and Polity* 5, no. 3 (2001) and Lynn A. Staeheli, Eleonore Kofman and Linda J. Peake, eds, *Mapping Women, Making Politics: Feminist Perspectives on Political Geography.* (London and New York: Routledge, 2003). Also, for a discussion on immigration as geopolitics, see the special issue of *Political Geography* 21 (2002).

3. Ernst Spaan, *Labour Circulation and Socioeconomic Transformation: The Case of East Java, Indonesia* (Groningen: Rijksuniversiteit Groningen, 1999); hereafter cited in text as Spaan (1999).

4. Jessop (1990: 261), cited in Jim Glassman, "State Power Beyond the 'Territorial Trap': The Internationalization of the State," *Political Geography* 18 (1999): 677; hereafter cited in text as Jessop (1990).

5. Nakertrans. Indonesian government website for transmigration and the labor force. http://www.nakertrans.go.id/berita_penting/2001/September/BP010917.htm (last accessed 8 July 2003); hereafter cited in text as Nakertrans (2003).

6. Christine B.N. Chin, "Walls of Silence and Late Twentieth Century Representations of the Foreign Female Domestic Worker: The Case of Filipina and Indonesian Female Servants in Malaysia," *International Migration Review* 31, no. 2 (1997): 353–85.

7. For an overview, see Katie Willis and Brenda Yeoh, eds., *Gender and Migration* (Cheltenham, UK and Northampton, MA: Edward Elgar Publishing Limited, 2000).

8. cf. Shirlena Huang and Brenda S. A. Yeoh, "Ties that Bind: State Policy and Migrant Female Domestic Helpers in Singapore," *Geoforum* 27 (1996): 479–93; hereafter cited in text as Huang and Yeoh (1996).

9. Also see Christine B.N. Chin, *In Service and Servitude: Foreign Female Domestic Workers and the Malaysian "Modernity" Project* (New York: Columbia University Press, 1998), hereafter cited in text as Chin (1998); Christine B.N. Chin,"The State and the 'State' in Globalization: Social Order and Economic Restructuring in Malaysia," *Third World Quarterly* 21, no. 6 (2000): 1035–57.

10. e.g., Christine DiStefano, *Configurations of Masculinity: A Feminist Perspective on Modern Political Theory* (Ithaca, New York and London: Cornell University Press, 1991); Catharine A. MacKinnon, *Toward a Feminist Theory of the State* (Cambridge, MA: Harvard University Press, 1989).

11. Rebecca Elmhirst, "Learning the Ways of the Priyayi: Domestic Servants and the Mediation of Modernity in Jakarta, Indonesia." In *Gender, Migration and Domestic Service,* ed. Janet Henshall Momsen, 242–62 (London and New York: Routledge, 1999).

12. Shirin Rai, "Women and the State in the Third World." In *Women and Politics in the Third World,* ed. Haleh Afshar, 25–39 (London and New York: Routledge, 1996).

13. Kathryn Robinson, "Gender, Islam, and Nationality: Indonesian Domestic Servants in the Middle East." In *Home and Hegemony: Domestic Service and Identity Politics in South and Southeast Asia,* eds. Kathleen M. Adams and Sara Dickey, 249–82 (Ann Arbor, MI: University of Michigan Press, 2000), hereafter cited in text as Robinson (2000); Eleanor Abdella Doumato, *Getting God's Ear: Women, Islam, and Healing in Saudi Arabia and the Gulf* (New

York: Columbia University Press, 2000), hereafter cited in text as Doumato (2000).

14. cf. Huang and Yeoh (1996); Janet Henshall Momsen, ed., *Gender, Migration and Domestic Service* (London and New York: Routledge, 1999); Geraldine Pratt, "From Registered Nurse to Registered Nanny: Discursive Geographies of Filipina Domestic Workers in Vancouver, BC," *Economic Geography* 75, no. 3 (1999): 215–36.

15. Kathryn Robinson, "Housemaids: The Effects of Gender and Culture in the Internal and International Migration of Indonesian Women." In *Intersexions: Gender, Class, Culture, Ethnicity,* eds. Gillian Bottomley, Marie M. De Lepervanche, and Jeannie Martin, 33–51 (Sydney: Allen and Unwin, 1991); hereafter cited in text as Robinson (1991).

16. Aris Ananta, Daksini Kartowibowo, Nur Hadi Wiyono, and Chotib. "The Impact of the Economic Crisis on International Migration: The Case of Indonesia," *Asian Pacific Migration Journal* 7, nos. 2–3 (1998): 313–38; hereafter cited in text as Ananta, et al. (1998).

17. Rashid Amjad, "Philippines and Indonesia: On the Way to a Migration Transition," *Asian and Pacific Migration Journal* 5, nos. 2–3 (1996): 335; hereafter cited in text as Amjad (1996).

18. Graeme Hugo. "Labour Export from Indonesia." *ASEAN Economic Bulletin* 12, no. 2 (1995): 280; hereafter cited in text as Hugo (1995).

19. As early as the late 1980s, migrants were also destined for sites throughout the Middle East, Southeast Asia, and East Asia. It is likely that the numbers of undocumented emigrants increased for all destinations after the beginning of the Indonesian financial crisis, as growing numbers of people sought income abroad. But the numbers of documented emigrants fell during the same period, in part because the cost of documentation and travel became prohibitive for many prospective migrants. Further, many overseas contract workers, particularly in Malaysia, have been forcefully repatriated and housed in refugee camps, as the economies of the receiving countries have not provided the surplus necessary to continue to pay overseas workers (Ananta et al., 1998). As this article goes to press in November of 2003, newspaper reports indicate that the Saudi government has stopped providing visas to Indonesian workers (Pikiran Rakyat, April 16, 2003).

20. Rianto Adi, *Migrasi internasional tenaga kerja Indonesia: harapan dan kenyataan* (International Migration of Indonesian Migrant Workers: Expectation and Reality) (Jakarta: Pusat Penelitian Unika Atma Jaya, 1995): 131, as cited in Spaan (1999): 159; hereafter cited in text as Adi (1995).

21. Rusdi Tagaroa and Encop Sofia. *Buruh migran Indonesia: Mencari keadilan* (Indonesian Migrant Workers: Searching for Justice). Bekasi: Lembaga advokasi buruh migran—sololidaritas perempuan (Migrant Workers Advocacy Institute—Women's Solidarity, 2002); hereafter cited in text as Tagaroa and Sofia (2002).

22. Spaan (1999); Riwanto Tirtosudarmo, *Indonesian Domestic Workers in Saudi Arabia* (Mimeograph, Leiden, the Netherlands: International Institute of Asian Studies, 2000).

23. Suzanne Brenner, *The Domestication of Desire: Women, Wealth, and Modernity in Java* (Princeton, NJ: Princeton University Press, 1998).

24. Krishna Sen, "Indonesian Women at Work: Reframing the Subject." In *Gender and Power in Affluent Asia*, eds. Krishna Sen and Maila Stivens, 35–62 (New York: Routledge, 1998); hereafter cited in text as Sen (1998).

25. Saraswati Sunindyo, "Murder, Gender, and the Media: Sexualizing Politics and Violence." In *Fantasizing the Feminine in Indonesia*, ed. Laurie J. Sears

(Durham and London: Duke University Press, 1996): 125; hereafter cited in text as Sunindyo (1996).

26. Madawi al-Rasheed, *A History of Saudi Arabia* (Cambridge and New York: Cambridge University Press, 2002): 151–152; hereafter cited in text as al-Rasheed (2002).

27. J. Birks, I. Seccombe, I., and C. Sinclair, "Labour Migration in the Arab Gulf States: Patterns, Trends, and Prospects," *International Migration* 26, no. 3 (1998): 267–86.

28. Tri Nuke Pujiastuti, "The Experience of Overseas Workers from Indonesia." Unpublished MA thesis, Department of Geographical and Environmental Studies, University of Adelaide, Australia, 2000; hereafter cited in text as Pujiastuti (2000).

29. W.A. Shadid, E.J.A.M. Spaan, and J.D. Speckmann, "Labour Migration and the Policy of the Gulf States." In *Labour Migration to the Middle East: From Sri Lanka to the Gulf,* eds. F. Eelans, T. Schampers, & J. D. Speckman, 63–86 (London and New York: Kegan Paul, 1992); Pujiastuti (2000).

30. Anthony H. Cordesman, *Saudi Arabia: Guarding the Desert Kingdom* (Boulder, CO: Westview, 1997).

31. Eleanor Abdella Doumato, *Getting God's Ear: Women, Islam, and Healing in Saudi Arabia and the Gulf* (New York: Columbia University Press, 2000): 22; hereafter cited in text as Doumato (2000).

32. Eleanor Abdella Doumato, "Women and Work in Saudi Arabia: How Flexible are Islamic Margins?" *Middle East Journal* 53, no. 4 (1999): 569; hereafter cited in text as Doumato (1999).

33. Georg Stauth, *Politics and Cultures of Islamization in Southeast Asia: Indonesia and Malaysia in the Nineteen-nineties* (New Brunswick and London: Transaction Publishers, 2002). The role of religion in the history of the formation of the Saudi state is beyond the scope of this article, but see al-Rasheed (2002) for a nuanced account.

34. Eleanor Abdella Doumato, "Education in Saudi Arabia: Gender, Jobs, and the Price of Religion." In *Women and Globalization in the Arab Middle East: Gender, Economy, and Society,* eds. Eleanor Abdella Doumato, Marsha Pripstein Posusney, 239–78 (Boulder, CO and London: Lynne Reiner Publishers, 2003).

35. Caroline Nagel, "Contemporary Scholarship and the Demystification—and Re-Mystification—of 'Muslim Women,'" *Arab World Geographer* 4, no. 1 (2001): 63–72.

36. Joni Seager, "The Short Curious Half-Life of 'Official Concern' About Women's Rights," *Environment & Planning* 34, no. 1 (2003): 1.

37. Riwanto Tirtosudarmo, *Indonesian Domestic Workers in Saudi Arabia* (Mimeograph, Leiden, the Netherlands: International Institute of Asian Studies, 2000); hereafter cited in text as Tirtosudarmo (2000).

38. *Republika,* October 31, 1997, as cited in Ananta et al. (1998): 332.

39. *The Jakarta Post,* May 6, 1998, cited in Ananta et al. (1998): 332.

40. Benedict Anderson, ed., *Violence and the State in Suharto's Indonesia* (Ithaca, New York: Southeast Asia Program Publications, Cornell University, 2001).

41. Richa Nagar, Vicky Lawson, Linda McDowell, and Susan Hanson. "Locating Globalization: Feminist (Re)Readings of the Subjects and Spaces of Globalization." http://www.clarku.edu:80/departments/geography/leir/4feminists.htm (accessed January 10, 2007) 20, emphasis added.

# 6 Domains of Empowerment

## Women in Micro-Credit Groups Negotiating with Multiple Patriarchies

*Lakshmi Lingam*[1]

The 1980s saw a shift in developmental approaches from redistribution and basic needs to structural adjustment and market-oriented economic reforms. The introduction of economic austerity measures, declines in support and subsidies to the social sector, and increased emphasis on privatization led to serious setbacks in survival and livelihoods of a large majority of people. During the 1990s, a "new poverty agenda" surfaced in World Bank's *World Development Report 1990* as a counterpart to the "Washington consensus" on structural reforms. Income generating programs targeting poverty reduction through micro-credit were deployed as part of the new social safety nets. Micro-credit has since been incorporated in the Poverty Reduction Strategy Papers of the World Bank and the International Monetary Fund.[2]

The promotion of women in micro-credit programs is seen as a sound policy imperative. Justification of female membership in micro-credit has highlighted a three fold purpose: Facilitating effective household-level poverty reduction, providing the space and means for the empowerment of women clients, and enabling viability of lending institutions. The term "empowerment," first used by feminists of the South engaged with grass-roots women to indicate change in power relations in favor of women, has increasingly come to be used in the micro-credit and micro-finance sector. The terms "autonomy," "empowerment," "control," and "agency" have acquired significance in literature as projected results of participation in micro-credit groups. While evidently there is a broad consensus on the significance of women's empowerment and contours of the definition of empowerment, indicators to measure it is are still debated. Some studies focus on "outcome" and others on "process" indicators. Research, though at times contradictory, seems to indicate that women in micro-credit programs are negotiating for changes in various social and economic hierarchies that they confront.

Given the competing claims of success that are made by NGOs and government agencies about micro-credit programs and their impacts on women's empowerment, the present paper shares the results of a study conducted in selected villages in Andhra Pradesh, South India. The paper briefly reviews micro-credit and empowerment linkages, provides background information on the study location, and elaborates on the domains of women's empower-ment as experienced by them in interaction with the state, community, and household levels. The paper then critically examines the conceptual crevices in assumptions about the homogeneity of poor women and the promise of micro-credit for poverty-alleviation and transforming gender relations.

## MICRO-CREDIT AND EMPOWERMENT CLAIMS

Research emerging from innovative initiatives in India and Bangladesh identifies the potential benefits of micro-credit as women's ownership of productive assets and newly found agency, articulation, and mobility.[3] The process of empowerment changes power relations in favor of those who have exercised little power over their own lives. Definitions of empower-ment encompass change in the material and ideological arenas and women's collective "power to" bring about these changes externally as well as their "power within" to believe in their own ability to do so. Transformation of consciousness, in addition to control over different resources, is important.[4] Three inter-related dimensions are needed to make this possible: access to and control over resources to create the preconditions for the exercise of choice, active agency to exercise choices, and achievements that are the outcomes of choices.[5] Women's "strategic life choices,"[6] are manifested in various outcomes such as improvements in child survival, acceptance of contraception, and decline in domestic violence. Mosedale (2005) summa-rizes these as "women achieving a change that expands options not only for themselves but also for women in general both now and in the future."[7]

Studies in the field of micro-credit and empowerment, seen together or independently, variously measure the success of the micro-credit program by outcomes or process indicators that seem to indicate women's agency. Stud-ies that focus on micro-credit define the success of women's groups (SHGs) in terms of effective group savings, regularity of meetings, maintenance of record books, loan repayments without defaults, building capital, and set-ting up micro enterprises, and consider this success a proxy for empower-ment. Demographic and population studies use individual proxy indicators to measure empowerment like education, employment, property holding, or participation in a SHG and correlate them to outcome indicators like child survival, acceptance of small family norm, or health seeking behavior. Studies that examine the effect of participation in a SHG on household-level decision-making or autonomy to make independent decisions posit their questions as process measures of empowerment.[8]

Mayoux (1999) categorized approaches to micro- finance and gender as:[9]

- Financial sustainability paradigm:[10] The goal is provision of finan-cially self-sustainable micro-finance services to large numbers of poor people, particularly micro-entrepreneurs and small entrepreneurs.

- Poverty alleviation paradigm: The goal is reducing poverty among the poorest, increasing well being and community development. The focus is on small savings and loan provision for consumption and production, group formation, etc. This paradigm justifies some level of subsidy for programs working with particular client groups or in particular contexts.
- Feminist paradigm: The underlying concerns are gender equality and women's human rights. Micro-finance is promoted as an entry point in a wider strategy for women's economic and socio-political empowerment. The focus is on gender awareness and feminist organization.

These paradigms all assume that women's access to microfinance will set off mutually reinforcing "virtuous spirals" that increase their economic, social, legal, and political empowerment. Each has a different focus on how gender relations are addressed within the program.

In a recent paper, Mayoux (2006) challenges assumptions about the automatic benefits of micro-finance for women.[11] For example, high repayment levels do not necessarily indicate that women have used the loans themselves. Men may take the loans from women or women may choose to invest loans according to men's priorities. Likewise, high demand for loans by women may be a sign of social pressure to obtain resources for in-laws or husbands rather than an indicator of empowerment. Thus a study by Goetz and Sen Gupta (1996) in Bangladesh found that with an increase in loan amounts, investments were typically made in "male" activities and women had decreased control over the management of these loans.[12] The sociocultural constraints on women accessing markets for sales also compel women to mediate their small businesses through men, effectively reiterating the male prerogative over knowledge and mobility. Other research disagrees, however. Rather than see the funding of male activities as a problem, a study of an unsuccessful micro-enterprise program in India reiterates the need to make men part of the solution to help women address poverty as well as gender issues.[13]

There is growing critique of the potential of participation in micro-credit groups for changing gender relations. Feminist and other writings critical of the "instrumentality" embedded in the mobilization of women into micro-credit and self-help groups argue that "money proves an inadequate currency for changing gender relations."[14] Micro-credit programs that are successful in terms of loan repayment rates and growing membership do not appear to be challenging existing social hierarchies of caste, class, ethnicity, and gender; on the contrary, they may be legitimating these hierarchies.[15] Batliwala and Dhanraj (2004) point out that mass creation of women's self-help groups nurtures a "depoliticized collective action" that does not threaten the power structures and political order.[16] Whether claims for structural transformation can be made at all is a question. Kabeer (2005) observes that there are no magic bullets, no panaceas, no readymade formulas, and no blueprints for structural transformation. According to her, "micro-credit may at most provide a safety net for the poor rather than a ladder out of poverty."[17]

Women's experience of violence is seen as a negative fallout of participation in micro-credit groups by some researchers. However, others interpret the occurrence of violence as an indicator of resistance to male order.[18] Apart from variations in interpretations of the findings, Kabeer (2001) points out the need to contextualize conceptualizations in an understanding of relations of dependence, interdependence, and autonomy which determine different process trajectories.[19] Autonomous control over resources may be a measure of empowerment according to a researcher, while it may not be the same for women. The question of culture specificity in the ways women make or do not make choices and the difficulty of measuring culture-specific choices with external parameters has been highlighted by Kabeer (1999).[20] She pointed out the importance of capturing subjective explanations given by women themselves to understand women's negotiations of gender relations within the household and the community.

These are among the issues debated in the literature pertaining to the methodology for measuring the success of micro-finance initiatives and women's empowerment. It is the contention of this paper that women are handling multiple patriarchies—the state, community, caste, and households—at their own pace; or, as one woman described it, "one step at a time." Women are differentially positioned based on their age, caste, class, and marital status and do not always identify through a group identity or gender identity. This adds to the complexity to be explored in this paper.

## ABOUT THE STUDY

The arguments for this paper emerge from a study conducted in three villages in Mehboobnagar[21] District of Andhra Pradesh,[22] a southern state in India. Three villages from three *Mandals* (administrative clusters consisting of ten or more villages) taking three different approaches to women's programs were chosen for study:

- Village 1 has a women's empowerment program called "Mahila Samata" (Education for Women's Equality) that is managed by an autonomous government-supported body and is funded by the Dutch government. In this village women from the lowest castes, (shepherd and Scheduled Castes[23]), have been mobilized into *sanghas* (collectives). Mahila Samakhya gives precedence to social mobilization, education (know/understand/analyze the structures of oppression), group formation, information and self-development (enhancing self-esteem and confidence, bargaining/negotiating).
- Village 2 has poverty-reduction self-help groups, popularly known as *Velugu* (light) groups, funded by the World Bank. The program

is called Indira Pragati Padam (IPP). Its initial priority was to mobilize Scheduled Caste and Scheduled Tribe[24] women but now includes women of other castes as well. Each group member contributes one rupee each day to the group savings.

- Village 3 has a welfare-oriented program known as *Podupu Lakshmi* (*podupu* means savings and *lakshmi* is the name of the goddess of wealth). Women members form neighborhood savings groups of eighteen to twenty participants. The groups are generally made of semiliterate women of slightly higher caste groups (legally designated as Other Backward Castes[25]) who can draw savings by maneuvering household budgets or carry on a home-based income-generating activity like managing milch cattle or petty lending.

Since early 2004, the governmental departments managing the poverty reduction and welfare programs have merged, so officials see these programs as being the same while the women do not. In each village, the mobilization of women started during the last five years, and each village also had other ongoing government initiatives. In Village 1 presently all three programs coexist, though women draw their primary affiliation to the Samata *sangha*.

The study used both quantitative and qualitative methods to collect information from the program machinery, the village people, and women in the SHGs. An interview schedule covered personal and household details. The schedule also attempted to capture mobility patterns within and beyond the village for various activities, (alone, with other women, family members), changes experienced in the household and community, and decision-making in the household regarding domestic work, purchase of agricultural and non-agricultural assets, place of delivery, children's education, marriage age, and marriage gifts.

The data were collected in August and September 2004 when I stayed in the three villages with a team of field investigators. Focus-group discussions and village meetings were conducted during a follow-up trip in January 2005. A total of 300 women from three villages were interviewed of which 88 percent are members of SHGs and 12 percent are women who are not part of any SHGs. Of the total, 69 percent were below age 40, 85 percent were currently married, 92 percent were illiterate, and the majority belonged to Backward Castes and Scheduled Castes. The respondents predominantly belonged to landless households and were dependent on agricultural and nonagricultural wage work.

## Different Programs but Similar Results

Despite the different modes of mobilization in the three programs, the womens' responses to several questions pertaining to their perceived changes in public and aspects of their private lives were not significantly different (See Table 6–1). The discussions with the women leaders[26] of SHGs, however, indicated differences in women's awareness of gender issues and in what they saw as their collective role in changing this. Women from the village were mobilized by the feminist-oriented organization prioritized issues related to early marriage age, girl-child education, women's health, and domestic violence. On the other

Table 6–1 Percentage Distribution of Changes Perceived by SHG Women

| Changes in | Village 1 (Feminist-orientedOriented) (N=81) | | | Village 2 (Poverty Alleviation) (N=93) | | | Village 3 (Welfare-Oriented) (N = 91) | | |
|---|---|---|---|---|---|---|---|---|---|
| | In-creased | De-creased | Just the Same | In-creased | De-creased | Just the Same | In-creased | De-creased | Just the Same |
| **Public Domain Issues** | | | | | | | | | |
| Able to speak to outsiders | 75 (92.4) | 1 (1.2) | 6 (7.4) | 81 (87.1) | 1 (1.1) | 10 (10.7) | 89 (97.8) | —— | 2 (2.2) |
| Interest in commu-nity and village matters | 56 (69.1) | 3 (3.7) | 21 (25.9) | 66 (70.9) | 1 (1.1) | 25 (26.9) | 77 (84.6) | 3 (3.3) | 10 (10.9) |
| **Personal & Private Domain Issues** | | | | | | | | | |
| Feel Confi-dent | 75 (92.4) | 1 (1.2) | 5 (6.2) | 81 (87.1) | 1 (1.1) | 10 (10.7) | 89 (97.8) | — | 2 (2.2) |
| Able to manage money | 69 (85.2) | 2 (2.5) | 10 (12.3) | 68 (73.1) | — | 24 (25.8) | 88 (96.7) | — | |
| Your work-load | 50 (61.7) | 17 (20.9) | 14 (17.3) | 67 (72.0) | 18 (19.3) | 8 (8.6) | 67 (73.6) | 21 (23.1) | 2 (2.2) |
| Leisure time | 22 (27.1) | 47 (58.0) | 12 (14.8) | 19 (20.4) | 67 (72.0) | 7 (7.5) | 27 (29.7) | 59 (64.8) | 4 (4.4) |
| Quantity and quality of food | 74 (91.4) | | 7 (8.6) | 82 (88.2) | | 11 (11.8) | 71 (78.0) | 1 (1.1) | 18 (19.8) |
| Family income | 40 (49.4) | 28 (34.5) | 13 (16.0) | 35 (37.6) | 52 (55.9) | 5 (5.4) | 32 (35.2) | 52 (57.1) | 7 (7.7) |
| Family debt | 30 (37.0) | 34 (41.9) | 17 (20.9) | 52 (55.9) | 35 (37.6) | 5 (5.4) | 54 (59.3) | 32 (35.2) | 5 (5.5) |

hand, the women that were mobilized under the welfare and poverty alleviation models were focused on savings, repayment, group norms, and credit.

Lack of major differences in the findings between the three villages, despite the different mobilization methodologies, point to two possible explanations:

1. In the larger policy environment, government has placed its emphasis on educating girls, increasing the age at marriage, reducing child labor, providing scholarships to girls, and enrolling women in welfare programs, to name a few. While the performance of programs may vary across villages, government efforts are omnipresent. Practically all departments of the government enlist the support of women's SHGs to implement or monitor programs or to introduce new initiatives. Women are seen as enthusiastic and reliable grassroots workers.
2. There are limitations in the process-indicator questions used to measure women's empowerment. Also, quantitative methodologies do not capture women's perceptions in nuanced or in subjective ways. The arenas of control or decision-making that typically come under the scanner of questionnaires are at the lower end of the patriarchal bastion and are easy to negotiate and loosen. Issues like being able to purchase a *sari* or a piece of jewelry or visit a natal village without the permission of the husband or a senior member, do not pose a major threat to gender relations in lower-caste households or among communities where women are not secluded. Questions about the purchase of consumer items or jewelry are more indicative of availability of liquid cash than empowerment. Similar observations were made by a study in Vietnam.[27] Therefore, in response to a question on purchase of jewelry, many women quipped, "Give us the money first, and then we will buy and show you." Some women mentioned that it is such a rare occasion to be able to buy jewelry that they would like to enjoy it with their husband or family.

## DOMAINS OF EMPOWERMENT

Empowerment programs with different entry points—for example, addressing access to material resources *or* ideological matters—address issues in a piecemeal manner. The poverty alleviation and welfare-oriented programs implicitly expect women to individually renegotiate the ideological arena. Feminist-oriented mobilizations that address ideological issues like girls' education, marriage age, and domestic violence marginally address gender relations within the domestic domain, caste-based inequalities in the community, and official policies of marginalization by the state. Seemingly there is a distinction that programs make about empowering women by facilitating their public-domain roles and leaving the equations of their private-domain roles untouched. In other words, the "gender practical interests" are addressed and the "strategic gender interests" are outside the realm of mobilization.[28]

I assert that the positive changes that women experience in the public domain cannot be assumed to transform the other domains of women's lives simultaneously or automatically. The pace may be different and can be linked to how women drive it and their awareness of it. In many villages, my field observations indicate that women who take up leadership roles in the SHG or in the affairs of the village are more likely to be older women past procreative and caring commitments, single or widowed women, or women who have adult daughters or daughters-in-law to take care of domestic work. Women who negotiate for power in the public domain are also women who have better bargaining power within the family and have alternative persons to deliver social reproduction work. They take on active leadership roles within the *sanghas,* are open to attending training programs, and display readiness to spearhead change. They are much more supportive of increasing the marriage age for girls to eighteen years, acceptance of a small family norm, and institutional deliveries for their daughters and daughters-in-law.

Individual women within the SHGs show different patterns of empowerment in terms of: public vs. private empowerment, collective vs. individual empowerment, and joint vs. autonomous empowerment. These varied levels of women's empowerment are entwined with the rigidity or flexibility of each of the various institutions—the state, community, and household in a society that represents the co-existence of multiple patriarchies.[29]

## Public-Domain Empowerment (Within Limits!): Interaction with the State

Women in all of the villages expressed the changes they experienced from being part of collectives as increases in *dhairyam* (self-confidence) and *thelivi* (awareness). Table 6–1 presents the data on women's perceived changes in the public and private domains of their lives. In all three villages, women mentioned that their confidence in speaking to outsiders and their interest in the village and community matters had increased. The ability to interact with and question unsatisfactory performance of government officials, whether hospital staff or school teachers, was explained by the women as a reflection of their *dhairyam.* In a context where women previously had seldom expressed their rights as citizens beyond casting a vote according to the will of the men or their caste collective, this shift is palpable. Women say they have discovered their voices. Of the three programs, the women from the village that had a successful welfare program recorded higher percentages of all positive improvements in their questions. This is closely linked to the fact that the *Podupu Lakshmi* program is one of the oldest in addressing women's requirements for income-generating programs.

Women often reveal their identity as *sangha* members in their conversations with government staff or officials. Many of them are well aware that they can make a written complaint to the District Collector if they perceive that bureaucracy is stalling their demands. This practice was part of the *Janmabhoomi* (land of birth) campaigns of the earlier state government (Telugu Desam Party), which introduced the concepts of people's participation in governance and accountability of the bureaucracy to the people.[30] Several state programs established community-based committees for operationalizing concepts of social audit and accountability. Women are a significant part of these committees and play an active role. Women's SHGs along with community-based users' committees were and are identified as community-based oversight committees that monitor government programs. This has opened new avenues of negotiation with the state and the emergence of women's political agency outside the framework of democratic electoral politics.

There are competing development programs that seek the attention of women to make a difference in their lives. It is noteworthy to observe how households mediate their coping strategies through women's participation in these programs. (This will be discussed in the household section). In Village 1 women belong to the *sangha* as well as micro-credit groups. A woman leader associated with both programs said to me: "Ikkada anta akkal, paiselu levu; akkada anta paiselu, akkal ledu" ("Here—there is a lot of awareness and ideas but there is no money. There—there is money but no awareness and ideas.") Evidently, "rational" choices are made through "rational" assessments.

## Community-Level Empowerment

Women's collective interventions and agency are, at this point, limited to public-domain negotiations with institutions. The village women in one of the villages mentioned that they had collectively demanded that their *Panchayat* (village council) provide amenities like drinking water and street lighting. The *Panchayat* had arranged to dig a bore well and lay pipelines for drinking water. Households pay a small fee for the service. Women are proud of their achievement and often invoke collective protest as a strategy to resolve their problems. Women mentioned that men in the village seek their help to approach government officials for village-related development works or for community mobilization, e.g., to raise funds to construct a temple. In response to questions about being responsible at the household and community levels, women mentioned that they were aware of getting overburdened with public domain roles, but at the time they wished to put to good use the newfound legitimacy within and outside the village that emerges from their collective strength. It appears that the women at this juncture understand their rights as "citizens" and are claiming them, at least in limited ways.

As long as women's newly found public role is not threatening the caste, class, or gender order it is somewhat tolerated. In Village 1, women mentioned that they had organized a separate flag-hoisting ceremony at the women's *sangha* office a few years ago. The women were reprimanded for taking their "freedom beyond limits," because the flag-hoisting has traditionally been held only on the premises of the *Panchayat* (village council office) and the school. Although men in private poke fun at women's newfound visibility, collectively they tolerate women's mobilization "within certain limits".

In certain villages in the Mehbubnagar district, *sangha* women directly confronted upper- caste interests in maintaining cultural practices like dedicating young girls as *joginis*.[31] The women were abused by upper-caste men and told that the party in power had changed so they would have to close their *sanghas;* it was the men's turn to rule. Men generally maintain a close watch on the proceedings of the women's meetings. They frequently support women's activities, accompany them to the bank if necessary, and carry out some errands for the SHGs, but also indirectly intervene in the outcomes of the meetings through the women members of the household.

Because access to credit is easier for women than men, male resistance to women's public-domain participation is on the decline. However, the shrinking possibilities for men to receive loans for agriculture and allied activities are leading to male resentment of government policies and backlash against women's programs in several villages. There seems to be an obvious conceptual gap in assuming that micro-credit can reduce poverty and improve women's status within households, while men from poor households face, albeit in less complex ways, disempowerment, loss of livelihoods, and lack of lifestyle options, as indicated by the growing agrarian distress manifested in farmers' suicides in many regions of Andhra Pradesh.[32]

Key informant interviews with men of lower- and middle-caste groups who were considered to be opinion leaders revealed skepticism about government strategies to mobilize women at the cost of neglecting male farmers in terms of access to credit, agricultural extension services, and market support. Both men and women pointed out that the SHG movement is useful but it still does not address the issue of employment opportunities for the youth, many of whom are first-generation literates. There are no rural industries that can employ young people. Educated and uneducated youth migrate to distant cities to work on construction sites for lack of avenues for work within or close to the village.

## Empowerment in Personal and Private Domains: Household Decision-Making

Women across all villages reported an increase in their influence on household decision making, their ability to manage money, and their personal confidence. It is noteworthy that women from all villages mentioned that their workload has increased and their leisure has reduced. Women explained that "Times are hard; we have to work hard to make ends meet." Also, participation in village level activities and SHGs entails attending meetings and training programs outside of the village.

Decision-making within households is linked to the composition of families in all three villages. Where senior members such as a mother-in-law are present in the family, decisions are made by older members until the daughter-in-law attains seniority. Even younger men have to abide by authority or negotiate their way. I have observed that where a mother-in-law and daughter-in-law are both members of an SHG, it is the mother-in-law who attends the meetings, not the daughter-in-law. The daughter-in-law has the responsibility of cooking and caring for children, which the mother-in-law has graduated from. Responses to several questions about purchases of assets (small and large, agricultural and nonagricultural) indicated that decisions are made by men or by men and women together. Women's autonomous decisions on most family matters are rare unless it is a household headed by a woman. In response to question on "whether women are able to influence decisions on all matters or only on some matters," 86 percent women mentioned that they are able to influence on some matters, and 14 percent mentioned on all matters.

Women reported that decisions about marriage and dowry gifts were often made by community elders who were consulted for mediation to settle marriage liaisons. They said that the practice of dowry is not changing as a result of women's mobilization. With reference to the purposes for which loans were taken, 3.8 percent of the women mentioned dowry and marriage expenses (refer to Table 6–2). It is only in Village 1 that women did not mention taking loans for weddings and dowry expenses. It does not overrule the existence of dowry in the village, but shows that these loans have not been used for this purpose.

Women's loans from the SHGs have been spent towards agricultural investments (34 percent), household consumption (40 percent) and in income-earning activities[33] (26 percent) (refer to Table 6–2) indicating the significance of women's loans for reducing the deficiency in agricultural investment and expenditure on food and health. A few have purchased consumer goods. However, women's participation in farming-related decisions is generally limited. In farming households this is seen as a routine activity, because the same crops are grown each year and what is grown is linked to land quality, availability of water for irrigation, and, at times, the predicted market. Women contribute labor for cultivation, crop processing, and storage. They are more likely to intervene to influence how many bags of food grains are retained for domestic consumption.

It appears that women consider being part of the SHG as a household strategy rather than an opportunity to claim a share in household power. At the household level, women seem to be striving for joint decision-making with men rather than autonomy and control. They seek greater equality,

**Table 6–2** Purpose of Loans Taken from the SHG

| Purpose of loan | Village 1 (Lingampalli) | Village 2 (Pappireddy-guda) | Village 3 (Thadiparthi) | Total (%) |
|---|---|---|---|---|
| **I. Agriculture-Related Expenses** | | | | |
| Agriculture investment (crop) | 21 | 14 | 7 | 42 (22.6) |
| Purchase land | 3 | 2 | 1 | 06 (3.3) |
| Agriculture assets purchased | 3 | 1 | 1 | 05 (2.7) |
| Repaid another loan and agricultural investment | 2 | 1 | - | 03 (1.6) |
| For bore- well digging | 1 | 1 | 1 | 03 (1.6) |
| Agricultural assets and bore well | - | 1 | - | 01 (0.5) |
| **II. Household-Related Expenses** | | | | |
| Consumption | - | 17 | 10 | 27 (14.5) |
| Health expenditure | 1 | 13 | 8 | 22 (12) |
| Dowry/wedding | - | 4 | 3 | 07 (3.8) |
| Consumer assets purchased | 3 | 7 | 5 | 15 (6.4) |
| Consumption assets and agricultural investment | 1 | 2 | 1 | 04 (2) |
| **III. Non-Agricultural Investment** | | | | |
| Purchased milch cattle/ sheep/goat | 5 | 11 | 5 | 21 (11.5) |
| Started small business | 2 | 3 | 7 | 12 (6.5) |
| Given on lending | 1 | 3 | - | 04 (2) |
| Don't know | 4 | 4 | 3 | 11 (6) |
| Total | 47 | 84 | 52 | 186 (100) |

strengthened interdependence, and men's recognition of their contributions rather than autonomy in an individual sense.

*Personal Mobility*

Freedom of mobility is considered an important process indicator that facilitates women's ability to carry out activities of their choice. There are distinct differences in the mobility patterns of women who are members of SHGs as opposed to women who are not members of SHGs. Table 6–3 indicates that women undertake familial activities along with the men in their family. Women from all three villages expressed an increase in mobility outside the village for meeting government officials, transacting business at the bank, and attending training programs. All these activities are carried out by a small group of women, who take turns to undertake the tasks of the SHG, like visiting the bank, depositing money, getting passbooks updated, and discussing the possibility of bank loans; negotiating for government schemes; and attending training programs, village cluster meetings, and so on. Trips related to family activities like visiting places, purchasing small assets, or visiting hospitals are undertaken along with other family members or with the husband. Though women also travel alone or with children, this does not emerge as a major pattern in any of the villages.

*Gender Relations*

Experiences from India and other parts of the world show steady changes in gender norms and gender relations in the public and private domains in response to women's mobilization. To questions on perceived changes in gender relations, women gave the responses presented below. It should be noted that unlike several parts of northern India, southern India does not practice strict seclusion. Women from the low- and mid-range caste groups are visible in public and work on their own farms or as agricultural laborers.[34] Further, Mehboobnagar district is part of a historical region that had strong peasant revolts against the *Nizam* rulers immediately after India's independence. Women participated actively in this armed struggle.[35]

In rural areas, men and women express the measure of an event such as rainfall in terms of "*paise* to the *rupee*," which is a saying in India analogous to "like cents on the dollar." During my field study, in response to a question about the adequacy of rains during the season, most people said they had had "only 50 *paise* rain and at all the wrong times."[36] The survey asked women to use this idiom to measure the changes in their husbands' attitudes towards their contribution to the household and their participation in community-based social activities, their husbands' facilitation of their attendance at meetings, and actual sharing of household work, including male children's

**Table 6–3** Activity-Wise Mobility Pattern of SHG Women and Non-SHG Women

| | SHG Women | Non-SHG Women | Total |
|---|---|---|---|
| **To Attend Meetings** | | | |
| No | 26 (9.8) | 11 (32.4) | 37 (12.4) |
| Yes alone always | 6 (2.3) | 0 | 6 (2.0) |
| Yes alone sometimes | 56 (21.1) | 2 (5.8) | 58 (19.4) |
| Yes with other women | 162 (61.1) | 4 (11.8) | 166 (55.5) |
| Yes with husband/family | 7 (2.6) | 0 | 7 (2.3) |
| Others | 7 (2.6) | 1 (2.9) | 8 (2.7) |
| NA | 1 (0.4) | 16 (47.1) | 17 (5.7) |
| Total | 265 | 34 | 299 (100.0) |
| **To Market to Purchase Household Items** | | | |
| No | 14 (5.3) | 2 (5.8) | 16 (5.4) |
| Yes alone always | 24 (9.1) | 2 (5.8) | 26 (8.7) |
| Yes alone sometimes | 37 (13.9) | 6 (17.6) | 43 (14.4) |
| Yes with other women | 61 (23.0) | 8 (23.5) | 69 (23.1) |
| Yes with husband/family | 102 (38.5) | 12 (35.3) | 114 (38.1) |
| Others | 24 (9.1) | 1 (2.9) | 25 (8.3) |
| NA | 3 (1.1) | 3 (8.8) | 6 (2.0) |
| Total | 265 | 34 | 299 (100.0) |
| **To Market to Buy Agricultural Inputs and Seeds** | | | |
| No | 35 (13.2) | 3 (8.8) | 38 (12.7) |
| Yes alone always | 15 (5.7) | 0 | 15 (5.0) |
| Yes alone sometimes | 10 (3.8) | 1 (2.9) | 11 (3.7) |
| Yes with other women | 11 (4.1) | 1 (2.9) | 12 (4.0) |
| Yes with husband/family | 137 (51.7) | 18 (52.9) | 155 (51.8) |
| Others | 13 (4.9) | 2 (5.8) | 15 (5.0) |
| NA | 44 (16.6) | 9 (26.5) | 53 (17.7) |
| Total | 265 | 34 | 299 (100.0) |

*(continued)*

**Table 6–3** Activity-Wise Mobility Pattern of SHG Women and Non-SHG Women (continued)

| | SHG Women | Non-SHG Women | Total |
|---|---|---|---|
| **To Visit the Hospital for Children** | | | |
| No | 31 (11.7) | 3 (8.8) | 34 (11.4) |
| Yes alone always | 23 (8.7) | 1 (2.9) | 24 (8.0) |
| Yes alone sometimes | 28 (10.6) | 8 (23.5) | 36 (12.0) |
| Yes with other women | 10 (3.8) | 2 (5.8) | 12 (4.0) |
| Yes with husband/family | 155 (58.4) | 16 (47.1) | 171 (57.2) |
| Others | 9 (3.4) | 1 (2.9) | 10 (3.3) |
| NA | 9 (3.4) | 3 (8.8) | 12 (4.0) |
| Total | 265 | 34 | 299 (100.0) |
| **To Migrate to Work** | | | |
| No | 228 (86.0) | 20 (58.8) | 248 (82.9) |
| Yes alone always | 3 (1.1) | 0 | 3 (1.2) |
| Yes alone sometimes | 4 (1.5) | 3 (8.8) | 7 (2.3) |
| Yes with other women | 0 | 0 | 0 |
| Yes with husband/family | 28 (10.6) | 8 (23.5) | 36 (12.0) |
| Others | 0 | 1 (2.9) | 1 (0.3) |
| Not applicableA | 2 (0.7) | 2 (5.8) | 4 (1.3) |
| Total | 265 | 34 | 299 (100.0) |

Note: Multiple answers were given in the "Others" category.

learning to do domestic work. The attempt was to understand changes in gender relations and division of labor within households that can contribute to sustainable change. The data are presented in Table 6–4.

The majority of women reported a 50-paise change in men's appreciation of their contributions to the household; a 25-paise change in men facilitating women's participation in SHG activities; a 50-paise increase in actual sharing of domestic work; and a 25- or 50-paise reduction of anger and irritation. One woman commented, "In the beginning he used to do a lot of *lolli* (petty quarreling and nagging); now he does not." In one village, the women have collectively constructed a *sangha* office. One woman said that if her husband quarrels too much she will threaten to go and stay in the *sangha* office, and she also has the support of the other women in doing this. She says that, because of this, her husband is afraid that all of the women will quarrel with him. All

Table 6–4 Women's Perceptions of Changes in Gender Relations: Rupee Ratio

| A. | How many "paise in a rupee" is your husband? | 25ps. | 50ps. | 75ps. | Total |
|---|---|---|---|---|---|
| | | % | % | % | % |
| 1. | Willing to share work in the family? | 13 | 79 | 8 | 100 |
| 2. | Actually doing domestic work? | 31 | 65 | 4 | 100 |
| 3. | Giving a larger share of earnings for the household? | 12 | 77 | 11 | 100 |
| 4. | Appreciating your contribution to the family? | 17 | 76 | 7 | 100 |
| 5. | Appreciating your participation in social/community-based social activities? | 36 | 65 | 4 | 100 |
| 6. | Facilitating your attending of meetings and trips outside the village? | 56 | 37 | 7 | 100 |
| 7. | Not expressing anger and irritation towards you? | 38 | 40 | 22 | 100 |
| B. | How many paise in a rupee are male children learning household work? | 64 | 31 | 5 | 100 |
| C. | How many paise in a rupee do you attribute these changes to the SHG/sangha? | 24 | 70 | 6 | 100 |

of the women mentioned that the men are afraid to oppose them; they see that women are talking sense and are doing good work instead of gossiping.[37]

It is important to note that while men are willing to share doing domestic work there is some resistance to facilitating women's participation in SHG. Women are expected to complete all of the household tasks and attend the group meetings. Normally the meetings are held at 9 pm to help women who go for paid work during the day to attend the meetings. I expected that the sons of those women members, who are learning to perform domestic work, would sow the seeds for future changes in the gender division of work. However, 64 percent of the women reported only a 25-pais increase in the number of boys learning domestic work. They often giggled at this question, pointing to deep-seated women's perceptions of gender roles as "natural" and "appropriate" for women.

*Crevices in the Empowerment Processes:*
*Poor Women are Not a Homogenous Group*

Women experience different kinds of exclusion in the formation and functioning of SHGs. Extremely poor households (with no regular earnings or able bodied members), migrant households, and old women face exclusion. Village 1 has several old women in the *sangha* because their membership fee is less than 10 *rupees* a month (about 25 cents) and there is no focus on savings, credit, and repayments.

Exclusion on the basis of caste, and resistance to collectivization cutting across caste lines, was evident in the villages. While gender relations are going through nominal changes, caste hierarchies, differences, and hostilities among the poor are resistant to change. All of the village-level SHG meetings that were held as a preamble to the study involved women from all caste groups. In Village 1 we did not notice any overt physical distance being maintained by Other Backward Castes (OBC) women from the lower castes, whereas in the other two villages all the OBC women not only maintained distance but also had serious conflicts. During the course of introductions, while women from the lower castes stood up, put their palms together (to indicate reverence), gave their name and the name of their *sangha,* and conveyed their greetings, the OBC women sat in their places and gave only their names and the names of their *sangha.* After the meeting, one OBC woman asked, "How can we fold our hands in front of people who are lower caste and work for wages on our fields?" Women come into these meetings with a caste and family identity, not with a gender identity.

Poor women are not a homogeneous group, hence sisterhood among the poor is not simple and straightforward. The expectation that women can be mobilized as a class of poor women undermines the reality that gender is embedded within multiple social stratifiers like caste, ethnicity, religion, and race. The convergence of poverty-reduction and welfare approaches over the last two years in all districts is producing palpable tensions in the villages. Earlier, women were not only mobilized through different programs with differing program goals but were also mobilized as different caste groups. Tensions over choice of leaders for the Village Development Organization[38] (VDO) that allocates development funds provided by the IPP have grown between different caste groups within the same village. These tensions are underplayed by the community coordinators (NGO staff). There are attempts to "discipline women and communities" and functionally cobble together "social cohesion" among the poor as a class without working on the deep-seated caste differences. This is a bigger challenge that is not amenable to solution by micro-credit programs.

## Womens' Empowerment in the Midst of Growing Agrarian Crises

Research on farmers' suicides points to the growing distress among the agrarian classes, an effect of individualization, a process of socioeconomic "estrangement" in the context of rapid economic transformation.[39] The declining share of agriculture in the gross state domestic product (GSDP) since the 1980s;[40] the high cost of cultivation, diminishing productivity, and low returns; weak support from government; growing underemployment;

increase in indebtedness of farm households; and recurrent farmers' suicides form the backdrop for the mobilization of women in Andhra Pradesh.[41] Access to loans and small capital provides elbow room for women and households, but it is not seen as a solution to poverty. Loans for consumption and health expenditures, referred to in the literature as "consumption smoothing," highlights how these loans provide a straw to stay afloat in a cash-strapped situation (see Table 6–2). SHG loans do not create livelihood options that substitute for the need to migrate to cities for work. Emigration to the cities is still a major strategy for several households who do not find joining SHGs a viable alternative.

Women's empowerment through micro-credit and self-help groups provides a glimmer of hope in the midst of growing poverty and declining livelihoods. Mobilization and solidarity of women are being cobbled together within the context of extreme economic adversity and growing urban-rural inequalities. While women are collectivized for purposes of savings and credit, they are simultaneously individualized to handle the impacts of neoliberal policies at the household level.[42] Wives of farmers who commit suicide bear the major brunt of agrarian crises coupled with caste and gender inequities.[43]

## CONCLUSIONS

Empowerment of women in limited ways is not tenable within a local and global context of exclusion, marginalization, and impoverishment resulting from trade regimes and macroeconomic policies. This paper has attempted to intervene in the existing discourses on measuring women's empowerment with indicators that are purely located at the household or individual level. If the disempowerment of individuals and households is a structural phenomenon (due to class, caste, gender, and state policies) located at various levels (household, community, markets, and the state) then empowerment should also address and affect all these institutions.

Much of the literature tends to view poor women as a homogenous group and considers women's empowerment in isolation from men. This paper highlights the limited gains that women make by being members of self-help groups and directs attention to two questions: Can women's empowerment happen within a larger context that is disempowering? And, can exclusive program focus on women help change gender- and caste-based inequalities? To both these questions, the field-based observations and the data posit negative responses.

## NOTES

1. I would like to sincerely thank the Fulbright Program, the United States Educational Foundation in India (USEFI), and the Council for International

Exchange of Scholars (CIES) for giving me the opportunity to conduct this study and interact with scholars as part of the Fulbright New Century Scholar Program (2004–2005). Special thanks to Dr. Jayati Lal and the Institute for Research on Women and Gender, University of Michigan (UMICH) for inviting me to spend time as a Visiting Scholar at Ann Arbor. The time at UMICH was valuable in many ways. I would like to thank the Tata Institute of Social Sciences for giving me all the requisite support and to Neera Desai who contributed to the conceptualization of the field research. This study would not have been possible without the support of the village women, field staff, AP Mahila Samata Society, Society for the Elimination of Rural Poverty, Department of Rural Development, Government of AP and the Naandhi Foundation. I owe my gratitude to Carolyn Elliott for her provocative questions and valuable comments which strengthened this paper manifold.

2. Heloise Weber, "The Imposition of a Global Development Architecture: The Example of Micro-credit," *Review of International Studies* 28 (2002): 537–55.
3. Marilyn Carr, Martha Chen, and Renana Jhabvala, *Speaking Out: Women's Economic Empowerment in South Asia* (New Delhi, India: Vistaar Publications, 1996); Piush Antony, *Towards Empowerment: Experiences of Organizing Women Workers* (New Delhi: International Labour Organization, 2001); and Govind Kelkar, Dev Nathan, and Rownok Jahan, "Redefining Women's 'Samman:' Microcredit and Gender Relations in Rural Bangladesh," *Economic and Political Weekly,* XXXIX, no. 32 (August 7, 2004): 3627–40.
4. Srilatha Batliwala, *Empowerment of Women in South Asia: Concepts and Practices* (New Delhi, India: Asian South Pacific Bureau of Adult Education and FAO, 1993).
5. Kabeer, N. "Resources, Agency, Achievements: Reflections on the Measurement of Women's Empowerment" in Sida (2001). *Discussing Women's Empowerment: Theory and Practice,* 17–57 (accessed July 11, 2007) at http://www.sida.se/shared/jsp/download.jsp?f=sidastudies+No3.pdfda=2080.
6. "Strategic life choices" include whether to marry, whom to marry, whether to have children, how many children, freedom of movement, political participation, etc.
7. Sarah Mosedale, "Assessing Women's Empowerment: Towards a Conceptual Framework," *Journal of International Development* 17 (2005): 252.
8. Anju Malhotra, Sidney Ruth Schuler, and Carol Boender, "Measuring Women's Empowerment as a Variable in International Development." Background paper prepared for the World Bank Workshop on Poverty and Gender: New Perspectives. Gender and Development Group. Washington, DC: World Bank, 2002; Deepa Narayan, ed., *Measuring Empowerment: Cross-disciplinary Perspectives.* The International Bank for Reconstruction and Development/The World Bank (New Delhi: Oxford University Press, 2006).
9. Linda Mayoux, *Micro-Finance and the Empowerment of Women: A Review of the Key Issues* (International Labor Organization, 1999).
10. Mayoux refers to approaches as "paradigms," the assumption being that they emerge from widely different underlying assumptions that determine the strategies. However, I have reservations about calling them paradigms. In the context of this study the financial sustainability and poverty alleviation approaches, though they have differences in program design and delivery, do not have major differences in their approach to gender or poverty.
11. Linda Mayoux, "Women's Empowerment through Sustainable Micro-Finance: Rethinking 'Best Practice,'" discussion draft, February 2006. http://www.genfinance.info/Documents/Mayoux_Backgroundpaper.pdf (accessed May 11, 2007).

12. Anne Marie Goetz and Rina Sen Gupta, "Who Takes the Credit? Gender, Power and Control over Loan Use in Rural Credit Programmes in Bangladesh," *World Development* 24, no. 1 (1994): 45–63.
13. Fiona Leach and Shashikala Sitaram. "Microfiance and Women's Empowerment: A Lesson from India." *Development in Practice* 12, no. 5 (November 2002): 575–88.
14. Cecile Jackson, "Rescuing Gender from the Poverty Trap," *World Development* 24, no. 3 (1996): 491.
15. Jude L. Fernando and Alan W. Heston, eds., "The Role of NGOs: Charity and Empowerment." *The Annals of the American Academy of Political and Social Science* 554, no. 1 (November 1997).
16. Srilatha Batliwala and Deepa Dhanraj, "Gender Myths that Instrumentalise Women: A View from the Indian Frontline," *Institute of Development Studies Bulletin* 35, no. 4 (October 11–18 , 2004).
17. Naila Kabeer, "Is Microfinance a 'Magic Bullet' for Women's Empowerment? Analysis of Findings from South Asia," *Economic and Political Weekly* XL, nos. 44–45 (October 29, 2005): 4718.
18. Sidney Ruth Schuler, Syed M. Hashemi, A.P. Riley, and A. Akhter, "Credit Programs, Patriarchy and Men's Violence against Women in Rural Bangladesh," *Social Science and Medicine* 43, no. 12 (1996): 1729–42.
19. Kabeer, N. "Conflicts Over Credit: Re-evaluating the Empowerment Potential of Loans to Women in Rural Bangledesh." *World Development* vol. 29 No.1. January 2001, 63–84.
20. Naila Kabeer, *The Conditions and Consequences of Choice: Reflections on the Measurement of Women's Empowerment,* UNRISD Discussion Paper, no. 108 (Geneva, Switzerland: UNRISD, 1999).
21. Mehboobnagar is one of the poorest districts in AP, with small and marginal landholding farming households. Several coarse food grains have always been produced in this region as dryland rain-fed crops. The past few decades have witnessed a steady shift to rice, a marketable crop, which requires irrigation. In the absence of canals and other sources of irrigation, all the villages in this district tap underground water sources to raise wet crops. At the time of the study, scanty rainfall for the third consecutive year had placed considerable strain on the farming community. For generations, seasonal migration to Mumbai, Hyderabad, and different parts of the country has been an important survival strategy for landless households in this and neighboring districts. In recent years, deaths due to HIV/AIDS, a fallout of male migration, have been on the rise.
22. Andhra Pradesh (AP) is known as a significant information technology hub. The state was unambiguously a laboratory for neoliberal World Bank policies over the past ten years under the close management of a former Chief Minister, Narla Chandra Babu Naidu of the Telugu Desam Party (TDP), who was popularly known in the business media as the "CEO of Andhra Pradesh." Along with several economic restructuring policies the state also introduced innovative governance initiatives in democratic decentralization, e-governance, and campaign-based approaches to development initiatives. In line with the neoliberal paradigm, women's and girls' development were high on the agenda, and women were positioned in the forefront of all social sector government programs.
23. The Scheduled Castes are a collection of Indian social groups who historically were at the bottom of the Hindu caste hierarchy. After independence, the Constitution of India in 1950 created a scheduled list of castes for purposes of affirmative action. The Scheduled Castes are now also collectively referred to as the Dalits.

24. Scheduled Tribes are the indigenous tribes who have also been listed in the Constitution of India for purposes of affirmative action.
25. Other Backward Castes (OBCs) are the socially and educationally Backward Caste groups who are above the Scheduled Castes in the caste hierarchy. This population of both Hindu and non-Hindu groups constitutes over 52 percent of the Indian population. However, not all communities within the OBC are covered by reservations or affirmative action.
26. In Village 1 the *sangha* had only two leaders to represent all of the members in the village. In the other two villages, each SHG has two leaders, and all of the SHGs form a Village Organization (VO), which in turn chooses two leaders to represent the groups.
27. Diana Santillan, Sidney Ruth Schuler, Hoang Tu Anh, Tran Hung Minh, Quach Thu Trang, and Nguyen Minh Duc, "Developing Indicators to Assess Women's Empowerment in Vietnam," *Development in Practice* 14, no. 4 (June 2004): 534 -49.
28. The terms "gender practical interests" and "strategic gender interests" were first coined in 1985 by Maxine Molyneux. These concepts helped to develop gender planning and policy development tools. Gender practical interests and gender practical needs refer to what women and men perceive as immediate necessities such as water, shelter, food, and health care. Strategic gender interests refer to interventions that focus on fundamental issues related to women's—or less often, men's—subordination and gender inequities. Strategic gender interests are long-term, usually not material, and are often related to structural changes in society regarding women's status and equity. They include legislation for equal rights, reproductive choice, and increased participation in decision-making. See: Maxine Molyneux, "Mobilization without Emancipation? Women's Interests, the State, and Revolution in Nicaragua," *Feminist Studies* 11, no. 2 (1985): 227–54.
29. The term "multiple patriarchies" was used by Kumkum Sangari in a discussion on the validity of an argument for a uniform civil code in India within a context of legal, religious pluralisms, and customary domains. The existence of caste divisions, different modes of production, different familial types—patrilineal and matrilineal—and their complex articulation with regional histories and religions have contributed to multiple patriarchies in India. I would consider the state, markets, community, and household as institutions that represent multiple patriarchies in interaction with each other. Their prescriptions and practices are gendered and these are contested and negotiated. See: Kumkum Sangari, "Politics of Diversity: Religious Communities and Multiple Patriarchies," *Economic and Political Weekly* XXX, no. 51 (December 23, 1995): 3287–3310 and no. 52 (December 30, 1995): 3381- 9.
30. The Janmabhoomi program borrows its inspiration from a South Korean program called *Saemoul Undong* and a Malaysian program called *Bhoomiputra*.
31. The practice of dedicating girls as *joginis* exists in the border districts of Andhra Pradesh and Karnataka. Young girls below the age of fifteen are dedicated in service to God in a ritual in which they are married to a local deity. Generally an upper-caste man will patronize the dedication and in return will claim physical rights—sexual and labor—over the girl, with no commitment to the children that are born through these liaisons. The girl continues to stay with her parents and contributes to the economic survival of the family. Indirectly the family seeks economic support from upper-caste men through such practices.
32. Commission on Farmers' Welfare. *Final Report of the Commission on Farmers' Welfare.* http://macroscan.com/pol/apr05/pdf/Full_Report_Commission_Farmer_AP.pdf (accessed May 11, 2007). (2004). Over the last decade, the state

and central governments drastically reduced subsidies to the agriculture sector and exposed the farmers to market volatility and private profiteering, and did not generate non-agricultural economic activities. The burden has disproportionately fallen on small and marginal farmers and tenant farmers leading to numbers of suicides among farmers in Andhra Pradesh as well as several other states in India.

33. The program in Village 1 is not linked to savings and credit; however, women belong to SHGs as part of the *Podupu Lakshmi* program. Therefore, they have given information on loans taken from within those groups.

34. The total female work-participation rate in India, according to the 2001 Census, is 25.68 percent, and the corresponding statistic for Andhra Pradesh is 34.93 percent.

35. Stree Shakti Sanghatana, *"We Are Making History . . ." Life Stories of Women in the Telengana People's Struggle* (New Delhi: Kali for Women, 1989).

36. While this looks like evidence of an idiom based on money, it is not clear when this expression began. Similar expressions were reported by Integrated Health Management (IHM), Pachod, Maharashtra, which statistically validated the use of what it calls *Pachod Paisa* in place of Likert's scale (Kapadia-Kundu and Dyalchand 2005).

37. It would be interesting to study the changes that men perceive among themselves as a result of women's participation in SHGs.

38. In the Indira Pragati Padam (IPP) program all the SHGs within a village are collectivized into a Village Development Organization. All SHGs have to contribute a membership fund. Two women are chosen as leaders (first and second) of the organization. These leaders are members of a federation, which is a collective of women leaders from every ten villages. Community development funds are allocated by the IPP.

39. B.B. Mohanty, "'We are Like the Living Dead:' Farmer Suicides in Maharashtra, Western India," *Journal of Peasant Studies* 32, no. 2 (2005): 244–76.

40. The share of the agriculture sector in the GSDP, which was 53 percent in 1960–1961, has dwindled to about 13 percent in 2002–2003. The most rapid declines were after the 1980s (Rao and Suri 2006).

41. P. Narasimha Rao and K.C. Suri. "Dimensions of Agrarian Distress in Andhra Pradesh." *Economic and Political Weekly* XLI, no. 16 (April 22, 2006): 1546–52.

42. Suicide of farmers, I would consider, is an extreme expression of this "individualization."

43. The gender aspects of farmers' suicides have not been adequately studied. The author is currently exploring this problem.

# Part II
# Politicized Religions and Citizenship

# 7 Gender, Nation, and the Dilemmas of Citizenship

## The Case of the Marriage Acts of Trinidad and Tobago

*Rhoda Reddock*[1]

Like many other parts of the Americas, the Caribbean is a region of migrants, forced or voluntary. With the exception of a marginalised minority of indigenous peoples, still fighting for visibility and recognition, issues of citizenship—legal, political, economic, cultural, and symbolic—are constant in the day-to-day negotiations of everyday life. The history of postcolonial multiethnic Trinidad and Tobago can be characterised as a continuous struggle for inclusion by all groups, for the security of belonging, for recognition, and for rights to the benefits of citizenship. State responses to demands by leaders of ethnic and religious collectivities have resulted in what can only be defined as a form of multiculturalism, although this has never been a position publicly acknowledged as official policy. These demands and the state responses have been used to provide the feelings of inclusion, belonging, and recognition that citizenship claims, both material and symbolic. But each group's demand usually results in parallel demands or counterdemands by other groups.

This chapter is part of a larger work that is concerned with the gendered character of relations between the various ethnic groups in Trinidad and Tobago and the ways in which the experiences and aspirations of women and men are differently implicated, often with complex results and problematic outcomes. It focuses specifically on the four marriage laws that have emerged in Trinidad and Tobago over the twentieth century: the Marriage Act, the Hindu Marriage Act, the Muslim Marriage Act, and most recently the Orisa Marriage Act. The case of the marriage acts in Trinidad and Tobago is examined as one example of the ways in which the responses of the colonial and postcolonial state have contributed to a growing multiculturalism. It illustrates the symbolic importance of difference and recognition in contexts of ethnic diversity and postcolonialism and the important symbolic roles of women and marriage in such situations.

## CITIZENSHIP IN MULTIETHNIC, POSTCOLONIAL SOCIETIES

The issue of citizenship, although not always recognised as such, has been crucial to postcolonial multiethnic societies seeking to forge a nation-state in the wake of the end of formal colonialism. Citizenship has been particularly fraught in postcolonial societies where the conflictual legacies of empire and its practices of mass labour migration, divide-and-rule politics, and political favouritism continue to shape their present. With the dismantling of the old empires, as noted by Stuart Hall, many new multiethnic and multicultural nation-states were created. Efforts at nation building have had to take place in contexts of extensive poverty and underdevelopment, deepening global inequality, and an unregulated neoliberal economic world order. Increasingly, crises in these societies assume a multicultural or ethnicised form[2] where groups demand full citizenship based on the recognition of their difference. Hall sees today's ethnic problems as having their root in the colonial experience and notes,

> The movement from colonization to post-colonial times does *not* imply that the problems of colonialism have been resolved, or replaced by some conflict-free era. Rather the "post-colonial" marks the passage from one historical power-configuration or conjuncture to another. Problems of dependency, underdevelopment and marginalization, typical of the "high" colonial period, persist into the post-colonial. However these relations are *resumed* in a new configuration. (Hall 2000, 212–213)

Feminist analyses of cultural and political contestation in multiethnic postcolonial contexts in the economic South such as Fiji, Sri Lanka, South Africa, Malaysia, Mauritius, South Africa, and Singapore are limited. These countries share histories of British colonialism: large-scale immigration, the racialisation of nonwhite subordinated groups, forced labour systems, multiethnicity, and to varying degrees, the plantation. The colonial plantation system was the common characteristic of all of these territories. Populations from various parts of the world were brought together for the profitable production of cash crops for British economic expansion. The descendants of these populations struggle with the legacy of these experiences. Yet we have been unable to learn from each other in dealing with this problematic legacy. It is hoped that this chapter can contribute to a larger discussion within and between such societies.

The emergence internationally of the new identity politics of the late twentieth century has seen a shift from an emphasis solely on political and economic justice for oppressed groups to a focus on multicultural citizenship.[3] There is a new recognition of the need for the culture of the mainstream to be more inclusive and to represent the diversity of all constituents. Anthias and Yuval-Davis argue that in this context of identity politics, culture has become heavily ideologised: "It has become a kind of symbolic system prone to conscious manipulation through politics." There is an increasing awareness by a number of the world's inhabitants "that they *have a culture*," and where this is problematic, they can "create one."[4]

Hobson and Lister note the emergence of the term *recognition* to capture this dimension of citizenship and suggest, "Implicit in this discourse is a new construction of justice that contends that non-recognition not only inflicts harm on groups and individuals, but also is a form of oppression." Lack of recognition, they suggest, "implies exclusion and marginalisation from 'full participation' in the community; thus recognition struggles are struggles for participation and influence over the boundaries and meaning of citizenship."[5]

In these contexts varying versions of multiculturalism have been used to provide the feelings of inclusion, belonging, and recognition that citizenship claims to deliver. Multiculturalist claims often are most significant in areas related to religious practice but also in areas related to control over women such as marriage. On one hand, multiculturalism forces dominant economic, social, and cultural groups to acknowledge the heterogeneity of their society or nation and the existence of others; in other words, as observed by Homi Bhaba, multiculturalism "destablises the rhetoric of the homogeneity of the nation."[6] However, Stuart Hall points out dangers in this mode of politics. He distinguishes between the multicultural and multiculturalism. The former he describes as "the social characteristics and problems of governance posed by any society in which different cultural communities live together and attempt to build a common life while retaining something of their 'original' identity." *Multiculturalism,* on the other hand, refers to strategies and policies adopted to govern and manage the problems of diversity and multiplicity that multicultural societies throw up (Hall 2000, 209). The problem with multiculturalism is the tendency for it to be converted into a political doctrine, a formal singularity that is fixed into a cemented condition (Hall 2000, 8), no longer dynamic and fluid. Therefore, it is necessary to be vigilantly aware of the double-edged nature of citizenship claims and of multiculturalism, which are not only emancipatory and socially progressive but often can be exclusionary and deny the diversity of interests within collectivities. Yuval-Davis and Werbner specifically call attention to

> the gendered pitfalls of multiculturalism, which often excludes the interests of women and economically disadvantaged groups, by privileging cultural, regional or national divisions. We need to challenge the corporatising tendencies of pluralist policies which obscure class, gendered and racial disadvantages and ignore the predicaments experienced by the disabled, by non-citizens and by stigmatised minorities. (Yuval-Davis and Werbner 1997, 30)

Viewing ethnic or religious communities as homogenous results in power being located in the hands of male (and upper-class) "community leaders." This results in the reification of cultural communities, ignoring the diverse voices within groups and the transfer of power to unelected "traditional communal male elders" (Yuval-Davis and Werbner 1997, 18).

The marriage acts in Trinidad and Tobago have all these effects. They acknowledge the religious diversity of the population and provide male religious leaders of representative communities with symbolic leadership. In the course of doing so, however, they compromise the citizenship of women.

## THE COLONIAL EXPERIENCE OF ETHNICITY AND GENDER

Racial and ethnic stereotypes defined and shaped by European and Euro-American colonial and cultural hegemony continue to influence interethnic relations in the Caribbean today. Historically, populations from various parts of the world were brought together for the profitable production of cash crops for British economic expansion. The descendants of these populations struggle today with the legacy of these experiences, especially the structural inequalities and feelings of low self-esteem and self-worth.

With the exception of a minority of descendants of the indigenous populations (locally called Caribs), the Trinidad and Tobago population is the result of a number of migrations, forced and otherwise. According to the 2000 census, the rest of the population consists primarily of descendants of enslaved and free Africans, including demobilised African American soldiers and migrants from other Caribbean territories (37.5 percent) and indentured labourers from the Indian subcontinent and more recent Indian migrants (40.0 percent).[7] Also in the population mix is a variety of smaller groups including descendants of indentured Portuguese (mainly from Madeira) and Chinese; more recent immigrants from Hong Kong and China, Lebanon, and Syria; descendants of the European plantocracy and colonial officials and more recent Euro-American and European migrants; and mixtures of all the above, including named hybrid categories such as *Spanish* and *dougla* (20.5 percent).[8] Not surprisingly, attempts to codify ethnic groups for purposes of data collection and analysis are fraught with difficulties that include problems of definition and individual identity as well as social and political factors that contribute to these processes.

Because of its late entrance into plantation production (late eighteenth century), labour shortage was a recurring problem in Trinidad and Tobago. This was heightened during the last years of slavery, when the eighteen-hour workday was reduced to nine hours. Brereton identifies the ways in which the stereotype of the "lazy nigger" emerged at the time of emancipation in Africa, the United States, and the West Indies, becoming "an integral element in Victorian attitudes to race."[9] She quotes British novelist Anthony Trollope, who stated,

> The Negro will never work unless compelled to do so; that is the Negro who can boast of unmixed African blood. He is as strong as a bull, as hardy as a mule, docile as a dog when conscious of a master. . . . . He can work without pain and without annoyance. But he will never work as long as he can sleep and eat without it.[10]

Aisha Khan, in her review of the statements of colonial observers and travel writers on Indian immigrant labour brought to the region in the late nineteenth century to replace the emancipated slave population, underscores the ways in which Europeanness was used as a yardstick to measure worth. She quotes William Agnew Paton's description of Indian migrants:

"The coolly men . . . except for blackness, their faces are characteristically European. Their features are the features of thin and emaciated Italians, Frenchmen, Englishmen—in a word Caucasians." She cites another Victorian traveller, Alfred Radford, who reported that the "coolies" of Trinidad "were not black. I could easily take them for great gentlemen."[11] Khan goes further to show how a discourse of Indian and African "natural antipathy" emerged within colonial discourse, a narrative that has continued in the postcolonial period. She notes that colonial writing on the Caribbean was influenced by similar ideas in Africa and India, and she cites H. V. P. Bronkhurst, a British observer in Trinidad who remarked in 1883, "No wonder that the two races [Indian and African] do not, and it is to be feared never will amalgamate; that the Coolie, shocked by the unfortunate awkwardness of gesture and vulgarity of manners of the average Negro, and still more of the Negress, looks on them as savages, while the Negro, in his turn, hates the Coolie as a hard-working interloper, and despises him as a heathen" (cited in Khan 2004, 57). This narrative continues in the postcolonial period.

Black ex-slave women were of particular concern to colonial observers. The Caribbean slave experience, I have argued elsewhere, constructed them as labourers and not as wives or mothers. These women's resistance to the colonial system and to nineteenth-century attempts to introduce versions of maternalism and wifehood resulted in a degree of autonomy, sexual and otherwise, that was not visible in other parts of the colonial world.[12] Writing in 1870, during his visit to Port of Spain, Trinidad, Charles Kingsley reported, "I feel that a stranger would feel a shock . . . at the first sight of the average negro woman of Port of Spain, especially the younger. Their masculine figures, their ungainly gestures, their loud and sudden laughter, even when walking alone and their general coarseness shocks and must shock."[13]

This negative construction of Afro-Trinidadian womanhood suggests that this degree of autonomy and control over their lives was unacceptable. Negative stereotypes reflect badly not only on women but also on men and the entire community. Therefore, it is not surprising that Indo-Caribbean womanhood was constructed in opposition to the imagined Afro-Caribbean women and vice versa.[14] In a related argument, Tejaswini Niranjana suggests that elite anxiety about the urban Afro-Trinidadian woman in the nineteenth century, or even the rural Creole woman, arose from their image as independent in both sexual and economic terms. The Indian woman entering Caribbean society in the aftermath of slavery had to be constructed oppositionally in order to make up for the lost control over African women's labour and, one may add, sexuality.[15] Indo-Trinidadian notions of ethnic purity and, by extension, cultural superiority rely on control of women's sexuality, she suggests. Current contrasts between the "chaste, pure" Indo-Trinidadian woman and the "unchaste, impure, loose" Afro-Trinidadian woman reflect the ways in which colonialists' constructions continue to shape postcolonial racial constructs and ideologies of racialized gender.

Although ethnicity can be seen as a basis for the celebration of identity, Utterwulghe notes that it also has a pathological dimension. It is this pathological potential of ethnicity that provides the possibility for social and political manipulation. Writing on the Rwandan genocide, he argues that myths of the past, based on conscious and subconscious fears, contribute to feelings of insecurity in the present and the future.[16] In order to understand the various groups' relations to each other, therefore, it is necessary to understand their relations with and valuing by their colonial power. It should be noted that within this mythologized history, women often had a particular place, something Utterwulghe does not examine.

The historical context of contestation in Trinidad and Tobago, as in other multiethnic postcolonial societies, is one where racial and ethnic stereotypes defined and shaped by European and Euro-American colonial and cultural hegemony continue to influence interethnic relations. Thus Brackette Williams could conclude in relation to multiethnic Guyana (formerly British Guiana),

> There is ample evidence to suggest that in Guiana subordinated ethnic segments accepted European cultural domination in practice and . . . utilized racial stereotypes derived from this elite stratum to compete for and to justify their rights to certain economic and political benefits. . . . . This image was reinforced by formal and informal administrative policies that encouraged group competition and a notion that political representation along ethnic lines was essential to protect the interests of the different groups.[17]

As Williams observes, these ideologies of race and gender have also become inscribed in the formal and informal political and economic ordering of societies such as Guyana and Trinidad and Tobago, which ensure their reproduction from one era to the next.

## ETHNICITY AND MARRIAGE IN TRINIDAD AND TOBAGO

The Caribbean traditionally has been characterised by lower rates of marriage than other parts of the world, although these tend to be higher in Guyana and Trinidad and Tobago because of the higher rates of marriage among the Indian-descended population. Nevertheless, according to the 2000 census, in Trinidad and Tobago only 38 percent of women fifteen years and over were living in married unions; 30 percent had never had a husband or common-law partner, and 10.2 percent lived in common-law unions (Trinidad and Tobago Census 2000).

Caribbean social scientists have noted varying attitudes toward marriage among different Caribbean populations, resulting in different patterns of marriage and unions.[18] They have identified a complex and contradictory relationship toward formal legal marriage, especially among the African-descended populations, the result of many factors including the fact that slaves were not allowed to marry during slavery. Marriage remains an ideal for many because of the hegemonic acceptance of religious ideals and the desire for improved social status. However, flexibility around this institution, especially among the majority Afro-Caribbean population, allows a range of alternative practices such as never marrying, visiting unions, common-law (free) unions, and the easy acceptance of children born outside marriage. These practices are now available to the wider population. Legal marriage therefore is viewed paradoxically as the ideal marital form, but it is also resisted as the form that allows the greatest measure of male dominance and decrease in the freedom and mobility of women. Marriage is perceived as desirable by the Afro-Trinidadian lower-class women, but they entertain it only subject to the fulfillment of other social and economic requirements.[19]

In this context, Smith and Jayawardena observed as early as 1959 that in then–British Guiana, the elaborate Indo-Guyanese marriage ritual and male dominance had become important symbols of group difference from the rest of the society, whose approaches to marriage were much less structured and where women had a greater degree of autonomy.[20] Although marriage remains an important rite of passage for the women and men in the Indo-Caribbean populations, already in the 1950s when marriage ages were much lower, there was a high rate of dissolution of first marriages, with second nonlegal or common-law unions being formed outside marriage (Braithwaite and Roberts 1962). The struggle for recognition of Hindu and Muslim marriages therefore represented more than simply the right to marry legally. It was also a struggle for the recognition of difference and the codification of male privilege within private and public familial space.

## GENDER, CITIZENSHIP, AND MARRIAGE

Controls over marriage and women's sexuality are important mechanisms in maintaining the boundaries of ethnic and national citizenship. Thus historian Nancy Cott explains marriage as

> the vehicle through which the apparatus of state can shape the gender order . . . as well as an institution that sculpt[s] the body politic; it is a mechanism for distributing the responsibilities of citizenship, its perquisites and rights, for legitimating both private and public authority, and for disciplining the production and reproduction of "the people."[21]

Not surprisingly, therefore, when groups demand inclusion in the imagining of the nation-state but in a manner that ensures their ethnic distinctiveness, women, marriage, and control over them become important markers of difference.

Feminist scholars highlight the many ways in which gender is intricately woven into the construction of national and ethnic identities. Anthias and Yuval-Davis (1992) explore this in detail, noting that women are constructed as biological reproducers of the members of national collectivities, reproducers of the boundaries of national groups through restrictions on their marital and sexual relations, active transmitters and producers of national culture, symbolic signifiers of national difference, and active participants in national struggle (cited in McClintock 1995, 355). Marriage is one effective way to manage and monitor these processes.

To understand these links, feminist scholars have moved the discourse on citizenship beyond its roots in the struggle for political rights narrowly defined and the relationship to the state. Just as they have reconceptualised politics to incorporate everyday struggles and negotiations around the body, sexuality, and gender relations, they have redefined citizenship. Following T. H. Marshall, who defined citizenship as "full membership in the community," they see it as a multilayered concept. Political subjects and social actors have diverse interests and are often involved in more than one political or social collectivity, the boundaries of which could be local, ethnic, national, or global (Yuval-Davis and Werbner 1997, 5). Thus women may be members of religious and ethnic collectivities and at the same time see the need for struggle to change their status as women. Membership in one community may have critical effects on membership in others. Where the marriage regime does not provide them with full and equal membership in their ethnic or religious group, it diminishes their citizenship status within the wider nation-state.

## GENDER, RELIGION, AND MULTICULTURALISM: THE CASE OF THE MARRIAGE ACTS

The marriage acts of Trinidad and Tobago represent one of the earliest mechanisms of the colonial state to respond to the pressures of this multicultural society. Calls for the legalisation of Hindu and Muslim marriages were among the early demands of the East Indian National Association, founded in 1897 in Princes Town in south Trinidad. This issue was included in their petition forwarded by the governor to the undersecretary of state for the colonies.[22] In the early twentieth century a new organisation, the East Indian National Council, comprising mainly Christian Indo-Trinidadians, joined this call. The argument was that marriages that occurred under Muslim and Hindu rites were not recognised by the existing civil law despite the ostentatious rituals that marked them. If the marriages were not subsequently registered, they were considered null and void. In other words, Hindu and Muslim leaders could not become marriage officers in their own right.

Although this demand was seen as particularly important for purposes of inheritance, historian J. C. Jha questioned its significance at this time, when the majority of Indians showed little concern for these legal trappings. The majority of them were still agricultural labourers who had little to pass on to their progeny. Not surprisingly, therefore, the majority of the Indian population in Trinidad initially remained apathetic to the marriage issue.[23] It was an issue for the nationalists, however, as a mark of recognition and distinctiveness for the wealthy few. It was also an issue for Muslims because it threatened the loss of their right to four wives (Jha 1982, 113). By the turn of the century, when Indians began to acquire property, some in lieu of their return passage to India, the problem of a rightful inheritor became more important. As they began to aspire for higher positions in society, the status of illegitimacy for children of unrecognised marriages became a concern. Many Indian and lower-class African boys were denied acceptance to the state and religious boys' secondary schools that facilitated social mobility (Jha 1982, 129–132).

In 1905, Abdul Aziz, leader of the East Indian National Association, led a delegation to the governor demanding the legalisation of Islamic marriages. But it was not until 1936 that the Muslim Marriage Ordinance of 1935 was passed (Jha 1982, 129–132). Although the campaign began simultaneously, the Hindu Marriage Act was not passed until 1945, nearly ten years after the Muslim Marriage Act. This delay resulted from competing demands among Hindu leaders. In 1924, for example, a draft bill was prepared but rejected by conservative sections of the Hindu community (Jha 1982, 129). In the 1930s and 1940s non-Sanatanist Hindu sects such as the Arya Pratinidhi Sabha made representations for the age of consent for females to be fourteen years instead of the twelve years advocated by the Sanatan Dharma Board of Control (Jha 1982, 132). Not surprisingly, the voices of Indo-Trinidadian women, Hindu or Muslim, were absent from all the debates.

Little consideration was given to similar marriage laws for Afro-Trinidadian citizens because there was no public demand. The totalitarian impact of the slave system had demonised African religious and cultural practices and pushed them underground, where they continued to develop in various forms and adapt to their new environment. This was particularly significant in Trinidad and Tobago as Free Africans who had not experienced the dehumanising and totalising cultural effects of the slave system were imported into Trinidad and Tobago in the last years of slavery.[24] These migrations revitalised African religious and cultural traditions in many parts of the islands. In 1883, however, an ordinance banning drumming was passed, with significant impact on African religious practice. It was followed in 1917 by the Shouters Prohibition Ordinance, which made practice of the Spiritual Baptist faith, an Afro-Christian religion, illegal. Only after years of struggle was this ordinance repealed in 1951.[25] The practice of "Shango" or Orisa, a Yoruba-based religious tradition, has been the most lasting African religious survival of this era. It experienced a revival in the late twentieth century.

In the first decade of the twenty-first century, Trinidad and Tobago has four marriage acts in operation: the Marriage Act, first promulgated in

1923; the Muslim Marriage and Divorce Act of 1961, which replaced the ordinance of 1936; the Hindu Marriage Act of 1945; and the more recent Orisa Marriage Act of 1999. There is also a Cohabitational Relationships Act, passed in 1998. Each of the four marriage acts includes detailed rules of acceptability, the registration of marriage officers, forms for application, and registration. All include clauses on legitimacy, although illegitimacy is no longer an official legal category because of the Status of Children Act.

## Marriage Act No. 13 of 1945

The Marriage Act of 1945 is effectively both the Christian marriage act and the civil marriage act, although this is not mentioned in its title. This act allows the solemnisation of marriages by Christian marriage officers (usually ministers of religion) or district registrars, usually magistrates. Paragraph 7, dealing with marriage officers, states,

> 7(1) The President, or any person duly authorised by him may grant licences to such persons being ministers of any Christian religion, as the President or such authorised person may, in his discretion, think fit, to be Marriage Officers, and without assigning any reason for doing, cancel any such licence. (Paragraph 7[1], p. 5)

Although this act has been amended at least eleven times, the last in 1980, this religious proviso still stands. Additionally, although the age of consent for both men and women is fixed at eighteen years, the minimum age of marriage is not stated in the act, although it may be implied. Legally therefore, the minimum age of marriage according to this act is as established in the English common law, which establishes the minimum ages of marriage as fourteen years for males and twelve years for females. This is amazing, bearing in mind that in England itself this law was changed and the minimum age of marriage increased in 1929.[26]

For people under eighteen who want to marry, even after so many amendments, the permission of the father is still required; if no father is available then the lawful guardian or guardians may give consent. Only where there is no guardian, and if the mother is unmarried, may the mother give consent. The relevant text is as follows:

> The father, if living, of any party to an intended marriage under eighteen years of age (such party not being a widower or widow), or if the father is dead then the guardian or guardians of the person of the party so under age lawfully appointed, or one of them, and in case there is no such guardian then the mother of such party if unmarried, and if there is no mother unmarried then the guardian or guardians of the person appointed by the High Court, if any, or one of them, has authority to give consent to the marriage of such party, and such consent is hereby

required for the marriage of such party so under age, unless there is no person authorised to give such consent. (Paragraph 23, p. 11)

Although it is unclear why mothers have so little authority in this matter or why this has received so little concern over the years, the answer probably lies in the legal concept of guardianship, which was not granted to women until recently. Additionally, Christianity predominates among the African-descended and mixed populations, where marriage under eighteen years is not prevalent.

It is also baffling that despite amendments, the degrees of allowable consanguinity are still those "according to the Law of England in force on 30 August 1962, the day of national independence from England" (Paragraph 36(2), p. 16). One concludes that the Marriage Act is not secular but primarily patriarchal, Christian, and colonial. This undoubtedly fuelled the demands for additional marriage ordinances.

## Muslim Marriage and Divorce Act No. 7 of 1961

The existing Muslim Marriage and Divorce Act is the only one of the acts in which the word *divorce* is included in the title. The current act, last amended in November 1980, prohibits the contraction or registration of polygamous marriage. However, it allows either party to apply for the dissolution or annulment of the marriage. In contrast with the Marriage Act, which does not state a minimum age of marriage, this act specifies a minimum age of marriage of sixteen for males and twelve for females. As in the Marriage Act, consent for marriage of underage people can be given by the mother only if the father or other lawful guardian or guardians are dead or not otherwise available (p. 6). However, there is no qualification regarding the marital status of the mother.

Unlike in the Marriage Act, the prohibited degrees of consanguinity or affinity are as according to Islamic Law (p. 7). Additionally, divorce officers, similar to marriage officers, are appointed within the various Islamic religious bodies, and either party may apply to the body to which they belong for a divorce.

The sample registration forms attached to the Muslim Act also reflect early twentieth century thinking on women's place. No columns were included on the marriage or divorce certificates for wife's occupation, yet these continue to be the official documents used.

## The Hindu Marriage Act of 1945

In this act, the prohibited degrees of consanguinity or affinity are according to Hindu law. Although a minimum age of marriage is established at fourteen for females and eighteen for males, parental consent is not required for females after age sixteen (Hindu Marriage Act, p. 6). Interestingly, efforts by the Hindu

Women's Organisation in the 1990s to increase the age of legal marriage for women have failed. As in the other acts, mothers may give consent only when a father, guardian, or guardians are dead or unavailable. Here as well, the official sample forms do not include a column for the wife's occupation.

Reflecting the influence of colonial Christianity in Trinidad and Tobago, it should be noted that although each piece of legislation reproduces as much as possible the distinctiveness of the religious tradition, the language and terms used continue to be tinged with the language of Christianity, as illustrated in Paragraph 9 of the Hindu Marriage Act: "*(a)* that each of the parties shall belong to and profess the Hindu faith or religion; . . . *(d)* that the marriage shall be solemnized by a Marriage Officer in accordance with the rites of the Hindu religion and with the provision of this Act" (p. 6).

## The Orisa Marriage Act of 1999

The most recent of these acts, the Orisa Marriage Act of 1999, is the result of the contemporary revalidation of African religious traditions. This act was passed at a time when the country was governed by a predominantly Indo-Trinidadian government, a government clearly more sympathetic to the concerns of non-Christian religious traditions. It was during this period also that a public holiday was declared to commemorate the repeal of the Shouters Prohibition Ordinance, the law that had prohibited the practice of that Afro-Christian religion. These developments marked the assertion of more clearly African nationalist interests over those of the Creole nationalist tradition, which had become identified with Christianity.

The Orisa Marriage Act is a child of the late twentieth century but also reflects the less patriarchal character of this tradition in the diaspora, where women have had a stronger leadership role in African-derived religious traditions than in the Christian, Islamic, and Hindu traditions. For example, the language of this act is much more gender inclusive, a marriage officer may be "a Priest or Priestess," and mothers or fathers may give consent to underage marriage in the absence of the father or other male guardian: "The required consent to marriage by a minor shall be given by the mother or father of the minor and if the mother and father are dead, by the guardian or guardians appointed for the purpose by the President" (Orisa Marriage Act 1999, p. 208).

The minimum age of marriage age for females is sixteen and for males it is eighteen, and on the sample marriage certificate information about the wife's occupation is requested, although not in the same detail as for the husband. Interestingly, the prohibited degrees of consanguinity and affinity are as established in the Marriage Act.

## The Cohabitational Relationships Act

In 1998, the Cohabitational Relationships Act was passed in Trinidad and Tobago. For the first time the country formally recognised the existence of intimate, consensual, heterosexual nonlegal unions and put forward mechanisms for registration, "protection" of spouses or partners, and resolution of conflict or disputes occasioned by the end of a union by death, separation, or other cause.

For many this development was long overdue. The practice of common-law, consensual, or concubinage relationships has been well studied and documented by anthropologists and sociologists of the Caribbean throughout the twentieth century. Although recognised by demographers in 1943 in the collection of fertility-related data on women, this form of union had remained legally unrecognised in the region despite its frequency. The act emerged from contemporary recognition that significant proportions of the Trinidad and Tobago population never marry or choose to live in cohabitational consensual relationships after a first failed marriage or widowhood. It is particularly significant for people of African descent and for Hindus, because widow remarriage is not allowed under the Hindu Marriage Act. This act is the only truly secular act; religious considerations are excluded.

## THE MARRIAGE ACTS: SYMBOLIC CONSTRUCTIONS OF DIFFERENCE

The existence of these different marriage acts is one example of the continuous efforts of the Trinidad and Tobago state to manage diverse ethnic, cultural, and religious demands for recognition, citizenship, and inclusion in the idea of the nation. They also reflect clearly the ways in which such demands for recognition often carry specific implications for women and other internal differences of power. It is significant that the acts, especially the first three, continue to exist in their essentially patriarchal form, despite other laws enacted since the late 1970s that have introduced greater levels of equality between women and men and strengthened child protection.

The Status of Children Act of 1981, for example, equated the rights of the mother and father in the areas of custody once paternity has been established. This is for children born in or out of wedlock. Before this only men had custody for children in the existing common law. This act was reinforced by the 1981 Family Law (Guardianship and Custody) Act, which provided women with the powers of guardianship that were previously vested only in men. It is the earlier situation, in which women lacked guardianship over their children, that is still reflected in the first three marriage acts discussed here. In the event of the dissolution of a marriage, all groups have to access the same Matrimonial Proceedings and Property Act of 1988 No. 2 of 1972 for property settlement. Although, as mentioned earlier, these acts all allow child marriage, the Sexual Offences Act of 1986 sets the legal age of sexual consent at sixteen except if parties are lawfully married. At the same time the Children (Amendment) No. 68 of

2000 established eighteen as the upper limit of childhood, in conformity with the United Nations Convention on the Rights of the Child.[27] However, this was never proclaimed, so the age limit of sixteen remains.[28]

In 1998 a government-appointed committee was established to review all the marriage laws and the proposed Orisa Marriage Bill and make recommendations for harmonisation. The committee was mandated to address four main areas, including age and consent. The legal subcommittee recommended the following: that laws related to marriage be harmonised into one marriage act, that there be uniformity in the divisions of the marriage districts, that the age of capacity for a female to marry be raised to sixteen for all religions, and that de facto guardians be recognised as people capable of giving consent (T&T Report to CRC 2003, 88). This legal document was used as basis for further committee deliberations and consultations in 1999 and 2000. In the end there was no consensus. According to the Report to the CRC, "One of the issues which remained contentious following these consultations was the proposed harmonisation of the minimum age of marriage under the different statutes. The official position of representatives of the Muslim and Hindu groups was that the minimum ages represented in the Muslim and Hindu Marriage Acts should not be altered, largely because of their traditional beliefs" (T&T Report to CRC 2003, 88).

Not surprisingly, therefore, the legal age of marriage in the Muslim Marriage and Divorce Act emerged as an issue when in January 2002, Trinidad and Tobago presented its Initial, Second and Third Report to the United Nations Committee on the Convention on the Elimination of All Forms of Discrimination Against Women.[29] In their response the commissioners enquired about the following:

> On the difference in the marital age and the law under the Hindu and Muslim Marriage Act [sic], she noted that the Convention prohibited child marriage as did the Convention on the Rights of the Child. Was the Government addressing that problem? Child marriage was also a health issue. The Constitution respected family life and privacy. Was there any mention of introducing reform on the basis of the public good, recognizing that child marriage was not permissible under international obligations and was contrary to the girl-child['s] health needs?[30]

The commissioners went on to ask about the proportion of Muslim women under the age of sixteen who actually got married. They noted,

> The Muslim marriage age was 12 years, whereas the compulsory school age under the education act was between 6 and 12 years, meaning that every child up to 12 must attend school. Had the Muslim Marriage act taken the cue from the minimum age set by the Education Act? Assuming that it had, now the country had a new education policy, would

Trinidad and Tobago think of making secondary education compulsory and raise the minimum marriage age to 18 with the hope that no girl below the age of 18 would drop out of school? . . . Another speaker saw a contradiction between the marriage age under the Muslim law and the criminal provisions of the sexual offences act, which set the age at 14. Was it then considered rape in marriage? (CEDAW 2002a)

In their concluding report to the government of Trinidad and Tobago, the CEDAW commissioners included among their overall recommendations the following:

39. The Committee is disturbed that child marriages are sanctioned under several of the legal regimes regulating marriage. The Committee notes that such marriages are prohibited by article 16, paragraph 2, of the Convention, and that such marriages have serious consequences for girls, including with regard to health.[31]

In response to questions raised by the United Nations Committee on CEDAW in 2002, the Trinidad and Tobago delegation reported that "the disparity in the ages of marriage under the Hindu and Muslim marriage acts had been addressed in consultations with the representatives of those religions, but no agreement had been reached on raising those ages. A consultative committee had been established by the Government to address that problem, which had drafted a miscellaneous provisions marriage bill. Since there was now no consensus as to a uniform age of marriage in the country, the draft bill had never been presented to Parliament" (CEDAW 2002b).

In the Government's Second Periodic Report on the Convention on the Rights of the Child it was noted that child marriage did occur, although the numbers were small. In 1997, 1998, and 1999 the numbers of marriages of females under fifteen years old were 15, 16, and 7, respectively, whereas for all marriages of females seventeen years and under were 587, 579, and 549, respectively, suggesting a steady decline (T&T Report to CRC 2003, 89).[32]

More recently, in 2005, in its shadow report to United Nations Commission on the Rights of the Child (CRC), the Trinidad and Tobago Coalition on the Rights of the Child, a nongovernment organisation, noted that all four marriage acts violated both the Convention on the Rights of the Child and the CEDAW, conventions ratified by the government of Trinidad and Tobago. In highlighting this point the coalition called on the judiciary to

take a stand on the issue of age of marriage in the interest of the girl child in particular. Failure to do so means that the exploitation of girls and young women continues to be legitimized within the framework of domestic law.
    With regard to the failure to achieve consensus within the Hindu and Muslim community that would bring about an increase in the age of

marriage, due consideration must be given to "who" the parties to the decision making process are. In a society where positions of power within political, religious, cultural and social organizations are still largely held by men and patriarchal views and positions are articulated and maintained the human rights of women and girls continue to be marginalized.[33]

The continued existence of provisions in the marriage acts that conflict with new legislation suggests that they continue to be of great symbolic importance. This was evident in the resistance to changing the age of marriage for women in the Muslim and Hindu marriage acts.[34] These acts maintain distinct axes of patriarchal power and recognition along religious and ethnic lines; therefore, religious leaders (mainly male) have resisted efforts to bring them in line with other legislative changes and new thinking on women's rights. The contention that the value of these acts is primarily symbolic is supported by the fact that few child marriages actually occur. The fact that they do occur continues to be cause for concern, however. What other reason could be suggested for the maintenance of the status quo in the acts, except their importance as a symbol of patriarchal control over the women of one's group?

In the multicultural context of Trinidad and Tobago, patriarchal claims based on religious and ethnic diversity are also evident in other areas, such as in the control over shelters for battered women. After the establishment of two shelters by women's movement activists in the 1980s and 1990s, at least three religious-run shelters—Hindu, Muslim, and fundamentalist Christian—came into existence.[35] So although the multicultural character of Trinidad and Tobago is definitely an achievement worthy of celebration, this model of multiculturalism is one that delivers women into the control of their male religious and ethnic leaders.

## CONCLUSION

The marriage acts are but one example of the ways in which Trinidad and Tobago has sought to manage its diversity. They are also evidence of an incremental multiculturalism that has emerged without the official declaration of such a policy. The policy has developed in a piecemeal way in response to religious and ethnic demands and claims by primarily male leaders. The three earlier acts have been subject to changes and amendments over the years, but though superseded by more recent legislation and by social change such as the actual age of marriage, they remain symbols of group distinctiveness and recognition as well as of patriarchal cultural control.

## NOTES

1. I would like to acknowledge the support of the Fulbright New Century Scholars Program which facilitated the development of this paper. Early ideas were

presented to my working group and I received useful feedback. I also received feedback from Andrea Friedman who was the discussant for this paper at the Global Feminisms Conference organised at Washington University, St. Louis in April 2006. The comments of the editor Carolyn Elliott were also useful during the final stages of writing the paper. Special thanks go to my legal advisors Gaietry Pargass and Lynette Seebaran-Suite.

2. Stuart Hall, "The Multi-Cultural Moment." In *Un/Settled Multiculturalisms*, ed. Barnor Hesse (London: Zed Books, 2000): 212; hereafter cited in text as Hall (2000).

3. Will Kymlicka, *Multicultural Citizenship* (Oxford: Oxford University Press, 1995).

4. Floya Anthias and Nira Yuval-Davis, *Racialized Boundaries: Race, Nation, Gender, Colour and Class and the Anti-Racist Struggle* (London: Routledge, 1992): 10.

5. Barbara Hobson and Ruth Lister, "Citizenship." In *Contested Concepts in Gender and Social Politics*, eds. Barbara Hobson, Jane Lewis, and Birte Siim (Cheltenham, UK: Edward Elgar, 2002): 40.

6. Cited in Nira Yuval-Davis and Pnina Werbner, eds. *Women, Citizenship and Difference* (London: Zed Books, 1997); hereafter cited in text as Yuval-Davis and Werbner (1997).

7. The Republic of Trinidad and Tobago Central Statistical Office. *Population and Housing Census* (2000), http://cso.gov.tt/census2000; hereafter cited in text as Trinidad and Tobago Census (2000) (accessed 24, February 2006).

8. *Spanish* was originally used to refer to the descendants of peons, Venezuelan peasants who worked in the cocoa and coffee estates of the Northern Range in Trinidad; it is often used to refer to people of mixed ancestry of similar appearance. *Dougla* refers to persons of mixed African and Indian ancestry, normally first generation or with similar appearance.

9. Brereton, Bridget. *A History of Modern Trinidad* (London, Kingston and Pat, Spain, Heineman) 1981, 79–89. Ann McClintock also documents the emergence of an "intricate discourse on idleness and sloth" in colonial South Africa as a mechanism to legitimise land plunder and alter precolonial habits of labour. See Ann McClintock, *Imperial Leather: Race, Gender and Sexuality in the Colonial Contest* (New York: Routledge, 1995): 252; hereafter cited in text as McClintock (1995).

10. Cited in Bridget Brereton, *Race Relations in Colonial Trinidad: 1870–1900* (Cambridge: Cambridge University Press, 1979): 147.

11. Aisha Khan, *Callaloo Nation: Metaphors of Race and Religious Identity Among South Asians in Trinidad* (Durham, NC: Duke University Press, 2004): 48; hereafter cited in text as Khan (2004).

12. Rhoda Reddock, "Women and Slavery in the Caribbean: A Feminist Perspective," *Latin American Perspectives* 12, no. 1 (1985): 63–80.

13. Charles Kingsley, *At Last: A Christmas in the West Indies* (London: Macmillan, 1896): 71.

14. Rhoda Reddock, "Conceptualizing Difference in Caribbean Feminist Thought." In *New Caribbean Thought*, eds. Brian Meeks and Folke Lindhal (Kingston, Jamaica: The UWI Press, 2001).

15. Tejaswini Naranjana, "'Left to the Imagination': Indian Nationalisms and Female Sexuality in Trinidad," *Public Culture* 11, no. 1 (1999): 236.

16. Steve Utterwulghe, "Rwanda's Protracted Social Conflict: Considering the Subjective Perspective in Conflict Resolution Strategies," *Online Journal of Peace and Conflict Resolution*, Issue 2.3 (August 1999): 6, http://www.trinstitute.org/ojpcr/p2_3utter.htm. (accessed 4, September 2005)

17. Brackette Williams, *Stains on My Name, War in My Veins: Guyana and the Politics of Cultural Struggle* (Durham, NC: Duke University Press, 1991): 159.
18. Lloyd Braithwaite and George Roberts, "Mating Among East Indian and Non-Indian Women in Trinidad," *Social and Economic Studies* 11, no. 3 (1962): 203–240; hereafter cited in text as Braithwaite and Roberts (1962).
19. Rhoda Reddock, Roanna Gopaul, Paula Morgan, and Elsa Leo-Rhynie, *Women and Family in the Caribbean: Historical and Contemporary Considerations* (Georgetown, Guyana: CARICOM Secretariat, 1999): 15.
20. Although this study focussed on Guyana, I find it speaks to the situation in Trinidad and Tobago. See R. T. Smith and Chandra Jayawardena, "Marriage and Family Amongst East Indians in British Guiana," *Social and Economic Studies* 8 (1959): 321–376.
21. Nancy F. Cott, *Public Vows: A History of Marriage and the Nation* (Cambridge, MA: Harvard University Press, 2000): 3–5. This reference was brought to my attention by Andrea Freidman.
22. Gerard Tikasingh, "Toward the Formulation of the Indian View of History: The Representation of Indian Opinion in Trinidad 1900–1921." In *East Indians in the Caribbean: Colonialism and the Struggle for Identity*, eds. Bridget Brereton and Winston Dookeran (New York: Kraus International, 1982): 14.
23. J. C. Jha, "The Background to the Legalization of Non-Christian Marriage in Trinidad and Tobago." In *East Indians in the Caribbean: Colonialism and the Struggle for Identity*, eds. Bridget Brereton and Winston Dookeran (New York: Kraus International Publications, 1982): 121; hereafter cited in text as Jha (1982).
24. These included the Yoruba, Congo, Rada, Fulani, Mandingo, Igbo, Coromanti, and Ashanti peoples. Warner-Lewis notes that the Yoruba were particularly significant and culturally arrogant and transplanted their legal systems to the region. See Maureen Warner-Lewis, *Guinea's Other Suns: The African Dynamic in Trinidad Culture* (Dover, MA: The Majority Press, 1991): 21–22.
25. March 30, Shouter Baptist Liberation Day, is now a public holiday to commemorate the repeal of this ordinance. This day was first marked in 1996.
26. I thank attorney at law Gaietry Pargass for this information.
27. Republic of Trinidad and Tobago, Ministry of the Attorney General. *Second Periodic Report of the Republic of Trinidad and Tobago: Convention on the Rights of the Child* (Human Rights Unit, Port of Spain, June 2003): 81; hereafter cited in text as T&T Report to CRC (2003).
28. However, the age of majority for voting, entering into contracts, and other purposes is eighteen (Attorney at Law Gaietry Pargass).
29. CEDAW, the United Nations document dealing with discrimination against women.
30. United Nations CEDAW, "Experts Welcome Positive Aspects of Trinidad and Tobago's Anti-Discrimination Measures but Stress Gender-Based Constraints." UN Press Release WOM/1310 (2002a); hereafter cited in text as CEDAW (2002a).
31. United Nations CEDAW. "Committee on the Elimination of Discrimination Against Women Concludes Consideration of Trinidad and Tobago Report." UN Press Release WOM/1316 (2002b); hereafter cited in text as CEDAW (2002b).
32. The similar figures for males under seventeen for those years were 87, 68, and 88. No males were married under fifteen years of age.
33. Trinidad and Tobago Coalition on the Rights of the Child. *NGO Comments on Trinidad and Tobago Second Periodic Report Under the Convention on the Rights of the Child* (April 2005): 8.
34. I thank family law practitioner Lynette Seebaran-Suite for these insights.
35. Claims for recognition are evident even in the politics of public holidays.

# 8 Constructing the Female Muslim Citizen

## Law as a Site of Struggle for Inclusion and Exclusion

*Titia Loenen*

Worldwide, tensions between "Islam" and "the West" have increased tremendously in the last decade. The events of September 11, 2001, in the United States, the wars in Afghanistan and Iraq, and the Danish cartoon crisis are dramatic manifestations of these tensions. In Western critiques of Islam, the presumed inferior position of women in Islam often provides one of the pivotal points for disqualifying Islamic norms and values. Muslim women living in Western countries, who are mainly immigrants or of immigrant descent, may find themselves in a double or rather triple bind, caught at the intersection of race, sex, and religion.[1] European discussions on banning the Islamic headscarf from public schools are a case in point.[2]

In this chapter I explore the ways in which Muslim women often are constructed in these discussions as, in certain ways, "failed" citizens who may be excluded from certain positions in society. Citizenship in this context is not understood in a formal way in terms of nationality but, following T. H. Marshall, as "a status bestowed on those who are full members of a community. All who possess the status are equal with respect to the rights and duties with which the status is endowed."[3] Rights and equality figure prominently in this notion of citizenship.[4]

I will particularly focus on the role of law in this construction. In the European context, courts often play a major role because of their competence to assess the compatibility of legislation and practices with national or international and European human rights provisions such as nondiscrimination and freedom of religion. A case study dealing with headscarves in the public classroom will show the crucial difference it makes as to how this issue is approached in legal terms and the effects this has on the inclusion or exclusion of Muslim women from full citizenship.

In the following I briefly sketch some characteristics of the European headscarf debates and subsequently discuss two legal cases dealing with Muslim teachers in public schools, who were not allowed to wear headscarves in the classroom. In the first case this prohibition was upheld as a lawful limitation on her rights; in the second case it was deemed a violation of those rights. The chapter concludes with a comparison and evaluation of the different approaches taken in both cases, their consequences in terms of recognizing Muslim women in Europe as full citizens, and how this may affect their empowerment.

## EUROPEAN DEBATES ON THE HEADSCARF

French plans to prohibit pupils at public schools from wearing headscarves in school attracted worldwide attention in 2003. In 2004 a legal ban on wearing any "ostentatious religious symbols" at primary and secondary school was enacted.[5] The French discussion did not take place in isolation, for similar issues have been hotly debated in other western European countries. Thus in Germany controversies reached a peak around a Muslim teacher who brought legal proceedings against a public school that did not allow her to wear a headscarf in front of the classroom.[6] In the Netherlands, headscarf issues received exceptional media attention when a law student was refused a job as a law clerk because she was not willing to put away her headscarf during court sessions.[7]

In this chapter I limit myself to the issue of prohibiting public school teachers from wearing a headscarf in school. Taking a closer look at the European discussions, three arguments to support such a prohibition stand out.

### Separation of Church and State

The first argument concerns the principle of the separation of church and state, or rather of the separation of religion and state. Although this principle is interpreted in different ways in Europe, the interpretation I refer to here considers any manifestation of religion in the public state sphere to present an infringement of the required neutrality of the state toward all religions and beliefs. It requires adherence to uniform and neutral standards in this sphere, relegating manifestations of religion or other personal convictions to the private sphere. In the privacy of one's home and in private associations everyone is free to live according to whatever religion or belief one wishes, but in the public sphere everyone has to abide by the uniform standards set by the state. In this reading, wearing any religious symbols in public schools, not just headscarves, is considered to jeopardize this state neutrality. The French ban on all ostentatious religious symbols reflects this idea.[8]

Most European countries do not share this very strict requirement of state secularism, although it is certainly receiving more attention these days because of discussions about the place of Islam in European societies. Some European countries, such as the United Kingdom, Sweden, Norway, and Greece, still have remnants of an established church.[9] Other systems adhering to a "separation of church and state" model, such as the Netherlands and Germany, may at the same time embrace a pluralistic approach to religion in the public sphere. In those countries the state is not allowed to impose any religious convictions on its citizens, yet this does not mean the state sphere has to be rigorously nonreligious. In their understanding of state neutrality or secularism, the obligation this principle puts on the state is not to ban all religion and religious expressions from the public state sphere but to guarantee equal treatment of religions and other beliefs. Thus in the Netherlands the state funds denominational schools on an equal basis with public schools. Muslims have profited from this arrangement by having been able to establish an increasing number of Islamic schools. Pupils in the Netherlands and Germany are free to wear religious symbols such as headscarves, kippas, or crucifixes in the public school classroom. Thus the principle of state neutrality means quite different things across European countries.

## Sex Equality

Sex equality is the second major reason put forward to place restrictions on wearing a headscarf in public schools. This argument perceives the headscarf as a symbol of the inferior position of women in Islam. Because the state cannot condone sex discrimination, a public school cannot be allowed to send out such a message through its teachers. In France, the sex equality argument figured prominently in the report of the so-called Stasi Commission, which advised the French government on the headscarf issue after extensive consultations with all groups and interests involved.[10] The commission repeatedly referred to pressure being imposed on Muslim women and girls to wear a headscarf (Stasi 2003, 31–32, 38–39). This reading of the headscarf as oppressive to women is highly contested. The issue seems to cut right across traditional political divides, finding, for instance, feminist supporters and opponents.[11]

Empirical research makes it clear that wearing a headscarf may have very different meanings for different people.[12] And even on an individual level a headscarf need not represent a single thing. Thus, headscarves are sometimes worn as a sign of support for a political Islam, as a symbol of opposition to assimilationist politics, as a manifestation of piety, or indeed as an expression of women's subservient position to men. In Western Europe, attention is often given to the search for identity by immigrant groups seeking a place in their new home country. Muslim groups and Muslim women are no exception in this respect, and Islam often plays an important role in this process. For Muslim women living in traditional communities, wearing a headscarf may also provide more space for emancipation. Wearing a headscarf in education or work may show that they can live emancipated lives without forgoing their Islamic identity.[13] In this respect, it becomes even more crucial to know what the headscarf represents, empirically, in the reality of people's lives.

The German constitutional court underlined the different meanings a headscarf may represent in its decision in the case *Ludin*. It specifically countered the position that wearing a headscarf is a shorthand for oppressive views on women, noting that for many young women in Germany a headscarf may very well be a freely chosen means to live self-determined lives without having to break away from their culture of origin.[14]

## Public Order

A third important argument against allowing a teacher in a public school to wear a headscarf stems from concerns of public order. The headscarf is quite often associated with fundamentalist Islamic views and political Islam. Therefore, the threat radical Islam poses is projected on the headscarf more generally. This runs parallel with the French notion that women and girls are being pressured into wearing a headscarf by their radical Islamic relatives. Given these tensions, fear exists that the presence of headscarves in school may lead to unrest and resentment on the school grounds, thus endangering the "school peace" that is needed to guarantee children a good educational environment. This argument was emphasized in Stasi (2003) and more generally in the French discussions on the headscarf (Gemie, 2004). The Stasi Commission even characterizes the headscarf issue as having changed from an issue of freedom of conscience into one of public order.[15] The public order argument was also referred to by the German Constitutional Court as a possibly valid reason for placing restrictions on religious dress in public schools, although the German court did not accept it in the case at hand because no concrete danger was shown to exist.[16]

The three arguments show the interplay of issues of religion, sex, and race. The first argument is directed at religious expressions of whatever kind, yet the setting and the emergence of the debates in Europe cannot leave any doubt that they were triggered by concerns surrounding the integration of an increasing number of Muslim immigrants of non-Western origin, who are bound to stay and claim acceptance as full citizens in European societies. It is not religion that is perceived as problematic but Islam.[17] Given the different ethnic and cultural background of most Muslim groups, racial factors in the broad sense I use here are clearly implied as well. In this context, the sex equality argument takes on a peculiar position. On one hand it is brought into the discussion as a sincere concern, which, if valid, may provide a legitimate reason for curbing religious expressions. On the other hand, it seems to be used quite opportunistically as a convenient argument for Islam- or immigrant-bashing by right-wing groups who have never been known as staunch defenders of women's rights.

We now turn to two legal cases concerning Muslim teachers who complained that their rights were infringed because they were not allowed to wear headscarves in the classroom.

## LEGAL CASES CONCERNING HEADSCARVES IN THE CLASSROOM

### The Case of *Dahlab Versus Switzerland* for the European Court of Human Rights[18]

Dahlab was a teacher at a public primary school, teaching children between four and eight years of age. At some point she converted from Catholicism to Islam and subsequently started to wear a headscarf. For several years nothing happened. As far as the facts of the case disclose, Dahlab functioned as she should, and no complaints were filed by pupils or parents against her wearing a headscarf in class. Only when the situation came to the attention of the director general of primary education of the *Kanton* where she worked did she get into trouble. The director general considered wearing a headscarf a religious expression, jeopardizing the denominational neutrality the state has to uphold in public schools to protect the religious beliefs of pupils and parents and to ensure religious harmony. Dahlab was ordered to put away her headscarf during classes and was dismissed when she refused to do so. She complained that this dismissal infringed her right to freedom of religion. After balancing the rights at stake, the Swiss federal court upheld the decision by giving priority to the right of the pupils to receive education in a religiously neutral environment. Dahlab then brought her complaint to the European Court of Human Rights (ECHR or European Court).[19]

The ECHR decision of February 15, 2001, turned on the question of whether the limitation of Dahlab's right to freedom of religion was "necessary in a democratic society" to achieve the legitimate aim of guaranteeing the denominational neutrality of the state, to protect the religious beliefs of the pupils and parents, and to preserve religious harmony.[20] The ECHR concluded that this is indeed the case. The ECHR did not give any weight to the fact that Dahlab had been working for more than three years wearing a headscarf without complaints by either parents or the school board. The court then turned to the question of the impact of a teacher wearing a clearly religious sign such as a headscarf on the freedom of conscience and religion of the pupils. Although the court recognized the difficulty of assessing this impact, it continued with a sweeping statement about the message a headscarf may broadcast to the pupils, especially pupils who are only four to eight years old and thus more easily influenced than older children: "In those circumstances, it cannot be denied outright that the wearing of a headscarf might have some kind of proselytizing effect, seeing that it appears to be imposed on women by a precept which is laid down in the Koran and which, as the Federal Court noted, is hard to square with the principle of gender equality. It therefore appears difficult to reconcile the wearing of an Islamic headscarf with the message of tolerance, respect for others and, above all, equality and non-discrimination that all teachers in a democratic society must convey to their pupils."[21]

The Court's linking the question of the teacher's required neutrality to the question of gender equality and more generally to notions of tolerance, respect, and equality is surprising, for the Swiss Court had identified the problem of a teacher wearing a headscarf as one of religious expression. It referred to the headscarf's possibly negative meaning for women's equality only in a sideline. The ECHR took this ascribed meaning and message of wearing a headscarf as the decisive argument to justify prohibiting a teacher to wear a headscarf in the public classroom. Thus the ECHR found that it is not the religious argument but the sex equality argument that justifies curbing this religious manifestation.

## The Case of the Dutch Student Teacher[22]

A similar Dutch case, which was decided in 1999, concerned a student teacher at a public primary school who was not allowed by the school authorities to wear her headscarf in class. As in the case of Dahlab, the argument turned on the required neutrality of the state. Because public education must respect all religions and denominations, teachers must have an open attitude toward different convictions and beliefs. This means teachers should be very reluctant in expressly manifesting their adherence to a particular religion or conviction. This is all the more so, the school authorities added,

> in case a way of dressing identifies a person with a group which does not only live according to strict opinions themselves, but which also has shown little tolerance towards persons with different opinions within the same religion. It seems evident that an Islamic woman, who considers it her duty to wear the headscarf even in the intimacy of her classroom, bears witness of holding very stringent opinions, also in comparison with the large majority of her fellow-believers, and may thus be perceived as threatening to other women and girls of the same religion, who mostly achieved the right to a freer way of living with difficulty.[23]

The student teacher filed a complaint about this decision with the Dutch Equal Treatment Commission. This semijudicial body supervises the Dutch General Equal Treatment Act, which covers discrimination on a number of grounds, including race, sex, and religion. Although its decisions are not legally binding, the case law of the commission is an important source of jurisprudence.

In assessing whether the exclusion of the student teacher amounts to discrimination on the basis of religion, the Equal Treatment Commission was very brief. The commission affirmed the legitimacy of requiring public school teachers to have and display an open attitude toward all convictions and beliefs. To decide whether the student teacher complied with this requirement, however, the commission found it was not legitimate for the school to presume from her wearing a headscarf that this open attitude was missing. The school should have inquired after the actual opinions and ideas of the teacher instead.

## COMPARISON AND EVALUATION

If we compare the two cases, the most striking difference concerns the way in which the legal bodies assessed the meaning to be attributed to wearing a headscarf in front of the class. The ECHR started from a sweeping general statement about the meaning of the headscarf as a Koranic precept for women that is "hard to reconcile" with a message of tolerance, respect, and nondiscrimination. It did not give any clue as to the sources for this conclusion, suggesting it to be something self-evident or of general knowledge. In a November 2005 case concerning a Turkish ban on wearing headscarves and other religious symbols at Turkish universities, the ECHR confirmed its negative reading of the headscarf by referring to the statement made in *Dahlab* without taking back anything.[24]

As we have seen before, this is definitely not the case, as was acknowledged by the German constitutional court. If anything, research shows that the headscarf has multiple meanings and cannot be reduced to a single, essentialized one. The ECHR approach seriously reduces the citizenship status of Muslim women who wear a headscarf. It perceives them as passive bearers of what the court supposes to be their community's culture and religion instead of human agents in their own right who could have an individual view of the meaning of the headscarf and make a deliberate and free choice to wear it. Through this mechanism it attributes opinions and attitudes to them that are clearly incompatible with the underlying values of the European democracies. It classifies them de facto as failed citizens who may therefore be excluded from important public functions such as being a public school teacher. There can be little doubt the same will apply to many other public functions in the police or the judiciary. Their basic civil rights are seriously affected.[25]

On the other hand, the Dutch Equal Treatment Commission did not accept an approach starting from unsubstantiated presumptions about the meaning of wearing a headscarf. In its principled reasoning it requires public authorities to assess, on an *individualized* basis, what the headscarf means *for this particular teacher*: Does it distract from the neutral and open attitude she is appropriately required to demonstrate toward all religions and beliefs as a public school teacher? To find out, the school authorities have to (and are allowed to) make an individual inquiry. In fact, this is something they have to do regarding any person aspiring to teach in public schools, including those who dress in a religiously neutral way. It is part of each interview with job applicants. This approach leaves the option open to exclude any person wearing a headscarf who wears it because of fundamentalist, intolerant convictions. But the justification in such a situation would not derive from her headscarf as such but from her intolerant convictions.

It seems evident that the approach by the Equal Treatment Commission is more empowering to women. The commission recognizes Muslim women's agency in wearing a headscarf instead of seeing them, by definition, as victims of their own community's ideas on women. Furthermore, the commission does not fall into the trap of prejudice by stereotyping Islam as such as incompatible with notions of sex equality and tolerance. The approach by the Equal Treatment Commission thus seems clearly preferable. It is significant to note that nothing in the European Convention on Human Rights would prohibit the ECHR from embracing the approach. On the contrary, as Judge Tulkens contended in her dissenting opinion in the case of *Sahin*, it would be more in line with its general case law, in which the court time and again emphasizes that any limitation of rights protected by the European Convention on Human Rights must be done with respect to the particular applicant, not in any general or abstract sense.[26]

## CONSEQUENCES OF AN INDIVIDUALIZED ASSESSMENT

Does an individualized and contextual assessment of whether wearing a religious symbol such as a headscarf is compatible with the required neutral attitude of a public school teacher mean that "anything goes" in terms of wearing religious symbols in class? This question is not an academic one given the discussions in the Netherlands concerning the *niqab* or *burqa,* which some Muslim women wear in public.[27] In December 2005 anxiety over the perceived lack of Muslim integration resulted in a sweeping motion by a majority in the Dutch Parliament requesting the Dutch government to enact a ban on wearing a *burqa* in public.[28] In November 2006 the government decided to pursue this issue and started working on the legal hurdles to take.[29] In the United Kingdom, the *niqab* received tremendous media attention when Jack Straw, a leading Labour politician, spoke out against women wearing a *niqab* because it is in his view a "visible statement of separateness" and hampers community relations.[30] At about the same time a United Kingdom employment tribunal decided a Muslim teacher at a primary school was rightfully suspended from her job when she refused to remove her face-covering veil in the classroom. She has appealed to an employment appeals tribunal.[31]

I will limit myself here to the question whether a ban on face-covering veils such as the *niqab* can and should be imposed on public school teachers or whether a teacher should be allowed to wear a *burqa* or *niqab,* just like a headscarf.

Applying the individualized test highlighted earlier, one would have to ask whether the individual woman involved lacks the required open and neutral attitude toward all religions and beliefs. Although specific empirical research on the motives for wearing a *burqa* or *niqab* in Western Europe seems to be lacking, at least in the Netherlands, wearing a face-covering

veil appears to be more closely linked to a strict adherence to rigidly ortho-
dox interpretations of Islam than the headscarf. Thus it is less likely that a
woman wearing a face-covering veil will pass the test of having the required
open-mindedness. If this were shown to be true, one could perhaps argue
that a woman wearing a *burqa* or *niqab* provides a prima facie case of lacking the required open attitude toward other religions and convictions.

Whether this holds true or not, the *burqa* and *niqab* raise some other
concerns that may be even more important. These were brought forward
in another case before the Dutch Equal Treatment Commission that concerned two young, *niqab*-wearing women attending a vocational school.[32]
They consented to leave off their face-covering veils during lessons but not
elsewhere on the entire school complex, as required by the school authorities. Their complaint to the Equal Treatment Commission was unsuccessful.
The commission's argument in upholding the ban concerned the negative
influence that a face-covering veil has on communication by eliminating its
nonverbal aspects. Good communication was deemed crucial for providing
a good educational environment that is not limited to classroom lessons but
extends to all other activities on the school grounds.

The commission did not go into the question how this type of dress relates
to sex equality. This seems a relevant point to me as well. Wearing a *burqa*
or *niqab* is much harder to square with equality than wearing a headscarf
because it seems closely related to notions and practices of sex segregation.
This is born out by the case mentioned earlier. One of the students was working as a trainee at a day care center, where without her *niqab* she refused to
talk to male parents bringing or fetching their children.[33] Sex segregation, like
racial segregation, is highly problematic from an equality perspective.

If a student is not allowed to wear a *niqab* or *burqa* for communication
purposes, the argument would be even stronger in the case of a teacher.
Thus, allowing a public school teacher to wear a headscarf need not imply
blanket permission for other, more restrictive religious attire such as a *niqab*
or *burqa*.

## CONCLUDING REMARKS

The discussion of the two headscarf cases shows that law can play a powerful role in constructing notions of citizenship and processes of inclusion
and exclusion. The case study also demonstrates that courts may have much
leeway in deciding such issues. Much depends on how they use their legal
competence. On one hand, the ECHR reduced Muslim women's citizenship
status by attributing an essentialized and very negative meaning to wearing
a headscarf. This is all the more disquieting as it flies in the face of empirical research available on this subject. This denial of their agency has disempowering effects, for it deprives a large group of Muslim women of their
right to equal access to public functions. On the other hand, the Dutch Equal

Treatment Commission, by demanding an individualized assessment of what a headscarf represents, regards Muslim women as responsible agents who can, but also should, account for their convictions and actions. As such, the commission's approach is more empowering to women and thus preferable.

I realize that this approach implies drawing lines of inclusion and exclusion and of deciding who is to be recognized as a full citizen. If a Muslim woman (or any other person) does not demonstrate the required open and neutral attitude toward her pupils, she is not fit to be a school teacher in a public school in the commission's books and may be excluded from such a position. Other arguments may come into play when more restrictive forms of religious dress such as the *niqab* or *burqa* are involved. At the end of the day, attaining full citizenship status in western European states depends on embracing the core values of those democracies. Although it may be difficult to decide what those core values are in concrete detail, tolerance toward other people's beliefs and convictions is undoubtedly one of them.

## NOTES

1. I use *race* here as in the United Nations Convention on the Elimination of All Forms of Racial Discrimination, as including "colour, descent, or national or ethnic origin" (Article 1, Section 1).
2. The terms differ between countries: *foulard* or *voile* (France), *veil* or *hijab* (United Kingdom), and *Kopftuch* (Germany), for example. Because discussions focus on the headscarf and not on other forms of veiling, I use *headscarf* throughout this chapter to avoid confusion.
3. T. H. Marshall, "Citizenship and Social Class." In *Class, Citizenship and Social Development. Essays by T. H. Marshall* (Westport, CT: Greenwood Press, 1976), 84.
4. See Ruth Lister, "Citizenship: Towards a Feminist Synthesis," *Feminist Review* 57 (1997): 29.
5. Law 2004–228 of March 15, 2004. For an overview of the French discussion, see Sharif Gemie, "Actualité. Stasi's Republic: The School and the 'Veil': December 2003–March 2004," *Modern & Contemporary France* 12 (2004): 387–397, hereafter cited in text as Gemie (2004); and T. Jeremy Gunn, "Religious Freedom and *Laïcité*: A Comparison of the United States and France," *Brigham Young University Law Review* (2004): 419–505.
6. *Ludin,* Bundesverfassungsgericht, September 24, 2003, 2BvR 1436/02, http://www.bundesverfassungsgericht.delentscheidungen/rs20030924_2bur143602.html, hereafter cited in text as *Ludin* (2003). For an overview of the German discussion, see Matthias Mahlmann, "Religious Tolerance, Pluralist Society and the Neutrality of the State: The Federal Constitutional Court's Decision in the Headscarf Case," *German Law Journal* 4, no. 11 (November 1, 2003). http://www.germanlawjournal.com/article.php?id=331. Last accessed 13, July 2007.
7. For an overview of the Dutch discussions see Sawitri Saharso, "Headscarves: A Comparison of Public Thought and Public Policy in Germany and the Netherlands," CRISPP paper, January 2005. http://www.essex.ac.uk/ECpR/events/generalconference/budapest/papers/4/8/saharso.pdf. Last accessed 13 July 2007.
8. In France this model of state–religion relationship is called *laïcité*.
9. For an overview, see S. van Bijsterveld, *Godsdienstvrijheid in Europees Perspectief* (Freedom of Religion from a European Perspective) (Deventer: WEJ Tjeenk Willink, 1998), 34–35.

10. Commission Stasi (Commission de Réflexion sur l'Application du Principe de Laïcité dans la République), *Rapport au Président de la République,* December 11, 2003. http://lesrapports.ladocumentationfrancaise.fr/BRP/034007 25/000. pdf. Last visit 13 July, 2007; hereafter cited in text as Stasi (2003).

11. For a discussion of the clashes between feminist groups in France, see Bronwyn Winter, "Secularism Aboard the *Titanic:* Feminists and the Debate over the Hijab in France," *Feminist Studies* 32 (2006): 279–298.

12. For the United Kingdom, see Claire Dwyer, "Veiled Meanings: Young British Muslim Women and the Negotiation of Differences" *Gender, Place and Culture* 6 (1999): 5–26; for France, see Caitlin Killian, "The Other Side of the Veil: North African Women in France Respond to the Headscarf Affair," *Gender & Society* 17 (2003): 567–590.

13. See more extensively on the position and identity of Islamic groups in western Europe, including the position of women: Silvio Ferrari and Anthony Bradney, eds., *Islam and European Legal Systems* (Dartmouth/Ashgate: Aldershot, 2000); and Steven Vertovec and Ceri Peach, eds., *Islam in Europe: The Politics of Religion and Community* (London: Macmillan Press, 1997).

14. "Die Forschungsergebnisse zeigen jedoch, dass die Deutung des Kopftuchs nicht auf ein Zeichen gesellschaftlicher Unterdrückung der Frau verkurzt werden darf. Vielmehr kann das Kopftuch für junge muslimische Frauen auch ein frei gewähltes Mittel sein, um ohne Bruch mit der Herkunfstkultur ein selbstbestimmtes Leben zu führen." Case *Ludin* (2003), Section 52.

15. "La Commission, après avoir entendu les positions des uns et des autres, estime qu'aujourd'hui la question n'est plus la liberté de conscience, mais l'ordre public. Le contexte a changé en quelques années. Les tensions et les affrontements dans les établissements autour de questions religieuses sont devenus trop fréquents" (Stasi 2003, 39).

16. *Ludin* (2003), Section 58.

17. In this respect, the symbolic weight of the headscarf turns it into an "overdetermined sign," as Najmabadi calls it, and discards its historical contingency. See Afsaneh Najmabadi, "Gender and Secularism of Modernity: How Can a Muslim Woman Be French?" *Feminist Studies* 32 (2006): 239–255.

18. ECHR, February 15, 2001, *Dahlab v. Switzerland* (decision on admissibility), appl. no. 42393/98. http://www.hudoc.echr.coe/int/.

19. The ECHR supervises application of the European Convention on Human Rights by the States Parties to the Convention. People who have exhausted domestic remedies can bring their complaints about infringements of their rights under the convention to the ECHR. The convention covers all major civil and political rights. The decisions of the ECHR are legally binding.

20. According to Article 9, Section 2 of the European Convention of Human Rights, "Freedom to manifest one's religion or beliefs shall be subject only to such limitations as are prescribed by law and are necessary in a democratic society in the interests of public safety, for the protection of public order, health or morals, or for the protection of the rights and freedoms of others."

21. *Dahlab v. Switzerland* (2001).

22. *Oordeel* 99–18, published in T. Loenen, ed., *Gelijke behandeling: Oordelen en commentaar 1999* (Equal Treatment: Decisions and Comments 1999). (Deventer: Kluwer, 2000). The *oordelen* or decisions of the commission are not legally binding or enforceable. They are available in Dutch only.

23. The translation is mine. The original Dutch reads, "Die noodzaak tot terughoudendheid geldt te meer als het gaat om een wijze van kleden die de betrokkene vereenzelvigt met een groepering, die niet alleen voor zichzelf zeer strenge opvattingen naleeft, maar ook weinig blijk geeft van tolerantie ten opzichte van andersdenkenden binnen dezelfde religie. Het lijkt evident dat

een Islamitische vrouw die zelfs in de beslotenheid van het eigen klaslokaal meent de hoofddoek te moeten dragen, ook in vergelijking met de grote meer-derheid van haar geloofsgenoten, getuigt van zeer stringente opvattingen en daarmee impliciet bedreigend kan overkomen op de vrouwen en meisjes van dezelfde godsdienst, die zich veelal met grote moeite het recht op een vrijere leefwijze hebben verworven."

24. See Section 111 of the judgment. The case dealt with a complaint by a student. The ECHR upheld the ban; see ECHR November 10, 2005 (Grand Cham-ber), *Sahin v. Turkey,* http://www.hudoc.echr.coe.int/. This is an even more far-reaching and questionable limitation of the freedom of religion because students do not hold public positions.
25. The right of citizens to be appointed to public functions on an equal basis is guaranteed as a constitutional right in and the Netherlands; for Germany, see Article 33, Section 2 of the German *Grundgesetz,* and for the Netherlands see Article 3 of the Dutch *Grondwet.*
26. Dissenting opinion of Judge Tulkens in *Sahin v. Turkey* (2005), Section 7.
27. A *niqab* is a veil that covers the face entirely except for a small slit for the eyes. A *burqa* also covers the full face, but sight is made possible by a gauze at the level of the eyes.
28. Motion *Wilders* of October 10, 2005, *Kamerstukken II* 2005/06, 29754, no. 41, carried on December 21, 2005.
29. To circumvent legal (human rights) objections to a *burqa* ban as such, it intends to create a general prohibition on face-covering attire in public for purposes of safety and security. See "Algemeen verbod gezichtsbedekkende kleding" http://www.justitie.nl/actueel/nieuwsberichten/archief-2006/2006/algemeen-vertod.gezichtsbedekkende-kleding.aspx?op=34&cs=578 (last accessed 13 July 2007; available in Dutch only) and "Netherlands Moves Toward Total Ban on Muslim Veils," *Guardian* (November 11, 2006). Since then nothing much has happened. Given the change in government in 2007 (the current one having a more left wing signature), it seems unlikely the Govenrment will be keen on pursuing these plans, though it may be forced to do so as, just before finalizing this article, on 12 July 2007, a right wing member of Parliament put forward a bill to criminalize wearing a *burqa* or *niqab* in public. See http://www.nos.nl/nosjournaal/artikelen/2007/7/120707_Goerka.html.(Accessed 13 July 2007).
30. "Dangerous Attack or Fair Point? Straw Veil Row Deepens. Minister's Remarks Fuel Claims of Islamophobia Crisis," *Guardian* (October 7, 2006). http://www.guardian.co.uk/.
31. "Tribunal Dismisses Case of Muslim Woman Ordered Not to Teach in Veil," *Guardian* (October 20, 2006). http://www.guardian.co.uk/.
32. *Oordeel* 2003–40. http://www.cgb.nl.
33. *Oordeel* 2003–40, Section 2.8. http://www.cgb.nl.

# 9 *Shari'ah* Activism in Nigeria Under *Hudud*

## Margot Badran[1]

In 1999, the year of the return to democracy in Nigeria after years of military dictatorship, the contender for governor of Zamfara, the state with the highest poverty and lowest literacy in the North, pledged to place *hudud* or Islamic laws of crime and punishment into statutory law. This move was billed as a "return to the shari'ah."[2] By 2002, twelve out of thirty-six states had instituted *hudud* laws. Under these laws sex outside marriage, or *zina,* was criminalized and for the guilty could bring the ultimate penalty of death by stoning; amputations were prescribed for crimes of theft.[3] Human rights activists and feminist activists in Nigeria, who had seen the disastrous effects of *hudud* in other countries over the past decades, worried that women and the poor would fall victim to these laws.[4]

As feared, it was not long before women were accused of *zina* (adultery) and brought before shari'ah courts. In what became two high-profile cases, Safiyatu Husseini of Sokoto and Amina Lawal of Katsina, both from northern states with majority Muslim populations, were summarily convicted and sentenced to death by stoning in the lower shari'ah courts. These quickly became high-profile cases, locally and globally. It did not escape attention that it was *women,* and more precisely *poor* women, who were brought before the law, whereas the men involved simply absconded. Nigerian women activists, Muslims and non-Muslims alike, together with some male supporters immediately swung into action. Through their non-government organization, Baobab for Women's Human Rights and the Women's Rights and Protection Association (WRAPA), activists offered the two women legal assistance and simultaneously mounted wide publicity campaigns. The accused were eventually acquitted in higher shari'ah courts of appeal in their respective states—Safiyatu Husseini in 2002 and Amina Lawal in 2003—as a result of scrupulous application of *fiqh* (Islamic jurisprudence). It was in the Islamic legal system that the women were both convicted and, through the strenuous work of Nigerian activists, acquitted. However, Westerners who protested through petitions and via the media—until Nigerian activists asked them to stop as their support became counterproductive, especially when laced with expressions of Islamophobia—took credit for the victory as a triumph of (Western) secular discourse. This is not to suggest that the glare of the global media—Western and beyond—was without positive influence, however.

The campaigns women mounted to see justice done to Amina Lawal and Safiyatu Husseini, through legal teams organized to defend their rights before higher shari'ah courts and the public advocacy and debates that they stimulated, constitute a stunning manifestation of Islamic feminism at work. Did this activism and its positive outcomes provoke or further enhance Islamic feminist consciousness—the awareness of Qur'an-based women's rights as *insan*, as human beings? Did the successful campaigns catalyze intensified debates in Nigeria around issues of gender justice and social justice, mobilizing Islamic discourse to empower Muslim women and erode oppressive ideas about and treatment of women in the name of Islam? To seek answers to such questions I went to Nigeria early in 2005 to meet women.[5]

In this chapter I discuss briefly how the women's activism around the *zina* cases made an important contribution to the ongoing project of Islamic feminism; however, my main interest is to explore how this activist campaign catalyzed a longer-term unfolding of Islamic feminism. I seek answers to these questions through the results of interviews and conversations with Muslim women I met in Nigeria. I place this in the context of global Islamic feminist discourse and practice. Muslim women in various locations move in strikingly parallel ways as well as along divergent paths and in different time frames in elaborating and activating Islamic feminism.

## BEFORE "THE RETURN" TO SHARI'AH

Since the late 1970s, and especially since the 1980s, two diametrically opposed discourses on women and gender generated by Muslims have circulated transnationally. One discourse, initially spread mainly by men as Islamists or advocates of political Islam, also called Islamic fundamentalists, was a patriarchal discourse in the language of Islam supporting male domination and protection of women in a system of unequal gender rights laying stress on women's family roles. The other was a gender egalitarian discourse generated by Muslim women as feminists and human rights advocates that stressed women's rights and public roles in the multiple and intersecting discourses of Islamic modernism, (Muslims') secular feminism, human rights, and democracy.

The 1990s saw the appearance of the new Islamic feminist discourse, based on women scholars' new Qur'anic interpretation articulating the full equality of women and men across the public–private spectrum. This Islamic feminist discourse, backed by this new exegetical work, elaborated a more radical notion of gender equality than Muslim women's secular feminisms, which had typically acquiesced in the notion of equity or balanced gender roles in the private or family sphere. The early secular feminist movements in Muslim majority societies that first arose in the early twentieth century, fighting battles on multiple fronts, found it easier to make headway pushing for full equality in the public sphere. They accepted the new Islamic modernist approaches to ameliorating injustices in the family by pushing for optimal performance of gender-differentiated roles.[6] It would take time for societal changes and higher levels of training before women could embark on a more radical interpretation of their own, as happened toward the end of the twentieth century. With the turn of the twenty-first century, the patriarchal and egalitarian discourses of Islam and their respective proponents were on a high-stakes collision course.

In the early 1980s in different parts of the globe, Muslim women, joined by some non-Muslims, began to consolidate a transnational feminist and human rights culture when they formed the network called Women Living Under Muslim Laws (WLUML). It began informally when Algerian women objected to not being consulted about the draft for a new Muslim family law in Algeria. Formally established in 1984, WLUML has engaged in advocacy and lobbying work around questions of laws and their implementation, issuing alerts and circulating petitions on behalf of women suffering victimization. It undertook a long-term project to gather data on laws and women's experience in Muslim societies around the world, which resulted in the publication of *Knowing Our Rights: Women, Family, Laws and Customs in the Muslim World* in 2003, with a third edition published in December 2006.[7] The women who began WLUML were secular feminists and human rights advocates who used international discourses and who familiarized themselves with the various legal discourses, including religious jurisprudence, found in the societies where they operated. With the development of Islamic feminist discourse in the 1990s they accessed its insights and methods as well.[8]

As Muslim women were consolidating this transnational feminist network culture, the transnational movement of political Islam was spreading globally. Islamism, which had begun to surface in parts of the Muslim world in the 1970s, made its appearance in northern Nigeria toward the end of that decade through a group called the Jama'atu Izalat al-Bid'a wa Iqamat al Sunna, or the Society for the Eradication of Innovation and the Establishment of Tradition.[9] The Izala movement has been called neo-fundamentalist because it did not challenge the state (as did fundamentalist movements such as the Egyptian-founded Muslim Brothers) but rather civil society and especially Sufi trends, advocating legal reform (or a return to Islamic laws). At the core of its reformist project was spreading its own brand of Islamic education, and to that end it created Islamic schools throughout the north to teach religious subjects along with what in Nigeria are called Western subjects (elsewhere often called modern subjects) to males and females alike. An unintentional result of these neo-fundamentalists' mission of teaching the religious sciences and the Arabic language was to open the way for questioning Izala's reactionary patriarchal attitude to Islam. A young woman I spoke with after she completed her studies in an Izala-run school went on to give women lessons in religion in her home, where she introduced them to a gender egalitarian approach to Islam. While operating as an outspoken feminist education activist—and she is not shy about claiming this label— she continued her Islamic religious studies at the university.[10]

During this same period, Nigerian women were creating their own associations and spearheading their own education initiatives. In 1985, Muslim women from around the country with ties to the Muslim Sisters Organization and other Islamic associations came together to establish the Federation of Muslim Women's Organizations of Nigeria (FOMWAN), with Aisha Lemu as its first head or *amirah*. Its main purpose was to provide schooling for Muslim girls in a curriculum that combined Islamic and Western subjects. Although FOMWAN laid stress on education and an overall religious formation, it also provided health training and services in its various outreach programs. This grassroots association celebrated its twentieth anniversary in 2005 in a large conference in the nation's capital, Abuja.[11] Its current head is activist, writer, and journalist Bilkisu Yusuf.

Nigerian women, Muslims and Christians together, were also forming human rights and women's rights organizations in the 1990s. I mention, as examples, the two organizations that came to the rescue of the women accused in the two *zina* cases. Baobab for Women's Human Rights was established in 1996 under the leadership of Ayesha Imam, a founding member of WLUML.[12] Although autonomous, the organization has ties with WLUML. Three years later in 1999, the year the first *hudud* laws were announced, WRAPA was founded, with activist Saudatu Mahdi assuming the position of secretary general. Human rights and feminist activists used multiple discourses, seeing human rights, democracy, and progressive religious discourse as mutually reinforcing women's rights and human rights, gender justice and social justice.

Muslim women operating more fully within an Islamic framework, such as the FOMWAN women, and those functioning within multiple frameworks, such as Baobab and WRAPA members, were not adversarial, but their focus and their projects differed. From talking with women from both groups it appears that around the turn of the twenty-first century and especially in the aftermath of the *zina* cases these two groups were converging more and more in their concerns about issues of women, state, and society. The problematic verdicts issued by the lower shari'ah courts in the *zina* cases and the impressive backing by women activists from Baobab and WRAPA through the mobilization of *fiqh* readings have galvanized women across a broad spectrum in support of a common quest for gender justice and social justice in the aftermath of the instituting of *hudud* laws.

## ISLAMIC FEMINISM

Islamic feminism is a global discourse that is continually fed by the local, while the global discourse likewise animates the local. In the 1990s a new feminist paradigm in the language of Islam caught the attention of Muslim women in different locations, themselves feminists, who often unknown to each other started to call it Islamic feminism. They were noticing and naming a feminist discourse and practice grounded in rereadings of the Qur'an, seeking rights and justice for women, and for men, in the totality of their existence. Women interpreters enunciated two key concepts of Islamic feminism: gender equality and social justice. They were fundamental ideals that were to be applied in everyday life across the public–private continuum.[13]

With its paramount grounding in religious discourse, Islamic feminism did not reject or replace what has been known as Muslims' secular feminisms, expressed in the discourses of Islamic modernism, secular nationalism, and humanitarian and later human rights. Islamic feminism elaborated the principle of gender equality as part and parcel of all equalities within Islamic discourse as its paramount discourse. It can be seen as building on and extending the Islamic modernist strand of Muslims' multivocal secular feminism.[14] In her book *Qur'an and Woman: Reading the Sacred Text from a Woman's Perspective,* African American Amina Wadud elaborated the notions of gender equality and social justice and made clear their necessary intersection.[15] Her work has provided powerful support in the form of strong Islamic argumentation in the struggle for the implementation of equality and justice across lines of race, gender, and class.

Patriarchal ideas articulated in the language of Islam have subverted the practice of gender equality and social justice that the Qur'an puts forward. Pakistani American Asma Barlas faced the problem head on when she defined patriarchy and unmasked its invidious work in eroding the notion and practice of Qu'ranic equality of human beings (*insan*) irrespective of their physical attributes (e.g., anatomy, skin color) and various socially constructed differences. Removal of the structures of inequality that patriarchy sustains is fundamental to the project of understanding and practicing equality. Asma Barlas's *"Believing Women" in Islam: Unreading Patriarchal Interpretations of the Qur'an,* the outcome of work begun in the 1990s, was published in 2002.[16]

Other scholars concerned about inequitable or problematic laws enacted in the name of Islam turned their attention to Islamic jurisprudence or *fiqh,* derived from interpretation of the Qur'an and other sources such as *hadith* (sayings and deeds attributed to the Prophet Muhammad). Ziba Mir-Hosseini, a London-based scholar from Iran, scrutinized *fiqh* and its application in the enacting of Muslim personal status codes, also called family law, in statutory law.[17] These codes, claiming firm grounding in Islamic jurisprudence, have instituted laws that support a patriarchal family structure.

Complicating the reform of *fiqh*-backed laws, commonly called shari'ah laws and often simply "the shari'ah" (as the elision of *fiqh* and shari'ah as divinely guided "path" illustrates), is the widely held belief that to alter the

Muslim personal status or family laws is to tamper with the sacred. This has long been an effective way to inhibit people from engaging in critique and attempts to recast *fiqh*-based laws. This is not to say, however, that there have not been serious and sustained movements by feminists to reform *fiqh*-based Muslim family law nor that no successes have been achieved.[18]

Islamic feminists have taken pains to make the distinction between the shari'ah as the path discerned from the Qur'an that Muslims are exhorted to follow in life (shari'ah as divine inspiration and guiding principles) and so-called shari'ah laws (laws deriving from understandings of *fiqh* that are man-made and therefore open to questioning and change). The shari'ah, as the path indicated in scripture as the word of God, is sacred but must be ascertained through human effort. By stressing the distinction between man-made laws and the divine path, Islamic feminists strive to remove an obstacle in the way of those who feared, indeed were encouraged to fear, that they might be challenging divine law if they questioned *fiqh* and laws deriving from it.[19]

## SHARI'AH AS PATH AND AS POLITICS

In Nigeria with the politicization of the shari'ah, the distinction between shari'ah as "the path" and shari'ah as man-made law was expediently kept blurred by states that came to be called the shari'ah states after instituting *hudud* laws and declaring "a return to the shari'ah."[20] Although the label "shari'ah states" was originally conferred by non-Muslims to refer to states that had instituted *hudud* laws and then taken up by the media, it was soon brandished by the so-called shari'ah states themselves as if in confirmation of their self-arrogated task to reestablish the shari'ah.

It is important to note that the notion of the "shari'ah state" as a state within a sovereign state is peculiar to Nigeria. A "shari'ah state" should not be confused with a sovereign "Islamic state," declaring its constitution and all of its laws to be based on the shari'ah. Unlike in the self-styled Islamic states, the notion of the "shari'ah state" in Nigeria simply pivoted around the institution of *hudud* laws, a law-and-order approach to Islam.

By making the claim and igniting hope for a new coming of shari'ah to be ushered in through the "gate of *hudud*," state authorities set themselves on a course they did not chart. In short, they misread the politics. The rapid and zealous implementation of *hudud*, witnessed by the condemnations of the two poor women in the *zina* cases, flung open a Pandora's box of confusions and contractions swirling around "the shari'ah" and actions taken in its name and vividly linked two kinds of oppressions: that of women and that of the poor. With the explosion of the two *zina* cases, women who came to the rescue of their condemned sisters put forward another definition of shari'ah and opened up a fresh look at *fiqh*.

## HUDUD

*Hudud* have remained traditionally operative but never codified in Saudi Arabia. Long surpassed by secular laws in most Muslim societies, *hudud* were reinstated in codified form in the late 1970s and early 1980s in Iran, Pakistan, and Sudan with the imposition of Islamist regimes.[21] The imposition of *hudud* elicited strong opposition among women inside and outside these countries. Women as human rights activists and secular feminists in Pakistan through Shirgat Gah (which began as a women's resource center in 1975 with ties to WLUML) and through the Women's Action Forum (created in 1981) have fought the abuses perpetrated against women through aggressive campaigns of public protest and exposure and letter-writing and petition campaigns and continue to do so today with a certain amount of success.[22] Meanwhile, Iranian women at home and in diaspora have mounted vigorous protests on behalf of women victimized under the *hudud* laws. The network called Nisa Meydaan, or Women's Field, which includes long-term activists and lawyers such as Shirin Ebadi and Mihrangaz Kar and scholars such as Ziba Mir-Hosseini and Val Moghadam, is currently engaged in a vigorous transnational initiative called the "Stop Stoning Forever Campaign."[23] Pakistani and Iranian activists have made extensive use of the WLUML network to support women condemned under the *hudud* laws and to expose and discuss the laws per se.

When the *hudud* laws were proclaimed in Nigeria, Nigerian women activists who had gained exposure to the workings of *hudud* laws in other countries and had supported the causes of women victimized under *hudud* laws were well experienced, well networked, and poised to act.

## TWO *ZINA* CASES IN NIGERIA

Women-headed defense teams composed primarily of women lawyers along with specialists in jurisprudence and Arabists who were assembled by Baobab and WRAPA appealed the cases of Safiyatu Husseini and Amina Lawal in the higher shari'ah courts. The shari'ah court system (both the lower and higher courts) had been accustomed to hearing personal status cases (or cases relating to family law and inheritance) only since the early twentieth century, when *hudud* (which previously had never been codified in Nigeria although practiced in what were called "*qadi*'s courts") had been outlawed under the British. With independence in 1960s a national criminal code was enacted. Close and routine familiarity with Islamic jurisprudence concerning *hudud* was lacking, as was a recent history of precedents. In appealing the cases, the women-headed defense teams laid out details of *fiqh* demonstrating the stringent requirements of evidence and strict procedures that had to be followed in *hudud* cases to protect the cause of justice. The cases that resulted in acquittals constituted an impressive public display of "learning through legal action," or "walking through *fiqh*." The acquittals were a triumph of the principles of Islamic equality and justice over patriarchal inequities. To date there have been no more convictions for *zina* and accordingly no capital punishment carried out. In the Federation of Nigeria, although capital punishment is on the books its implementation has fallen into abeyance.[24]

Whereas classical *fiqh* (consolidated during the formation of the major schools of jurisprudence in the ninth and tenth centuries) shored up a patriarchal model of the family, classical jurisprudence took a strikingly gender egalitarian approach to crime and punishment. Requirements of evidence and procedures were to be strictly applied to both women and men. It has been suggested that the penalty of death by stoning for those guilty of *zina* was prescribed for both sexes, and it was so onerous that the punishment was meant to act as a deterrent, not a weapon to be easily wielded, especially against the vulnerable. It rankled when judges in the lower shari'ah courts handed down quick guilty verdicts to the two women accused of *zina,* while the men involved were never brought before the courts, and that the convicted were poor women. It clearly did not signal the advent of social justice that the state-directed "return to the shari'ah" promised. People linked oppression against women and oppression of the poor. They began to insist that social and economic justice should prevail as part of living by the shari'ah before *hudud* was instituted.

The cooperation between Muslim and Christian women in the *zina* cased occasioned a strengthening of transcommunal activism in support of justice and equality in Nigeria. Backing the cause of justice in the shari'ah courts was not of necessity linked to a religious identity or faith position, as the support of Nigerian Christian activists acting on behalf of their endangered Nigerian and Muslim sisters illustrated. The activists shared common understandings of justice and equality, irrespective of their religious affiliations. This has seldom been noticed as observers have been quick to circulate instances of interreligious strife rather than cooperation, especially around issues of women and gender.[25]

## NIGERIAN MUSLIM WOMEN'S NARRATIVES

To understand the long-term impact of the activism around these two *zina* cases and the support initiated by women as part of the elaboration project of Islamic feminism, I spoke with women in the Muslim-majority states of the north, where *hudud* laws were in force, and with women in the Middle Belt, where Muslims were not in the majority and *hudud* laws were nonexistent. I conducted fifty interviews in February and March 2004 in six of the twelve northern states with *hudud* laws: Kano, Katsina, Sokoto, Kaduna, Niger State, and Zamfara, and with women in Plateau State in the Middle Belt, where Muslims and Christians are roughly equal in number, to get the views of those living in states without *hudud*.[26] The overall mix of people I talked with included some men and a few Christians whom I met more by chance than by design.

My interlocutors (as I prefer to call them because the interviews resembled conversations with a vibrant give and take) were middle-class women living and working in major cities. They included activists, academics, lawyers, journalists, writers, teachers, government employees, and some students. They represented mainly two generations: those in their mid-forties and fifties, including some in their sixties who brought some historical depth to the current debates, and those generally in their thirties. Their views inform the core of this chapter. A few encounters with students in their twenties pointed to preoccupations of a third generation that would form an intriguing new project.

During my research I participated in two conferences where I had interactions with Muslims and Christians and with women and men: the Conference on Christian–Muslim Relations in Zamfara in March 2005 and the Conference on Promoting Women's Rights Through Shari'ah in Northern Nigeria, sponsored by the Centre for Islamic Legal Studies at Ahmadu Bello University in Zaria.[27] On an earlier visit to Nigeria I participated in the International Conference on the Implementation of Shari'ah in a Democracy: The Nigerian Experience, held in Abuja. My presentation, "Ongoing *Tafsir* on Men and Women in Islam: Constructions and Practices of Democracy and Social Justice"—in which I spoke about Islamic feminist discourse, focusing mainly on Amina Wadud and Asma Barlas—exposed me to the passions and perils the subject evokes.[28] These experiences in public forums were instructive and helpful in contextualizing my more private discussions with women.

In this chapter, as always, I am careful to make the distinction between Islamic feminism as a named discourse and Islamic feminist as an assumed identity. In my encounters in northern Nigeria and the Middle Belt I did not find reference made to Islamic feminism as an explicit discourse, nor did I find people who called themselves Islamic feminists. Moreover, I discovered that the terms *feminism* and *feminist* were not in general circulation and that they were highly controversial, so to use such terms publicly would be provocative and counterproductive. However, I did find what I recognized as Islamic feminist questions, concerns, ideas, and forms of activism.

Therefore, in speaking of Islamic feminism or Islamic feminists in Nigeria I use the terms in a purely analytical sense. I use these terms in order to be able to place the ideas and experience of Nigerians in the context of the global phenomenon of Islamic feminism and to discuss Nigerian expressions of Islamic feminism and their important transnational contributions. To protect their privacy, I will not identify women by name. However, I shall quote some of their words to give readers direct access to their expressive voices. All the women I quote are activists, and I identify them further simply by profession.

## WOMEN AND THE ("RETURN TO") THE SHARI'AH

You have to know shari'ah before you can implement it. We thought
that because of the enormous protection that Islam gives women that
this is what would obtain. Muslim women thought the shari'ah states
would give us this. [But] it was like we were at the receiving end. This
issue of adultery and sentencing only women to death, even the manner
in which it was done, made us feel that the shari'ah was against women,
which is not true. We feel maybe because it is a male-dominated society
and because of selfish reasons that women only are at the receiving end.
(professor)[29]

We are not quarreling with the shari'ah as a concept, but we are quarreling with the implementation. Regarding our men: Why is it for you
shari'ah implementation is about women being "proper"? If we are going to get what the shari'ah stands for then we will be better off. We are
going to hold you accountable. We are going to say the shari'ah should
be implemented with social justice. (professor)

Men hijack the shari'ah to the detriment of women. (professor)

If the rich get off and the poor "get the shari'ah on them," there will
definitely be a problem. (student)

If we practice shari'ah people will live in peace because some will not
acquire too much wealth while others live in poverty. If the shari'ah is
practiced as it should be, there will be more space for women in the
society. (professor)

During the time of the two *zina* cases women's attention was riveted on
*hudud*, but in the aftermath of the acquittals attention shifted more broadly
to discussion of the shar'iah.[30] Some two years after the second acquittal the
subject of the shari'ah kept coming up in my conversations with women. As
these quotations indicate, women repeatedly spoke of how the male-defined
shari'ah (or the "state-defined" shari'ah) was constructed and deployed
to the detriment of women and the poor. They expressed no doubt that
this was in contradiction with the Qur'anic message. The *zina* cases were a
wrenching example for women of the willingness to scapegoat women and
the poor. Women pointed out publicly (as increasingly men did as well) that
in the context of Islam *hudud* should be put in force only in a society where
the social and economic well-being of all categories of people prevail; only
then is it possible that justice might be served under *hudud*.

Concerning the state-announced "return to shari'ah," women repeated
that the shari'ah had always been integral to Muslim life in Nigeria and
important in their own lives. What was important was how the shari'ah was

understood by Muslims and to what they were "returning." In conversations women showed that they had a firm idea how patriarchal thinking had intruded into the egalitarian message of the Qur'an, thereby skewing understanding and practice of the shari'ah. The women repeatedly insisted that access to formal training in religion should be widespread among women so they could understand the shari'ah for themselves and be part of its broader articulation and practice.

Many women confided that they were not in favor of the *hudud,* and certainly not in conditions in which social and economic justice did not prevail, but with *hudud* laws already on the books they would continue their vigilant struggle for justice within the existing legal framework. Women thus chose to contest not the laws as such but rather their applications. They also did not address head-on the question of the broader idea of a state-backed shari'ah. This was a wise tactic and probably their only real option, for women, as they told me, had far less public space to debate and dissent than men. In a conference on Comparative Perspectives on Shari'ah in Nigeria at the University of Jos in January 2004, when Abdullahi An-Naim, a renowned Sudanese scholar of law and Islamic jurisprudence, argued against the notion of a state-backed shari'ah, he was met with an explosive outcry.[31]

Women found more space to confront discrimination and injustice to women in the context of the shari'ah court than in the public arena at large. It was in the context of the courts that women brought different knowledge and understanding to bear. This was a stunning case of women's activism as Islamic knowledge production. It did not escape public attention that it was women who took the initiative in coming to the defense of the accused, who were also women. Women assembled the defense teams that consisted mainly (but not only) of women lawyers and specialists, who successfully took the cases of the condemned women to the higher shari'ah courts, where only men presided. Women's voices were heard through their legal defense teams in the context of the shari'ah court system, where their solidly *fiqh*-backed arguments won the day. This underscored the notion of women as human beings (*insan*) capable of defending justice and not simply a category in need of protection or as a group of weak, deficient, and vulnerable human beings.

This usurpation of the right in the Nigerian common law system for women to act as judges, and indeed in an Islamic system (for it is patriarchal convention rather than Islamic jurisprudence that prevents women from being judges), leaves the adjudication of criminal cases in an Islamic legal context solely in the hands of men. In certain other Muslim societies, such as Iran, Sudan, and Morocco, women have been able to be judges, and more recently, as a result of the persistence of Muslim women's feminist activist struggle, women in Egypt have been allowed to be judges.[32]

The legal activism on the part of Nigerian women demonstrated that women were quicker to support—and to rally support for—the vulnerable and victimized than most men. Through their activism women not only saved other women from further victimization but served as examples of empowerment to their sisters.

It was also widely apparent that Muslim and Christian women as Nigerians worked together in the defense of their fellow citizens. One Muslim said, "I am a human rights activist. I believe in human rights because Islam has a charter. I am working with other human rights organizations because in the end we are all Nigerian. [I struggle] if my right is denied, the same with my Christian counterpart, so we are all working for human rights, but I have guidance from my religion concerning what human rights is." Another Muslim activist woman said of the Christian supporters, "The Christians did not come out as Christians but as women." I have noted elsewhere that among the binaries Islamic feminism breaks down is opposition between Muslims and non-Muslims and between the secular and the religious.

## NEED FOR NEW INTERPRETATION

> We are looking beyond old interpretations and static ways of doing things and at the need to engage with today. What will happen if Muslim women are not carried along as things are developing? The Qur'an gives women space, the right to participation, consultation. There is a tendency to use the cultural perspective to belittle women, to deny the consultation of women, making them irrelevant when it comes to decision making, making them virtual minors who cannot take decisions, who need to have others take decisions for them. Are men addressing all the issues we want them to address? Aren't women best placed to examine things from a woman's perspective? (writer)

> A problem with a lot of the *tafsir* is that it has been done centuries back. They were mainly made by scholars who had never encountered another culture so that they were operating with an understanding only of their own people. Because in Islam knowledge is a vibrant thing, ideally it should be a continuous looking at what others have done and adding to it, not just closing down and saying that's it. (professor)

> Until now the question of *ijtihad* [independent reasoning in approach to religious texts] has been kept silent. It has not been made public. (professor)

In conversations women repeatedly stressed need for women themselves to conduct interpretation of the Qur'an and *fiqh*, the core project of Islamic feminism. The two *zina* cases made dramatically clear the need for gender-sensitive readings of religious sources.

Some women who have been university professors since the 1980s explained that two decades ago they had pointed to the need for women to engage in religious interpretation. They find themselves reiterating this again today. The idea that women could read the Qur'an and other religious texts for themselves remains highly threatening to most people, especially because it could lead to the assumption of authority in religious matters on the part of women. A younger activist claimed that the trials of the two women "sensitized people to do research. The trials aroused their curiosity." She insisted that "the debates help in enlightening individuals and to push them to find out for themselves what shari'ah entails."

A young woman professor declared quite simply, "Patriarchal ideas are presented as Islamic. You read the Qur'an and find most of what they are preaching is not in the Qur'an." She repeated a point that several other women made about the lack of public space in which they can debate issues of women and Islam. She confided, "You [women] risk being called Western, radical, or even having a fatwa put on you." Speaking not only of women she continued, "Our people are now beginning to perceive the heavy dose of religious prescription they are given and that at the same time those dispensing it are not applying it to themselves." This is an example of the disenchantment I heard voiced a few years earlier from the state-heralded "return to the shari'ah" in the wake of the *zina* cases. Women and the poor became the touchstone of society's protracted wait for justice.

How to take the analysis into public space and make it operative? Repeatedly women spoke about the problem of being ostracized if they were too outspoken in public about their views on "sensitive issues" such as women and the shari'ah. I heard the term "no-go area" often in relation to controversial subjects and was plainly told that men have far more leeway to dissent in public than women. Although women have greater space to speak out in the contexts of universities and certain nongovernment organizations, they are still more constrained than men are. One activist and former university professor said, "It is a social precept that Islam does not allow women to question, to condemn." Another professor and activist exclaimed, "Until now the question of *ijtihad* or critical intellectual inquiry into religious sources has been kept silent. It has not been made public."

## RECUPERATING A LOCAL FEMALE TRADITION OF SCHOLARSHIP AND AUTHORITY

Claiming a line of scholarly women in the Islamic tradition is important for contemporaries in establishing legitimacy and authority as women in the field of religious learning. Compiling histories of Muslim women of the past as models and inspiration for present-day women is integral to the project of Muslim women's feminisms. The genre of biographical dictionary holds a central place in Islamic scholarship. Pakistani activists and Shirgat Gah members Farida Shaheed and Aisha Shaheed made a recent contribution to this genre when they published *Great Ancestors: Women Asserting Their*

*Rights in Muslim Contexts,* which includes an essay on the illustrious Nigerian woman Nana Asma'u.[33]

Muslim women in Nigeria today who are not finding it easy to occupy a place in the ranks of *ulemah* or Islamic scholars as Qur'anic interpreters or specialists in *fiqh* and other Islamic sciences can claim Nana Asma'u (1793–1864) as a revered female ancestor and renowned Islamic scholar and teacher and through her claim legitimacy for the work of contemporary women as religious scholars. Nana Asma'u, who came from a family of women and men who were religious scholars, was the daughter of Osman Dan Fodio, leader of the religious revival and founder of the Sokoto Caliphate.[34] She is well known for playing a key role in the spread of the Islamic revival and especially in the education of women.

FOMWAN dedicated the cover story "Muslim Women Scholars" in its journal *The Muslim Woman* in celebration of its twentieth anniversary in 2005 to promote the education, including religious education, of women.[35] Sa'idiyya Umar, FOMWAN member and director of the Center for Hausa Studies at Uthman Dan Fodio University in Sokoto, sees in the *yantaru* movement that Nana Asma'u led, bringing schooling in religion and other subjects to women in villages far and wide, a model that FOMWAN continues today in its mission to provide religious formation and education for Muslim women throughout the country.[36] Laying claim to her past, Asmau Joda, activist and member of Baobab, asserted, "In my Fulani community women have for centuries had a long tradition of being religious scholars. Asma'u, daughter of Osman Dan Fodio, was appointed in charge of religious affairs by her brother Muhammad Bello." She insisted, "We have to re-read our histories."[37]

## CLAIMING A DEPATRIARCHALIZED ISLAM

It was evident in private conversations between women that the recent trials had triggered renewed debates about gender equality and social justice as principles found in the Qur'an but lacking in society, indicating an accelerated impatience with the lack of delivery of promises that the acclaimed "return to the shari'ah" held out and the kind of oppression that can come with so-called law reform. The debates and activism around the *zina* cases produced a heightened Islamic feminist consciousness. They led to a clash of consciousnesses in Nigeria: an Islamic feminist consciousness and the Islamist or neofundamentalist consciousness. They represented very different approaches to the shari'ah and to the law. The challenge for women is to move from analysis to action in the arena of the community and society at large, and not in the restricted atmosphere of the shari'ah courts. How can women construct a functioning depatriarchalized Islam?

Islamic feminism, by whatever name, in Nigeria as elsewhere is a work in progress. Nigerian Muslim women are aware of the challenge of moving themselves and the culture beyond patriarchy claiming to be Islamic into the space where an egalitarian Islam is operative. From what I observed in Nigeria it seems that a process is under way that cannot be reversed. It also appears that the road ahead to a depatriarchalized Islam there, as elsewhere, will be long and full of perils. However, the Nigerian success story in the *zina* cases and the debates about Islam and the shari'ah, and about equality and justice, is a salient chapter in the local and global Islamic feminist narrative.

## NOTES

1. It is a pleasure to express my thanks for the support that made this research both possible and enriching. I am grateful to the Fulbright New Century Scholars program for inviting me to be part of the cohort of scholars in 2003–2004 around the theme of global women's empowerment. I thank Ayesha Imam for facilitating my affiliation with Baobab during the course of my project and for members with whom I corresponded and met in person. I am grateful to Habu Muhammad, whom I met when he was a Fulbright scholar at the Program of African Studies in Northwestern University and who was very helpful in introducing me to people in Kano, where he teaches at Bayero University in the Department of Political Science. I am grateful to Haruna Wakili, director of Mambaya House, and Ismaila Zango, deputy director, and the professors at Bayero University for their warm welcome and help during my stay in Kano. I thank Hamidu Bobboyi, then director of Arewa House, for the hospitality he extended and Aisha Lemu and her husband, Sheikh Lemu, for having me as their guest in Minna. I thank my colleague and friend Muhammad Sane Umar for our many conversations both in Evanston and in Jos, where he was most helpful during my stay, as was Philip Ostien of the University of Jos. I thank all the women with whom I had extended interview-conversations for sharing their knowledge and for their candor and wit. They are at the center of this work. I also wish to thank Carolyn Elliott, who was a superb leader of the New Century Scholar group and who has been helpful to all of us right up to the final editing of this volume. I appreciate the keen eye she brought to my chapter.

2. See Philip Ostien, Jamila M. Nasir, and Franz Kogelmann, eds., *Comparative Perspectives on the Shari'ah in Nigeria* (Ibadan, Nigeria: Spectrum Books, 2005). This is a collection of papers from a conference on the shari'ah held in Jos in 2004 as part of a year-long project undertaken by the University of Jos and the University of Bayreuth, Germany, under the rubric "The Shari'ah Debate and the Shaping of Muslim and Christian Identities in Northern Nigeria."

3. For a stunning analysis of *zina* and contextualization of *hudud*, see Charmaine Pereira, *"Zina* and Transgressive Heterosexuality in Northern Nigeria." *Feminist Africa: Sexual Cultures* 5 (2005), 52–80.

4. The network Women Living Under Muslim Laws has circulated a huge amount of information on women suffering under *hudud* laws, as have women's association in different countries where *hudud* laws are in effect, such as Iran and Pakistan.

5. I wrote an article about my encounters, "Liberties of the Faithful," *Al Ahram Weekly* (May 19–25, 2005) that has been published in a slightly different form in Margot Badran, *Feminism Beyond East and West: New Gender Talk and Practice in Global Islam* (New Delhi: Global Media Publications, 2006): 67–76.

6. See Margot Badran, *Feminists, Islam, and Nation: Gender and the Making of Modern Egypt* (Princeton, NJ: Princeton University Press, 1995).

7. WLUML, *Knowing Our Rights: Women, Family, Laws and Customs in the Muslim World* (New Delhi: Zubaan, 2003).

8. On WLUML see Farida Shaheed (one of the founding members), "Networking for Change: The Role of Women's Groups in Initiating Dialogue on Women's Issues." In *Faith and Freedom*, ed. Mahnaz Afkhami (Syracuse, NY: Syracuse University Press, 1995); and Valentine M. Moghadam, *Globalizing Women: Transnational Feminist Networks* (Baltimore: The Johns Hopkins University Press, 2005).

9. Sanusi Lamido Sanusi, "Fundamentalist Groups and the Nigerian Legal System: Some Reflections" *Warning Signs of Fundamentalism,* Women Living Under Muslim Laws (WLUML), (London: December 2004) 79–82, provides telling insights into the movement and its implications. For a detailed study of the Izala movement see Ousmane Kane, *Muslim Modernity in Postcolonial Nigeria: The Society for the Removal of Innovation and Reinstatement of Tradition* (Leiden, The Netherlands: Brill, 2003). The reader will note two different translations of this group's name; in the text I have preferred to use the one provided by Sanusi.

10. Muhammad Sane Umar discusses this young woman (preserving her anonymity) in "Mass Islamic Education and Emergence of Female 'Ulema' in Northern Nigeria: Background, Trends, and Consequences." In *The Transmission of Learning in Islamic Africa,* ed. Scott S. Reese (Leiden, The Netherlands: Brill, 2004).

11. For a self-profiled history of FOMWAN and its present structure and work, see "FOMWAN: Twenty Years of Service to Islam," *FOMWAN* (2005). It is now under the leadership of its fifth head or *amirah,* Bilkisu Yusuf.

12. *Baobab for Women's Human Rights and Sharia Implementation in Nigeria: The Journey So Far* (Lagos, Nigeria: Baobab, 2003).

13. I looked at Islamic feminism in a talk in Cairo in 2002 and another one in Cairo in 2006. These are, respectively, "Islamic Feminism: What's in a Name?" and "Islamic Feminism Revisited," available on the Web site of *Al Ahram Weekly* (http://www.ahram.org.eg/weekly) (last accessed July 7, 2007), where they were first published, and in *Feminism Beyond East and West* (2006): 23–42.

14. I have discussed the confluences of Muslim women's secular feminisms in "Locating Feminisms: The Collapse of Secular and Religious Discourses in the Muslim Mashriq," *Agenda* (South African feminist journal, special issue on African feminisms), 59 (2001): 41–57; and "Between Secular Feminism and Islamic Feminism: Reflections on the Middle East and Beyond," *Journal of Middle East Women's Studies* (inaugural issue, January 2005): 6–28.

15. Amina Wadud, *Qur'an and Woman: Rereading the Sacred Text from a Woman's Perspective* (New York: Oxford University Press, 1999).

16. Asma Barlas, *"Believing Women" in Islam: Unreading Patriarchal Interpretations of the Qur'an* (Austin: University of Texas Press, 2002).

17. Ziba Mir-Hosseini, *The Religious Debate in Contemporary Iran* (Princeton, NJ: Princeton University Press, 1999) and *Marriage on Trial: A Study of Family Law, Iran and Morocco* (New York: I.B. Tauris, 2000).

18. The most recent example is the reform of the Moroccan Mudawwana in 2004, which is now the most progressive shari'ah-backed Muslim family law. The earliest feminist efforts to reform Muslim personal status law go back to early twentieth-century Egypt, where the battle has been sustained but the gains minimal.

19. For a concise clarification of this, see Ziba Mir-Hosseini, "Muslim Women's Quest for Equality: Between Islamic Law and Feminism," *Critical Inquiry* (Summer 2006): 629–645.

20. On "the return to the shari'ah" in Nigeria, see Philip Ostien et al. (2005).

21. For a general exposition of *hudud,* see Cherif Bassiouni, ed., *The Islamic Criminal Justice System* (New York: Oceana, 1980).

22. See Khawar Mumtaz and Farida Shaheed, *Women of Pakistan: Two Steps Forward, One Step Backward?* (London: Zed, 1987); Anita Weiss, ed., "Implications of the Islamization Program for Women." In *Islamic Reassertion in Pakistan: The Application of Islamic Laws in a Modern State* (Syracuse, NY: Syracuse University Press, 1986); and Anita Weiss, "Women's Action Forum." In *The Oxford Encyclopedia of the Modern Islamic World,* vol. 4 (Oxford: Oxford University Press, 1995): 346–348. Shahla Haeri deals with the *hudud* and Islamization process initiated by the state in *No Shame for the Sun: Lives of Professional Pakistani Women* (Syracuse, NY: Syracuse University Press, 2002).

23. See http://www.meydaan.org and Soheila Vahdati, "Stop Stonings in Iran, but Don't Confuse the Issue" *Women's eNews* (January 4, 2007).

24. I am grateful for Richard Joseph and Ndubisi Obiorah for confirming this observation.

25. On transcommunal cooperation see Ayesha Imam, "Fighting the Political (Ab)Use of Religion in Nigeria: Baobab for Women's Human Rights, Allies, and Others." In *Fundamentalism: Warning Signs, Law, Media and Resistances,* eds. Ayesha Imam, Jenny Morgan, and Nira Yuval-Davis, eds. http://www.wluml.org (December 2004).

26. I originally wanted to speak with women of more modest backgrounds from villages and major cities, but for a number of reasons this was beyond my reach.

27. In the Conference on Christian–Muslim Relations I was invited to give a presentation and encouraged to be an active participant. I received an invitation from the organizers to attend the Conference on Promoting Women's Rights Through Shari'ah in Northern Nigeria, where I was strictly an observer in the plenary sessions, although I contributed in the breakout session. In the first conference in Zamfara women and men intermixed in the seating; in the Kaduna conference women and men were arranged in parallel groups in the hall.

28. My presentation provoked both critical and favorable responses, more the former than the latter.

29. All the activists I interviewed are women from various professions. I include quotations because the women's words are pithy and powerful. Purely summarizing their thoughts and arguments does not convey the same force.

30. Although my focus is on the debates as I gleaned them through interviews, conversations, group discussions, and conferences, much has been written in the press and learned publications. FOMWAN dedicated a special issue of *The Muslim Woman* to the theme "Sharia Implementation in Nigeria," vol. 8, 2003. In keeping with FOMWAN's education mission, stress is laid on the importance of education in understanding and living by the shari'ah.

31. See his paper, "The Future of *Shari'ah* and the Debate in Northern Nigeria." In *Comparative Perspectives on the Shari'ah in Nigeria,* eds. Philip Ostien, Jamila M. Nasir, and Franz Kogelmann, 327–357 (Ibadan, Nigeria: Spectrum Books, 2005).

32. This adverse effect of the enactment of *hudud* has yet to be widely noticed. A woman lawyer, activist, and daughter of a former grand *qadi* said in an interview, "If a woman can adjudicate under common law I do not see any reason why she cannot do so as well under shari'ah law."

33. Farida Shaheed and Aisha Shaheed, eds., *Great Ancestors: Women Asserting Their Rights in Muslim Contexts* (Lahore, Pakistan: Shirgat Gah, 2004); for essay on "Nana Asma'u, see pp 51–54.

34. For an analysis of Asma'u's scholarly work and poetry in the context of Muslim intellectual and political life, see Beverly Mack, "Muslim Women's Knowledge

Production in the Greater Maghreb." In *Gender and Islam in Africa,* ed. Margot Badran (Leiden: Brill, 2007). For the first full-length biography see Jean Boyd, *The Caliph's Sister* (London: Frank Cass, 1989), and on her oeuvre see Jean Boyd and Beverly Mack, *The Collected Works of Nana Asma'u bint Shehu Usman Dan Fodio 1793–1864* (East Lansing: Michigan State University Press, 1997).

35. "Muslim Women Scholars," *The Muslim Woman* 9 (2005), 9–10.
36. Sa'idiyya Umar, "Nana Asma'u the Great Scholar," *The Muslim Woman* 9 (2005), 8–17.
37. Interview with Yoginder Sikand. http://www.islaminterfaith.org (accessed Dec. 15, 2006).

# 10 The Land of Real Men and Real Women

## Gender and EU Accession in Three Polish Weeklies

*Agnieszka Graff*[1]

In the period before and immediately after Poland's accession to the European Union (May 1, 2004) Polish media were overflowing with "gender talk." On the radio one would hear randomly placed banter about "natural differences between the sexes" (in fact, a new station, FM 94, was established in 2002 with "real men" in mind). Almost any event discussed on the evening news could spark a comment such as "this is what women are like" or "men cannot help but be men." Magazines and newspapers provided an abundance of images featuring manly men and womanly women, as well as departures from such norm, notably drag queens from the Berlin Love Parades.

This article looks at a small portion of this broader phenomenon, examining a selection of gender-focused stories and images published in three mainstream political weeklies—*Polityka, Wprost,* and *Newsweek Polska*—between the spring of 2002 and the summer of 2005.[2] My first aim is to demonstrate the abundance of "gender talk" in the three magazines. Second, I show that around May 2004 discourse on gender difference intensified abruptly, particularly in the conservative *Wprost,* which was featuring stories about femininity and/or masculinity every other week in this period. The phenomenon observed here is highly formulaic, so a major part of this study is devoted to defining the formula and interpreting its significance. My purpose is to suggest a link between the media's obsessive concern with gender and the process of Poland's EU accession. I argue that anxieties evoked by Poland's EU accession have been projected onto, and resolved within, the realm of gender. In a final section, I return to the three weeklies, suggesting a typology of gendered nationalisms. In elaborating this argument, I refer to various theorizations of gender and nationalism,[3] including a recent Polish contribution to this debate.[4]

## LISTENING TO GENDER TALK

*Polityka, Newsweek,* and *Wprost* represent the mainstream of Polish print media; they are the top three opinion weeklies on the market in terms of distribution, selling between 130,000 and 165,000 copies per week.[5] On the spectrum of political views they range from liberal or progressive and pro-EU (*Polityka*) to neoliberal and neoconservative (*Wprost*), with *Newsweek* somewhat uneasily trying to occupy a neutral space where various views of social phenomena are examined from a "common sense" point of view. As I will show, however, common sense in Poland tends to be conservative, especially where gender issues are concerned. Despite the differences between the weeklies, there is one striking similarity: In the period that interests us here all three presented a consistently pro-EU line, supporting Poland's accession and encouraging readers to vote "yes" in the June 2003 referendum.[6]

Between April 2002 and May 2005 the magazines asked a number of worried questions about gender roles, sexuality, and reproduction in Poland. Here is a representative sample of cover stories: "What Does a Man Want Today? To Remain Themselves, Men Increasingly Take Up Femininity"[7] (*Newsweek*, April 21, 2002) (Figure 10.1), "How to Raise a Child on Weekends. Working Mothers Besieged by Good Advice" (*Polityka*, February 7, 2004), "SHE works, HE does not. How the Shock on the Labor Market Destabilized the Traditional Polish Family" (*Newsweek*, June 1, 2003) (Figure 10.2), "Special Protection for Women. Who Needs the Government Gender Equality Program?" (*Newsweek*, September 7, 2004), and "More Freedom—But What About Sex? New Research on Erotic Lives of Polish Women" (*Newsweek*, May 24, 2004).

In the spring and summer of 2004 the spotlight was on reproduction: "If We Want to Be a Healthy Society—Let's Make Babies" (*Polityka*, August 14, 2004) (Figure 10.3) and "The Last Parents. Dramatic Decline in Polish Population" (*Wprost*, April 11, 2004) (Figure 10.4). In the summer of 2003 the largely progressive *Polityka* wrote about intolerance toward sexual minorities ("Homo-Condemnation," August 9, 2003). A year later the weekly turned its attention specifically to lesbians ("When a Woman Loves a Woman," September 4, 2004). In March 2003 the magazine featured a group of feminists on its cover ("Women's Rebellion. Polish Feminists Take to the Streets," March 8, 2003). Meanwhile, *Wprost* was concerned about the way sexual minorities and feminists "terrorize" the "normal" majority ("The Terror of Equality," June 13, 2004). On a more optimistic note, the magazines were preoccupied with the prospect of Poland having a female president (*Polityka*, September 13, 2003) and with Polish women's skills in various lines of business—vastly superior, according to *Wprost*, to those of women in Western countries ("What Polish Women Can Do," November 30, 2003). Finally—a theme to which we will return—soon after Poland's EU accession, *Wprost* reassured its readers, announcing "The Return of the Real Man" (May 30, 2004) (Figure 10.5). Nevertheless, the magazines were soon worrying again about "The Unfaithful Wife" (*Newsweek*, July 26, 2004) and the results of her philandering ("Am I the Daddy? 12 Thousand Polish Men Have Taken DNA Tests to Find Out," *Wprost*, February 13, 2005).

**Figure 10.1.** Newsweek Cover (21 April 2002). "What Does a Man Today Want?"

Each of the articles comes with an image, for they are all cover stories. In each case, the front page features a photograph of (usually anonymous) men and women, ultramasculine and ultrafeminine, respectively. Many of the *Wprost* covers can be described as quasipornographic: Of the sixteen gender-focused

LATO Polacy wykupują Chorwację   MATNIA 2 Łapiński i jego związki z FOZZ

www.newsweek.pl

**Newsweek** POLSKA

22/2003 1.06.03

**Wstrząs**
na rynku
pracy
zachwiał
tradycyjną
polską
rodziną
—
**43%**
badanych
zna rodziny,
w których
kariera żony
stała się
ważniejsza

**41%**
mężczyzn
uważa wyższe
zarobki żony
za stan
normalny

**ONA PRACUJE ON NIE**

Figure 10.2. Newsweek cover (1 June 2003). "SHE Works; HE Does Not."

covers that appeared between June 2002 and May 2005, six featured air-brushed nude bodies. In four cases these are bodies of both sexes; in two, all we get is a female body, enlarged, with focus on buttocks or breasts, the head carefully left out of the frame (May 25, 2003; April 4, 2004). The couples are arranged in poses resembling sexual acts, the woman clearly "on top,"

PSYCHOLODZY W **NERWACH** DYPLOMACI **DO WYMIANY** **CO WOLNO** PROBOSZCZOM

TYGODNIK
Nr 33 (2465)
14 sierpnia 2004
(Aug 14. 2004)
cena 4,50 zł
(w tym 7% VAT)
Nr indeksu
369195
www.polityka.com.pl

**POLITYKA**

Jacek Żakowski apeluje:

Jeśli chcemy
być zdrowym
społeczeństwem

**Róbmy dzieci!**

**Figure 10.3.** Polityka cover (14 August 2004). "If We Want to be a Healthy Society: Let's Make Children."

dominating the man. In the most explicit image, the woman is riding the man like a horse, holding the reins rather tightly (July 14, 2002). Such images were more than magazine covers to be enjoyed in private. On the contrary, they received enormous public visibility. Displayed on newsstands the week a

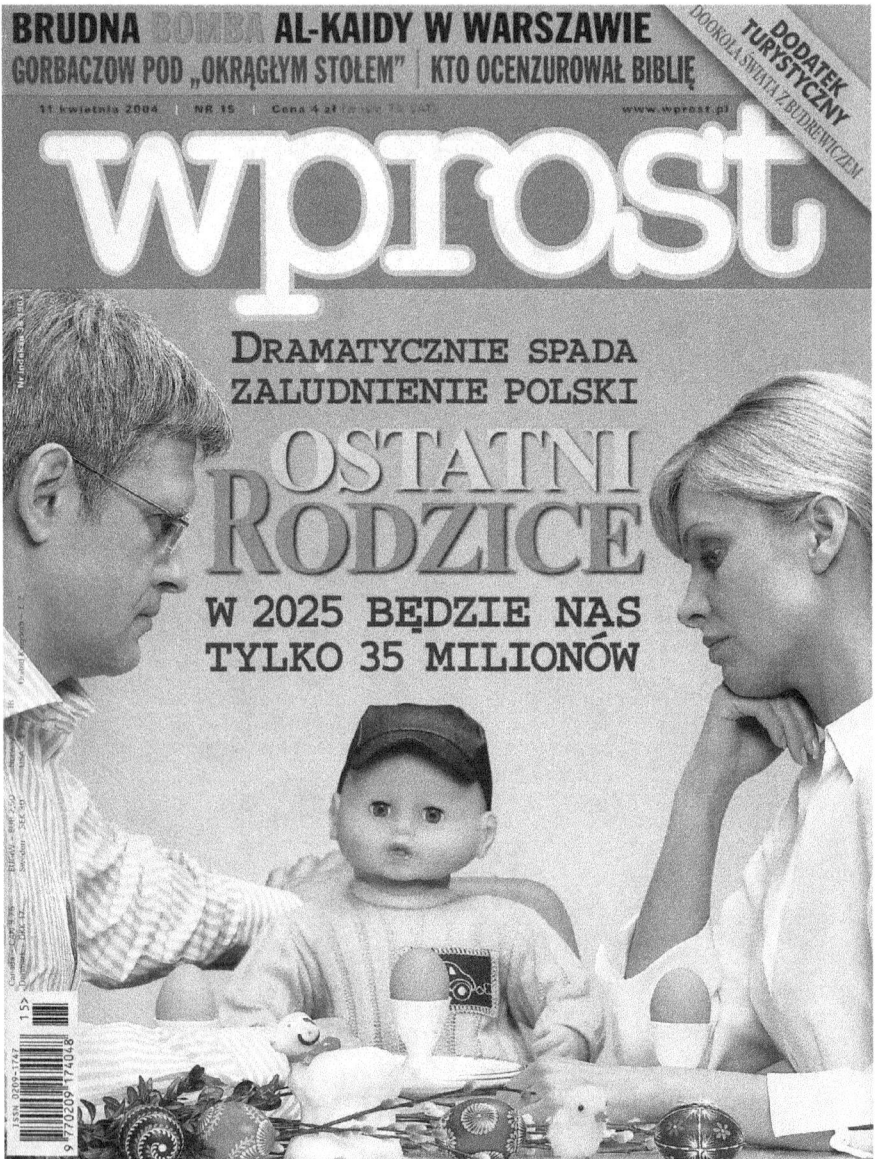

**Figure 10.4.** Wprost cover (11 April 2004). "The Last Parents. Dramatic Decline in Polish Population." (authors: Marek Król and Tomasz Strzyzewski)

given magazine came out, they lingered in various waiting rooms for months afterwards. More importantly perhaps, they occupied public space, especially in urban centers, in the form of large posters advertising the weeklies.

**Figure 10.5.** Wprost cover (30 May 2004). "The Return of the Real Man." (authors: Marek Król and Tomasz Strzyzewski.

What does this deluge of stereotypical, and sometimes pornographic, imagery signify? The easy answer is that the magazines in question compete for mainstream readership, and everyone knows that sex sells. Another explanation is that the weeklies are providing a representation of social reality; after all, Poland is going through a major shift in gender relations, a "renegotiation of the sexual contract," as one sociologist calls it.⁸ A third response—one I relied on in my own thinking until recently—is to rely on the concept of backlash.⁹ Most of the articles are only marginally concerned with social reality; more often, they engage in myth making, in revealing "eternal truths" about men and women. These "truths" are naturalizations of inequality. Many pieces of "gender news" in Polish media are recycled versions of fad-driven stories from Western, mostly American, media of the last three decades. They exemplify the rhetoric described in Faludi's *Backlash:* Women want to have it all, but we know this is impossible; men would gladly welcome equality, but women really love to be dominated; equality is a great thing, but children suffer, and so on.

These explanations are satisfactory in many ways, but they cannot account for the intensification of "gender talk" in the period of EU accession (i.e., in the spring of 2004). This was especially pronounced in the one magazine that was Euro-skeptical (though never explicitly opposed to EU accession): *Wprost.* My sixteen gender-focused *Wprost* covers come from period of thirty-six months, during which a total of 151 issues appeared (nos. 1019–1170). This amounts to 10.6 percent, or roughly one in nine covers devoted to gender in these three years. Yet five of the sixteen appeared between early April and mid-June 2004, which makes precisely 50 percent of *Wprost*'s covers in this period.

The jump is even more astounding if we consider the context. Poland was voluntarily giving up much of its autonomy as a state in order to join the European community of nations; meanwhile, *Wprost* was focusing its attention on men, women, and the games they play (or do not play) with each other. The stories progressed as follows: "E-Sexphilia" (April 4, 2004), on the disturbing implications of Internet sex; "The Last Parents" (April 11, 2004), on the impending demographic catastrophe caused by excessive professional ambitions of women; "To Marry a Pole" (May 16, 2004), on the rising demand for Poles of both sexes on the European marriage market; "The Return of the Real Man" (May 30, 2004), on the demise of feminism and inevitability of patriarchy; and finally "The Dictatorship of Equality" (June 13, 2004), about sexual minorities and feminists who engage in "cultural terrorism" in the name of "political correctness." Poland's EU accession took place on May 1, between *Wprost*'s jeremiad on falling birth rates and its proud announcement that Poles are desired as wives and husbands.

## GENDER TALK AS DISPLACED NATIONALISM

*Wprost*'s optimistic announcement of "The Return of the Real Man" is no more and no less fact-based than its anxiety about the unsatisfactory nature of Internet sex or the "crisis of masculinity" that troubled *Newsweek* two years earlier. Rather than search for gender realities behind the gender myths, I want to argue that the stories are symptoms of a process that is not really, or at least not primarily, about gender. In my view, the media's preoccupation with masculinity, femininity, and sexual orientation is tied to Poland's EU accession, a link that becomes apparent once we focus on the structure of the stories rather than try to identify the social realities they claim to describe. A highly formulaic narrative emerges from the mass of articles I have examined. The master story unfolds as follows: Things used to be "normal" and "natural," men and women used to know who they are, but sex roles in Poland—indeed, worldwide—are in crisis today, so that the future looks bleak. Nonetheless, the natural order (i.e., male domination) will soon be restored. This structure appears in many of the individual articles, but it can also be traced on an intratextual level: The progression of *Wprost* articles in April–May 2004 also roughly reproduces the sequence. It is hardly a coincidence that "The Return of the Real Man" was announced a week after EU accession. The consoling narrative about an orderly past, the present crisis, and an imminent restoration of order in the realm of gender relations can be read as a displaced narrative about collective identity, an effort to contain ambivalence and anxiety about European integration. EU accession symbolizes a broader set of issues here: the ongoing systemic transformation, the pressures of globalization, and the resulting diminution of Poland's autonomy as a nation-state a mere decade and a half after this autonomy was restored.

The link I diagnose here is not unique to Poland, of course. Many scholars, focusing on a variety of cultural and historical contexts, have examined the close ties between discourses about gender and those that define national, racial, or ethnic identity.[10] There is also an ongoing debate within feminist theory about tensions and alliances that arise, because of the gendered nature of ethnic identity, between feminism and multiculturalism.[11] The central insight and departure point of these various studies is that the seemingly neutral liberal discourse on citizenship notoriously excludes women,[12] and nationalist discourses tend to be heavily gendered in ways that limit women's agency, particularly in the spheres of sexuality and reproduction. To quote Anthias and Yuval-Davis,

> Women do not only teach and transfer the cultural and ideological traditions of ethnic and national groups. Very often they constitute their actual symbolic figuration. The nation as a loved woman in danger or as a mother who lost her sons in battle is a frequent part of the particular nationalist discourse in national liberation struggles or other forms of national conflicts when men are called to fight 'for the sake of our women and children' or to 'defend their honour.' Often the distinction between one ethnic group and another is constituted centrally by the sexual behavior of women.[13]

Nation and gender are both culturally constructed categories; moreover, they construct each other via notions of what is "natural" and what is "cultural." The negotiation of gender difference and the advancement of nationalism are parallel processes: Ideologies that naturalize gender tend to naturalize race and ethnicity as well. As Mosse (1985, 1–47, 133–153) elaborates, the history of nationalism is deeply enmeshed in the development of another powerful discourse: that of "respectability," the bourgeois ethos that idealizes moderation, control of passion, discipline, and purity. In Europe both ideologies reached their peak influence in the early nineteenth century. Significantly, both nationalism and respectability cohered around an ideal of "manliness," young and virile but chaste. Nationalism excluded all that was "unmanly" (particularly homosexuality), and sexual stigma often was projected onto the ethnic or racial other (as in the attribution of homosexuality to Jews in Nazi Germany). As Yuval-Davis (1998) and others have shown, women are rarely vilified as outsiders, but they rarely attain the position of full participants of national processes. Their role is primarily that of biological reproducers and bearers of culture, and the nation itself is allegorically represented as a woman. Whether this woman is imagined as young or old, fertile or infertile, safe or in permanent danger, says a lot about a given group's self-image. Following Boehmer, McClintock (1996, 261) argues that "the male role in the nationalist scenario is typically 'metonymic.'" Men are examples, parts of the whole called nation; women, on the other hand, are placed in a "metaphoric" or symbolic relation to the collectivity. "Excluded from direct action as national citizens, women are subsumed symbolically into the national body politic as its boundary and metaphoric limit."

In our three weeklies it is often not just woman that serves as metaphor for nation but rather woman as half of a couple, where the other half might be present, implied, or conspicuously absent. *Wprost*'s images of couples with the woman in the dominant position can be read as an expression of anxiety that EU membership will disturb "natural" social hierarchies. In this context it is useful to call up Joan W. Scott's argument that at the center of French identity resides the idea of complementarity of the sexes, the image of a heterosexual couple in erotic tension, with the woman responsive to the desiring male gaze. Scott rereads French universalism, arguing that the preoccupation with headscarves in schools and the tendency to call them "veils" result from the gendered and (hetero)sexualized construction of French national identity.[14] A similar dynamic seems to be at work in the Polish fantasy about the gender order in crisis. The difference is that Polish "gender talk" places more emphasis on fertility and reproduction, whereas the French discourse on national identity seems to rely more on norms concerning eroticism.

The idea of woman's problematic relationship to nationhood and citizenship has been taken up by several Polish scholars in recent years, often in relation to the history of anti-Semitism in Poland.[15] Janion (2004, 15), one of Poland's most renowned public intellectuals, argues that we are in the midst of a convulsive "farewell to Poland," to the romantic and peculiarly gendered mythology that has ruled our collective imagination for more than 200 years: "Poland has been represented as an allegory, symbol, myth. The motherland's body was usually a body filled with suffering, pain, misery—a body in chains, in stocks, pushed into an open grave, even crucified. She has died before our eyes, but we knew she would be resurrected. She sent her sons to their death in the name of this resurrection, and they went willingly. Dressed in dark flowing robes, this mother in deep mourning awakened in us dread and terror, but also a sense of pity, a quivering, fearful sort of love."

According to Janion, Poland-the-dying-mother-of-us-all has evolved into a grotesque caricature of her former self. Conservative politicians now in power believe in keeping the corpse alive, but the youngest generation of Polish writers, artists, and intellectuals is bidding an impatient and often disrespectful farewell to nationalist ideology. Janion cites a number of recent essays and novels in which the phantasmic body of Poland turns out to be ludicrous, pitiful, and contemptible. There is nothing romantic about the disillusion; it is a symptom of the bankruptcy of national ideology. Yet the time of crisis has the merit of making the ties between gender and nation-hood grotesquely conspicuous.

## FROM "SEX-MISSION" (1983) TO "E-SEXPHILIA" (2004)

A few years ago I proposed an account of the link between gender and transition from communism based on a reading of a particular cultural text: *Sex-mission*,[16] a popular Polish science fiction comedy released in 1983.[17] I argued that our recent history has been told through an extended gendered metaphor: State socialism was imagined as a totalitarian matriarchy with no private sphere and no intimacy, a world of castrated men and overbearing women. *Sex-mission* is merely the best-known representation of this popular fantasy. The movie is a political allegory with the communist state shown as an underground world inhabited solely by women, ruled by an absurdly inept feminist–totalitarian regime, and held in place thanks to a lie: the claim that the earth above is uninhabitable because of nuclear radiation. The woman who rules this state, known as Her Excellency, later turns out to be a homosexual man who had resorted to a life of cross-dressing because of his terror of women. The "normal" (i.e., heterosexual and patriarchal) world order is restored by two brave men who find themselves trapped in the land of feminists. Their struggle—clearly that of two "dissidents"—is the plot of the film and the source of its humor. Victory comes when the heroes seduce two of the women and sabotage the feminist baby factory so that it produces a male infant. The underground world—a sort of undifferentiated subterranean womb—can now be abandoned, and life can begin aboveground, with the two sexes in their proper spheres. The film's closing frame is a still: the newborn male's sexual organ in close-up.

In the 1990s, the transition to democracy established itself in collective consciousness as the remasculinization of national culture, allegedly feminized by state socialism. As British political scientist Peggy Watson argues, "The political exclusion of women as distinct from men—their reconfiguration as a 'minority'—. . . [is] constitutive of the democratization of Eastern Europe. In the West 'backlash' is a name some have given to intimations of this built-in democratic exclusion."[18] The logic of recovery from *Sex-mission* has required women's contribution to Solidarity to be forgotten[19] so that transition to democracy could be coded as restoration of a patriarchy. Backlash against women's rights was legitimized within a narrative of return to normalcy and national sovereignty. Traditional gender roles became a guarantee of stability in an otherwise unstable world.

The present analysis of "gender talk" found in Polish media of 2002–2005 shows that the central myth of *Sex-mission* was recycled yet again during the period of EU accession. This time it was not communism but the influence of the EU that was represented as a reversal of gender roles. In the eyes of conservative commentators, EU legislation on gender equality and sexual minority rights was a sign of weakness and effeminacy; it was suggested that the Polish attitude toward the EU should be more manly. The following quotation comes from a *Wprost* editorial, printed in the "E-Sexphilia" issue (April 4, 2004, 3), a month before accession. It is a scathing criticism of those who want to deal gently with the EU, that is, those who support the draft of the Constitutional Treaty debated at the time:

> Have the impression that the great love of the members of the Party of the White Flag for the real Europeans (those based in Paris and Berlin) is a lot like sex performed without a real partner. . . . . The Euro-constitution and the European lobby in Paris and Berlin are very much like orgazmotrons (devices for reaching orgasm). In contact with them, the Polish hyper-Europeans are achieving virtual orgasms, which is to say they are really Euro-masturbating.

The metaphor linking EU accession and sex is so overdeveloped here that it slides into a grotesque catachresis. If enthusiasm for the EU is a form of masturbation, then a tough negotiating position becomes proper heterosexual intercourse, penetration and all, with Poland in the active role. The building blocks for this bizarre metaphor are provided by the issue's cover story on the European fad of sex without partners. Westerners, we are told, are all but addicted to the use of the Internet for sexual pleasure. The title of this article, "E-Sexphilia," is an obvious allusion to *Sex-mission* (in Polish, *seksmisja, seksfilia*). When the editorial links both to Poland's EU accession, the implications are clear: The EU turns out to be a threat to Poland's autonomy comparable to Soviet domination. Poland is again threatened by the feminine element; only a prompt return to virility can save us.

The sexualization of nationalist categories is rarely as explicit as in the aforementioned example, but it is hardly a coincidence that pictures in my collection project anxiety about both hierarchy and reproduction. Consider the following images featured on covers of the three weeklies:

- Woman in business suit with child but no man (*Polityka,* February 7, 2004)
- Man with a baby but no woman (*Newsweek,* April 21, 2002)
- Many babies, no parents to be seen (*Polityka,* August 14, 2004)
- Man, woman, and plastic doll (instead of child) at breakfast table against a sickly green background (*Wprost,* April 11, 2004)
- Tall woman dressed for success towering over an incompetent man (no child) (*Newsweek,* June 1, 2003)

Also worthy of special mention are two images of gender reversal:

- The presidential couple portrayed with swapped bodies. The result clearly is more catastrophic for him than for her; the first lady looks quite attractive, if somewhat bulky, as a man, but the president is ridiculous as a woman, complete with a woman's sexy legs and shoes (*Polityka,* April 13, 2003, 23; illustration of an article on Jolanta Kwaśniewska's presidential ambitions).
- A somewhat dazed-looking woman nursing a grown man in a business suit, small enough to fit in her arms (*Wprost,* March 9, 2003, 60; illustrating an article on women's excessive power in Polish society) (Figure 10.6).

All these images represent departure from an implied norm in family relations. All are anxious and worried. They speak eloquently of lack, dissatisfaction, imbalance, and the yearning for a natural order. Finally, they rely on the addressee's ability to call up such an order or norm: a fantasy of familial bliss, a heterosexual, clearly differentiated and hierarchical couple with many children. A series of such reassuring images is presented inside the cover story on childlessness and imminent demographic catastrophe in the April 11, 2004, issue of *Wprost* (p. 24). We are to accept the large Polish family as the healthy alternative to the man–woman–plastic doll trio on the cover. The article itself draws a clear link between having many children, being a Polish patriot, and faring well in the capitalist market. According to the author, the traditional family—stay-at-home mom, dad driven to succeed by the need to "feed" his brood, numerous children educated to be real patriots—constitutes "the best capital" and a "perfect micro-market." In short, a patriarchal family serves one well in a "liberal economy." Enemies of such a family are also mentioned: they include Lenin, Hitler, Stalin, Mao, and Pol Pot, as well as socialists and "feminist ideology." Today, we are told, the family remains under threat in Europe (as opposed to the United States) because of high taxes and the excesses of the welfare state (which makes reliance on loved ones redundant). Significantly, this article appeared in *Wprost* three weeks before Poland's EU accession.

Conservatism and neoliberalism coexist in perfect harmony here in a nationalist framework: "The autonomous family," resilient, capable of reproducing

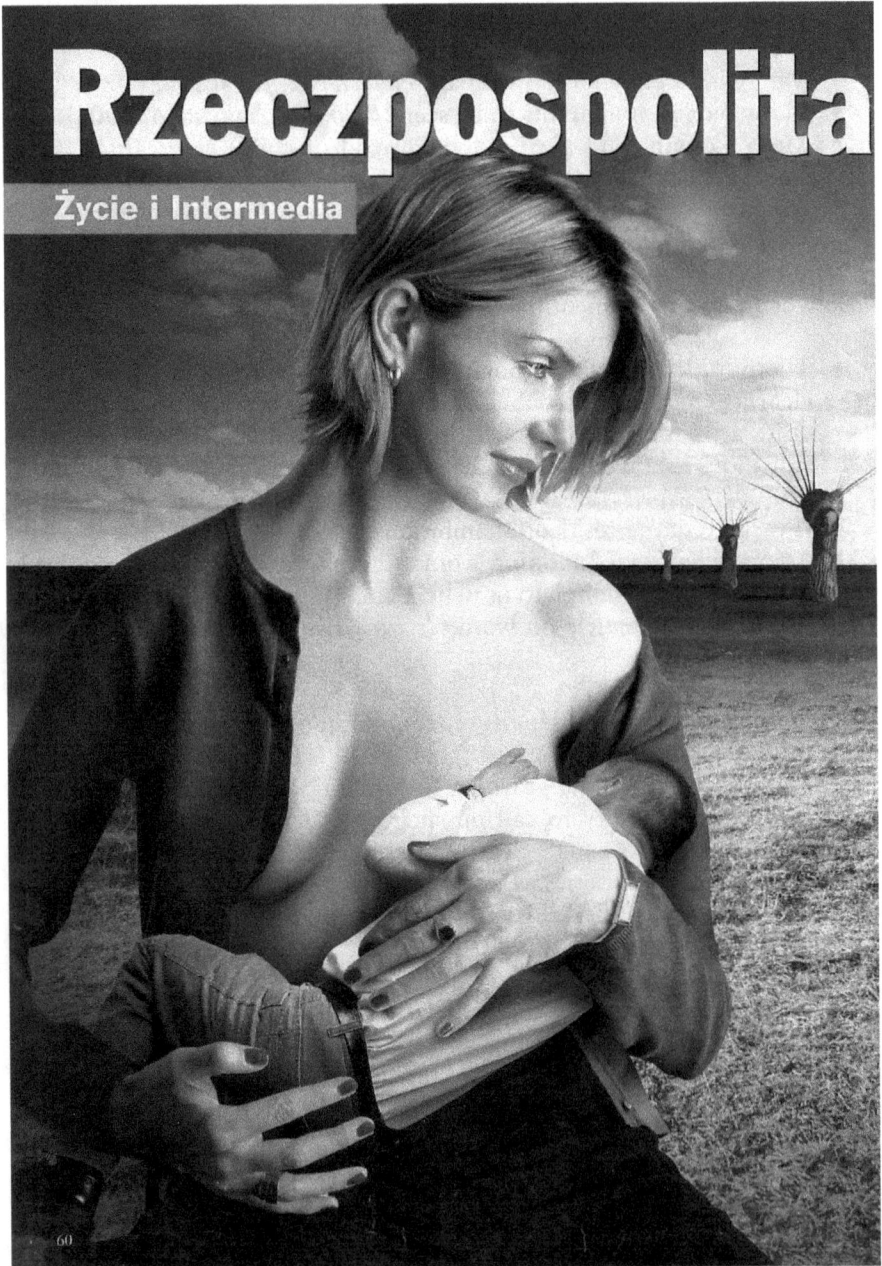

**Figure 10.6.** Wprost, illustration of "Rzeczpospolita Babska," article on women's dominant role in Polish culture (9 March 2003) (image by Igor Morski, based on photograph by Maciej Mankowski)

itself as capital, is clearly a metaphor for the desired state of the nation. Self-less motherhood (i.e., women relegated to the private sphere) turns out to be the sole guarantee for community, patriotism, national survival, and, last but not least, the growth of capital. When women work, warns the author, the family is in danger of being ruptured by "internal competition, which often leads to conflict." References to the United States, viewed as the embodiment of traditionalism and economic well-being, help construct a fantasy of Poland's "healthy independence" within the "unhealthy" body of the EU. We are to resist European effeminacy by building a sturdy alliance with the manly America. Arguably, the United States *Wprost* idealizes here is a deeply anachronistic vision, a "happy housewife" postcard from the 1950s. However, it is worth remembering that the idea of domesticated women and aggressive market-oriented men is equally anachronistic with regard to today's Poland, a country where most women (71 percent) agree that to work for pay is to have more social respect, a mere 2 percent believe that homemakers are respected, and almost half the population names "partnership" as the preferred model of marriage (Fuszara 2002, 17–18).

*Wprost* provided an even happier ending to its gender drama in the last issue of May 2004. "The Return of the Real Man" takes us on a speedy tour of world history, from the Amazons; through feminism, parthenogenesis, and cloning, to the "newest research," which proves that "serious problems are caused by ignoring the role of sperm in procreation"; and finally the recent realization that women's emancipation constitutes a grave health hazard. But help is on the way. A Belgian theologian is cited as saying, "It is important and healthy for women, for families, for societies, that we are dealing with the return of the human male, almost from the dead." The cover features heterosexual (though childless) harmony. The man, placed well above the woman, looks proudly and sternly ahead, into the future; the woman, teeth bared in a submissive smile, turns her trusting gaze up toward her mate. We may have joined the sickly, gender-troubled EU, but we remain a land of manly men and submissive, adoring women.

Admittedly, *Wprost* is the most conservative of the three magazines; it promotes a mixture of neoliberalism, nativism, and ethnonationalism embraced by neither of the other two. Nonetheless, the view of gender featured in all three magazines shares a common structure. There is a blissful era of order and "tradition" somewhere in the past, a crisis and reversal in the present, and finally—this part is prominent in *Wprost,* suggested in *Newsweek,* and usually absent in *Polityka*—the promise of a restored gender order. Gender is given an aura of newsworthiness in these stories, but the sense of drama and change is undercut by the conclusion that, in the end, gender roles have an eternal, timeless nature. There is a tension between making gender seem dynamic and insisting that it is not, a contradiction that can be read as articulation of anxiety about Polish national identity in a period of upheaval and change. The antifeminist message is driven by a need to maintain the fiction of a constant, timeless national spirit while accepting the dramatic change that is, in fact, taking place. The patriarchal family is viewed as an oasis of stability, a safe haven outside history. This explains why in the period of EU negotiations, resistance to women's rights (especially in the realm of reproduction) came to function as a marker of Poland's "cultural specificity."

## THREE VISIONS OF GENDER, THREE VERSIONS OF NATIONALISM

This study has downplayed the differences between the three weeklies, emphasizing the underlying common narrative. It is now time to acknowledge the variations. I mentioned earlier that *Wprost*'s imagery was in many cases quasipornographic, with recurring visions of women dominating men. *Newsweek*'s gender obsession in the same period was less intense (only ten cover stories in total, compared with *Wprost*'s sixteen) and less focused on eroticism and domination. Five covers include some nudity, but none are as explicit as *Wprost*'s copulation images. Only one cover—the one asking whether women's erotic lives are hurt by too much freedom—shows a nude female body in a pose suggesting orgasm (May 24, 2004). In the three covers that feature couples, women are shown as more in control than men or as perhaps in control of the men: They are positioned higher in the image, take up more space, and seem more alert (May 16, 2003; March 22, 2004; April 31, 2004).

What sets *Newsweek* apart from the other two magazines is its intense interest in masculinity: Five cover stories look at the crisis of masculinity, with the covers featuring images of men, either feminized (April 14, 2002; July 28, 2002; January 13, 2003) or ultramasculine (October 13, 2003). *Polityka*'s coverage of gender was generous (twenty-four issues with cover stories on gender-related topics) but different in nature from the other two journals. In each case there was an issue or problem at stake, never sex difference as such; many of the stories were based on concern with women's rights and well-being (e.g., anorexia, June 15, 2002; sexism in advertising, August 10, 2002; rise in women's alcoholism, July 26, 2003; the taboo of menopause, April 2, 2005).

A few of *Polityka*'s covers feature nude couples (February 15, 2003; November 8, 2003) or scantily dressed women (June 28, 2003), and there is a close-up of female buttocks (September 27, 2003), but none of these images can be described as pornographic. What is striking about many of the pictures is their carefully wrought symmetry: Men and women are given equal amount of space, neither is shown as dominant. In an image illustrating marital struggles over money, for instance, faces are positioned opposite each other, shouting, both equally aggressive (December 6, 2003). *Polityka*'s interest in gender, though intense and presented in "women's rights" frame, is nonetheless entirely separate from its general journalism.

Each magazine supported EU accession, but each did so in a different ideological framework. I argue that these disparities are vividly reflected in the way gender was discussed and visualized. Yuval-Davis's (1998, 21–24) typology of nationalisms, introduced in *Gender and Nation,* can be helpful in accounting for these differences. *Wprost* appears to promote an idea of nation that follows roughly the *Volknation* tradition, which is focused on kinship and maintenance of clear boundaries. Within this tradition, to cite Yuval-Davis (1998, 21), "the myth of common origin or shared blood/genes tends to construct the most exclusionary/homogeneous visions of 'the nation.'" Unlike the ultra–right wing press in Poland (openly hostile to EU accession), *Wprost* was rarely explicit in formulating a hard-line nationalistic position. Resistance to EU membership was suggested via the magazine's reliance on sociobiology, its use of nudity (sexual problems invariably associated with Western culture), and its aggressive homophobia (homosexuality was described as sick, unnatural, and non-Polish, an import from Germany). Whenever gender was in focus, the magazine turned to biological reproduction, characteristic of the *Volknation* discourse. Both women's reproductive rights and gay rights are presented as an imposition from the outside, a threat to Poland's biological welfare and political stability. Europe is portrayed as "feminized" and perverted (in contrast to the manly and virile United States).

*Newsweek* comes out somewhat bland in comparison to *Wprost*. Though increasingly conservative, the magazine tends to present an uninhabited trust in what it considers "modern" (Western, European) while insisting that Polishness is fully compatible with modernity. *Newsweek*'s stories about gender are framed in culturalist terms (i.e. as human interest stories rather than ideological jeremiads). Whereas *Wprost* resorts to categories such as "nature," "instinct," "violation of natural law," or "sex wars," *Newsweek* speaks cautiously of "traditional roles," "deeply rooted cultural conventions," "new habits," or "conflicting interests." Nonetheless, the phrase "traditional Polish family" is used in a manner that suggests something timeless, eternal, and impervious to change. It is against this timeless constant that "changes in roles" are juxtaposed. This framing corresponds to Yuval-Davis's (1998, 21) theorization of *Kulturnation*, the national project that constructs "the symbolic heritage provided by language and/or religion and/or other customs and traditions . . . as 'the essence' of 'the nation.'" Although such a construction allows assimilation, adds Yuval-Davis, it has little tolerance for "'nonorganic' diversity."

*Newsweek* appears deeply ambivalent about the desired limits of such tolerance and the definition of what might pass for "organic." Part of the problem is structural: The magazine is forever asking "real people" what they think and how they feel about their lives. Not surprisingly, some turn out to be happy, some not, some are adjusting to "new roles," others resist and resent them. The framing of these mixed experiences on the part of editors tends to be conservative and sometimes undercuts the message of the actual article. For instance, the May 2003 cover story on role reversal in families, where "she works and he does not . . . it is the woman who goes hunting and brings home food," has a surprisingly progressive conclusion: "If the man has to take care of the home for a while, the crown will not fall off his head." However, this paean to male adaptability is undercut by three short, virulently antifeminist articles placed in the same issue and by the magazine's cover showing us what a couple with "reversed roles" might look like (see Figure 10.2). The woman in the photograph is "dressed to kill" in a red power suit, defiant, one high-heeled foot lifted for departure. The man—barefoot, slouching, sitting on the ground right by her, coffee mug and magazine in hand—seems stagnant and aimless. In short, he is emasculated by her success. For all the seeming progressivism of its coverage of gender, *Newsweek* frames it in such a way as to project a far more ambivalent message. Cultural change is all very well, but we need to maintain traditional forms of cultural reproduction. What fool would marry the woman in red?

The most progressive of the three weeklies, *Polityka,* can be said to engage in a future-oriented *Staatsnation* discourse, with nation defined by a civic project (Yuval-Davis 1998, 21). This project is liberal, universalistic, and by definition opposed to discrimination. *Wprost*'s notion of "tyranny of tolerance" would be unthinkable in *Polityka.* The question remains, however, about the limits of inclusive universalism: To what extent are women or sexual and ethnic minorities construed as part of the project? As feminist critics argue, the problem with classical liberal theories of citizenship lies in their presumption that all citizens have equal status, which makes actual inequalities derived from gender, class, or other contexts seem irrelevant.[20] Despite occasional in-depth treatment of women's issues (and rare but thoughtful coverage of the situation of sexual, racial, and ethnic minorities), *Polityka* is liberal in this classical sense: It fails to integrate its position on minorities and inequality into its notion of citizenship as such. Inequalities are subject of special concern, but articles on the future of Polish society often are written as if white and largely middle-class heterosexual men made up the whole of the body politic. A report on Poland's anticipated future, published by *Polityka* at the turn of the twenty-first century, tells the story of a certain Adam, the prototypical Pole whose life is being predicted (December 30, 2000). The text and all illustrations focus on the growing and aging Adam, with the existence of women briefly acknowledged when he decides it is time to get married. Another amusing example of this "gender blind" approach is the issue of *Polityka* focusing on the overgrooming of upper-class Polish children: The cover features a photograph of six little boys (September 30, 2003).

## CONCLUSION

The three magazines do not simply present different views of men and women as members of society. Rather, they produce distinct visions of gender within specific discourses on nation and state. A restrictive frame, focused on heterosexuality and fertility, is characteristic of nationalistic *Wprost; Newsweek* uses a culturalist framework, which seems flexible but is in fact firmly grounded in a very specific notion of tradition; and the liberal *Polityka* occasionally embraces feminist arguments on gender but fails to integrate them into its broader agenda. Each of the three frameworks carries a mixed message about women's changing position in society, one that reflects the mixture of pride and shame characteristic of Polish attitudes toward history and national identity. On one hand, women's supposedly new liberated status is an inherent threat to national stability; it leads to demographic disaster and role reversal, and it threatens the natural order. On the other hand, there is the proud image of Polish women as strong and successful—stronger and more successful than their Western counterparts.

It is important to recall the political context in which mainstream (i.e., pro-EU) media operated in this period. Ambivalence about accession was largely unacknowledged because of the need to mobilize readers in the face of a rising anti-EU sentiment on the populist and nationalist right. Weeklies such as *Newsweek, Polityka,* and *Wprost* simply could not afford to endanger the accession process. In effect, the mainstream press was carefully self-censored. First, newspapers and magazines were urging their readers to say "yes" in the EU referendum. Next, during the crisis in negotiations that followed, they insisted that, whatever the glitches, accession would still benefit everyone. Given this self-imposed censorship, the narrative of "gender crisis" followed by the "return of the real man" seems highly functional, not as a statement on gender but as an effort to construct a notion of national identity stable enough to accommodate EU accession. All three magazines—even the notoriously conservative and Euro-skeptical *Wprost*—supported Poland's "yes" to EU membership. Whatever reservations they had were safely displaced onto, and resolved within, the arena of "gender talk." We will never know the extent to which this contributed to the success of the referendum.[21]

One last image from my collection seems worthy of mention in conclusion: the *Polityka* cover on the day of Poland's EU accession (May 1, 2004) (Figure 10.7). It is a cartoon by well-known satirist Andrzej Mleczko, captioned "Poland Returns to Europe." In the drawing, a grotesque parade of clowns, priests, crooks, and peasants is led by a much larger figure of a plump naked woman bearing the Polish national flag. All but two of the figures in the crowd representing Polish society are male (the exceptions are two nuns). This image both embodies and deconstructs the politics of liberal "gender blindness" exemplified by *Polityka* and, more broadly, by Poland's elites. Mleczko mocks the refusal to take women seriously as citizens and the readiness to elevate them as symbols of the nation. The cartoon caricatures the very dynamic that Yuval-Davis (1998), McClintock (1996), Janion (2004), and others analyze in their work. Women are not included (metonymically) as members of the collectivity; instead, they are perceived (metaphorically) as the embodiment of the nation as such. To drive the point home, Mleczko colors his metaphor pink, leaving the elements of the metonymy black and white. Women are not imagined as citizens of the state, but the nation is persistently imagined as a woman, one who leads us—with all our obsessions, weaknesses, and complexes—back to Europe.

**Figure 10.7.** Polityka cover (1 May 2004). "Poland Returns to Europe" (cartoon by Andrzej Mleczko)

NOTES

1. An early version of this chapter was presented and discussed in November 2004 at the "Gender in Transition: Women in Europe" workshop organized by the New York University Center for European Studies and the Network of East–West Women. The author would like to thank the organizers and participants of this meeting for their encouragement and useful comments, particularly Ann Snitow, Sonia Jaffe-Robbins, Elzbieta Matynia, and Magdalena Grabowska.

2. Online archives of each are available as follows. *Newsweek,* http://news-week.redakcja.pl/sklep/dostep.asp (articles and covers, paid access), or http://newsweek.redakcja.pl/wydania/ (covers only, free access); *Polityka,* http://www.polityka.pl/archive/do/registry/articleSearch (articles only, paid access; covers available on request from internet@polityka.com.pl); and *Wprost,* http://archiwum.wprost.pl/ (articles, free access), or http://archiwum.wprost.pl/okladki/ (covers, free access).
3. Ann McClintock, "No Longer in a Future Heaven: Nationalism, Gender and Race." In *Becoming National,* eds. Geoff Eley and Ronald Grigor Suny, 260–284 (Oxford: Oxford University Press, 1996), hereafter cited in text as McClintock (1996); George Mosse, *Nationalism and Sexuality. Middle Class Morality and Sexual Norms in Modern Europe* (Madison: The University of Wisconsin Press, 1985), hereafter cited in text as Mosse (1985); and Nira Yuval-Davis, *Gender and Nation* (London: Sage, 1998), hereafter cited in text as Yuval-Davis (1998).
4. Maria Janion, "Rozstać się z Polską," *Gazeta Wyborcza* 20 (October 2004): 14–16; hereafter cited in text as Janion (2004).
5. Approximate average sales as recorded in February 2006: 165,000 copies (*Polityka*), 140,000 (*Newsweek Polska*), and 130,000 (*Wprost*) (Report of Press Distribution Control Union ZKPD) "Spada sprzedaż tygodników epinii." Press, 11 May 2006 http://www.press.pl/newsy/pokaz.php?id=5943 (accessed 16 June 2006).
6. "Referendum 2003," "Referendum ogólnokrajowe w sprawie wyrazenia zgody na ratyfikacje Traktatu dotyczacego przystapienia Rzeczypospolitej Polskiej do Unii Europejskiej," Panstwowa Komisja Wyborcza. http://referendum.pkw.gov.pl/sww/kraj/indexA.html (access: 16 June 2006).
7. All Polish titles and quotations in A. Graff's translation.
8. Małgorzata Fuszara, "Zmiany w świadomości kobiet w Polsce w latach dziewięćdziesiątych." In *Kobiety w Polsce na przełomie wieków. Nowy kontrakt płci?,* ed. Małgorzata Fuszara, 13–38 (Warszawa: Instytut Spraw Publicznych, 2002); hereafter cited in text as Fuszara (2002).
9. Susan Faludi, *Backlash: The Undeclared War Against American Women* (New York: Anchor, 1991).
10. J. M. Coetzee, "Apartheid Thinking," in *Giving Offense: Essays on Censorship,* 163–184 (Chicago: Chicago University Press, 1996); Geraldine Heng and Janadas Devan, "State Fatherhood: The Politics of Nationalism, Sexuality, and Race in Singapore." In *Nationalisms and Sexualities,* ed. Andrew Parker, Mary Russo, Doris Sommer, and Patricia Yaeger, 343–364 (New York: Routledge, 1992); Orly Lubin, "'Gone Soldiers': Feminism and the Military in Israel," *The Journal of Israeli History* 21, nos. 1–2 (spring/autumn 2002): 164–192; Patricia Stamp, "Burying Otieno: The Politics of Gender and Ethnicity in Kenya," *Signs* 16, no. 4 (1991): 351–388; McClintock (1996); Mosse (1985); and Yuval-Davis (1998).
11. M. Jacqui Alexander and Chandra Talpade Mohanty, eds., *Feminist Genealogies, Colonial Legacies, Democratic Futures* (New York: Routledge, 1997); Reina Lewis and Sara Mills, eds., *Feminist Postcolonial Theory: A Reader* (New York: Routledge, 2003); Susan Okin, Joshua Cohen, Mathew Howard, and Martha Nussbaum, eds., *Is Multiculturalism Bad for Women?* (Princeton, NJ: Princeton University Press, 1999); and Anne Phillips, "Multiculturalism, Universalism and the Claims of Democracy," Paper No. 7 for United Nations Research Institute for Social Development project "Gender Justice, Development and Rights" (Geneva: UNSRID, 2001): 4–23.
12. Ruth Lister, "Dialectics of Citizenship," *Hypatia* 12, no. 4 (1997): 6–26; Kate Nash, "Feminism and Contemporary Liberal Citizenship: The Undecidability of 'Women,'" *Citizenship Studies* 15, no. 3 (2001): 255–268, hereafter cited in text as Nash (2001); Carole Pateman, *The Disorder of Women* (Cambridge,

UK: Polity Press, 1989), hereafter cited in text as Pateman (1989); and Sylvia Walby, "Is Citizenship Gendered?" *Sociology: The Journal of the British Sociological Association* 28, no. 2 (1994): 279–295.

13. Floya Anthias and Nira Yuval-Davis, "Women and the Nation State." In *Nationalism: The Reader,* ed. John Hutchinson and Anthony D. Smith, 312–316 (Oxford: Oxford University Press, 1994), at 315.
14. Joan Wallach Scott, "French Universalism in Crisis," Public lecture. New School University, Dean's Forum, November 11, 2004.
15. Janion (2004); Ewa Hauser, "Traditions of Patriotism, Questions of Gender: The Case of Poland," *Genders* 22 (fall 1995): 78–105; Elżbieta Matynia, "Provincializing Global Feminism: The Polish Case," *Social Research* 70, no. 2 (summer 2003): 499–530; and Bożena Umińska, *Postać z cieniem. Portrety Żydówek w polskiej literaturze* (Warsaw: Sic!, 2001).
16. Machulski, Juliusz. *Seksmisja* [Sexmission] (Poland, 1983); Director: Juliusz Machulski. Starring: Olgierd Łukaszewicz, Jerzy Stuhr. Screenplay by: Jolanta Hartwig-Sosnowska; Pawel Hajny; Juliusz Machulski.
17. Agnieszka Graff, *Świat bez Kobiet* (Warsaw: W.A.B., 2001): 14–32.
18. Peggy Watson, "(Anti)feminism After Communism." In *Who's Afraid of Feminism? Seeing Through the Backlash,* ed. Ann Oakley and Juliet Mitchell, 144–161 (New York: The New Press, 1997), at 146–147.
19. Shana Penn, *Solidarity's Secret. The Women Who Defeated Communism in Poland* (Ann Arbor: The University of Michigan Press, 2005).
20. Barbara Hobson and Ruth Lister, "Citizenship." In *Contested Concepts in Gender and Social Politics,* eds. Barbara Hobson, Jane Lewis, and Birte Siim, 23–53 (Cheltenham, UK: Edward Elgar, 2002), at 36–39; Nash (2001); Pateman (1989); Yuval-Davis (1998, 69–92).
21. Official results of the June 2003 Accession Referendum, as announced by the National Election Committee, with a 58.85 percent rate of participation: 77.45 percent of the voters supported EU accession, 22.55 percent opposed it (cited in "Referendum 2003").

# Part III
# Gender Violence and Masculinities

# 11 Sexual Violence Against Women and the Experience of Truth Commissions

*Julissa Mantilla Falcon[1]*

Truth commissions have been established in many countries to investigate gross human rights abuses, explain their causes, analyze their impact on society, and develop proposals to avoid repetition of abuse. In general, these are bodies of investigation set up by states in order to protect and enforce the rights to truth, justice, and reparations for victims. In some cases, they also have the objective of promoting reconciliation inside the society and are known as truth and reconciliation commissions.

Although each truth commission responds to different realities, they share some common characteristics: They have a mandate stating the crimes and abuses to be investigated, they investigate gross past abuses, they do not act as prosecutors or judicial officers, and they are temporary. At the end of their work, they prepare a report that compiles the facts and makes proposals for reparation and institutional reforms.[2] Usually, the mandate is issued in the peace accord or by the decree or law that creates the truth commission.

Historically, truth commissions have not incorporated a gender perspective in their mandates or composition. Moreover, sexual violence as a gender-based crime has not been considered as a subject of investigation for most truth commissions. This chapter seeks to explain the evolution of law defining sexual violence as a gender-based crime and the importance of including it in the mandate of a truth commission, citing the experiences in several countries.

## SEXUAL VIOLENCE AGAINST WOMEN UNDER INTERNATIONAL HUMAN RIGHTS LAW

Sexual violence against women was not been considered a human rights violation in the main treaties and documents of international human rights law. These are general treaties signed by large numbers of countries that stipulate two sets of rights: civil and political rights and economic, social, and cultural rights.[3] Later, several treaties about specific human rights violations such as torture,[4] slavery and traffic of people,[5] and the elimination of the discrimination against women[6] were signed. However, there are still no treaties that focus on violence against women. When states ratify treaties they assume international obligations and may be liable for international responsibility if they do not comply with those obligations. In the case of human rights treaties, states have the obligation to prevent and investigate human rights violations, punishing the perpetrators and compensating the victims.

Instead, human rights law dealing with the subordination of women and gender-based crimes has evolved through other kinds of documents and international resolutions. Gradually, an edifice of law has been built through reports of the United Nations commissions and special rapporteurs, regional systems, international criminal courts, and truth commissions. Women's organizations and international case law have contributed to this evolution.

A major step forward was taken by the Second World Conference of Human Rights (1993). Its Vienna Declaration stated that rights of women and girls are human rights and shall be protected and recognized internationally. The conference highlighted the importance of eliminating violence against women in public and private life, all forms of sexual harassment, exploitation and trafficking of women, and sexist prejudices in the administration of justice. It also argued for the eradication of any conflicts that arise between the rights of women and prejudicial consequences of traditional practices and customs, cultural prejudices, and religious extremism. Furthermore, it argued that violations of human rights of women in armed conflicts are violations of fundamental principles of international human rights law and humanitarian law. The conference[7] insisted that various kinds of crimes—murders, systematic violations, sexual slavery, and forced pregnancies—require an effective response.[8]

United Nations agencies and mechanisms have made a commitment to the human rights of women. The Committee for the Elimination of Discrimination Against Women (CEDAW), established in 1979, included sex-based violence in its definition of discrimination against women as follows: "violence directed to women because they are women or because women are affected in a disproportionate way." This definition includes acts that cause physical, mental, or sexual harm or suffering, threats, coercion, and other forms of privation of liberty.[9] Moreover, CEDAW stated that rural women are at risk of violence because of the persistence of traditional attitudes related to the subordination of women in many rural communities.

Extraconventional mechanisms of international human rights law have included violence against women in their reports and strategies of work. One of the most effective has been the appointment of Special Rapporteurs to make visible the situation of women. For instance, the resolution of the Commission on Human Rights that created the Special Rapporteur on Contemporary Forms of Slavery (1998) condemns the violations of rights of women in armed conflicts, establishing that these are violations of humanitarian law and asking for "an efficient response to such kind of violations, particularly to murders, systematic rapes, sexual slavery and forced pregnancy."[10]

In 1994, the United Nations also appointed a Special Rapporteur on Violence Against Women because of "the continuous and endemic characteristic of violence against women."[11] This appointment was decided in the 50th Session of the Commission on Human Rights as a way of condemning all acts of violence against women and girls. The commission emphasized

> the duty of Governments to refrain from engaging in violence against women and to exercise due diligence to prevent, investigate and, in accordance with national legislation, punish acts of violence against women and to take appropriate and effective action concerning acts of violence against women, whether those acts are perpetrated by the State, by private persons or by armed groups or warring factions, and to provide access to just and effective remedies and specialized, including medical, assistance to victims.[12]

The mandate of the special rapporteur allows her to seek and receive information on violence against women, its causes and consequences; to recommend measures to eliminate violence against women; to work closely with other United Nations bodies to ensure that their reports include regular and systematic information on human rights violations affecting women; and to cooperate closely with the Commission on the Status of Women.

The various international regional treaties also included violence against women in their purview. However, the 1994 Inter American Convention on the Prevention, Punishment and Eradication of Violence Against Women (Convention of Belém do Pará) is the only treaty that considers violence against women as a human rights violation. According to this convention, violence against women includes any act or conduct, based on gender, that causes death or physical, sexual, or psychological harm or suffering to women, whether in the public or the private sphere. Violence against women includes physical, sexual, and psychological violence.[13] Acts of violence include the following:

- Physical, sexual, and psychological violence occurring in the family, including battering, sexual abuse of female children in the household, dowry-related violence, marital rape, female genital mutilation and other traditional practices harmful to women, nonspousal violence, and violence related to exploitation
- Physical, sexual, and psychological violence occurring in the general community, including rape, sexual abuse, sexual harassment, and intimidation at work, in educational institutions, and elsewhere, trafficking in women, and forced prostitution
- Physical, sexual, and psychological violence perpetrated or condoned by the state, wherever it occurs[14]

The breadth of the convention's definition to include acts in the family and in the community is very significant. Moreover, the convention holds the state responsible not only if the perpetrators are official representatives but also if they are private citizens and the state has failed to exercise due diligence. To fulfill this duty the state must not only establish effective remedies for victims of violence but also develop preventive measures.

## Sexual Violence as Torture

Where sexual violence happens along with other human rights violations, investigators often prioritize these other violations over the abuses against women. Therefore, a significant step was taken when the Inter American Convention established a precedent for analysis of sexual violence as a form of torture, thus including sexual violence in the human rights framework. The precedent was established by the 1996 report of the case *Raquel Martín de Mejía v. Peru,*[15] which concluded that rape constitutes a breach of the American Convention of Human Rights and the Inter American Convention to Prevent and Punish Torture.

This case concerned Fernando Mejía Egocheaga and his wife, Raquel Martín de Mejía. Dr. Mejía Egocheaga was a lawyer, journalist, and political activist as the chairman of the Provincial Committee of Izquierda Unida (United Left). In his law practice, Dr. Mejía Egocheaga concentrated on defending the rights to land of the most disadvantaged groups in Peru. In his political activity, he planned to run for mayor of Oxapampa and later possibly to make a bid for a seat in Congress. Mrs. Raquel Martín de Mejía was a teacher and worked as principal of a school for the handicapped.

In June 1989 Sendero Luminoso (Shining Path) terrorists in Posuzo, a town not far from Oxapampa, killed several soldiers. A few days later about 100 military personnel from the "Batallón Nueve de Diciembre," based in Huancayo, were helicoptered into Oxapampa to conduct counterinsurgency operations in the region.[16] On June 15, 1989, a group of men with their faces covered by ski masks and carrying submachine guns suddenly turned up at the Mejías' home and demanded to see Dr. Mejía Egocheaga. When he opened the door, six men wearing military uniforms went in. One of them struck Dr. Mejía Egocheaga with his weapon and another ordered him into a yellow government-owned pickup. Fifteen minutes later, a group of militaries with their faces covered again showed up at the Mejías' house. One of them went into the house, asked for Dr. Mejía Egocheaga's identity documents, and then raped Mrs. Mejía. About twenty minutes later the same person returned to the Mejías' home and raped her again.

The Inter American Commission on Human Rights (IACHR) decided to presume the facts of the case to be true, given the culture of violence in Peru, as noted in several reports that it referenced:

- In his 1992 report, the Special Rapporteur Against Torture appointed by the United Nations Human Rights Commission noted that in

Peru, in the areas under the state of emergency, military personnel frequently resorted to sexual abuse.

- In his 1993 report, the rapporteur stated that in the areas under a state of emergency, rape seemed to be used as a form of intimidation or punishment against groups of civilians suspected of collaborating with the insurgent groups.
- The Amnesty International report in 1991 denounced the existence of an extended practice of rapes committed by military personnel in Peru.
- The Human Rights Watch Report of 1993 reported that rape is a common practice in Peru.

Moreover, the IACHR noted that there were not effective domestic remedies in Peru through which a victim of sexual abuse by members of the security forces could obtain an impartial investigation of the events and punishment of those guilty.

The IACHR then established that the sexual violence committed was a form of torture. It defined three elements of torture:

- It must be an intentional act through which physical and mental pain and suffering are inflicted on a person.
- It must be committed with a purpose.
- It must be committed by a public official or by a private person acting at the instigation of the former.

Regarding the first element, the commission declared that rape is a physical and mental abuse that is perpetrated as an act of violence. Mrs. Mejí was a victim of rape, said the IACHR, "and in consequence of an act of violence that cause[d] her physical and mental pain and suffering." Related to the second element, the IACHR noted that Raquel Mejía was raped with the aim of punishing her personally and intimidating her. Concerning the third requirement, Mrs. Mejía was raped by a member of the security forces accompanied by a large group of soldiers.

Having established that the three elements of the definition of torture were present in the case under consideration, the commission concluded that the Peruvian state is responsible for violation of Article 5 of the American Convention. This case constitutes one of the most important international precedents in the analysis of sexual violence as a form of torture.

## Sexual Violence During Armed Conflicts: International Humanitarian Law

Humanitarian law establishes that sexual violence should be understood as an infraction of the minimum norms of humanity during international and internal armed conflict. For international conflicts, the Fourth Geneva Convention of 1949 and Protocol I established that rape and sexual abuses are forbidden. In the case of internal armed conflict, the prohibition is found in Article 3 of the Geneva Conventions and in Protocol II.

However, violence against women during periods of armed conflict has generally been viewed as a side effect of the central battle. Only in the past decade after the Vienna Declaration of 1993, the Fourth World Conference on Women in Beijing in 1995, and rulings by international courts on Rwanda and the former Yugoslavia has violence against women during armed conflict come to be considered a violation of human rights and a crime against humanity.[17]

United Nations Resolution 1325[18] on Women, Peace and Security, passed in 2000, expresses the Security Council's concern that women and children account for the vast majority of those adversely affected by armed conflict and calls for full implementation of international humanitarian and human rights law protecting the rights of women and girls during and after conflicts. The resolution urges states to ensure increased representation of women at all decision-making levels in national, regional, and international institutions and in mechanisms for the prevention, management, and resolution of conflict. It also calls on states to take special measures to protect women and girls from gender-based violence, particularly rape and other forms of sexual abuse, and all other forms of violence in situations of armed conflict. Finally, it argues that states are responsible for putting an end to impunity and prosecuting those responsible for genocide, crimes against humanity, and war crimes, including those relating to sexual violence against women and girls. It stresses the need to exclude these crimes, where feasible, from amnesty provisions.[19]

The International Committee of the Red Cross (ICRC) has also identified other results of armed conflict that affect the human rights of women. Women who have to assume responsibility for their own and their families' survival or to search for relatives who were disappeared often are placed in insecure or dangerous situations. Others must deal with the impact of having husbands and partners in prison. The ICRC report argues that sexual violence is frequently used in those contexts as a form of torture intended to degrade, intimidate, and defeat specific groups of the population and to make them leave.[20]

## Sexual Violence and International Criminal Law

Finally, in international criminal law, the Draft Code of Crimes Against the Peace and Security of Mankind of 1996[21] included rape, forced prostitution, and other sexual abuses as crimes against humanity (Article 18, j), as well as other inhumane acts that severely damage physical or mental integrity, health, or human dignity, such as mutilation and severe bodily harm. The Commentary on the Draft Code[22] highlights that the General Assembly of the United Nations unanimously reaffirmed that rape constitutes a crime against humanity under certain circumstances.[23]

Later the case law of the Ad Hoc Tribunals for Yugoslavia and Rwanda recognized sexual violence as a war crime and a crime against humanity. These tribunals found that sexual violence could constitute genocide, slavery, torture, and other cruel, inhuman, or degrading treatment or punishment.[24] The International Criminal Tribunal for Rwanda made the first judgment that recognizes rape and sexual violence as constitutive acts of genocide in the sentencing of the Akayesu case. This judgment includes a broad definition of rape as a physical invasion of a sexual nature, freeing it from mechanical descriptions and a requirement of vaginal penetration by the penis. Other important advances are that forced nudity was recognized as a form of inhumane treatment, and rape was recognized as a form of torture.[25]

The International Criminal Tribunal for the former Yugoslavia (ITFY) also contributed significantly to the definition of rape under international criminal law. The ITFY stated that rape is a forcible act, that is, the act is "accomplished by force or threats of force against the victim or a third person, such threats being express or implied and must place the victim in reasonable fear that he, she or a third person will be subjected to violence, detention, duress or psychological oppression." It is significant that *force* is broadly interpreted and includes rendering the victim helpless.[26]

In another case, the ITFY sustained that "the basic underlying principle common to [the national legal systems surveyed] is that sexual penetration will constitute rape if it is not truly voluntary or consensual on the part of the victim. ... The full range of [the relevant] provisions ... suggest that the true common denominator which unifies the various systems may be a wider or more basic principle of penalizing violations of sexual autonomy."[27] The ITFY concluded that the "sexual autonomy is violated wherever the person subjected to the act has not freely agreed to it or is otherwise not a voluntary participant. The absence of genuine and freely given consent or voluntary participation may be evidenced by the presence of various factors such as force, threats of force, or taking advantage of a person who is unable to resist."[28]

Later in 1998, the Statute of the International Criminal Court included sexual violence as a crime against humanity in Article 7 and as a war crime in Article 8.[29] As scholar Rhonda Copelon has highlighted, the Rome Statute names "a broad range of sexual and reproductive violence crimes—rape, sexual slavery including trafficking, forced pregnancy, enforced prostitution, enforced sterilization, and other serious sexual violence—as among the gravest crimes of war." When these crimes are committed as part of a widespread or systematic attack on a civilian population, these are crimes against humanity in times of peace as well as war and by nonstate actors as well as officials.[30]

Furthermore, the Rome Statute diminishes the potential for retraumatization of the victims during trials.[31] Copelon notes that the "evidentiary rules minimize some of the worst traditional features of rape trials, including distrust of women's testimony and humiliation through cross-examination about consent or their sexual histories."[32] This provides a model for national legislations to be updated.

## SEXUAL VIOLENCE AND THE TRUTH AND RECONCILIATION COMMISSIONS

As we have seen, recognition of sexual violence as a human rights violation, a war crime, and a crime against humanity has been a long and slow process. Failure to acknowledge the real dimensions and impact of sexual violence against women has been reflected in the reports of the truth commissions around the world. Most truth commissions have not included gender-based crimes in their mandates, investigations, and reports, but there have been some exceptions.

An important experience came from Latin America when the Guatemalan Commission of Historical Clarification (1994–1999)[33] was established at the conclusion of a thirty-year conflict. This entity was the first one to include a special concern with women's human rights and gender-based violence. Its final report included a chapter on sexual violence against women, which it found to be a widespread and systematic practice used as a terrorist weapon.[34] The report explains the difficulties interviewers faced in collecting information because affected women did not talk about sexual abuses. Despite these obstacles the report presents cases of rape, forced abortion, and sexual violence against pregnant women, among other abuses. It reports that in many of these instances, sexual violence against women was used for the purpose of humiliating and offending men.

In South Africa[35] (1995–1998) a truth and reconciliation commission was created to investigate the human rights abuses and crimes committed during the apartheid era. The male structure of the commission did not facilitate the collection of women' stories and voices.[36] However, at the insistence of some female commissioners and activists, the commission organized three public hearings to highlight the abuses that affected women's rights. The Gender Research Project of the Centre for Applied Legal Studies (CALS) at the University of the Witwatersrand and of the Centre for the Study of Violence and Reconciliation prepared a submission to the commission highlighting the importance of gender in a truth and reconciliation process. This document argues that women's experience cannot be understood in isolation from men's and must be seen in the context of their roles and status in society.[37] In cases of sexual violence, the submission explained that women found it very difficult to admit that it happened and often denied the facts. According to the CALS testimony, of nearly 9,000 cases of violations, only nine women claimed they had been raped.[38]

Analyzing cases of torture from a gender perspective, the CALS submission suggested that the purposes of torture of men and women differed. Sexual torture of men was aimed to induce sexual perversity and abolish political power, whereas sexual torture of women sought to induce shame and guilt.[39] Specific modes of torturing women were to withhold medical care and to attack women's identity as women or mothers ("You are irresponsible, you are an unnatural woman, an unnatural mother").

The final report, issued in October 1998, recognized that the commission's definition of "gross violation of human rights" resulted in blindness to the types of abuse experienced predominantly by women.[40] Therefore, it included a special chapter on the hearings on women.[41] This highlighted that women were silent on sexual abuse, noting that a majority of the women spoke as relatives and dependents of men who had directly suffered human rights violations, whereas most of the men spoke as direct victims.[42] The commission concluded that the state was responsible for the ill treatment of women in custody. They were sexually abused by security forces, suffered from withholding of medical attention, food, and water, received threats against their families and children, and were humiliated around biological functions such as menstruation and childbirth.[43]

A truth and reconciliation commission was created in Sierra Leone in 2002–2004 after the armed conflict there. This was an especially offensive case in which even the peacekeepers of the United Nations Mission in Sierra Leone had sexually exploited women, including soliciting child prostitutes.[44] Furthermore, a 2002 report by Physicians for Human Rights showed that internally displaced women and girls were victims of rape, sexual violence, and other gross human rights violations.[45]

With this background, the commission was explicitly charged by the Lome Agreement, which ended the conflict, with giving "special attention to the subject of sexual abuses and to the experiences of children within the armed conflict."[46] However, there were no more references to the general situation of sexual violence against women or to gender.

Former commissioners from the South African truth and reconciliation commission with experience in gender issues were among the commissioners in Sierra Leone. They stressed the need for a gender perspective in the investigative process. The United Nations Development Fund for Women and the Nairobi-based Urgent Action Fund[47] conducted a training program focused on international law related to sexual violence and methods for interviewing rape victims and supporting and protecting female witnesses. Attendance by the commissioners and relevant staff sent a strong message within the whole institution "that the issue of gender violence was an institutional priority."[48]

As in South Africa, civil society organizations played an important role in the proceedings. The Coalition on Women's Human Rights in Conflict Situations[49] submitted a report to the commission highlighting the impact of sexual violence on women during the conflict.[50]

The final report, released on October 5, 2004, includes a chapter titled "Women and the Armed Conflict" that describes the violations suffered by women in Sierra Leone.[51] The report concluded that women and girls became targets for sexual abuses during the conflict[52] by all armed groups. The abuses included killings, rape, sexual slavery, slave labor, abduction, assault, amputation, forced pregnancy, torture, trafficking, and mutilation. Rape and sexual slavery were committed almost exclusively against females.

The commission made specific recommendations to redress the marginalization of women in Sierra Leone, calling on communities to make special efforts to encourage acceptance of the survivors of rape and sexual violence. The problem of customary law was also addressed. The commission called on the government to end the practice of forcing rape victims to marry the aggressor or accept monetary compensation for these crimes.[53]

One of the most recent cases is the Truth and Reconciliation Commission of Liberia, established in 2005 by the Liberian National Transitional Legislative Assembly. Its mandate reflects the gradual progress made in past commissions in addressing problems of gender-based violence. The Liberian commission was charged with adopting "mechanisms and procedures to address the experiences of women, children and vulnerable groups, paying particular attention to gender based violations, as well as to the issue of child soldiers."[54] Moreover, the act states that the commission shall consider and be sensitive to issues of human rights violations, gender, and gender-based violence and ensure that no one with a known record of human rights violations is employed by the commission. It also states that gender mainstreaming shall characterize its work, operations, and functions, ensuring "that women are fully represented and staffed at all levels of the work of the TRC and that special mechanisms are employed to handle women and children victims and perpetrators, not only to protect their dignity and safety but also to avoid re-traumatization."[55]

Furthermore, the act provides that the commission's work shall help to restore the dignity of victims and promote reconciliation, giving special attention to the issues of sexual and gender-based violence. Special programs are to be created for children and women living under burdens of trauma, stigmatization, neglect, shame, and threats and others in difficult circumstances who may want to recount their stories either in privacy or in public, subject to the discretion of the commission. For this purpose, the commission is to employ specialists in children's and women's rights.[56]

This act establishes an important precedent for future truth commissions. Although it is too soon to analyze the work of the Liberian Truth and Reconciliation Commission, its effectiveness should be monitored by academics and activists.

## THE PERUVIAN TRUTH AND RECONCILIATION COMMISSION

The Peruvian Truth and Reconciliation Commission (2001–2003) was created after the armed conflict between the government and Shining Path and other subversive groups (1980–2000). When the commission started its work, Peruvian society was not aware of cases of sexual violence committed against women during the armed conflict. There were no previous national reports on the subject, although there were well-prepared reports and studies of torture, forced disappearances, and arbitrary executions. Therefore, the mandate did not include investigation of the cases of sexual violence.

However, the Peruvian commission used the final reports of Guatemala and South Africa as precedents, along with rulings from the international criminal tribunals from Yugoslavia and Rwanda. These provided important information about how victims of sexual violence typically react, the challenges that the commission would face, and the best ways to incorporate a gender approach to its work. The conclusions of the Guatemalan final report were used as a starting point because of the similarities between the Peruvian and the Guatemalan armed conflicts. For example, the Guatemalan report explained how men and women were separated before being killed: Men were killed first while women were raped and then killed. This information provided a hypothesis for Peruvian investigators about differences in massacres depending on whether men or women were involved. From the South African experience, the Peruvian commission learned about women victims' difficulties in denouncing sexual abuse and the importance of differentiating how human rights violations affect men and women.

Benefiting from advances in international law, the commission adopted a very broad definition of sexual violence as

> the realization of a sexual act against one or more persons or when a person is forced to realize a sexual act by force or threat of force or through coercion caused by fear of violence, intimidation, detention, psychological oppression or abuse of power used against that person or other persons, or taking advantage of a coercive environment or the inability of the person to freely consent.[57]

With this definition, the Peruvian commission could investigate not only cases of rape but also forced marriage, forced abortions, forced nudity, sexual blackmail, and sexual slavery, among other forms of sexual violence.

## Some Strategies

Because the investigation of sexual violence cases was not planned from the beginning or included in the mandate, the Peruvian commission had to develop some important strategies:

- They created a Gender Unit in order to incorporate a gender perspective in taking and analyzing testimonies and coordinating with local organizations.

- The Gender Unit organized training sessions for commission personnel to develop sensitivity to gender-based crimes, especially sexual violence.
- An oversight group inside the commission was created to guarantee the incorporation of the gender perspective throughout the commission offices, in countryside offices as well as in the main Lima office.
- Flyers, posters, and radio programs were prepared explaining that sexual violence is a human rights violation and should be denounced.
- A support group including representatives of human rights and women's nongovernment organizations was created to discuss the need to incorporate special chapters on sexual violence and gender in the final report.

## The Final Report[58]

The final report of the Peruvian Truth and Reconciliation Commission was released on August 28, 2003. As a result of the strategies outlined earlier, it included important findings on sexual violence and women's roles in armed conflict. A chapter on gender recognized that the previous situation of inequality and discrimination against women remained during the armed conflict. It also noted that the conflict transformed gender roles as women assumed responsibility for family survival and for dealing with the displacement of whole populations escaping from the conflict.[59]

Concerning the cases of sexual violence, the commission recognized the same type of underreporting of the cases because of victims' feelings of guilt and shame as in previous truth commission reports. Most of the cases of sexual violence happened in the context of other human rights violations (such as massacres, arbitrary detentions, summary executions, and torture) that tend to overshadow cases of sexual violence.

One of the most important conclusions of the Peruvian commission is that sexual violence against women was a widespread crime committed by state agents. These crimes included rape, sexual blackmail, sexual slavery, sexual mutilation, sexual molestation, sexual humiliation, forced prostitution, forced pregnancy, and forced nudity. Sexual violence in the context of arbitrary detentions and forced disappearances was a practice in some military bases and police stations and was not investigated or punished. Women in jail were also victims of sexual violence, not only by the agents in charge but also by the doctors who could verify the sexual abuse.

On the other hand, the Peruvian commission found cases of rape, forced marriage, and forced abortions in the camps of Shining Path, one of the subversive groups.[60] This was an important finding that countered the false assumption common among Peruvians that subversives (*senderistas*) do not rape women. There were also cases of Shining Path members forced to have sexual relationships with the other members of the group.

The final report includes a Comprehensive Plan for Reparations that highlights the importance of the gender perspective and the need for equal participation of men and women in the implementation of the plan. The commission demanded that in all circumstances the abuses and crimes against women be explicitly mentioned. It proposed economic reparations for victims of rape and children born after rape.[61]

The commission report was very important in Peruvian society because it brought forward evidence about sexual violence during the armed conflict that was unknown and surrounded by impunity. However, the commission did not find evidence requiring criminal prosecutions against state agents that committed sexual abuses. Regrettably, the impunity surrounding sexual violence against women continued, not only because the victims felt ashamed but also because the state did not encourage women to file complaints. In the rare cases in which women filed a complaint, their voices were not heard.

## The Peru Truth and Reconciliation Commission and Women's Search for Justice

After the commission released its report, it filed forty-seven cases of human rights violations before the Peruvian National Prosecutor. There were two cases of sexual violence among them. Although this seems like very few cases, it bears noting that the special investigations unit, in charge of the filing cases, did not plan to file any such cases at all.[62] The two cases filed were the following:

- Magdalena Monteza (1992). She was a student illegally detained by the army and later raped during the interrogation. She became pregnant after being abused. The case was temporarily closed by the prosecutor because the rapist could not be identified.
- The Manta and Vilca (1984–1998) cases. These are rural towns where women frequently submitted to sexual violence by militaries controlling the zone.

Currently, these cases are not getting enough attention by judicial authorities. The problem is not only army interference with the investigations but also lack of legal aid for the victims.[63] Moreover, there are legal problems related to the lack of a definition of sexual violence in the national criminal code, difficulties in collecting evidence given the time that has elapsed, lack of training in international human rights law, and the gender of judicial authorities. Furthermore, in many cases victims have already started new families and do not want to reveal what happened, or their communities forbid them to give testimony in order to avoid shame.[64]

This experience has shown the importance of updating national legislation to incorporate international law and precedents. Judicial authorities must receive training to understand that sexual violence is a crime for which perpetrators must be punished.

## CONCLUSION

It has taken a long time for sexual violence against women to be considered a human rights violation and an international crime. International documents and resolutions, advanced rulings, and the work of academics and activists have contributed to this process. Truth commissions are a good example of this evolution. Although the majority of truth commissions did not include sexual violence cases in their mandates, the Guatemalan, South African, Peruvian, Sierra Leone, and Liberian Truth Commissions provide a new model. However, there is still much work to do.

First, it is very difficult for women to denounce these acts or even talk about them. They feel ashamed and do not understand that they are not responsible for the aggression. Moreover, women are afraid that both the perpetrators and their own communities and families may stigmatize them. They are more likely to identify themselves as relatives of male victims, neglecting their own stories and suffering.

Judicial authorities and police officers lack sensitivity in taking care of their complaints. The late recognition of sexual violence against women as a human rights violation by international human rights law has affected the prosecution of these crimes. Many investigations and reports do not analyze the specific cases of sexual violence as such. In some cases they are not included at all, and in others the violations are subsumed under other human rights violations.

Lawmakers must follow and respect international laws, recognizing that violence against women is gender-based violence that must always be investigated, condemned, and punished.[65] States should ratify international treaties on the matter and fulfill their international obligation to prevent human rights violations, investigate these cases, punish those responsible, and compensate the victims.[66] National legislation should be updated accordingly.

Finally, international standards should be followed in the prosecution of sexual violence, including the collection of evidence, the testimonies of victims, and the protection of witnesses. These are not easy tasks, but justice and compassion demand nothing less.

## NOTES

1. I would like to thank the New Century Scholars Program for supporting my investigation. I also would like to thank Sofia Donaires and Oscar Sandoval, former students and research assistants who helped me with data collection.

2. For more information, see Priscilla Heyner, *Unspeakable Truths: Confronting State Terror and Atrocity* (New York: Routledge, 2001).
3. Universal Declaration of Human Rights (UDHR, 1948), Articles 2 and 5; American Declaration of Rights and Duties of Men (ADHR, 1948), Article II; the International Covenant on Civil and Political Rights (ICCP, 1966), Articles 7, 10, and 26; American Convention on Human Rights (AC, 1969), Articles 1, 6, and 11.
4. Convention Against Torture and Other Cruel, Inhuman or Degrading Treatment or Punishment (1984).
5. Supplementary Convention on the Abolition of Slavery, the Slave Trade, and Institutions and Practices Similar to Slavery (1956) and the Protocol to Prevent, Suppress and Punish Trafficking in Persons, Especially Women and Children, Supplementing the United Nations Convention Against Transnational Organized Crime, G.A. res. 55/25, annex II, 55 U.N. GAOR Suppl. (No. 49) at 60, U.N. Doc. A/45/49 (Vol. I) (2001).
6. Convention on the Elimination of All Forms of Discrimination Against Women (CEDAW) (1979).
7. Declaration and Platform of Action, Vienna, Paragraph 28.
8. Julie Mertus and Pamela Goldberg, "Perspective on Women and International Human Rights After the Vienna Declaration: The Inside/Outside Construct," *New York University Journal of International Law and Politics* 26 (1994): 201.
9. General Recommendation 19 (1992), Convention on the Elimination of All Forms of Discrimination Against Women (1979).
10. Commission on Human Rights, "Contemporary Forms of Slavery." http://www.hri.ca/forthereCord1998/documentation/commission/e-cn4-sub2–1998–13.htm (accessed November 22, 2006).
11. Resolution 1994/45, Commission on Human Rights, United Nations E/CN.4/RES/1994/45, 56 session, March 4, 1994.
12. Office of the United Nations High Commissioner for Human Rights, "Special Rapporteur on Violence Against Women, Its Causes and Consequences," http://www.ohchr.org/english/issues/women/rapporteur/ (accessed December 20, 2006).
13. Article 1, Convention on the Prevention, Punishment and Eradication of Violence Against Women, "Convention of Belém do Pará" (1994).
14. *Report of the Fourth World Conference on Women of United Nations* (Beijing, September 4–15, 1995), A/CONF.177/20.
15. Report No. 5/96, Caso 10.970, Raquel Martín de Mejía, Perú, March 1996.
16. Ibid.
17. Platform of Beijing (1995), Section D. This section focused particularly on women belonging to minorities and indigenous women, whom it found to constitute most of the victims.
18. United Nations Security Council Resolution 1325 on Women, Peace and Security (S/RES/1325), October 31, 2000; hereafter cited in text as United Nations Security Council Resolution 1325.
19. Ibid.
20. Charlotte Lindsey, "The Impact of Armed Conflict on Women," http://www.reliefweb.int/library/documents/2001/icrc-women-17oct.pdf (accessed January 15, 2006).
21. *Draft Code of Crimes Against Peace and Security of Mankind* (Draft Code 1996), International Law Commission, Session 48.
22. United Nations, *Draft Code of Crimes Against the Peace and Security of Mankind with Commentaries* (1995), http://untreaty.un.org/ilc/texts/instruments/english/commentaries/7_4_1996.pdf (accessed January 10, 2006).

23. Rape and Abuse of Women in the Areas of Armed Conflict in the Former Yugoslavia, G.A. res. 50/192, U.N. Doc. A/RES/50/192 (1995).
24. Special Rapporteur on Women, Report 57. In High Commissioner of Human Rights, "Rights of Women," Bogotá, December 2002, Paragraph 21.
25. Rhonda Copelon, "Gender Crimes as War Crimes: Integrating Crimes Against Women into International Criminal Law," *McGill Law Journal* 46 (2000): 217–240; cited hereafter in text as Copelon (2000).
26. *Prosecutor v. Anto Furundžija* (case no. IT-95–17/1-T, judgment of December 10, 1998).
27. *Prosecutor v. Kunarac, Kovač and Vuković* (case no. IT-96–23, judgment of February 22, 2001).
28. Ibid.
29. "Article 7: Crimes against humanity

For the purpose of this statute, 'crime against humanity' means any of the following acts when committed as part of a widespread or systematic attack directed against any civilian population, with knowledge of the attack: . . .

(g) Rape, sexual slavery, enforced prostitution, forced pregnancy, enforced sterilization, or any other form of sexual violence of comparable gravity; . . .

Article 8: War crimes . . .

2. For the purpose of this Statute, "war crimes" means: . . .

(xxii) Committing rape, sexual slavery, enforced prostitution, forced pregnancy, as defined in article 7, paragraph 2 (f), enforced sterilization, or any other form of sexual violence also constituting a grave breach of the Geneva Conventions; . . .

(c)   In the case of an armed conflict not of an international character, serious violations of article 3 common to the four Geneva Conventions of 12 August 1949, namely, any of the following acts committed against persons taking no active part in the hostilities, including members of armed forces who have laid down their arms and those placed hors de combat by sickness, wounds, detention or any other cause: . . .

(vi)   Committing rape, sexual slavery, enforced prostitution, forced pregnancy, as defined in article 7, paragraph 2 (f), enforced sterilization, and any other form of sexual violence also constituting a serious violation of article 3 common to the four Geneva Conventions."
30. Copelon (2000, 235).
31. Rhonda Copelon, "Achieving Women's Full Citizenship." In *Carnegie Council of Ethics and International Affairs,* "Violence Against Women," Human Rights Dialogue, Series 2, No. 10 (Fall 2003): 20–21.
32. Ibid., 20.
33. Juan Hernández Pico, *Memoria del silencio: Un informe estremecedor. Para la memoria de los mártires,* http://www.uca.edu.ni/koinonia/relat/206.htm (accessed September 2002).
34. Comisión para el Esclarecimiento Histórico. Guatemala: Memoria del Silencio, Chapter II, Volume 3.
35. World Bank, *Gender, Justice and Truth Commissions* (Washington, DC: World Bank, 2006): 11; hereafter cited in text as World Bank (2006).
36. Fiona Ross, *Bearing Witness: Women and the Truth and Reconciliation Commission in South Africa* (London: Anthropology, Culture and Society, 2003).
37. Truth and Reconciliation Commission, Women's Hearing, July 29, 1997. Participation of Dr. Sheila Meintjies, http://www.doj.gov.za/trc/special/women/meintjie.htm (accessed September 12, 2006).
38. Ibid.

39. Ibid.
40. South African Truth and Reconciliation Commission, Volume 4, Chapter 10, Special Hearing: Women, http://www.stanford.edu/class/history48q/Documents/EMBARGO/4chap10.htm (accessed December 2005).
41. South African Truth and Reconciliation Commission, Volume 4, Chapter 10, http://www.doj.gov.za/trc/trc_frameset.htm (accessed July 14, 2007).
42. Ibid., Paragraph 6.
43. Final Report of the Truth and Reconciliation Commission, Volume 5, Chapter 6, http://www.stanford.edu/class/history48q/Documents/EMBARGO/5chap6.htm (accessed December 12, 2006).
44. Binaifer Nowrojee, "Making the Invisible War Crime Visible: Postconflict Justice for Sierra Leone's Rape Victims," *Harvard Human Rights Journal* 18 (2005): 92; hereafter cited in text as Nowrojee (2005).
45. Physicians for Human Rights, *War-Related Sexual Violence in Sierra Leone. A Population-Based Assessment* (Cambridge, MA: PHR, 2002).
46. The Truth and Reconciliation Commission Act 2000, http://www.sierra-leone.org/trc-documents.html (accessed November 24, 2006).
47. The Urgent Action Fund collaborates with female activists in three primary contexts: peace building in situations of armed conflict, escalating violence, or politically volatile environments; potentially precedent-setting legal and legislative actions; and protection of female human rights defenders (http://www.urgentactionfund.org/) (accessed July 12, 2007).
48. Nowrojee (2005, 93).
49. This coalition was created to promote the adequate prosecution of perpetrators of gender violence in transitional justice systems based in Africa, in order to create precedents that recognize violence against women in conflicts and help find ways to obtain justice for women survivors of sexual violence (http://www.womensrightscoalition.org/) (accessed July 12, 2007).
50. *Submission by the Coalition for Women's Human Rights in Conflict Situations to the Truth and Reconciliation Commission,* http://www.womensrightscoalition.org/site/advocacyDossiers/sierraLeoneTR/submissiontotr.php (accessed November 24, 2006).
51. *The Final Report of the Truth and Reconciliation Commission of the Sierra Leone,* Volume 3B, Chapter 3: "Women and the Armed Conflict," http://trcsierraleone.org/drwebsite/publish/v3b-c3.shtml (accessed July 12, 2007).
52. Women's International League for Peace and Freedom, http://www.peacewomen.org/news/SierraLeone/newsarchive03/truthcommission.html (accessed July 13, 2007).
53. World Bank (2006).
54. Truth and Reconciliation Commission (TRC) of Liberia Act, May 12, 2005, Section 4, a.
55. Ibid., Section 24.
56. Ibid., Article 8.
57. *Informe Comisión de la Verdad y Reconciliación del Perú,* http://www.cverdad.org.pe (accessed November 22, 2006).
58. Ibid.
59. Reporte Secretario General, Sr. Francis M. Deng, "Intensificación de la promoción y el fomento de los derechos humanos y de las libertades fundamentales, en particular la cuestión del programa y los métodos de trabajo de la Comisión de derechos humanos, éxodos en masa y personas desplazadas. Los desplazados internos," Comisión de Derechos Humanos-ECOSOC, 52° período de sesiones, E/CN.4/1996/52/Add. 1.
60. *Informe Comisión de la Verdad y Reconciliación del Perú,* http://www.cverdad.org.pe (accessed November 22, 2006).

61. *Programa Integral de Repaciones de la Comisión de la Verdad y Reconcili-ación del Perú*, http://www.cverdad.org.pe/ifinal/index.php (accessed November 22, 2007).
62. I remember a conversation with the chief of this unit who told me that gender was not one of the criteria to file a case. However, after the efforts of the Gender Unit this situation has changed.
63. Of 1,512 victims currently involved in judicial proceedings, 1,148 lack legal counsel (World Bank 2006, 16).
64. Julissa Mantilla, "La Comisión de la Verdad y Reconciliación del Perú: Principales logros y hallazgos," *Revista IIDH 43* (June 2006): 338.
65. Julissa Mantilla, "War Crimes," *Latinamerica Press* 38, no 7 (April 19, 2006): 7.
66. Velasquez Rodriguez Case, judgment of July 29, 1988, Inter-Am.Ct.H.R. (Ser. C) No. 4 (1988).

# 12 Rape, Trauma, and Meaning

*Nicola Gavey*[1]

There is no difference between being raped
and being run over by a truck
except that afterward men ask if you enjoyed it.

—Marge Piercy, *Rape Poem* (1985)[2]

It is almost regarded as a truism today that rape is traumatic. But this under-standing, which we now accept as so evidently true, has a very short his-tory. The turning point came only in the 1970s. Before this time, women's experiences of rape[3] were largely hidden from public view. A woman's suf-fering—her sense, quite possibly, of having been "run over by a truck"—was a form of experience and knowledge banished to the private domain. Representations of rape and its impact in the public domain were instead restricted to those knowable from what could be considered a man's point of view. In places such as the United States and New Zealand, both popular cultural and legitimated professional knowledge about the nature of rape were sharply limited by assumptions that fundamentally dis-identified with the victim. Rape was often portrayed as sexy, or invited by the woman, and any suggestion of negative consequences was just as likely to be attributed to preexisting weakness in the woman's character, just as the rape itself was likely to be seen as at least in part her fault.[4] As Sutherland and Scherl noted in 1970, not only had little attention been paid to "the victim's adjustment following sexual assault" in the medical and psychological literature, but "specific references to the young woman most frequently discuss the pos-sibility of her conscious or unconscious participation in the incident."[5]

Over the course of the 1970s, these dominant notions about rape and about its impact were turned on their head. Through the efforts of femi-nist activists, researchers, and mental health workers, minimizing discourses about rape gave way to discourses that emphasized its inherent harm.[6] As French historian Georges Vigarello noted, "the reference to an inner trauma . . . became one of the main criteria for asserting the gravity of the crime: no longer the moral or social impact of the tragedy, or the insult or degrada-tion, but the shattering of a consciousness, a psychological suffering whose intensity was measured by its duration, even its irreversibility."[7] But what we mean by *trauma* is not at all clear, and indeed it is used in various, arguably contradictory ways. Beyond its flexible use to refer to both harmful events and actions themselves as well as to people's responses to them, there are contradictory tensions in terms of how this (post)traumatic response is understood. Sometimes the term is used in a vague and almost metaphorical sense to refer to unspecified forms of psychological pain and suffering. In the psy-disciplines, however, trauma has a much more precise meaning.[8]

In this chapter I briefly outline this meaning and the ways in which it is brought to bear in representations of the trauma of rape in the psy-disciplines. I argue that within these models the meaning of rape is inadvertently reduced to a fear of death.[9] Through reference to some women's accounts of their experience of rape I show that the potential meaning of rape is much more and/or less than this, raising questions about the appropriateness of using a trauma paradigm as the overarching way of making sense of the impact of rape.

A "rape trauma syndrome" was originally identified by Ann Burgess and Lynda Holmstrom (1974) on the basis of their observations and interviews with ninety-two women who had presented to a hospital emergency department following the experience of "forcible rape." They described a pattern (with variations) of behavioral, somatic, and psychological responses, distinguishing those that occurred in the acute phase immediately after the rape from longer-term effects. Burgess and Holmstrom (1974, 982) described rape trauma syndrome as "an acute stress reaction to a life-threatening situation,"[10] noting that women's primary reaction to rape was fear for their lives: "Victims stated that it was not the rape that was so upsetting as much as the feeling that they would be killed as a result of the assault" (Burgess and Holmstrom 1974, 983).[11]

In the period since publication of this highly influential study, research on trauma more generally has mushroomed. Two almost paradoxical trends have emerged. On one hand, the notion of trauma has entered public discourse as a sort of one-word lexicon for any form of psychological pain and suffering seen to be caused by experiences in the world. As Derek Summerfield (2001, 96) put it, "In Western societies the conflation of distress with 'trauma' increasingly has a naturalistic feel; it has become part of everyday descriptions of life's vicissitudes." Medical and scientific discourse, on the other hand, has moved toward more exacting definitions of trauma, increasingly theorizing it as a particular kind of psychobiological response to life-threatening events.[12] Such definitions have been taken up by influential theorist–clinicians writing about trauma. "Unlike commonplace misfortunes," according to feminist psychiatrist Judith Herman, "traumatic events generally involve threats to life or bodily integrity, or a close personal encounter with violence and death."[13] In an even stronger statement, psychotherapist Babette Rothschild strongly emphasizes the necessary component of "threat to life and limb" in any definition of trauma and cautions against overuse of the term to refer to other kinds of distressing events.[14]

This emphasis on the terrifying, potentially life-threatening nature of the trauma is consistent with the requirements of a medicalized lens that has produced the diagnostic category of posttraumatic stress disorder (PTSD).[15] In this model, there are three key domains of posttraumatic impact: hyperarousal (such as an exaggerated startle response, difficulty concentrating, sleep disruption, and irritability), forms of reexperiencing, or what Herman (1992) calls intrusion (experiences of psychologically reliving or reenacting the trauma, such as intrusive distressing memories, dreams, or flashbacks), and avoidance or constriction (such as psychological numbing, detachment, memory impairment, and the suppression of thoughts about the trauma and avoidance of related situations).[16]

The role of fear is key in this model. Increasingly scientists have focused on the neurobiological mechanisms through which the experience of intense fear in a situation over which one has limited or no control can lead to persistent forms distress and other difficulties (along a continuum that includes PTSD). Because fear and terror are the two emotions most commonly attributed to women facing rape, it is unsurprising that such approaches have been applied to understanding its impact. In a neurobiological model, according to David Lisak, this means "rape victims" will be left with "a permanently altered brain. As part of its legacy, trauma leaves its victims with fear networks etched into the amygdala, networks that can be triggered by a multitude of cues that would ordinarily not evoke fear."[17]

Although Burgess and Holmstrom (1974) did not explicitly make such a generalizing claim, a notion that rape *is* (as opposed to *can be*) life threatening was for some time tenaciously repeated despite the antirape movement's concurrent insistence on recognizing that rape takes a variety of forms.[18] Deborah Rose, for instance, stated in 1986 that "every rape victim experiences literally the threat of loss of life."[19] It is less common now to find explicit claims that rape is inherently life threatening.[20] Nevertheless, formulations of the kind of trauma experienced following rape often remain explicitly referenced to the pattern of response identified by Burgess and Holmstrom (1974) (based on their research with women portrayed as having faced this kind of life-threatening rape),[21] or they otherwise explicitly invoke posttraumatic stress disorder, which has largely displaced and subsumed the notion of rape trauma syndrome.[22] In some cases the term *trauma* is used simply as an implicit shorthand reference to posttraumatic stress.

Thus, an unexamined and paradoxical thread runs through much of the writing about the trauma of rape: a mismatch between the shifts in our understanding of what rape *is* and the trends in understanding what rape *does* to women. At the same time as we have come to accept that a man's forced penile penetration of a woman's vagina in the absence of her consent is rape regardless of the presence of physical violence or of the nature of their relationship, we have persevered with a relatively narrow model of trauma that was derived from the experiences of women who had been subject specifically to life-threatening forms of rape. If anything, the field's loyal commitment to highlighting the posttraumatic response (as *the* response to rape) has intensified, probably because of the cachet of psychobiological approaches to trauma, which can be seen as conveying scientific legitimation to victims' suffering.

In the psy-literature on rape, many authors do recognize the heterogeneity of rape, and many provide nuanced and qualified accounts of the different ways in which different women respond to rape. Nevertheless, there is a dominant "standard story" about the impact of rape that tends to float up for attention from the more murky sea of partial, sometimes contradictory research facts. The standard story that headlines even some of the most careful work in the area is about "*the* trauma of rape,"[23] which implicitly if not explicitly keeps alive a myth that there is one kind of fairly uniform response to rape. In some cases the effects of rape are portrayed in ways that defy theoretical consistency. In one work on "the trauma of acquaintance rape," for instance, there is a disconnection between reports of women's own descriptions of the impact of sexual assault on their lives, which seem predominantly to highlight relational difficulties associated with trust, intimacy, and anger; and the authors' claim in an adjacent section that "the impact of acquaintance rape on a victim may be seen from the diagnostic perspective of posttraumatic stress disorder."[24] Of course it is possible that acquaintance rape, just like rape committed by any category of perpetrator, could occur under conditions that spark a wide range of possible reactions, from those that look like posttraumatic stress to those that have a quite different quality. What is generally missing in the literature, however, is some kind of reflexive recognition that the nature and experience of rape can be so diverse that the more exacting notions of trauma not only might not always provide the best fit but might occlude consideration of the form and complexity of some women's experiences.

As I have already emphasized, the experience of overwhelming fear is both central to the original formulation of rape trauma syndrome and a requirement for its theoretical successor, PTSD. How then should we make sense of the possible kinds of impact of those forms of rape in which fear of physical violence and death is not part of the picture? As part of a broader project on contemporary understandings about the impact of rape, I have interviewed twenty-five women[25] about their experience of rape and, more particularly, the impact or place of that rape in their lives. As a group these women had a very diverse range of experiences, both in terms of the nature of the rape itself and the place of that rape in the wider context of their lives. The experiences included a horrific prolonged, tortuous, and life-threatening attack by a stranger in a woman's home, as well as other violent rapes, some in classic stranger scenarios, others by men known to the women. The place that rape played in their lives varied enormously in complex and often not obvious ways. I had some sense of the negative (although not exclusively so) impact of rape for all the women I interviewed. Although, with the possible exception of one woman, none identified their experience of rape as the worst thing that had happened in their lives.

As I was interviewing, one of the dimensions that I became particularly interested in was the place of fear during a woman's experience of rape. Certainly there was no necessary relationship between the presence of fear and whether or not the man was known to the woman. Hayley, one of the several women who spoke about the terror they had felt, was violently raped by her former partner. I include part of her articulate narrative here as a sort of antidote to the possibility that my overall argument could be read as failing to recognize the extreme horror of such violent rapes. Although feminists have debated the political efficacy of "speaking out" about the truth of women's pain and "sexual suffering" as the way toward social change,[26] one of the messages from Herman's (1992) analysis is about the importance of not allowing knowledge of such horrors to be repressed from social consciousness.

*Nicola:* You said in the diary [which Hayley had shown me before our interview] that um, you'd never been so scared in your life.

*Hayley:* No because I honestly thought I was going to die. [*Nicola:* Yeah, yeah] Yeah. And I mean this was somebody who had hit me [*Nicola:* Mm] with his fists in the past but I never felt on those occasions that he was actually going to *kill* me, [*Nicola:* Mm] but *this* time I *did* feel that he was going to kill me.

*Nicola:* Mm, and do you remember how the um fear, was it terror or was it, would you describe it as, would that be an accurate word for it or?

*Hayley:* Yeah panic [*Nicola:* Mm] total panic. Yeah because um . . . I was completely pinned down, I couldn't [*Nicola:* Yeah] move, I couldn't, you know, and it's the most *horrible* feeling [*Nicola:* Mm] it's sort of like being trapped in a coffin I suppose, [*Nicola:* Mm] you just can't move, [*Nicola:* Mm] and you just feel utterly utterly helpless.

*Nicola:* Can you remember what the um experience of that panic was like in your body? What- what impact, what sort of, the way that actually, um?

*Hayley:* Well, [*sigh*] I- I suppose, you know people talk about white fear [*Nicola:* Yeah] and it's like that, like your *whole* blood system has been turned to ice. You- you actually feel cold and, [*Nicola:* Mm] but it doesn't last very long and you feel well everything inside of you, um, has gone sort of cold and numb, and then it goes away and- and comes back again. [*Nicola:* Mm] Mm. I suppose that's what people feel like when they're, when they *are* about to die, [*Nicola:* Mm] yeah.[27]

Hayley's portrayal of the violent rape she experienced, and her description of the "white terror" she felt in the face of possible death, suggest a situation and response that are highly consistent with the kind of event that trauma theorists postulate can trigger a posttraumatic stress reaction. As in Hayley's experience, sometimes rape is accomplished through physical violence and/or through the immobilizing effects of terror in response to the threat of life-threatening violence; sometimes as part of a horrific web of cruel and sadistic torture.

Sometimes, however, the context of rape does not appear to contain any of these elements, and rape is accomplished more through a breach of good faith. In such cases, a woman might be taken by surprise within a set of situational conditions and a compressed temporality that do not allow room for or promote fear. Some of the women I interviewed described rapes in which fear apparently was either not present at all or not a prominent feature of their response at the time. Some trauma theorists describe the phenomenon of a stress-induced altered consciousness in which people may feel no fear or pain, despite being in a situation of severe and imminent threat.[28] Yet these women's accounts gave no suggestion that their absent or relatively low fear was related to this kind of psychobiological survival response.

Sharon, for example, was raped when she was twenty-two or twenty-three by a very good friend on the floor of his lounge after they had shared dinner together. After making some sexual advances that she declined, "he ended up pushing me down face first on the ground, and, lying on- on my back with his arm holding my face down onto the ground"; . . . "I was basically biting the carpet and I was screaming and my face was like [*Nicola:* Mm] ground into the carpet" as he forcefully raped her from behind.

*Nicola:* . . . do you remember whether you experienced fear in- in- at- in- in that moment?

*Sharon:* No, I don't think I, no. It was more disbelief [*Nicola:* Mm] more than anything. Um . . . no I don't, I don't, I wasn't afraid, [*Nicola:* Mm] I wasn't afraid of him. Um and when it was over I wasn't afraid of him.

*Nicola:* Mm. You weren't afraid-

*Sharon:* I knew that if I stayed in the house he wouldn't hurt me. [*Nicola:* Yeah] I wasn't, yeah, um, yeah no I don't, [*Nicola:* Mm] no, don't remember feeling scared or, [*Nicola:* Mm] yeah.

Similarly, Jackie who was raped when she was seventeen or eighteen by an acquaintance on a blind double date described it as an experience that was "scary but not terrifying at all." She was entrapped by this man in his house; he "tore the crotch of the stockings out," forcibly raped her, leaving her with "bruises all *over* me" the next day.

*Jackie:* . . . it's like, cor this guy's doing this to me and I don't want it you know it's- it's, it was scary but not terrifying at all because I knew that it would work out it would be okay, it would be okay I just knew that it would.

*Nicola:*   Do you think, you- you, was it um, was it in part you had no fear that he would hurt you beyond that? Did you-

*Jackie:*   I never ever felt that he would um, beat me up or, I never felt that he'd kill me, I never felt [*Nicola:* Yeah] that, not at all. Um . . . no I didn't think that he'd beat me up or anything like that I, no I didn't.

Later, when I asked her, "What sort of effect do you think it had on you at the time?" she replied,

*Jackie:*   Well I've *thought* about that and I actually don't think it's had *any* effect on me, I don't have *any* trouble [*Nicola:* Mm] um . . . sexual or anything like that I've got no problems there.

As she had already explained earlier in the interview,

And you know it wasn't- wasn't what he *did* to me, my biggest fear was . . . [*crying*] was my family, was them finding out because in those days it was like, if anything like that happened to you, it was your fault, [*Nicola:* Mm] you were to blame, [*Nicola:* Mm] *you* looked a certain way, you shouldn't have worn a dress [*Nicola:* Right]

If we take Jackie's claim at face value, and we would surely have to be careful not to, then her story suggests that not only is rape not inherently life threatening (which is widely understood) but also that rape may not, in and of itself, always be experienced as extremely harmful. Although this possibility is clearly evident in the fine print of any study on the psychological effects of rape, the standard story, as I have already noted, is one that highlights the trauma of rape (understandably, given the recent past in which the potential harm of rape was ignored, minimized, and denied). Notably, what was upsetting to Jackie about this experience was the potential for her family to find out that she had been raped and thus for her to lose control over the way in which she was marked by the gendered cultural meanings around rape. Such meanings were prone at the time (more than thirty years ago) to invoke constructions of women's dangerous lurking sexuality, thus not only blaming the victim for the rape in the first place but stigmatizing her as "that" kind of (bad, sexually wanton) woman.

I met Leanne midway through the interviews I was conducting. When Leanne first made contact on the phone, she said, "I find it hard to say I was raped. It was clear that I didn't want to, but he went ahead anyway." The man who raped her, when she was nineteen, was her boyfriend at the time and later became her husband. She wondered whether she would be a suitable interviewee because her experience was, in her words, "in the lesser range." Her story stood out because of a striking and compelling juxtaposition. On one hand her account was of a "simple" rape (to use

Susan Estrich's term),[29] the kind of rape that some men and women have
been unwilling to see as rape, despite meeting a technical definition, and
the kind of rape that might generally be regarded as at the "lesser" end
of a scale of seriousness and harmfulness. On the other hand, Leanne's
narrative about the dramatic life-changing impact of the rape detailed a
trajectory of harm that was one of the most poignantly rendered and clear
cut of those of any of the women I interviewed.

*Leanne:*  Well I've . . . I, I've never kind of referred to it as rape before,
um or well I, well I maybe have done, very early on but um . . .
basically um, I'd met this guy a couple of times and we ended
up in bed and- [*laugh*] and I told him that [*Nicola:* Mm] um I
didn't want sex and I'd made it really clear. Um, and I made it
clear to the point that he responded to me that he understood
and um, then he went ahead anyway. And although it wasn't,
you know it wasn't violent or forceful it um . . . I came from
a mentality that um . . . I- I came from quite a strict Catholic
upbringing, and I really had in my mindset that- that there
was virginity and then there was not virginity and- and that so
much of your self-worth was hooked up in that . . . [*Nicola:* Mm]
that it- it was, just you know that split second that moment
changed everything, [*Nicola:* Mm] um, and that there was no,
there was no going back. Um, so that- hard part . . . was not
the action itself it was really, from- from that moment on how
I labeled myself, [*Nicola:* Mm] and the fact that um, he didn't
understand at *all* where I was coming from, [*Nicola:* Mm] had
no concept of it.

Although Leanne said that the rape was not "forceful," it was still forced
in the sense that he "went ahead anyway" in direct contravention of her
"really clear" communication to him that she "didn't want sex." In the
context of some consenting sexual engagement, his unwelcome sexual
imposition (the rape) undoubtedly required only light force. It is not difficult to imagine that he was probably positioned in such a way that
only one or two moves were necessary to simply push his penis into her
vagina. His transgression to the point of rape was made possible, it seems,
because the scene was one in which she was utterly unprepared for the
need to resist; she was disarmed by trust and a certain amount of naïveté,
perhaps.[30] (Leanne had described herself as "quite naïve," having previously had only a relationship with a boy who respected and shared her
religious values about sex.) These conditions provided psychological and
temporal qualities to the event that allowed little room for effective resistance to rape. A little while later in the interview, Leanne described her
reaction at the time of the rape, which, like Sharon's, was characterized
more by disbelief than by fear.[31]

*Nicola:* So you remember much detail about the- the moment that it happened and- and how you kind of felt when- when he went ahead
anyway and-

*Leanne:* Um, yeah I do. Um . . . I- I probably just, I probably remember tho- you know that moment or those couple of minutes
more than anything else. [*Nicola:* Mm] Um, yeah I just . . .
I- I think I was just stunned and I was just . . . disbelief and I,
yeah . . . just silent really [*Nicola:* Mm] and, and I- I just . . .
I remember, I remember crying but, you know not from pain
or anything else just from, just, and I think he was asleep and
I just like rolled over and cried but . . . again it wasn't really,
it wasn't, yeah the moment was just disbelief actually [*Nicola:*
Mm] just- just stunned that, [*Nicola:* Mm] I kind of felt like I'd
been deceived or something, mm.

The nature of the impact of this rape for Leanne was not of the kind that
ushered into experience a constellation of posttraumatic symptoms that
were the neurobiological trace of her response to traumatic stress. Rather,
it brought about a more existential psychological crisis whereby she lost
confidence in her whole system of religious values and beliefs and her sense
of who she was in that system of meaning.[32] Because of the importance of
virginity to her sense of herself as a good and moral person, the experience
of having it taken from her left her struggling with the kind of woman she
had become. Although very reflexive about the way in which this event that
might "seem such an inconsequential thing to *most* people," had affected
her, she nevertheless struggled with self-judgment:

How are you *meant* to feel about yourself, [*Nicola:* Mm] kind of thing
like are you then a, you know scarlet woman or something? And- and
that kind of, I *felt* like that but I knew I'd, I knew I *wasn't* that [*Nicola:*
Mm] but I, didn't know how to reconcile it, so.

Not only was Leanne's identity completely disrupted by the rape, but the
future course of her life took shape in that moment, sending her along a
path in which her choices and opportunities were curtailed and in which she
had to struggle not to lose her whole sense of self. Left feeling fundamentally
"unworthy," she ended up marrying the man who raped her, even though
she had persistent doubts, at least in part "because of that action because,
um, I didn't feel worthy of anyone else."

As Cathy Reissman eloquently demonstrates, bearing witness through
the research process is a complex business that requires an openness to
seeing and hearing experiences and realities that do not fit always with our
preexisting models and agendas.[33] The same is true in relation to the clinical realm, where therapy and support are offered to women. The dominant
model of rape trauma derived from Burgess and Holmstrom's early work

has been important in challenging misogynist, victim-blaming, and mini-mizing discourses about rape. But is this comparatively new framework of meaning fluid and flexible enough to allow us to bear adequate witness to all women who have experienced rape and other forms of sexual violence, including but not limited to those who have experienced terrorizing, life-threatening forms of rape? Or might it have become so hegemonic that it has taken hold in a way that fosters a certain blindness to its own limita-tions? If that is the case, then we perhaps risk doing further (symbolic) violence to the experiences of some of the women for whom we seek to promote recognition, care, and justice. Accounts of women such as Leanne are important for illuminating how rape can have profound and disabling meanings beyond those allowed for in the dominant trauma paradigm. However, as Leanne commented after our interview, once the tape recorder had been turned off, "with rape crisis and the like you feel like you have to be a certain kind of way to have any credibility."

Beyond this important issue of theoretical adequacy and accountabil-ity lies another set of questions regarding the politics of trauma. Leanne also said after the interview that it can be difficult to accept how "such a *simple* thing can have such a *strong* effect." That such a thing can seem simple is in itself surely a sign of the normalization and naturalization of men's sexual entitlement and women's relative lack of sexual auton-omy. As such it is a reminder that rape is made possible through forms of cultural scaffolding (Gavey 2005) that privilege men and disempower women. Despite the best intentions of pioneers such as Judith Herman, who emphasized the social and political dimensions of trauma (in relation to rape and trauma more generally), I suggest that an increasingly bio-medicalized trauma paradigm directs our attention away from the social and the political. So seductive is the challenge of unlocking the neurobio-logical secrets of the traumatized psyche that this inner intrigue becomes the almost exclusive focus of attention for those interested in trauma.[34] However, feminists know that the challenge of stopping rape is not going to be advanced by solving such questions alone. For this reason we will need to take care that a trauma lens does not totally eclipse a feminist lens, which remains so necessary for highlighting the critical nexus of gender and power that we need to dismantle on the way.

## NOTES

1. I would like to acknowledge and thank all the women I interviewed for my broader project on rape narratives for giving me the privilege of hearing their personal and moving stories. I would like to thank Fulbright for their gener-ous support of the inspired New Century Scholars (NCS) program, which provided the most stimulating, challenging, and enriching context in which to pursue understandings and action toward the global empowerment of women. I thank all of my NCS colleagues for their engaging and inspiring company. I also thank Dr. Mary Harvey for her generous hospitality when I was a visiting

scholar during part of my NCS year at the Victims of Violence Program and Department of Psychiatry, Harvard Medical School. I am also grateful to the Marsden Fund of the Royal Society of New Zealand and to The University of Auckland for funding my wider project on rape narratives. Many thanks also to Carolyn Elliott for helpful feedback on this chapter.

2. Marge Piercy, "Rape Poem." In *Violence Against Women: A Critique of the Sociobiology of Rape*, eds. Suzanne R. Sunday and Ethel Tobach (New York: Gordian Press, 1985).

3. My focus on the rape of women by is not meant to imply that men and children do not also get raped.

4. See for example Nicola Gavey, *Just Sex? The Cultural Scaffolding of Rape* (London and New York: Routledge, 2005); hereafter cited in text as Gavey (2005).

5. Sandra Sutherland and Donald Scherl, "Patterns of Response Among Victims of Rape," *American Journal of Orthopsychiatry* 40, no. 3 (1970): 503–511, at 503. See also Ann Wolbert Burgess and Lynda Lytle Holmstrom, "Rape Trauma Syndrome," *American Journal of Psychiatry* 131 (1974): 981–986; hereafter cited in text as Burgess and Holmstrom (1974); Elaine Hilberman, "Rape: 'The Ultimate Violation of the Self,'" *American Journal of Psychiatry* 133, no. 4 (1976): 436–437; Kurt Weis and Sandra S. Borges, "Victimology and Rape: The Case of the Legitimate Victim," *Issues in Criminology* 8, no. 2 (1973): 71–115.

6. For further discussion of recent historical shifts in Western discourse on rape, see Gavey (2005), and for a more general historical analysis of the feminist antirape movement in the United States, see Maria Bevacqua, *Rape on the Public Agenda: Feminism and the Politics of Sexual Assault* (Boston: Northeastern University Press, 2000). Of course, minimizing, victim-blaming discourses of rape have not vanished, but they no longer drive the dominant public story about rape.

7. Georges Vigarello, *A History of Rape: Sexual Violence in France from the 16th to the 20th Century* (Cambridge, UK: Polity, 2001), 209.

8. Following Nikolas Rose, *psy* is used as an umbrella term to refer collectively to disciplines such as psychology, psychiatry, and closely related fields such as counseling. See Nikolas Rose, *Inventing Ourselves: Psychology, Power, and Personhood* (Cambridge: Cambridge University Press, 1998).

9. Trauma is written about in a variety of ways, and some feminist writers and others in the humanities often use the term *trauma* in a looser way. However, it seems clear that Western medicalized psychobiological understandings of trauma are increasingly gaining dominance. See Nimisha Patel, "Clinical Psychology: Reinforcing Inequalities or Facilitating Empowerment?" *The International Journal of Human Rights* 7, no. 1 (2003): 16–39; Derek Summerfield, "The Invention of Post-Traumatic Stress Disorder and the Social Usefulness of a Psychiatric Category," *British Medical Journal* 322 (2001): 95–98; hereafter cited in text as Summerfield (2001).

10. When we consider that Burgess and Holmstrom's research was based on work with women who presented to a hospital emergency department of a city hospital, it is not surprising that these were women who were more likely (than women in general who have experienced rape) to have encountered life-threatening rapes. One subsequent study on the prevalence of rape by Mary Koss and her colleagues found that only 5 percent of the rapes identified by women were revealed to victim support services, only 5 percent were reported to the police, and 42 percent were never revealed to anyone. See Mary P. Koss, Christine A. Gidycz, and Nadine Wisniewski, "The Scope of Rape: Incidence and Prevalence of Sexual Aggression and Victimization in a National Sample of Higher

Education Students," *Journal of Consulting & Clinical Psychology* 55, no. 2 (1987): 162–170. It is also interesting to notice that in an earlier publication, although the term *psychological trauma* was used in passing, it was not the dominant framework used for describing the "crisis with either psychological or social consequences" that rape represented for most of the women in their sample. The term *trauma* was more prominently used, as might be expected in a nursing journal at that time, to refer to forms of physical trauma. See Ann Wolbert Burgess and Lynda Lytle Holmstrom, "The Rape Victim in the Emergency Ward," *American Journal of Nursing* 73, no. 10 (1973): 1740–1745; hereafter cited in text as Burgess and Holmstrom (1973).

11. See also Burgess and Holmstrom (1973).
12. I am basing this claim on English-language sources from predominantly Western countries. According to some, trauma is a normal response to an extraordinarily horrible event; in the growing literature on posttraumatic stress disorder (PTSD), however, others argue that the syndrome of persisting symptoms severe enough to qualify for a diagnosis of PTSD is a psychiatric illness, "far more than a simple extension of the normative stress response." See Alexander C. McFarlane, "The Prevalence and Longitudinal Course of PTSD: Implications for the Neurobiological Models of PTSD," *Annals of the New York Academy of Sciences* 821, no. 1 (1997): 10–23, at 20. For further discussion, see Rachel Yehuda and Alexander C. McFarlane, "Conflict Between Current Knowledge About Posttraumatic Stress Disorder and Its Original Conceptual Basis," *American Journal of Psychiatry* 152, no. 12 (1995): 1705–1713.
13. Judith Lewis Herman, *Trauma and Recovery* (New York: Basic Books, 1992), 33; hereafter cited in text as Herman (1992). (Rape is one of the key examples Herman writes about.)
14. Fieldnotes, July 21, 2003, taken during attendance at Babette Rothschild, *The Mind and Body of Trauma: Understanding Traumatic Memory & PTSD.* One-day professional workshop presented by Doctors for Sexual Abuse Care, Auckland, New Zealand, 2004. (See also Babette Rothschild, *The Body Remembers: The Psychophysiology of Trauma and Trauma Treatment* (New York: W.W. Norton, 2000); hereafter cited in text as Rothschild (2000). For concern about overuse of the category of PTSD and the term *trauma* see also Richard J. McNally, *Remembering Trauma* (Cambridge, MA: Belknap Press of Harvard University Press, 2003); and Roger K. Pitman, "Overview of Biological Themes in PTSD," *Annals of the New York Academy of Sciences* 821, no. 1 (1997): 1–9; hereafter cited in text as Pitman (1997).
15. American Psychiatric Association, *Diagnostic and Statistical Manual of Mental Disorders,* 4th ed. (Washington, DC: American Psychiatric Association, 1994); hereafter cited in text as APA (1994).
16. See APA (1994), Herman (1992), Pitman (1997).
17. David Lisak, "The Neurobiology of Trauma," unpublished paper, 2002, http://www.nowldef.org/html/njep/dvd/pdf/neurobiology.pdf (accessed October 31, 2003): 3.
18. In fact, Burgess and Holmstrom's (1974) identification of the patterns of response they called rape trauma syndrome was based on observations and interviews with the ninety-two adult women within their larger study who had experienced what they called "forcible rape," not the additional seventeen adult women whom the authors thought were victims of some other kind of circumstance (for further discussion, see Lynda Lytle Holmstrom and Ann Wolbert Burgess, *"The Victim of Rape: Institutional Reactions* (New Brunswick, NJ: Transaction Publishers, 1983). It is possible that in a contemporary context some of those women might have been considered to have also experienced rape.

19. Deborah S. Rose, "'Worse Than Death': Psychodynamics of Rape Victims and the Need for Psychotherapy," *American Journal of Psychiatry* 143, no. 7 (1986): 817–824, at 818.

20. The notion that rape is inherently life-threatening is still in circulation, however. For example, in a section on the emotional needs of the rape victim in a currently available online curriculum on rape, it is noted, "They may or may not be physically injured but all have been through a life threatening situation and will need time and support to recover." See Marcia Cohen and Sherrie H. McKenna, *Rape: Psychology, Prevention and Impact*, Vol. III (New Haven, CT: Yale–New Haven Teachers Institute, 1981), http://www. yale.edu/ynhti/curriculum/units/1981/3/81.03.06.x.html (accessed January 11, 2007). (Although originally published in 1981, this fact is not highlighted for people coming upon the resource through a keyword-directed Web search.)

21. As Wikipedia tells us, "Rape Trauma Syndrome is [not *can be*] experienced by rape victims and can be divided into phases." See "Rape." *Wikipedia: The Free Encyclopedia*, http://en.wikipedia.org/wiki/Rape (accessed January 8, 2007).

22. By 1991, for instance, Edna Foa and her colleagues were noting that "the psychological sequelae of rape have been conceptualized as posttraumatic stress disorder." See Edna B. Foa, Barbara O. Rothbaum, David S. Riggs, and Tamera B. Murdock, "Treatment of Posttraumatic Stress Disorder in Rape Victims: A Comparison Between Cognitive–Behavioral Procedures and Counseling," *Journal of Consulting and Clinical Psychology* 59, no. 5 (1991): 715–723, at 715.

23. For example, Mary P. Koss and Mary R. Harvey, *The Rape Victim: Clinical and Community Interventions*, 2nd ed. (Newbury Park, CA: Sage, 1991). See also Jenny Petrak, "The Psychological Impact of Sexual Assault." In *The Trauma of Sexual Assault: Treatment, Prevention and Practice*, eds. Jenny Petrak and Barbara Hedge (Chichester, UK: John Wiley & Sons, 2002).

24. Vernon R. Wiehe and Ann L. Richards, *Intimate Betrayal: Understanding and Responding to the Trauma of Acquaintance Rape* (Thousand Oaks, CA: Sage, 1995): 51.

25. I interviewed twenty-two women in New Zealand and three women in the Boston area of the United States. Four of the New Zealand women were also interviewed a second time. The majority of participants were recruited through a suburban newspaper article. The ages of the women quoted here, at the time of their interviews, were Hayley (forty-eight), Sharon (thirty-six), Jackie (fifty), and Leanne (thirty-four) (these names are pseudonyms). Interviews were transcribed in full, recording all words and utterances.

26. Renee Heberle, "Deconstructive Strategies and the Movement Against Sexual Violence," *Hypatia* 11, no. 4 (1996): 63–76. For further feminist critique of a trauma model or the construct of PTSD, see Gavey (2005); Sharon Lamb, "Constructing the Victim: Popular Images and Lasting Labels." In *New Versions of Victims: Feminist Struggles with the Concept*, ed. Sharon Lamb (New York: New York University Press, 1999); and Jeanne Marecek, "Trauma Talk in Feminist Clinical Practice." In *New Versions of Victims: Feminist Struggles with the Concept*, ed. Sharon Lamb (New York: New York University Press, 1999).

27. The interview extracts quoted in this chapter are taken from the original transcripts, and have not been edited. Short pauses are denoted by three dots [ . . . ]; a hanging hyphen indicates an abrupt end to a train of speech; a speaker's emphasis is shown in italics.

28. For example, Rothschild (2000, 10) and Herman (1992, 42–43).

29. Susan Estrich, *Real Rape* (Cambridge, MA: Harvard University Press, 1987). As Estrich discusses, it has also been historically difficult to get a serious hearing for such rapes in the criminal justice system. See also Gavey (2005).

30. Admittedly I am making some interpretive presumptions here, on the basis of Leanne's fuller narrative. In the interests of maintaining rapport and taking a moral and political position in relation to the hearing of women's testimonies of rape, there are some questions that I did not ask (such as about her opportunities for or attempts at physical resistance). To have done so in the context of her particular narrative would have immediately invoked echoes of the historically powerful cultural skepticism about the impossibility of raping an unwilling woman, and I was unwilling to risk inviting or intensifying her vulnerability or sense of being judged by doing so.

31. Burgess and Holmstrom (1974, 982) note that "the impact of rape may be so severe that feelings of shock or disbelief are expressed." However, the nature of the disbelief described by Sharon and Leanne seemed more akin to the reaction to a betrayal rather than fear; both emphasized that they had not experienced any fear for their life or further physical violence.

32. It is interesting to note that cognitive scientist Jennifer Freyd, who coined the term "betrayal trauma," has developed a two-dimensional model of traumatic events that takes account of the possibility that terror or fear and social betrayal exist on orthogonal dimensions, both of which may be present in varying degrees. Although this model might accommodate some more of the features of experiences such as Leanne's, it is also noteworthy that Freyd cites rape as an example that might simultaneously involve betrayal and be life threatening, thus (although not explicitly claiming that this is the case) retaining the presumption of rape as life threatening. See Jennifer J. Freyd, "Betrayal Trauma: Traumatic Amnesia as an Adaptive Response to Childhood Abuse." *Ethics & Behavior* 4, no. 4 (1994): 307–329; and Jennifer J. Freyd, "What Is a Betrayal Trauma? What Is Betrayal Trauma Theory?" http://dynamic.uoregon.edu/~jjf/defineBT.html (accessed January 13, 2007).

33. Catherine Kohler Reissman, "Doing Justice: Positioning the Interpreter in Narrative Work." In *Strategic Narrative: New Perspectives on the Power of Personal and Cultural Stories,* ed. Wendy Patterson (Lanham, MD: Lexington Books, 2002).

34. My analysis is not intended to deny that many women may experience the aftermath of rape in ways that conform to a trauma model and/or that some may indeed find comfort in the knowledge provided by this framework for making sense of their experiences. See Susan J. Brison, *Aftermath: Violence and the Remaking of a Self* (Princeton, NJ: Princeton University Press, 2002).

# 13 Understanding Masculinities, Empowering Women

## What Have Boys in Ghana Got to Do with It?

*Akosua Adomako Ampofo and
John Boateng[1]*

Since the late 1990s, a number of significant developments have helped push the issues of masculinity, culture, and power to the fore in the public discourse on women's empowerment in Ghana. Since 1998, Ghana has recorded increasing reports of violence against women and mostly female children by men in a variety of situations, including brutal serial and spousal killings of women that generated headlines and attention in the public domain from 2000 to 2002. The spousal killings have been "justified" under different framings of male rights and privilege. Media reports, for example, suggest that the wife-killings are frequently related to husbands' constructions of their roles as family heads and providers, women's failures to accord men their due respect by seeking permission before embarking on certain ventures, or perceptions about women's sexuality.[2]

The urgency of understanding masculinity has escalated with the epidemic of HIV/AIDS. There is a growing consensus that the behavior of some men and boys is largely driving the epidemic in sub-Saharan Africa. In many settings males have a dominant role in deciding the nature and context of sex, and whether condoms are used.[3] About half of all people infected with HIV are younger than 25 years. Teenage girls in sub-Saharan region are five times more likely to be infected than boys, and 62 percent of young people aged 15 to 24 who are HIV-positive live in sub-Saharan Africa.[4] Given the nature of the transition from HIV infection to AIDS, the high incidence of AIDS among young people in their twenties indicates that many contracted HIV before age twenty. The younger people are when they become sexually active, the more likely they are to have several sexual partners, and the more likely they are to be exposed to STDs including HIV. Children under the age of fourteen represent the so-called "window of hope" for managing HIV/AIDS because they have generally not begun their sexual lives could be encouraged to postpone the onset of sexual activity, and have better control over their sexuality when they do.

We believe that men and women, but especially boys and men, must undergo transformations if we are to see more equal gender relations, and that men in particular must understand how masculinity operates and what it does to women and men. When men are led to intimate perspectives on men, often through the eyes of other men, they are better equipped to recognise so-called hegemonic masculinities and their deleterious effects on women, children, and other men.[5] In this paper we seek to open a window on some of the meanings of manhood among boys aged between 11 and 15 in the hope that this will expand our understanding of masculinities and contribute to the development of "new men."[6]

The term "masculinity" is a collective gender identity, not a natural attribute. It is socially constructed and fluid, resulting in diverse forms across different times and contexts, and mediated by class, race, ethnicity, religion, age, geographic location, and other local factors. Therefore it is more appropriate to refer to *masculinities*.[7] Masculinity defines how boys and men should behave, be treated, dress, appear and succeed, and the attitudes and qualities they should have.[8] The study of masculinities is an effort to make sense of the relationships between individual males and groups of males as well as between males and females. Morrell (1998) notes that it is through the investigation of these masculine points of view that a platform for the deconstruction of stereotypical masculinities and the reconstruction of new norms can be formed.[9]

While much work has been done on adolescent sexual behaviours, focusing on their so-called "risky" behaviours, less attention has been paid to understanding *how* young people construct their gender identities, and how these constructions might be related to sexual and other lifestyle choices. Styles of gender and sexual interaction between males and females are rehearsed during adolescence. Research carried out with adolescent boys around the world suggests that viewing women as sexual objects, using coercion to obtain sex, and viewing sex as a performance-oriented perspective begins in adolescence or even in childhood and may continue into adulthood.[10] At the same time a handful of studies suggest that this is also the time when boys and young men learn to challenge normative, hegemonic forms of masculinity and to construct less hegemonic notions and expectations.[11] Understanding these alternative masculinities can help suggest possibilities for transformation of particular kinds of masculinities.

In this paper we explore some of the meanings of masculinity—of being a boy or a man—as presented by thirty boys aged between the ages of eleven and fifteen, generally before they would have begun sexual activity. They are from two communities in the Eastern Region of Ghana, one of which has a matrilineal heritage and the other a patrilineal one. These data form part of a larger study in which we conducted in-depth interviews with fifty-eight students, twenty-eight girls, and thirty boys, who were selected following preliminary analysis of survey findings from among those categorised as having an "egalitarian," "average," or "male dominant" orientation.[12] All of the boys whose responses are discussed below also participated in a survey of all first-year Junior Secondary School students in the towns.

## UNDERSTANDING MASCULINITIES

Theories of masculinity are important for understanding the social legitimization among both males and females of the unequal treatment of women. These conceptual arrangements allow us to understand the different kinds of masculinities, to make sense of the power aspects of masculinity, and thus to suggest how specific constructions might be used as models to transform more hegemonic forms of masculinities.

Hegemonic masculinity is the dominant form of masculinity in a society and pertains to the relations of cultural domination by men. Hegemonic masculinity presents a version of how men should behave, and the cultural idea of how putative "real men" do behave (Morrell, 1998). In addition to being oppressive for women, hegemonic masculinity silences other masculinities, placing them in opposition to itself and depriving them of currency or legitimacy. Boys and men who fail to live up to this form of masculinity may be ridiculed as being feminized. In Akan, the dominant language in Ghana, they are referred to as *bemaa-basia,* "female-man."

Nonetheless, there have always existed, and continue to exist, other forms of masculinity. Several studies describe individual men who contest these hegemonic forms, despite ridicule or physical threats.[13] Narismulu and Mamphele both describe young men who defy peer constructions of masculinity in their rough township neighbourhoods in the new post-apartheid South Africa. They reflect sensitivity and concern not only towards women but also towards other men. Suttner's examination of masculinities in the ANC reveals diverse models that "disrupt what is the . . . conduct expected of male heroes."[14] Suttner describes Sobizana Mngqikana, a freedom fighter who sheds tears because he is hurt by a slight from his comrades. Work on male-male sexual relations also reveals that men who are "gay," or who have sex with men, destabilize gender scripts not only because of abnormal sexual practices, but also by displaying unmanly or feminine traits in modes of dress or gestures for example.[15]

Reknowned Nigerian novelist Chinua Achebe writes of the pain inflicted by hegemonic masculinity in Igbo society and shows alternative forms. In his famous novel *Things Fall Apart* (1958), Achebe's character Okonkwo is a patriot who rules his household with an iron hand.[16] Wives and children, even adult children, are expected to fall in line with his commands. Okonkwo acts this way in part to compensate for his own father's perceived weakness. His father Unoka died in debt and humiliation when Okonkwo was very young. Shame for his father and fear of failure drive Okonkwo to work tirelessly. Nwoye is Okonkwo's sensitive and thoughtful, but also less ambitious, son by his first wife and Okonkwo has high expectations for him. Fearing that Nwoye will turn out like his own father, Unoka, Okonkwo is severe with his son. He wants Nwoye to grow up into a tough, prosperous young man "capable of ruling his father's household when he is dead and gone to join the ancestors." Young Nwoye, however, prefers listening to female-oriented stories, such as those about the tortoise or the bird Eneke, to stories of violence and bloodshed that seek to inculcate notions of masculine bravery and control.

In Nwoye, Achebe shows us an alternative masculinity, one crushed by Okonkwo's dominance. Yet Okonkwo's hegemonic masculinity and obsession with being a "real" Igbo man becomes his undoing. His harshness and insensitivity in sacrificing his son's best friend, a young boy given to the village as tribute in war, drive his son away. Okonkwo's recklessness ultimately leads to his exile from his beloved village and home. Another character in the novel, Okonkwo's elderly and wise uncle, shows another counterpoint to hegemonic masculinity. In Okonkwo's eventual submission to his uncle's authority Achebe shows the possibility of an alternate, and gentler, masculinity.

The stratification of gender roles is passed down through the generations. Among the Akan of Ghana a son does not inherit from his father, but fathers are expected to set up their male children in life through training, giving of gifts such as land and guns, and helping their sons to marry their first wife. Sons are usually apprenticed to either the father himself or to a master craftsman, orator, or statesman. During this apprenticeship process definitions of appropriate masculinity are transmitted. Approved or encouraged male characteristics include virility, strength, authority, power, and leadership; the ability to offer protection and sustenance, intelligence and wisdom; and the ability to bear physical and emotional pain. Girls are taught to defer to men and boys as stronger, wiser, and more responsible, while boys are taught to lead and control women.[17] A boy who does not measure up to prescribed expectations is branded a *bema-basia*, meaning "man-woman." Conversely, a girl who veers into the domains prescribed for boys is branded *babasia-kokonin,* meaning "woman-cock" or "male-woman" (Adomako Ampofo, 2001).

Proverbs are used to explain and describe gender differences. Amoah (1991) and Rattray (1927) cite several that portray men as brave and authoritative over events and circumstances:[18]

> If the gun lets out its bullets, it is the man who receives them on his chest.
> Even if a woman buys a gun or a drum it leans against a man's hut.
> The hen also knows that it is dawn, but it allows the cock to announce it.

In daily discourse these sayings endorse masculine inclinations in boys and reinforce gender positions (Adomako Ampofo, 2001).

Feminist research on decision-making between spouses, domestic gender role arrangements, and sexual and reproductive behaviours in Africa indicates that male dominance remains pervasive and accepted in Ghana and much of sub-Saharan Africa. Studies on gender-based violence, for example, show that male violence against females is common and that many women seem to accept violence from intimate partners as inherent in the relationship.[19] It shows that male-against-female violence erupts when women fail to seek permission from their partners before taking "major" decisions such as going on a journey, engaging in a new economic activity, or even visiting a friend (Coker-Appiah and Cusack, 1999). A "real" man also does not tolerate his wife questioning him about his sexual adventures, or worse, refusing to have sex with him afterward.[20] Although women frequently end up as victims of violence, men are also under a great deal of pressure to fit the hegemonic norm of what it means to be a man, and the attendant frustrations are linked to stress and gender-based violence.[21]

What do all males have in common? In what ways do they differ in their conceptions of manhood? Why are men the way they are? How and when are particular masculinities constructed and used? Most importantly, how can the answers gleaned be used to promote more gender equitable attitudes between men and women? This paper presents a small window into the deconstruction of masculinities.

## GHANAIAN BOYS AND MANHOOD

In this section we discuss issues related to domestic gender roles, reproductive decision-making, and permission-seeking from interviews with boys in Ghana. We discuss the following questions we asked the boys: how do constructions of acceptable tasks at home change with adolescence, who has the right in a sexual partnership to initiate and refuse sexual activity, and do men have the right to discipline women who do not seek permission before undertaking various ventures?

## Gender Roles

The boys' responses to our questions concerning household tasks show that they are beginning to identify these tasks with notions of masculinity that differentiate them from girls, many of which they had been required to perform as a younger child.

"I am a boy, so I do not carry rubbish to the dumpster or cook in the kitchen; my sister, however, can carry rubbish to the dumpster and she can cook."

"They (the girls) have to cook for the boys but the boys don't have to cook for the girls."

"I'm a poor cook, but it's okay; after all, I'm a boy. Therefore, I do not need to cook for anybody but myself."

Three areas of domestic work that boys no longer partake of emerge as important markers in the transition to manhood: cooking and kitchen work, doing the laundry, and sweeping. Most of the boys clearly believe that kitchen work is a female role and their absence from this activity marks them as "not female," or "male."

> "Don't you see that, in the house, boys don't normally cook. So when they cook they will be laughed at and people will say that you like food."

> "Let's say that when you are born a woman. If your mother is cooking, you will see that her daughter is always with her so that she can teach her how to cook. So it is the woman who must cook."

> "It is because it is the womens' job. Let's say that we know that, when it comes to sweeping, it is the women that know how to sweep."

> "When boys participate in cleaning the house or doing laundry, it is only to help the girls in their female duties. When the boys do laundry, they only wash their own clothes, or perhaps those of an older male such as a father's or uncle's."

> "When we are staying on our own, like now that we are in our own father's house, when we [the boys] finish eating we leave our plates for the girls to wash, and the girls sweep the house and others. Then when there is some weeding to be done, we weed so that the girls will rest. And there are times, like Saturdays, when we wash all our things. If we clean the room then we help the girls and we all do it."

> "Sometimes the woman knows she can wash, but as for men they can't wash well. But let me say that if you are not married then you can wash your own clothes if you are a man. But a man will only wash his own things. Sometimes if a man says that he is washing, he cannot wash, lets say, his mother's things."

There are some boys, however, who reject these gendered divisions of labor:

> "As for cooking, the girls can do it and we the boys too can do it too."

Some boys go further to provide a more qualified understanding. One, for example, went into a detailed description of an equal division of labour in a scenario where he becomes a doctor and his mother-in-law is visiting. If his wife's mother reprimands her for being lazy and a bad wife for letting her husband do the kitchen work, he would defend her saying, "We are the same."

Often, however, this appreciation of doing household chores is guided purely by pragmatic considerations of how an unmarried man would organise his life:

"The work has to be shared that way so that when the boys grow up and they are not yet married, they can do certain basic things like cooking on their own before they marry."

One boy talked about what he would teach his children—in this case, his sons:

> I will want to teach all of them (my children). . . . . Maybe some will not marry directly when they grow, maybe they will work for sometime before. So since he is working . . . maybe he will want to live alone. . . . . He will not get any woman who will cook for him or wash his things for him. So if he does not learn these things he will have problems.

Nonetheless, in teaching his son to cook another boy says he will make sure:

> "If he learns, I will not let him learn more than a girl."

The boys make a significant distinction between the chores appropriate to women and men in a premarital relationship and in a marital one. Marriage is different from dating with regard to the couple's commitment, and therefore the expectations they can have of each other. There are roles women are required to perform in the home, such as cooking, which the boys acknowledge could not be insisted upon before marriage because the man has not formally married the woman. Women may choose to perform these domestic roles, but their partners (boyfriends or betrothed partners) have no power to enforce them:

> "With some couples, the woman may do all their house chores. So if you are free, you can tell her to come and wash your things for you because she is your friend. She can too; if she wants to come and wash your things for you, she can."

With regard to marriage, the boys we interviewed understood that the husband assumes the responsibility for providing money and other resources to support the woman he has married. They expected the husband to work outside the home while the wife stays at home, cooks, and does her husband's laundry:

> "The women would have to do the cooking because it is the men who go to work and bring the money, so they shouldn't do the cooking."

Some boys are quite clear that a wife's place is to serve her husband:

> "Because he is the one that, when everything is at home, he makes sure that every thing is in place. So when some men marry, they marry a

woman in order for her to serve them. So he should not let the woman sit down and and proceed to serve her, the woman must rather serve him."

However, the boys concede that a responsible and caring man will help with her duties when necessary. Not only will this ease the wife's burden, it will save the husband, who is the head of the home, from disgrace in the event that visitors show up.

*Respondent*: Okay, just because the house chores are for the woman that does not mean that you should leave everything to the woman. You should be able to help her. You do that so that all of the house chores will be perfect. Sometimes when you leave everything to the women, there are things that she may not be able to do. But when people come to the house they will not insult only the woman, they will insult all of you. So you should be able to help her so that you all work. . . . It is your duty to help her.

*Interviewer*: So if your son grows and his wife is not sick and is at home, does he have to cook for her?

*R*: As for that, it does not mean that when the woman is at home it is the man who will cook. It is the woman who cooks for the man. Maybe she is tired when she returns from work or the work that she does is a lot. Then he can help her to cook.

*I*: And what if she is not tired; she is not sick and is at home?

*R*: Then he must not cook whilst the woman sits down.

The concept of a male role in housework as a helper that does a favour or a kindness to the woman seems firmly lodged in the ideology of many of the boys.

## Reproductive Decision-making

Reproductive decision-making is a contentious area for many couples, with disagreements leading to so-called "unwanted" or "mistimed" births for many women.[22] We asked boys about the marital decisions concerning the decision to have children, the decision to stop having children, using contraceptives, and having sex. They displayed a high level of pragmatism, generally according women the final say when it came to stop having children, and according men the final say when it came to continuing to have children. This is consistent with the preferences of older men (Adomako Ampofo, 2004), suggesting that ideas about masculinity remain linked to concepts of biological fatherhood. In a scenario where a couple already has one or more children and the wife wants to stop childbearing or delay having another child while her husband wants to continue having children, boys think that the wife's opinion should count more than the husband's because it is her body that would carry the child. However, if a woman wants a child but her husband wants to delay the birth of the child or stop having children altogether, boys think that his decision should count because they recognise that the husband is the one who will provide for the child.

> "The man should be responsible for family planning in the marriage."

Women who are not willing to "give" men the children they need can be divorced, or the man can take a second wife.

> "If the man insists on having a child and the woman also says no, and if the man gets angry, the man can divorce the woman and look for another."

> "What I will say to the woman is that, if she says she is tired and she does not want to have any more children, she should allow the man to go and marry another woman he can have a son with. If she does not want [to bear him a child] then she should understand what he is saying."

Additionally, if a woman is being ridiculed for being childless, when it is her husband who wants to delay childbearing, the husband should be considerate. Boys recognise the important ways in which biological parenthood is tied to a normal identity. However, when the interviewer linked cessation of childbearing to a man's ability, or lack of ability, to take care of more children, the boys revert the decision-making power to the husband.

> "The woman does not have the power . . . because [having children] is part of the benefit that you get from the money you provided for performing the customary rites. It is the man who will take care of the children."

When the interviewer introduced the caveat that the wife had assured her husband she could look after the child, some boys said it is okay to have another child even though the husband feels financially challenged, and that this does not diminish the husband's power.

*Interviewer:* When you say that, it means that it is the woman who has gotten power over the issue?

*Respondent:* What I mean is that you have given her the power. You mean that you don't have money to take care of the child if she gives birth again. And she also means that even if you don't have money to take care of the child, she has money that she will use to help you take care of the two children.

There are many boys who had earlier supported clear gender divisions in the allocation of household work, who recommend discussion and compromise on matters of reproduction, such as when the woman wants a child and the man is not ready. Or they recognise that unwanted pregnancies and children may be experienced by women more profoundly than by men. Here boys acknowledge that, although the husband has a titular headship position, his wife has a more valuable or sensible position on certain issues that he should acknowledge.

> "The woman should be responsible for family planning because if she does not make sure that they have family planning she can get pregnant."

> "Maybe, I can tell the woman to be patient a bit, and if in time I get some money we can have children."

> "You are saying that the woman wants a child and the man says no, the man should go and see a doctor or a nurse to discuss the issue [about family planning]."

Or, in the reverse case, when the man wants a child but his wife is not ready:

> "Maybe it will help both of you [to postpone childbirth], so you will have to be patient with her."
>
> *Interviewer*: So, regarding the man, you want to say that he does not have much power in the marriage?
>
> *Respondent*: He does, but sometimes he has to listen to what the woman says. Sometimes what the woman says is also valuable and so he has to listen, because it will help both of them.

Very few respondents reported that they ever had sex, and even among these experiences, some had been non-consensual or one-time occurrences. Thus we pursued questions about sexual activity with a great deal of caution. It may be because the boys are not yet sexually active and have not begun to engage in peer discourse around actual sexual experiences or manhood and sexuality that they claim a high level of respect for women's decisions about sex. This presents a unique opportunity to reinforce the notion that men and women have equal rights and desires in sexual activity.

We asked the boys how they would deal with a situation in which a wife did not want to have sex, or turned away from her husband's advances because she was tired. It was heartening to us to hear answers like the following:

> "You have the chance and she also has the chance. So if she says that she is tired you have to respect that."

We also presented the reverse scenario when the wife wanted sex and the husband didn't and the boys gave similar responses, none of them indicating that it was an unlikely scenario.[23]

## Permission Seeking and Violence

Boys agree that wives should seek permission from their husbands before they travel, visit parents, embark on business ventures, or make any other plans. It is the status of marriage that confers these rights or power on a man—a power he does not have and cannot enforce as long as he has not married a woman. These expectations do not hold for girlfriends, even if the couple plan to get married.

> "Since you are friends she can tell you that she is going. She will not ask you for permission because since you are not married. *She is not under you*. But if you have married then *she is under you* so she can ask you for permission. And you are not a father that she has to come and ask if she can go somewhere or not. But you are friends so she can come and tell you that she is going to see her father (emphasis added)."

> "If you say she shouldn't go, she can choose to go and not to go because you have not married her."

> "You didn't give birth to her . . . you have not married her, she is just your friend."

It seems that boys see marriage as transforming a woman's status from "friend" to "dependent," and that the role of guardian is transferred from her father or mother to her husband. This guardianship position comes with the right to grant a wife permission to undertake particular activities. The transformation in status is typically explained by the simple fact that the man married the woman.

> "The reason why the man can go without permission is that he *married* the woman and not vice versa, so whereas the man can go somewhere with authority, the woman cannot do likewise (emphasis added)."

> "She has to ask for permission because now that you have married her she is *under* you. Her parents know that she is under you (emphasis added)."

> "If the wife wants to go on a business trip, she needs to ask permission . . . because a wife must obey whatever her husband tells her . . . because it is the man who spent all those monies in marrying her. So if the man says something and she doesn't listen he can go an inform her parents."

If a wife fails to seek permission her husband reserves the right to issue a verbal warning. If she refuses to heed the warning, the man has the right to punish her by doing something else to make her listen, reporting her to her parents, or in rare cases, beating her. While most of the boys reject the use of violence in relationships, especially in premarital relationships, where an act of violence was linked to transgressions that defy male headship—such as "disobedience" or failure to seek permission from a spouse—they sometimes considered it legitimate. A boy who earlier said that a man could not beat a girlfriend for whom customary rites had not been performed, justified beatings for married couples.

*Interviewer*:   Could I have beaten her if we were married?
*R*:                  Please, yes.
*I*:                   What is the justification?
*R*:                  Because you have paid so much for her to be your wife.

Violence is justified by a few on the basis of "love," much as one would discipline a loved child to keep it from straying.[24] Says another boy:

*Respondent*:   If she doesn't listen and she goes, you can divorce her.
*Interviewer*:   You said formerly too that you could beat her?
*R*:                  Yes, if you love her, you can beat her. But if you are quick tempered, you will sack her.
*I*:                   That means that you will sack her if you don't love her, but if you love her, you will beat her?
*R*:                  Yes, because you may feel sorry for her so you will just get angry and beat her up. And there are times, when you get too angry, you will divorce her by going to present a drink to her family.

Husbands, on the other hand, are under no compulsion to ask permission from their wives. A considerate and responsible man will, however, inform his wife, or discuss his plans with her.

> "You are telling her about your plans because, you being the man, she cannot tell you what to do."

Although this same boy feels that it is only appropriate for a man to show respect towards his wife by sharing his decision to do something or go somewhere with her, he feels that the man does not need a woman's permission. Even if she disapproves and requests that her husband not do what he has planned, this boy still feels that the husband can still proceed and his wife can neither prevent nor punish him. Indeed, the mere fact that a man tells his partner about a decision he has taken should be accepted by his wife as a sign of respect for her. Thereafter, she is not expected to question the decision but to gratefully acknowledge the fact that he chose to share it with her.

*Interviewer*:   The man [also] must ask permission from her?
*Respondent*:  Yes.

I:      [And] if she says no?

R:    Then you can leave in anger.

I:      When I defy her and go. Can she beat me when I come back?

R:    Please, no.

I:      Why?

R:    Because you are a man. So if she beats you, you will also beat her back and the whole thing will turn into something else. She can't beat you up, because you went in to marry her but she did not go to marry the man.

Politically correct adults might be more reticent in categorically stating that men have more power than women, even when this power difference is manifested in their relationships in concrete ways—but the interviewed boys are less constrained.

"In marriage, the man has the power."

This power a husband has over his wife is reflected even in the responses of the boys who oppose violence. These boys suggest alternatives such as reporting an errant wife to her parents, threatening her, and ultimately, divorce, but inherent in the discourse is the idea that a wife is a minor, a child who needs to be frightened into obedience by the threat of sanctions or withdrawal of privileges:

*Interviewer:*  Is it good that the man beat the wife when the woman has done something he does not like?

*Respondent:*  No even if it is not good [what the woman has done], the man should not beat the woman.

I:      If he says something and the woman does not listen, and then he says it again and the woman does not listen, what can the man do?

R:    He should correct her.

I:      He corrected her and the woman did not listen.

R:    Then the man can frighten her and tell her that if she does not take care he will beat her . . . Then he will beat her, and he should get close and reprimand her. Then she will be frightened.

I:      So he can beat her?

R:    No, he should not beat her. But he should frighten her.

I:      She has asked for permission and you said "don't go" and she goes [anyway]. Now can I beat her?

R:    You don't have the right to beat her. You have to go and tell her parents what she does

I:      Can't I hit her a few times?

R:    There is no need to hit her at all.

I:              So what about all the many things I paid to her father?

R:              Okay, it was paid to show that the woman is with you; the woman is *under you*. That does not give you the right ... to beat her (emphasis added).

The few boys who feel that it is not necessary for a woman to ask permission either link this to a woman's economic autonomy ("After all it is her own money.") or see the idea of seeking "permission" as a courtesy that, once sought, a husband is obliged to allow.

## DOES MASCULINITY MATTER?

The boys in our study attach meanings to manhood that differ in the extent to which they reflect hegemonic masculinities. The boys are clearest about the differences in gender identity identified with household tasks as one travels from boyhood to manhood, especially upon attaining the status of being married. Typical female chores such as cooking, cleaning, and laundry must be forsaken, or only performed in a helping capacity or if one is still single. Not only does marriage free men from the mundane responsibilities of household management, it also confirms manhood in the sense that one moves up from "female" and "boyish" tasks to manly ones.

The boys recognise masculinity as something to be achieved, or a place to arrive at, in stages, and over time it must be won and defended. They see the transition from being single to marriage as a status enhancer for men and a sign that one has taken on more responsibility, while women see marriage as simply a transfer from one authority figure, or set of authority figures (her parents), to another (the husband). Male authority derives not simply from being a man, but from the fact that men marry women, and not vice versa. Men are the prize awarded to worthy women—the good husband is the reward for having been a good girl.[25]

If boys are conditioned to see marriage as a major step in the trajectory towards manhood, with its attendant privileges relative to women, boys can be expected to seek marriage and to enforce these gender divisions when they are married. Yet the finding that some boys do not see marriage in this way suggests that alternative models can be introduced and reinforced. Even among the boys with hegemonic notions about what it means to be a man, none constructed the alternative, less-dominant form of masculinity as a deviant, or less normative or legitimate, form such as the "female-man." That is to say, while many boys support a form of masculinity that portrays men as strong and in charge, they do not reject a softer form for other men who choose it. This is particularly hopeful.

Whatever form of masculinity the Ghanaian boys accept, however, they all recognise masculinity as imbued with power. The boys are in no doubt that men have more power and authority than women.

# NOTES

1. The research for this paper was funded with a grant from the World Health Organization (WHO, Special Programme of Research, Development and Research Training in Human Reproduction). The authors would also like to thank Ama Pinkrah, University of Ghana, for her assistance with sorting and coding data files.

   This chapter is a modified version of an earlier paper titled "Multiple Meanings of Manhood among boys in Ghana" that was presented at the conference "From Boys to Men," University of the Western Cape, 26–28 January 2005 in Cape Town and will appear in a book edited by Kopano Ratele and Tammy Shefer.
2. In November of 2000 the first author joined women's organizations in Ghana in a demonstration in Accra to protest the serial killings and the failure of the government to identify and arrest the perpetrator(s). During the march some men we met on the way assured us that so long as they were men and we were women they would "discipline" us if we were out of line.
3. Akosua Adomako Ampofo, "'When Men Speak, Women Listen: Gender Socialization and Young Adolescents' Attitudes to Sexual and Reproductive Issues." *African Journal of Reproductive Health* 5, no. 3 (2001): 196–212, hereafter cited in text as Adomako Ampofo (2001); Akosua Adomako Ampofo, Osman Alhassan, Francis Ankrah, Deborah Atobrah and Moses Dortey, *Sexual Exploitation of Children in the City of Accra* (Accra, Ghana: UNICEF, 2007); F. Nii-Amoo Dodoo, "Men Matter: Additive and Interactive Gender Preferences, and Reproductive Behavior in Kenya," *Demography* 359, no. 2 (1998): 229–42, hereafter cited in text as Dodoo (1998); Rivers and Aggleton (1999).
4. UNAIDS, *2006 Report on the Global AIDS Epidemic: Executive Summary,* A UNAIDS 10th Anniversary Special Edition (Geneva, Switzerland: Joint United Nations Programme on HIV/AIDS, 2006): 5.
5. For example, Camara Laye's (1954) descriptions of his initiation and circumcision experience in his book *The African Child* had a profound impact on the students in Adomako Ampofo's "Men and Masculinities" class. Students recognised that a practice intended to serve as a transition from boyhood to manhood can be fraught with anxieties and fear for the initiate. See: Camara Laye, *The African Child* (London and Glasgow: Collins, 1954).
6. Organizations such as GETNET in South Africa have been working with men and women in organisations to catalyse new masculinities that are caring, supportive, non-violent and responsible. See: Robert Morrell, "Men, Movements and Gender Transformation in South Africa," *Journal of Men's Studies* 10, issue 3 (2002): 309; hereafter cited in text as Morrell (2002).
7. Robert W. Connell, "Masculinities and Globalisation," *Men and Masculinities* 1 (1998): 3–23; Lisa A. Lindsay and Stefan F. Miescher, *Men and Masculinities in Modern Africa* (Portsmouth, NH: Heinemann, 2003); Robert Morrell, "Of Boys and Men: Masculinity and Gender in Southern African Studies," *Journal of Southern African Studies* 24, no. 4 (1998): 605–30, hereafter cited in text as Morrell (1998); and Kopano Ratele, "Contradictions in Constructions of Masculinity," *News* from the Nordic Africa Institute, 2002, hereafter cited in text as Ratele (2002).
8. Kamla Bhasin, *Exploring Masculinity* (New Delhi, India: Women Unlimited, 2004).
9. The idea of studying men and masculinities is still viewed with scepticism, if not outright dismissal, in many academic programmes in Africa. Unlike in Europe and North America, it is largely female scholars who have examined

these issues. A notable exception is South Africa where male scholars such as Morrell (1998, 2002) and Ratele (2002) have written on aspects of the constructions of masculinity.

10. Adomako Ampofo (2001); also: Shireen Jejeebhoy, "Adolescent Sexual and Reproductive Behavior: A Review of Evidence from India." ICRW Working Paper, no. 3 (Washington, DC: International Center for Research on Women, 1996).

11. Morrell (1998); Gary Barker, "Gender Equitable Boys in a Gender Equitable World: Reflections from Qualitative Research and Program Development with Young Men in Rio de Janeiro, Brazil." *Sexual and Relationship Therapy* 15, no. 3 (2000); Jesus Ramirez-Valles, Marc A. Zimmerman, and Michael D. Newcomb, "Sexual Risk Behavior among Youth: Modeling the Influence of Prosocial Activities and Socioeconomic Factors," *Journal of Health and Social Behavior* 39, no. 3 (1998): 237–53.

12. The Principal Investigators, Akosua Adomako Ampofo and Francis N. Dodoo interviewed girls and boys respectively, and also interviewed a subsample of mothers and fathers of the children in 2002.

13. See Adomako Ampofo (2001); Ramphele Mamphele, "Teach Me How to Be a Man: An Exploration of the Definition of Masculinity." In *Violence and Subjectivity,* eds. Veena Das, Arthur Kleinman, Mamphele Ramphele and Pamela Reynolds, 102–19 (California: University of California Press, 1997); and Priya Narismulu, "'Now I am Suffering, I've Got No Place to Stay:' Experiences of Insecurity in a Durban Shack Settlement." Paper presented at the Conference on Uncertainty in Contemporary African Lives at the MS Training Centre for Development Cooperation, Arusha, Tanzania, April 9–11, 2003.

14. Raymond Suttner, "Masculinities in the ANC-led Liberation Movement." Paper presented at the conference "From Boys to Men," University of the Western Cape, Cape Town, South Africa (26–28 January 2005): 21.

15. See, for example, Marc Epprecht's work, DATE, on male-male sexualities in Southern Africa: Marc Epprecht, "Male-Male Sexuality in Lesotho: Two Conversations," *Journal of Men's Studies* 10, no. 3 (2002): 373–89.

16. Chinua Achebe, *Things Fall Apart* (Oxford: Heinemann, 1958).

17. Women are generally understood to acquire wisdom and even supernatural insights as they age, for example, priestesses. This is reflected in our talk of "consulting the wise, old woman". Men, however, do not require the characteristics of age or the position of priesthood to attain such influence.

18. Elisabeth Amoah, "Femaleness: Akan Concepts and Practices." In *Women, Religion and Sexuality: Studies on the Impact of Religious Teaching on Women,* ed. Jeanne Becher, 129–53 (Philadelphia: Trinity Press International, 1991); and Robert S. Rattray, *Religious Art in Ashanti* (Oxford: Clarendon Press, 1927).

19. Dorcas Coker-Appiah and Kathy Cusack, *Violence against Women and Children in Ghana* (Accra, Ghana: Gender Studies and Human Rights Documentation Centre, 1999), hereafter cited in text as Coker-Appiah and Cusack (1999); and Akosua Adomako Ampofo and Mansah Prah, "You May Beat Your Wife, But Not Too Much: The Cultural Context of Violence in Ghana." In *Violence against Women in Ghana,* eds. Kathy Cusack and Takyiwaa Manuh (Accra, Ghana: Gender Studies and Human Rights Documentation Centre, forthcoming).

20. For example, a December 20, 2004 report by the Ghana News Agency titled, "Man Kills Wife for Denying Him Sex" describes how Kwaku Boateng was alleged to have shot his wife Adwoa Kyeraa for denying him sex. Apparently there had been a number of "misunderstandings" between the couple over Kwaku's "amorous adventures," and on the day in question Adwoa refused

to have sex with Kwaku fearing he might infect her with the HIV virus. In anger Kwaku "took his single-barrelled gun and shot the woman dead in the bedroom at close range."

21. Akosua Adomako Ampofo. "'*By God's Grace I Had a Boy.*' Whose 'Unmet Need' and 'Dis/Agreement' About Childbearing among Ghanaian Couples." In *Rethinking Sexualities in Contexts of Gender,* ed. Signe Arnfred (Uppsala, Sweden: Nordic Africa Institute, 2004): 115–38, hereafter cited in text as Adomako Ampofo (2004); Jeff Hearn, "The Problems Boys and Men Create, the Problems Boys and Men Experience." Paper presented at the conference "From Boys to Men," University of the Western Cape, Cape Town, South Africa, 26–28 January 2005; and Marcia Inhorn, "'The Worms Are Weak:' Male Infertility and Patriarchal Paradoxes in Egypt," *Men and Masculinities* 5 (2003): 238–58.

22. Adomako Ampofo (2004); and Dodoo (1998).

23. There was only one boy who, having said that a man who didn't want to have sex (presumably because he linked sex with pregnancy) should go and buy a condom or let his wife use the pill, recommended force to be used if the wife was the unwilling partner: "Then you may really have to force her so that she might think that when she doesn't yield you might go out and take another woman and leave her."

24. In his book, *Nine Years at the Gold Coast,* the Reverend Dennis Kemp notes that, in a bible class when "attention was drawn to St Paul's admonition respecting treatment of wives . . . it was unmistakably evident that some of the members felt that St. Paul was lavish in his gallantry . . . and that a woman will not believe that her husband loves her unless he flogs her occasionally." After all they had learned that "Whom the Lord loveth, he chasteneth" and "Do I not love my wife?" See Dennis Kemp, *Nine Years at the Gold Coast* (London, New York: Macmillan, 1898): 67.

25. There are also several proverbs noting that a man who finds a (good) wife has found a treasure, or that marriage is a good station for a man to enter into.

# 14 The Truth Will Set Us Free

## Religion, Violence, and Women's Empowerment in Latin America

*Monica Maher*

Though religion has often been used as a major tool in the oppression of women for millennia, it is now being reinterpreted as a critical source of women's empowerment. Women in growing numbers are re-reading religious traditions from their collective experiences and perspectives. In doing so, they are reclaiming the foundations of their faiths and setting themselves free of dogma that has served to hide the truth of their historical and contemporary capacities for action. Religious teachings that portray women as naturally inferior and morally weak, fulfilled only in complement to men, are being increasingly exposed as stereotypes based on ignorance and illusion. Such stereotypes are being challenged as the basis of the power inequalities that underlie violence against women.

This essay will explore new perspectives on religion, violence, and women's empowerment in contemporary Latin America with a case study from Honduras. First, it will give background on the issue of religion and women's empowerment, focusing on Latin American feminist theology. Secondly, it will describe the Mercy Weaver of Dreams Program in northern Honduras, a grassroots Catholic women's organization that aims to empower women not only economically and politically but also spiritually. The process of spiritual empowerment will be examined in depth, followed by discussion of connections to daily struggles, including those to combat rising levels of feminicide.

## RELIGION AND WOMEN'S EMPOWERMENT

Religion has become increasingly prominent in public discourses and political debates internationally, often including issues of women's empowerment. Religious justifications for violence against women and for denying women's rights are still common in many places around the world. In recognition of this fact, United Nations' documents of the last two decades, such as the 1993 Declaration on the Elimination of Violence against Women and the 1995 Beijing Platform for Action, specify that states should not renege on their obligations to honor women's rights on the basis of arguments that invoke religion, culture, or tradition.[1]

At the same time, feminist scholars have increasingly begun to address the role of religions as important transnational forces in the world and in the lives of many women, urging an approach to religion that recognizes its complexity and potential positive contribution to women's rights. This has included recognition of the diversity not just among, but internal to, religions. Feminist philosopher Martha Nussbaum for example, describes the "diversity" and "dynamism" within religious traditions, encouraging humanist feminists and political liberals to do the same as part of a more effective political strategy that does not write off religion as necessarily reactionary.[2] Similarly, feminist lawyer Lynne Freedman asserts that recognizing "the certain importance that religious belief and practice has for millions of women around the world is one of the most important challenges for the human rights and reproductive health movements today."[3] This necessarily entails breaking the "myth of a monolithic homogeneous" religion and embracing the diverse ways distinct cultural, ethnic, and religious identities influence women's choices (Freedman, 1996: 59, 66).

The recognition of the complexity of both women's multiple identities, including religious belonging, and religious traditions themselves has led to increasing challenge of the supposed irreconcilable rift between religion and women's rights. Feminists are acknowledging religion as an internally contested and shifting cultural terrain like any other, a site of conflict in which many women struggle for increasing voice and authority. According to Ayesha Imam, Chief of the Culture, Gender, and Human Rights Branch of the United Nations Fund for Population Activities and core member of Women Living Under Muslim Laws, "Human rights approaches need to move beyond the notion of culture (including religion) as a static barrier to human rights" to recognize "potential resources as well as obstacles."[4] Indeed, as Wendy Chavkin asserts, the dichotomy between universal rights and culture and religion is "neither nuanced nor necessary" but reflects an essentialist stance that betrays the truth of both rights and religion as fluid constructs.[5] An either/or approach feeds into religious extremists' political purpose to lay claim to the so-called "fundamentals" of a religion as its unique and final voice. Religion is not reducible to something fixed but is in constant change within institutions and individuals.

Today, women are increasingly reclaiming their role as creative leaders in remaking religious traditions across the world. Feminist scholars have turned to exploring this phenomenon, affirming the diversities of women's religious practices and beliefs. Their scholarship offers insight into the imaginative flexibility and range of women's religious interpretations and actions in negotiating their moral and social agency in the face of multiple patriarchies[6].

## Latin American Feminist Theology

Christian feminist scholars and activists around the world have been challenging patriarchal expressions of Christianity for several decades, rethinking and rewriting theologies and ethics based on women's experiences and wisdom. In Latin America, the "long-standing trajectory of feminist experience and struggle" is the "primary source and point of reference" for feminist theology.[7] In Latin America, feminist theology arose in the 1970s within the context of liberation theology which emphasized economic justice and the preferential option for the poor, inspiring many women to participate in base Christian communities and popular social and political movements. Liberation theology relied heavily on Marxist analysis, tending to reduce all social conflict to that of class, considering gender and race conflicts as secondary problems that would resolve themselves through class struggle. Critiques of patriarchy and the social sins of sexism and racism within church and society were largely absent; little attention was given to newer socialist thinkers, such as feminist socialists, and to the theologies of women.[8] These oversights served as the catalysts for the development of feminist theology in Latin America, where feminism is "old and "fertile" dating back to the early 1900s (Aquino, 1998: 93, 95). As Mexican Catholic feminist theologian, Pilar Aquino, asserts, "Liberation theology has a fundamental lack: the absence of reflection on the historical and spiritual experience of woman and their efforts to transform the systems destroying their lives and humanity."[9]

Because of its origins in liberation theology, Latin-American feminist theology is grounded in a strong critique of colonization and neo-colonization, of global economic and political injustice. It takes as its primary lens of interpretation the experiences of poor women "struggling against patriarchal power relationships in the present context of the world market economy" (Aquino, 1998: 105). Other key thematic principles include valorization of daily life and the body, and a non-sacrificial form of redemption (Aquino, 1998: 104–5).[10]

Aquino and Costa Rican feminist liberation theologian, Elsa Tamez, have highlighted key moments or phases of Latin American feminist theology, corresponding to historic meetings of Latin American women theologians in each of the past three decades.[11] At the first meeting, held in Puebla, Mexico in 1979, Christian women gathered to systematize their experiences as women within the struggle for liberation on the continent. The conference document, "Latin American Women, Church, and Theology," recognized that the experiences and visions of women were omitted from liberation theology and urged "incorporation of women within the theological endeavor (Aquino, 1998: 99)." The second meeting in 1985 in Buenos Aires, Argentina, entitled "Latin American Theological Encounter from the Perspective of Woman," emphasized that it wasn't enough to assume the presence of women under the general category of "the poor," but that it was necessary to affirm the "specific face of the poor." Participants acknowledged the existence of a "double struggle" for women against oppressions of both class and sex, the necessity of reading the Bible from the perspective of women and of questioning not just the context in which the Bible is read, but the context of the text itself (Tamez, 1998: 127, 130). The third meeting in Rio de Janeiro, Brazil in 1993 on the theme of, "Spirituality for Life: Women Against Violence," included recognition of the need for a more systematic appropriation and application of gender theories in women's theological work, the methodological interconnection of race, class and sex/gender in critical social and theological analysis, and the importance of Latin American indigenous and black feminist theologies (Aquino, 1998: 101). This moment marked explicit embrace of the term "feminist" theology (Tamez, 1998: 133).

Brazilian Catholic ecofeminist theologian Sister Ivone Gebara describes three phases of Latin American feminist theology in terms of an evolution in theological emphasis. During the first phase, the late 70s to the mid-80s, the main focus of the struggle for liberation was on rediscovery of the leadership roles of women in the Bible. This corresponded to women's discovery of their oppression as historic subjects in the Church, theology, and the Bible. In the second phase, the mid-80s to the early 90s, attention was on the "feminization of theological concepts," including discovery of the "feminine" face of God. In the third phase, from the early 90s to the present, the call is for the full reconstruction of theological paradigms.[12] As Elsa Tamez asserts, " We are aware of the radical nature of this challenge, which means reworking, or rather reinventing, the whole of Christian theology."[13]

Gebara characterizes the work of the first two stages as "patriarchal feminism"[14] which actually reinscribes gender stereotypes by uncritically incorporating the patriarchal philosophical frameworks of liberation theology. Only in the last phase of "critical feminism" or "holistic ecofeminism" does a thorough feminist reconstruction of theology begin, which addresses Christianity's anthropological and cosmological foundations (Gebara, 1993: 46). Such a theology represents an attempt to "overcome all kinds of dualism that have characterized the Christian tradition and have blamed, in a very particular way, woman's body" (Gebara, 1995: 41). In contrast to the dualistic and one-dimensionality of androcentric theology, ecofeminist theology is characterized by a vision of reality as unitary, relational, and pluridimensional,[15] reflective of the insights of modern physics and the new cosmology.[16]

The three stages of Latin American feminist theology are not necessarily exclusive and chronological, according to Tamez and Gebara, but often co-exist and overlap depending on the particular country, group, and history.[17] Gebara herself is the most celebrated theologian of the last stage of holistic ecofeminism. One of the most creative voices of the continent, she was silenced for two years in 1994 by the Vatican for her radical theology and public stance on the decriminalization of abortion in Brazil.[18] Her writing, teaching, and activism have greatly influenced women throughout the continent, giving words to what many had been feeling and challenging unquestioned assumptions, including about the Bible.

Indeed, Gebara (1995: 84) recognizes that "the Bible is not only an inspiring force of liberation, but also principally a legitimizing force for a series of oppressions;" one must "denounce and overcome" such oppressions and try "to destroy images, language and symbols" that maintain women's subordination to men. Indeed, a feminist Biblical hermeneutic seeks both the sources of and alternatives for economic and political injustice justified by texts (Gebara, 1995: 41). This requires critical thinking and questioning,[19] involving the de-contextualization and re-contextualization of the texts (Gebara, 1995: 36) and a concerted effort to "recuperate the historical memory" of women, an "invisible and subversive memory" of those rendered inferior as historical subjects (Gebara, 1995: 84). The text "turns into our accomplice . . . a useful tool for our cause," read from the point of view of "our own interests" (Gebara, 1995: 36). Such a Biblical hermeneutic is not just a theoretical pursuit but is "above all, a new practice of life" (Gebara, 1995: 43).

Because the Bible, introduced during colonization, is part of five centuries of Latin American history, part of "our historical flesh,"[20] a radically new re-reading offers a critical opportunity for remaking the flesh, personally and communally. This is particularly relevant in the case of rural women, especially the poorest, who "bear in their flesh the scars of the rejection of their bodies, of the guilty verdict pronounced on their flesh by the patriarchal system which has formed them" (Gebara, 1993: 172). A feminist Biblical re-reading challenges dualistic patriarchal categories, allows for an understanding of the inter-relatedness of all persons and things, reflecting a "moral posture which does not close in on itself but is capable of entering into a contemplative and admiring attitude before the wonder that we are and grasp" (Gebara, 1995: 42). A feminist reading thus is an "invitation to open ourselves to the Spirit that lives in us," a Spirit of "the unexpected, surprises, and above all, hope" (Gebara, 1995: 87).

Gebara has inspired hope and surprise through her own teaching, guiding women through Biblical re-readings, prodding them to discover another relationship to the text, their histories, their tradition, the cosmos, and themselves. This has often included re-reading the creation stories of Genesis, particularly of Adam, Eve and the fall,[21] a story Gebara asserts to be "the basic myth supporting prejudice against women" (Gebara 2002: 5). Traditional theology, based on a particular interpretation of Genesis, asserts there are two distinct human natures by sex and associates women more closely with evil, in fact "all but identifies woman with evil as if women incarnate evil" (Gebara, 2002: 4).

In her activism with grassroots women's groups, Gebara has been closely connected to the Collective Con-spirando of Santiago, Chile. Dedicated to women's popular education on issues of ecofeminism, spirituality and theology, Con-spirando has worked since 1991 to uncover and replace the religious myths, stories, and archetypes that underlie violence against women and women's oppression generally, drawing upon feminist scholarship from Latin America as well as North America and Europe. Con-spirando's work has greatly facilitated the development of networking among progressive faith-based women's groups in the continent and the deepening of ecofeminist theological reflection. In addition to sponsoring workshops, seminars and encounters the collective publishes a quarterly magazine, whose editorial board includes Gebara. One of the more recent and popular issues of *Conspirando* magazine, sparked by feminist theological research and attention of the popular media, compiled the reflections of women's groups throughout Latin America on the historical Biblical figure of Mary Magdalene.[22]

Feminist theological scholarship and activism of teachers like Gebara and organizations like Con-spirando are key examples of the feminist religious activism of the continent, a movement aimed at both social and ecclesiastical transformation. This movement is grounded in the experiences and struggles of many grassroots groups throughout Latin America like the Mercy Weaver of Dreams Program in Honduras, whose daily work on women's empowerment incorporates the perspectives of spirituality, theology, and religion. Less visible at the regional level, the hands-on work of such groups are the basis of the changes that are occurring throughout the continent with respect to religion, to women's increasing voice in Christian discourse, and praxis.

It is with Dream Weavers that I worked for three months in 2004 doing participatory research on the topic of religion and women's empowerment.[23] The research involved co-facilitating spaces for theological reflection in Honduras with Dream Weavers Program Director, Mercy Associate and feminist theologian Carmen Manuela Del Cid.[24] Together, we attended Conspirando's Latin American Encounter on Ecofeminist Spirituality and Ethics in Chile in January 2005. Research methodologies also included open-ended individual and group interviews, conversation, and accompaniment, and collection of published and unpublished documentation. It is to the work of the Mercy Weaver of Dreams that we now turn, in order to explore the ways such a grassroots group incorporates religion and spirituality into its programs as one indispensable dimension of women's empowerment.

## THE MERCY WEAVER OF DREAMS PROGRAM

The Mercy Weaver of Dreams Program (Programa de la Misericordia Tejedora de Sueños), known simply as Dream Weavers, emerged in the aftermath of Hurricane Mitch to address the increasing poverty of women in and around the northern industrial capital of San Pedro Sula. From its beginnings in 1999, its services have focused on "women's political, economic, social and spiritual empowerment," operating in conjunction with the women's cooperative, Cooperative Mixta Feminina Limitada (COMFEL). Both Dream Weavers and COMFEL are initiatives of the Catholic Sisters and Associates of Mercy of Honduras. As such, Dream Weavers reflects the vision of the Mercy Sisters, operative in Honduras for almost fifty years, to "act in solidarity with the poor, especially women and children" and to "build a society where women enjoy fullness of life and equality in church and society."[25] Dream Weavers shares this vision with Mercy Sisters in nine countries of Latin America, who gathered for regional meetings in Honduras in early 2004. During the meetings, Ivone Gebara lead theological reflection and offered a public forum on feminist theology sponsored by the Mercy community.

The general objective of the Dream Weavers Program is "to create gender awareness and political and spiritual practices that aim to change the structures that sustain gender inequality." Specifically, this means "to accompany women's groups in order to strengthen their organizational initiatives and leadership capacity," "to promote economic autonomy . . . in cooperation with (the women's cooperative) COMFEL," and "to facilitate spiritual formation from a critical feminist Christian perspective." The latter has included a series of annual or biannual four-day retreats for women. Other ongoing activities involve a variety of popular education workshops for women's groups on: gender, human rights, citizenship, self-esteem, sexuality, spirituality, domestic violence, STDs, HIV/AIDS, yoga/tai chi, computer training, and income-saving and generating skills such as sewing, cosmetology, floristry, baking, craft- making. To date, Dream Weavers has reached over 1,000 women of the most economically marginalized neighborhoods of San Pedro Sula.[26]

Dream Weavers places a high priority on organization and education of women in the process of personal and structural transformation. Its Creed begins with this statement of faith: "We believe in women (and) in the power of their struggles . . ." The Creed continues, "We believe that when grassroots women . . . know their rights and understand their reality of gender and class oppression, the transformation of unjust structures is made possible." Spirituality plays an important role: "We believe . . . women have the capacity to live a creative spirituality that recognizes the dignity and value of alternatives that privilege human and planetary life." The role of solidarity in spiritual awakening and social transformation is critical. The Creed ends: "When each woman discovers within herself the inner power capable of transforming the world, she runs to give the good news to her sisters."

The National Women's Institute (INAM) in Honduras, the official government agency for women, describes empowerment in a similar fashion in its trainings for women, referring to a "spiritual power," an "inner power." INAM workshop materials on "Women and Democracy" which aim at greater civil participation of women, define empowerment as "an inner strength (or force) in people," "a process" through which "women use this inner power to exercise their citizenship, defend their rights, increase their self-esteem and construct their identity."[27]

Dream Weavers arose out of the realization of women working at the cooperative, COMFEL, that economic empowerment in the form of loans and technical assistance was not enough. Cooperative members needed training and support to learn how to dream, to visualize something more and to believe in their capacity to realize their visions. Without such support, many remained caught in the dictates of their family or community, unable to act on their own behalf with their new access to money. Therefore, greater financial independence was not sufficient but had to be integrated with social support and spiritual training in the ability to dream, the discovery of inner power.

Support in learning to dream is critical in a context like Honduras of increasing absolute poverty and criminal violence, marked by continuous insecurity and the struggle to survive, leading often to desperation among women of the urban barrios. Del Cid, Director of Dream Weavers, often refers to the situation as one of "collective depression" in which women feel that they have no control over their lives, no options. Indeed, the industrial valley of San Pedro Sula has experienced great social dislocation and pressure including increased gangs, organized crime, narco-trafficking, rapid urbanization, rural migration, neoliberal economic globalization and the proliferation of multinational factories or maquilas in free trade zones that employ mainly young women.

The sense of insecurity has been reinforced in northern Honduras by rising levels of feminicide, particularly of economically marginalized and young women, reflective of a tragic trend throughout the continent.[28] In just the first six months of 2003, 146 women lost their lives in the San Pedro Sula Valley to shooting and stabbing (71), alleged accidents (42) and undetermined causes (33).[29] In 2003 and 2004, there were about 300 reported cases of feminicide in Honduras as a whole.[30] Although homicide rates have gone up overall in the country, these crimes have stood out for their brutality, the perception by police of the culpability of victims, and the minimal efforts to investigate.[31] Victims are often raped or otherwise tortured before death, and sometimes dismembered and mutilated after death. Extensive media coverage often reinforces the sense of trauma and lack of safety by offering graphic descriptions and images of women's bodies in a kind of public sensationalism.

For Del Cid, the rising wave of feminicide is rooted in a "crisis of masculinity" which is in fact a "reflection of a crisis of a whole political, economic and ideological-religious system sustained on oppression of sex, race and class." At a time when more and more, especially young and rural, women are entering public spaces of work and social organization to support impoverished extended families, the murders create a climate of palpable fear, adding a sense of great physical insecurity to the existing insecurity of increasing poverty. Del Cid believes, "the deaths are an effort to convince us that the safest place for us is the house." With the shifting of gender roles away from those supported by traditional teaching in which "masculine domination and control" have "become legitimized as the will of God," feminicide serves as a way of "punishing all of us women who in some way are leaving behind the canons established and legitimized by the divine order" (Del Cid, 2003).

In the face of such intense social pressures and insecurities, how is women's empowerment realized? Specifically, how does Dream Weavers facilitate the spiritual transformation in women in which they realize their "inner power" to work together toward social change? How do women begin to unleash their imaginations, weave their dreams, and live out their visions of equality?

## The Spiritual Empowerment Process: The Truth Will Set Us Free

Insights into these questions can be gained by examining one of Dream Weavers' retreats that had the most impact on participants: "Memorias Peligrosas, Mujeres Poderosas" ("Dangerous Memories, Powerful Women"). This four-day retreat took place in northern Honduras from July 1st through the 4th of 2004 with twenty participants, a cross-generational gathering of members of women's groups from San Pedro Sula's economically marginalized neighborhoods, literate women of educational levels ranging from second grade through high school. The majority were Catholic. All were affiliated with Dream Weavers, and many had attended one of five previous retreats. There was thus a foundation for working together, a sense of trust and connection to ongoing daily life and real struggles to improve their political and economic conditions. Like all retreats, this one was based on a participatory and embodied methodology that began with women's own ideas and experiences and included individual and group work, silence, ritual, drawing, dance, song, and critical reflection.

The retreat six months prior, "Relationships Between Women," had addressed various definitions of power and power relationships. There, women had expressed interest to explore in greater depth the concept of *poder desde* or "power from within," suggesting it as the topic of the next retreat. The "Dangerous Memories, Powerful Women" gathering thus began with a discussion of *poder desde,* inviting participants to define the term. Descriptions included: inner strength, energy, desire, what you can do and be, clarity of thought, great inner potential that allows us to develop ourselves and help others, strength and courage to confront any situation and govern oneself, the ability to say yes or no, a positive force that comes from deeply within, the ability to decide on an action, courage for a constant struggle, action for oneself and others, to maintain standing through difficulties, and capacity to attain one's goals.

Women concluded that the key words to describe *poder desde* were: inner force, clarity, inner potential, strength, courage, decision-making capacity, the ability to achieve our goals. The focus was on action, decision-making, daily life and ongoing struggle, perseverance and resistance. Indeed, the Spanish word *poder* is a noun meaning "power" and a verb meaning "to be able to." Therefore, within its definition is the sense of potential action and agency toward.

The workshop unmasked the social myths surrounding gender roles in which "one learns that protagonism is of man; he is the one who has to act." Participants attested that women come to believe that they are: useless, weak, incapable, only for the house, crybabies, lazy, dependent, gossipers, spenders, quiet, deaf, obedient, submissive, without rights to study or play sports, unable to think, and virgins obliged to fidelity. This is the result of social conditioning in the family, school, church, and political system. Participants compared these descriptions of women with their own everyday lives, realizing that they are in fact often more responsible for the family, and are communicative, capable, strong, committed, intelligent, concerned, and sensitive. Indeed, women act everyday, struggling hard for their daily survival. The internalized ideology of weakness serves to rob them of their voice and confidence.

Critical analysis of society's depiction of women continued in the workshop with discussion of female Biblical figures, starting with the mythical character Eve of the creation story of Genesis 2 and 3. Participants noted that Eve is said to be responsible for the evil in the world, "because of her, sin enters the world." Because of her, "if you don't feel pain, you are not a woman." Women began to question this depiction, noting Eve's strengths . . . she was curious, had desire for knowledge, struggled alone, gave birth alone, and knew how to get ahead without anyone. She was decisive, free to choose. Thus, women began to approach the Biblical text in new ways, questioning traditional interpretations, reading with new eyes of suspicion and a budding creative imagination based on their own experiences of both oppression and agency. As Del Cid encourages women in doing critical feminist interpretation, "We read the Bible in order to illuminate our life . . . Now we need to do it in reverse, learn to read our life in order to illuminate the Bible."[32]

Theological reflection centered on knowledge, curiosity and women, viewing the serpent as an ancient symbol of wisdom and generosity. Women struggled to answer the question: What was Eve's sin? This seemed particularly relevant since "the disobedience of Eve is used to re-enforce the obedience of women today and in all of history." Del Cid led women through the discernment, "The sin of Eve brought her to learn of an unknown world. What was Eve looking for? Knowledge. Is it bad to want to know? No. What is forbidden to us? Knowledge, we are . . . seeing the echoes until today. We are looking at the beginning of patriarchy. . . . ." Although Eve is associated with sexuality, remembered for tempting Adam, women concluded that "the sin of Eve is not a sexual sin, but one of knowledge." They challenged whether it was a sin to want to know and noted that the text tells a story written by men in a patriarchal era. Such Biblical narratives and their interpretations carry consequences for women that reinforce present day patriarchy. According to Del Cid: "In the story of Adam and Eve is the justification for the oppression and discrimination against us as women, we are always the guilty ones, even with rape and abuse. And we always feel guilty. It is a historical guilt that comes from the story of Eve." Participants emerged from the discussion asserting women's right, like Eve, to question, to think, to doubt, to have suspicions, to have inner power and to act with that power.

Retreat participants thus reformulated traditional interpretations of Biblical texts like Genesis 2–3 in such a way that they became inspiring stories about women's agency. In addition, they looked for neighboring Biblical narratives for a message of women's dignity. They discussed the often forgotten fact that there are two creation stories in the Bible, Genesis 1 as well as Genesis 2–3. Yet "why is the story that is most emphasized that of Eve? They want to put everything on women." Del Cid noted that, "In the first story of creation all is good, God created man and woman in God's image and likeness, at the same time God created them, all was very good. But this story is not spoken of much." Therefore, while critiquing patriarchal expressions of Biblical theology, participants also located resources for a theology of women's equality in the Genesis creation stories about original human nature. And with an attitude of suspicion, they discussed why the first creation story, which portrays woman as made in the divine image, is not widely taught.

Discussion of socioreligious depictions of women included not only the mythical figure of Eve of the Genesis 2–3 but also historical Biblical figures of early Christian history, among them Mary Magdalene. Participants described her to be known in popular society as: an adulteress, a sinner, humiliated (at Jesus feet), rejected, having seven bad spirits (that Jesus removed). They expressed their own opinions that she was: a great protagonist, the first witness of the Resurrection, free, courageous, independent, self-confident, one who learned how to love, in the company of Jesus, and capable of continuing forward. The retreat was able to capitalize on prevailing publicity regarding powerful women in the early history of the Christian Church by replaying a recently aired TV documentary reporting revelatory new theological scholarship on the historical leadership of Mary Magdalene. It described her role as the first Apostle, indeed the Apostle of the Apostles, and the discovery of her repressed text, the Gospel of Mary Magdalene.

This information had a profound impact on many women's views of themselves and their relationship to the Catholic Church and its teachings. Unlike the discussion of Eve, by considering non-canonical sources, the discussion of Mary Magdalene went beyond critiquing and reformulating familiar Biblical textual interpretations to challenging the very definitions and limits of the Bible itself. Women spoke of Maria Magdalene as the one who founded the Church, was the first at Jesus' tomb and Resurrection, was the first preacher and the person most intimately connected to Jesus, and who had her own Gospel that is now finally being studied, but also who was recast as a prostitute and a repentant sinner. Participants identified with the way that Mary Magdalene had been misrepresented in history, reporting that they too were unrecognized protagonists. They asked, "How many times have we been accused of something we are not," and "We have always been in history but it has been erased."

At the height of the discussion, Del Cid suddenly and passionately exclaimed, "Do you know what this means?!!" She explained that the Church had been based on a lie, the lie of solely male leadership, the lie that Peter was the Rock, when in reality women have been the foundation and leaders from the beginning. These hidden historical and religious truths, now coming to light, are a shocking wake-up call for women who suddenly realize the truth of their own strengths and leadership capacities. Jesus' words as recounted in the Gospel of John—"You will know the truth, and the truth will set you free,"[33]—take on new meaning in this context.[34] This context is freedom from historical and theological manipulation, and freedom for women to embrace the truth of who they are.

Del Cid explained why memories are dangerous and important, "Memories tell us who we are, connect us to our power . . . this power that has knowledge of our own history." Indeed, participants asserted a result of the retreat was to "discover ourselves" as inheritors of "a great positive power that we have had from long ago but had not recognized." The words freedom and clarity emerged strongly during the retreat, a clarity of faith resulting from a new form of discernment based on women's historical and contemporary experiences. A song about woman's freedom, competence, and strength sung with fervor repeatedly reinforced this theme. So did the participants' final words: "For centuries we have been carrying guilt that we don't have. . . . . We have taken off the blindfold and see with clarity," and "Today we have taken off this blindfold in order to set our powers free."

How do women exercise this power? What is the impact of the spiritual training and theological reflection on their agency? Is there a connection with women's daily lives and with broader social struggles?

## Connections to Daily Struggles

Women's testimonies attest to a correlation between the training and their daily life, between the new insights and their behavior. In an extended evaluation of retreats with those who had attended most regularly,[35] participants agreed that the time together gave them a renewed sense of energy and hope to work on their own behalf, struggling for their dignity within family, paid work, church, and community situations. Some women left abusive home situations, and others approached them with a sense of greater calm and detachment, knowing that they were not responsible for others actions. One woman reported immediately confronting a boss for compensation due and persevering with determination until successful. A few spoke up for greater opportunities for girls and women within their local schools and churches. Most affirmed a new sense of joy and commitment to work with other women in community groups. One woman even organized a women's rally to pressure the local government to open a municipal women's center, and then became the center's coordinator.

Women's experiences of putting their power together to challenge and change structures of injustice has been affirmed and reinforced through a women's network of the North Coast, El Foro de Mujeres por la Vida, the Forum of Women for Life. The Forum coalesced in 2003 among women of diverse organizations, including human and labor rights groups, to express solidarity with the women of Iraq at the beginning of the U.S. invasion. Later that year, propelled by the brutal murder and dismemberment of a young Honduran woman by her husband, a white U.S. citizen,[36] the Forum began to address the rising levels of feminicide in northern Honduras. This included a demonstration in front of the cathedral, a public panel and press conference, and an eighteen-month course for grassroots activists on women, gender, and human rights. More recently, the Forum has taken public stands on other issues such as the death penalty and migration/immigration. As a founding member of the Forum, Dream Weavers has been very involved from the onset and has encouraged its staff and program participants to take part in public actions. Therefore, many have an ongoing and immediate experience through the Forum of women's collective organizing for social justice.

In July 2004, soon after the "Dangerous Memories, Powerful Women" retreat, the Dream Weavers staff and retreat participants brought the discussion of Mary Magdalene to the Forum, including replaying the documentary. As in the retreat, there was fervent response from the more than fourty women attending the Forum session and a sense of dramatic connection to everyday struggles in the history of Mary Magdalene. The topic of women's public leadership was particularly relevant as a national campaign was underway to secure a 30 percent quota in the representation of women from all levels of government office. Attendees spoke of current popular and political discourse that seeks to discredit women's public leadership by criticizing them on sexual grounds as promiscuous and amoral prostitutes. Participants noted how the many victims of feminicide were also often called prostitutes and blamed for their crimes. Indeed, in the face of rising violence in Honduras, there is increasing public support for social cleansing, clearing the streets and society of sex workers, prostitutes and homosexuals, those deemed immoral and easily scapegoated for general social disorder and demise.

The perception of feminicide victims' basic immorality and complicity in their own murders perhaps may explain, in part, the lack of public outcry and action against these crimes as human rights violations. Official religious authorities, both evangelical and Roman Catholic, have also been largely silent—even though they have been active in many other campaigns for both conservative and progressive causes. The Catholic Church is known for its strong public stands against the death penalty, neoliberal globalization and rising levels of absolute poverty, human rights abuses against gang members, and rising levels of violence generally.

Religious emphasis on women as guilty sinners, especially with respect to sexuality, not as intelligent leaders and historical actors, provides an ideological foundation for feminicide and the lack of serious attention to it. This historical and theological manipulation leads most tragically in Honduras to women believing in the irrelevancy of their lives, their lives as part of an easily dispensable, "throw away" culture (Del Cid, 2005: 23). This ideology, supported by prevailing religious narratives and inaction, must be and is being questioned. The connection between violence, religion, and women's empowerment is critical.

In challenging what they have been taught as final and certain truth about female nature and the historical religious tradition, women often begin to question authorities, finding their voices in political activism toward justice for women. In the case of the Forum's ongoing focus on feminicide, this has involved demanding state attention, investigation, and prosecution. Many of the Forum's members are also involved in addressing human rights abuses of women workers of multinational factories or *maquilas*. Many of the women are participants in the myriad of other secular trainings that enhance women's energy, confidence, and collective self-esteem. But the religious component is often the most shocking (even the Bible is a source of support for machismo?!), and liberating, a catalyzing last straw of insight, the turning point in responding.

The real power of religious re-interpretation lies in approaching differently that which has been promulgated as absolute, fixed, and unchanging truth. In Del Cid's words, "Theoretically, they have made us believe something, but the reality says something else."[37] When women realize what they have been taught as absolute and sacred is itself changing, dependent on human interpretation, then the whole world opens up. Their own perspectives, voices, and experiences—indeed their entire lives, become important again in their eyes. Freedom becomes real freedom. This is freedom like no other, freedom from the deepest chains and shackles on the human psyche and spirit—freedom to be fully human, deeply spiritual, rational, and powerful.

Sometimes questioning the unquestionable leaves women a bit shell shocked, rudderless, because what they believed to be so certain is seen suddenly as contingent and open for interpretation like all other human teachings. At one workshop on Biblical feminist hermeneutics, a woman couldn't sleep the first night after examining misogynist Biblical texts and wondering whether these could be called the "Word of God." It literally turned her world upside down. And yet, together, women regain their grounding in the retreats and workshops, through listening to their own truths, deep-seated doubts they have never dared to share, questions that connect to a profound intuition. Participants realize that not one person or institution holds the absolute truth, but that truth emerges through a group discernment process based on their own experiences and realities—a collective wisdom.

In the process, women began to develop a new understanding and relationship to the divine. They began to recognize God in new forms and new places, in themselves, in everyday life—everywhere. When asked in a 2004 Dream Weavers workshop to describe God, the participants' responses were: Internal wisdom, 50 percent father and 50 percent mother, the sun, doors and windows, hope, my help, the air I breathe, always with me, feel but don't see, love, and power on earth.[38] In this way, women don't lose God altogether, they lose a certain image and relationship to God. The image slowly shifts away from a God who robs them of their agency and demands endless sacrifice, like the wrathful and abusive male God of Genesis 2–3 who punishes Eve with submission to her husband and pain in childbirth, condemning all subsequent women to suffer. Women gradually develop a relationship to God as a loving presence, recover a memory of their body and spirit being made in divine likeness, discover God embodied within, remember who they are, and recover their power. Indeed, women realize, through recovery of historical collective memory, that we have always had power. Freer of an abusive and punishing God, women more easily challenge external authorities who no longer reflect their image of a fear-inspiring God because they now experience God as inner wisdom, love, and power.

As mentioned, this path of spiritual empowerment and theological reflection is filled with paradox and contradiction that is not resolved quickly or easily. In one workshop that used a mirror to encourage women to see themselves as people with strength and dignity, one participant reacted by gasping and covering her face, and another looked around the mirror in search of the person with dignity. As Del Cid explains in her training, the process is cyclical and filled with clarity and confusion. Women take off a blindfold and see clearly, then new questions come. These questions are embraced in workshops as a guide to the path made in the walking. This is a spirituality that encourages risk-taking in making new starts, accepts human imperfection and cyclical growth, and emphasizes compassionate solidarity within the love and mercy of God and life as a call to happiness not suffering.[39]

What are the implications of the Dream Weaver Program experience for understanding women's empowerment? Most strikingly, empowerment involves a shift in perception. Here women have realized that they already are leaders and protagonists in the family and community—women with agency and power from the beginning of time. This shift in perception, a spiritual empowerment, has resulted in action. With the new awareness, women take on even stronger public roles, negotiate with more confidence, and find ways to work together. The challenge is to approach womens' empowerment as a process that is not intended to change women, but to unmask internalized illusion to reveal who women are and have always been. Empowerment is more about taking away than adding; it involves stripping away false ideologies to unleash women's creativity and wisdom, allowing women to be fully human, powerful and imperfect.

In the case of participants of the Mercy Weaver of Dreams Program in Honduras, "the truth that sets us free" is a revelation about the falsehood of women's inferior moral nature and about the legacy of women's moral and religious agency and leadership. It is not a truth of absolute dogma but of historical collective wisdom, the revelation of patriarchal religious teaching about women as based on lies, historical manipulation, and repression of information. These revelations are a source of great empowerment for women unleashing wonder, joy, energy, and vision toward affirmation of their current protagonism. The truth of women's historical leadership unmasks the myth of the natural inferiority or second-class status of women, questions the long-standing Christian association through history of women with weakness, evil and sexual immorality, and encourages women to live out spiritualities based in the tradition that support women's well being, happiness, and moral agency. These are spiritualities of empowerment that encourage women to be, to think and to act as human—sacred people.

## NOTES

1. The 1993 Declaration on the Elimination of Violence Against Women (Article 4) and the 1995 Beijing Platform for Action (Chapter IV, 124a) assert in relation to violence against women that states should not invoke "custom, tradition, or religious considerations to avoid their obligations with respect to its elimination."
2. Martha Nussbaum, *Women and Human Development: The Capabilities Approach* (Cambridge: Cambridge University Press, 2000), 181–182.
3. Lynn Freedman, "The Challenge of Fundamentalisms," *Reproductive Health Matters,* no. 8 (November 26, 1996): 66; hereafter cited in text as Freedman (1996).
4. Ayesha M. Imam, "Women's Reproductive and Sexual Rights and the Offense of Zina in Muslim Laws in Nigeria," *Where Human Rights Begin: Health, Sexuality, and Women in the New Millennium,* eds. Wendy Chavkin and Ellen Chesler (New Brunswick, NJ: Rutgers University Press, 2005), 67.
5. Wendy Chavkin, "Conclusion," *Where Human Rights Begin,* 274–75. Chavkin is referring here to the article of Ayesha M. Imam and that of Jessica Horn, "Not Culture But Gender: Reconceptualizing Female Genital Mutilation/Cutting" in that volume.
6. One cross-cultural, multi-country study that reflects such a creative approach to religion is that of the International Reproductive Rights Research Action Group (IRRAG). It portrays the varying extents to which grassroots Muslim women in Egypt and Catholic women in Brazil and Mexico, for example, assert their religious authority in everyday life, interpreting their traditions in ways that support their demands for certain aspects of their sexual and reproductive rights, and claiming their entitlements to sexual and reproductive rights in ways that support their religious identities. Rosalind Pollack Petchesky and Karen Judd eds. *Negotiating Reproductive Rights: Women's Perspectives across Countries and Cultures,* IRRAG (London: Zed Books/St. Martin's Press, 1998).
7. María Pilar Aquino, "Latin American Feminist Theology," *Journal of Feminist Studies in Religion* 14, no. 1 (Spring 1998): 92; hereafter cited in text as Aquino (1998).
8. María José F. Rosado Nunes, "Women's Voices in Latin American Theology," *The Power of Naming: A Concilium Reader in Feminist Liberation Theology,* ed. Elisabeth Schussler Fiorenza. (Maryknoll, NY: Orbis Books, 1996), 19.
9. María Pilar Aquino, *Our Cry for Life: Feminist Theology from Latin America* (Maryknoll, NY: Orbis Books, 1993), 64.
10. Elsa Tamez, "Hermenéutica Feminista de la Liberación: Una Mirada Retrospectiva," *Cristianismo y Sociedad* No.135–136 (Guayaquil, Ecuador, 1998), 133; hereafter cited in text as Tamez (1998).

11. These were organized by the Ecumenical Association of Third World Theologians (EATWOT). See Aquino (1998) and Tamez (1998). The latter was a lecture delivered by Tamez at the EATWOT Conference of Latin American Women Theologians, Rio de Janeiro, Brazil, December 1993.
12. Ivone Gebara, "Ecofeminismo holístico: entrevista con Ivone Gebara," interview by Mary Judith Ress, *Con-spirando* No. 4. (June 1993): 44–45; hereafter cited in text as Gebara (1993).
13. As cited in Mary Judith Ress, *Without a Vision, the People Perish: Reflections on Latin American Ecofeminist Theology* (Santiago, Chile: The Con-spirando Collective, 2003), 20; hereafter cited in text as Ress (2003). Judy Ress offers a comprehensive and clear systematization of the stages of Latin American feminist theology as described by Tamez and Gebara, and as lived out in her own work in the region, 14–25.
14. Ivone Gebara, *Teología al Ritmo de Mujer* (Madrid: San Pablo, 1995), 38; hereafter cited in text as Gebara (1995).
15. Ivone Gebara, *As incomodos filhas de Eva na igreja da América Latina* (São Paulo: Edições *Latina,* 1989), 12–15.
16. See, for example, Brian Swimme and Thomas Berry, *The Universe Story: From the Primordial Flaring Forth to the Ecozoic Era—A Celebration of the Unfolding of the Cosmos* (San Francisco: Harper Collins, 1992).
17. Ress (2003): 20, paraphrasing Gebara; Tamez (1998): 134.
18. For more on her stand on abortion and her silencing, see Ivone Gebara, "The Abortion Debate in Brazil," *Journal of Feminist Studies in Religion* (fall 1995): 129–135.
19. Ivone Gebara, *Out of the Depths: Women's Experience of Evil and Salvation* (Minneapolis: Fortress Press, 2002), 6; hereafter cited in text as Gebara (2002).
20. Ivone Gebara, "The Face of Transcendence as a Challenge to the Reading of the Bible in Latin America," *Searching the Scriptures* Vol. I., ed. Elisabeth Schussler Fiorenza (New York: Crossroad, 1993), 172; hereafter cited in text as Gebara (1993).
21. For example, at the two-week seminar, "Mas all de la violencia: solidaridad y ecofeminism," "Beyond Violence: Solidarity and Ecofeminism," part of the "Shared Garden" project co-sponsored by Colectivo Con-spirando, the Women's Alliance of Theology, Ethics and Ritual of Washington, D.C. and Gebara's team, Colectivo Pe No Chao of Recife, Brazil, held in Santiago, Chile, January 27 to February 8, 1997.
22. *Con-spirando,* No. 49 (Spring 2005.) This magazine issue was prompted by the wide popularity and controversy of the novel by Dan Brown and the movie, *The Da Vinci Code,* and by research on Mary Magdalene by feminist scholars of early Christian history such as Harvard Professor Karen King.
23. My relationship to the Mercy Weaver of Dreams Program dates back to 2000 when Director Del Cid invited me to collaborate with the new program by co-facilitating annual or biannual retreats for women.
24. Carmen Manuela Del Cid, a former Sister of Mercy, was one of the first women to receive a master's degree in theology from the Universidad Centroamericana José Simeón Cañas (UCA), the well-known Central American Catholic University run by Jesuits in El Salvador. She was awarded the degree in 1994 after completing her thesis on feminist liberation theology.
25. From the Vision Statement of the Sisters of Mercy of the Americas.
26. As stated in the Mercy Weaver of Dreams Program brochure, summer 2006.
27. Instituto Nacional de la Mujer de Honduras, "Taller 'Mujer y Democracia': Quién dijo que la Política no es cosa de Mujeres?" San Pedro Sula, Cortés, June 19 and 20, 2004, Embajada de Los Países Bajos.

28. For current statistical and analytical information on this crisis which is affecting the continent, including Guatemala, Mexico, El Salvador, Costa Rica, Dominican Republic, Colombia, Argentina, Peru, and Chile, see: http://www. isis.cl/Feminicidio, a site maintained by Isis International/Chile which includes a database. Mexican anthropologist and parliamentarian, Marcela Lagarde, provides the conceptual framework for the term, "feminicide," which she coined (from the term "femicide") to refer to the "genocide" of women; Marcela Lagarde y de los Rios, "Por la vida y la libertad de las mujeres: Fin al feminicidio" Dia V-Juárez, February 2004, http://www.isis.cl/Feminicidio/ Juarez/pag/quessfem.htm, 7, (accessed January 8, 2005).

29. "Investigación: Encuentran otras dos mujeres muertas," *La Prensa*, San Pedro Sula, Honduras, July 20, 2003, Sección Pasiones, 44.

30. Carmen Manuela Del Cid, "Feminicidio en Honduras," presentation at the panel on "Crossing Boundaries: the Politics of 'Femicides' in the Americas," International Forum of the Association of Women's Rights in Development (AWID), Bangkok, Thailand, October 27, 2005. Del Cid cites 163 reported cases in 2003, 130 in 2004, and 170 in 2005; these statistics were gathered from the major daily newspapers and include girls and adult women. Boletina Dignas Solidarias (Associación de Mujeres por la Dignidad y la Vida) cites more than 300 feminicides in Honduras between 2003 and 2004, Boletina Electrónica No. 50, November 2004, San Salvador, El Salvador, http://www. isis.cl/Feminicidio/doc/ (accessed January 31, 2006).

31. Carmen Manuela Del Cid, "La justificación de la violencia desde la perspectiva teológica," paper presented at the panel, "Las Causas del Feminicidio," Foro de Mujeres por la Vida," San Pedro Sula, Honduras, July 30, 2003; hereafter cited in text as Del Cid (2003).

32. Del Cid at the Dream Weavers' Workshop, "Mujeres en el Movimiento de la Sabiduría: Interpretación Crítico-Feminista de la Biblia," San Pedro Sula, Honduras, 4 November 2004. Besides Ivone Gebara's work, this workshop grew out of the groundbreaking critical feminist scholarship of Biblical scholar and Harvard Professor, Elisabeth Schüssler Fiorenza, whose work, *Wisdom Ways: Introducing Feminist Biblical Interpretation* (Maryknoll, NY: Orbis Books, 2001) is available in translation at the local Catholic theological library as *Los caminos de la Sabiduría: Una introducción a la interpretación feminista de la Biblia,* trad. José Manuel Lozano Gotor (Maliaño, España: Editorial Sal Terrae, Santandar, 2004).

33. John 8:31–32: "To the Jews who had believed him, Jesus said, 'If you hold to my teaching, you are really my disciples. Then you will know the truth, and the truth will set you free.'" *The NIV Study Bible, New International Version* (Grand Rapids: Zondervan, 1985).

34. Del Cid points out the new significance of these words in her article on the workshop submitted to *Con-spirando* for their issue on Mary Magdalene: Carmen Manuela Del Cid, "Memorias Peligrosas . . . Mujeres Poderosas," *Con-spirando,* No. 49 (Spring 2005): 22–24; hereafter cited in text as Del Cid (2005).

35. The evaluation was carried out as a three-day retreat on May 30 to June 1, 2006 in San Pedro Sula, Honduras, facilitated by Carmen Manuela Del Cid and Monica Maher.

36. Martha Isabel Moncada, age 26, was murdered by her husband, age 46, Andrew Stephan Gole, a U.S. citizen, in Tegucigalpa, Honduras, fifteen days after filing a report on April 28, 2003 of domestic violence with public authorities. Feminists were outraged that no action had yet been taken to protect her life. See "Lentitud de la DGIC selló el destino de Martha Moncada," *El Tiempo,* San Pedro Sula, Honduras, on May 14, 2003, sección el Pais,

4. Also, in the same newspaper edition, see "Sospecha de familiares: Por un millón de dolares el gringo habría descruartizado a su esposa," and "Family members' suspicion: For a million dollars the gringo dismembered his wife." Daily newspapers reported the demonstration of the Forum of Women for Life held about ten days later. See "Reclaman por impunidad en asesinatos contra mujeres," *El Tiempo,* San Pedro Sula, Honduras May 25 of 2003, sección El Pais, pg. 8; and "Mujeres exigen justicia y respeto a sus derechos," *La Prensa,* San Pedro Sula, Honduras, sección Raices, May 25, 2003, 8.

37. As stated at the meeting of the Forum of Women for Life, San Pedro Sula, Honduras, July 10, 2004.

38. Mercy Weaver of Dreams Workshop, "Mujeres en el Movimiento de la Sabiduría: Interpretación Crítico-Feminista de la Biblia," San Pedro Sula, Honduras, November 4–6, 2004.

39. These themes emerge regularly in collective sharing on spirituality of the Mercy community, including during the gathering of Mercy Sisters and Associates in San Pedro Sula, September 25, 2004.

Part IV
# Sexual Autonomy and Global Politics

# 15 Women, Culture, and HIV/AIDS in Sub-Saharan Africa

## What Does the "Empowerment" Discourse Leave Out?

*Kawango E. Agot*[1]

In this paper, I examine the concept of empowerment as *the* means proposed by the international donor agencies to alleviate suffering among the poor in the developing world, particularly women and other vulnerable populations. I am concerned with how the term is defined and used, how it is measured, and how useful the measurement is for understanding how widows in Kenya, as a case study, confront issues around HIV and AIDS within prevailing cultural norms. Using findings from a study we carried out in Kenya in 2004–2005, I discuss how problematic it is to apply the framework of "empowerment" to challenge the circumstances in which most women in sub-Saharan Africa live and act, circumstances that predispose them to either being infected or infecting their sexual partners with HIV. More specifically, I explore how widows from the Luo ethnic community in western Kenya conceptualize empowerment within the context of societal norms and expectations of two sexual behaviors in widowhood, sexual cleansing and inheritance.

Sexual cleansing refers to one-time ritual sex that a brother-in-law or other male performs with a widow after the burial of her husband.[2] It is often carried out between two to six months post-burial, sometimes longer, to unlink the widow from the ghost of her husband and reintegrate her fully into the community (Agot, 2001). An uncleansed widow is perceived as impure and her movements and social interactions are restricted and monitored.[3] She may not participate in key community functions, such as life cycle ceremonies of close family members (birth, marriage, and death), food production processes (cultivation, planting, and harvesting) and construction of homes, among others.

Cleansing is often followed by inheritance, a practice where a brother-in-law assumes social and economic responsibility for a widow after she has been cleansed. Sometimes, the brother-in-law cleanses the widow and then proceeds to inherit her; other times, both the cleanser and the inheritor are men not related to the late husband. For widows of childbearing age, sex often constitutes an integral part of inheritance, for both companionship and recreation. It also serves the purpose of having a partner with whom to observe the cultural requirements of sexual performance to mark the community functions mentioned above (Mboya, 1997; Agot, 2005; Luginaah,et al, 2005). For the most part, decisions around sexual cleansing and inheritance involve participation of close and extended family members, who sometimes put pressure on widows to be inherited (Mboya, 1997; Okeyo and Allen, 1994; Agot, 2005; Luginaah, 2005).

## INTERNATIONAL DEVELOPMENT AGENCIES AND THE DISCOURSE OF EMPOWERMENT

In the view of key international development agencies, notably the World Bank, WHO, UNIFEM and UNAIDS, the universal remedy to women's emancipation from subordination is encapsulated in one word: empowerment. According to the Bank's World Development Report of 2000/2001,[4] empowerment is considered one of the three pillars of poverty and vulnerability reduction (the other two being promoting opportunity and enhancing security). The Bank defines empowerment as enhancing an individual's or group's capacity to make choices and transform those choices into desired actions and outcomes (Alsop and Heinsohn, 2005). An empowered person or group is presented as one that possesses the capacity to make effective choices and act on them to achieve desired outcomes. The capacity to make an effective choice is primarily influenced by agency (personal ability and asset base to envisage and purposively make meaningful choices) and opportunity structure (the formal and informal contexts within which one operates, including laws, regulatory frameworks, and norms governing behavior). In the context of this paper, agency is used to mean ability to recognize positions of disempowerment and capacity to take corrective action, including overt or covert resistance to the status quo. Opportunity or supportive structure is used to refer to systems that create an environment which is either facilitative of or inhibitive to widows taking up opportunities to improve life of self and family. Both agency and opportunity structures can be enabled or created through external facilitation, but must ultimately be owned by the targeted population.

The Bank (Holland and Brook, 2004) and others (for example, Rowlands)[5] recommend that any program for empowerment develop clear outcome measures that correlate its activities with specific indicators defining the end product to be achieved by an empowered person or group. They view empowerment as a stage model or progression from passive access to institutions and resources to active participation, influence, and ultimately, control (Holland & Brook, 2004: 94). While I concur that it is essential to operationalize empowerment and measure its success against some preset outcome indicators, I do not subscribe to such "end product" view as *the* way to assess the impact of an "empowerment" program. I see the raising of consciousness to make individuals and groups aware of and appreciate available options as a pre-requisite for action. This view of empowerment cannot be captured by only "standardizable, observable, and measurable" time-bound indicators as proposed by the Bank; there is need for a more nuanced method of probing feelings and attitudes that drive the decisions people make. Within the context of women and HIV in Africa, as I shall discuss in the next section, both process and "end product" are equally important in determining who is empowered and who is not.

To conceptualize the various trajectories of empowerment, I propose moving away from visualizing an empowered individual as one who has reached a final finish line, toward viewing empowerment as comprising multiple paths that are context-specific and without designated destinations. Each path brings with it a measure of empowerment in so far as one has moved—independently or aided—from a place one considers disempowering to a place where one can feel, and act, with more autonomy. Once this new "place" is reached, more avenues for further or different forms of empowerment open up. For instance, two people in the same neighborhood could be in comparable economic and social places, yet feel very differently about their personal empowerment. The Bank[6] now recognizes this complexity, and points out that empowerment is a multidimensional and dynamic phenomenon that changes according to context, circumstances, and interests. What it does not adequately explain, however, is how to collect information that captures this fluidity.

A recent report of the Bank (Alsop and Heinsohn, 2005) and Rowlands (1997) recommends "performance indicators" to capture the "degree of empowerment" by recording whether a subject has the opportunity to make a choice, whether the person actually uses the opportunity to choose, and once the choice is made, whether it brings the desired outcome. The concept of opportunity to choose is, however, more complex than this formulation suggests. In considering whether a woman has an opportunity to make a choice, we need to be concerned, as a starting point, with whether she is aware of the range of choices available to her. For example, women with access to credit facilities are often considered by development agencies as empowered on the assumption that increased participation in the economic sphere will lead to, or at least facilitate, their empowerment. Yet in Bangladesh where Osmani looked at the effect of access to credit on women's empowerment, she observed that women who had access to credit still felt that unequal access to food between men and women in a family was justified, an opinion similar to women without access to credit. Borrowers did not seem to have been empowered enough to alter the traditional pattern of intra-household allocation of consumption.[7] The author attributes this to centuries of cultural conditioning that cannot be undone by less than a decade's involvement in income-generating activities. On the other hand Coleman reported that research across the globe has shown that women with access to micro-financing got more involved in family decision-making, were more politically and legally aware, participated more in public affairs, and suffered less domestic violence.[8] These contrasting studies suggest that where there are strong cultures contraindicating women's autonomy, more than money and education are needed to empower women. For them to become aware of choices presented by new opportunities such as credit, the cultural conditioning that leads them to accept unfairness and inequality must be systematically undone. As long as the cultural conditioning remains in place, they do not have the capacity to make an effective choice.

Further, we must look beyond where opportunities are chosen to see whether the choice brings the desired result. To a seeker of family planning services, a pregnancy delayed or stopped is a choice made. For this to be a more meaningful measure of empowerment however, we also need to know whether this outcome translates into some long-term empowerment indicator, such as improvements in the health status of the woman or in the welfare of her children. The Bank (Alsop and Heinsohn, 2005) cites as an example a woman who wants to send her daughter to school and then considers the questions this decision would elicit, such as; is there a school for the daughter to go to—that is, does the option exist to make a choice, does she actually make the decision to send the daughter to school—that is, is the option to choose utilized, and does the daughter actually attend the school—that is, if the choice was made, what results were achieved? In this illustration, school attendance might be considered an achievement if the woman was only interested in getting her daughter to school. For long-term empowerment however, we need to ask further questions, such as; did she complete her schooling to a reasonable degree or was she, as many school going girls, a casualty of attrition, and did going to school enable her to get commensurate gainful employment?

A challenging example is provided by the experience of Female Genital Cutting (FGC). An increasing number of educated women (and men) are unable to get economic returns from their investment in education. While programs targeting increasing school enrollment of the girl-child may record some success in terms of an "education for empowerment" indicator, they fail the "income for empowerment" test when education does not translate into improvements in income levels. As a result of this growing disparity, women view marriage and motherhood as alternative achievements. Looking attractive and marriageable, and pleasing their husbands in marriage, become their new goals for survival in life. Nypan found in Tanzania that as families found it increasingly difficult to pay the rising school fees and job opportunities for educated youths became even more scarce, there was a resurgence of FGC during the late 1980s.[9] The declining economic value and social status of school education prompted young women—often against the will of their educated and unexcised mothers—to view this initiation as a means of enhancing their social standing and marriage prospects. While international media and global feminists see FGC as disempowering to all women at all times, these educated young women perceived FGC as empowering and giving them some sense of self worth and the assurance of a future where education had failed. This underscores the interpretative nature and context-specificity of the concept of empowerment.

Additionally, international controversy over FGC has largely cast girls and women as victims, but according to Thomas, adolescent Kenyan girls' efforts to excise each other because FGC was banned situate girls and women as central actors (Thomas, 2000). Similarly, Shell-Duncan and colleagues quoted a woman from a community in Kenya that practices FGC as saying, "in your place this [not being excised] might be fine, but for Rendille women, circumcision is the only thing that separates us from animals."[10] Despite awareness of the potential risk of HIV infection and transmission, the Rendille view the risks of "circumcision" as worth taking in light of the implications for marriageability and other social benefits that accrue. Women and girls perpetuate these practices as a survival fallback position when all else has failed.

This raises a key question regarding empowerment in environments that provide few opportunities to women. In exercising apparent choice, are they not just conflating cultural conformity with empowerment? Viewed reflectively, this underscores the extreme depths cultural conditioning can go, which a single generation of education is incapable of undoing. Further, it demonstrates that achievements by programs that target just a single form of empowerment tool (e.g., education) but leave out other attendant core areas (e.g., economics), or those that target just a few members of a community but leave out a large majority, are bound to be undermined, or even reversed, as the case with FGC has demonstrated.

The illustrations cited above reveal another important point, that the role of individual decision-making in conceptions of empowerment is shortsighted in contexts where cultural conformity is a key underlying determinant of people's behavior. The World Bank conception of women's empowerment envisages collective as well as individual empowerment, but its implicit notion of collective is a grouping of individuals joining together for a shared goal. In contrast, women often see themselves, and are treated by men, as primarily members of an organic unit such as the family or the community, with their personal interests subordinated to group goals. The conceptual challenge is to articulate a notion of empowerment that recognizes the significant role of relationships in women's lives. To be useful internationally, the concept of empowerment cannot rest on an implicit assumption of individual autonomy. But in recognizing relationships the concept must differentiate subordination and self-sacrifice from positive, constructive, self-including engagement in a relationship.


## METHODS

In this section, I describe the methods and results of a pilot study in which we investigated how widows perceived empowerment within the context of the cultural practices of widow-cleansing and widow inheritance. The pilot study that informed this paper was an offshoot of a five-year parent study investigating the association between widow inheritance and HIV infection in Kenya, known locally as the HIV/AIDS Widow Inheritance (HAWI) Study. In the parent study, we screened close to 2400 widows for HIV and 62 percent tested positive. Of those who had HIV, over 80 percent had had sex since the death of the husband, mainly through the cultural practices of sexual cleaning and inheritance. This study provided evidence that due to these cultural norms and in a background of such a high proportion of widows who are HIV-positive, widows form a critical core transmitter group in this community. The prevalence of inheritance was similar among HIV-positive and HIV-negative widows, suggesting that while HIV-negative widows are at a risk of being infected through the two practices, those who are HIV-positive also risk transmitting the virus to the inheritors or cleansers.

In the pilot study,[11] we facilitated the setting up of post-test support groups to provide widows with what we labeled empowerment forums, with the goal of increasing the widows' autonomy in decision-making around sexual cleansing and inheritance. Specifically, we disseminated information on reproductive and sexual health issues; facilitated peer education and counseling to make widows feel supported and valued by self and others; educated them on the importance of seeking prompt care and treatment for HIV and related opportunistic infections; strategized with them on safe sex practices within the context of sexual norms around widowhood; trained them on how to disclose their HIV status, write wills, and prepare loved ones for possible bereavement; urged them to practice inheritance and sexual cleansing safely or consider discarding the practices altogether; and provided training in income-generating activities.

To recruit participants, invitations to widows interested in being part of a post-test support group were announced on posters, by word of mouth at the HAWI clinic, by staff during field outreach activities, and through relevant community gatekeepers. The community gatekeepers were invited for a goal-setting meeting and trained in forming HIV/AIDS support groups using a manual developed by Society of Women and AIDS in Kenya (SWAK). Fourteen support groups were formed, with membership ranging between twenty-five and eighty and a total membership of over 800 widows. Leaders of the groups convened at Bondo town monthly for the first three months and every two months thereafter to share progress and challenges with each other and with the project administration (Figure 15–1 across shows one such meeting).

Expert speakers were invited periodically: An obstetrician/gynecologist discussed issues around childbearing among HIV-positive women, a clinical officer talked about prevention and management of opportunistic infections, and a field worker with the Centers for Disease Control and Prevention (CDC) and SWAK provided information on nutrition, positive living, safe drinking water, detrimental cultural practices, writing of wills, and disclosure.

Exchange visits were encouraged among members and leaders. Active, extroverted HIV-positive members who had disclosed their status publicly were

Figure 15.1.

facilitated to visit other groups and share their personal experiences, including the benefits of and challenges to disclosure. Two trainings on disclosure of status, positive living, writing of wills, and memory projects were organized for selected members by SWAK, and training on home-based care was provided by I-Cross, Kenya. Upon return, those who were trained shared what they learned with other members of their groups. The project also facilitated initial visits of fourty-three widows to a facility providing free antiretroviral (anti-HIV) drugs, but due to the high cost of public transportation, fewer than ten widows were able to continue with the treatment. In addition, the project facilitated the registration of the groups with SWAK and worked with each group to develop a constitution, which was required for registration with the Ministry of Culture and Social Services. Registration with SWAK gave the groups free access to the trainings offered by the society, while registration with the Ministry made them eligible to apply for government funds for grassroots activities.

Though we collected data on socioeconomic and demographic characteristics (age, income, education), as well as on sexual and other behaviors (sexual partnerships, transactional sex, condom use, will-writing, disclosure of HIV status, etc), I base this paper on in-depth interviews with 101 study participants from the pilot study. In collecting life histories of these widows, we were interested in whether participants felt empowered by the activities of the program. We also explored how the widows defined and conceptualized empowerment generally and within the context of widowhood, HIV, and the sexual norms of inheritance and cleansing. Figures 15–2a and 15–2b are interview scenes. Figure 15–2a is in the home of one of the very needy widows; the widow in the white t-shirt (bottom left) was preparing porridge for her family (inheritor—in white shirt leaning on a pole, and two children) when the study team arrived. Our field team coordinator (in yellow t-shirt) is getting instructions from her on how to proceed with preparing the porridge while she gets interviewed away from the family by a female staff in the project vehicle (parked back left). In Figure 15–2b, the client is being interviewed at her workplace.

Figure 15.2a.

Figure 15.2b.

## IN THE WIDOW'S SHOES: TOWARDS A CRITIQUE
## OF THE EMPOWERMENT DISCOURSE

Before starting to collect data, we attempted to translate the word "empowerment" and found it highly problematic. After eliciting suggestions, we asked the participants to back-translate the words suggested and found the meanings did not quite capture the term "empowerment" as conceptualized in the English language. The most frequently suggested words and their back-translations were: *tegno* (strength/maturity), *teko* (strength/energy), *chir* (boldness/courage), *mijing'o* (authority/drive/boldness/self-confidence, from within). After much deliberation, we settled for *mijing'o* as the closest translation, recognizing that the project findings must be viewed in the context of this linguistic limitation.

Participants' responses to questions about what constitutes "empowerment" reveal the following common themes: having the capacity to enhance one's ability to afford basic needs (36 percent); motivation or encouragement of an individual to address life issues (30 percent); ability and drive to set and achieve one's goals in life and to shape one's destiny (18 percent); and becoming enlightened through education or knowledge acquisition (15 percent). One respondent said: "Empowerment is inner strength." When asked if the "inner strength" is acquired at birth or in the course of growing up or in adulthood, she responded:

> I think it is from birth throughout [life]. Because there are people who even if you teach them all you can you are wasting your time because they were born with reduced brain. It is not easy for such people to have [acquire] inner strength. They are weak throughout. When you are growing up, the teaching you get can make you have inner strength. If your family gives you responsibility and supports you to think [for yourself], you grow up dong things on your own. And you feel bold. I think if you are also lucky to join groups that can build you [up] like workshops and meetings for women, these add you strength. You see, to have inner strength you must build it throughout your life. Many people help you but you must also try. (An elementary school teacher.)

Their choices of words/phrases (build capacity, enhance, motivate, encourage, ability to achieve, and enlighten) suggest a conception of empowerment as being enabled to take charge of one's own life. While this points to existence of opportunity structure, it falls somewhat short of laying out the need for laws, regulations, and norms to guarantee that achievements are arising from conducive structural systems and not merely vertical. Also, we do not see much of personal agency displayed here; instead, we read women's receptive response to external influences. However, there is a level of agency exhibited in the quotation, that whereas external support is critical, personal efforts and interest must also be demonstrated.

When asked specifically about women's empowerment, the respondents focused on three main themes: encourage, motivate, and improve women's ability to overcome limitations or to perform better in life (51 percent), enhance women's economic achievement and involvement in income generating activities (21 percent), and enable women to be independent and know their rights (16 percent). A respondent from the fishing industry said:

> For me, empowerment of women means women are able to do things for themselves. People in the [Kenyan] government should provide women [with] ability to earn a living. They should give us proper jobs to do. Like me I don't like what I am doing but what do I do? The men use you before they give you fish. If you refuse, you don't get fish and your children sleep hungry. If you tell them you are unwell, they don't believe you. So for me, to have empowerment is to have ways of helping your family. I mean clean ways.

To be empowered women need an environment where they can work freely to improve their circumstances, as well as opportunities to move towards the goal. An enabling environment (e.g., laws that do not prohibit women from seeking employment) should be accompanied by concrete opportunities that can be taken up; otherwise they serve no purpose as they do not translate into improvements in women's lives.

Moving from defining the abstract concept of "empowerment" to visualizing the kind of women whom respondents considered empowered, 63 percent identified empowered women as those who have attained an economic indicator (a successful business, economic stability, ability to support self and family, or being salaried) while 23 percent considered empowered women as those with children who are successful in life. There is no suggestion in these responses of dependence on men or on others. Within the context of a supportive environment, the widows identified empowered women as those who are successful in their own right and by their own (albeit enabled) efforts. One respondent commented that: "I am empowered when I am able to support my children and myself. This means I don't beg or wait to be given. I don't like to be given things *fwaaahh* (just like that). But [throws hands up as if in resignation], what choice do we have? We have to beg these people [gesturing with her head towards the in-laws' houses]. And they set rules that you must obey before they can help you."

These views resonate with the definition of empowerment as a process that cannot be done to or for women, but has to emerge from within them. When development agencies such as the World Bank propose that empowerment be identified with a measurable outcome such as household food supply or provision of water, the means by which these outcomes are to be made available is not clear. In my view, the means is what constitutes empowerment, not the outcomes. Empowerment is not the end product in terms of food in the store or safe water in the tank; it is the knowledge and assurance that you have the means (environment and opportunity) and ability (agency) to obtain the food or safe water whenever it is needed. If food were made available through food aid, for example, then the recipient would have food but remain disempowered, because if the aid were withdrawn, she would return to the original condition of lack.

Moving closer to the widows' personal lives, we presented scenarios to enable the respondents to assess their own empowerment. Out of the 101 respondents, 44 percent said they did not consider themselves empowered and 56 percent felt empowered. Those who considered themselves empowered defined their status mostly in terms of having children, shelter, water, land, fuel wood, and clothing—in that order. When asked to mention what they thought would make them more empowered, those who did not consider themselves empowered mentioned adequate food, shelter, land, cattle, children, and access to healthcare. Lastly, we asked which empowerment indicators they would wish to have or have more of. This time access to healthcare topped the list, followed by cattle, education for children, and food.

> Health is the biggest [most important] thing. Because when you are healthy, you can do all the things you want. When you are sickly like me here, even if you gave me cattle or land, I cannot look after them until I feel better. Maybe I will sell them to treat myself. Or eat before I die. Let us agree that to be empowered one needs to be healthy first. Secondly, you need to have your own things that you can use, not things you have to ask someone for permission first then use. In my mind, this is the person who is empowered. (A small-scale businesswoman who had closed her shop for three months because she was unwell.)

More than half of the women interviewed were HIV-positive, which is probably why healthcare emerged as an urgent need. We see a shift from more abstract terminologies such as capacity building, enhancement, and so on, to children and possession of or access to tangible basic needs and property. This lends supports to a context-based conception of empowerment as relative, fluid and reflecting needs prevailing at the time. It is worth noting, however, that no respondent defined an outcome of empowerment in terms of agency per se, for agency without opportunity would not address their basic needs.

With regard to their inheritance status, 24 percent of our respondents had never been inherited, 41 percent had been inherited previously and 35 percent were inherited at the time of the interview. When asked under what circumstances they would swap position (if uninherited widows would want to be inherited and vice-versa), twenty-seven of the thirty-five widows who were inherited at the time of the study preferred to remain so. They gave various reasons: the social and economic support they were receiving from the inheritors; to make it easy to observe sexual rituals without having to look elsewhere for a stranger (for details, see Agot, 2001); so as not to risk having their children, land and other property confiscated by in-laws; because it is approved by their churches; to have more children; and for companionship and fulfillment of sexual needs. Asked if they would still prefer to remain inherited if they were economically stable and assured of not losing their property and children, the number did not drop as expected. Most of them would still prefer to remain inherited so as to keep their children or other family members from being affected by *chira*.[12] When asked why, a client challenged the interviewer that: "Whom do I leave inheritance for? Do you want my children to die? To be killed by *chira*? You are also a Luo. Or are you a *Jamwa* [non-Luo] that you don't remember your roots? Even if it is AIDS, I have lived for over 30 years and the future of my children is what is important."

As I argued previously, empowered women are not necessarily those who wish to or can separate their personal needs from familial or societal obligations. In the context of our study, choosing inheritance because of responsibilities to family and to the larger community should be seen as compatible with empowerment as defined in the language of these women. In other words, empowerment should not be seen as characterizing only Western-style autonomous individuals. This argument, however, works only for women who are choosing inheritance because of family and who see themselves as empowered by their choice. Those who choose inheritance simply to conform to traditions do not fall in this category.

Almost all widows who had a history of being inherited but were no longer inherited at the time of interview (n = 42) did not wish to resume the relationship or start a new one. This notwithstanding, almost half of them continued to observe the required sexual rituals (having sex to mark key social events such as rites of passage of close family members). The widows viewed this arrangement as being more liberating in that it released them from duties and responsibilities of taking care of an inheritor, while allowing them to "protect" their children and other family members from *chira* by doing the rituals.

> Me, after I had been cleansed, I sent away the man. He didn't want to go, I think because he wanted to enjoy my things. Now I am free. If I am faced with a taboo that requires that I have sex, I look for someone of my choice. When it is over, he goes. You know, this has made me take care of my children without any headache from anyone. I still observe the tradition [of sexual ritual] but no man makes noise at me or my children.

With regard to the relationship between empowerment and inheritance status, of the thirty-five respondents who were inherited at the time of the study, twenty-three (66 percent) felt they were less empowered compared to when they were not inherited, ten (29 percent) felt more empowered in their current inheritance status, and two (6 percent) felt no difference. A little over half of the forty-two respondents who had been inherited but had quit by the time of the study also felt they were less empowered during the time they were inherited. The reasons they cited were: being answerable to someone who was not their husband, instability of inheritors such that one was always unsure of their next move, and inheritors who felt they had a right to sleep with other widows while they are with you. Asked why they got inherited in the first place, they cited various external pressures from immediate and extended family members, conformity with culture, and for a few, economic and social support from the inheritors.

In sum, the majority of the widows—both inherited and uninherited—felt that inheritance was disempowering, yet 76 percent had a history of being inherited, including 35 percent of the respondents who were inherited at the time of the study. Moreover, 87 percent of the 35 widows who were inherited preferred to remain in the relationship even when offered economic stability and legal protection of children and property. A theme threading through the paper is that responsibility to one's community often takes precedence over duty to self, such that empowerment discourse makes sense only if it is crafted in response to community as well as individual needs.

## IMPACT OF THE SUB-STUDY AND CONCLUSIONS

From our sub-study, several conclusions can be reached. One, all respondents had full knowledge that sexual cleansing and inheritance could feasibly increase their risk for HIV infection or transmission, yet 76 percent were, or had been, inherited. The majority found the practice disempowering, but went ahead and conformed to the cultural requirement in order to "protect" their families from perceived adverse effects of failing to be inherited (collectively referred to as *chira*). In the sub-study, the strategy we used to address the issue of *chira* was to equip the widows with information that made them critically weigh the consequences of *chira* vis-à-vis that of contracting or transmitting HIV, and provided them with forums to debate these issues amongst themselves and decide on a way forward. In building this awareness we sought to address generations of cultural conditioning and how to debunk some of these entrenched beliefs. The result was that widows were able to come up with several safe alternatives to inheritance, including symbolic inheritance, use of condom, HIV counseling, and testing of the widow and the inheritor prior to starting a relationship, sticking with one inheritor, or relying on support from the church to counter the belief in *chira*. For example, in Figure 15–3 below widows are preparing a skit depicting deaths from identical causes in two different families; one where the widow was inherited and another where the widow did not observe the practice. The interpretation of the villagers was that the widow who was not inherited died from *chira* while the one who observed the practice died from witchcraft or other causes. The message being conveyed here was that death and other misfortunes occur equally to those who are inherited as well as those who are not, and that inheritance does not necessarily provide insulation from tragedies or general mishaps.

**Figure 15.3.**

Also, 27 percent of the 101 respondents interviewed said they would prefer to remain in their relationships because of economic and social benefits,
an indication that with economic emancipation and social support, these
widows would probably make a choice against being inherited. Our program
provided training on income generation and peer counseling and education
to boost the economic and social standing of the widows and free them from
the hold of their in-laws and other members of their extended families. In
doing so, we provided an enabling environment which saw fourteen groups
being formed with a total membership of over 800, with leaders elected by
the members and empowered by the HAWI project to run the activities of
their respective groups. The result was that most groups continued to be
active one year after the end of direct involvement by HAWI and with no
funding from outside sources. I view this as empowerment from within.

Three, the widows defined empowerment in terms of real economic and
social needs, as well as access to legal protection over their children and
property. Fear of being disinherited and of having their children confiscated
made some widows succumb to pressured inheritance, a testimony that until
the government puts in place a functional legal system to protect the widows, attempts at address sexual cleansing and inheritance of widows as risk
behaviors for HIV infection will continue to be undermined.

In summary, in the absence of alternative fallback in terms of social, economic, and legal recourse, widows and other vulnerable women will continue to play a key role in perpetuating practices that work to undermine

their own autonomy. When basic survival is at stake, widows will continue to conflate empowerment with access to means of survival. To many widows, inheritance has served as this means, and consequently been nourished this way. Our role in addressing the empowerment of widows should, as a matter of necessity, recognize that factors external to the widows often compel them to remain or become inherited, suggesting that if these factors were removed or minimized, the widows would redefine empowerment in terms that do not include cultural conformity.

## NOTES

1. Many thanks to those who made the research informing this paper successful: Financial support from the Fulbright Program's 2004–2005 New Century Scholars Program (administered by the Council for International Exchange of Scholars), professional support from Profs. Carolyn Elliott and Lucy Jarosz, field logistics by study staff (Jesses Asewe, Jacob Odhiambo, Lilian Ouma, Juliana Okello, Jullie Juma, Beatrice Otieno, Nya Malo, Nya Ndori), University of Washington's Department of Geography for providing the opportunity for the exchange visit, and all participants without whom the study would not have been carried out. I am truly grateful.
2. Kawango E. Agot, "Widow Inheritance and HIV/AIDS Interventions in Sub-Saharan Africa: Contrasting Conceptualizations of 'Risk' and 'Vulnerability'" (Ph.D. diss., University of Washington, 2001), hereafter cited in text as Agot (2001); Kawango E. Agot, "HIV/AIDS Interventions and the Politics of the African Woman's Body." In *A Companion to Feminist Geography*, eds. Lise Nelson and Joni Seager (London: McMillan Publishers, 2005), hereafter cited in text as Agot (2005); Paul Mboya, *Luo Kitgi gi Timbegi: A Handbook of Luo Customs* (Kisumu: Anyange Press, 1997), hereafter cited in text as Mboya (1997); Isaac Luginaah, David Elkins, Eleanor Maticka-Tyndale, Tamara Landry, and Mercy Mathui, "Challenges of a Pandemic: HIV/AIDS-Related Problems Affecting Kenyan Widows," *Social Science & Medicine* 60, no. 6 (2005): 1219–28, hereafter cited in text as Luginaah, et al. (2005).
3. Tom Mboya Okeyo, and Ann K. Allen, "Influence on Widow Inheritance on the Epidemiology of AIDS in Africa," *African Journal of Medical Practice* 1, no. 1 (1994): 20–5, hereafter cited in text as Okeyo and Allen (1994); Agot (2001, 2005), Luginaah, et al. (2005).
4. Ruth Alsop, and Nina Heinsohn. "Measuring Empowerment in Practice: Structuring Analysis and Framing Indicators." *World Bank Policy Research Working Group paper 3510*. (Washington, DC: World Bank, February 2005), hereafter cited in text as Alsop and Heinsohn (2005); Jeremy Holland, and Simon Brook. "Measuring Empowerment: Country Indicators." In *Power, Rights, and Poverty: Concepts and Connections*, ed. Ruth Alsop. A working meetings sponsored by DFID and the World Bank, March 23–24, 2004 (Washington, DC: The World Bank), hereafter cited in text as Holland and Brook (2004)
5. Jo Rowlands. *Questioning Empowerment: Working with Women in Honduras* (Oxford: Oxfam, 1997).
6. Fruzsina Csaszar, "Understanding the Concept of Power." In *Power, Rights, and Poverty: Concepts and Connections*, ed. Ruth Alsop. A working meeting sponsored by DFID and the World Bank, March 23–24, 2004 (Washington, DC: The World Bank).

7. Lutfun N. Khan Osmani, "Impact of Credit on the Relative Well-Being of Women: Evidence from the Grameen Bank," *IDS Bulletin* 29, no. 4 (1998): 30–8.
8. Isobel Coleman, "The Payoff from Women's Rights," *Foreign Affairs* (May/June 2004). http://www.foreignaffairs.org/20040501faessay83308/isobel-coleman/the-payoff-from-women-s-rights.html (accessed December 30, 2006).
9. Nypan (1991), in Lynn Thomas, "*Ngaitana* (I Will Circumcise Myself)": Lessons from Colonial Campaigns to Ban Excision in Meru, Kenya. In *Female "Circumcision" in Africa: Culture, Controversy, and Change,* eds. Bettina Shell-Duncan and Ylva Hernlund, 129–50 (Boulder: Lynne Reinner Publishers, 2000); cited hereafter as Thomas (2000).
10. Betinna Shell-Duncan, and Ylva Hernlund. Female "Circumcision" in Africa: Dimensions of the Practice and Debates." In *Female "Circumcision" in Africa: Culture, Controversy, and Change,* eds. Bettina Shell-Duncan and Ylva Hernlund, 1–40 (Boulder: Lynne Reinner Publishers, 2000).
11. Ethical approval for the study was obtained from Kenyatta National Hospital Ethics Review Committee (Approval #P48/4/2004).
12. *Chira* is a chronic wasting, often terminal, condition perceived to be associated with breaching of sexual and other relational taboos. Besides wasting, other classic signs and symptoms include persistent cough, vomiting, diarrhea, thinning of hair texture, loss of hair, and generalized tiredness and depression (Agot, 2005). Because of the similarities in the signs and symptoms between *chira* and AIDS, the two are often conflated.

# 16 Age of Consent Law and Moral Order
## The Criminalization of Youth Sexual Relationships in Uganda

*Shanti A. Parikh[1]*

*"They arrested me for loving a schoolgirl"*

In December 1998, 20-year-old Yahaya Waigongolo[2] of Iganga town in eastern Uganda was arrested and later convicted of having sexual intercourse with a minor, a criminal offense called "defilement." According to Section 123 of the Ugandan Penal Code (cap 106) as amended in 1990, a male of any age who has sexual intercourse with a female under the age of eighteen, whether she consents or not, is guilty of defilement. It is a criminal offense carrying a maximum penalty of death by hanging.[3] The victim in this case, whom I will call Lydia, was a seventeen-year-old schoolgirl living in a middle-class section of town that bordered Yahaya's one-roomed housing row. The two young lovers had been involved in a liaison for about nine months before the arrest. They colluded to keep the affair hidden from the girl's strict father. Her father asked Lydia's stepmother to increase surveillance over the adolescent after he noticed her waning interest in school and in her childhood friends, as well as a decrease in her typical playfulness with her younger step-siblings. Lydia's increasingly visible signs of pregnancy, such as loose-fitting clothes and nausea, sent an already protective father into a state of rage, culminating in his determined efforts to find out who impregnated his daughter. Afraid that her father's anger would result in violence against her and perhaps her stepmother, Lydia easily gave up the name of her lover.

Early the next morning, two police met Yahaya at a distribution depot in town where he worked as a manual laborer loading and unloading cargo. The young man was handcuffed and escorted to the police station, inciting a wave of morning excitement and gossip in town. After being accused of defiling and impregnating the young girl, Yahaya claimed in his own defense that a week ago he had given the girl's stepmother 65,000 shillings (about US$ 40) for medical expenses and explained that he would continue to provide financial assistance to the baby. "Work has been slow," he pleaded, "but I will provide assistance when I get paid."[4] The girl's positive identification and Yahaya's promise to provide child support were adequate evidence to charge Yahaya with defilement.

The case sped quickly through the judicial system, and Yahaya was sentenced to twenty-six months in a state prison for capital offenders. About four months before his release, his sentence was extended by six months after the father claimed that Yahaya had defied court orders by communicating with his daughter through a letter delivered by a friend. The father brought a letter to the court to show that Yahaya was defiant and non-remorseful. Neither Yahaya nor Lydia were given an opportunity to respond to the charges. When I spoke with Yahaya in June 2002, he had been out of prison for eight months and was looking for work in Iganga town. "They arrested me," Yahaya began the narrative of his criminal conviction, "for loving a girl who was in school." Although he told me he was no longer in a relationship with Lydia, my assistant and I could not tell if his answer was a scripted attempt to protect himself from further incrimination.

Yahaya was one of many young men in Uganda imprisoned during the mid-1990s and early-2000s for having sexual relations with teenage girls under the age of eighteen. In 1990, women reformers fought a legislative battle to increase the age of consent from fourteen to eighteen and revised the maximum punishment to death by hanging. Advocates of the law believed that increasing and enforcing the age of consent would empower girls by protecting them from sexual exploitation and abuse. Borrowing from international human rights frameworks, women reformers believed that the age of consent law provided a rights-based empowerment strategy for addressing the disproportionately high HIV rates among young women and reversing the trend of out-of-wedlock teenage pregnancies. The law was intended to prosecute and deter middle-aged sugar daddies, pedophiles, organizers of child sex labor, and parents who arranged childhood marriages. Reformers hoped to challenge male sexual privilege, create new ways of thinking about who has sexual access to young females, and provide girls with a period of time during which they could obtain an education and safely mature into young adults.[5]

Their goals were somewhat met. On the one hand, the aggressive anti-defilement campaigns launched in the early 1990s lead to a dramatic increase in reported defilement cases. In Iganga, reported defilement cases rose from zero in 1990 to over 50 percent of all criminal cases in 1998, according to the Chief Magistrate's court registry (see Figure 16–1). On the other hand, while reported cases increased, the law was overwhelmingly being used to arrest young men, a group not expressly targeted by the law's advocates. Specifically, the average age of males charged with defilement in Iganga was 21.5-years old.[6] Based on anecdotal evidence and non-governmental (NGO) reports, the same phenomenon was occurring throughout Uganda. Sugar daddies and pedophiles, the intended targets of the law, often settled cases out of court with police and sometimes families, escaping formal legal punishment and imprisonment.

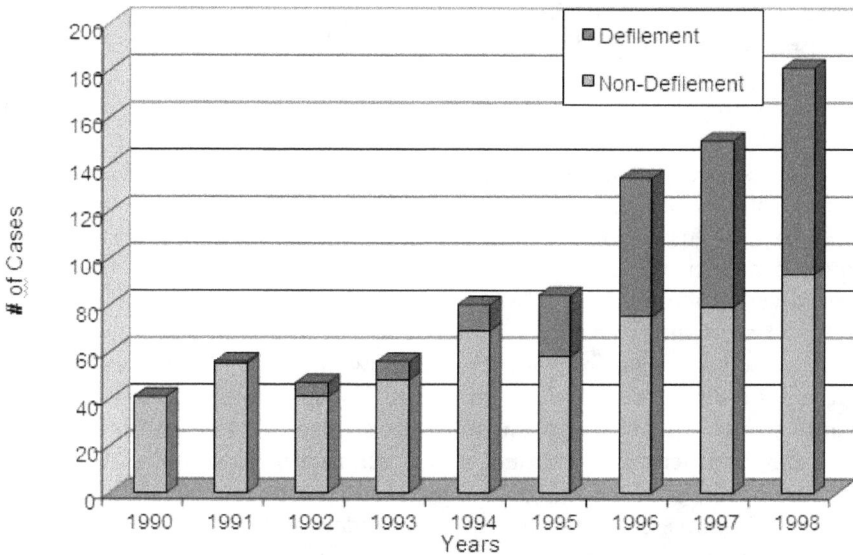

**Figure 16.1.**

Stories about young men being arrested for having underage girlfriends circulated almost daily throughout local communities and in the media, leading many people to believe that young men were indeed the prime target of the law. Schoolboys and other young men I interviewed expressed fear about being arrested for having relationships with classmates and young women. Moreover, fear of punishment emerged as a dominant theme in boys' love letters.[7] In a love letter I collected in 1999, a seventeen-year-old schoolboy wrote to his sixteen-year-old love interest:

> I didn't mean [for] you to decide whether to give up or to go on. But asked you to suggest which method can we play when carrying our love affairs in order to avoid being netted by your parents, who are bitterly in need of netting me.

Other letters bore warnings such as "burn this letter after reading" or "destroy this letter," so that incriminating evidence of the courtship would not exist.

During children's rights workshops I facilitated in 2002 and 2004 sponsored by Save the Children (Denmark), participants from rights agencies expressed similar anxieties about the law, complaining that the defilement cases involving consensual liaisons between young lovers were clogging the judicial system. They believed these cases served to distract the public and legal resources from the law's intended aim of prosecuting and deterring pedophiles and sugar daddies.

Based on ethnographic research, I ask the following questions. First, why is a law that was intended to empower young women being used to systematically regulate youth relationships, when it is commonly recognized in Uganda that older men and sugar daddies are the greatest perpetrators of sexual abuse and among the greatest factors fueling the HIV epidemic among young women? Second, what does this unintended use of the Defilement Law tell us about the universality of human rights frameworks and how the notion of rights gets refracted through local histories, meanings, and power structures?

My intent is not to argue against the use of international human rights frameworks for securing women's empowerment and gender equality. Rather, as a feminist scholar and advocate, I propose that we must critically examine the complex and unintended consequences of our empowerment strategies. Furthermore, we must seek a nuanced understanding of historically produced local meanings of rights and current anxieties within communities. My investigations into the unintended uses of the Defilement Law reveal deep anxieties about female sexual agency, generational tensions, and the prolonged effects of poverty and widespread unemployment of young men. A major finding of this study is that the universalist, feminist discourse of human rights is in conflict with, or complicated by, the class-based agendas of parents, local police, and other local leaders.

## FROM CULTURAL RELATIVISM TO POWER: THE ETHNOGRAPHY OF HUMAN RIGHTS

My analysis for this article engages with theoretical and methodological debates surrounding the ethnography of human rights. Hence, I will begin with a brief historical overview of anthropological perspectives on and approaches to the notion of human rights. Over the last few decades, human rights has emerged as the standard international framework through which arguments are made for protecting individuals from repressive states; arguing against certain cultural practices; providing for health care, housing, safety, and formal education; and legitimizing the claims of historically disenfranchised groups. The pursuit of human rights is commonly presented as an avenue for achieving modernity by setting the stage for freedom and securing individual autonomy, and hence fostering politically active and economically productive citizens. At the same time, two main critiques of the human rights movement have emerged. One suggests that the movement is closely aligned with social evolutionary assumptions—that societies move from primitive to civilized by adopting Western notions and ideas. The second critique focuses on the tension between claims of universality and respect for diversity.

Anthropology has had a precarious history with the notion of human rights.[8] During deliberations to adopt the 1948 Universal Declaration of Human Rights (UDHR), the American Anthropological Association, a socially progressive and internationally-aware group within the U.S., submitted a statement expressing its opposition to the declaration. The association's contention was not that certain rights did not apply to peoples around the world. Rather, Melville Herskowitz and other authors of the argued against the UDHR on the basis that it was both Eurocentric and potentially conducive to a new form of Western colonial domination. A few decades later, anthropological critiques of the UDHR used a cultural relativist standpoint, positing that it failed to account for variations in cultural and religious values. Throughout those earlier years, anthropologists found themselves in a quagmire. They considered themselves advocates for the often disenfranchised and colonized groups with whom they did research, but they found the Eurocentric rhetoric of human rights advocates to be patronizing.

More recently, given the increasing number of women and historically disenfranchised groups entering the profession of anthropology, and also given the rise of international declarations advancing the rights of specific groups (such as women, children, and indigenous groups), the discipline has more comfortably embraced the human rights framework. Many anthropologists publicly recognize the potential transformative power of the international rights framework in addressing violations against people with whom we work.[9] However, anthropologists and feminists argue for the need to investigate ways in which various players manipulate and interpret human rights concepts to achieve certain aims. Beverly Stoeltje summarizes these trends by arguing that the ethnography of human rights has moved from a discussion in which cultural specificity was seen as contradicting universal notions of human rights to one "in which the pursuit of human rights is approached as itself a cultural process that impinges on human subjects and subjectivities in multiple and contradictory ways."[10]

Rather than viewing human rights as either at odds with cultural beliefs ("cultural relativism") or as rooted in universal principles of social justice, the new critical legal anthropology pays particular attention to the myriad ways in which legal discourses and ideologies of rights are articulated in everyday practices and power relations in the pursuit of specific aims.[11] Informed by Foucault's theory of power, these approaches focus on how institutions that generate and circulate discourses of rights—the mass media, legal aid agencies, law enforcement, or other arbitration venues—act as powerful interlocutors through which global and national ideologies of rights are negotiated, contested, and adapted on the local level. These interlocutors play a crucial role in authorizing, legitimizing, and normalizing certain types of sexual relationships while simultaneously criminalizing, marginalizing, and pathologizing others through continual surveillance and censure.[12]

In this article, I build on these recent bodies of literature by demonstrating how a rights-based law intended to protect young females in Uganda from sexual exploitation is deployed in local settings in ways that reinforce and uphold, rather than change, patriarchal control over the female body. When refracted through local power structures, the pursuit of human rights may play out in unexpected ways. Ironically, whereas older people and men are often portrayed as reluctant to embrace modernist notions of women's rights, they are precisely the ones who creatively appropriate the Defilement Law. They do so partly because the law provides them a state technology for reasserting their perceived traditional authority that has faded over the last fifty years.

## HISTORICIZING ADOLESCENT FEMALE SEXUALITY IN IGANGA: RESEARCH SETTING AND METHODS

This article is based on several research trips taken between 1996 and 2005 to the Iganga town region.[13] The town of Iganga is the rapidly growing administrative and economic center for the Iganga district in southeastern Uganda. It lies 120 kilometers to the northeast of Kampala, the capital, and along the Trans-Africa highway, a major international artery populated with truck stops and towns with high rates of HIV infection.[14] Before British colonial rule began in the late 1800s, the Basoga ethnic group of Iganga lived in dispersed lineage groups and relied primarily on subsistence farming and livestock activities. Today, to meet the cash needs of an increasingly monetized economy, most households supplement farming with a combination of low-profit activities such as shop keeping, manual labor, driving bicycle or motorcycle taxis, trading, or repair work. Having a salaried position elevates a person's socioeconomic status, but these positions are more readily available to men. Residents view the availability of modern lifestyles (such as formal education and commercial leisure) and luxury goods (such as televisions, mobile phones, refrigerators, and cars) as desirable indicators of progress. However, access to cash income in Iganga has not kept pace with changing consumer demands, creating tensions between parents and children and increased stratification among households.[15]

A priority for both parents and youth is formal education. Whereas parents view their children's education as a key to family social mobility and public status, young people believe that education provides a route out of rural poverty and access to modern identities, non-kin social networks, and eventually luxury goods. In reality, however, persistent poverty severely limits young people's access to education, and it is common for youth to have many interruptions in their schooling. Young people that I interviewed frequently took a term or a year off from schooling if their parents did not have enough money for school fees, a situation particularly common for girls. This situation sometimes leads girls into transactional, sex-for-money relationships with older men. Sugar daddy relationships and perceived adolescent female sexual agency were highly contentious topics among residents. In some cases, parents would disapprove of but silently ignore suspicions of such liaisons, as the man was, in a sense, assisting the entire household.

As observers of Africa have noted, residents hold paradoxical feelings about education. While parents want their children to attend school, education is often blamed for corrupting and spoiling youth by introducing them to ideas and people outside the kinship network and community settings. This tension between youth and adults is most clearly apparent in youth sexual relationships. As one elder remarked, "Our young people today have gone crazy. And our girls! Parts, parts, parts [vagina, vagina, vagina] everywhere." At the heart of this common critique are concerns about the loss of the role of kin in the sexual learning and marital processes.[16]

The ideal Basoga marriage system is exogamous and revolves around the exchange of bridewealth from the groom's family to the bride's family. As with other patrilineal groups in Africa, legitimate sexual access to a young woman is negotiated through her father.[17] Anything else is considered theft, a crime committed by one man against another. The exchange of bridewealth legitimately transfers rights over a young woman's sexuality (and labor) from her father to her new husband. Family involvement in selecting and publicly approving sexual liaisons is paramount for the family's reputation and the harmonious functioning of a new marital union. Schooling and other socioeconomic changes are seen as disrupting ideal routes to marriage.

Over the last fifty years, monetization of the economy, Christianization, ideas about modernity brought in by the media, and formal education have altered the sexual expectations and experiences of young people. While oral histories I collected from elders indicate that in the past young people did have romantic and sexual liaisons before marriage, these liaisons were hidden from adults and the expectation was that they might not result in marriage. Without a doubt, dating has become a standard practice among young people, causing great anxiety among adults. As will be explored later, the Defilement Law becomes a way for parents to regain some of their historical power in the negotiation of sexual liaisons of daughters and at the same time express their disapproval of youth dating.

I used ethnographic research methods to understand how the intended use of the Defilement Law is situated within this local context of anxiety over female sexual agency and youth dating. Ethnographic research based on extended stays in the community and participant observation provides a more intricate understanding of everyday life than is often attainable through "official" data, including court documents or state records, interviews with elites or leaders, and research surveys. Complex social phenomena, particularly those involving private topics such as sexuality, require fine attention to how people say things are (*ideology*), what people actually do (*experiences and individual agency*), and how people perceive their experiences (*situated subjectivities*).

I interviewed seven young men who had been arrested for defilement. When possible, I also interviewed the young women who were considered, by the law, the victims in the case. Legal cases involving illicit or taboo topics quickly take on their own life, becoming "social facts" existing outside of the case itself. Therefore, I also gathered local narratives about several defilement cases in Iganga that had become part of the town's semi-public discussion, or gossip. In order to understand the perspectives of national and local players working on issues of defilement and sexual offenses, I interviewed women's and children's rights advocates, magistrates and judges, court registrars, and legal scholars and practitioners. My understanding of historical changes in Iganga was constructed from numerous life histories with elders, the 1950s research of anthropologist Lloyd Fallers, and other works done in Iganga by anthropologists and historians.[18]

In addition to interviews, my research assistants and I collected stories about defilement and sexual liaisons from the mass media and popular culture. We also gathered information from the Iganga Magistrate Court registry, recording the number of cases in each of the five criminal categories, ages of the alleged perpetrator and victim (when available), and the judicial action in each case. We did the same for cases taken to the Probate (family) office, which handled family and domestic disputes. Cases of child support brought by women or the parents of young women made up over 50 percent of all domestic and family matters taken to the office. I had a chance to observe the proceedings of a few of these cases that were brought by fathers seeking child support for their pregnant teenage daughters. I did not, however, observe any criminal proceedings of defilement cases.

## THE DEFILEMENT LAW: CONSTRUCTING INNOCENT GIRLS AND PREDATORY SUGAR DADDIES

In the early 1900s during British colonial rule, the Defilement Law was adopted in Uganda as part of a larger colonial project to civilize Africans. Following British law, the age of consent for females was set at fourteen. While other laws pertaining to sexual and domestic matters were used during colonial times to justify the British civilizing mission and establish certain gender relations,[19] I found no evidence that the Defilement Law was commonly used during colonial or post-independence times. Rather, oral histories I collected suggest that sexual violations were typically determined, handled, and adjudicated between families or by local authorities.

The age of consent law remained relatively unused until the early 1990s, when women reformers and children's rights advocates collaborated with international donors to begin an aggressive anti-defilement campaign. The 1990 bill to increase the age of consent and the aggressive campaigns were part of a series of radical legal moves by women reformers to challenge historical structures of patriarchy that granted males cultural rights over the female body.

Women reformers' aggressive attacks on male sexual privilege generated a flurry of public cynicism and opposition.[20] Miria Matembe, an outspoken Member of Parliament and controversial women's rights advocate, became a favorite target of counterattacks. Matembe was used as the public symbol of "the war against men." In an article entitled "Women Demand Castration for Men over Sex Abuse," Matemba's now famous quote appeared: "Men are in possession of a potentially dangerous instrument which should be cut off unless it is properly used."[21] A satirical cartoon appeared in the same newspaper a few days later showing a scared older man with his hands tied with rope at the entrance of an office called the "Castration Center." The thin man is greeted by two women, one holding a large pair of scissors, the other wielding a machete (Figure 16–2). His pre-pubescent accuser stands next to him in equal fear and confusion as the man prepares for his impending castration.

Directly below this provocative and emotive cartoon is a letter to the editor bearing the title, "School girls provoke." The juxtaposition of the

**OPINION: School girls provoke**

Figure 16.2.

emasculating cartoon and the editorial about seductive adolescent females represents one type of anxiety about the age of consent. As this cartoon demonstrates, the anti-defilement campaign is portrayed as a war against men. But men, according to proponents of this view, are not perpetrators of sexual exploitation. Rather, they are the victims of adolescent female sexual seduction and the innocent targets of feminist attacks. Women activists are portrayed as emotional, irrational, and jealous of sexually attractive, nubile younger females. Thus, younger females are constructed as Uganda's new breed of self-interested *femmes fatales*.

Another critique against widely enforcing the age of consent portrayed the law as an attempt of the national government to interfere in private and local matters. This national interference, it was argued, shows a lack of respect for community autonomy, a lack of trust in the ability of local leaders to protect their own residents, and hence a throwback to earlier colonial days. Invocations of culture, tradition, and community self-determination emerged as common rationalizations for not meddling in private disputes concerning the age of consent.

Amidst the heated public criticism and opposition, the campaign that eventually won public acceptance was based on the image of the innocent girl-child. The symbol of the innocent child distracted the public from allegations that the law was a direct attack on men and on historical (and, thus, "natural") gender roles. The campaign tapped into the international tide of discourses and funding surrounding human rights and innocent childhood.[22] This international legal tide offered the anti-defilement campaign financial and technical support from international donors. Aligning the anti-defilement movement with global rights discourses also provided a framework for reconfiguring notions of childhood and women's rights in Uganda. Nationally, the campaign folded neatly into the national discourse on modernity and human rights being promoted by President Yoweri Museveni's socially progressive agenda.[23]

Fundamentally, the anti-defilement campaigns were an attack on "tradition" by policymakers motivated to make Uganda, and more specifically Ugandan women, "modern." Female reformers vocally attacked customs they considered archaic and backward, such as arranged marriages of girls and forced marriage. They sought to protect girls not only from older men, but also from parents who use bridewealth acquired through the marriage of a daughter as a source of income or who lend out daughters for domestic service in order to pay off debts. Increasing and enforcing the age of consent, according to advocates of the law, would shield young females by legally lengthening their childhood, thereby providing them a protected environment within which to mature physically and emotionally and develop skills that would ensure greater economic and social independence from males. During this extended time, young females could be shaped into modern women.

By positioning females under the age of eighteen within the protected status of children, advocates attempted to repackage girls as lacking the ability to resist male sexual advances. Defilement, as constructed by women activists, was woven into various seduction narratives in which innocent girls are trying to overcome great odds at home, in the community, and at school. If a girl goes astray, it is not of her own will, but because her innocence was violated. She was defiled, either by being married off, seduced by a man, or impregnated and ruthlessly left to suffer. As the next section demonstrates, however, women reformers and communities may have had different ideas about which girls were protected under the law.

## COMPETING CLASS AGENDAS:
## NOT ALL GIRLS ARE EQUALLY INNOCENT

When I began research in 1996 in Iganga, the Defilement Law was common knowledge among residents. Six years into the campaign, posters depicting a young female, usually adolescent, being preyed upon by a stalking drunkard or a sugar daddy, with a caption such as "Protect Your Friends," were regularly seen in government buildings and health clinics around the dusty agrarian town (see Figures 16–3 and 16–4). Another common theme featured a pre-pubescent girl being lured by a man holding a piece of candy or a friendly smile. The colorful print campaigns sponsored by various HIV/AIDS

Figure 16.3.

Figure 16.4.

and child advocacy NGOs had made their way to the walls of the make-shift, one-room, local council offices in the outlying villages. Gossip about local cases easily spread within gathering places, and rarely did I hear great shock about the numerous defilement stories reported in the media. Instead, residents would comment that defilement cases were more frequent today than in the past. However, I suspect this was more a function of increased attention than increased frequency. Given its relatively recent insertion into public discourse, I was struck by how easily the Defilement Law fit into the local landscape, especially since male sexual advances towards younger females had been historically commonplace.

Local narratives about defilement cases involving adolescent girls stimulated critical reflection about female sexual agency and about the age at which a female becomes responsible for her sexual actions.[24] Through these debates, class emerged as a key determinant in the culpability and innocence of the male and female involved in the case. Whereas residents of Iganga were generally aware that Uganda's new legal and public discourse expanded childhood to the age of eighteen, they held complex views about the blanket characterization of adolescent females as "children." Historically, the transition from child to adult depended less on chronological age and more on reproductive, economic, and social factors. The economic status of the girl and her family inevitably underwrote perceptions about her maturation and sexual responsibility. A resource-poor girl not attending school was perceived as making a transition out of the child category sooner than a girl from a middle-class family attending school. Likewise, a young female who has reproduced was considered taking on adult responsibilities and duties. Therefore, innocence and the state protection that accompanies the modern category of child—notions central to the reformers' conception of the Defilement Law—tended to be reserved for a young female who is considered a future modern woman and productive contributor to society. Girls of low economic and educational status, on the other hand, are perceived as sexually knowing, and therefore outside the protection of this law. Instead, residents often saw them as a possible burden to society because of unplanned pregnancies or dubious economic activity, such as commercial sex work.

This flexible social classification of the teenage girl—as an innocent child or a sexually knowing adult—has complicated local uses of the Defilement Law. Most residents of Iganga with whom I spoke held that relationships between pubescent females and older, middle-class, married males represent common historical uses of male power in the context of economic desperation and gender roles. Yet there was an increasingly vocal opinion, especially among older women, that these liaisons were becoming less acceptable, for they left the adolescent girl with limited social mobility and options.

The Defilement Law is phrased in terms of protecting "the girl-child," regardless of other aspects of identity. However, class is fundamental to social constructions of innocence, consent, and the meaning of youthful sexuality in a particular instance. The victim's degree of innocence is partly determined by her future earning potential; girls in school promise higher returns for their parents and society. Daughters from poorer families, it is often assumed in local and popular discourse, can be swayed easily into illicit sexual liaisons. Girls from wealthier families, whose family inheritance and social reputation are at stake, are often subject to tighter parental and kin surveillance. Class and educational attainment determine a female's access to sexual respectability within wider society. The image of the pure schoolgirl has become a salient symbol of Uganda's future.

Therefore, to return to my earlier example, through the lens of class Yahaya was guilty of having sexual intercourse not just with an underage girl, but with an underage schoolgirl, a female who represented Uganda's future. In contrast to Yahaya's case stands a complaint brought against a nineteen-year-old motorcycle repair apprentice, Roland, by the father of a pregnant teenager. Unlike Yahaya, Roland had impregnated a teenage girl, Sara, who had a history of sexual liaisons with men. She was "already spoiled," to borrow the common phrase of elders. Sara's father had taken Roland to the Probate Family Office to demand child support for her unborn child. When I asked the Probate Officer why she did not refer the case to the Magistrate Court as defilement, she remarked that the girl had already been "living as an adult," by which she meant both sexually active and earning her own money. The teenage girl had stopped schooling and had spent some time with her sister-in-law in another town working in a restaurant. Because Sara was no longer in school and working in a place deemed unsuitable for respectable females, she was seen as possessing the sexual agency of an adult. Hence, Sara was not entitled to the full protection of the Defilement Law.

A similar class dynamic occurs with male perpetrators. Although residents recognize the threat of sugar daddies, their economic status provides them with access to sexual privilege not accorded to poorer men. Their sexual behaviors might be considered deplorable, but this is trumped by the reality that they provide crucial economic support for a wide social and kin network. Unlike poor men who might have limited ability to support children they conceive out of wedlock, wealthier men can afford it. Hence, sugar daddies (for their wealth) and schoolgirls (for their future promise and purity) each represent Uganda's entrance into modernity. By the same token, unemployed or poor young men and out-of-school girls epitomize failure to achieve modernity and progress. The coupling of schoolgirls and their unemployed peers represents yet another quandary in Uganda, for these relationships threaten the social order by subverting historical expectations. I turn next to the quandary of youth sexual relationships.

## OMUTANGO: CONTROLLING DELINQUENT DAUGHTERS AND DISCIPLINING DEFIANT BOYS

Adults in Iganga echo the harsh commentary promulgated in Ugandan popular culture about the ways in which young females today use their sexuality for material gain. This common critique has left residents ambivalent about adolescent defilement cases. Many older residents feel that adolescent female sexual agency and the desire for modern goods have loosened social controls over sexuality. In the words of one elder, "Our girls have gotten out of hand. They give themselves away so cheaply." According to local convention, youth sexual relations defy notions of parental authority and are often classified under the Lusoga term *obwenzi*, or sexual promiscuity. *Obwenzi* generally refers to a common sexual behavior that threatens the perceived traditional moral order. The specific social meaning of *obwenzi* has shifted historically, given the wider context and the systems of sexual regulation under threat.

When anthropologist Lloyd Fallers conducted research in Iganga in the 1950s, *obwenzi* commonly referred to cases in which a man was accused of having sexual intercourse with another man's wife, or adultery. During Uganda's post-independence period in the mid-1960s, elders recall *obwenzi* accompanying feelings of social euphoria and spoke about sexual transgressions occurring at burials, weddings, and other community celebrations with dancing, music, and inter-generational and inter-clan interactions. In the 1970s, during Uganda's economically and socially turbulent period, *obwenzi* described unmarried women who engaged in long-distance trading and were sexually liberated because they were economically and socially unattached to a particular man. Today, *obwenzi* is frequently used to mean the exchange of sex for modern material goods, such as makeup, trousers, and beauty products, or cohabiting without the consent of parents. Moreover, it is equated with unconstrained sexual behaviors and low morals.[25] Whereas in the past *obwenzi* generally referred to adult sexual behaviors, gradually it has also come to include behaviors of young people, particularly girls who act without consent of their parents and males who do not adequately provide *omutango* (compensation) to the parents.

For parents in Iganga, there is a difference between delinquent daughters who engage in *obwenzi* and innocent daughters who are seduced by men of power. Elders frequently point to the shifting nature of marriage to underscore their dissatisfaction with changes in sexual relationships. A local proverb—"One who entices you away will not pay bridewealth"—reflects the deeply felt sentiment that females too easily enter sexual unions without the approval of their parents. "Parents today do not have control over their daughters," remarks a mother of six children. Another elder exclaimed, "Girls today go from one temporary marriage to another. They run off with men, get married without their parents' knowledge. They get divorced the next day and then marry someone else."

Female laxness about entering into sexual unions is perceived to have led to the decay of the betrothal process and, more significantly, to the declining importance of the family in that process. In the ideal past, parents of the girl would look for a man for her to marry soon after menarche, which marked the end of childhood. The threat and shame of getting pregnant in the father's home leads to intense surveillance over the girl. For elders, the ideal marriage is based on an agreement between the prospective groom and the father of the female, and ultimately between two kinship groups.

The key moment in this process is the highly formal ceremony between the two kin groups known as "the introduction" (*kwándhúla*), during which the two clans are formally introduced and endorse the union, final bride-wealth is negotiated, and gifts to relevant kin members are delivered. The gift exchange in sexual relationships still occurs, but it is now frequently between a girl and her suitor. The removal of the girl's family from this exchange, and the focus on the girl alone as beneficiary of the gift, lies at the heart of moral anxiety.[26]

The acceptance of the gift symbolizes parental consent. In that context, it becomes clear why the age of consent debate in Iganga is less about *age* than it is about *consent*. Historically, the concern was not about the consent of the girl but the consent of the parents, most often the father or another paternal clan member. Failure to get the consent of parents—regardless of the age of the girl or whether she consented—was considered the violation. Once violated, the girl is considered soiled and the parents can sue for damages done to them since, by elaboration, it is presumably more difficult to find her a husband and the bridewealth given for her will be less.

The use of the Defilement Law to address the issue of parental consent is evident in the case of a 14-year old girl who engaged in sexual relations with a teenage shop attendant. As part of the girl's evening chores, her parents sent her to town regularly to purchase goods and food. A young shop attendant often offered the unescorted girl free items and eventually invited her to his room, which was located behind the shop. One day after returning from town, the mother noticed that "the girl's way of walking has changed," and inquired about the change. The daughter evaded the topic of sexual intercourse, blaming her new stride on a boil between her legs. Concerned and suspicious, the mother took the girl to the doctor. After threats from her mother, at the doctor's office the girl finally revealed that she had been having sexual intercourse with the teenage shop attendant. The parents of the girl confronted the young man and his parents, explained that they were willing to forgive the boy and his parents, and asked them to pay a fine of 300,000 shillings (about US$170). When the parents of the young male refused the amount, the incensed girl's parents argued, "We have been kind enough to you. What kind of person are you? You have destroyed our girl and you are not being considerate." The girl's parents reported the case to the police, and the boy was arrested and eventually convicted of defilement.

In another case, the disgruntled parents first tried other venues to pressure the young man to either marry their daughter or support the child. Unfortunately for the boy, neither he nor his widowed mother had the money. The unsatisfied parents used the age of consent law as additional leverage against the young man. After pleadings from the daughter, the case was dropped and an agreement was made out of court. From the perspective of the parents in this case, it is better to get an out-of-court settlement or arrange for child support with the young man rather than have him in jail. For other young men such as Yahaya, however, the outcome of being a financially poor lover was not as pleasant.

Older residents in Iganga view recent social changes such as the shift from kinship to civil ties, education, and the perceived autonomy of young people as destroying the moral order. Their narratives about the sudden decline of the traditional betrothal process and the rise of youth sexual agency have become a common way for residents to explain the high prevalence of HIV and single mothers. Their solution to HIV, moral decline, and teenage pregnancy is to discipline delinquent daughters by curtailing their involvement with young lovers. The Defilement Law provides a way for expressing and resolving deep generational conflicts about youthful sexual agency and moral chaos. For many parents such as Lydia's, the Defilement Law restores some control over a daughter's sexual autonomy by punishing a suitor who, from the perspective of the parents, cannot provide adequate compensation to them or care for their daughter. Because defilement is a criminal offense, it is a crime against the state; parents technically receive no compensation as they did in the past under the rules of *omutango*. Hence, what many parents originally thought was re-instating their authority over their daughters in fact places final authority over their daughters with the state.[27] Just as reformers discovered how difficult it is to engineer social change in a desired direction, so too have older people in Iganga experienced unintended consequences of their actions.

## SEXUAL CITIZENSHIP: RETHINKING RIGHTS AND WOMEN'S EMPOWERMENT

In this article, I have examined how women reformers in Uganda fought for the enforcement of the Defilement Law as a strategy to empower girls by offering protection from sexual abuse and exploitation. As the law's advocates envisioned it, sugar daddies, pedophiles, and perpetrators of child sex slavery were the main targets of the law. While in Iganga, I witnessed how the anti-defilement campaigns did indeed change attitudes and public awareness about the sexual rights of girls and women. But I also saw many unintended consequences of the law. More often than not, the law was used to prosecute young men. This is not to suggest that none of these young men were sexual offenders, but almost all of the judges, women reformers, and other legal professionals with whom I spoke felt that boyfriends and consensual liaisons outnumbered male pedophiles in terms of arrests. As this article has shown, young people believed that boys were the ones being targeted by protective parents, teachers, and other authorities. Their crime was not just being boyfriends, but also being economically poor and hence undeserving suitors. I do not wish to ignore that youth relationships may be sites of abuse and gender inequalities, but the secrecy and anxiety surrounding youth sexual encounters certainly does not facilitate the development of sexually healthy individuals. Ultimately, the Defilement Law provides adults a powerful tool for asserting their authority over adolescent females and youth sexual relations. In this way, the very phenomenon that women reformers attempted to challenge—patriarchal control of female sexuality—has been strengthened and given legitimacy under the rights-based law.[28]

What do these findings tell us about human rights as a tool for women's empowerment? I am not proposing that we abandon the rights framework for advancing gender equality or other sorts of equality. Rather, I am concerned about uncritical applications of Westernized notions of human rights without considering other forms, understandings, and meanings of rights. While attending a recent professional conference in the U.S., I was struck by comments and assumptions made by dedicated and rightfully angry panelists who were incensed by the continued gender abuses occurring around the world. A representative from a U.S-based human rights agency declared that we (meaning feminists or perhaps the West) have to make sure that human rights are respected and observed around the world. When considering the panelist's comments in light of my findings in Iganga, four points about competing notions of rights come to mind.

First, I think parents in Iganga would contend that *their rights* have been violated when someone has had unauthorized sexual liaisons with one of their daughters, and that they, the parents, deserve compensation. Michelle Oberman argues in her historical analysis of U.S. law that the age of consent reflected the long-standing assumption that "virginity was so highly prized that a man who took a girl's virginity without her father's permission was considered to have committed a theft against the father." [29] In Uganda, it is precisely the idea that female sexuality belongs to a man that facilitated the widespread use of the Defilement Law, for most cases in Iganga were brought by fathers. Unauthorized sexual access to a female had been considered a violation against her male guardian, whether her father or husband. Second, what the passionate human rights advocate on the panel failed to recognize is that throughout sub-Saharan Africa and other parts of the world, rights are embedded within a dense bundle of social relations. These rights are intricately tied to the concepts of responsibility and duties to others. Hence, local constructions of women's rights are tied to their duties and responsibilities to their husbands, children, brothers, parents, and others. Often these responsibilities and duties are primary concerns to women.

Third, I propose that we rethink our epistemological approach to problems and solutions of gender inequality. In using universal frameworks and discourses, we must seek to understand how imported notions fit into local histories, power structures, and current anxieties. For instance, whereas women reformers in Uganda regard planned structural change as the *answer* to combating sexual abuse of girls, adults in Iganga see structural change as the *problem* fueling abuses of sexuality. As I have demonstrated, the climate in Uganda is marked by economic uncertainty, urbanization, and anxiety about HIV and out-of-wedlock teenage motherhood. Communities feel that older systems of regulation—including compensation, betrothal, and the marital process—have diminished, leading to a destabilized moral order. Furthermore, senior male authority has diminished considerably in the last fifty years, occasioned by the increase of wage labor, formal education, the shift from kinship to civic networks for access to resources, and the emergence of youth romantic relationships (Parikh 2001). Within the climate of these economic and social changes, the Defilement Law has become a way for senior males to regulate young girls' sexuality, control junior males' sexual pursuits, and end youth romantic relationships. In short, the law is being used to restore the marriage process, reinstate perceived traditional hierarchies governing access to female sexuality, and, in the process, criminalize adolescent relationships. Meanwhile, the law is being used by parents to assert their historical rights over children and to reclaim some of the economic benefits culturally entitled to parents.

My final point concerns the intersection of socioeconomic class and human rights. Specifically, responses to the Defilement Law show that notions of female sexual exploitation and male criminality are determined by class. The case of Yahaya and Lydia exemplifies how the interconnectedness of criminality, class, and generation is reproduced and strengthened through patterned local uses of the Defilement Law. Residents of Iganga almost unanimously agreed that Yahaya's sentence might not have been so harsh, or might not have been pursued by law enforcement, if there were not a perceived difference in class and future social mobility between the two lovers. Like other schoolgirls, Lydia represents the modern and educated class. Yahaya, the young manual laborer represents the backward, lower class. This triple helix of class, criminality, and age is promulgated through community awareness campaigns, the media, and local talk. In this way, local parents are at odds with policymakers about what economic class of men young girls need to be protected against. While policymakers want to protect girls from businessmen and sugar daddies, parents want to protect them from men of the lower class. In the end, the human rights tool has served as an answer to class anxiety and the effect it has on gender relations. Yet to empower women, the empowerment of their entire community within global systems of inequality needs to be taken seriously. While we see marginalized women as oppressed, they are surrounded by and in various social relations with men who are also oppressed by globalization, neo-liberalism, and poverty. A global empowerment of disenfranchised women must also seek to improve the situation of their men, be it their sons, husbands, lovers, brothers, or fathers.

## NOTES

1. Funding for this project was provided by Fulbright New Century Scholars Fellowship, Yale University International and Area Studies grants, and Leadership Alliance Fellowship from Brown University. I owe my greatest research

debt to residents of Iganga, FIDA-U (The Ugandan Association of Women Lawyers) and Save the Children (Denmark). While in Uganda I was affiliated with Makerere Institute for Social Research and had a relationship with the School of Public Health at Makerere University.

2. All names of parties involved in defilement cases have been changed to protect those involved.

3. Defilement is one of five criminal offenses. The other four offenses are murder, rape, robbery, and treason. As defilement is a capital offense, cases can only be adjudicated by one of the eight High Court circuits, the Court of Appeals, or the Supreme Court.

4. This story is based on interviews my research assistants and I conducted with Yahaya, a neighbor, the court registrar, and Lydia.

5. In the late 1980s, HIV/AIDS epidemiologic reports in Uganda showed that females ages 15–19 were disproportionately infected with HIV compared to their male counterparts by a ratio of 5-to-1 (Kamali, et al., 2000). Researchers and media reports have noted that sex between young females and older males was at the heart of this gender disparity (Frask-Blunt, 2002; Obbo, 1995; Schoef, 1992). In the early 1990s, the term "sugar daddies" began to appear as the standard word for older, married men who used their economic means to entice young women into sexual relationships.

Information about the intended perpetrators to be charged under the Defilement Law is based on interviews with women in various law reform and women's organizations. They were explicit about their target perpetrators for the Defilement Law. They also referred to the numerous studies about disproportionate rates of HIV and educational attainment between the sexes.

See Anatoli Kamali, Lucy Mary Carpenter, James Alexander Grover Whitworth, Robert Pool, Anthony Ruberantwari, and Amato Ojwiya, "Seven-year Trends in HIV-1 Infection Rates, and Changes in Sexual Behaviour, Among Adults in Rural Uganda," *AIDS* 14, no. 4 (2000): 427–34; Martha Frask-Blunt, "The Sugar Daddies' Kiss of Death," *Washington Post*, October 6, 2001; Christine Obbo, "Gender, Age and Class: Discourses on HIV Transmission and Control in Uganda." In *Culture and Sexual Risk: Anthropological Perspectives on AIDS.* Han ten Brummelhuis and Gilbert Herdt, eds. (Amsterdam: Gordon and Breach Publishers, 1995); and Brooke G. Schoepf, "Women at Risk: Case Studies from Zaire." In *The Time of AIDS: Social Analysis, Theory and Method*, Gilbert Herdt and Shirley Lindenbaum, eds., 259–86 (Newbury Park, CA: Sage Publications, 1992); hereafter cited in text as Schoepf (1992).

6. Shanti Parikh, "Sugar Daddies and Sexual Citizenship in Uganda: Rethinking 3rd Wave Feminism," *Black Renaissance / Renaissance Noir* 6, no. 1 (2004): 82–107.

7. Shanti Parikh, "Desire, Romance, and Regulation: Adolescent Sexuality in Uganda's Time of AIDS." Ph.D. diss., Yale University, 2001; hereafter cited in text as Parikh (2001).

8. For reviews of the anthropology of human rights, see Karen Engle, "From Skepticism to Embrace: Human Rights and the American Anthropological Association," *Human Rights Quarterly* 23 (2001): 536–60; Mahmood Mamdani, "Introduction." In *Beyond Rights Talk and Culture Talk: Comparative Essays on the Politics of Rights and Culture,* Mahmood Mamdani, ed., 1–13 (New York: St. Martin Press, 2000); Sally Engle Merry, "Human Rights and the Demonization of Culture (and Anthropology Along the Way)," *Polar: Political and Legal Anthropology Review* 26, no. 1 (2003): 55–77; and

Wilcomb E. Washburn, "Cultural Relativism, Human Rights, and the AAA," *American Anthropologist* 89, no.4 (1987): 939–43.

9. American Anthropological Association, *Declaration on Anthropology and Human Rights Committee for Human Rights* (American Anthropological Association, 1999); Diana J. Fox, "Women's Human Rights in Africa: Beyond the Debate over the Universality or Relativity of Human Rights," *African Studies Quarterly* 2, no. 3 (1998). http://web.africa.ufl.edu/asq/v2/v2i3a2.htm (last accessed January9, 2007); Dorothy L. Hodgson, "Women's Rights as Human Rights: Women in Law and Development in Africa (WiLDAF)," *Africa Today* 49, no. 2 (2002): 3–26; and Ellen Messer, "Anthropologists in a World with and Without Human Rights." In *Exotic No More: Anthropology on the Front Lines*, Jeremy MacClancy, ed., 319–37 (Chicago: University of Chicago Press, 2002).

10. Stoeltje, Beverly J. "Introduction to Women, Language, and Law in Africa II: Gender and Relations of Power." *Africa Today* 49, no. 2 (2002): xi.

11. See Jean Comaroff and John L. Comaroff, "Criminal Justice, Cultural Justice: The Limits of Liberalism and the Pragmatics of Difference in the New South Africa," *American Ethnologist* 31, no. 2 (2004): 188–204; Daniel M. Goldstein, "'In Our Own Hands-': Lynching, Justice, and the Law in Bolivia," *American Ethnologist* 30, no. 1 (2003): 22–43; Susan Hirsch, *Pronouncing & Persevering: Gender and the Discourses of Disputing in an African Islamic Court* (Chicago: University of Chicago Press, 1998); Sally Falk Moore, *Social Facts and Fabrications: "Customary" Law on Kilimanjaro, 1880–1980* (New York: Cambridge University Press, 1986); Dorothy L. Hodgson, "'My Daughter . . . Belongs to the Government Now:' Marriage, Maasai and the Tanzanian State," *Canadian Journal of African Studies* 30, no. 1 (1996): 107–23, hereafter cited in text as Hodgson (1996); Sally Engle Merry, "Spatial Governmentality and the New Urban Social Order: Controlling Gender Violence through Law," *American Anthropologist* 103, no. 1 (2001): 16–29; and Mindie Lazarus-Black, "Law and the Pragmatics of Inclusion: Governing Domestic Violence in Trinidad and Tobago," *American Ethnologist* 28, no. 2 (2001): 388–416.

12. Michel Foucault, *The History of Sexuality: An Introduction,* vol. 1 (New York: Vintage Press, 1978).

13. By the Iganga town region, I am referring to the town and outlying villages.

14. H. Pickering, M. Okongo, B. Nnalusiba, K. Bwanika, and J. Whitworth. "Sexual Networks in Uganda: Casual and Commercial Sex in a Trading Town." *AIDS Care,* 9 (1997): 199–207.

15. See James Ferguson, *Expectations of Modernity: Myths and Meanings of Urban Life on the Zambian Copperbelt* (Berkeley: University of California Press, 1999).

16. Shanti Parikh, "From Auntie to Disco: The Bifurcation of Risk and Pleasure in Sex Education in Uganda." In *Sex in Development: Science, Sexuality, and Morality in Global Perspective,* Vincanne Adams and Stacey L. Pigg, eds., 125–58 (Durham: Duke University Press, 2005).

17. Caroline Bledsoe and Gilles Pison, eds., *Nuptiality in Sub-Saharan Africa: Contemporary Anthropological and Demographic Perspectives* (New York: Oxford University Press, 1994); and David Parkin and David Nyamwaya, eds., *Transformations of African Marriage* (Manchester, UK and Wolfeboro, NH: Manchester University Press for the International African Institute, 1987).

18. Lloyd Fallers, *Bantu Bureaucracy: A Century of Political Evolution among the Basoga of Uganda* (Chicago: University of Chicago Press, 1965); Lloyd

Fallers, *Law without Precedent: Legal Ideas in Action in the Courts of Colonial Busoga* (Chicago: University of Chicago Press, 1969).

19. Jean Allman and Victoria B. Tashjian, *I Will Not Eat Stone: A Women's History of Colonial Asante* (Portsmouth, NH: Heinemann Press, 2000).

20. See Sylvia Tamale, *When Hens Begin to Crow: Gender and Parliamentary Politics in Uganda* (Boulder, CO: Westview Press, 1999); Aili Mari Tripp, *Women & Politics in Uganda* (Madison, WI: University of Wisconsin Press, 2000).

21. Jossy Muhangi, "Women Demand Castration for Men over Sex Abuse." In *The New Vision*, Kampala, Uganda, December 18, 1991.

22. These international forums included the World Summit for Children (1990), the World Conference on Education for All (1990), the World Conference on Human Rights (1993), the World Summit for Social Development (1995) and the Fourth World Conference on Women (1995). In a series of international forums, the 1989 International Convention on the Rights of the Child (CRC) received special attention.

23. E. Khiddu-Makubuya, "The Rule of Law and Human Rights in Uganda: The Missing Link." In *Changing Uganda: The Dilemmas of Structural Adjustment & Revolutionary Change,* Holder Bernt Hansen and Michael Twaddle, eds., 217–23 (London: James Currey, 1991); and M. Louise Pirouet, "Human Rights Issues in Museveni's Uganda." In *Changing Uganda: The Dilemmas of Structural Adjustment & Revolutionary Change,* Holder Bernt Hansen and Michael Twaddle, eds., 197–209 (London: James Currey, 1991).

24. Sylvia Tamale, "How Old is Old Enough? Defilement Law and the Age of Consent in Uganda," *East African Journal of Peace & Human Rights* 7, no. 1 (2001): 82–101.

25. Philip Setel, *Plague of Paradoxes: AIDS, Culture, and Demography in Northern Tanzania* (Chicago: University of Chicago Press, 1999); hereafter cited in text as Setel (1999).

26. There has been much recent academic and media attention to transactional nature of sexual relationships in Africa and the role this has played in the spread of HIV (e.g., Schoepf 1992, Setel 1999). Less attention has been given to how communities internally regulate or deal with this phenomena and the historical trajectory of this part of the sexual economy.

27. In an ethnographically rich article, Hodgson (1996) makes a similar analysis arguing that a female's biological, but generally absent, father did not have guardianship over his daughter in the court of law. The disgruntled father remarked, "My daughter belongs to the state now."

28. For similar analyses of how the age of consent law was used to manipulate an unintended social agenda is found among U.S. historians. See, for instance, Carolyn E. Cocca, "The Politics of Statutory Rape Laws: Adoption and Reinvention of Morality Policy in the States, 1971–1999," *Polity* 35, issue 1 (2002): 51–72; Elizabeth Hollenberg, "The Criminalization of Teenage Sex: Statutory Rape and the Politics of Teenage Motherhood," *Stanford Law and Policy Review* 10 (1999): 267–87; Mary E. Odem, *Delinquent Daughters: Protecting and Policing Adolescent Female Sexuality in the United States, 1885–1920* (Chapel Hill: The University of North Carolina Press, 1995); and Stephen Robertson, "Age of Consent Law and the Making of Modern Childhood in New York City, 1886–1921," *Journal of Social History* 35, no.4 (2002): 781–98.

29. Michelle Oberman, "Girls in the Master's House: Of Protection, Patriarchy and the Potential for Using the Master's Tools to Reconfigure Statutory Rape Law," *DePaul Law Review* 50 (2001): 799–826. For scholarship on kinship

and marriage in Africa that has long observed a similar pattern of male rights over female sexuality among patrilineal groups, see E.E. Evans-Pritchard, *Kinship and Marriage among the Nuer* (Oxford: Clarendon Press, 1951); Alfred Reginald Radcliffe-Brown and Daryll Forde, eds., *African Systems of Kinship and Marriage* (London: Oxford University Press, 1951); Meyer Fortes, ed., *Marriage in Tribal Societies* (Cambridge: Cambridge University Press, 1962); and Isaac Schapera, *Married Life in an African Tribe* (London: Faber and Faber, 1940).

# 17 Hijacking Global Feminism
## Feminists, the Catholic Church and the Family Planning Debacle in Peru

*Christina Ewig*[1]

From 1996 through 1998, the state-run family planning program in Peru carried out mass sterilization campaigns that targeted women in poor, primarily indigenous, rural communities. The program prioritized sterilization over other forms of contraception, performed surgical contraception under low-quality conditions that at times led to the death or serious injury of the patients, and often carried out the sterilizations without first obtaining voluntary, informed consent. The sheer number of these sterilizations (217,446 from 1996 through 1998) was achieved in part through a system of quotas that provided little incentive for high-quality care.[2] In late 1998, a feminist lawyer investigating abuses in state-run hospitals stumbled upon evidence of problems in the family planning program and began to disseminate her findings to the media. Her action initiated closer scrutiny and ultimately created demands for the program's reform.

Peru's problematic sterilization campaigns of the mid-1990s are in many ways an old story of the instrumental use of women by national planners and international organizations as a means of controlling population growth and promoting economic development. What is remarkable about Peru in 1996 is that these sterilization campaigns took place in strikingly new global and national contexts that appeared to favor women's reproductive rights. By the late 1990s a new credo of reproductive rights dominated global population efforts, and Peru had seemingly absorbed this discourse. In 1982, Peru ratified all articles of the United Nations Convention on the Elimination of All Forms of Discrimination Against Women (CEDAW), first adopted by the UN Assembly in 1979. The CEDAW promotes women's equality in political, social, and economic realms and it is the only human rights convention that affirms women's reproductive rights. At the 1993 UN Conference on Human Rights in Vienna and the 1995 Copenhagen World Summit for Social Development, feminist activists were successful for the first time in placing women's rights on the international human rights agenda, and women's poverty on the international development agenda. Women's movements were also influential at the 1994 International Conference on Population and Development (ICPD) held in Cairo and the United Nations 1995 Fourth World

Conference on Women in Beijing, conferences in which Peruvian feminists were active participants.

Peru's Family Planning Program was significantly reformed on the heels of the Cairo and Beijing conferences. Its guiding documents largely reflected the language and goals agreed upon at Cairo, including a commitment to reproductive health care, women's reproductive rights, and the promotion of gender equity. The program's focus on the poorest Peruvians had the potential to dramatically increase access to family planning methods in a country where previously the middle classes and the wealthy were the only ones privileged with access to contraception. In addition, feminists and the government had established a mechanism to monitor the implementation of the "Program of Action" agreed upon at Cairo; a corporative body called the *Mesa Tripartita de Seguimiento al Programa de Acción del Cairo* (Tripartite Board to Monitor the Cairo Program of Action), which included members from the state, civil society, and international institutions.

How, then was it that abuses reminiscent of past sterilization campaigns, such as those in Puerto Rico, India, and South Africa, could occur in the late 1990s when both international and national circumstances seemed specifically designed to prevent such abuses? In this article, I will show how the Fujimori administration in Peru hijacked the global feminist language developed at Cairo and instrumentally used Peruvian feminists themselves to push a traditional Malthusian population policy that placed national economic development above women's human rights.

The difference between the Peruvian case and similar programs in other countries in the past is that national political actors not only used women to achieve their population goals, but also appropriated national and global feminist discourses to legitimize their actions. Peru's experience with family planning alerts us to the increasingly complex ways that global and national feminist agendas can be coopted for non- or even anti-feminist goals. It also demonstrates the need for continual and critical monitoring of state actions by feminists, even when these actions may on the surface appear to be positive for women.

## CAIRO AND BEIJING

In 1994, the International Conference on Population and Development held in Cairo produced a significant change in the discourse around population issues. From the view of population control as a means to security and economic development, the international discussion shifted to an approach that considered women's reproductive rights and gender equity as well as population control and environmental impact.[3] Access to reproductive health services, for all men and women, was one objective of the accords, and reproductive rights were explicitly linked with human rights. At Cairo, reproductive health was defined as a state of complete physical, mental and social well-being and not merely the absence of disease or infirmity, in all matters relating to the reproductive system and to its functions and processes. Reproductive health therefore implies that people are able to have a satisfying and safe sex life and that they have the capability to reproduce and the freedom to decide if, when, and how often to do so. Implicit in this last condition are the right of men and women to be informed and to have access to safe, effective, affordable, and acceptable methods of family planning of their choice, as well as other methods of their choice for regulation of fertility which are not against the law, and the right of access to appropriate health-care services that will enable women to go safely through pregnancy and childbirth and provide couples with the best chance of having a healthy infant.[4]

The Cairo conference also stated that reproductive rights are "human rights." The Cairo accords clearly succeeded in placing women's reproductive health and rights onto the population agenda, and in dampening previous emphases on overpopulation.

Yet, does this shift at Cairo represent a true watershed, or is the population establishment skillfully invoking feminist discourse, while maintaining the same fundamental objective of population control? Anthropologist Ines Smyth (1998: 228–30) has suggested that the definition of "reproductive rights" for the population establishment differs from feminist understandings. She explains that, whereas "the notion of self-determination in childbearing" became central to feminist definitions of reproductive rights by the late 1980s, the population establishment in the early 1990s equated reproductive rights with consumer choice in family planning options. In other words, she argues that the population establishment interpreted reproductive rights as a form of free-marketeering rather than as a fundamental human right. Betsy Hartmann, Director of the Population and Development Program at Hampshire College, criticized the Cairo agreements as leaving open the way for narrow, technocratic interpretations of reproductive health.[5] Thus, feminist scholars expressed concern that fundamental concepts of international feminist discourse, such as reproductive rights, have been appropriated, manipulated, and used instrumentally by institutions and individuals for their own agendas.

Family planning policy in Peru under the administration of President Alberto Fujimori illustrates this instrumental pattern. The Fujimori administration utilized international feminist discourses on reproductive health and rights, and alliances with Peruvian feminists themselves, to cloak a traditional population control agenda.

Less than a year following the Cairo accords, during his second inauguration speech in 1995, Fujimori announced a major change in Peru's population policy. He proclaimed a concerted "struggle against poverty," and promised family planning would play a critical role in this new initiative. Fujimori's political power at this point was strong. Congress was newly reconstituted, following Fujimori's closure of that body and a brief rule by decree in 1992. Although Fujimori's self-coup in 1992 was viewed poorly by international observers, nationally the President was lauded for taking a forceful position against the worst economic crisis in Peru's history and against guerrilla insurgencies that had led a decade-old civil war.[6] Riding on this wave of popularity, President Fujimori reinforced his commitment to family planning. As the only male head of state to address the United Nations Fourth World Conference on Women in Beijing and "as part of its policy on social development and the fight against poverty," Fujimori announced that his "government has decided to carry out an integral strategy of family planning that confronts openly, for the first time in the history of our country, the serious lack of information and services available on the matter."[7] This announcement of expanded family planning was an attempt to win the favor of Peruvian feminists who had substantial national visibility in 1995 due to the conference and its preparatory meetings. Fujimori arrived at the Beijing conference at a critical moment—when conservative actors like the Catholic Church were attempting to roll back some of the rights established in the Cairo accords. His announcement at the conference led to what some observers have called "an implicit alliance" between Fujimori and some feminists in civil society, though others remained wary of the Fujimori agenda, which, overall, was mixed on women's issues.[8]

The Beijing speech also garnered Fujimori badly needed kudos from the international community. His outspoken support of women's reproductive rights appeared to be a democratic gesture, assuaging those countries that looked unfavorably upon Fujimori's closing of the Congress. After his 1992 self-coup, the United States Agency for International Development (USAID) had pulled funding for its two major health programs in Peru, one of which was family planning.[9] Fujimori's new policy served to shore up international alliances and win tacit approval, if not financial backing, for its program from important bi- and multilateral agencies, such as USAID.

At Beijing, the President, dressed in blue jeans and tennis shoes, not only shed the traditional formal attire of Presidents and UN delegates, but also shed Peru's traditional governmental alliance with the Catholic hierarchy on issues of artificial contraception. This significant expansion of family planning services in Peru was made possible by a long-standing conflict between the Fujimori government and the Peruvian Catholic hierarchy dating to rifts during Fujimori's 1990 election campaign. Although the Catholic hierarchy is opposed to artificial contraception in general, it particularly opposes surgical forms of contraception, which it views as mutilation of the body. Surgical sterilization had been illegal in Peru, except in cases where pregnancy was considered a mortal risk. But just days before the Beijing Women's Conference, in September 1995, after lively debate, the Fujimori-dominated Congress passed legislation that legalized "voluntary surgical contraception," creating more dissent between the church and the government.[10] Fujimori's Beijing announcement proceeded to take direct aim at the church, accusing "the Catholic hierarchy" of trying at all costs "to prevent the Peruvian State from carrying out a modern and rational policy of family planning" that would help "the poorest sectors of our population."[11]

This speech, portraying his government as modern and the church as irrational and backwards, heightened tensions between the two and led the Peruvian bishops to proclaim the government family planning initiative as a "satanic" proposal that would turn "the entire country into a whorehouse."[12] Despite this vehement Church opposition, the government proceeded to expand access to state-provided contraceptive services, including "voluntary" vasectomies and tubal ligations.

## REPRODUCTIVE HEALTH OR MALTHUSIAN CONTROL?

Despite conflicts with the Church, it is evident from Fujimori's placement of family planning within his broader "struggle against poverty" that he viewed family planning as a means to poverty reduction rather than to women's rights. However, his use of international feminist forums such as Beijing and his citation of feminist-influenced development accords created the impression that the policy would balance poverty reduction objectives with reproductive rights, especially since Fujimori explicitly cited the Cairo accords in legal documents pertaining to population policy in Peru.[13]

Peru's revised program, outlined in the document "Reproductive Health and Family Planning Program 1996–2000," was largely in line with the Program of Action agreed upon at Cairo. It was intended not only to revise Peru's earlier family planning policies but also to end the mismanagement and corruption that had led to the threat of termination by international aid agencies (Interview Anonymous 6). The revised plan followed Cairo in defining reproductive health as "the condition of complete physical, mental, and social well being that men and women require in order to develop reproductive functions with security during all periods of life."[14] This plan, in considering family planning a priority within overall reproductive health, modified the Cairo approach only in the reference to the Catholic concept of "responsible parenthood" and in the inclusion of "modern and secure" forms of contraception.

Peru's revised plan also echoed Cairo in naming gender equity as a goal to be achieved through equal rights for both sexes and "health services that will diminish the barriers that limit women's access to quality care" (MINSA, 1996: 30). The plan attempted to ensure warm interactions between caregivers and clients, high-quality attention, and respect for clients' self-determination within their cultural values (MINSA, 1996: 28–29). Finally, as already noted, for the first time, this family planning program included the option of sterilization as a contraceptive choice.

And yet, the document did contain some important flaws, which were later identified by Peru's *Defensoría del Pueblo* (human rights Ombudsperson's office).The *Defensoría* decided that program documents set goals that ran counter to full reproductive rights, and that inadequate resources were allocated.[15] Among fifteen goals for service provision, the *Defensoría* required a change in three in March 1998 after an investigation by the *Defensoría del Pueblo,* the Congress, and a special commission named by the Ministry of Health. The changes involved editing the goal of "reaching" 50 percent contraceptive coverage of all women in their fertile years and 70 percent of women in their fertile years in union, to "making the effort to reach" these same numbers of women. In the second change, the original goal of making contraception available to 60 percent of adolescent women in union was changed to also avoid unwanted adolescent pregnancies. The third change revised the goal of assuring that every woman who gives birth in a health establishment leave the establishment using some form of birth control, to individually counseling post-partum women on the family planning options available. Furthermore, Family Planning was isolated from programs that addressed other aspects of reproductive health, such as adolescent health, women's health care, infant care, AIDS, and other sexually transmitted diseases, and cervical cancer (MINSA, 1996: 19, 23). The revised family planning program seemed to reflect the Cairo agreements. In addition to the President's rhetoric about women's rights and the echo of the Cairo language, advertising for the family planning program appeared feminist in emphasizing the rights of women and couples to choose the number of their children. A newspaper ad for the program read: "There are those that still do not understand that Peruvian women, or the couples in Peru, have the right to choose."[16] These factors produced an image of a progressive government program that favored individual liberties and reproductive well being for women and men.

However, other government documents reveal that the upper echelons of the Fujimori government—the presidency and the prime minister's office—viewed family planning principally as a tool for economic development, with little regard for the promotion of reproductive health or rights. The fact that these high-level authorities privileged sterilization over other forms of contraception was not only contrary to the norms of reproductive health agreed upon at Cairo, which required a choice of contraceptive methods, but also exposed their orientation toward population control. An influential document entitled "Basic Social Policy Guidelines," developed in 1993 by the Prime Minister's staff, projected dramatic population growth for Peru and argued that this increase, if left unchecked, would outstrip the economy's ability to provide adequate employment and basic social services. Although this document does not offer a specific population control strategy, it does provide justification for such a policy based on economic and demographic trends.[17]

Another document, "Social Policy: Situation and Perspectives," discussed family planning services more explicitly, as one of a number of "goods" to be distributed to the neediest communities. This approach had the potential to expand access to family planning methods to the poor, who had not previously been served. However, the document also demonstrates the government's clear preference for sterilization over other methods of family planning: One of the thirteen indicators for success of social policies was the number of "people who opt for a permanent method of family planning."[18] No indicator for any other form of contraception was included. Thus, the number of surgical sterilizations performed became one of only thirteen criteria for the evaluation of the Fujimori administration's struggle against poverty.[19]

Clearly, the primary goals of the family planning program under Fujimori were economic growth and poverty reduction, not reproductive health and rights. The government logic was that a reduction in population would lead to an increase in GDP per capita. Thus, elite, primarily white, male policy makers sought control of women's bodies as a means to meet their goals of economic growth.

These policy goals contributed to the record of mounting abuses. The President pressured Family Planning Program staff to meet sterilization quotas, and the precarious working conditions of state health employees led to low quality care and human rights abuses. As the documents discussed above demonstrate, the state used the number of women sterilized as an indicator of successful poverty alleviation. According to former staff of the program, the family planning advisor, Dr. Eduardo Yong Motta, appointed by the President, would contact the program weekly to set increased quotas for surgical sterilizations. Furthermore, the President or Dr. Yong Motta would attend the program's weekly meetings to monitor achievement of the quotas (Interview Anonymous 6). Fujimori even met directly with subregional directors of the health system to promote local surgical sterilizations (Interview Anonymous 6).

Another factor contributing to heavy pressures to sterilize women was the precarious position of state health employees, who were largely hired on contracts that were renewed based on sterilization quotas. If quotas were not met, these employees risked losing their jobs[20] at a time when health professionals were abundant in Peru, but health-sector jobs were few. Furthermore, some were given financial incentives to meet or beat the quotas in local sterilization campaigns.[21]

Analysis of government propaganda reveals that it was not only *women's* bodies, but *poor and indigenous* women's bodies, that were the object of these campaigns and of Peru's family planning program more generally. Unlike the feminist-inspired ads described above, this second strand of propaganda was not distributed to the general Peruvian populace. Instead, it

**Figure 17.1.**

targeted the low income and poor clientele of state-run public health clinics, emphasizing that more children would cause greater poverty.

Posters and large calendars that hung in the waiting areas of state health clinics typically depicted two contrasting pictures side-by-side. In Lima's poor neighborhoods, the posters featured a happy, clean family with a boy and a girl, in a house with a neatly kept and green yard juxtaposed with a picture of a straw shack jammed with a family with many sad children in a dusty, dirty neighborhood (See Figure 17–1, contrasting pictures). The poster reads: "Only you can decide how many children to have." At times, these posters only showed the picture of squalid conditions, with the slogan: "For Life and Health. FAMILY PLANNING. Only you can decide."

The contrasting images of poor and middle-class urban life send the message that fertility control can lead to an elevation in class status. Lima is situated in a desert, and in some poor neighborhoods, water for cooking and bathing is brought in by truck, delivered, and stored in large metal drums. Only the wealthy could afford the irrigated green lawns, flowers, and trees depicted in the small family picture. The children in this family are dressed

**Figure 17.2.**

in school uniforms and hold books in their arms, indicating they have been able to pay the fees for uniforms and materials.

In a rural province in the department of Ayacucho, the billboard pictured in Figure 17–2 was clearly racialized. On the right side of the billboard, in the center of the "O" in the word "NO," a typical rural, highland indigenous family is depicted, with mother and daughter wearing traditional skirts and long, braided hair. The parents' faces express panic and exhaustion, apparently due to the five children surrounding them. The billboard contrasts this family of seven with a family of four who appear to be of European descent: The parents are tall and fair, and the mother's short-cropped, curly hair is blonde. The mother's Western-style dress is clearly impractical for the physically demanding agricultural work of rural Ayacucho. Finally, the better-off, white family has two boys and no girls. Girls in rural areas of Peru are less valued and are often considered a burden. This billboard implies that family planning could lead to only having sons.

The billboard telescopes a racialized message. By controlling one's fertility, one will "Live Happily" as the billboard states—and apparently simultaneously become white and lose indigenous cultural traditions. The proposed transformation is also gendered. In rural Peru, women protect and preserve indigenous cultural traditions, and only the mother and daughter in the pictured indigenous family maintain traditional dress. The proposed transition to "whiteness" then imposes a much greater burden on women, who have also been more resistant to giving up their cultural traditions.

Sterilization campaigns especially targeted poor, uneducated indigenous women who had little access to artificial contraception and who were easily deceived by staff members seeking to fulfill quotas or receive financial rewards. Not only did these conditions militate against genuinely voluntary and informed consent in reproductive health services, but they reflected the class and racial biases of the Peruvian elite, from whom policymakers were drawn.

## UNCOMFORTABLE ALLIES

In 1996 and 1997 Giulia Tamayo, a lawyer with the feminist human rights group, Latin American and Caribbean Committee for the Defense of Women's Rights (CLADEM), was the first to expose patient grievances with the government family planning program. Her report documents 243 cases of sterilization under questionable circumstances in nineteen departments, and led Peru's *Defensoría del Pueblo* to launch a full investigation of the program that identified[22] systematic deficiencies in gaining voluntary and informed consent for surgical sterilization. Of 157 cases investigated in 1999, fourty-one had no consent procedure at all. Of the ninety cases that took place when a consent procedure was part of the program's policy, it was not used by staff in seventy-one.[23] Finally, of the nineteen cases where the consent form was used, it was filled out properly only eleven times (Defensoría del Pueblo, *La Aplicación* II, 2000: 43–45). Consent forms and updated manuals on sterilization procedures were not prepared and distributed prior to the launching of the program, and when they were produced, they were not distributed to all health centers and posts in a timely manner, or sometimes at all.[24] Moreover, the *Defensoría* found twenty-seven different consent forms, many of which were confusing.[25]

The *Defensoría* investigated twenty-four cases of death or serious injury as a result of surgical sterilization and found the majority due to low-quality care: a lack of sanitary conditions and thus infection; poor medical practices, including damage to other bodily organs during the procedure; or a lack of follow-up care, among other reasons (Defensoría del Pueblo, *La Aplicación* II, 1999). From 1996 to 1998, the *Defensoría del Pueblo* documented sixteen deaths as a result of female sterilizations, or a rate of 7.35 deaths per every 100,000 operations.[26]

A few attempts were made to address the abuses in the family planning program, but members of the President's party or his ministers denied any wrongdoing. Two women congressional members (Beatriz Merino of Frente Independiente Moralizador and Anel Townsend of Unión Por el Perú), who had in the past supported women's political rights, demanded that the Women's Commission of the Congress take action and investigate the quotas for sterilizations and other abuses. The commission did begin an inquiry, including visits by commission members directly to health centers.[27] However, the head of this Commission, Luz Salgado, a staunch member of the President's party (Cambio 90/Nueva Mayoría), defended the program and vehemently denied the existence of quotas.[28] The Minister of Health did the same when called upon to testify.[29]

Thus, groups in civil society resorted primarily to outside means to demand change in the government family planning policy. An unusual alliance began to coalesce in opposition to the program: The Catholic hierarchy and Peruvian feminists. Juan Julio Wicht, a Peruvian priest and intellectual, active in debates on population, stated in an interview in 1998: "The institutions and parties are very debilitated. All that is left is the press and the media."[30] Few mechanisms of accountability did exist in Peru in 1998 and 99, because the Fujimori regime had grown increasingly authoritarian. For feminists, the task of responding to the government abuses was made more complex by their implicit alliance with Fujimori since Beijing and their explicit engagement with the state and international population agencies through the *Mesa Tripartita*.

The hierarchy of the Catholic Church, which had opposed the family planning program since the start, took advantage of the newspaper reports of program abuses to launch its own campaign against government provided family planning services. The Church hierarchy ferreted out stories of abuses in the family planning program and provided these to the media. Cardinal Augusto Vargas Alzamora appeared on television news and made regular statements to the major newspapers denouncing the family planning program.[31] Vargas and his successor Cardenal Luis Cipriani also used Sunday Masses to sway the public against the program and pressure the government. In addition, religiously conservative congressional members, such as Rafael Rey, a member of the conservative Catholic Opus Dei, demanded an investigation of the program on religious grounds.[32] Church agitation against the program led to the inclusion of "natural" family planning methods in the family planning program's array of contraceptive choices.

A number of factors compromised feminist responses to the abuses by the family planning program.[33] First, feminists faced the dilemma of speaking out against a program for whose expanded services they had advocated for decades. Criticizing the family planning program ran the risk of harming the cause of reproductive rights in the public eye and placed feminists in the unsavory position of apparent agreement with the Catholic hierarchy. Second, they faced the political problem of criticizing a very popular government. Third, feminists themselves were divided. While some backed the regime, most did not; and among Fujimori's feminist opponents, some felt that problems in the family planning program were secondary to the larger fight against an authoritarian regime.[34] Feminists' positions were further complicated by the involvement of Peru's three major feminist organizations—Manuela Ramos, Flora Tristán, and the Red Nacional de Promoción de la Mujer—in the *Mesa Tripartita*. These feminist organizations were caught in a web of political and financial relationships with the Peruvian state and the international population agencies. Their dependence both on good relations with the state and on financial support from international population agencies compromised their ability to speak out directly and quickly against abuses in the state family planning program.

The *Mesa Tripartita* was intended to represent the interests of the state, international institutions, and civil society in determining specific steps to carry forward the Cairo accords. The brainchild of the Latin American Women's Health Network, it was successfully implemented in Peru as a result of the combined efforts of the groups Flora Tristán and Manuela Ramos.[35] Its first steps, taken in 1997 and 1998, were to map out existing activities of the government, civil society, and international agencies in the field of reproductive health. The three sectors then prioritized which aspects of the Cairo agreements would be implemented immediately.[36] Finally, the *Mesa* developed indicators and mechanisms to monitor the implementation of the accords.

Some feminists felt that "the space decidedly allowed feminists to enter and present initiatives, or at least to promote debate and make proposals." Moreover, it was a means of holding the state accountable to the Cairo Accords.[37] The *Mesa* was seen by these sectors as a means to influence an authoritarian regime otherwise closed to input from civil society. Other feminists outside the *Mesa* disagreed with its premise altogether, arguing that reproductive rights should not be negotiated.

When abuses in the family planning program came to light, feminists on the *Mesa* had the difficult task of demanding government accountability while still preserving the institution as an important access point for information, communication and negotiation. Some feminists on the *Mesa* felt that their role was to defend the state family planning program. According to one, "[In the *Mesa Tripartita*] the majority of people did not have a clear idea of their role as 'civil society'; on the contrary, they had the idea that 'we are all part of the Family Planning Program' and therefore, the enemies of the Program are our enemies."[38] Manuela Ramos needed to maintain good relations with local government health offices for the success of its multi-million dollar reproductive health project, *Reprosalud,* while simultaneously defending women's rights. Moreover, *Reprosalud* was financed by USAID, which also sat on the *Mesa*. USAID, for its part, was concerned about the Peruvian family planning program, especially when its abuses were brought to light. However, as a bilateral agency, it was committed to working with the government to improve the program.[39] Due to Manuela's relationships with the state and USAID, speaking out against the family planning program was risky.[40] Similarly, the Red Nacional de Promoción de la Mujer received a good portion of its financing from UNFPA, which directed the *Mesa Tripartita*.[41] UNFPA's response to abuses in the family planning program, similar to USAID, was to work more closely with government administrators to improve the program, rather than critique it. According to some observers, the dependency of the Red Nacional on UNFPA financing moderated the feminist organization's approach.[42] Thus, for some feminists, the connection with the state and international agencies that the *Mesa* provided, while initially designed to empower feminists, instead undermined their autonomy and ability to speak critically.

The three feminist NGOs on the *Mesa* attempted to hold to a middle position between protecting advances in family planning and pushing the *Mesa* to respond to the problems in the program. Some followed the UNFPA lead and sought to use the *Mesa* to work with the government in improving its family planning practices. The feminist organizations debated whether each case of questionable sterilization ought to be brought to the *Mesa* for negotiation or whether new cases should be taken directly to the *Defensoría del Pueblo* for investigation.[43] Over time, and with pressure from other feminists, feminists on the *Mesa* became more outspoken. Representatives of Manuela Ramos, for example, eventually asked for the resignation of the Minister of Health. Overall, however, these feminist organizations responded to the abuses in family planning only slowly. The web of relations that they had with the state and international population agencies compromised their ability to hold the state accountable to the Cairo Accords.

Feminist groups not involved with the *Mesa* spoke out most strongly against the abuses in the family planning program. Some lobbied Congress to utilize its constitutional powers to oversee the ministries. Some supported the *Defensoría del Pueblo* in an effort to strengthen this institution as a mechanism of horizontal accountability.[44] The *Defensoría* documented the cases of death, uninformed consent, and other irregularities in the program. It made accurate information available and spoke out as an independent voice within the state, demanding an end to the sterilization campaigns, a waiting period prior to the surgeries, and the revision of some family planning documents. However, the *Defensoría*'s powers of enforcement were limited to publicizing and denouncing the government's errors.

Ultimately, CLADEM and a consortium of smaller Peruvian NGOs appealed to an international source of accountability, the United Nations. The UN Committee on Elimination of Discrimination Against Women, which oversees signatories' adherence to CEDAW, called upon Peru to justify its family planning policy, after receiving a critical report on the policy prepared by CLADEM's Lima office, the center for Reproductive Law and Policy in New York, and the Lima office of the Center for the Defense of Women's Rights (DEMUS).[45] The government sent representatives of the Women's Ministry to respond to the questioning. Although the UN action was effective in forcing the government to explain its actions publicly for the first time, this approach depended on Peru's voluntary agreement to the international accords with no guarantees for future compliance. The feminists who did speak out against the government did so in an increasingly authoritarian political context. By the late 1990s, the Fujimori government censored much of the media, and denied its opponents basic civil and

340   *Christina Ewig*

human rights. In 1998, Giulia Tamayo, the activist who first broke the story of abuses in the program and who was a central figure in bringing them to the attention of the CEDAW commission, was physically threatened, her home was broken into, and videos of testimonials that she had been gathering as evidence of wrongdoing in the family planning program were stolen.

Curiously absent from the debates over family planning in the 1990s were the voices of the women most affected. Poor, rural, and indigenous women did not collectively organize to voice their opinions on family planning policy. Instead, their voices were primarily heard in the individual testimonials collected by Tamayo and the *Defensoría del Pueblo*. The collective response of indigenous and peasant women came much later, in 2001, from the "Mujeres de Anta"—twelve peasant and *quechua*-speaking women of Anta in the department of Cuzco. Organized by the feminist umbrella organization Movimiento Amplio de Mujeres, these rural women traveled from Cuzco to Lima to demand compensation for the sterilization abuses that they suffered at the hands of the family planning program.[46]

Peru is notable among countries with large indigenous populations for its lack of an indigenous movement and organization. The strongest rural organizations to emerge in the 1990s were the *rondas campesinas,* or peasant militias, that were formed in self-defense against the threat of the revolutionary guerrilla movement called the Shining Path. The *rondas,* with their mostly male membership, did not address family planning policy, perhaps due to perceiving it as a personal and female issue. Furthermore, many of the *rondas* supported the Fujimori government. Finally, many rural and poor women, at least apparently, "prefer" sterilization as a contraceptive choice. In fact, a major argument in favor of Fujimori's family-planning program was that its emphasis on sterilization was a logical response to a large and long-standing unmet demand. Although there are no statistics to prove what the real demand for sterilization was, in a context of few alternatives and of material deprivation, some poor women in Peru as elsewhere in Latin America did see sterilization as a reliable method to end cycles of unwanted pregnancies.

## LEGACIES AND CONCLUSIONS

As a result of the efforts of feminist whistle-blowers, the proactive position of the *Defensoría del Pueblo,* as well as international agencies, Peru's Family Planning Program was substantially overhauled in 1999. Moreover, demand for family planning options continued to be strong in post-Fujimori Peru.[47] However, the Fujimori program's legacy of population control tactics did damage the cause of reproductive rights. In 2001, Peruvians elected Alejandro Toledo President of Peru by a very small margin, following President Fujimori's flight into exile due to a corruption scandal and following a brief transition under Valentín Paniagua. Due to his weak political support, Toledo sought allies among conservative Catholic politicians. Toledo's first two health ministers belonged to conservative sects; his first minister of health Luis Solari de la Fuente, to the Sodalicio de Vida Cristiana, and his second, Fernando Carbone Campoverde, to Opus Dei. Both Solari and Carbone actively sought to reduce reproductive rights in Peru, in part by taking advantage of the family planning scandals of the 1990s. In his writings prior to becoming Minister of Health, Solari asserted that a "social alliance" bound "Northern nations" with feminists interested in controlling birth rates.[48] In 2001, Solari introduced legislation, which never passed, that would have allowed health care providers "conscientious objection" to carrying out any medical act against their personal moral or ethical views (Chávez, 2004: 34). He also introduced successful legislation that made "The Day of the Unborn" an official national commemorative day (Chávez, 2004: 36).

When Fernando Carbone became minister, he re-opened the sterilization debate, claiming that under Fujimori there had been 300,000 cases of forced sterilization. His attempt to hold Fujimori accountable was based on questionable facts with an obvious underlying political agenda. Clearly Carbone sought to use the family planning scandal under Fujimori to severely weaken state family planning in Peru. Moreover, he did so by again invoking international rhetoric, this time of human rights: He labeled Fujimori's family planning actions as "genocide" and set up a "truth commission" to investigate them (Chávez, 2004: 44). Under Solari and Carbone, many health ministry personnel, including those who worked in reproductive health, were replaced by religious conservatives. Minister Carbone banned the use of the word "gender" in any health ministry documents, reflecting the Catholic hierarchy's opposition to the term.[49]

In its 2002 and 2005 investigative reports on family planning in Peru, the office of the *Defensoría del Pueblo* found that since 2001 there had been an increase in health establishments denying both access to surgical sterilization and full information on the range of contraceptive methods available. It also found that since 2001, stocks of contraception in state health establishments decreased and patients were being charged for contraception, in violation of Peruvian law.[50] Moreover, the *Defensoría* found that the Ministry had refused to make the emergency contraception pill (legalized in 2001 before Toledo took office) available in public health establishments.[51] Carbone also argued that intrauterine devices were abortive and attempted to remove them from public health centers (Chávez, 2004: 42). A Congressional Commission in 2002 called for making voluntary surgical sterilization again illegal (Chávez, 2004: 47). In 2003, the Health Ministry implemented a "Peru-Life Strategy" which emphasized the "rights" of the unborn (Chávez, 2004: 37). The effects of these policies became apparent in national statistics on contraceptive use in 2003 and 2004. Peruvians' use of all artificial forms of contraception dropped by 26 percent between 2002 and 2004. The dramatic drop is likely due to instances of illegal fees, some doctor's refusals to provide contraception, and perhaps most importantly Solari and Carbone's refusals to re-stock state contraceptive supplies.[52]

In 2003, feminists and public health activists successfully lobbied Toledo to remove Carbone from the Ministry. Again, rights language was invoked, this time to support sexual and reproductive rights. This second wave of battles over family planning again underlines how global human rights and feminist discourses were employed to shape national political agendas. The succeeding Health Minister, Dr. Pilar Mazetti who was appointed in 2003, actively repaired the damage done by her predecessors to state family planning programs. That damage was extensive: religious conservatives gained direct power within the Ministry of Health and significantly weakened the state family planning program. Their influence on public and governmental attitudes outlasted the conservative ministers.

The family planning debacle in Peru raises theoretical questions in three areas: first, the relationship between feminists and the state and the viability of mixed state-civil society- international institutions like the *Mesa Tripartita;* second, the relationship between urban, middle class feminists and poor, indigenous women; and third, the consequences of the instrumental use of global feminist language.

In terms of state-feminist relations, the family planning debacle demonstrates the need for multiple feminist locations. Although the Peruvian feminists that participated in the *Mesa* were constrained by their relationship with the state and international population agencies, the same relationships allowed them access to information on state policy and practices. In the increasingly authoritarian context of Peru in the late 1990s, the ties that feminists forged with the state were in fact some of the only bridges that existed between the state and Peruvian civil society. The *Mesa* was therefore a key point for information and negotiation that other groups, such as labor unions, lacked altogether. Yet, as this case study has made clear, participation in the *Mesa* also muted the extent to which these feminists could be critical. On the other hand, feminists outside the *Mesa,* who were free of compromises with state and international agencies, were key in bringing international attention to the national problem of sterilization campaigns. In what Margaret Keck and Kathryn Sikkink call the "boomerang pattern' these feminists responded to an authoritarian national context by using international mechanisms to pressure the state.[53] I conclude, therefore, that both pragmatic feminist groups that are willing to interact with the state, and autonomous radical feminist groups able to strongly criticize state actions are essential to the success of feminist policy positions.[54]

In Peru's family planning program, as I have shown, a hidden population control agenda was masked by the disingenuous use of feminist discourse. Recognition of this agenda was not obtained through administrative monitoring but through actual observations of the program in action in remote rural villages. Such efforts require state cooperation coupled with an autonomous base for investigation and contestation as well as a willingness to move beyond the urban centers to observe the effects of policies in remote areas. The fact that it took over a year for abuses in the family planning program to be discovered indicates a lack of connection between Peruvian feminist NGOs and the rural, indigenous women they hoped to serve. Peruvian feminists are concentrated in Lima, and poor and indigenous women are poorly represented in the feminist movement, whereas government co-optation of feminist discourse was facilitated by feminists' own relative privilege.

The events surrounding the family planning program in Peru demonstrate the complex ways in which conservative forces can appropriate feminist discourses disseminated in the global and national arenas and even manipulate feminists themselves. The Peruvian case may be sobering but we must keep in mind what Rosalind Petchesky aptly notes: although transnational activists often find their words and work appropriated, their work and words have also opened up "new strategic possibilities."[55] Advances in reproductive rights have been made in Peru, in large part due to the work of transnational and national activists. The fact that these gains have been tempered by opponents is the inescapable reality of politics. For feminists, appropriation of feminist discourse requires a continual effort to be precise about their own definitions, to critically observe the usage of these discourses, and to be willing to hold those who use these discourses accountable to their political intentions. Feminists must be on the leading edge of either defending or redefining particular concepts before others redefine them in undesirable ways.

## NOTES

1. I appreciate the generous financial support of the Fulbright Foundation, the Institute for the Study of World Politics, the Ford Foundation and the Duke University-University of North Carolina Program in Latin American Studies that made this research possible. I am grateful to the many people in Peru who contributed to this article by sharing their time and insights. For comments on early drafts, I thank Bonnie Shepard, Cynthia McClintock, Michelle Mouton, Jessica Fields, Anne Eckman, Maxine Eichner, Carisa Showden, Merike Blofield, Anne Marie Choup, Jonathan Hartlyn, and William Jones. I received helpful comments when I presented versions at the International Congress of the Latin American Studies Association in Miami in 2000, the Cayetano Heredia University School of Public Health in 2000, and the Institute for Research on Women at Rutgers University in 2001. I thank Kiran Asher for suggesting the term "hijacking." I thank Nancy Palomino and Ruth Iguiñiz for their helpful comments on the final draft. Finally, I am grateful to the anonymous reviewers and editors of *Feminist Studies* for their extensive and thoughtful comments. (A longer version of this chapter was published in the Fall 2006 issue of *Feminist Studies*).

2. Defensoría del Pueblo, *La Aplicación de la Anticoncepción Quirúrgica y los Derechos Reproductivos,* II, Casos Investigados por la Defensoría del Pueblo. Informe Defensorial 27. (Lima: Defensoría del Pueblo, 1999), 289.
3. See Sandra D. Lane, "From Population Control to Reproductive Health: An Emerging Policy Agenda," *Social Science and Medicine* 39 (1994): 1303–14; Ines Smyth, "Gender Analysis of Family Planning: Beyond the 'Feminist vs. Population Control' Debate." In *Feminist Visions of Development: Gender Analysis and Policy,* eds. Cecile Jackson and Ruth Pearson (London: Routledge, 1998), 217–38, hereafter cited in text as Smyth (1998); and Harriet B. Presser and Gita Sen, *Women's Empowerment and Demographic Processes: Moving Beyond Cairo* (New York: Oxford University Press, 2000).
4. Programme of Action of the International Conference on Population and Development. Chapter VII "Reproductive Rights and Reproductive Health," (Cairo, 1994) http://www.unfpa.org/icpd/icpd_poa.htm#ch7 (forthcoming access info).
5. Betsy Hartmann, *Reproductive Rights and Wrongs: The Global Politics of Population Contro,* revised edition (Boston: South End Press, 1995), 136–9.
6. In 1990 Peru was experiencing the worst economic crisis of its history, with inflation at 7.650 percent per year. Instituto Nacional de Estadística e Informática, *Perú: Compendio Estadístico 1991–2* (Lima: Instituto Nacional de Estadística e Informática, 1992).
7. From the original speech in Spanish delivered by President Fujimori to the United Nations IV Conference on Women, September 15, 1995, Beijing, China. My thanks to UN staff for the fax of the original speech in Spanish, and to Heather Roff for her assistance in obtaining it from the UN. English translations are by the author.
8. Rosa María Alfaro, *Agendas Públicas de Género. Inicios de una Nueva Etapa Pública: Entre Dificultades, Dilemas y Avances* (Lima: Consultoría de Inserción e Impacto de las Contrapartes de la Fundación Ford, 1996), cited in Barrig, "La Persistencia." I am indebted to Nancy Palomino for her insights into Peruvian feminists' reactions to Fujimori at the Beijing conference. Regarding the mixed record of the Fujimori administration on women's issues, at Beijing alone, while the President's speech clearly supported women's reproductive rights, other members of the President's cabinet supported conservative positions at the conference, and Peru signed the Beijing Platform for Action with reservations.
9. Interview with former official of the Family Planning Program, Anonymous 6, 12 August 1998, Lima; hereafter cited in text as Interview Anonymous 6. All interviews are by the author.
10. Voluntary surgical contraception was legalized through modification of the National Population Policy (Law 346), passed September 7, 1995, days before the Beijing conference. The Congressional debate on the law included conflict with the Catholic Church and discussion of poverty alleviation objectives (Congressional debates in *Diario de Debates* Primera Legislatura Ordinaria de 1995. Jueves, 7 de setiembre de 1995, 463–535).
11. President Fujimori to the United Nations IV Conference on Women.
12. Quotes by bishops in "Peru's Family Planning Fight Forgets the Poor," *National Catholic Reporter* 31 (October 6, 1995): 11.
13. See, for example, Decreto Supremo No. 055–97-PCM, the law that created COORDIPLAN, as well as follow-up legislation, D.S. 011–98-PROMUDEH.
14. Ministerio de Salud, "Programa de Salud Reproductiva y Planificación Familiar," (Lima: MINSA, UNFPA, Enero, January 1996), 5; hereafter cited in text as MINSA (1996).
15. See MINSA (1996): 26–27 for original wording and Ministerial Resolutions 089–98-SA/DM and 076–98-SA/DM for the changes.

16. Ads like this ran frequently in 1998. The line quoted is from a full-page ad that ran in 3A *El Sol* 21 January 1998.
17. "Lineamientos Básicos de la Política Social," (Lima: Primer Ministro, November 1993).
18. "Política Social: Situación y Perspectiva a Agosto 1997," Documento de Trabajo. 21–08–97. Internal report of the Comisión Interministerial de Asuntos Sociales. Un-numbered page in Appendix E titled: "Comisión Interministerial de Asuntos Sociales: Indicadores de Seguimiento." Neither tubal ligation or vasectomies are technically irreversible. However, the surgery required to reverse these procedures is essentially unavailable to the poor in Peru.
19. One former family planning staff member also indicated to me that surgical sterilization was considered to be a more cost-effective means of providing family planning (Interview Anonymous 6). Barrig (1999) also found this connection.
20. See "Médico admite campaña del gobierno," A14, *El Comercio*, February 23, 1998 and "Denuncian en EE.UU. plan de esterilización," 3A, *El Sol*, February 25, 1998 for doctors' testimonies of these contract obligations.
21. These campaigns and financial incentives were documented in the three volumes of reports published by the Defensoría del Pueblo: *Anticoncepción Quirúrgica Voluntaria*, vol. I, Casos Investigados por la Defensoría del Pueblo, Informe Defensorial 7 (Lima: Defensoría del Pueblo, 1998); *La Aplicación de la Anticoncepción Quirúrgica y los Derechos Reproductivos* II, hereafter cited in text as Defensoría del Pueblo, *La Aplicación* II (1999); and *La Aplicación* III, Casos Investigados por la Defensoría del Pueblo, Informe Defensorial 69, (Lima: Defensoría del Pueblo, 2002);. They were also well-documented in Peruvian newspapers, and I witnessed financial incentives to staff during site visits to rural health centers in 1999.
22. CLADEM, *Nada Personal: Reporte de Derechos Humanos sobre la Aplicación de la Anticoncepción Quirúrgica en el Perú, 1996–1998* (Lima: CLADEM, 1999).
23. The twenty-six remaining cases involved complaints about procedures that did not require consent.
24. Defensoría del Pueblo, *La Aplicación* II (2000) and interview with health center nurse midwife, Anonymous 26, February 23, 1999, Ayacucho.
25. Personal communication, *Defensoría* staff member Julissa Mantilla, January 20, 1999, Lima.
26. Defensoría del Pueblo, *La Aplicación* II (1999): 289. For comparison, the risk ratio of tubal ligation in the United States is 3.9 per 100,000 procedures. Vasectomies carry a much lower risk of 1 per 100,000. See Gregory L. Smith, George P. Taylor, and Kevin F. Smith, "Comparative Risks and Costs of Male and Female Sterilization," *American Journal of Public Health* 75, no. 4 (1985): 370–4.
27. "Comisión de la Mujer visitó centros de salud," A4, *El Comercio*, 26 January 1998.
28. "Congresistas piden investigar compañas de esterilización," A4, *El Comercio*, 13 January 1998.
29. Presentations by Minister of Health Marino Costa Bauer before the Commissions of Health, Population, and the Family and Women, Human Development and Sports, January 16, 1998 and March 10, 1998 respectively. See also "Entrevista a Marino Costa Bauer," *El Comercio*, April 3, 1998.
30. Interview with Juan Julio Wicht 13 November 1998, Lima.
31. Cardinal Vargas was interviewed on the show "Panorama" of Panamerican Television, April 12, 1998 (Easter). See also "La ley divina está por encima de las leyes humanas," A9 *El Comercio*, 8 May 1998. On Cipriani see "La sociedad debe proteger la vida," 11 *Cambio*, April 5, 1999.

32. "Demandan que se paralicen campañas de esterilización," A4 *El Comercio,* January 26, 1998.
33. My analysis of feminist responses to the Fujimori family planning program has benefited from comments from and conversations with Ana Güezmes, Nancy Palomino, Susana Chávez, Maria Jennie Dador (all previously members of Peruvian feminist organizations) in Peru during June 2005. Also important were interviews with Celeste Cambria and Frescia Carrasco in 1998, former representatives of Flora Tristán and Manuela Ramos respectively, to the Mesa Tripartita.
34. Interview with Ana Güezmes, June 28, 2005, Lima. This position was particularly strong among feminists in Flora Tristán.
35. Interview with Frescia Carrasco of Manuela Ramos, March 16, 1998, Lima.
36. Interview with Celeste Cambria Rosset of Flora Tristán, April 15, 1998, Lima, and interview Carrasco 1998.
37. Interview Carrasco.
38. Quoted in Barrig (1999).
39. Personal communication with USAID official in Lima, July 2000.
40. Reprosalud was a multiyear reproductive health project financed by USAID, and was the largest sum ever granted to an NGO in Peru. Members of Manuela that I interviewed in June of 2005 disagreed on whether Reprosalud hampered Manuela's response to government abuses; some felt this was not an issue, others felt that there were fears that speaking out would harm Manuela's relationship with local health offices.
41. Interview Rogelio Fernandez Castilla, UNFPA-Peru Representative, May 16, 1998.
42. Observation by Nancy Palomino, June 2005.
43. Personal communication, María Jennie Dador, June 20, 2005, Lima.
44. Personal communication, Giulia Tamayo, April 20, 1998, Lima.
45. CLADEM/CRLP/DEMUS, "Derechos Sexuales y Reproductivos de las Mujeres en el Perú," Reporte Sombra, elaborado para la Décimo Novena Sesión del Comité para la Eliminación de Todas las Formas de Discriminación Contra la Mujer (June 1998). See also the UN proceedings.
46. María Esther Mogollón, "Peruanas esterilizadas por la fuerza reclaman justicia," *Cimac Noticias,* 2003. http://www.cimacnoticias.com/noticias/03mar/03030504.html (forthcoming access info). In response to the Mujeres de Anta, President Toledo granted women negatively affected by the sterilization campaigns free state health insurance under the *Seguro Integral de Salud* (Integral Health Insurance Plan).
47. In 2000, 25.5 percent of sexually active women were inadequately protected against unwanted pregnancy (INEI, *Encuesta Nacional Demográfica de Salud Familiar,* Lima: Instituto Nacional de Estadística e Informática, 1996 and 2000).
48. Susana A. Chávez, *Cuando el Fundamentalismo Se Apodera de las Políticas Públicas: Políticas de Salud Sexual y Reproductiva en el Perú en el Período Julio 2001-Junio 2003,* (Lima: Flora Tristan, 2004), 33; hereafter cited in text as Chávez (2004).
49. In a visit to Peru in 2002 in which I lectured to a group of Health Ministry personnel, the conservative orientations were clear. Informants from the Health Ministry informed me on this visit that the use of the word "gender" was prohibited by the Minister. See also Chávez (2004).
50. Defensoría del Pueblo, *La Aplicación* III (2002), and *Supervisión de los Servicios de Planificación Familiar* IV, Casos Investigados por la Defensoría del Pueblo, Informe Defensorial 90 (Lima: Defensoría del Pueblo, 2005).

51. Defensoría del Pueblo, *Anticoncepción Oral De Emergencia*. Informe Defensorial 78. (Lima: Defensoría del Pueblo, 2004).
52. Defensoría del Pueblo, *Supervisión de los Servicios* (2005), 46–7. Percentage calculated from raw figures provided by the Defensoría: 1,411,646 in 2002 to 1,047,521 in 2004.
53. Margaret Keck and Kathryn Sikkink, *Activists Beyond Borders: Advocacy Networks in International Politics* (Ithaca, NY: Cornell University Press, 1998).
54. Geertje Lycklama à Nijeholt, Joke Sweibel, and Virginia Vargas, "The Global Institutional Framework: The Long March to Beijing." In *Women's Movements and Public Policy in Europe, Latin America, and the Caribbean,* eds. Geertje Lycklama à Nijeholt, Virginia Vargas and Saskia Wieringa, (New York and London: Garland Publishing, 1998), 25–48; Dorothy McBride Stetson and Amy Mazur, eds. *Comparative State Feminism* (Thousand Oaks: Sage, 1995).
55. Rosalind Pollack Petchesky, *Global Prescriptions: Gendering Health and Human Rights* (New York: Zed Books, 2003), 27.

# Works Cited

Acharya, Keshab P., Nara Bahadur Thapa, and Shiva Sharma. *Economic Liberalization in Nepal: Sequence and Process.* Kathmandu, Nepal: OXFAM GB-Nepal, 1998.

Acharya, Meena. "Changing Gender Status—Achievements and Challenges." In *Population Monogram of Nepal.* Kathmandu, Nepal: CBS, 2003b.

Acharya, Meena. "Global Integration of Subsistence Economies and Women's Empowerment: An Experience from Nepal." In *Globalization, Governance and Gender,* eds. Isabella Bakker and Rachel Silvey. NY: Routledge, forthcoming, 2006.

Acharya, Meena. *Labor Market Developments and Poverty in Nepal: With Special Opportunities for Women.* Kathmandu, Nepal: Tanka Prasad Acharya Memorial Foundation, 2000.

Acharya, Meena. "The Economic Foundations of the Current Socio-Political Crisis in Nepal." In *Nepal Tomorrow: Voices and Visions,* ed. D.B. Gurung. Kathmandu, Nepal: Koselee Prakashan, 2003a.

Acharya, Meena, and Lynn Bennett. *An Aggregate Analysis and Summary of 8 Village Studies: The Status of Women in Nepal,* vol. 2, part 9. Kathmandu, Nepal: CEDA, 1981.

Acharya, Meena, and Puspa Ghimire. "Gender Indicators of Equality, Inclusion and Poverty Reduction for Measuring Program/Project Effectiveness." *Economic and Political Weekly* 40, nos. 44 and 45 (2005): 4719–28.

Acharya, Meena, Yuba Raj Khatiwada, and Shankar Aryal. *Structural Adjustment Policies and Poverty Eradication.* Kathmandu, Nepal: Institute for Integrated Studies, 2003.

Achebe, Chinua. *Things Fall Apart.* Oxford: Heinemann, 1958.

Acker, Joan. "Inequality Regimes: Gender, Class, and Race in Organizations." *Gender & Society* 20 (August 2006): 441–64.

Ackerly, Brooke A. "Testing the Tools of Development: Credit Programmes, Loan Involvement, and Women's Empowerment." *IDS Bulletin* 26, no. 3 (1995): 56–68.

Adi, Rianto. *Migrasi internasional tenaga kerja Indonesia: Harapan dan kenyataan* (International Migration of Indonesian Migrant Workers: Expectation and Reality). Jakarta, Indonesia: Pusat Penelitian Unika Atma Jaya, 1995.

Adomako Ampofo, Akosua. "Framing Knowledge, Forming Behaviour: African Women's AIDS-Protection Strategies." *African Journal of Reproductive Health* 2, no. 2 (1998): 151–74.

Adomako Ampofo, Akosua. "'When Men Speak, Women Listen: Gender Socialization and Young Adolescents' Attitudes to Sexual and Reproductive Issues." *African Journal of Reproductive Health* 5, no. 3 (2001): 196–212.

Adomako Ampofo, Akosua. "'By God's Grace I had a Boy.' Whose 'Unmet Need' and 'Dis/Agreement' About Childbearing About Ghanaian Couples." In *Rethinking*

*Sexualities in Contexts of Gender,* ed. Signe Arnfred, 115–38. Uppsala, Sweden: Nordic Africa Institute, 2004.

Adomako Ampofo, Akosua, Osman Alhassan, Francis Ankrah, Deborah Atobrah, and Moses Dortey. *Sexual Exploitation of Children in the City of Accra.* Accra, Ghana: UNICEF, 2007.

Adomako Ampofo, Akosua and Mansah Prah. "You May Beat Your Wife, But Not Too Much: The Cultural Context of Violence in Ghana." In *Violence Against Women in Ghana,* eds. Kathy Cusack and Takyiwaa Manuh (Accra, Ghana: Gender Studies on Human Rights Documentation Centre: forthcoming).

Agot, Kawango E. "Widow Inheritance and HIV/AIDS Interventions in Sub-Saharan Africa: Contrasting Conceptualizations of 'Risk' and 'Vulnerability.'" Ph.D. diss., University of Washington, 2001.

Agot, Kawango E. "HIV/AIDS Interventions and the Politics of the African Woman's Body." In *A Companion to Feminist Geography,* eds. Lise Nelson and Joni Seager. London: McMillan Publishers, 2005.

Ahmed, Fauzia Erfan. "The Rise of the Bangladesh Garment Industry: Globalization, Women Workers, and Voice." *NWSA Journal* 16, no. 2 (2004): 34–45.

Alexander, M. Jacqui, and Chandra Talpade Mohanty, eds. *Feminist Genealogies, Colonial Legacies, Democratic Futures.* New York: Routledge, 1997.

Alfaro, Rosa María. *Agendas Públicas de Género. Inicios de una Nueva Etapa Pública: Entre Dificultades, Dilemas y Avances.* Consultoría de Inserción e Impacto de las Contrapartes de la Fundación Ford. Lima, 1996. Photocopy.

"Algemeen verbod gezichtsbedekkende kleding." http://www.justitie.nl/actueel/nieuwsberichten/archief-2006/algemeen-verbodgezichtstedekkende-kleding.aspx?=34&cs=578. Last accessed 13 July 2007.

Ali, Shaheen Sardar. "Women's Rights CEDAW and International Human Rights Debates: Toward Empowerment?" In *Rethinking Empowerment: Gender and Development in a Global/Local World,* eds. Jane L. Parpart, Shirin Rai, and Kathleen Staudt. London: Routledge, 2002.

All-China Women's Federation. *A Review of the Social Status of Women in China.* Beijing, China: New World Press, 1995.

Allman, Jean, and Victoria B. Tashjian. *I Will Not Eat Stone: A Women's History of Colonial Asante.* Portsmouth, NH: Heinemann Press, 2000.

Al-Rasheed, Madawi. *A History of Saudi Arabia.* Cambridge and New York: Cambridge University Press, 2002.

Alsop, Ruth, and Nina Heinsohn. "Measuring Empowerment in Practice: Structuring Analysis and Framing Indicators." *World Bank Policy Research Working Paper 3510* (February 2005).

American Anthropological Association. *Declaration on Anthropology and Human Rights Committee for Human Rights.* American Anthropological Association, 1999.

American Psychiatric Association. *Diagnostic and Statistical Manual of Mental Disorders,* 4th ed. Washington, DC: American Psychiatric Association, 1994.

Amjad, Rashid. "Philippines and Indonesia: On the Way to a Migration Transition." *Asian and Pacific Migration Journal* 5, nos. 2–3 (1996): 339–66.

Amoah, Elisabeth. "Femaleness: Akan Concepts and Practices." In *Women, Religion and Sexuality: Studies on the Impact of Religious Teaching on Women,* ed. Jeanne Becher, 129–53. Philadelphia: Trinity Press International, 1991.

Ananta, Aris, Daksini Kartowibowo, Nur Hadi Wiyono, and Chotib. "The Impact of the Economic Crisis on International Migration: The Case of Indonesia." *Asian Pacific Migration Journal* 7, nos. 2–3 (1998): 313–38.

Anderson, Benedict, ed. *Violence and the State in Suharto's Indonesia.* Ithaca, New York: Southeast Asia Program Publications, Cornell University, 2001.

Andors, Phyllis. "Women and Work in Shenzhen." *Bulletin of Concerned Asian Scholars* 20, no. 3 (1988): 22–41.

An-Naim, Abdullahi. "The Future of *Shari'ah* and the Debate in Northern Nigeria." In *Comparative Perspectives on the Shari'ah in Nigeria,* eds. Philip Ostien, Jamila M. Nasir, and Franz Kogelmann. Ibadan, Nigeria: Spectrum Books, 2005.

Anthias, Floya, and Nira Yuval-Davis. *Racialized Boundaries: Race, Nation, Gender, Colour and Class and the Anti-Racist Struggle.* London: Routledge, 1992.

Anthias, Floya, and Nira Yuval Davis. "Women and the Nation State." In *Nationalism: The Reader,* eds. John Hutchinson and Anthony D. Smith, 312–6. Oxford: Oxford University Press, 1994.

Antony, Piush. *Towards Empowerment: Experiences of Organizing Women Workers.* New Delhi: International Labour Organization, 2001.

Aquino, María Pilar. "Latin American Feminist Theology." *Journal of Feminist Studies in Religion* 14, no. 1 (Spring 1998): 89–107.

Aquino, María Pilar. *Our Cry for Life: Feminist Theology from Latin America,* trans. Dinah Livingstone. Maryknoll, NY: Orbis Books, 1993.

Asghedom, Amanuel Andebrhan. "The Impact of War on the Role of Women" Unpublished paper presented to Fulbright NCS Program, April 2005.

Badran, Margot. "Ongoing *Tafsir* on Men and Women in Islam: Constructions and Practices of Democracy and Social Justice." Unpublished paper.

Badran, Margot. "Between Secular Feminism and Islamic Feminism: Reflections on the Middle East and Beyond." *Journal of Middle East Women's Studies* 1 (January 2005): 6–28.

Badran, Margot. *Feminism Beyond East and West: New Gender Talk and Practice in Global Islam.* New Delhi: Global Media Publications, 2006.

Badran, Margot. *Feminists, Islam, and Nation: Gender and the Making of Modern Egypt.* Princeton: Princeton University Press, 1995.

Badran, Margot. "Locating Feminisms: The Collapse of Secular and Religious Discourses in the Muslim Mashriq." *Agenda* 59 (2001): 41–57.

Badran, Margot. "Liberties of the Faithful." *Al Ahram Weekly* (May 19–25, 2005).

Baker, Michael, Jonathan Gruber, and Kevin Milligan. "Universal Childcare, Maternal Labor Supply and Family Well-Being." NBER Working Paper No. 11832 (December 2005).

Bakker, Isabella, ed. *The Strategic Silence: Gender and Economic Policy.* London: Zed Books, 1994.

Bakker, Isabella, and Stephen Gill. *Power, Production and Social Reproduction: Human Insecurity in the Global Political Economy.* New York: Palgrave Macmillan, 2003.

Balakrishnan, Radhika, ed. *The Hidden Assembly Line: Gender Dynamics of Subcontracted Work in a Global Economy.* Bloomfield, CT: Kumarian Press, 2002.

Ball, Terence, and Richard Dagger. *Political Ideologies and the Democratic Ideal.* New York: HarperCollins, 1991.

Banerjee, Nirmala. "Between the Devil and the Deep Sea: Shrinking Options for Women in Contemporary India." In *The Violence of Development,* ed. Karin Kapadia. New Delhi: Kali for Women, 2002.

Banerjee, Nirmala, ed. *Indian Women in a Changing Industrial Scenario.* New Delhi: Sage Publications, 1991.

*Baobab for Women's Human Rights and Sharia Implementation in Nigeria: The Journey So Far.* Lagos: Baobab, 2003.

Barker, Gary. "Gender Equitable Boys in a Gender Equitable World: Reflections from Qualitative Research and Program Development with Young Men in Rio de Janeiro, Brazil." *Sexual and Relationship Therapy* 15, no. 3 (2000).

Barlas, Asma. *"Believing Women" in Islam: Undreading Patriarchal Interpretations of the Qur'an.* Austin: University of Texas Press, 2002.

Barrig, Maruja. "La Persistencia de la Memoria: Feminismo y Estado en el Peru de los 90." Lima: Proyecto Sociedad Civil y Gobernabilidad Democrática en los Andes y el Cono Sur, Fundación Ford, 1999. Photocopy.

Bashevkin, Sylvia. *Welfare Hot Buttons: Women, Work, and Social Policy Reform.* Toronto: University of Toronto Press, 2002.

Bassiouni, Cherif. *The Islamic Criminal Justice System.* London and New York: Oceana, 1980.

Batliwala, Srilatha. *Empowerment of Women in South Asia: Concepts and Practices.* New Delhi: Asian South Pacific Bureau of Adult Education and FAO, 1993.

Batliwala, Srilatha. "The Meaning of Women's Empowerment: New Concepts from Action." In *Population Policies Reconsidered: Health, Empowerment and Rights,* eds. Gita Sen, A. Germain, and L.C. Chen. Cambridge, MA: Harvard University Press, 1994.

Batliwala, Srilatha, and Deepa Dhanraj. "Gender Myths that Instrumentalise Women: A View from the Indian Frontline." *Institute of Development Studies Bulletin* 35, no. 4 (October 11–18, 2004).

Beckett, Katherine, and Bruce Western. "Governing Social Marginality: Welfare, Incarceration, and the Transformation of State Policy." In *Mass Imprisonment: Social Causes and Consequences,* ed. David Garland. London: Sage Publications, 2001.

Beneria, Lourdes, and Martha Roldan. *The Crossroads of Class and Gender.* Chicago, IL: University of Chicago Press, 1987.

Bennett, Lynn. *Dangerous Wives and Sacred Sisters: Social and Symbolic Roles of High Caste Women in Nepal.* New York: Columbia University Press, 1993.

Bennett, Lynn, and Kishore Gajurel. *Negotiating Social Change: Gender, Caste and Ethnic Dimensions of Empowerment and Social Inclusion in Rural Nepal.* Kathmandu, Nepal: World Bank (November Draft), 2004.

Bevacqua, Maria. *Rape on the Public Agenda: Feminism and the Politics of Sexual Assault.* Boston: Northeastern University Press, 2000.

Bhasin, Kamla. *Exploring Masculinity.* New Delhi: Women Unlimited, 2004.

Bhasin, Kamala, and Dhar Sunita. *Joining Hands to Develop Women Power, a Report of a South Asian Workshop on Gender and Sustainable Development.* Koitta, Bangladesh, 1998.

Bijsterveld, S. van. *Godsdienstvrijheid in Europees Perspectief* (Freedom of Religion in a European Perspective). Deventer: WEJ Tjeenk Willink, 1998.

Birks, J., I. Seccombe, and C. Sinclair. "Labour Migration in the Arab Gulf States: Patterns, Trends, and Prospects." *International Migration* 26, no. 3 (1998): 267–86.

Bisnath, Savitri, and Diane Elson. "Women's Empowerment Revisited." *Background paper, Progress of the World's Women.* UNIFEM, 2003. http://www.unifem.undp.org/progressww/empower.html (last accessed October 2006).

Bledsoe, Caroline, and Gilles Pison, eds. *Nuptiality in Sub-Saharan Africa: Contemporary Anthropological and Demographic Perspectives.* New York: Oxford University Press, 1994.

Boyd, Jean. *The Caliph's Sister.* London: Frank Cass, 1989.

Boyd, Jean, and Beverly Mack. *The Collected Works of Nana Asma'u bint Shehu Usman Dan Fodio 1793–1864.* East Lansing, Michigan: Michigan University Press, 1997.

Boyd, Monica. "Family and Personal Networks in International Migration: Recent Developments and New Agendas." *International Migration Review* 23 (Autumn 1989): 638–70.

Braithwaithe, Lloyd, and George Roberts. "Mating Among East Indian and Non-Indian Women in Trinidad." *Social and Economic Studies* 11, no. 3 (1962): 203–40.

Brenner, Suzanne. *The Domestication of Desire: Women, Wealth, and Modernity in Java.* Princeton, NJ: Princeton University Press, 1998.

Brereton, Bridget. *A History of Modern Trinidad*. London, Kingston, and Port of Spain, Heineman, 1981.

Brereton, Bridget. *Race Relations in Colonial Trinidad: 1870–1900*. Cambridge: Cambridge University Press, 1979.

Brison, Susan J. *Aftermath: Violence and the Remaking of a Self*. Princeton and Oxford: Princeton University Press, 2002.

Brownmiller, Susan. *Against Our Will: Men, Women and Rape*. New York: Simon and Schuster, 1976.

Brücker, Herbert. "Can International Migration Solve the Problems of European Labour Markets?" *Economic Survey of Europe*. Geneva, UN Economic Commission for Europe, Economic Analysis Division, 2002.

Burgess, Ann Wolbert, and Lynda Lytle Holmstrom. "The Rape Victim in the Emergency Ward." *American Journal of Nursing* 73, no. 10 (1973): 1740–5.

Burgess, Ann Wolbert, and Lynda Lytle Holmstrom. "Rape Trauma Syndrome." *American Journal of Psychiatry* 131 (1974): 981–6.

Carlen, Pat. *Women's Imprisonment*. London: Routledge, 1983.

Carr, Marilyn, Martha Chen, and Renana Jhabvala, eds. *Speaking Out: Women's Empowerment in South Asia*. (New Dehli, India: Vistaar Public Press, 1996)

Castles, Francis G. "The World Turned Upside Down: Below Replacement Fertility, Changing Preferences and Family-friendly Public Policy in 21 OECD Countries." *Journal of European Social Policy* 13 (2003): 209–27.

CBC News Online. "The Assisted Human Reproduction Act." *Indepth: Genetics and Reproduction*. Canadian Broadcasting Company, 2004.

CDC (California Department of Corrections). "Joint Venture Employers." *Joint Venture Program* (June 1994).

Central Bureau of Statistics/NPC. *Nepal Labor Force Survey*. Kathmandu, Nepal: HMG, 1999.

Central Bureau of Statistics/NPC. *Nepal Living Standards Survey, 2003/2004*, vols. 1 and 2. Kathmandu, Nepal: HMG, 2004.

Central Bureau of Statistics/NPC. *Population Census 2001, The National Report*. Kathmandu, Nepal: HMG, 2001.

Chanana, Karuna. "Female Sexuality and Education of Hindu Girls in India." In *Sociology and Gender*, ed. Sharmila Rege. New Delhi: Sage Publications, 2003.

Chant, Sylvia. "Contributions of a Gender Perspective to the Analysis of Poverty." In *Women and Gender Equity in Development Theory and Practice: Institutions, Resources and Mobilization*, eds. Jane S. Jaquette and Gale Summerfield. Durham, NC: Duke University Press, 2006.

Chesnais, Jean-Claude. "Fertility, Family, and Social Policy." *Population & Development Review* 22 (1996): 729–39.

Chávez A., Susana. *Cuando el Fundamentalismo Se Apodera de las Políticas Públicas: Políticas de Salud Sexual y Reproductiva en el Perú en el Período Julio 2001-Junio 2003*. Lima: Flora Tristan, 2004.

Chavkin, Wendy. "Conclusion." In *Where Human Rights Begin: Health, Sexuality, and Women in the New Millennium*, eds. Wendy Chavkin and Ellen Chesler. New Brunswick, NJ: Rutgers University Press, 2005.

Chesney-Lind, Meda. "Rethinking Women's Imprisonment." In *The Criminal Justice System and Women*, eds. Barbara Price and Natalie Skoloff. New York: McGraw-Hill, 1995.

Chin, Christine B.N. *In Service and Servitude: Foreign Female Domestic Workers and the Malaysian "Modernity" Project*. New York: Columbia University Press, 1998.

Chin, Christine B.N. "The State and the 'State' in Globalization: Social Order and Economic Restructuring in Malaysia." *Third World Quarterly* 21, no. 6 (2000): 1035–57.

Chin, Christine B.N. "Walls of Silence and Late Twentieth Century Representations of the Foreign Female Domestic Worker: The Case of Filipina and Indonesian Female Servants in Malaysia." *International Migration Review* 31, no. 2 (1997): 353–85.

Chivers, C.J. "Putin Urges Plan to Reverse Slide in the Birth Rate." *The New York Times,* (May 11, 2006, late edition).

Chow, Esther Ngan-ling. "Gendered Migratio, Patterns, Space and Citizenship" *Gender, Place, and Culture* special issue 'Seeking Gender Justice: Reflections, Dialogue and Strategic Action, forthcoming.

Chow, Esther Ngan-ling. "Economic Reforms, Gendered Migration, and Women's Employment in the Manufacturing Industries of South China: A Preliminary Analysis." Paper presented at the World Congress of Sociology, sponsored by the International Sociological Association, Montreal, Canada, July 1998.

Chow, Esther Ngan-ling. "Gender Matters." *International Journal of Sociology* 18 (September 2003): 443–60.

Chow, Esther Ngan-ling. "The Citizenship Divide: The Politics of Space and Activism: The Organizing of Migrant Workers in Urban China." Paper presented at RC-32, Research Committee on Women in Society at the ISA World Congress of Sociology, Durban, South Africa, July 2006.

Chow, Esther Ngan-ling. "The Feminization of Survival: Is Migration a Household Strategy or an Individual Rational Choice?" Paper presented at the Mid-year Meeting of the Sociologists for Women in Society in San Juan, Puerto Rico, 2006.

Chow, Esther Ngan-ling. "Paid work, Income Control, and Remittance: Empowering Migrant Workers in South China." Paper presented at annual meeting, the American Sociological Association, New York City, 2007.

CLADEM. *Nada Personal: Reporte de Derechos Humanos sobre la Aplicación de la Anticoncepción Quirúrgica en el Perú, 1996–1998.* Lima: CLADEM, 1999.

CLADEM/CRLP/DEMUS. "Derechos Sexuales y Reproductivos de las Mujeres en el Perú." Reporte Sombra, elaborado para la Décimo Novena Sesión del Comité para la Eliminación de Todas las Formas de Discriminación Contra la Mujer. (June 1998).

The Clearinghouse on International Developments in Child, Youth and Family Policies. *Issue Brief.* New York: Columbia University (Spring 2002). <http://www.childpolicyintl.org/issuebrief/issuebrief5table1.pdf (accessed April 12, 2006).

Clement, Grace. *Care, Autonomy and Justice: Feminism and the Ethic of Care.* Boulder, CO: Westview Press, 1996.

Cocca, Carolyn E. "The Politics of Statutory Rape Laws: Adoption and Reinvention of Morality Policy in the States, 1971–1999." *Polity* 35, issue 1 (2002): 51–72.

Coetzee, J. M. "Apartheid Thinking," *Giving Offense: Essays on Censorship,* 163–84. Chicago: Chicago University Press, 1996.Cohen, Marcia, and Sherrie H. McKenna. *Rape: Psychology, Prevention and Impact,* vol. III. New Haven, CT: Yale-New Haven Teachers Institute, 1981. http://www.yale.edu/ynhti/curriculum/units/1981/3/81.03.06.x.html (accessed January 11, 2007).

Coker-Appiah, Dorcas, and Kathy Cusack. *Violence against Women and Children in Ghana.* Accra, Ghana: Gender Studies and Human Rights Documentation Centre, 1999.

Coleman, Isobel. "The Payoff from Women's Rights." *Foreign Affairs* (May/June 2004). http://www.foreignaffairs.org/20040501faessay83308/isobel-coleman/the-payoff-from-women-s-rights.html (accessed December 30, 2006).

Comaroff, Jean, and John L. Comaroff. "Criminal Justice, Cultural Justice: The Limits of Liberalism and the Pragmatics of Difference in the New South Africa." *American Ethnologist* 31, no. 2 (2004): 188–204.

"Comisión de la Mujer visitó centros de salud." *El Comercio,* A4. (January 26, 1998).

Commission on Farmers' Welfare. *Final Report of the Commission on Farmers' Welfare.* http://macroscan.com/pol/apr05/pdf/Full_Report_Commission_Farmer_AP.pdf (accessed May 11, 2007).

Commission Stasi (Commission de réflexion sur l'application du principe de laïcité dans la République). *Rapport au Président de la République,* (December 11, 2003). http://www.ladocumentationfrancaise.fr/brp/034000725/0000.pdf. (Accessed 13 July 2007.)

"Congresistas piden investigar compañas de esterilización," *El Comercio,* A4. (January 13, 1998).

Connell, Robert W. "Masculinities and Globalisation." *Men and Masculinities* 1 (1998): 3–23.

Connell, Robert W. "The State, Gender, and Sexual Politics: Theory and Appraisal." *Theory and Society* 19 (1990): 507–44.

Copelon, Rhonda. "Gender Crimes as War Crimes: Integrating Crimes against Women into International Criminal Law." *McGill Law Journal* 46 (2000): 217–40.

Copelon, Rhonda. "Achieving Women's Full Citizenship." *Carnegie Council of Ethics and International Affairs,* "Violence against Women," Human Rights Dialogue, series 2, no. 10 (Fall 2003): 20–1.

Cordesman, Anthony H. *Saudi Arabia: Guarding the Desert Kingdom.* Boulder, CO: Westview, 1997.

Cott, Nancy F. *Public Vows: A History of Marriage and the Nation.* Cambridge: Harvard University Press, 2000.

Cruikshank, Barbara. *The Will to Empower.* Cornell University Press, 1999.

Csaszar, Fruzsina. "Understanding the Concept of Power." In *Power, Rights, and Poverty: Concepts and Connections,* ed. Ruth Alsop. A working meeting sponsored by DFID and the World Bank, March 23–24, 2004. Washington, DC: The World Bank.

"Dangerous Attack or Fair Point? Straw Veil Row Deepens. Minister's Remarks Fuel Claims of Islamophobia Crisis," *Guardian* (October 7, 2006). http://www.guardian.co.uk/.

Davis, Angela. *Are Prisons Obsolete?* New York: Seven Stories Press, 2003.

Defensoría del Pueblo. *Anticoncepción Quirúrgica Voluntaria,* vol. I, Casos Investigados por la Defensoría del Pueblo. Lima: Defensoría del Pueblo, 1998.

Defensoría del Pueblo. *La Aplicación de la Anticoncepción Quirúrgica y los Derechos Reproductivos,* vol. II, Casos Investigados por la Defensoría del Pueblo. Lima: Defensoría del Pueblo, 1999.

Defensoría del Pueblo. *La Aplicación de la Anticoncepción Quirúrgica y los Derechos Reproductivos* III, Casos Investigados por la Defensoría del Pueblo, Informe Defensorial. Lima: Defensoría del Pueblo, 2002.

Defensoría del Pueblo. *Anticoncepción Oral De Emergencia.* Informe Defensorial 78. Lima: Defensoría del Pueblo, 2004.

Defensoría del Pueblo. *Supervisión de los Servicios de Planificación Familiar* IV, Casos Investigados por la Defensoría del Pueblo, Informe Defensorial 90. Lima: Defensoría del Pueblo, 2005.

Del Cid, Carmen Manuela. "La justificación de la violencia desde la perspectiva teológica," paper presented at the panel, "Las Causas del Feminicidio," Foro de Mujeres por la Vida," San Pedro Sula, Honduras, July 30, 2003.

Del Cid, Carman Manuela. *Los caminos de la Sabiduría: Una introducción a la interpretación feminista de la Biblia,* trad. José Manuel Lozano Gotor (Maliaño, España: Editorial Sal Terrae, Santandar, 2004).

Del Cid, Carmen Manuela. "Memorias Peligrosas ... Mujeres Poderosas," *Conspirando,* No. 49 (Spring 2005): 22–24.

Del Cid, Carman Manuela. "Mujeres en el Movimiento de la Sabiduría: Interpretación Crítico-Feminista de la Biblia," Presentation at the Dream Weavers' Workshop, San Pedro Sula, Honduras, November 4, 2004.

Deng, Francis M., Sr., Secretario General. *"Intensificación de la promoción y el fomento de los derechos humanos y de las libertades fundamentales, en particular la cuestión del programa y los métodos de trabajo de la Comisión de derechos humanos, éxodos en masa y personas desplazadas. Los desplazados internos,"* Comisión de derechos humanos-ECOSOC, 52° período de sesiones, E/CN.4/1996/52/Add.1.

"Denuncian en EE.UU. plan de esterilización," *El Sol*, 3A. (February 25, 1998).

DFID/World Bank. *Citizens With (Without) Rights: Nepal Gender and Social Exclusion Assessment,* final draft. Kathmandu, Nepal: DFID/World Bank, June 2005.

DiStefano, Christine. *Configurations of Masculinity: A Feminist Perspective on Modern Political Theory.* Ithaca, New York and London: Cornell University Press, 1991.

Division for Gender Equality. "The Equal Opportunities Act is Now More Stringent." *New Life: A Gender Equality Magazine for New Parents* (2001).

Dodoo, F. Nii-Amoo. "Men Matter: Additive and Interactive Gender Preferences, and Reproductive Behavior in Kenya." *Demography* 359, no. 2 (1998): 229–42.

Domanick, Joe. *Cruel Justice: Three Strikes and the Politics of Crime in America's Golden State.* Berkeley: University of California Press, 2004.

Doumato, Eleanor Abdella. "Education in Saudi Arabia: Gender, Jobs, and the Price of Religion." In *Women and Globalization in the Arab Middle East: Gender, Economy, and Society,* eds. Eleanor Abdella Doumato and Marsha Pripstein Posusney, 239–78. Boulder, CO and London: Lynne Reiner Publishers, 2003.

Doumato, Eleanor Abdella. *Getting God's Ear: Women, Islam, and Healing in Saudi Arabia and the Gulf.* New York: Columbia University Press, 2000.

Doumato, Eleanor Abdella. "Women and Work in Saudi Arabia: How Flexible are Islamic Margins?" *Middle East Journal* 53, no. 4 (1999): 568–83.

Downes, David. "The *Macho* Penal Economy: Mass Incarceration in the United States—A European Perspective." In *Mass Imprisonment: Social Causes and Consequences,* ed. David Garland. London: Sage Publications, 2001.

Dunson, David B., Bernardo Colombo, and Donna D. Baird. "Changes with Age in the Level and Duration of Fertility in the Menstrual Cycle." *Human Reproduction* 17 (2002): 1399–1403.

Dwyer, Claire. "Veiled Meanings: Young British Muslim Women and the Negotiation of Differences." *Gender, Place and Culture* 6 (1999): 5–26.

East Coast Assisted Parenting. http://www.russiansurrogacy.com/ (accessed September 7, 2006).

Elmhirst, Rebecca. "Learning the Ways of the Priyayi: Domestic Servants and the Mediation of Modernity in Jakarta, Indonesia." In *Gender, Migration and Domestic Service,* ed. Janet Henshall Momsen, 242–62. London and New York: Routledge, 1999.

Engle, Karen. "From Skepticism to Embrace: Human Rights and the American Anthropological Association." *Human Rights Quarterly* 23 (2001): 536–60.

"Entrevista a Marino Costa Bauer." *El Comercio*. (April 3, 1998.)

Epprecht, Marc. "Male-Male Sexuality in Lesotho: Two Conversations." *Journal of Men's Studies* 10, no. 3 (2002): 373–89.

Epstein, Helen, and Julia Kim. "AIDS and the Power of Women." *New York Review of Books* (February 15, 2007): 39–41.

Estrich, Susan. *Real Rape*. Cambridge, MA: Harvard University Press, 1987.

EUROPA. The European Job Mobility Portal (EURES). http://europa.eu.int/eures/main.jsp?acro=lw&lang=en&catId=490&parentId=0 (accessed June 26, 2006).

EUROPA. Population and Social Conditions. Eurostat, 2006. http://epp.eurostat. ec.europa.eu/ (accessed June 26, 2006).

Evans, M.I., L. Littmann, L.S. Louis, L. LeBlanc, J. Addis, M.P. Johnson, and K.S. Moghissi. "Evolving Patterns of Iatrogenic Multifetal Pregnancy Generation: Implication for the Aggressiveness of Infertility Treatments." *American Journal of Obstetrics and Gynecology* 172 (1995): 1750–5.

Evans-Pritchard, E.E. *Kinship and Marriage Among the Nuer.* Oxford: Clarendon Press, 1951.

Ewig, Christina. "Reproduction, Re-reform and the Reconfigured State: Feminists and Neoliberal Health Reforms in Chile." In *Social Reproduction and Global Transformations: From the Everyday to the Global,* eds. Isabella Bakker and Rachel Silvey. NY: Routledge, forthcoming.

Eyal, Gil, and Joanna Bockman. "Eastern Europe as a Laboratory of Economic Knowledge: The Transnational Roots of Neo-Liberalism." *American Journal of Sociology* 103, no. 2 (2004): 310–52.

Fallers, Lloyd. *Bantu Bureaucracy: A Century of Political Evolution Among the Basoga of Uganda.* Chicago: University of Chicago Press, 1965.

Fallers, Lloyd. *Law Without Precedent: Legal Ideas in Action in the Courts of Colonial Busoga.* Chicago: University of Chicago Press, 1969.

Faludi, Susan. *Backlash: The Undeclared War Against American Women,* New York: Anchor, 1991.

Ferguson, James. *Expectations of Modernity: Myths and Meanings of Urban Life on the Zambian Copperbelt.* Berkeley: University of California Press, 1999.

Fernando, Jude L., and Alan W. Heston, eds. "The Role of NGOs: Charity and Empowerment." *The Annals of the American Academy of Political and Social Science* 554, no. 1 (November 1997).

Ferrari, Silvio, and Anthony Bradney, eds. *Islam and European Legal Systems.* Dartmouth/Ashgate: Aldershot, 2000.

Fineschi, V., M. Neri, and E. Turillazzi. "The New Italian Law on Assisted Reproduction Technology," Law 40/2004. *Journal of Medical Ethics* 31 (2005): 536–9.

Floro, Maria, and Hella Hoppe. "Towards Globalization with a Human Face: Engendering Policy Coherence for Development." In *Social Reproduction and Global Transformation: From the Everyday to the Global,* eds. Isabella Bakker and Rachel Silvey. NY: Routledge, forthcoming.

Foa, Edna B., Barbara O. Rothbaum, David S. Riggs, and Tamera B. Murdock. "Treatment of Posttraumatic Stress Disorder in Rape Victims: A Comparison between Cognitive-Behavioral Procedures and Counseling. *Journal of Consulting and Clinical Psychology* 59, no. 5 (1991): 715–23.

Folbre, Nancy. *The Invisible Heart,* New York: New York Press, 2001.

FOMWAN special edition, "Sharia Implementation in Nigeria." *The Muslim Women* 8 (2003).

"FOMWAN: Twenty Years of Service to Islam." *FOMWAN* (2005).

Foot, David K., Richard A. Loreto, and Thomas W. McCormack. "Demographic Trends in Canada, 1996–2006: Implications for the Public and Private Sectors." In *Canada in the 21st Century.* Ottawa: Industry Canada Research Publications, 1998.

Fortes, Meyer, ed. *Marriage in Tribal Societies.* Cambridge: Cambridge University Press, 1962.

Foucault, Michel. *The History of Sexuality: An Introduction,* vol. 1. New York: Vintage Press, 1978.

Fox, Colleen M. "Changing Japanese Employment Patterns and Women's Participation: Anticipating the Implications of Employment Trends." *Manoa Journal* 3 (1994): 1–5.

Fox, Diana J. "Women's Human Rights in Africa: Beyond the Debate over the Universality or Relativity of Human Rights." *African Studies Quarterly* 2, no. 3

(1998). http://web.africa.ufl.edu/asq/v2/v2i3a2.htm (last accessed January 19, 2007).

Fox, Kathryn. "Changing Violent Minds: Discursive Correction and Resistance in the Cognitive Treatment of Violent Offenders in Prison." *Social Problems* 46, no. 1 (1999a): 88–103.

Fox, Kathryn. "Reproducing Criminal Types: Cognitive Treatment for Violent Offenders in Prison." *The Sociological Quarterly* 40, no. 3 (1999b): 435–53.

Frank, O., P. Bianchi, and A. Campana. "The End of Fertility: Age, Fecundity and Fecundability in Women." *Journal of Biosocial Science* 26 (1994): 349–68.

Frankenberg, Elizabeth, and Duncan Thomas. *Measuring Power*. Food Consumption and Nutrition Division Discussion Paper No. 113. Washington, DC: International Food Policy Research Institute, 2001.

Fraser, Nancy. *Unruly Practices*. Minneapolis: University of Minnesota Press, 1989.

Fraser, Nancy. *Justice Interruptus*. New York: Verso, 1997.

Frask-Blunt, Martha. "The Sugar Daddies' Kiss of Death." *Washington Post,* October 6, 2001.

Freedman, Estelle. *Their Sisters' Keeps: Women's Prison Reform in America, 1830–1930*. Ann Arbor: University of Michigan Press, 1981.

Freedman, Lynn. "The Challenge of Fundamentalisms." *Reproductive Health Matters,* no. 8 (November 16, 1996): 66.

Freyd, Jennifer, J. "Betrayal Trauma: Traumatic Amnesia as an Adaptive Response to Childhood Abuse." *Ethics & Behavior* 4, no. 4 (1994): 307–29.

Freyd, Jennifer, J. "What is a Betrayal Trauma? What is Betrayal Trauma Theory?" http://dynamic.uoregon.edu/~jjf/defineBT.html (accessed January 13, 2007).

Frohmann, Alicia, and Teresa Valdés. "Democracy in the Country and in the Home: The Women's Movement in Chile." In *The Challenge of Local Feminisms,* ed. Amrita Basu, 276–301. Boulder, CO: Westview Press, 1995.

Fuszara, Małgorzata. "Zmiany w świadomości kobiet w Polsce w latach dziewięćdziesiątych." *Kobiety w Polsce na przełomie wieków. Nowy kontrakt płci?,* ed. Małgorzata Fuszara, 13–38. Warszawa: Instytut Spraw Publicznych, 2002.

FWLD. *Shadow Report to CEDAW Monitoring Committee, Nepal*. Kathmandu, Nepal: Forum for Women, Law and Development, 2003.

Gal, Susan, and Gail Kligman. *The Politics of Gender after Socialism*. Princeton: Princeton University Press, 2000.

Garland, David. *The Culture of Control: Crime and Social Order in Contemporary Society*. Chicago: University of Chicago Press, 2001.

Garland, David. "Introduction: The Meaning of Mass Imprisonment" In *Mass Imprisonment: Social Causes and Consequences,* ed. David Garland. London: Sage Publications, 2001.

Gartner, Rosemary, and Candace Kruttschnitt. "A Brief History of Doing Time: The California Institution for Women in the 1960s and the 1990s." *Law & Society Review* 38, no. 2 (2004): 267–303.

Gavey, Nicola. *Just Sex? The Cultural Scaffolding of Rape*. New York and London: Routledge, 2005.

GDS/FES. *Women in Garment Industries,* Kathmandu, Nepal: GDS/FES, 1997.

Gebara, Ivone. "The Abortion Debate in Brazil." *Journal of Feminist Studies in Religion* (Fall 1995): 129–135.

Gebara, Ivone. *As incomodos filhas de Eva na igreja da América Latina*. São Paulo: Edições *Latina,* 1989.

Gebara, Ivone. "Ecofeminismo holístico: entrevista con Ivone Gebara," interview by Mary Judith Ress, *Con-spirando* No. 4. (June1993): 44–45.

Gebara, Ivone. "The Face of Transcendence as a Challenge to the Reading of the Bible in Latin America." In *Searching the Scriptures,* vol. I., ed. Elisabeth Schussler Fiorenza. New York: Crossroad, 1993.

Gebara, Ivone. *Teología al Ritmo de Mujer.* Madrid: San Pablo, 1995.

Gebara, Ivone. *Out of the Depths: Women's Experience of Evil and Salvation.* Minneapolis: Fortress Press, 2002.

GEFONT. "Search for Alternatives." Kathmandu, Nepal: GEFONT, 2003.

Gemie, Sharif. "Actualité. Stasi's Republic: The School and the 'Veil': December 2003-March 2004." *Modern & Contemporary France* 12 (2004): 387–97.

Giddens, Anthony. *Central Problems in Social Theory: Action, Structure and Contradiction in Social Analysis.* London: Macmillan, 1979.

Glassman, Jim. "State Power Beyond the 'Territorial Trap': The Internationalization of the State." *Political Geography* 18 (1999): 669–96.

Gleicher, Norbert, Denise M. Oleske, Ilan Tur-Kespa, Andrea Vidali, and Vishvanath Karande. "Reducing the Risk of High-Order Multiple Pregnancy After Ovarian Stimulation with Gonadotropins." *New England Journal of Medicine* 343 (2000): 2–7.

Goetz, Anne Marie, and Rina Sen Gupta. "Who Takes the Credit? Gender, Power, and Control over Loan Use in Rural Credit Programs in Bangladesh." *World Development* 24, no. 1 (1996): 45–63.

Goldstein, Daniel M. "'In Our Own Hands': Lynching, Justice, and the Law in Bolivia." *American Ethnologist* 30, no. 1 (2003): 22–43.

Graff, Agnieszka. *Świat bez Kobiet.* Warszawa: W.A.B., 2001.

Grammuck, Sherri and Patricia R. Pessar. *Between Two Islands: Dominican International Migration.* Berkeley: University of California Press, 1991.

Grasmuck, Sherri and Rosario Espinal. "Market Success or Female Autonomy? Income, Ideology, and Empowerment Among Microentrepreneurs in the Dominican Republic." *Gender & Society* 14 (April 2000): 231–55.

Grenova, Martina. "Slovakia's Booming Fertility Tourism." *Insight Central Europe,* June 2, 2006.

Grewal, Inderpal, and Caren Kaplan. "Introduction: Transnational Feminist Practices and Questions of Postmodernity." In *Scattered Hegemonies: Postmodernity and Transnational Feminist Practices,* eds. Inderpal Grewal and Caren Kaplan. Minneapolis: University of Minnesota Press, 1994.

Gunn, T. Jeremy. "Religious Freedom and *Laïcité*: A Comparison of the United States and France." *Brigham Young University Law Review* (2004): 419–505.

Gurung, Jeannette D., ed. *Searching for Women's Voices in the Hindu Kush Himalayas.* Kathmandu, Nepal: ICIMOD, 1999.

Haberland, Nicole, and Diana Measham, eds. *Responding to Cairo: Case Studies of Changing Practice in Reproductive Health and Family Planning.* New York: Population Council, 2002.

Haeri, Shahla. *No Shame for the Sun: Lives of Professional Pakistani Women.* Syracuse: Syracuse University Press, 2002.

Hall, Stuart. "The Multi-Cultural Moment." In *Un/Settled Multiculturalisms,* ed. Barnor Hesse. London: Zed Books, 2000.

Haney, Lynne. "Gender, Welfare, and States of Punishment." *Social Politics* 11 (2004): 3.

Haney, Lynne. "Homeboys, Babies, Men in Suits: The State and the Reproduction of Male Dominance." *American Sociological Review* 61 (1996): 779–93.

Haney, Lynne. *Inventing the Needy: Gender and the Politics of Welfare in Hungary.* Berkeley, CA: University of California Press, 2002.

Hannah-Moffat, Kelly. "Losing Ground: Gendered Knowledges, Parole Risk, and Responsibility." *Social Politics* 11 (2004): 3.

Hannah-Moffat, Kelly. *Punishment in Disguise: Penal Governance and Federal Imprisonment of Women in Canada.* Toronto: University of Toronto Press, 2001.

Hartmann, Betsy. *Reproductive Rights and Wrongs: The Global Politics of Population Contro* (revised edition). Boston: South End Press, 1995.

Hashemi, Syed M., Sidney Ruth Schuler, and Ann P. Riley. "Rural Credit Programs and Women's Empowerment in Bangladesh." *World Development* 24, no. 4 (1996): 635–53.

Hauser, Ewa. "Traditions of Patriotism, Questions of Gender: The Case of Poland," *Genders* 22 (Fall 1995): 78–105.

Hays, Sharon. *Flat Broke with Children: Women in the Age of Welfare Reform.* New York: Oxford University Press, 2003.

Hearn, Jeff. "The Problems Boys and Men Create, the Problems Boys and Men Experience." Paper presented at the conference "From Boys to Men," University of the Western Cape, Cape Town, South Africa, January 26–28, 2005.

Heberle, Renee. "Deconstructive Strategies and the Movement Against Sexual Violence." *Hypatia* 11, no. 4 (1996): 63–76.

Heng, Geraldine, and Janadas Devan. "State Fatherhood: The Politics of Nationalism, Sexuality, and Race in Singapore." In *Nationalisms and Sexualities,* eds. Andrew Parker, Mary Russo, Doris Sommer, and Patricia Yaeger, 343–64. New York: Routledge, 1992.

Herman, Judith Lewis. *Trauma and Recovery.* New York: Basic Books, 1992.

Hernández Pico, J., Memoria del silencio: Un Informe estremecedor. Para la memoria de los mártires. http://www.uca.edu.ni/koinonia/relat/206.htm (accessed September 2002).

Herrara, Gioconda. "States, Work and Social Reproduction through the Lens of Migrant Experience: Ecuadorian Domestic Workers in Madrid." In *Social Reproduction and Global Transformation: From the Everyday to the Global,* eds. Isabella Bakker and Rachel Silvey. NY: Routledge, forthcoming.

Heymann, Jody, Alison Earle, Stephanie Simmons, Stephanie S. Breslow, and April Kuehnoff. *The Work, Family, and Equity Index: Where Does the United States Stand Globally?* Boston, MA: The Project on Global Working Families, 2004.

Heyner, Priscilla. *Unspeakable Truths: Confronting State Terror and Atrocity.* New York: Routledge, 2001.

Hilberman, Elaine. "Rape: 'The Ultimate Violation of the Self.'" *American Journal of Psychiatry* 133, no. 4 (1976): 436–7.

Hirsch, Susan. *Pronouncing & Persevering: Gender and the Discourses of Disputing in an African Islamic Court.* Chicago: University of Chicago Press, 1998.

Hobson, Barbara, and Ruth Lister. "Citizenship." In *Contested Concepts in Gender and Social Politics,* eds. Barbara Hobson, Jane Lewis and Birte Siim, 23–53. Cheltenham, UK: Edward Elgar, 2002.

Hodgson, Dorothy L. "'My Daughter . . . Belongs to the Government Now:' Marriage, Maasai and the Tanzanian State." *Canadian Journal of African Studies* 30, no. 1 (1996): 107–23.

Hodgson, Dorothy L. "Women's Rights as Human Rights: Women in Law and Development in Africa (WiLDAF)." *Africa Today* 49, no. 2 (2002): 3–26.

Holland, Jeremy, and Simon Brook. "Measuring Empowerment: Country Indicators." In *Power, Rights, and Poverty: Concepts and Connections,* ed. Ruth Alsop. A working meeting sponsored by DFID and the World Bank, March 23–24, 2004. Washington, DC: The World Bank.

Hollenberg, Elizabeth. "The Criminalization of Teenage Sex: Statutory Rape and the Politics of Teenage Motherhood." *Stanford Law and Policy Review* 10 (1999): 267–87.

Holmstrom, Lynda Lytle, and Ann Wolbert Burgess. *The Victim of Rape: Institutional Reactions.* New Brunswick and London: Transaction Publishers, 1983.
Hondagneu-Sotelo, Pierrette. *Gendered Transitions: Mexican Experience of Immigration.* Berkeley, CA: University of California Press, 1994.
Horowitz, Asher, and Gad Horowitz. *"Everywhere They are in Chains:" Political Theory from Rousseau to Marx.* Scarborough, Ontario: Nelson Canada, 1988.
Huang, Shirlena, and Brenda S. A. Yeoh. "Ties that Bind: State Policy and Migrant Female Domestic Helpers in Singapore." *Geoforum* 27 (1996): 479–93.
Hughes, E.G., and M. Giacomini. "Funding In-Vitro Fertilization Treatment for Persistent Subfertility: The Pain and the Politics." *Fertility and Sterility* 76 (2001): 431–42.
Hugo, Graeme. "Labour Export from Indonesia." *ASEAN Economic Bulletin* 12, no. 2 (1995): 275–98.
Imam, Ayesha M. "Fighting the Political (Ab)Use of Religion in Nigeria: BAOBAB for Women's Human Rights, Allies, and Others." In *Fundamentalism: Warning Signs, Law, Media and Resistances*, eds. Ayesha Imam, Jenny Morgan, and Nira Yuval-Davis. http://www.wluml.org (accessed December 2004).
Imam, Ayesha M. "Women's Reproductive and Sexual Rights and the Offense of Zina in Muslim Laws in Nigeria." In *Where Human Rights Begin: Health, Sexuality, and Women in the New Millennium*, eds. Wendy Chavkin and Ellen Chesler. New Brunswick, NJ: Rutgers University Press, 2005.
INEI. *Perú: Compendio Estadístico 1991–2.* Lima: Instituto Nacional de Información y Estadísticas, 1992.
INEI. *Encuesta Nacional Demográfica de Salud Familiar (ENDES).* Lima: Instituto Nacional de Información y Estadísticas, 1996.
INEI. *Encuesta Nacional Demográfica de Salud Familiar (ENDES).* Lima: Instituto Nacional de Información y Estadísticas, 2000.
Inhorn, Marcia. "'The Worms Are Weak': Male Infertility and Patriarchal Paradoxes in Egypt." *Men and Masculinities* 5 (2003): 238–58.
Instituto Nacional de la Mujer de Honduras, "Taller 'Mujer y Democracia': Quién dijo que la Política no es cosa de Mujeres?" San Pedro Sula, Cortés, June 19–20, 2004, Embajada de Los Países Bajos.
INSTRAW (International Research and Training Institute for the Advanced of Women). *The Migration of Women: Methodological Issues of the Measurement and Analysis of Internal and International Migration.* Santo Domingo, Dominican Republic: United Nations, 1994.
"Investigación: Encuentran otras dos mujeres muertas," *La Prensa,* San Pedro Sula, Honduras, July 20, 2003, Sección Pasiones, 44.
Istituti di Medicina della Riproduzione ed Endocrinologia. http://www.ivf-institut.cz/IT/default.htm (accessed September 7, 2006).
Jackson, Cecile. "Rescuing Gender from the Poverty Trap." *World Development* 24, no. 3 (1996): 489–504.
Janion, Maria. "Rozstać się z Polską," *Gazeta Wyborcza* 20 (October 2004): 14–16.
Jaquette, Jane S., and Kathleen A. Staudt. "Gender and Politics in U.S. Population Policy." In *Political Interests of Gender,* eds. Kathleen Jones and Anna Jonasdottir. London: Sage Press, 1998.
Jejeebhoy, Shireen. "Adolescent Sexual and Reproductive Behavior: A Review of Evidence from India." ICRW Working Paper, no. 3. Washington, DC: International Center for Research on Women, 1996.
Jejeebhoy, Shireen J. "Women's Autonomy in Rural India: Its Dimensions, Determinants, and the Influence of Context." In *Women's Empowerment and Demographic Processes: Moving Beyond Cairo,* eds. Harriet Presser and Gita Sen. New York: Oxford University Press, 2000.

Jha, J.C. "The Background to the Legalization of Non-Christian Marriage in Trinidad and Tobago." In *East Indians in the Caribbean: Colonialism and the Struggle for Identity*, eds. Bridget Brereton and Winston Dookeran. New York: Kraus International Publications, 1982.

Judd, Ellen R. *Gender and Power in Rural North China*. Stanford, CA: Stanford University Press, 1994.

Kabeer, Naila. "Conflicts over Credit: Re-evaluating the Empowerment Potential of Loans to Women in Rural Bangladesh." *World Development* 29, no.1 (2001): 63–84.

Kabeer, Naila. *The Conditions and Consequences of Choice: Reflections on the Measurement of Women's Empowerment*, UNRISD Discussion Paper, no. 108. Geneva, Switzerland: UNRISD, 1999.

Kabeer, Naila. *The Power to Choose: Bangladesh Women and Labour Market Decisions in London and Dhaka*. London: Verso, 2000.

Kabeer, Naila. *Inclusive Citizenship: Meanings and Expressions*. New York: Zed Press, 2005.

Kabeer, Naila. "Is Microfinance a 'Magic Bullet' for Women's Empowerment? Analysis of Findings from South Asia." *Economic and Political Weekly* XL, nos. 44–45 (October 29, 2005): 4709–18.

Kabeer, Naila. "Reflections on the Measurement of Women's Empowerment." In *Discussing Women's Empowerment: Theory and Practice*. Sida Studies 3. Stockholm, Sweden: Swedish International Development Cooperation Agency, 2001.

Kabeer, Naila. *Reversed Realities: Gender Hierarchies in Development Thought*. London: Verso Press, 1994.

Kabeer, Naila. "Women, Wages and Intra-household Power Relations in Urban Bangladesh." *Development and Change* 28 (1997): 261–302.

Kabeer, Naila and Ramya Subrahmanian. *Institutions, Relations and Outcomes*. New Delhi: Kali for Women, 1999.

Kamali, Anatoli, Lucy Mary Carpenter, James Alexander Grover Whitworth, Robert Pool, Anthony Ruberantwari, and Amato Ojwiya. "Seven-year Trends in HIV-1 Infection Rates, and Changes in Sexual Behaviour, Among Adults in Rural Uganda." *AIDS* 14, no. 4 (2000): 427–34.

Kanaiaupuni, Shawn Malia. "Reframing the Migration Question: An Analysis of Men, Women, and Gender in Mexico." *Social Forces* (June 2000): 1311–48.

Kane, Ousmane. *Muslim Modernity in Postcolonial Nigeria: The Society for the Removal of Innovation and Reinstatement of Tradition*. Leiden: Brill, 2003.

Kann, Mark. "Penitence for the Privileged: Manhood, Race, and Penitentiaries in Early America." In *Prison Masculinities*, eds. Don Sabo, Terry Kupers, and Willie London. Philadelphia: Temple University Press, 2001.

Kapadia-Kundu, N., and A. Dyalchand. "The Pachod Paisa Scale: A New Scale for Measuring Attitudes, Client Satisfaction, Beliefs and Intentions." Unpublished paper. Pachod, India: Integrated Health Management, 2005.

Keck, Margaret E., and Kathryn Sikkink. *Activists Beyond Borders: Advocacy Networks in International Politics*. Ithaca, NY: Cornell University Press, 1998.

Kelkar, Govind, Dev Nathan, and Rownok Jahan. "Redefining Women's 'Samman': Microcredit and Gender Relations in Rural Bangladesh." *Economic and Political Weekly* XXXIX, no. 32 (August 7, 2004): 3627–40.

Kemp, Dennis. *Nine Years at the Gold Coast*. London, New York: Macmillan, 1898.

Khan, Aisha. *Callaloo Nation: Metaphors of Race and Religious Identity among South Asians in Trinidad*. Durham, NC and London: Duke University Press, 2004.

Khiddu-Makubuya, E. "The Rule of Law and Human Rights in Uganda: The Missing Link." In *Changing Uganda: The Dilemmas of Structural Adjustment &*

*Revolutionary Change,* eds., Holder Bernt Hansen and Michael Twaddle, 217–23. London: James Currey, 1991.

Killian, Caitlin. "The Other Side of the Veil. North African Women in France Respond to the Headscarf Affair." *Gender & Society* 17 (2003): 567–90.

Kingsley, Charles. *At Last: A Christmas in the West Indies.* London: Macmillan, 1896.

Kirkwood, Julietta. *Ser Política en Chile: Las Feministas y los Partidos.* Santiago: FLACSO, 1986.

Kishsor, Sunita. "Empowerment of Women in Egypt and Links to the Survival and Health of Their Infants." In *Women's Empowerment and Demographic Processes: Moving Beyond Cairo,* eds. Harriet Presser and Gita Sen. New York: Oxford University Press, 2000.

Klemetti, Reija, Tiina Sevon, Mika Gissler, and Elina Hemminki. "Complications of IVF and Ovulation Induction." *Human Reproduction* 20 (2005): 3293–300.

Klip, H., F.E.V. Leeuwen, R. Schats, and C.W. Burger. "Risk of Benign Gynecological Diseases and Hormonal Disorders According to Responsiveness to Ovarian Stimulation in IVF: A Follow-Up Study of 8714 Women." *Human Reproduction* 18 (2003): 1951–8.

Kofman, Eleonore, and Linda Peake. "Into the 1990s: A Gendered Agenda for Political Geography." *Political Geography Quarterly* 9, no. 4 (1990): 313–36.

Kohler, Hans-Peter, Francesco C. Billari, José Antonio Ortega. "The Emergence of Lowest-Low Fertility in Europe During the 1990s." *Population and Development Review* 28 (2002): 599–639.

Kosmogonia. http://www.kosmogania.gr/italian/italian/main.htm (accessed September 7, 2006).

Koss, Mary P., Christine A. Gidycz, and Nadine Wisniewski. "The Scope of Rape: Incidence and Prevalence of Sexual Aggression and Victimization in a National Sample of Higher Education Students." *Journal of Consulting & Clinical Psychology* 55, no. 2 (1987): 162–70.

Koss, Mary P., and Mary R. Harvey. *The Rape Victim: Clinical and Community Interventions,* 2nd ed. Newbury Park: Sage Publications, 1991.

Kymlicka, Will. *Multicultural Citizenship.* Oxford: Oxford University Press, 1995.

Lagarde y de los Rios, Marcela. "Por la vida y la libertad de las mujeres: Fin al feminicidio" Dia V-Juárez, February 2004, http://www.isis.cl/Feminicidio/Juarez/pag/quessfem.htm (accessed January 8, 2005).

Lamb, Sharon. "Constructing the Victim: Popular Images and Lasting Labels." In *New Versions of Victims: Feminist Struggles with the Concept,* ed. Sharon Lamb. New York and London: New York University Press, 1999.

Lane, Sandra D. "From Population Control to Reproductive Health: An Emerging Policy Agenda." *Social Science and Medicine* 39 (1994): 1303–14.

Laroque, Guy, and Bernard Salanié. "Fertility and Financial Incentives in France." *CESifo Economic Studies* 50 (2004): 423–50.

Laye, Camara. *The African Child.* London and Glasgow: Collins, 1954.

Lazarus-Black, Mindie. "Law and the Pragmatics of Inclusion: Governing Domestic Violence in Trinidad and Tobago." *American Ethnologist* 28, no. 2 (2001): 388–416.

Leach, Fiona, and Shashikala Sitaram. "Microfinance and Women's Empowerment: A Lesson from India." *Development in Practice* 12, no. 5 (November 2002): 575–88.

Lewis, Reina, and Sara Mills, eds. *Feminist Postcolonial Theory. A Reader.* New York: Routledge, 2003.

Library of Congress. "Czechoslovakia—Health and Social Welfare." *Country Studies.* Washington DC: Library of Congress, 2006.

Lim, Linda. "Women's Work in Export Factories: The Politics of a Cause." In *Persistent Inequalities: Women and World Development,* ed. Irene Tinker. New York: Oxford University Press, 1990.

Lin, Nan. *Social Capital: Theory and Research*. New York: Cambridge University Press, 2001.

Lindsay, Lisa A., and Stefan F. Miescher. *Men and Masculinities in Modern Africa*. Portsmouth, NH: Heinemann, 2003.

Lindsey, Charlotte Lindsey. "The Impact of Armed Conflict on Women." http://www.reliefweb.int/library/documents/2001/icrc-women-17oct.pdf (accessed 15 January 2006).

"Lineamientos Básicos de la Política Social." Primer Ministro, Lima. (November 1993).

Lisak, David. "The Neurobiology of Trauma." Unpublished paper, 2002. http://www.nowldef.org/html/njep/dvd/pdf/neurobiology.pdf (accessed October 31, 2003).

Lister, Ruth. "Citizenship: Towards a Feminist Synthesis." *Feminist Review* 57 (1997): 28–48.

Lister, Ruth. "Dialectics of Citizenship." *Hypatia* 12, no. 4 (1997): 6–26.

Little, Deborah. "Independent Workers, Dependent Mothers: Discourse, Resistance, and AFDC Workfare Programs." *Social Politics* 6 (1999): 161–202.

Lochhead, Clarence. "The Trend Toward Delayed First Childbirth: Health and Social Implications." *Isuma* 1 (2000): 41–4.

Loenen, T. (Ed.), *Gelijke behandeling: Oordelen en commentaar 1999* (Equal Treatment: Decisions and Comments 1999). (Deventer: Kluwer, 2000).

Loscocco, Karyn A., and Xun Wang. "Gender Segregation in China." *Sociology and Social Research* 76 (1992): 118–26.

Lubin, Orly. "'Gone Soldiers' Feminism and the Military in Israel." *The Journal of Israeli History* 21, nos. 1–2 (Spring/Autumn 2002): 164–92.

*Ludin*, Bundesverfassungsgericht, September 24, 2003, 2BvR 1436/02, http://www.bundesverfassungsgericht.de/.

Luginaah, Isaac, David Elkins, Eleanor Maticka-Tyndale, Tamara Landry, and Mercy Mathui. "Challenges of a Pandemic: HIV/AIDS-Related Problems Affecting Kenyan Widows." *Social Science & Medicine* 60, no. 6 (2005): 1219–28.

Lycklama à Nijeholt, Geertje, Joke Sweibel, and Virginia Vargas. "The Global Institutional Framework: The Long March to Beijing." In *Women's Movements and Public Policy in Europe, Latin America, and the Caribbean*, eds. Geertje Lycklama à Nijeholt, Virginia Vargas and Saskia Wieringa, 25–48. New York and London: Garland Publishing, Inc., 1998.

Lynch, Mona. "Rehabilitation as Rhetoric: The Ideal of Reformation in Contemporary Parole Discourse and Practices." *Punishment and Society* 2 (2000): 40–65.

McClintock, Ann. *Imperial Leather: Race, Gender and Sexuality in the Colonial Contest*. New York: Routledge, 1995.

McClintock, Ann. "No Longer in a Future Heaven: Nationalism, Gender and Race." In *Becoming National*, eds. Geoff Eley and Ronald Grigor Suny, 260–284. Oxford: Oxford University Press, 1996.

McCorkel, Jill. "Criminally Dependent? Gender, Punishment, and the Rhetoric of Welfare Reform." *Social Politics* 11 (2004): 386–410.

McDonald, Peter. "The 'Toolbox' of Public Policies to Impact on Fertility: A Global View." *Low Fertility, Families, and Public Policies*. Sevilla: European Observatory on Family Matters, 2000.

McFarlane, Alexander C. "The Prevalence and Longitudinal Course of PTSD: Implications for the Neurobiological Models of PTSD." *Annals of the New York Academy of Sciences* 821, no. 1 (1997): 10–23.

McKim, Allison. "Getting Gut-Level: Punishment, Gender, and Therapeutic Governance." Paper presented at the Annual Meeting of the American Sociological Association, session on Gender and Incarceration, August 2006.

McNally, Richard J. *Remembering Trauma*. Cambridge, MA and London: Belknap Press of Harvard University Press, 2003.

Machulski, Juliusz. *Seksmisja* [Sexmission] (Poland, 1983); Director: Juliusz Machulski. Starring: Olgierd Lukaszewicz, Jerzy Stuhr. Screenplay by: Jolanta Hartwig-Sosnowska; Pawel Hajny; Juliusz Machulski.

Mack, Beverly. "Muslim Women's Knowledge Production in the Greater Maghreb." In *Gender and Islam in Africa*, ed. Margot Badran. Leiden: Brill, 2007.

MacKinnon, Catharine A. *Toward a Feminist Theory of the State*. Cambridge, MA: Harvard University Press, 1989.

Mahlmann, Matthias. "Religious Tolerance, Pluralist Society and the Neutrality of the State: The Federal Constitutional Court's Decision in the Headscarf Case." *German Law Journal* 4, no. 11 (November 1, 2003). http://www.germanlawjournal.com/article.php?id=331. Accessed 13 July 2007.

Malhotra, Anju, and Mark Mather. "Do Schooling and Work Empower Women in Developing Countries? Gender and Domestic Decisions in Sri Lanka." *Sociological Forum* 12, no. 4 (1997): 599–630.

Malhotra, Anju, Sidney Ruth Schuler, and Carol Boender, "Measuring Women's Empowerment as a Variable in International Development." Background paper prepared for the World Bank Workshop on Poverty and Gender: New Perspectives. Gender and Development Group. Washington, DC: World Bank, 2002.

Mamdani, Mahmood. "Introduction." In *Beyond Rights Talk and Culture Talk: Comparative Essays on the Politics of Rights and Culture*, Mahmood Mamdani, ed., 1–13. New York: St. Martin Press, 2000.

Mamphele, Ramphele. "Teach Me How to Be a Man: An Exploration of the Definition of Masculinity." In *Violence and Subjectivity*, eds. Veena Das, Arthur Kleinman, Mamphele Ramphele and Pamela Reynolds, 102–19. California: University of California Press, 1997.

"Man Kills Wife for Denying Him Sex." *Ghana News Agency*, December 20, 2004.

Mantilla, Julissa. "La Comisión de la Verdad y Reconciliación del Perú: Principales logros y hallazgos." *Revista IIDH 43* (June 2006): 338.

Mantilla, Julissa. "War Crimes." *Latinamerica Press* 38, no. 7 (April 19, 2006): 7.

Marecek, Jeanne. "Trauma Talk in Feminist Clinical Practice." In *New Versions of Victims: Feminist Struggles with the Concept*, ed. Sharon Lamb. New York and London: New York University Press, 1999.

Marshall, T.H. "Citizenship and Social Class." In *Class, Citizenship and Social Development. Essays by T.H. Marshall*. Westport: Greenwood Press, 1976.

Mason, Karen Oppenheim, and Ann-Magritt Jensen, eds. *Gender and Family Change in Industrialized Countries*. New York, Oxford University Press, 1995.

Massey, Douglas S., et al. "Theories of International Migration Theory: A Review and Appraisal," *Population and Development Review* 20, no. 4 (1993): 699–751.

Matynia, Elżbieta. "Provinicializing Global Feminism: The Polish Case." *Social Research* 70, no. 2 (Summer 2003): 499–530.

Mayoux, Linda. "Micro-Finance and the Empowerment of Women: A Review of the Key Issues." *International Labor Organization*, 1999.

Mayoux, Linda. "Tackling the Down Side: Social Capital, Women's Empowerment and Micro-Finance in Cameroon." *Development and Change* 32 (2001): 435–64.

Mayoux, Linda. "Women's Empowerment through Sustainable Micro-Finance: Rethinking 'Best Practice.'" Discussion draft, February 2006. http://www.genfinance.info/Documents/Mayoux_Backgroundpaper.pdf (accessed July 11, 2007).

Mboya, Paul. *Luo Kitgi gi Timbegi: A Handbook of Luo Customs*. Kisumu: Anyange Press, 1997.

"Médico admite campaña del gobierno," *El Comercio*, A14. (February 23, 1998).

Merry, Sally Engle. "Human Rights and the Demonization of Culture (and Anthropology Along the Way)." *Polar: Political and Legal Anthropology Review* 26, no. 1 (2003): 55–77.

Merry, Sally Engle. "Spatial Governmentality and the New Urban Social Order: Controlling Gender Violence through Law." *American Anthropologist* 103, no. 1 (2001): 16–29.

Mertus, Julie, and Pamela Goldberg. "Perspective on Women and International Human Rights after the Vienna Declaration: The Inside/Outside Construct." *New York University Journal of International Law and Politics* 26 (1994): 201.

Messer, Ellen. "Anthropologists in a World with and Without Human Rights." In *Exotic No More: Anthropology on the Front Lines,* ed. Jeremy MacClancy, 319–37. Chicago: University of Chicago Press, 2002.

Mies, Maria. *Patriarchy and Accumulation on a World Scale.* London: Zed Books, 1986.

Milligan, Kevin. "Quebec's Baby Bonus: Can Public Policy Raise Fertility?" *Backgrounder.* Toronto: C.D. Howe Institute, 2002.

Mincer, Jacob. "Family Migration Decisions." *Journal of Political Economy* 86 (1978): 749–73.

Minister of Industry. "Canada's Demographic Situation: Fertility of Immigrant Women." *The Daily.* Statistics Canada, 2003.

Ministerio de Salud (MINSA). "Programa de Salud Reproductiva y Planificación Familiar." Lima: MINSA, UNFPA (Enero), 1996.

Ministry of Health and Social Affairs. Swedish Family Policy. Regeringen, 2003.

Mir-Hosseini, Ziba. *Marriage on Trial: A Study of Family Law, Iran and Morocco.* New York: I.B. Tauris, 2000.

Mir-Hosseini, Ziba. "Muslim Women's Quest for Equality: Between Islamic Law and Feminism." *Critical Inquiry* (Summer 2006): 629–45.

Mir-Hosseini, Ziba. *The Religious Debate in Contemporary Iran.* Princeton: Princeton University Press, 1999.

Moghadam, Valentine M. *Globalizing Women: Transnational Feminist Networks.* Baltimore: Johns Hopkins Press, 2005.

Moghadam, Valentine M. ed., *Identity Politics and Women: Cultural Reassertions and Feminisms in International Perspective.* Boulder: Westview Press, 1994.

Mogollón, María Esther. "Peruanas esterilizadas por la fuerza reclaman justicia." Cimac noticias, 2003. http://www.cimacnoticias.com/noticias/03mar/03030504.html (last accessed June 6, 2005).

Mohanty, B.B."'We are Like the Living Dead': Farmer Suicides in Maharashtra, Western India." *Journal of Peasant Studies* 32, no. 2 (2005): 244–76.

MOHP/HMG, New Era and ORC Macro. *Nepal Demographic Health Survey.* Kathmandu, Nepal, 2001.

Molyneux, Maxine D. "Mobilization Without Emancipation? Women's Interests, State, and Revolution in Nicaragua." *Feminist Studies* 11 (1985): 227–54.

Momsen, Janet Henshall, ed. *Gender, Migration and Domestic Service.* London and New York: Routledge, 1999.

Montpetit, Éric. "Public Consultations in Policy Network Environments: The Case of Assisted Reproductive Technology Policy in Canada." *Canadian Public Policy* 29 (2003): 95–110.

Moore, Sally Falk. *Social Facts and Fabrications: "Customary" Law on Kilimanjaro, 1880–1980.* New York: Cambridge University Press, 1986.

Morrell, Robert. "Men, Movements and Gender Transformation in South Africa." *Journal of Men's Studies* 10, issue 3 (2002): 309.

Morrell, Robert. "Of Boys and Men: Masculinity and Gender in Southern African Studies." *Journal of Southern African Studies* 24, no. 4 (1998): 605–30.

Mosedale, Sarah. "Assessing Women's Empowerment: Towards a Conceptual Framework." *Journal of International Development* 17 (2005): 243–57.

Moser, Caroline. *Gender Planning and Development: Theory, Practice and Training.* New York: Routledge, 1993.

Mosse, George. *Nationalism and Sexuality. Middle Class Morality and Sexual Norms in Modern Europe.* Madison: The University of Wisconsin Press, 1985.

Muhangi, Jossy. "Women Demand Castration for Men over Sex Abuse." In *The New Vision,* Kampala, Uganda, December 18, 1991.

Mumtaz, Khawar, and Farida Shaheed. *Women of Pakistan: Two Steps Forward, One Step Backward?* London and Karachi: Zed, 1987.

Murphy, Rachel. *How Migrant Labor Is Changing Rural China.* Cambridge: Cambridge University Press, 2002.

"Muslim Women Scholars," *The Muslim Woman* 9 (2005), 9–10.

Nagar, Richa, Victoria Lawson, Linda McDowell, and Susan Hanson. "Locating Globalization: Feminist (Re)Readings of the Subjects and Spaces of Globalization." http://www.clarku.edu:80/departments/geography/leir/4feminists.htm (accessed January 10, 2007).

Nagel, Caroline. "Contemporary Scholarship and the Demystification—and Re-Mystification—of 'Muslim Women.'" *Arab World Geographer* 4, no. 1 (2001): 63–72.

Najmabadi, Afsaneh. "Gender and Secularism of Modernity: How Can a Muslim Woman be French?" *Feminist Studies* 32 (2006): 239–55.

Nakertrans. Indonesian government website for transmigration and the labor force. http://www.nakertrans.go.id/berita_penting/2001/September/BP010917.htm (accessed July 8, 2003).

Naranjana, Tejaswini. "'Left to the Imagination:' Indian Nationalisms and Female Sexuality in Trinidad," *Public Culture* 11, no. 1 (1999): 223–43.

Narasimha, Rao P., and K.C. Suri. "Dimensions of Agrarian Distress in Andhra Pradesh." *Economic and Political Weekly* XLI, no.16 (April 22, 2006): 1546–52.

Narayan, Deepa, ed. *Measuring Empowerment: Cross-disciplinary Perspectives.* The International Bank for Reconstruction and Development/The World Bank. New Delhi: Oxford University Press, 2006.

Narismulu, Priya. "'Now I am Suffering, I've Got No Place to Stay:' Experiences of Insecurity in a Durban Shack Settlement." Paper presented at the Conference on Uncertainty in Contemporary African Lives at the MS Training Centre for Development Cooperation, Arusha, Tanzania, April 9–11, 2003.

Nash, Kate. "Feminism and Contemporary Liberal Citizenship: The Undecidability of 'Women.'" *Citizenship Studies* 15, no. 3 (2001): 255–68.

NCS Scholars. "Final Presentation: Negotiating Citizenship and Diversity: Gender, Nation, Diaspora." New York, April 2005.

Nepal Rastra Bank. *Multipurpose Household Budget Survey: A Study on Income Distribution, Employment and Consumption Patterns in Nepal.* Kathmandu, Nepal: Nepal Rastra Bank, 1988.

Nepal Rastra Bank. *Quarterly Economic Bulletin* (Mid-October), vol. XXXX, no. 1. Kathmandu, Nepal, 2005.

"Netherlands Moves Toward Total Ban on Muslim Veils," *Guardian* (November 11, 2006).

New ERA. *A Situation Analysis of Sex Work and Trafficking in Nepal with Reference to Children,* October 1996 issue. Submitted to UNICEF, Nepal (mimeograph), 1998.

*The NIV Study Bible, New International Version.* (Grand Rapids: Zondervan, 1985).

North, Liisa, and John D. Cameron, *Rural Progress Rural Decay: Neoliberal Adjustment Policies and Local Initiatives* (Bloomfield, CA: Kumarian, 2003).

Nowrojee, Binaifer. "Making the Invisible War Crime Visible: Postconflict Justice for Sierra Leone's Rape Victims." *Harvard Human Rights Journal* 18 (2005): 85–105.

NPC/UNDP. *Nepal Human Development Report 2004: Empowerment and Poverty Reduction.* Kathmandu, Nepal: United Nations Development Program, 2004.

Nussbaum, Martha. *Women and Human Development: The Capabilities Approach.* Cambridge: Cambridge University Press, 2000.

Nyoboe, Anderson A., L. Gianaroli, and K.G. Nygren. "Assisted Reproductive Technology in Europe, 2000." Results generated registers by ESHRE. *Human Reproduction* 19 (2004): 490–503.

O'Malley, Pat. "Risk, Power, and Crime Prevention." *Economy and Society* 21 (1992): 252–75.

O'Malley, Pat. "Volatile and Contradictory Punishment." *Theoretical Criminology* 3 (1996): 175–96.

Obbo, Christine. "Gender, Age and Class: Discourses on HIV Transmission and Control in Uganda. In *Culture and Sexual Risk: Anthropological Perspectives on AIDS*. eds. Han ten Brummelhuis and Gilbert Herdt, Amsterdam: Gordon and Breach Publishers, 1995.

Oberman, Michelle. "Girls in the Master's House: Of Protection, Patriarchy and the Potential for Using the Master's Tools to Reconfigure Statutory Rape Law." *DePaul Law Review* 50 (2001): 799–826.

Odem, Mary E. *Delinquent Daughters: Protecting and Policing Adolescent Female Sexuality in the United States, 1885–1920*. Chapel Hill: The University of North Carolina Press, 1995.

OECD. "Babies and Bosses: Balancing Work and Family Life." *Policy Brief*. Paris: Organisation for Economic Cooperation and Development, 2005.

Office of the United Nations High Commissioner for Human Rights, "Special Rapporteur on Violence against Women, its Causes and Consequences." http://www.ohchr.org/english/issues/women/rapporteur/ (accessed December 20, 2006).

Okeyo, Tom Mboya, and Ann K. Allen. "Influence on Widow Inheritance on the Epidemiology of AIDS in Africa." *African Journal of Medical Practice* 1, no. 1 (1994): 20–5.

Okin, Susan Moller. *Justice, Gender and the Family*. New York: Basic Books, 1999.

Okin, Susan Moller, Joshua Cohen, Mathew Howard, and Martha Nussbaum, eds. *Is Multiculturalism Bad for Women?* New Jersey: Princeton University Press, 1999.

Orloff, Ann. "Gender in the Welfare State." *Annual Review of Sociology* 22 (1996): 51–78.

Osmani, Lutfun N. Khan. "Impact of Credit on the Relative Well-Being of Women: Evidence from the Grameen Bank." *IDS Bulletin* 29, no. 4 (1998): 30–8.

Ostien, Philip, Jamila M. Nasir, and Franz Kogelmann. *Comparative Perspectives on the Shari'ah in Nigeria*. Ibadan, Nigeria: Spectrum Books, 2005.

Oxaal, Zoe, with Sally Baden. *Gender and Empowerment: Definitions, Approaches and Implications for Policy*. Bridge Report No. 40. Sussex: Institute of Development Studies, 1997.

Parenti, Christian. "Rehabilitating Prison Labor: The Uses of Imprisoned Masculinities." In *Prison Masculinities*, eds. Don Sabo, Terry Kupers, and Willie London. Philadelphia: Temple University Press, 2001.

Parikh, Shanti. "Desire, Romance, and Regulation: Adolescent Sexuality in Uganda's Time of AIDS." Ph.D. diss., Yale University, 2001.

Parikh, Shanti. "From Auntie to Disco: The Bifurcation of Risk and Pleasure in Sex Education in Uganda." In *Sex in Development: Science, Sexuality, and Morality in Global Perspective*, eds. Vincanne Adams and Stacey L. Pigg, 125–58. Durham: Duke University Press, 2005.

Parikh, Shanti. "Sugar Daddies and Sexual Citizenship in Uganda: Rethinking 3rd Wave Feminism." *Black Renaissance/Renaissance Noir* 6, no. 1 (2004): 82–107.

Parkin, David, and David Nyamwaya, eds. *Transformations of African Marriage*. Manchester, UK and Wolfeboro, NH: Manchester University Press for the International African Institute, 1987.

Parpart, Jane L., Shirin Rai, and Kathleen A. Staudt eds. *Rethinking Empowerment: Gender and Development in a Global/local World*. New York: Routledge, 2002.

Patel, Nimisha. "Clinical Psychology: Reinforcing Inequalities or Facilitating Empowerment?" *The International Journal of Human Rights* 7, no. 1 (2003): 16–39.

Pateman, Carole. *The Disorder of Women.* Cambridge: Polity Press, 1989.

Peck. Jamie. *Workfare States.* New York: Guilford Press, 2001.

Penn, Shana. *Solidarity's Secret. The Women Who Defeated Communism in Poland.* Ann Arbor: The University of Michigan Press, 2005.

Pereira, Charmaine. "Zina and Transgressive Heterosexuality in Northern Nigeria." *Feminist Africa: Sexual Cultures* 5 (2005), 52–80.

"Peru's Family Planning Fight Forgets the Poor." *National Catholic Reporter* 31 (October 6, 1995): 11.

Petchesky, Rosalind Pollack, and Karen Judd, eds. *Negotiating Reproductive Rights: Women's Perspectives Across Countries and Cultures,* IRRAG. London: Zed Books/St. Martin's Press, l998.

Petrak, Jenny. "The Psychological Impact of Sexual Assault." In *The Trauma of Sexual Assault: Treatment, Prevention and Practice,* eds. Jenny Petrak and Barbara Hedge. Chichester, England: John Wiley & Sons, 2002.

Phillips, Anne. "Multiculturalism, Universalism and the Claims of Democracy," Paper no. 7 for UNSRID project "Gender Justice, Development and Rights." Geneva: UNSRID (2001): 4–23.

Physicians for Human Rights. *War-Related Sexual Violence in Sierra Leone. A Population-Based Assessment.* USA: PHR, 2002.

Pickering H., M. Okongo, B. Nnalusiba, K. Bwanika, and J. Whitworth. "Sexual Networks in Uganda: Casual and Commercial Sex in a Trading Town." *AIDS Care,* 9 (1997): 199–207.

Piercy, Marge. "Rape Poem." In *Violence against Women: A Critique of the Sociobiology of Rape,* eds. Suzanne R. Sunday and Ethel Tobach. New York: Gordian Press, 1985.

Pikiran Rakyat (*People's Thoughts,* newspaper). Saudi Arabia akhirnya setop visa TKI (Saudi Arabia Finally Stops Giving Visas to Indonesian Workers). http://www.pikiran-rakyat.com/cetak/0403/16/0107.htm (accessed November 10, 2003).

Pirouet, M. Louise. "Human Rights Issues in Museveni's Uganda." In *Changing Uganda: The Dilemmas of Structural Adjustment & Revolutionary Change,* eds. Holder Bernt Hansen and Michael Twaddle, 197–209. London: James Currey, 1991.

Pitman, Roger K. "Overview of Biological Themes in PTSD." *Annals of the New York Academy of Sciences* 821, no. 1 (1997): 1–9.

Polanyi, Karl. *The Great Transformation.* Boston: Beacon Press, 1957.

Pollard, Michael S., and Zheng Wu. "Divergence of Marriage Patterns in Quebec and Elsewhere in Canada." *Population & Development Review* 24 (1998): 329–56.

"Política Social: Situación y Perspectiva a Agosto 1997," Documento de Trabajo. Internal report of the Comisión Interministerial de Asuntos Sociales. (August 21, 1997).

Pratt, Geraldine. "From Registered Nurse to Registered Nanny: Discursive Geographies of Filipina Domestic Workers in Vancouver, BC." *Economic Geography* 75, no. 3 (1999): 215–36.

Presser, Harriet B., and Gita Sen. eds. *Women's Empowerment and Demographic Processes: Moving Beyond Cairo.* New York: Oxford University Press, 2000.

Programme of Action of the International Conference on Population and Development. Chapter VII, "Reproductive Rights and Reproductive Health." Cairo, 1994. http://www.unfpa.org/icpd/icpd_poa.htm#ch7 (last accessed November 4, 2003).

Pujiastuti, Tri Nuke. "The Experience of Overseas Workers from Indonesia." Unpublished MA thesis, Department of Geographical and Environmental Studies, University of Adelaide, Australia, 2000.

Radcliffe-Brown, Alfred Reginald, and Daryll Forde, eds. *African Systems of Kinship and Marriage.* London: Oxford University Press, 1951.

Rafter, Nicole Hahn. *Partial Justice: Women, Prisons, and Social Control.* New Brunswick: Transaction Books, 1990.

Rai, Shirin M. *Gender and Political Economy of Development.* Cambridge: Polity Press, 2002.

Rai, Shirin. "Women and the State in the Third World." In *Women and Politics in the Third World,* ed. Haleh Afshar, 25–39. London and New York: Routledge, 1996.

Ramirez-Valles, Jesus, Marc A. Zimmerman, and Michael D. Newcomb. "Sexual Risk Behavior among Youth: Modeling the Influence of Prosocial Activities and Socioeconomic Factors." *Journal of Health and Social Behavior* 39, no. 3 (1998): 237–53.

"Rape." *Wikipedia: The Free Encyclopedia.* http://en.wikipedia.org/wiki/Rape (accessed January 8, 2007).

Ratele, Kopano. "Contradictions in Constructions of Masculinity." *News from the Nordic Africa Institute,* 2002.

Rattray, Robert S. *Religious Art in Ashanti.* Oxford: Clarendon Press, 1927.

Reddock, Rhoda. "Conceptualizing Difference in Caribbean Feminist Thought." In *New Caribbean Thought,* eds. Brian Meeks and Folke Lindhal. Kingston, Jamaica: The UWI Press, 2001.

Reddock, Rhoda. "Women and Slavery in the Caribbean: A Feminist Perspective." *Latin American Perspectives* 12, no. 1 (1985): 63–80.

Reddock, Rhoda, Roanna Gopaul, Paula Morgan, and Elsa Leo-Rhynie. *Women and Family in the Caribbean: Historical and Contemporary Considerations.* Georgetown: CARICOM Secretariat, 1999.

"Referendum 2003," "Referendum ogólnokrajowe w sprawie wyrazenia zgody na ratyfikacje Traktatu dotyczacego przystapienia Rzeczypospolitej Polskiej do Unii Europejskiej," Panstwowa Komisja Wyborcza. http://referendum.pkw.gov.pl/sww/kraj/indexA.html (access: 16 June 2006).

Reissman, Catherine Kohler. "Doing Justice: Positioning the Interpreter in Narrative Work." In *Strategic Narrative: New Perspectives on the Power of Personal and Cultural Stories,* ed. Wendy Patterson. Lanham: Lexington Books, 2002.

Republic of Trinidad and Tobago. *Cohabitational Relationships Act, No. 30 of 1998.* Government Printer, Port of Spain, 1998.

Republic of Trinidad and Tobago. *The Hindu Marriage Act No. 13 of 1945.* Government Printer, Port of Spain, 1945.

Republic of Trinidad and Tobago. *The Muslim Marriage and Divorce Act, No. 7 of 1961.* Government Printer, Port of Spain, 1961.

Republic of Trinidad and Tobago. *Marriage Act, No. 32 of 1996.* Government Printer, Port of Spain, 1996.

Republic of Trinidad and Tobago Central Statistical Office. *Population and Housing Census (2002).* http://cso.gov.tt/census2000 (Accessed 24 February 2006).

Republic of Trinidad and Tobago, Ministry of the Attorney General. *Second Periodic Report of the Republic of Trinidad and Tobago: Convention on the Rights of the Child.* Human Rights Unit, Port of Spain, June 2003.

Republic of Trinidad and Tobago. *The Orisa Marriage Act, No. 22 of 1999.* Government Printer, Port of Spain, 1999.

Ress, Mary Judith. *Without a Vision, the People Perish: Reflections on Latin American Ecofeminist Theology.* Santiago, Chile: The Con-spirando Collective, 2003.

Rhodes, Lorna. *Total Confinement: Madness and Reason in the Maximum Security Prison.* Berkeley: University of California Press, 2004.

Robertson, John A. "Protecting Embryos and Burdening Women: Assisted Reproduction in Italy." *Human Reproduction* 19 (2004): 1693–6.

Robertson, Stephen. "Age of Consent Law and the Making of Modern Childhood in New York City, 1886–1921." *Journal of Social History* 35, no. 4 (2002): 781–98.

Robinson, Kathryn. "Gender, Islam, and Nationality: Indonesian Domestic Servants in the Middle East." In *Home and Hegemony: Domestic Service and Identity Politics in South and Southeast Asia,* eds. Kathleen M. Adams and Sara Dickey, 249–82. Ann Arbor, MI: University of Michigan Press, 2000.

Robinson, Kathryn. "Housemaids: The Effects of Gender and Culture in the Internal and International Migration of Indonesian Women." In *Intersexions: Gender, Class, Culture, Ethnicity,* eds. Gillian Bottomley, Marie M. De Lepervanche, and Jeannie Martin, 33–51. Sydney: Allen and Unwin, 1991.

Rosado Nunes, Maria José F. "Women's Voices in Latin American Theology." In *The Power of Naming: A Concilium Reader in Feminist Liberation Theology,* ed. Elisabeth Schussler Fiorenza. Maryknoll, NY: Orbis Books, 1996.

Rose, Deborah S. "'Worse than Death:' Psychodynamics of Rape Victims and the Need for Psychotherapy." *American Journal of Psychiatry* 143, no. 7 (1986): 817–24.

Rose, Nikolas. *Inventing Ourselves: Psychology, Power, and Personhood.* Cambridge: Cambridge University Press, 1998.

Rose, Nikolas. *Powers of Freedom.* New York: Cambridge, 1999.

Ross, Fiona Ross. *Bearing Witness: Women and the Truth and Reconciliation Commission in South Africa.* London: Anthropology, Culture and Society, 2003.

Rothschild, Babette. *The Body Remembers: The Psychophysiology of Trauma and Trauma Treatment.* New York and London: W.W. Norton, 2000.

Rothschild, Babette. *The Mind and Body of Trauma: Understanding Traumatic Memory & PTSD.* One-day professional workshop, presented by Doctors for Sexual Abuse Care. Auckland, New Zealand, 2004.

Rowlands, Jo. "Empowerment Examined." *Development in Practice 5,* no. 2 (1995): 101–7.

Rowlands, Jo. *Questioning Empowerment: Working with Women in Honduras.* Oxford: Oxfam, 1997.

SAATHI and the Asia Foundation. *A Situation Analysis of Violence Against Women and Girls in Nepal.* Kathmandu, Nepal, 1997.

Saharso, Sawitri. "Headscarves: A Comparison of Public Thought and Public Policy in Germany and the Netherlands." CRISPP paper, January 2005. http://www.essex.ac.uk/ECpR/events/generalconference/budapest/papers/4/8/saharso.pdf (Accessed 13 July 2007).

SAHAVAGI. *Gender Equality and Empowerment of Women: An Update.* Submitted to UNFPA, Kathmandu, Nepal, forthcoming July 2007.

Salaff, Janet W. *Working Daughters of Hong Kong.* Cambridge: Cambridge University Press, 1981.

Saldeen, Pia, and Per Sundström. "Would Legislation Imposing a Single Embryo Transfer be a Feasible Way to Reduce the Rate of Multiple Pregnancies after IVF? *Human Reproduction* 20 (2005): 4–8.

SAMANTA. *A Study on Linkages between Domestic Violence and Pregnancy.* Kathmandu, Nepal, 2005.

Sanatorium Helios. http://www.sanatoriumhelios.cz/index_italian.html (Accessed July 8, 2006).

Sandel, Michael J. *Democracy's Discontents.* Cambridge, MA: Harvard University Press, 1996.

Sangari, Kumkum. "Politics of Diversity: Religious Communities and Multiple Patriarchies." *Economic and Political Weekly* XXX, no. 51 (December 23, 1995): 3287–3310 and no. 52 (December 30, 1995): 3381- 9.

Santillan, Diana, Sidney Ruth Schuler, Hoang Tu Anh, Tran Hung Minh, Quach Thu Trang, and Nguyen Minh Duc. "Developing Indicators to Assess Women's Empowerment in Vietnam." *Development in Practice* 14, no. 4 (June 2004): 534–49.

Sanusi, Lamido. "Fundamentalist Groups and the Nigerian Legal System: Some Reflections." *Warning Signs of Fundamentalism*, Women Living Under Muslim Laws (WLUML). (London: Dec 2004), 79–82.

Sarkar, Tanika, and Urvashi Butalia, eds. *Women and Right-Wing Movements: Indian Experiences*. London: Zed Books, 1996.

Sassen, Saskia. *Globalization and Its Discontents*. New York: The New Press, 1998.

Schapera, Isaac. Married Life in an African Tribe. London: Faber and Faber, 1940.

Schoepf, Brooke G. "Women at Risk: Case Studies from Zaire." In *The Time of AIDS: Social Analysis, Theory and Method,* eds. Gilbert Herdt and Shirley Lindenbaum, 259–86. Newbury Park, CA: Sage Publications, 1992.

Schuler, Sidney Ruth, Syed M. Hashemi. "Credit Programs, Women's Empowerment, and Contraceptive Use in Rural Bangladesh." *Studies in Family Planning* 25, no. 2 (1994): 65–76.

Schuler, Sidney Ruth, Syed M. Hashemi, A.P. Riley, and A. Akhter. "Credit Programs, Patriarchy and Men's Violence against Women in Rural Bangladesh." *Social Science and Medicine* 43, no. 12 (1996): 1729–42.

Schüssler Fiorenza, Elisabeth. *Wisdom Ways: Introducing Feminist Biblical Interpretation*. Maryknoll, NY: Orbis Books, 2001.

Scott, James C. *Weapons of the Weak: Everyday Forms of Peasant Resistance*. New Haven, CT and London: Yale University Press, 1985.

Scott, Joan Wallach, "French Universalism in Crisis." Public lecture. New School University, Dean's Forum, November 11, 2004.

Scott, Joan Wallach. "Gender: A Useful Category of Analysis." In *Feminism and History*, ed. Joan Wallach Scott. Oxford: Oxford University Press, 1996.

Seager, Joni. "The Short Curious Half-Life of 'Official Concern' About Women's Rights." *Environment & Planning A* 34, no. 1 (2003): 1–4.

Sen, Gita, and Caren Grown. *Development, Crises, and Alternative Visions: Third World Women's Perspectives*. New York: Monthly Review Press, 1987.

Sen, Krishna. "Indonesian Women at Work: Reframing the Subject." In *Gender and Power in Affluent Asia,* eds. Krishna Sen and Maila Stivens, 35–62. New York: Routledge, 1998.

Setel, Philip. *Plague of Paradoxes: AIDS, Culture, and Demography in Northern Tanzania*. Chicago: University of Chicago Press, 1999.

Sexuality Health Group Final NCS Plenary Presentation. "Using Feminist Critiques of Human Rights and Sexual Autonomy to Assess and Inform HIV/AIDS Interventions," New York, April 2005.

Shadid, W.A., E.J.A.M. Spaan, and J.D. Speckmann. "Labour Migration and the Policy of the Gulf States." In *Labour Migration to the Middle East: From Sri Lanka to the Gulf,* eds. F. Eelans, T. Schampers, & J. D. Speckman, 63–86. London and New York: Kegan Paul, 1992.

Shaheed, Farida. "Networking for Change: The Role of Women's Groups in Initiating Dialogue on Women's Issues." In *Faith and Freedom,* ed. Mahnaz Afkhami. Syracuse: Syracuse University Press, 1995.

Shaheed, Farida, and Aisha Shaheed. "Nana Asma 'u (1795–1865)." In *Great Ancestors: Women Asserting their Rights in Muslim Contexts,* ed. Farida Shaheed with Aisha Shaheed. Lahore, Pakistan: Shirgat Gah, 2004.

Shell-Duncan, Bettina, and Ylva Hernlund. "Female 'Circumcision' in Africa: Dimensions of the Practice and Debates" In *Female "Circumcision" in Africa: Culture, Controversy, and Change,* eds. Bettina Shell-Duncan and Ylva Hernlund, 1–40. Boulder, CO: Lynne Reinner Publishers, 2000.

Shevell, Tracy, Fergal D. Malone, John Vidaver, T. Flint Porter, David A. Luthy, Christine H. Comstock, Gary D. Hankins, Keith Eddleman, Siobhan Dolan, Lorraine Dugoff, Sabrina Craigo, Ilan E. Timor, Stephen R. Carr, Honor M. Wolfe, Diana W. Bianchi, Mary E. D'Alton, for the FASTER Research Consortium.

"Assisted Reproductive Technology and Pregnancy Outcome." *Obstetrics & Gynecology* 106 (2005): 1039–45.

Sikand, Yoginder. Interview with Asmau Joda on Islam and Women's Rights. http://www.islaminterfaith.org (accessed December 15, 2006).

Silvey, Rachel. "Managing Migration: Reproducing Gendered Insecurity at the Indonesian Border." In *Social Reproduction and Global Transformations: From the Everyday to the Global*, eds. Isabella Bakker and Rachel Silvey. NY: Routledge, forthcoming.

Smith, Gregory L., George P. Taylor, and Kevin F. Smith. "Comparative Risks and Costs of Male and Female Sterilization." *American Journal of Public Health* 75 (1995): 370–4.

Smith, R.T., and Chandra Jayawardena. "Marriage and Family amongst East Indians in British Guiana." *Social and Economic Studies* 8 (1959): 321–76.

Smyth, Ines. "Gender Analysis of Family Planning: Beyond the 'Feminist vs. Population Control' Debate." In *Feminist Visions of Development: Gender Analysis and Policy*, eds. Cecile Jackson and Ruth Pearson, 217–38. London: Routledge, 1998.

Sorrentino, Constance. "The Changing Family in International Perspective." *Monthly Labor Review* 113 (1990): 41–58.

Spaan, Ernst. *Labour Circulation and Socioeconomic Transformation: The Case of East Java, Indonesia.* Groningen: Rijksuniversiteit Groningen, 1999.

"Spada sprzedaż tygodników opinii." *Press*, May 11, 2006. http://www.press.pl/newsy/pokaz.php?id=5943 (access: 15 June 2006).

Special Rapporteur on Women, Report 57. In *High Commissioner of Human Rights, "Rights of Women."* Bogotá: December 2002, par. 21.

Stacey, Judith. *Patriarchy and Socialist Revolution in China.* Berkeley, CA: University of California Press, 1983.

Staeheli, Lynn A., Eleonore Kofman, and Linda J. Peake, eds. "Introduction." In *Mapping Women, Making Politics: Feminist Perspectives on Political Geography.* New York: Routledge, 2004.

Stamp, Patricia. "Burying Otieno: The Politics of Gender and Ethnicity in Kenya." *Signs* 16, no. 4 (1991): 351–88.

Stauth, Georg. *Politics and Cultures of Islamization in Southeast Asia: Indonesia and Malaysia in the Nineteen-nineties.* New Brunswick and London: Transaction Publishers, 2002.

Stetson, Dorothy McBride, and Amy Mazur, eds. *Comparative State Feminism.* Thousand Oaks, CA: Sage Publications, 1995.

Stoeltje, Beverly J. "Introduction to Women, Language, and Law in Africa II: Gender and Relations of Power." *Africa Today* 49, no. 2 (2002): vii-xiv.

Stree Shakti Sanghatana. *"We Are Making History . . ." Life Stories of Women in the Telengana People's Struggle.* New Delhi: Kali for Women, 1989.

Stromquist, Nelly P. "The Theoretical and Practical Bases for Empowerment." *Women, Education and Empowerment: Pathways Towards Autonomy*, ed. Carolyn Medel-Anonuevo. Report of the International Seminar held at UIE. Hamburg, Germany, and Paris: UNESCO, 1995.

Submission by the Coalition for Women's Human Rights in Conflict Situations to the Truth and Reconciliation. http://www.womensrightscoalition.org/site/advocacyDossiers/sierraLeoneTR/submissiontotr.php (accessed November 24, 2006).

Summerfield, Derek. "The Invention of Post-Traumatic Stress Disorder and the Social Usefulness of a Psychiatric Category." *British Medical Journal* 322 (2001): 95–8.

Sunindyo, Saraswati. "Murder, Gender, and the Media: Sexualizing Politics and Violence." In *Fantasizing the Feminine in Indonesia*, ed. Laurie J. Sears, 120–39. Durham and London: Duke University Press, 1996.

Sutherland, Sandra, and Donald Scherl. "Patterns of Response among Victims of Rape." *American Journal of Orthopsychiatry* 40, no. 3 (1970): 503–11.

Suttner, Raymond. "Masculinities in the ANC-led Liberation Movement." Paper presented at the conference "From Boys to Men," University of the Western Cape, Cape Town, South Africa, January 26–28, 2005.

Sutton, John. "Imprisonment and Social Classification in Five Common-Law Democracies." *American Journal of Sociology* 106 (2000): 350–386.

Sutton, John. "Imprisonment in Affluent Western Democracies." *American Sociological Review* 69, no. 2 (2004): 170–89.

Government of Sweden, Act on In Vitro Fertilization—Lang (1988:711) om befruktning utan för kroppen.

Swimme, Brian, and Thomas Berry. *The Universe Story: From the Primordial Flaring Forth to the Ecozoic Era—A Celebration of the Unfolding of the Cosmos.* San Francisco: Harper Collins, 1992.

Tagaroa, Rusdi, and Encop Sofia. *Buruh migran Indonesia: Mencari keadilan* (Indonesian Migrant Workers: Searching for Justice). Bekasi: Lembaga advokasi buruh migran—sololidaritas perempuan (Migrant Workers Advocacy Institute—Women's Solidarity), 2002.

Tamale, Sylvia. "How Old is Old Enough? Defilement Law and the Age of Consent in Uganda." *East African Journal of Peace & Human Rights* 7, no. 1 (2001): 82–101.

Tamale, Sylvia. *When Hens Begin to Crow: Gender and Parliamentary Politics in Uganda.* Boulder, CO: Westview Press, 1999.

Tamez, Elsa. "Hermenéutica Feminista de la Liberación: Una Mirada Retrospectiva," *Cristianismo y Sociedad* No.135–136. Guayaquil, Ecuador, 1998.

Tan, Shen. "At the Pearl River Delta: The Relations of Women Migrants to Foreign Invested Enterprises and Local Government." Paper presented at the Annual Meeting of the American Sociological Association in San Francisco, 1998a.

Tan, Shen. "Gender Differences in the Migration of Rural Labor." *Sociological Studies* 1 (1998b): 70–76.

Tanka Prasad Acharya Memorial Foundation. *Analysis of Caste, Ethnicity and Gender Data from 2001 Population Census in Preparation for Poverty Mapping and Wider PRSP Monitoring.* Report submitted to DFID, Kathmandu, Nepal in 2005. Unpublished.

Thomas, Lynn "*Ngaitana* (I Will Circumcise Myself):" Lessons from Colonial Campaigns to Ban Excision in Meru, Kenya." In *Female "Circumcision" in Africa: Culture, Controversy, and Change,* eds. Bettina Shell-Duncan and Ylva Hernlund, 129–50. Boulder, CO: Lynne Reinner Publishers, 2000.

Tikasingh, Gerard. "Toward the Formulation of the Indian View of History: The Representation of Indian Opinion in Trinidad 1900-1921." In *East Indians in the Caribbean: Colonialism and the Struggle for Identity,* eds. Bridget Brereton and Winston Dookeran. New York: Kraus International, 1982.

Tirtosudarmo, Riwanto. *Indonesian Domestic Workers in Saudi Arabia.* Mimeograph, Leiden, the Netherlands: International Institute of Asian Studies, 2000.

Tóth, Herta, Violetta Zentai, and Andrea Krizsán. *Hungary Country Report: Women, Integration, and Prison.* Final report prepared for the EU Project "Women, Integration, and Prison" (MIP), 2005.

"Tribunal Dismisses Case of Muslim Woman Ordered Not to Teach in Veil," *Guardian* (October 20, 2006). http://www.guardian.co.uk/.

Trinidad and Tobago Coalition on the Rights of the Child. NGO Comments on Trinidad and Tobago Second Periodic Report under the Convention on the Rights of the Child, April 2005.

Tripp, Aili Mari. *Women & Politics in Uganda.* Madison, WI: University of Wisconsin Press, 2000.

Truth and Reconciliation Commission, Women's Hearing, July 29, 1997. Participation of Dr. Sheila Meintjies. http://www.doj.gov.za/trc/special/women/meintjie.htm (accessed September 12, 2006).

Turone, Fabio. "New Law Forces Italian Couple with Genetic Disease to Implant all their IVF Embryos." *British Medical Journal* 328 (2004): 1334.

Umar, Muhammad Sane. "Mass Islamic Education and Emergence of Female 'Ulema' in Northern Nigeria: Background, Trends, and Consequences." In *The Transmission of Learning in Islamic Africa,* ed. Scott S. Reese. Leiden: Brill, 2004.

Umar, Sa'idiyya. "Nana Asma'u the Great Scholar." *The Muslim Woman* 9 (2005), 8–17.

Umińska, Bożena. *Postać z cieniem. Portrety Żydówek w polskiej literaturze.* Warszawa: Sic!, 2001.

UNAIDS. *2006 Report on the Global AIDS Epidemic: Executive Summary.* A UNAIDS 10th Anniversary Special Edition. Geneva, Switzerland: Joint United Nations Programme on HIV/AIDS, 2006.

UNDP. *Human Development Report.* New York: United Nations, 2005.

UNIFEM/NIDS. *Nepali Women and Foreign Labour Migration.* Kathmandu, Nepal: UNIFEM/Nepal Institute of Development Studies, 2006.

United Nations. *Abortion Policies: A Global Review.* New York: Population Division of the United Nations Secretariat, 2002.

United Nations. *Beijing Declaration and Platform for Action.* Fourth World Conference on Women, 1995.

United Nations. *World Population Prospects: The 2004 Revision and World Urbanization Prospects: The 2003 Revision.* New York: Population Division of the Department of Economic and Social Affairs of the United Nations Secretariat, 2004.

United Nations CEDAW. "Committee On the Elimination of Discrimination against Women Concludes Consideration of Trinidad and Tobago Report." UN Press Release WOM/1316, 2002b.

United Nations CEDAW. "Experts Welcome Positive Aspects of Trinidad and Tobago's Anti-Discimination Measures but Stress Gender-based Constraints." UN Press Release WOM/1310, 2002a.

United Nations Population Fund (UNFPA). *State of World Population 2006: A Passage to Hope, Women and International Migration.* New York: UNFPA, 2006.

Utterwulghe, Steve. "Rwanda's Protracted Social Conflict: Considering the Subjective Perspective in Conflict Resolution Strategies." *Online Journal of Peace and Conflict Resolution,* Issue 2.3 (August 1999). http://www.trinstitute.org/ojpcr/p2_3utter.htm (accessed 4 September 2005).

Vahdati, Soheila. "Stop Stonings in Iran, But Don't Confuse the Issue." *Women's eNews* (January 4, 2007).

Venn, A., L. Watson, J. Lumley, G. Giles, C. King, and D. Healy. "Breast and Ovarian Cancer Incidence after Infertility and In Vitro Fertilisation." *Lancet* 346 (1995): 995–1000.

Vertovec, Steven, and Ceri Peach, eds. *Islam in Europe. The Politics of Religion and Community.* London: Macmillan Press, 1997.

Vigarello, Georges. *A History of Rape: Sexual Violence in France from the 16th to the 20th Century.* Cambridge, UK: Polity, 2001.

Wacquant, Loic. "The Curious Eclipse of Prison Ethnography in the Age of Mass Incarceration." *Ethnography* 3, no. 4 (2002): 371–97.

Wacquant, Loic. "Deadly Symbiosis: When Ghetto and Prison Meet and Mesh." In *Mass Imprisonment: Social Causes and Consequences,* ed. David Garland. London: SAGE Publications, 2001.

Wacquant, Loic. "How Penal Common Sense Comes to Europeans: Notes on the Transatlantic Diffusion of Neoliberal Doxa." *European Societies* 1–3 (1999): 319–52.

Wadud, Amina. *Qur'an and Woman: Rereading the Sacred Text from a Woman's Perspective.* New York: Oxford University Press, 1999.

Walby, Sylvia. "Is Citizenship Gendered?" *Sociology–the Journal of the British Sociological Association* 28, no. 2 (1994): 279–95.

Warner-Lewis, Maureen. *Guinea's Other Suns: The African Dynamic in Trinidad Culture.* Dover, MA: The Majority Press, 1991.

Washburn, Wilcomb E. "Cultural Relativism, Human Rights, and the AAA." *American Anthropologist* 89, no. 4 (1987): 939–43.

Watson, Peggy. "(Anti)feminism after Communism." In *Who's Afraid of Feminism? Seeing through the Backlash,* eds. Ann Oakley and Juliet Mitchell, 144–61. New York: The New Press, 1997.

Waylen, Georgina. "Women and Democratization: Conceptualizing Gender Relations in Transition Politics." *World Politics* 46, no. 3 (April 1994): 327–54.

Weber, Heloise. "The Imposition of a Global Development Architecture: The Example of Micro-credit." *Review of International Studies* 28 (2002): 537–55.

Weiner, Elaine. "No (Wo)Man's Land: The Post-Socialist Purgatory of Czech Female Factory Workers." *Social Problems* 52, no. 4 (2005): 572–92.

Weis, Kurt, and Sandra S. Borges. "Victimology and Rape: The Case of the Legitimate Victim." *Issues in Criminology* 8, no. 2 (1973): 71–115.

Weiss, Anita. "Implications of the Islamization Program for Women." In *Islamic Reassertion in Pakistan: The Application of Islamic Laws in a Modern State,* ed. Anita Weiss. Syracuse: Syracuse University Press, 1986.

Weiss, Anita. "Women's Action Forum." In *The Oxford Encyclopedia of the Modern Islamic World,* vol. 4. New York and Oxford: Oxford University Press, 1995.

Wichterich, Christa. *The Globalized Woman.* London/New York: Zed Books, 2002.

Wiehe, Vernon R, and Ann L Richards. *Intimate Betrayal: Understanding and Responding to the Trauma of Acquaintance Rape.* Thousand Oaks, CA: Sage Publications, 1995.

Williams, Brackette. *Stains on My Name: War in my Veins: Guyana and the Politics of Cultural Struggle.* Durham, NC: Duke University Press, 1991.

Willis, Katie, and Brenda Yeoh, eds. *Gender and Migration.* Cheltenham, UK and Northampton, MA: Edward Elgar Publishing Limited, 2000.

Winter, Bronwyn. "Secularism Aboard the Titanic: Feminists and the Debate Over the Hijab in France" *Feminist Studies* 32 (2006): 279–98.

WLUML. *Knowing Our Rights: Women, Family, Laws and Customs in the Muslim World.* New Delhi: Zubaan, 2003.

World Bank. *Gender, Justice and Truth Commissions.* Washington DC: World Bank, 2006.

World Bank. *Poverty Trends in Nepal between 1995–96 and 2003–04: Background Paper for Nepal Poverty Assessment.* Presented May 12, 2005. Kathmandu, Nepal: World Bank. Unpublished.

Yehuda, Rachel, and Alexander C. McFarlane. "Conflict between Current Knowledge about Posttraumatic Stress Disorder and its Original Conceptual Basis." *American Journal of Psychiatry* 152, no. 12 (1995): 1705–13.

Yuval-Davis, Nira. *Gender and Nation.* London: Sage Publications, 1998.

Yuval-Davis, Nira. "Women, Citizenship and Difference." *Feminist Review* 57 (1997): 4–28.

Yuval-Davis, Nira, and Pnina Werbner, eds. *Women, Citizenship and Difference.* London: Zed Books, 1997.

Zegers-Hochschild, Fernando. "The Latin American Registry of Assisted Reproduction." In *Current Practices and Controversies in Assisted Reproduction,* eds. Effy Vayena, Patrick J. Rowe, and P. David Griffin. Geneva, Switzerland: World Health Organization, 2004.

# Contributors

**Carolyn M. Elliott** is Professor Emerita of Political Science at the University of Vermont. She was the founding director of the Center for Research on Women at Wellesley College and organized the first academic conference on Women and Development, which yielded "Women and National Development," a special issue of *Signs*. She also served as the President of the Association for Women's Rights in Development, an international professional association. Her publications on women include "Theories of Development: An Assessment," *Women and Education in the Third World: Comparative Perspectives,* and "Women's Family Histories."

**Meena Acharya** is an economist, feminist scholar, researcher, and writer in Nepali and English. Currently she is the general secretary of Tanka Prasad Acharya Memorial Foundation. She is well known for highlighting issues of poverty, development policy, and gender concerns in Nepalese society. Internationally, she has made pioneering contributions in the development of a methodology for the measurement of women's work and contributions to GDP. Her most recent publications include "Engendering the Budgetary System in Nepal," "Structural Adjustment and Poverty Eradication in Nepal," and "Labor Market Development and Poverty." She has also worked in the World Bank and provided consulting services to several United Nations organizations, including DESA/UN, UNDP, and UNIFEM.

**Akosua Adomako Ampofo** is Associate Professor of African Studies and Head of the Centre for Gender Studies and Advocacy at the University of Ghana. Her scholarship focuses on population and health issues in development, constructions of masculinity and femininity, gender-based violence, and race and gender in Africa. She is a member of AAWORD (the Association of African Women for Research and Development); Netright (the Network for Women's Rights, Ghana); The Domestic Violence Bill Coalition, and The Women's Caucus of the African Studies Association, of which she was co-convenor between 2004 and 2006. Her recent publications include "When Men Speak Women Listen: Gender Socialisation and Young Adolescents' Attitudes toward Sexual and Reproductive Issues," and "Does

Women's Education Matter? A Case Study of Reproductive Decision-Making in Ghana."

**Kawango E. Agot** is Coordinator of the UNIM Project, a study investigating the association between male circumcision and HIV infection among young men. She is also the Director of Impact-RDO, a local NGO working to improve the reproductive and sexual health of vulnerable populations in Kenya. Having earned a Ph.D. in Medical Geography and an M.P.H. in Epidemiology, her major research interest is in the cultural and behavioral risk factors for HIV infection and transmission, particularly in women. Her recent publications include "Male Circumcision in Siaya and Bondo Districts, Kenya: A Prospective Cohort Study to Assess Behavioral Disinhibition Following Circumcision," and "HIV/AIDS Interventions and the Politics of the African Woman's Body."

**Margot Badran**, a historian of the Middle East and Islamic Societies and specialist in gender studies, is Senior Fellow at the Prince Alwaleed ibn Talal Center for Muslim Christian Understanding, Georgetown University. She is the author of *Feminism Beyond East and West: New Gender Talk and Practice in Global Islam, Feminists, Islam and Nation: Gender and the Making of Modern Egypt* and co-editor of *Opening the Gates: An Anthology of Arab Feminist Writing*. She has two books forthcoming in 2007, *Islam and Feminism: Secular and Religious Convergences* and *Gender and Islam in Africa* (of which she is editor).

**John Boateng** received his Ph.D. in Agricultural and Extension Education from Pennsylvania State University and is currently a post-doctoral scholar in Cooperative Extension at the College of Agricultural Sciences, Pennsylvania State University. His research interests include extension marketing, impacts of urbanization on women's health, adolescence social responsibility, and integration of health and agricultural interventions.

**Wendy Chavkin** is Professor of Public Health and Obstetrics-Gynecology at Columbia University. She has written extensively on women's reproductive health issues and is editor and contributing author for *Double Exposure* and *Where Human Rights Begin*. She has served as Editor-in-Chief of the Journal of the American Medical Women's Association and Director of the Bureau for Maternity Services and Family Planning in New York City. She was Director of the Soros Reproductive Health and Rights Fellowship and is currently the Columbia University advisor for the Ibis Fellowship in Abortion and Reproductive Health, and chair of Physicians for Reproductive Choice and Health.

**Esther Ngan-ling Chow** is Professor of Sociology at the American University in Washington. Her interests are the interactions of class, gender and sexuality, citizenship, migration, globalization, and activism for social change and global justice. She is engaged in a major study to examine the impact of economic development on migration, work, family, and rural development in China. Her recent publications include *Transforming Gender and Development in East Asia*, "Gender, Globalization and Social Change in the 21st Century," and "Gendered Migration, Politics of Space and Citizenship: The Case of Women Migrant Workers in South China."

**Christina Ewig** is Assistant Professor of Women's Studies at the University of Wisconsin-Madison. A political scientist, she researches gender and social policy in Latin America, both historically and under neoliberalism. Her current research is a cross-national study of health sector reforms in Peru, Chile, Mexico, and Colombia. She is the author of "Piecemeal but Innovative: Health Sector Reform in Peru" and "Global Processes, Local Consequences: Gender Equity and Health Sector Reform in Peru."

**Nicola Gavey** is Associate Professor of Psychology at the University of Auckland, New Zealand. Trained as a clinical psychologist, she is interested in critically examining the cultural support for rape and heterosexual coercion in Western society. She has researched other issues relating to women's health and well being, including an analysis of the social implications of Viagra. Her recent book, *Just Sex? The Cultural Scaffolding of Rape* won the Association for Women in Psychology's Distinguished Publication Award.

**Agnieszka Graff** is Assistant Professor of American Studies at the University of Warsaw. She is researching the rhetorical strategies of modern American feminism as viewed from the East European perspective. A scholar and activist in Poland, she has published extensively on gender in Polish public life in both scholarly and political journals, and the mainstream press. Her recent publications in English include "Lost between the Waves? The Paradoxes of Feminist Chronology and Activism in Contemporary Poland" and "We Are (Not All) Homophobes: A Report from Poland."

**Lynne Haney** is Associate Professor of Sociology at New York University. She has published ethnographic research on gender and the welfare state in both the U.S. and Hungary. She is writing a book examining the gendered meanings of incarceration and the linkages between state systems of welfare and punishment in these countries. Her book *Inventing the Needy* won the American Sociological Association's 2003 Distinguished Book Award in Sex and Gender and the 2004 Award for Best Book in Political Sociology.

**Lakshmi Lingam** is Professor and Chair of the Centre for Women's Studies at the Tata Institute of Social Sciences in Mumbai, India. She has conducted research on women-headed households, sex-selective abortions, reproductive rights, women's health, migration, and structural adjustment policies and gender. She has contributed to gender and equity mainstreaming activities in the governments of the Indian states and to gender and equity issues in participatory action in Afghanistan. Among her publications are "Understanding Women's Health: A Reader," "Taking Stock: Women's Movement and the State," and "Gender, Households and Poverty: Tracking Mediations of Macro Adjustment Programmes."

**Titia Loenen** is Professor of Law and Gender at Utrecht University, Netherlands. Her research covers human rights, equality theory, international, European and comparative non-discrimination law, and family law. Her major interests are gender and multicultural issues. Among her publications are "Rethinking Sex Equality as a Human Right" and "Human Rights and Substantive or Inclusionary Equality."

**Monica Maher** is Visiting Assistant Professor of Social Ethics at Union Theological Seminary in New York City. Her research interests intersect the fields of social ethics and ecumenical studies in focusing on interreligious perspectives of women's moral agency in response to gender-based violence. She has recently published "Daring to Dream: Faith and Feminicide in Latin America" for a volume on religion and violence.

**Julissa Mantilla Falcon** is Professor of Law and Gender at the Catholic University of Peru. Her main interests are international human rights law, gender issues, and the human rights of women. She has done a comparative study of cases of sexual violence against women, focusing on those involving armed conflict. She has worked for the Peruvian Ombudsman Office for Human Rights investigating violations of reproductive rights in Peru, especially cases of forced sterilization, and was part of the legal team of the Peruvian Truth and Reconciliation Commission. Among her publications is "Sexual Violence against Women: The Findings of the Peruvian Truth and Reconciliation Commission."

**Shanti Parikh** is Assistant Professor of Anthropology at Washington University in St. Louis, Missouri. Her research focuses on the intersections of sex, gender, and power, and the political economy of sexuality. She has consulted on numerous sexual health and HIV projects. She has published material on youth sexuality, marital HIV risk, romance, and sex education in Uganda, and is completing her book *Regulating Romance: Youth, Sexuality, Power, and Globalization in Uganda's Time of AIDS*.

**Rhoda Reddock** is Professor and Head of the Centre for Gender and Development Studies at the University of the West Indies—St. Augustine campus. She is an activist in the Caribbean women's movement and founding member and first chair of the Caribbean Association for Feminist Research and

Action (CAFRA). A former chair of the Research Committee on Gender of the International Sociological Association, her publications include *Women, Labour and Politics in Trinidad and Tobago: A History,* which was named a CHOICE Outstanding Academic Book for 1995, *Plantation Women: International Experiences* (co-edited with Shobita Jain) Berg, Oxford, 1998 and the edited collection *Interrogating Caribbean Masculinities,* The UWI Press, Kingston, 2004.

**Rachel Silvey** is Associate Professor of Geography at the University of Toronto. Her research interests include gender and feminist geography, migration studies, and transnational Islam. Her work has appeared in the *Annals of Association of American Geographers, Progress in Human Geography, Gender, Place and Culture, the International Migration Review,* and elsewhere.

# Other Scholars in the NCS Program[1]

**Rabab Abdulhadi**
Director, Center for Arab-American Studies
University of Michigan
Dearborn, Michigan

>"From Self-Determination to Self Rule (and Back to Occupation): What Prospects for Palestinian Women?"

**Bolanle Adetoun**
Head, Gender Division
Economic Community of West African States
Abuja, Nigeria

>"Fostering Women's Empowerment: Gender and the HIV/AIDS Epidemic in Nigeria"

**Mona Ibrahim Ali,**
Associate Professor of English
American University in Cairo and Cairo University
Cairo, Egypt

>"New Feminism in the Making: Recent Trends in Gender Theories: A Reader"

**Amanuel Andebrhan Asghedom**
Director, Planning and Statistics
Ministry of Energy and Mines
Asmara, Eritrea

>"The Impact of War on the Role of Women"

**Kelly Askin**
Senior Legal Officer, International Justice
Open Society, Justice Initiative
New York, New York

>"Empowering Women through International Law and Process"

**Isabella Bakker**
Professor of Political Science
York University
Toronto, Canada

"Governance, Gender and Social Reproduction in an Era of Intensified Globalization"

**Fanny Mui-ching Cheung**
Professor and Chair, Department of Psychology
The Chinese University of Hong Kong
Hong Kong, China

"Work-Family Balance for Women in Chinese and US Societies: Implications for Enhancing Women's Leadership"

**Pregaluxmi Govender**
Associate
Africa Gender Institute, University of Capetown
Capetown, South Africa

"Towards a Global Politics of Love and Courage: Lessons from a Feminist Experiment in South Africa's First Democracy"

**Hella Hoppe**
Research Associate
Federation of Swiss Protestant Churches
Berne, Switzerland

"Engendering Globalization: Interlinking WTO/GATS and Financing for Development"

**Vesna Kesic**
Media Advisor
Office of the Ombudsperson for Gender Equality of Croatia
Zagreb, Croatia

"Gender Dimension of Transition, Conflict and Reconciliation: Women Recollecting and Reconstructing Memories"

**Imiya Mudiyanselage Kamala Liyanage**
Professor, Department of Political Science
University of Perdeniya
Peradeniya, Sri Lanka

"Research Strategies for Empowering Women in Local Governance in Sri Lanka: A Comparative Study Learning From India, the United States and Sweden"

**Olga Pyshchulina**
Principal Consultant, Department of Social Relations and Civil Society
National Instititute of Strategic Studies
Kyiv, Ukraine

"Trafficking in Human Beings and Illegal Migration as a Security Problem"

**Omar Sougou**
Associate Professor, Department of English
Gaston Berger University
Saint Louis, Senegal

"Transformational Creativity: Women Writing Resistance and Change"

## NOTES

1. Scholars are listed with their affiliation at the conclusion of the program in April 2005.

# Index

trauma, and nature of rape 10, 233–46
Trinidad and Tobago, marriage acts 6, 143–60
Trinidad and Tobago Coalition on the Rights
    of the Child 157–8
Trollope, Anthony 146
truth and reconciliation commissions 5,
    215–32
Tulkens, judge 168
Turkey, headscarf issue 167, 168

## U
Uganda, young people's sexual relationships
    10, 12, 303–25
Umar, Muhammad Sane 188n10
Umar, Sa'idiyya 186
UNAIDS 288
UNFPA 338–9
UNIFEM 288
United Kingdom: headscarf issue 162, 168;
    neoliberal penal system 29
United Nations: and liberalism 5; sexual
    violence 215–17, 218–19, 223;
    work/family reconciliation 47
United Nations Cairo document on repro-
    ductive rights *see* International
    Conference on Population and
    Development
United Nations Committee on the Elimina-
    tion of All Forms of Discrimina-
    tion against Women *see* CEDAW
United Nations Conference on Human
    Rights (Vienna, 1993) 216, 220,
    324n22, 327
United Nations Convention Against Torture
    and Other Cruel, Inhuman or
    Degrading Treatment or Punish-
    ment 229n4
United Nations Convention on the Elimina-
    tion of All Forms of Discrimina-
    tion against Women *see* CEDAW
United Nations Convention on the Rights of
    the Child 156, 157
United Nations Decade for Women 14
United Nations Declaration on the Elimina-
    tion of Violence against Women
    (1993) 265
United Nations Development Fund for
    Women 223
United Nations Human Rights Commission
    216–17, 218
United Nations Millennium Development
    Goals 5
United Nations Population Fund (UNFPA)
    338–9

United Nations Resolution 1325 on Women,
    Peace and Security (2000) 220
United Nations special rapporteurs 216–17,
    218–19
United Nations World Conference on
    Women *see* World Conference
    on Women
United States: age of consent law 320; ARTs
    48, 49; image in Polish press
    205, 207; migrants in 10, 11;
    nature of rape 233; neoliberal
    penal system 27–30, 32, 34, 35,
    36, 37, 38, 41n18, 43n28; Sep-
    tember 11, 2001 attacks 161
United States Agency for International
    Development 330, 338
Universal Declaration of Human Rights
    (UDHR)(1948) 307
universalism 48; and cultural relativism
    306–7
University of the Witwatersrand, Gender
    Research Project of the Cen-
    tre for Applied Legal Studies
    (CALS) 222–3
urbanization, and decline of birthrates 45
Urgent Action Fund 223
USAID 330, 338
utopian socialism 1
Utterwulghe, Steve 148

## V
Vargas Alzamora, Augusto, cardinal 337
victims, women as 37–8, 39
Vienna Declaration (1993) 216, 220
Vietnam, empowerment 125
Vigarello, George 233
Vilca case 227
violence: China 93; Ghana 250–1; Indone-
    sian migration to Saudi Arabia
    111–12, 113; masculinities in
    Ghana 10, 247, 250–1, 257–60,
    263n23; micro-credit in India
    120, 122, 124, 125; Nepal 67–8,
    69; religion in Latin America
    265, 269, 272; Trinidad and
    Tobago 158; *see also* sexual vio-
    lence and abuse
*Volksnation* tradition 207

## W
Wacquant, Loic 28, 29
Wadud, Amina 177, 181
war 8; sexual violence 216, 219–20, 223–8
war crimes 220, 221, 222